A History of Computing
in the Twentieth Century

Contributors

John Backus
Friedrich L. Bauer
Julian Bigelow
Garrett Birkhoff
Andrew D. Booth
Arthur W. Burks
J. C. Chu
Edsger W. Dijkstra
J. Presper Eckert, Jr.
Andrei P. Ershov
Robert R. Everett
I. J. Good
R. W. Hamming
A. S. Householder
Cuthbert C. Hurd
Harry D. Huskey
Donald E. Knuth
S. H. Lavington
D. H. Lehmer
John W. Mauchly

Kenneth O. May
N. Metropolis
Jan Rajchman
B. Randell
James E. Robertson
Mikhail R. Shura-Bura
Ralph J. Slutz
George R. Stibitz
Ryota Suekane
Antonin Svoboda
Erwin Tomash
Luis Trabb Pardo
Henry S. Tropp
S. M. Ulam
Mark B. Wells
M. V. Wilkes
J. H. Wilkinson
H. Zemanek
Konrad Zuse

International Reseach Conference on the History of Computing, Los Alamos Scientific Laboratory.

A History of Computing in the Twentieth Century

A collection of essays

Edited by

N. METROPOLIS
Los Alamos Scientific Laboratory
Los Alamos, New Mexico

J. HOWLETT
Oxford University
Oxford, England

GIAN-CARLO ROTA
Massachusetts Institute of Technology
Cambridge, Massachusetts
and
Los Alamos Scientific Laboratory
Los Alamos, New Mexico

 1980

ACADEMIC PRESS
A Subsidiary of Harcourt Brace Jovanovich, Publishers

New York   London   Toronto   Sydney   San Francisco

ACADEMIC PRESS, INC.
111 Fifth Avenue, New York, New York 10003

United Kingdom Edition published by
ACADEMIC PRESS, INC. (LONDON) LTD.
24/28 Oval Road, London NW1 7DX

Library of Congress Cataloging in Publication Data

International Research Conference on the History of
    Computing, Los Alamos Scientific Laboratory, 1976.
    A history of computing in the twentieth century.

    "The origins of digital computers: supplementary
bibliography, B. Randell": p.
       1. Computers––History––Congresses. 2. Electronic
data processing––History––Congresses. I. Metropolis,
Nicholas Constantine, Date. II. Howlett, Jack,
  Date   III. Rota, Gian Carlo, Date. IV. Title.
QA75.5.I63 1976   001.6'09   79–51683
ISBN 0–12–491650–3

To John R. Pasta

Contents

PART V   THE PLACES

List of Contributors

Numbers in parentheses indicate the pages on which the authors' contributions begin.

JOHN BACKUS (125), IBM Research Laboratory, San Jose, California 96193

FRIEDRICH L. BAUER (505), Institut für Informatik der Technischen Universität, D-8 München 2, Federal Republic of Germany

JULIAN BIGELOW (291), Institute for Advanced Study, Princeton, New Jersey 08540

GARRETT BIRKHOFF (21), Department of Mathematics, Harvard University, Cambridge, Massachusetts 02138

ANDREW D. BOOTH* (551), Lakehead University, Thunder Bay, Ontario P78 5E1, Canada

ARTHUR W. BURKS (311), Department of Computer and Communication Sciences, University of Michigan, Ann Arbor, Michigan 48104

J. C. CHU (345), 10 Baldwin Circle, Weston, Massachusetts 02193

EDSGER W. DIJKSTRA (563), Burroughs, Nuenen, The Netherlands

J. PRESPER ECKERT, JR. (525), Univac Division, Sperry Rand Corporation, Blue Bell, Pennsylvania 19422

ANDREI P. ERSHOV (137), Computing Center, Siberian Branch of the USSR Academy of Sciences, Novosibirsk 630090, USSR

ROBERT R. EVERETT (365), Mitre Corporation, Bedford, Massachusetts 01730

I. J. GOOD (31), Department of Statistics, Virginia Polytechnic Institute and State University, Blacksburg, Virginia 24061

* Retired.

R. W. HAMMING (3), Naval Postgraduate School, Monterey, California
    93940

A. S. HOUSEHOLDER* (385), Oak Ridge National Laboratory, Oak
    Ridge, Tennessee 37830

CUTHBERT C. HURD* (389), IBM, New York, New York 10017

HARRY D. HUSKEY (419), Division of Natural Sciences, University of
    California, Santa Cruz, California 95064

DONALD E. KNUTH (197), Computer Science Department, School of
    Humanities and Sciences, Stanford University, Stanford, California
    94305

S. H. LAVINGTON (433), Department of Computer Science, University
    of Manchester, Manchester M13 9PL, England

D. H. LEHMER (445), Department of Mathematics, University of Cali-
    fornia, Berkeley, California 94720

JOHN W. MAUCHLY† (541), Univac Division, Sperry Rand Corporation,
    Blue Bell, Pennsylvania 19422

KENNETH O. MAY† (11), Department of Mathematics, University of
    Toronto, Toronto, Ontario, Canada‡

N. METROPOLIS (457), Los Alamos Scientific Laboratory, Los Alamos,
    New Mexico 87544

JAN RAJCHMAN‡ (465), RCA Laboratories, David Sarnoff Research
    Center, Princeton, New Jersey 08540

B. RANDELL (47, 629), Computing Laboratory, University of Newcastle
    upon Tyne, Newcastle upon Tyne NE1 7RU, England

JAMES E. ROBERTSON (347), Department of Computer Science, Uni-
    versity of Illinois, Urbana, Illinois 61801

MIKHAIL R. SHURA-BURA (137), Institute for Applied Mathematics,
    The USSR Academy of Sciences, Moscow, USSR

RALPH J. SLUTZ (471), Environmental Research Laboratories, National
    Oceanic and Atmospheric Administration, Boulder, Colorado 80303

GEORGE R. STIBITZ (479), Department of Physiology, Dartmouth Medi-
    cal School, Hanover, New Hampshire 03755

RYOTA SUEKANE (575), Faculty of Engineering, Yamanashi University,
    Takeda-4 Kofu, Japan

ANTONIN SVOBODA (579), Computer Science Department, University
    of California, Los Angeles, California 90024

ERWIN TOMASH (485), Dataproducts Corporation, Woodland Hills, Cali-
    fornia 91365

LUIS TRABB PARDO (197), Computer Science Department, School of
    Humanities and Sciences, Stanford University, Stanford, California
    94305

* Retired.
† Deceased.
‡ Present address: Jan Rajchman, Inc., 268 Edgerstone Road, Princeton, New Jersey 08540.

HENRY S. TROPP (115), Department of Mathematics, Humboldt State University, Arcata, California 95521

S. M. ULAM (93), Department of Mathematics, University of Florida, Gainesville, Florida 32611

MARK B. WELLS (275), Los Alamos Scientific Laboratory, Los Alamos, New Mexico 97544

M. V. WILKES (497), Computer Laboratory, University of Cambridge, Cambridge CB2 3QG, England

J. H. WILKINSON (101), National Physical Laboratory, Teddington, Middlesex, England

H. ZEMANEK* (587), IBM, D-7030 Boeblingen, Federal Republic of Germany

KONRAD ZUSE (611), Im Haselgrund 21, 6418 Hünfeld, Federal Republic of Germany

* Present address: IBM Austria, A-1011 Wien, Austria.

Preface

"Historia magistra vitae, lux veritatis . . . ," we repeat to ourselves without conviction, and should like to go on believing. But scientific and technological history seem to belie this saying. The early version of an as yet ill-understood algorithm, the clumsy plan of an early engine, the pristine computer with its huge, superfluous circuits give us little inspiration to face the problems of our day. Technological advances appear as sudden, discontinuous leaps that cover all previous work with an impenetrable cobweb of obsolescence. It is left to the archeologist, not to the historian, to make his way across the tortuous maze of oblivion, and to retrieve at least an appearance of the lost artifact, an obtrusive contraption whose plans and photographs will serve to fill the glossy pages of coffee-table books.

Or so we are tempted to think when we look with secret boredom at the Carrollesque creations of a Babbage, at the megalomaniac plans of Geheimrat Leibniz, at the unconvincing fantasies of Leonardo da Vinci, or at the preposterous wheels of Raimond Lull. There is a point at which the study of the technological past turns into paleontology, and in the history of computation that point is uncomfortably close, and moving closer.

Why, then, a history of computing, no matter how recent the past recaptured? Couldn't it be honorably replaced by a compact commemorative plaque listing in gilded letters the names of the pioneers who made the computer age possible, God bless their souls? Are there any lessons to be learned from retelling and rereading the story of the computer and the rise of computer science?

First, some of the articles in this volume give useful factual information not to be found elsewhere. Randell's account of the COLOSSUS, until now a British top secret, is here made available for the first time; Ershov's, Shura-Bura's, and Svoboda's glimpses beyond the Iron Curtain are a novelty that will provide some exciting reading enjoyment.

The jumping on the bandwagon of the big corporations, belated as always, but done with all the flair and fanfare that would rekindle our wavering faith in the willingness of private enterprise to contribute to scientific research, is here amply documented. The reports of Everett on the MITRE Corporation, Hurd on IBM, Rajchman on RCA, Stibitz on Bell Labs, Tomash on Engineering Research Associates, Eckert and Mauchly on Sperry Rand, should set our capitalistic hearts to rest, at least until the next computer revolution.

The development of programming languages is perhaps the one chapter in this history that displays the dialectical development expected of intellectual history. Each new computer language is motivated by the preceding, and the mistakes of the past shine by their absence in the languages of the present. Backus's nitty-gritty list of early mistakes, Knuth's Olympian survey of early programming languages, Wells's reflections on the possibilities of algorithmic languages, Dijkstra's account of the implementation of ALGOL, Householder's tale of the triumphal stage entry of numerical algebra, are perhaps among the papers in this volume that will bear frequent rereading by all who have to navigate on the high seas of present-day programming. With this edifying objective in mind Hamming and May have written witty exhortations, urging us to preserve the fading records of our computer present.

The chatty, anecdotal accounts of Birkhoff, Good, Ulam, Wilkinson, Tropp, and Bigelow bring to life the pioneers of computing, and center stage is held by the personalities of the logician Alan Turing and mathematician John von Neumann. Few, except these giants, realized in the 1930s that the formalism of mathematical logic, considered by many a sterile exercise for philosophers and for mathematicians in search of a field, was instead the magic key to programming languages as well as to computer design.

For if there is a message that comes across in these essays, it is that the spark of life was given to computer science by a few men who displayed the vision gained elsewhere from a broad cultural background, and who were immune to the stupefying demands of some presumed relevance. The improbable symbolism of Peano, Russell, and Whitehead, the analysis of proofs by flowcharts spearheaded by Gentzen, the definition of computability by Church and Turing, all inventions motivated by the purest of mathematics, mark the beginning of the computer revolution.

Once more, we find a confirmation of the sentence Leonardo jotted despondently on one of those rambling sheets where he confided his innermost thoughts: "Theory is the captain, and application the soldier."

On a more practical plane, another unmistakable message emerges from these essays. Over the years, the constant and most reliable support of computer science—and of science generally—has been the defense establishment. While old men in congresses and parliaments would debate the allocation of a few thousand dollars, farsighted generals and admirals would not hesitate to divert substantial sums to help the oddballs in Princeton, Cambridge, and Los Alamos. Ever since Einstein wrote a letter to President

Roosevelt, our best friends have been in the branch of government concerned with defense. And now that the processing of intelligence data is rapidly reaching Byzantine complexity, we can learn from the past to appreciate another possible source of support that may be coming along.

"*Historia magistra vitae, lux veritatis. . . .*"

Los Alamos, New Mexico   N. METROPOLIS
27 April 1979   GIAN-CARLO ROTA

Acknowledgments

The original versions of these papers were presented at the International Research Conference on the History of Computing, held at the Los Alamos Scientific Laboratory (LASL), 10–15 June 1976. That conference had its inception in the recognition by J. Worlton, and his suggestion to N. Metropolis, that such a conference was urgently needed to record historical perspectives of computing pioneers during their lifetimes. That urgency has been unfortunately verified by the deaths of several of the conference attendees since the meeting was held. Support for the conference was provided through the good offices of John Pasta of the National Science Foundation, and Metropolis and Worlton became the principal investigators for this NSF project.

Harold Agnew, Director of LASL in 1976, recognized the importance of the conference and generously arranged for local support through LASL facilities and personnel. LASL personnel who contributed to the smooth running of the conference include Duane Harder, Marge McCormick, Carl Cuntz, and Robert Wellnitz.

The editorial work was carried out by J. Howlett under National Science Foundation Grant No. MCS-77-23744. The editors express special thanks to Michal Hakanson for the beautiful typing of the manuscript.

Part I

Introduction

We Would Know What They Thought
When They Did It

R. W. HAMMING

History apparently began with long lists of pharaohs, kings, rulers, etc., and the lengths of their reigns. Astronomy also in its early days consisted mainly in naming the stars and constellations. The more stars a person could name and identify the better an astronomer he was. Similarly, in many other fields of science the early stages involved giving names to things. Even in my youth doctors were taught the names of all the bones in the human body. These examples, and many others, show that man has an innate belief that giving a name to something gives him power over the thing itself. I believe that this is the reason that the early history tended so strongly to be lists of people and dates, with occasional details of what they did, and sometimes a brief biography.

We now recognize that the mere giving of names is not important; it is the ideas behind the things that matter. We are also slowly recognizing that the apparent accuracy of dates is misleading. Thus, when Gibbon gives 476 as the date when Rome fell, we realize that this is arbitrary to a high degree. Rome did not fall at one moment, nor does Gibbon so claim. It is merely convenient to have a definite date, but this convenience can be misleading.

Historians, like most experts, usually resent attempts to summarize their field of expertise. H. G. Wells's famous "History" is an example. Any universal history is usually resented by the experts who claim that their special field cannot be compressed. They prefer to claim that it cannot be done, that if a question is not precise, then there can be no real answer, indeed there

3

can be no real meaning. Common sense suggests that there is a valid, useful middle ground between the two extremes of vague generalities and precise details.

The history of firsts is also fraught with danger. Thus Gibbs discovered the Gibbs phenomenon in 1899, but it was published almost 50 years earlier, and lost. The recent fast Fourier transform, publicized by Cooley and Tukey, was published several times before, and lost. This should not be taken to mean that the person who adequately popularizes an idea should not be given credit for the idea. Again, in game theory the idea goes back to Borel, but the adequate popularization did not occur until von Neumann.

Gregor Mendel and his famous peas is another example of a discovery that was made and lost—but in this case the fame found its way back to the first man—or was he? Remember that Pascal has recently been displaced by Schickard!

But how about more recent dates? I have attended two computer dedication ceremonies at which the computer was going to be dismantled almost the next day and at best later assembled rather differently. What then does the dedication date of a computer mean? One has to look carefully before claiming that it means much!

We all know, of course, that many current history books have shifted from the who, what, and when to more cultural history. Thus not only are the histories interspersed with short biographical notes on individuals, but there are histories that treat not the individual but classes of people, not isolated events but trends like the industrial revolution, not definite dates but periods with vague beginnings and endings. Furthermore, we seem to be increasingly interested in the economic factors that lie behind events, in cultural trends like the spread of general education and literacy. Finally, we are gradually moving toward histories of ideas.

Why do we want the histories of ideas? As creative scientists we are more interested in the act of creation than we are in what is created. We have found that it is often easier to re-create something than it is to find it in the literature—it is certainly more fun! Faced with an almost infinite sea of details we resort to mastering the process of creation rather than the process of recall.

It has been said that if you want to master a field, then you should go to the masters and avoid the commentators. It is for this reason that I chose the title, "We would know what they thought when they did it." We wish to learn how to do great things ourselves rather than merely recall what others have done. Alas, historians almost always fail us in this matter.

Now to my first main point. It appears to me that the expert in a field usually prefers the classical form of history with its emphasis on who first did what and when he did it. Historians certainly prefer to write such histories. On the other hand, the outsider usually prefers the history of the *ideas* in the field—and he would like to have, but almost never gets, a history that adequately discusses how the idea arose and how rapidly it spread through the relevant population. Thus I have yet to find, although it may exist, a history that tells me how rapidly relativity and quantum mechanics spread throughout the existing population of physicists. Max Planck is reported to have said, "We did not convert them, we outlived them." This suggests that only a very small fraction of the currently living physicists accepted the new ideas, and it was only with the next generation of students that the concepts were widely understood and accepted.

Fortunately for us in the computer field, it is relatively easy to measure the spread of the *use* of computers. It has been true for much of the time that IBM has had about 70% of the market, and that most of its computers were on rental. Thus when I find that IBM made 1500 of the old 601 multiplying punches I can be reasonably sure that they were regularly in use. This is not true when I hear that someone sold 250 difference machines. Experience shows me that most old analog computing machines, from the Michelson Fourier analyzer to many other machines in various universities, merely sat there unused year after year. Thus not only are we in a reasonable position to make estimates of the total digital computing power available at any one date but we can be reasonably sure that much of this power was being used. How it was used and on what problems is another matter.

Now I do not want to claim that in the past the experts wrote only histories of who first did what and when, but I do claim that there has been a strong tendency toward this. E. T. Bell wrote the famous book "Men of Mathematics," but he also wrote "The Development of Mathematics," which, as its title indicates, tries to give a history of the ideas of mathematics. Either his heart was less in the second and he therefore wrote more poorly, or else mathematicians prefer the famous-men type of history since the first is widely seen on peoples' bookshelves and the second is comparatively rare.

To summarize so far, the histories of science I have read tend to emphasize the older type of history, while I believe there is clear evidence that what is wanted is the more cultural type of history, which treats of the development and spread of ideas, of computing equipment, and of their effects throughout the relevant population as well as in society in general.

The second point I wish to make is that by following the conventional rules history is remarkably biased. A statistician would say that history is asymptotically biased. Why do I say this? Conventional history requires positive proof, and rejects informed speculation. If there is no written record, or equivalent positive record, then something did not happen or was not understood. As a result of trying to play safe, almost all new material that is discovered shows that the past knew more than was given in the history books. The few exceptions occur when something is found to be a forgery or to be misdated. Otherwise new material generally shows, as I said, that the past knew more than we had given them credit for. The historian's rule of positive evidence produces systematically biased history.

Let me give a few examples of what I am calling informed speculation. I recall reading a beautifully illustrated book on cave painting in which the author remarks that the painters must have gone to a school of cave painting. To justify this claim the author observed that the style of painting was widespread both in area and in time, that the materials used were likewise uniform. And anyway, it wasn't gifted amateur painting. I looked again at the pictures and tried to imagine that local yokels painted then. No, they are not the paintings of talented amateurs; they are much too well done. I was forced to agree with the author that a school of cave painting was a reasonable thing to accept. But what else did that imply? Quite a lot to me.

Similarly, Stonehenge has gradually passed from being a rude structure built by clumsy oafs for primitive religious events to a rather sophisticated astronomical device. When you consider in great detail all the necessary things you would require if you had to build it at that time, then I believe you will gradually come to my opinion that there was more than a rude social structure behind the builders. I suspect that it took a great deal of social organization and knowledge to design, build, and maintain Stonehenge.

For many years the Egyptians were thought to have done their impressive stonework by brute strength and awkwardness. But consider the fact that the moving of an obelisk a few hundred feet taxed the abilities of the engineers at the end of the Renaissance. The problem was that the obelisk was so large that if it were supported only at both ends, it would break in the middle due to its own weight. Yet the Egyptians quarried it, moved it down the Nile, and set it up; the Romans took it down, moved it across the Mediterranean, and set it up. Let us recognize that the ancients must have known a great deal to have done what they did, and did not merely do it with masses of men.

I have long been interested in the cathedrals of the Middle Ages. Just looking at them I cannot believe they were built by dumb luck and by trial and error. As a result of remarks along these lines I went down to Princeton one afternoon to meet with some historians of the Middle Ages, and to discuss how much the builders must have known. The historians claimed that because they had the curriculum of the schools they therefore knew what the builders did and did not know. I remarked that if they thought that the Princeton University curriculum in mathematics has much relation to what we know and use in mathematics, then they were very wrong.

The historians claimed that since Beauvais fell down that proved that the builders had no adequate theory. I replied that the Tacoma bridge blew down but that does not prove we had no theory—only that the engineer had been careless.

Finally, they claimed that there were large cost overruns for many of the cathedrals. I remarked that the Sidney Opera House had a great cost over-run, and that the military was famous for cost overruns, but that this does not prove the lack of adequate theory.

Studies of the cathedrals by others indicate that they were remarkably well designed. The fact that they have lasted this long is obvious proof without making any technical studies.

I have long had a hobby of looking at old engineering feats, like old tun-nels, and speculating on what the builders *probably* knew and had technical control over. My conclusions are often at great variance from what I read in history books. When you further consider the social and economic climate that could produce the works you find further differences between what common sense suggests and books report. To repeat my point, the differ-ences arise from the historian's refusal to believe that the past knew more than the documents that have come down to us indicate. They refuse to apply informed common sense plus a feeling for practical engineering and to try to guess at probable states of information, technology, economics, and social organization.

The third main point I wish to bring up goes back to my title. Usually it is the history of the *ideas* in the field, rather than the isolated events, that inter-ests the outsider—and sometimes the insider too. The difficulty is that ideas are elusive, to say the least. The history of names, dates, and events is so easy, and apparently definite, that by comparison the history of ideas seems sloppy and therefore has been largely ignored.

To illustrate the difficulty of deciding when something is really under-stood, consider that many mathematicians have the experience of knowing a theorem and a proof for several years and then suddenly "understanding" the theorem in a new way. Occasionally there may be several of these epi-sodes of suddenly understanding what one had apparently known all along.

The example I shall take to illustrate the difficulty of measuring when an idea was first understood is the idea of the computer as a *symbol manipula-tor* rather than as a *number cruncher*. This was in a sense one of the decisive steps in the history of computing. Since ontogeny repeats phylogeny—the individual in his development repeats the steps, abbreviated of course, that the field went through—it is also a decisive step for each individual in the field.

One could claim that Turing, when he proved that the universal comput-ing machine could do anything any computer could do, must have under-stood the idea that computers are symbol-manipulating machines. A careful rereading of the famous Burks, Goldstine, and von Neumann report on pro-gramming [1] indicates to me that they thought of the computer as a number cruncher. There is simply no indication of general symbol manipulation. In the famous book on programming by Wilkes *et al.* [2] I found in Appendix D the germ of the idea of an interpreter. And it was from this source by careful, long study that I learned that computers were general symbol manipulators.

If they buried it in Appendix D did they understand what they had done? I doubt it!

When I came to apply this lesson to the new IBM 650 I devised a language (called simply L1) that was a three-address, floating-point arithmetic. The underlying language of the machine was of no influence in the design of the language. I believe I can say that at that moment I was clear about computers being symbol manipulators. Yet only a couple of years earlier when I wired much the same kind of language for an IBM CPC I had no such understanding. In the CPC case the nature of the computer itself dominated my thoughts, in the 650 case I designed the language I wanted without much regard to the computer.

An examination of the history of computing shows that around the years 1952–1954 many of us came to the same conclusion that the computer was more than a number cruncher. I recall Al Perlis remarking that a number of good scientists had for years been working with machines, and then suddenly got the message and went forth to preach the gospel. And I am sure they found much the same as I did, the audience would nod their heads, but one had the feeling that they were not understanding the message. The concept was hard to grasp when for years you had merely number crunched. Now it is fairly easy to grasp and the student easily takes this step that we hesitated so long to take. Yet he has to take it sometime.

Thus one sees that the understanding of an idea, let alone its spread into the relevant population, is hard to define, harder to measure, and almost impossible to prove. Yet, I say, this is what we want to know when we read the history of computing. Of course, the expert relishes the details, and the details must be there to serve as a basis for what is wanted, but the details themselves are not enough. The details should not be allowed to obscure the bigger picture. Again, we wish to grasp the act of creation itself, so that we can learn to create for ourselves.

My fourth point is easily stated. Just because you have lived through a period does not mean that you are competent to write a history of the period.

If you will but read a few books about history itself you will find that the writing of a good history is difficult and requires both training and talent. Indeed, having lived through some events may make it harder than if you merely came later and studied the period.

I have long had a saying, "Voyeurism is no substitute for experience." It applies not only to sex, but also to the field of science itself. A historian who merely reads about a field without getting deeply involved and making significant contributions himself is apt to be a mere voyeur. He will not understand the act of creation, and hence he will miss the essence of what we want—he will report only on what he understands, the name of the first person to do something, when he did it, and some surrounding circumstances. But the expert in the field, who does not get serious training in history, is apt to produce anecdotal stories rather than history.

If it takes two kinds of expertise to write a good history, and clearly there can be few people so talented, does this mean that I am against the writing of history? No! I am merely saying that is it not easily done. I hope that the Los Alamos conference marks the beginning of a serious attempt to write the history of what I believe is one of the greatest steps in the history of man—the creation, development, and mastery of the computer. And in saying this I hope that I have made it clear that there should be a great deal of emphasis on the creation, development, and spread of the ideas, rather than a mere enumeration of firsts, names, places, dates, numbers, speeds, etc. We want the real history of man and the computer.

REFERENCES

1. Burks, A. W., Goldstein, H. H., and von Neumann, J., "Preliminary Discussions of the Logical Design of an Electronic Computing Instrument," 2nd ed. Institute for Advanced Study, Princeton, New Jersey, 1947.
2. Wilkes, M. V., Wheeler, D. J., and Gill, S., "The Preparation of Programs for an Electronic Digital Computer." Addison-Wesley, Cambridge, Massachusetts, 1951.

NAVAL POSTGRADUATE SCHOOL
MONTEREY, CALIFORNIA*

* Formerly of Bell Laboratories, Murray Hill, New Jersey.

Historiography: A Perspective
for Computer Scientists

*KENNETH O. MAY**

Historians don't like sweeping generalizations, particularly when our students make them. But historians are generally more tolerant of this offence as the speaker gets more grey hairs. So I'm going to start off with a big generalization that probably will not hurt anyone's feelings. A little gimmick that I use in my history course is this: after a few weeks when students read a little bit about the general history of mathematics, I ask them to make a list of the twenty most important events in the history of mathematics. Their lists and mine lead to a lively discussion. On my list appears the modern computer as one of the very most important mathematical events of all time. I think that it would remain on even the shortest list that one could imagine. It would be a little difficult to make a list of one, but if one had three or four I think one would have to put it down. Of course I mean the development of computers, not the "invention of the computer" because it is meaningless to speak of the invention of the computer. Things are much more complicated than that: controversies over who invented something are usually unprofitable—these are complex events in which many people take part. Moreover, the "event" itself gets shifted as time goes on so that a particular aspect of

---

* Tragically, Professor May died suddenly on 1 December 1977, of a heart attack. This paper was constructed by his colleagues at Toronto from the tape record of his talk at the Los Alamos conference, with final editing by one of the editors of this volume (J. H.) and, in particular, by K. O. May's colleague, C. V. Jones.

the computer or computing changes its meaning with time. And so statements about who did what exactly first are not very meaningful.

But the computer, I think, is tremendously important. To say that it's one of the most important inventions in mathematics or in the history of mathematics would be an understatement. It would be closer to the truth to say that the development of the electronic computer is one of the major events not just in scientific history but in world history. And it's tempting to compare it with another event of more or less the same historic period: the release of atomic energy. I should be inclined to say with quite a bit of assurance that the historians of the future, if there are any, will agree with me that the computer is having and will have a bigger impact than atomic energy. I'm sure all will realize the significance of the "if." There is a possibility that release of atomic energy will have a bigger impact, but in that case there will be no historians to discuss the matter. Barring that possibility, it seems pretty plain that the computer is having a deeper effect on us because it seems to penetrate everywhere at every level. It penetrates at the technological level, and it penetrates at the level of scientific activity. It penetrates social activity, political activity, the way people are thinking. It's hard to think of any aspects of our lives that are not significantly influenced. For example, when electronic computers were coming in, I was interested in mathematical economics. It became obvious very quickly that the computer not only made possible some theoretical developments that hadn't been possible before, but, much more significant, it made possible a kind of centralized control and planning that had not been feasible before. And I'm sure this is only one of many ways in which it will have very big historical results.

One other general remark before I get down to business: I appreciate more and more that computers are a lot of fun. I've been very slow to get involved in any way myself with computers. I've been very cautious and suspicious about whether they would really help me with the information handling I was doing. For a long time I felt sure that the hand methods I was using were better and faster. Of course, if I had had unlimited funds, that would have been a different matter. I would occasionally check with people in our computer center, show them how I did things, and ask whether I could do it a little faster with computers. The answer was, "You'd better stick to your old-fashioned methods." But times are changing, and now although I'm not a computer scientist, I do have a computer terminal right in my office. This is not the most significant use of a computer, but it does substitute for one or two secretaries and for research assistants in a lot of things that I do. And in beginning to use the computer a little myself, I became more sympathetic with something I observed long ago—that computer people seemed to be a little bit nutty. They were gadget happy and got such a tremendous kick out of all the things that computers could do, the little things and big things. But now I really think that's great. I go around telling people what I can do the way everybody in the field seems to. Of course, every achiever in science or anything else enjoys what he's doing, but I think the computer people enjoy it even more than most.

My title is "Historiography." The term sometimes means the methods of history and sometimes the actual history of history. Methodology on the whole is a boring subject, and I don't intend to say very much about it. For one thing there is plenty of printed material available, and I have a strong feeling that we should take advantage of technological possibilities. Sometimes, people talk about how the computer is going to revolutionize our libraries and how the time will shortly come when there won't be books anymore. People will just get the computer to give them the information they want. I'm very skeptical about this because it's my observation that we have not yet utilized even the invention of printing. It no doubt will rise to the challenge of the computer.

There is great interest in computers and what they can do, but also interest now in telling the story, in telling the history. This is a very happy circumstance in my opinion. It indicates the maturity and sophistication of the field. Studying the past, it seems to me, is necessary for knowing what we are doing in any given field, or for understanding what the field is about.

My first comment is that one should distinguish between X and the history of X. The state of an art, science, or technology at any particular time is formulated by the people at that time for very specific purposes of that time. The background, the past, the development are very different things. One does not have in the past bits and pieces of the present as they now appear. That's not the way things develop. Things develop genetically. If you look at the historical background of a person to see how he developed from babyhood, you would not expect to find bits and pieces of the adult back there in the child. There was a time in the Middle Ages—and I've seen some wax models of this—where they thought that there was a tiny person in the embryo, and that he just got bigger. But we know now it's not at all like that. The fetus is not the same person, not the same thing back in the embryo, or as a child, as when it is an adult. It isn't just smaller or earlier, it's different. And this means that describing something from the current logical point of view is quite different from describing it historically. Historical description requires a time-lagged approach and means getting into understanding things as people understood them *then,* not as we understand them now.

The second point is that chronology is not the same thing as history. Chronology, which is simply what happened when, is the basis of history because if you try to write history without facts, then it's simply speculation and not to be taken very seriously. But on the other hand a mere list of who did what when is not history. History is processed data, facts organized and related. Similarly in physics, we don't think that a mere account of observations by a physicist is physics. It becomes science when it's interpreted, organized, and related to other parts of physics. In the same way, the chronological knowledge becomes history only when it's selected, analyzed, and accompanied with insight. This means that the history of computers ought to give insight not only into the history but also into the computer itself. It should give perspective by giving ideas about what the future developments might be, what the promising lines of development might be, and so on.

Now something about the role of computer scientists. I'm not sure that the term "computer scientist" is perfectly chosen, because it seems to me that the computer field is an amalgam of science and technology. Neither one is less important than the other. Maybe "computer people" is better, to cover both computer theorists and practitioners.

The most important thing here is that active people in the field have enough sense of history to realize that they should leave traces. This has not always happened in the history of science. One of the things said by his contemporaries about Gauss (one of the greatest mathematicians and probably *the* greatest calculator who ever lived) was that he covered his trail like a fox. And so it was very hard to know how he did things. Here was a man who calculated so rapidly in his head that all his life he did arithmetic from left to right instead of right to left. As he tells us, in doing all four operations from left to right he could calculate and write the numbers simultaneously. For addition he would write down one number and then as he wrote down the other he would look ahead far enough to anticipate the carries and include them as he wrote, so that he would just write down the answers as fast as he could write. It would be very nice if we knew more about this, but because he was too reticent, we don't. So, keep in mind that although a letter, a note, a diary, report, or a preliminary draft of a publication may be of no further interest to you and ready to be discarded, it might be very valuable in the future. So keep records. After all, people can throw it out later. It's impossible for an individual to assess the value of his own papers since they may have relevance to matters unknown to him.

The second thing that computer people can do is to talk and write about what they have done and are doing. It isn't enough in any science to do things; it's necessary to communicate what has been done. But I'm suggesting something more than the usual communication. Not only communicate your scientific results but also talk about how they arose, who was involved, all those things that are often unrecorded. We need memoirs. Reminiscences and memoirs that we have from the past are few and very valuable. So yield to any inclinations to reminisce.

And, finally, I should comment on participants becoming historians. There are pitfalls in this, of course, because people's memories are not precise. But that does not matter. The essence of historical scholarship is to use memoirs and other primary sources with discretion. And so a person who has participated shouldn't worry about the bias that he has because of his own participation. The historians will take care of that in due time by comparing sources, checking dates, and so on.

I'm not going to give a lot of unsolicited advice about how to do history. As I said, there is a tremendous literature, some of it very interesting, some philosophical, and some quite technical. There are manuals of historiography in general and for the history of mathematics in particular. There is an old one in Italian by Gino Loria, several by George Sarton, and a recent one of which I'm guilty, which is combined with a bibliography to help scholars avoid duplication ("Bibliography and Research Manual of the History of Mathematics," University of Toronto Press, Toronto, 1973). There is also the journal *Historia Mathematica*. Any scientist who wants to go into history should take the trouble to read some of these. But the main point is this: if you go into writing history, you should take it seriously. You shouldn't imagine that history is something to do when you're too tired to do something else. It's a discipline like any other. It has its own methods, criteria, techniques. Naturally, the historians are not as great as mathematicians or computer scientists, but in their own fumbling way they have developed their own field. One should see what they've developed and take advantage of it. By doing this, a competent person can certainly, without undue delay, learn the techniques and do excellent work.

Now, what I really want to put over is an idea, a point of view for which I do not claim originality. It may seem rather obvious. It relates to the place that the computer and computing has in mathematics and the history of mathematics in society. That place is, from a social point of view, still in doubt. It's a developing place. At first, in academic circles, computing appeared as something in the mathematics department. It might just as well have appeared in the engineering school; the hardware did appear there. Now it has become common, perhaps standard, for there to be separate departments of computer science. I think there is a tendency for computer science, or whatever we call it, to be much broader than simply a study of the electronic computer. It includes a big theoretical component relating to algorithms and automata, and a broad technology dealing with the whole field of information handling. This fits precisely into the way in which I think we should look at computing historically.

As I view it, and this is not the standard approach of historians of mathematics or of textbook writers, there are two great traditions in mathematics: the scientific tradition and the technological tradition, mathematical science and mathematical technology. Of course, computer science belongs, in my opinion, in the tradition of mathematical technology. This may trouble some mathematicians who feel that technology is a little less holy, a little lower in status, than science. But I don't have that prejudice; that's not the import of what I'm saying here.

The distinction I'm making is not at all the same as between pure and applied, because the regrettable and confused pure–applied distinction refers to the myth that there is some part of mathematics that has no application or is unconnected with the world, and another part that is applied. That is not what I'm talking about; both mathematical science and mathematical technology have theoretical components and applications. I think all of mathematics has applications; it is all applied. It's also not the same as the distinction between theory and practice, because mathematical technology, like all other branches of technology, has theory. There is a theoretical component of all branches of technology in addition to the intended application.

How is this technological tradition manifest? In prehistoric times, I see it represented by the beginnings of numeration, counting systems, the earliest arithmetic, the appreciation of art forms. Before any geometrical terminology there were many artifacts (products of primitive technology) that showed appreciation of things like symmetry and form. We observe the beginnings of mathematical science when people become curious about the properties of numbers that have been used for a long time, or when they begin to be interested in the logical, formal relations between geometric constructs. By Greek times all mathematics appears to be a mathematical science. You don't find any literature about mathematical technology, and this is why the historians neglect it.

The history of technology in general is not well documented. In fact, it's hardly documented at all. We know, for instance, that the invention of the stirrup and the efficient horse collar were perhaps two of the most important inventions and that they took place sometime in the Middle Ages. In Roman times a horse couldn't pull a load well, because the collar choked the horse, so the new collar made a tremendous difference to what they could do with horses. We don't know who invented these and other important things. Likewise we know very little about mathematical technology because it was transmitted from person to person with no surviving written record. For example, the abacus goes back in one form or another to prehistoric times. Yet never until very recently was there to be found a manual on the abacus, and no doubt the manuals of today will not be preserved.

Not so long ago there was dredged up out of the Aegean Sea, along with a number of other remains of a sunken ship off the island of Antikythera, some corroded lumps of bronze. Professor Derek de Solla Price has shown, after a detailed study including x-ray examination, that these were a calendrical computer, which simulated to a fair approximation the movements of the sun, moon, and the then-known planets. So the Greeks, at that early period, had a sophisticated calculating device, though not a computer in any modern sense of the word. But there is no mention of this anywhere in the literature of the period. Typically, scholars then, and later, were not interested in technology.

On its software side the tradition of mathematical technology might also be called the algorithmic tradition—that is, the tradition in which the focus is on solving problems, getting numerical answers. Algebra, in the traditional sense of a device for handling things symbolically, seems to me solidly a part of this algorithmic tradition. Other examples of software are formulas, numerical tables, and all the devices and methods of problem solving. All calculating devices—the abacus, the slide rule, mathematical instruments of all kinds, and calculating machines up to the modern computer—make up the hardware side of mathematical technology.

All this hardware and software developed steadily in history but without an elaborate literature, so that it doesn't appear in the historical record as a central thing. For example, it's often said that the Middle Ages were an absolute blank in the history of mathematics, that nothing much was done. This is not really true, because the methods of calculation made their greatest strides forward during precisely that period. The zero symbol first appeared in India in the eighth or ninth century. The decimal system of numeration came into Europe beginning in the tenth century. Algebra was being developed by the Arabs during the medieval period. Obviously that was a very productive period. It is said that nothing happened, because people think of mathematics only as a deductive, logical structure, and since that virtually stopped with the Greeks and picked up again only quite recently, they don't consider progress as having been made during that time.

If we look at the history of mathematics this way, it seems to me that one of the effects of the coming of the electronic computer is that for the first time mathematical technology becomes a consciously recognized discipline, a component of science and of technology, of the whole science–technology complex. Instead of being just a matter for practitioners who didn't seem to be in the mainstream, computing now becomes the Queen of Technology. I'm willing to grant it that title.

This is really something new. Computing becomes an important discipline in its own right. And, of course, we can see why. Calculation was just a chore that had a rather narrow scope, an uninteresting matter of calculating numerical answers. But now, the electronic computer has not only increased the capacity and speed of calculation but also enlarged the whole concept of what computing is. It is all of organized information handling, all algorithmic handling of data. And this, I think, is an illuminating way of looking at what is going on now. We are developing the most general, most abstract, and most effective methods of handling information. This is an almost complete analog of the role of mathematics. Mathematics is the collection of theoretical structures that have the characteristic of being the most abstract and most widely applicable. These structures, in computing as well as in mathematics, are more practical than any others just because of their abstractness. If this way of thinking about the matter is appropriate, it could be a rather useful way of looking at computer science and perhaps also a useful way of looking at computer policy questions. It certainly fits with the clear tendency for computer science to become an independent discipline, but one very closely linked with mathematics and with electronic and other technology. Of course, the value of this way of thinking can only be told by experience. In any case, I hope that the idea may be stimulating.

DEPARTMENT OF MATHEMATICS
UNIVERSITY OF TORONTO
TORONTO, ONTARIO, CANADA

Part II

The Human Side

Computing Developments 1935–1955, as Seen from Cambridge, U.S.A.

GARRETT BIRKHOFF

1. Prewar Years

The heroic years of computing developments began in the 1930s. During those years, Cambridge was a tranquil oasis in a world seething with troubles, providing support for two major computing activities. I shall begin by describing these. Although I was not personally involved in computing until after 1945, it was easy to be well informed about what was going on. This was easy in those days, because the scientific world was so small. By knowing 50 people and seeing them periodically, you could keep up superficially with almost everything that was worth knowing about.

The first major computing activity* that took place in Cambridge was the development by Vannevar Bush of the differential analyzer. Anyone who would like to learn about the differential analyzer should read Bush's own description [1] of what lay behind it. This acknowledges that British applied mathematicians, especially Kelvin and Maxwell, had thought of most of the relevant basic ideas. It was primarily technology, some Yankee ingenuity— Bush always liked to consider himself a Yankee inventor—that made it the success that it was.

Bush communicated frequently with Wiener—there was a lot of *esprit de*

---

* I am ignoring the *Nautical Almanac*, which played a very important role in the years 1855–1863.

21

corps in the small MIT of those days. In Wiener's own reminiscences, he claims that he foresaw the digital computer early and clearly, unlike Bush, who was totally absorbed by the analog computer and the continuum. This claim is interesting, and I hope that the facts will be cleared up by people who knew both men, before it is too late.

The differential analyzer was of course an analog machine, and we should all remember that all through the 1940s many scientists and engineers regarded analog computers as having at least the (still undemonstrated) potentialities of digital computers. The digital computer was identified in Cambridge, U.S.A., with Aiken's MARK I computer. Behind that there lay another connection with Kelvin, through Kelvin's participation in the planning of the transatlantic cable. Working on this also, without great academic training, was A. E. Kennelly, the discoverer and interpreter of the Kennelly–Heaviside layer.

Kennelly was comfortable enough through his Harvard salary and his consulting practice at the Harvard Engineering School to leave \$125,000 at his death for a professorship in applied mathematics. I learned of this only some years later, and have always wondered why the Harvard Mathematical Department did not lay claim to it. It should be possible to find out by examining the Harvard archives. Of course, Conant himself was mildly antimathematical. When he and Bush founded the National Defense Research Committee (NDRC), they saw no need for mathematics as such in the war effort.

The Kennelly bequest made it possible for Aiken to spend seven years at IBM developing the first automatic, large-scale calculator on an electromechanical basis, using a great deal of the IBM technology. Aiken did not always appreciate Thomas J. Watson, Sr., and all the cooperation he got from IBM. He told many fascinating anecdotes; one of them was about an IBM engineer of this period who was planning to implement binary division. When Aiken said, "You don't really have to do that because a/b is just $b^{-1}a$," the engineer replied, "Well, that's really very interesting. Just a minute." So he went over and took two numbers, a and b, computed the inverse of b, multiplied it by a, and compared the result with the quotient of a/b. When he found that they were indeed the same number, he said, "You're right; we'll go ahead."

Before leaving these early days I should like to say a little more about the peaceful, very small Harvard Engineering School at that time of the 1930s. Kennelly's successor was George Washington Pierce, who taught me electromagnetic theory. When I confessed that I had cut his classes, under the mistaken idea that he would be following his text, he generously lent me his personal course notes. Pierce was an inventive and practical pioneer, who collected \$2 million from the Bell Telephone Company in a patent suit. But he didn't see fit to endow a professorship; different individuals choose to spend their money in different ways!

The Harvard tradition from Pierce to Chaffee to Aiken, in electrical engineering and electromagnetic theory, was very direct, and had absolutely nothing to do with the Mathematics Department. I think that probably my father and I were among the few people in the Mathematics Department who liked to talk to these people in the 1930s and 1940s.

2. Wartime Years

I have been discussing the prewar period, to about 1942, and I should now like to shift into the period of the War. I think that in historical honesty we have to realize that it was dedication to the struggle against Hitlerism, and later to other problems of national defense, that provided the main driving force behind the development of the computer in the 1940s. It's absolutely impossible to understand it except in that context.

One of the great wartime and postwar computing centers was the Aberdeen Proving Ground, which had a differential analyzer, procured to help in computing range tables for exterior ballistics.

A very interesting historical digression could be made on this subject. Fortunately, Herman Goldstine has devoted considerable space to it in his book [2], because he knew Aberdeen. This was a great center of wartime activity, and on my weeks of vacations from Harvard I used to go down there. I was fortunate in having a desk in the office of R. H. Kent, where I saw and heard many things. I want to relate a few of them.

I'm not going to say much about the development of range tables, but my lowbrow impression as an observer was that range tables were not very useful in World War II. This is because it was not fixed-position trench warfare, it was mostly point-blank fire, often at a moving tank. As far as range tables were concerned, I think the most essential role was played by Jimmy Prevas. Prevas had at most a high school degree, but had one habit not shared by most of the mathematicians there carrying on the very distinguished tradition of Veblen and Bliss from World War I. Namely, he was always at the range where there were firings going on, keeping track of the wind and other relevant firing conditions. Whatever the theory behind the range tables, he made sure that the tables matched the firings for that particular day—when suitably corrected.

Perhaps those of us who are today engaged in computer simulation of other important phenomena may appreciate the importance of this kind of fine tuning, which has a very long history.

Aberdeen was a major center of wartime and postwar research; those of us who were there were well aware of the very fundamental developments at the nearby Moore School of Engineering at Pennsylvania, and that they had electronic machines which were fast but had very limited internal storage.

As regards von Neumann, here is just one anecdote. He came into Kent's office on one visit, with a program for calculating on the ENIAC a

one-dimensional model of 100 molecules to simulate a shock wave. He gave
a little seminar there to a small but select audience which included von
Kármán. After von Neumann finished, von Kármán said, "Well, Johnny,
that's very interesting. Of course you realize that Lagrange also used digital
models to simulate continuum mechanics." You could see from von Neumann's expression that although his scholarship was great, he was unaware
of the priority of Lagrange's "Mécanique Analytique."

I recall two interesting (for me) conversations with Aiken in 1944–1945,
when he was a lieutenant commander in our Navy. The first took place in the
Pullman washroom of the night train from Washington to Boston. This was a
place where many conversations occurred. You boarded the train at about
10:30 p.m. in Washington, and it arrived around 11:15 in Baltimore, where
you picked it up if you were at Aberdeen. Then if you weren't too tired you
might gossip with your Harvard and MIT friends. I suggested to Aiken there
that his new machine that was about to be dedicated could put the WPA*
tables out of business. Whether or not this had anything to do with it, in 1944
he was delighted to be ordered by an admiral to compute Bessel functions
whenever the MARK I was not otherwise occupied. Naturally, he received
this command with the greatest satisfaction.

The second conversation took place shortly after the war when Aiken's
MARK I was being formally dedicated in Cambridge as a present from IBM
to Harvard, and Thomas J. Watson, Sr., came up. If my recollection is correct, I rode with Aiken in a taxi from the lunch to the dedication. The astronomer Harlow Shapley was the prominent master of ceremonies. On the way,
trying to be interesting to Aiken, I made the remark as a strict amateur that I
felt the existence and uniqueness theorems of the mathematicians that the
physicists and applied mathematicians had spurned for decades were now
going to come into their own. What I had in mind was the concept of the
arithmetization of analysis, which had played a prominent role in motivating
the work of Weierstrass and others, now could receive a practical realization
because you could reduce so much to arithmetic. I doubt if Aiken was impressed, but I still think that my observation was important.

3. Postwar Developments

Another memorable recollection of von Neumann took place at the First
Canadian Mathematical Congress in 1945. I was unfortunate in speaking
right after von Neumann, and he for the first time unveiled his general ideas
about being able to solve problems numerically, which would defeat classical analysis, especially nonlinear partial differential equations arising from

* Works Project Administration: a classic set of mathematical tables hand computed during
1938–1948 as part of a project to provide work for unemployed mathematicians.

problems in fluid mechanics. The computer was to be a substitute for the wind tunnel. He was very inspiring; although L. F. Richardson may have had similar ideas in the 1920s, they were not supported by new ideas for computing hardware. I believe that it is today more efficient to use a computer than a wind tunnel in some transonic flow regimes. Whatever the truth is, it was a very hard act to follow, especially because just after von Neumann spoke someone got up and said this was the most exciting talk he had ever heard in his life. If you can imagine trying to speak right after such a remark you will appreciate my own feelings.*

Another speaker at that same meeting was Douglas Hartree, who spoke about using the differential analyzer to solve problems by the method of lines, a method that was developed later by Dorodnicyn. The use of an analog machine with enough arithmetic units to carry out the solution of a partial differential equation by "semidiscretization" represents, of course, a very important concept which has persisted.

There is a new package called a PDEPACK developed at the Lawrence Livermore Laboratories which tries to do the same thing. You can reduce many initial-value problems for partial differential equations to systems of ordinary differential equations, and these can be solved in principle by analog computers (e.g., by differential analyzers). It is hard to judge whether this is the right way to approach initial value problems even today, although, of course, today ordinary differential equations would be integrated on a digital machine.

Somewhat earlier, perhaps in 1944, von Neumann explained to me why he expected digital machines to be more effective than analog machines for scientific computation. By doubling the cost you can double the precision of a digital machine (number of significant decimal digits), whereas the cost of an analog machine increases by order of magnitude for even one additional decimal place. He said this to me in 1944, and I was immediately convinced by it. Von Neumann's observation was very helpful to me when David Young came to Harvard in 1946, and for the first time I ceased to be a mere observer and became a participant in the computing revolution that was taking place.

By 1947, David Young was looking for a thesis topic that would involve numerical methods. So I cast about in my mind and suggested automating the solution of Laplace's equation. I recalled being told by Walsh that the Dirichlet problem always had a solution. I was always arithmetically minded enough to be skeptical until I could see the solution, and in Walsh's lectures there was no indication given of how, given a particular set of boundary

---

* Von Neumann's own work is so well documented in his collected papers that I shall not reminisce about it further here. See, however, my article [3], which I am rewriting for publication as part of a monograph on "Numerical Fluid Mechanics."

values, you could determine the interior values. So I suggested to Young that he work on this problem.

This is a problem in scientific computing having a long background. In the plane, there is a very good five-point approximation concerning which many papers had been written by distinguished mathematicians, but mostly aimed at proving theorems, and not at computing. R. G. D. Richardson in 1917, Phillips and Wiener in 1922, Courant, Friedrichs, and Lewy in 1927 had all used this idea to prove that the Dirichlet problem was well posed, or well set, as one of the classical methods of proof. The stumbling block in applying this technique was simply that of solving large systems with simultaneous linear equations of a very particular sort. The matrix of coefficients was very sparse; it only had five nonzero entries in each row.

At the time I was unaware of the book of Kantorovich and Krylov, which was not translated into English until 1955. But it really would not have helped anyway: The main problem was not to get better difference approximations to the Laplace equation, but to solve the large system of simultaneous linear equations to which the five-point approximation led. My main concern at that time was the competition from analog methods, because there was also the electrolytic tank analogy. A whole laboratory in Paris was dedicated to the exploitation of this, and thanks to the Office of Naval Research I was able to invite Malavard from that laboratory for three months, to set up such an electrolytic tank at Harvard and use it to solve problems. I became convinced by firsthand experience that the electrolytic tank was a very delicate technique, and not really a long-range competitor to suitably planned digital computations, even for solving the Dirichlet problem.

The frontrunner among the existing methods was the relaxation method, which had been developed in England under the leadership of R. V. Southwell into a very successful technique, requiring three man-months per problem. I called on Sir Richard Southwell at Imperial College, London, and explained to him Young's thesis topic, and I told him what I wanted to do, which was to automate his ingenious method and have it so that a computer could apply it. From his wisdom as a senior scientific statesman he looked at me kindly and said, "That is absolutely impossible; the ingenuity of the human mind is much too great. Human beings get a feeling for their problems as they work with them; they develop intuitions which cannot be automated or communicated to a cold, heartless computer." After a suitable, graceful interval I left him, and went over to the other side of the hall, where I found a large drafting room in which each of ten or more graduate students was solving his own problem by pencil-and-paper arithmetic. Even desk computers were not needed: four or five digits were sufficient. Using erasers, better and better approximations having smaller and smaller "residuals" could be obtained! I said, "What do you really do?" They let me in on a secret: that they over-relaxed.

When I got back to Harvard I passed on this very valuable piece of information to David Young. Actually, his breakthrough in developing the successive over-relaxation (SOR) method, which lowered by an order of magnitude the cost of solving self-adjoint linear elliptic problems, was inspired by a numerical observation he made after computing on a desk computer all the eigenvalues of a 20×20 matrix for two processes; he observed that the second set of eigenvalues he got were the squares of the first set. It was a remarkable numerical coincidence! Then he started trying to figure out what the reason was, and this led to his theory of the SOR method for solving the Laplace equation.

Another aspect of Young's work seems worth mentioning, because our debt to European applied mathematicians was extreme during the whole period from 1935 to 1955. American mathematicians had shown their ability in pure mathematics in the decades 1895–1935, and had established themselves as equal in quality if not in numbers to their European colleagues, but they had largely neglected applied mathematics. Hilda Geiringer von Mises was very helpful in making Young realize that the theory of SOR applied rigorously not merely to the Laplace equation but also to general self-adjoint elliptic equations. His thesis was refereed several times, among others by her, and he had to rewrite it repeatedly before his exposition was considered suitable for publication in the *Transactions of the AMS*. Within two years after Young's thesis was written, and before it was published, it began to be used in industry and create employment for people who were in applications programming and numerical analysis.

All this took place from about 1945 to 1952. During these years there was another interesting event in Cambridge, and I should like to go back to Norbert Wiener. Here again I was a spectator; it must have been around 1946 or 1947. The rumor had spread that there were new computers that were like the human brain. Harvard sponsored a meeting in Emerson Hall at which the three principal speakers were von Neumann, Wiener, and Rashevsky. This was a public lecture, and the lecture room only held 500 people. There must have been 1000 more standing outside. The symposium was all about artificial intelligence, the computer and the brain, which is much more fascinating to the average person than solving the Laplace equation!

Some will remember, and I hope that an honest history will be written sometime, about McCulloch–Pitts theories and the widespread belief that the brain was some kind of a triggered neural network with all-or-none firing, and all that. The deep preprocessing and peripheral processing capabilities of the human brain were overlooked by the seers and prophets of the time. There was a feeling, I think, that this was the great wave of the future. Many of my friends kept asking me, "Aren't you afraid the computer will put mathematicians out of work?" Of course, this is the ambition of our friends, the people in artificial intelligence, but I have never quivered in terror at the thought.

I should like to say a few words about my recollections of Aiken as

Director of the Harvard Computation Laboratory. It was dedicated to discrete mathematics in spite of the computation of the Bessel functions, and Howard Aiken kept trying to induce me to work on relevant problems, particularly those involving Boolean algebra. He knew that I was under the illusion that I was an expert on Boolean algebra, and I must admit that at that time I thought it uninteresting because we could enumerate all finite Boolean algebras from the standpoint of modern algebra (i.e., up to isomorphism), and certainly you couldn't treat infinite Boolean algebras on a computer. Since then I have become somewhat wiser, I hope, and I realize that he was tackling a very deep problem in trying to find the shortest, simplest form for each Boolean polynomial, and to use it in the design of circuits. At the time I felt that it was something that would be very unrewarding for me.

Aiken had a very great gift for anticipating computer applications. I think his course in data processing was one of the first in the country. This was, I think, very forward looking of him; he saw that scientific computing was all very well, but that we must not put all our undergraduate and masters' candidates into numerical analysis and scientific computing or artificial intelligence; we must put many of them into data processing.

One of the things that should be emphasized here is the great change in our scientific and technological environment that has taken place in recent decades. I remember when Aiken was describing why he was giving the course in data processing and the great employment opportunities for M.A.s trained in it, he made the statement that in Oklahoma it cost maybe 3¢ a thousand cubic feet to produce natural gas, and 15¢ to bill the customer for it. We can see now, knowing what's happening to natural gas in the U.S., that the roles are soon going to be very much reversed.

Aiken was severely criticized behind his back by many people during these years for being so stodgy and sticking to electromechanical devices when there were electronic devices available. In this connection, I should like to quote Tony Oettinger, who talked to Aiken throughout that period. He claims that Aiken just felt that electronics (e.g., the Williams tube) was not sufficiently reliable. He was criticized from 1946 to 1952 and I think that the historians can settle whether it was in 1949 or 1951 that he became too conservative, but if we allow for the time between conceiving an idea, developing it into a practical design, getting money to support the building of a computer, and actually building it, perhaps things will fall into perspective. I suspect that Aiken was much less backward in his engineering thinking than many people claimed around 1950.

On the other hand, it is certainly true that he could be exceedingly disagreeable. Dean McGeorge Bundy told me that he had no trouble dealing with Aiken, because as soon as Aiken started pounding on the table Bundy pounded right back and Aiken got the point. I also recall a faculty committee on which I served, which was appointed to control Aiken and channel "his" computation laboratory into the general service of the faculty. It didn't take

Aiken more than one meeting to disrupt the faculty committee totally—it never had any control whatever on anything that he did.

4. Wider Trends

After the defeat of Hitler, the U.S. (along with Canada) was standing triumphant, virtually unscathed in a world in which most advanced countries were prostrate and in ashes. Its scientific preeminence was taken for granted, and most Americans thought of computing machines as almost a national monopoly. They had largely forgotten the tradition of European scientific superiority that had been generally accepted only a decade earlier. What is now known about ENIGMA and the Zuse machines should help to dispel this illusion.

By 1955, our country was entering an era when large-scale scientific computing came into widespread industrial use, having been up to then largely dedicated to problems of military science. Young's thesis was already taken up by Sheldon in 1952, and SOR began to be used in industry, I believe at General Electric. In 1954 the Bettis Atomic Power Laboratory got some IBM computers and they hired four Ph.D.s, among them Richard Varga. Varga had computed on desk machines for David Young—it was still a rather small scientific world—so at Bettis then they had four full-time mathematicians developing algorithms for use on IBM computers. Because programming languages were in their infancy, the algorithms that Varga and others developed had to be converted into machine language by professional programmers. Indeed, Varga had to bear the great cross of being told that the programmers couldn't be bothered with reprogramming some of his brilliant new algorithms, because it would disturb the reactor engineers too much to have changes made. I remember well his complaining to me about it.

I am dealing with the history of computing in the larger sense, and not with numerical analysis; I shall not go into the subsequent development of other competitors to the SOR method such as Alternate Directions Implicit (ADI), or the competition that went on between Knolls Atomic Power Laboratory at General Electric and Westinghouse with respect to which was the better method. I just want to make it clear that, by 1955, with the first commercial machines out, American industries, especially the nuclear industry but also the petroleum industry—which had been egged on by von Neumann: incidentally, he was an early consultant for the Standard Oil Development Company—were using computers and American industry has relied on them ever since. It provided employment to members of the Association for Computing Machinery, who became far more numerous than members of the American Mathematical Society, or even the Mathematical Association of America.

At Bettis, they still had in 1950 an analog network of copper bars with uniform conductivity for solving the Laplace equation and similar elliptic equations by analog methods. However, with the advent of commercial digital computers, analog machines faded permanently into the background as far as major industrial use was concerned. By the middle 1950s, the embryonic period of computers had ended; they were really substantially in their modern era.

GENERAL REFERENCES

"Bicentennial Tribute to American Mathematics" (Dalton Tarwater, ed.). Math. Assn. Amer., Washington, D.C., 1976.

G. Birkhoff and V. A. Dougalis, Numerical Fluid Dynamics (unpublished).

F. I. McShane, J. L. Kelley, and F. V. Reno, "Exterior Ballistics." Denver Univ. Press, Denver, Colorado, 1953. [See also *Math. Rev.* **15,** 657–659 (1954)].

J. von Neumann, "Collected Works," 6 vols. Pergamon, Oxford, 1961.

C. Reid, "Courant" (especially Chapter 27). Springer, New York, 1976.

S. M. Ulam, "Adventures of a Mathematician." Scribners, New York, 1976.

Norbert Wiener, "I Am a Mathematician." Doubleday, Garden City, New York, 1956.

Memorial papers on John von Neumann by Birkhoff and others, *Bull. Amer. Math. Soc.* **64,** No. 3, Part 2 (1958).

CITED REFERENCES

1. V. Bush, Instrumental analysis, *Bull. Amer. Math. Soc.* **42,** 649–669 (1946).

2. H. H. Goldstine, "The Computer from Pascal to von Neumann." Princeton Univ. Press, Princeton, New Jersey, 1972.

3. G. Birkhoff, Numerical hydrodynamics as a mathematical science, *Proc. Workshop Numer. Hydrodynam.* (L. M. Hunt, ed.), pp. 117–157. U.S. National Research Council, 1975.

DEPARTMENT OF MATHEMATICS
HARVARD UNIVERSITY
CAMBRIDGE, MASSACHUSETTS

Pioneering Work on Computers at Bletchley*

I. J. GOOD

This paper is related to the pioneering work on electronic computers at the Government Code and Cypher School at Bletchley, Buckinghamshire, during World War II. It is permissible to talk about this work because, in October 1975, photographs of COLOSSUS, one of the machines built during the war, were made available at the Public Record Office and Science Museum. Also three books have appeared related to the work done at Bletchley. The first was by Captain Winterbotham (1974), the second by Anthony Cave Brown (1975), and the third by William Stevenson (1976). All three books are very interesting, but they are concerned primarily with how the intelligence was used, and hardly at all with the methods by which it was obtained. The first two books mention another machine, the BOMBE, which was also used at Bletchley and which I shall mention again.

In this account I am handicapped in three different ways. In the first place my own knowledge is incomplete. For example, when we cryptanalysts broke a message we would not usually read the message ourselves, although we would sometimes read the first few letters to make sure there was no mistake. Instead, the keys to the message would be sent to the Intelligence Department, where the message would be deciphered and sometimes translated and where a selection would be made from the various decipherments for transmitting information to Churchill and to the armed forces.

* This paper was cleared by the British Cabinet Office in June 1976. It is essentially the text of an invited lecture given by Professor Good at the National Physical Laboratory, Teddington, England, on 28 April 1976, and is reproduced here by kind permission of the Director of the Laboratory.

I am also handicappd by my having been a *user* of machines much more than a designer, although the use affected the design. Thus, I know less about the engineering aspects than you might like to know. And my third handicap is that I have not been told that I may refer to the cryptanalytic techniques.

There were times at Bletchley when the future looked bleak for our cryptanalytic efforts. This was also true for the war effort as a whole, as you may remember from Churchill's famous "blood, tears, and sweat" speech. If you hated Hitler enough, you would fight on against fearful odds. You considered not just the small probability of success, but the large payoff if you were successful. Perhaps not everyone was like that. It was rumored that Denniston, who was at first head of Bletchley Park, and had done much for the organization, once said, "The Germans do not intend us to read their ciphers." Denniston was replaced by Commander Travis, whose personality was more that of a bulldog.

For the good of our morale, we were given a number of titbits about the results of our work.* For example, we were told it had led directly to the sinking of the Bismarck.† (I believe the historian Harry Hinsley in the translating Department, who is now a professor in Cambridge, was awarded an O.B.E. largely for that.) Also, there were times when Rommel did not receive any supplies in North Africa, because all his supply ships were being sunk as a consequence of our reading the Mediterranean ENIGMA. And obviously the reading of the U-boat traffic was tremendously valuable. Also, for the sake of our morale we were once visited by Churchill, who delivered a pep talk to a little crowd of us gathered around him on the grass. I recall that Turing was rather nervous about having to chat with Churchill. Much later another pep talk was given by Field Marshall Alexander in a hall with an audience of about a thousand. At one point he obtained a laugh by mimicking one of Montgomery's gestures.

Brian Randell, of the University of Newcastle, has prepared a long paper on the COLOSSUS, which he presented at the Los Alamos conference.‡ This paper by Randell was based on numerous interviews and is undoubtedly the best unclassified description of the history and some of the properties of the COLOSSUS. In fact, I have derived some of my information from his paper, so it's a fair exchange.

A full history of the work in Bletchley would require consulting numerous classified documents, together with further interviews with people who were allowed to be unconstrained by security considerations. Such a history might remain classified for some further time.

Owing to the rule of security known as "the need to know," which was

---

* After I wrote this report decryptions were made available to historians and a comprehensive evaluation of the effects of the cryptanalysis might be published before long.

† Included in this volume.

‡ But see the Addendum.

applied fairly rigorously during the war, there is probably no one person who could give a reasonably comprehensive account of any large project at Bletchley. People who were not at the top did not know much about matters that were not directly of their concern, and the people who *were* at the top were not fully aware of what was going on in their organization because of the complexity of the work, the advanced technology, the ingenuity, the mathematical ideas, and the variety of the cliquish technical jargon.

The easiest way to write this account is in chronological order in an autobiographical spirit. If I didn't use the autobiographical approach I wouldn't have enough to say, because I don't want to get entangled with the Official Secrets Act. In spite of the third of a century that has elapsed I think most of what I shall say is correct, especially when describing my own direct experiences. When I discuss other people's experiences I am more likely to make mistakes because, unlike Brian Randell, I have not interviewed them.

It may help to put the dates into perspective if I remind you that Britain declared war at 11:00 a.m. on 3 September 1939, and Germany capitulated on 8 May 1945. For about the first 20 months of the war I was a research mathematician in Cambridge studying under the distinguished mathematicians A. S. Besicovitch and G. H. Hardy. A number of scientists and mathematicians were on the so-called Reserve List and were not called up for military service. Perhaps the authorities remembered the poet Rupert Brook and the physicist Henry Moseley, who were both killed in 1915 in World War I. I believe the military mind in World War II was more enlightened about the use of trained minds. Or perhaps it was because World War I depended more on the Poor Bloody Infantry. At any rate, I did not join Bletchley Park, as it was called, until May 1941.

About two weeks before I went to Bletchley I met Milner-Barry at a chess match in London and I asked him whether he was at Bletchley working on German ciphers. His reply was, "No, my address is Room 47, Foreign Office." Two weeks later, when I joined Bletchley, I found he was head of a department called Hut 6, sure enough working on German ciphers.

At first, the official address at Bletchley was indeed Room 47, Foreign Office, Whitehall, London, but soon it became permissible to give one's private Bletchley address.

When I arrived at Bletchley I was met at the station by Hugh Alexander, the British chess champion. On the walk to the office Hugh revealed to me a number of secrets about the ENIGMA. Of course, we were not really supposed to talk about such things outside the precincts of the office. I shall never forget that sensational conversation. Incidentally, I think Alexander was one of the most intelligent people I've known, and I've known a lot of intelligent people.

Alexander at that time was the deputy head of a department run by the famous Alan Turing in a building known as Hut 8. The section or department contained about twelve mathematicians, four linguists, and a hundred women for mechanical clerical work, and some of them were very attractive. Turing used to refer jocularly to people who are forced to do mechanical operations as slaves. One of the clerks had a more analytical mind than the rest. She rose from the ranks and became one of the mathematical cryptanalysts. Her name was Joan Clarke. Turing was very friendly with her at one time.

Although there is a biography of Turing, written by his mother, perhaps a few words about him would be in order. When he attacked a problem he liked to start from first principles, and he was hardly influenced by received opinion. This attitude gave depth and originality to his thinking, and also it helped him to choose important problems. In discussions he was excitable, and his voice would rise to a high pitch, although he was not in the least quarrelsome. Between sentences he had a habit of saying ''Ah-ah-ah-ah-ah . . . ,'' which made it difficult to interrupt his line of thought, or even to have a line of thought of one's own!

In the first week of June each year he would get a bad attack of hay fever, and he would cycle to the office wearing a service gas mask to keep the pollen off. His bicycle had a fault: the chain would come off at regular intervals. Instead of having it mended he would count the number of times the pedals went round and would get off the bicycle in time to adjust the chain by hand. Another of his eccentricities was that he chained his mug to the radiator pipes to prevent its being stolen.

It was only after the war that we learned he was a homosexual. It was lucky the security people didn't know about it early on, because if they had known, he might not have obtained his clearance and we might have lost the war.

Our job in Hut 8 was to carry out certain complex cryptanalytic work and thus to prepare jobs for the machine known as the BOMBE, which was housed in another building. The name BOMBE was a bad code name because if it had leaked out to the Germans, we probably would have been blitzed to pieces.

Although I did not know it at first, the original ENIGMA was an unclassified machine (for enciphering plain language). It had, for example, been used by banks. Curiously enough I first learned this when I was billeted at Fenny Stratford, which was a small town close to Bletchley. Fenny Stratford was mainly distinguished by the presence of a tanning factory, which was probably both the smelliest and the ugliest building in England. From one perspective this building looked as if it had been hit by an oil bomb, although it was in fact undamaged. There was a retired banker named Burberry living in the hotel, and once he startled me by describing the ENIGMA which he had used in his bank. I probably said ''fascinating,'' and raised one eyebrow. Of course, I told him nothing about the work I was doing at the office!

The original ENIGMA machine is described in the well-known book by

David Kahn (1967). As Kahn points out, the ENIGMA was based on an earlier design by an American named Hebern. According to Kahn, Hebern was not properly compensated by the American government.

The main ingredient of the ENIGMA machine is a so-called rotor or hebern wheel. It is capable of rotating and it is wired so that the input alphabet is permuted to give an output alphabet. The original ENIGMA machine had three rotors in it together with a reflector so that the plain language letter would go through three rotors, then get reflected and come back through the same three rotors by a different route. Thus, for any fixed position of the rotors the original input alphabet would go through a succession of seven simple substitutions. Hence no letter could be enciphered as itself. But the whole effect of the machine was not merely a simple substitution since the wheels stepped in a certain way each time a letter was enciphered. The German military use of the ENIGMA was more complicated than this.

The ENIGMA was used both by the German Navy and the German Army. In Hut 8 we were only concerned with the naval ENIGMA. Hut 6 was concerned with other uses. The method of use was different in the Navy and Army so that this division of labor among the cryptanalysts was appropriate.

The U-boat ENIGMA had four rotors after a time instead of only three so it was more difficult to break.

The particular set of rotors in a machine was determined by daily keys. For example, the three rotors for the Mediterranean ENIGMA were selected from a set of eight, of permanently fixed wiring. Since the order in which they are put in the machine is relevant, the number of possible wheel orders was $8 \times 7 \times 6$. The wheel order was fixed for two days at a time. The number of initial settings for a message was about $26^3 = 17,576$ and moreover there was the additional plugboard which had $26!/(6!10!2^{10})$ possible states, changed daily. (See Kahn's photograph of the German ENIGMA in Fig. 1.) Thus, the number of possible initial states of the machine at the beginning of the message was about 9×10^{20}. For the U-boats it was about 10^{23}.

At this point it may be convenient to introduce a little terminology. The science of producing cipher systems is called cryptography, the science of attemping to break them is called cryptanalysis, and the two sciences combined are called cryptology. These words can be found, for example, in the third edition of the "Merriam–Webster Dictionary."

One might expect a cryptanalytic machine for working on a particular cryptographic machine to contain a fast model of it, or part of it, and this was true of the BOMBE. It obviously could not be sufficient merely to simulate the ENIGMA and to try all possible initial setups for a message because no machine even now would be capable of running through the 9×10^{20} possible states in a reasonable time. So there had to be some further ingenuity in the BOMBE. This I cannot describe, but I can say that Gordon Welch-

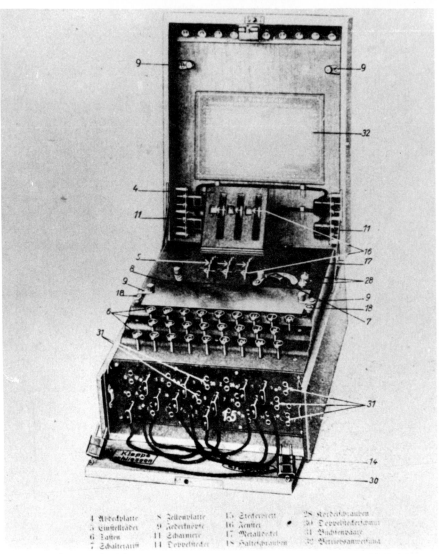

Figure 1 Photograph of the German ENIGMA machine. This photograph was kindly supplied by David Kahn, author of the well-known treatise *The Code Breakers* (Kahn, 1967), who used it also in his review of Winterbotham (1974) in the *New York Times Book Review* of 29 December 1974.

man had one of the basic ideas and Turing another one. My impression is that Turing's idea was one that might not have been thought of by anyone else for a long time, and it greatly increased the power of the BOMBE.

After I had been in Hut 8 for about a year Turing was sent to the U.S. for certain classified conferences, so that Alexander was in charge of the section. When Turing returned from America the authorities had decided to put him on another job, so that Alexander remained head of Hut 8 from that time until the end of the war. Alexander had a liking and ability for administration that Turing did not have. Alexander once said that the worst failing that an administrator could have was jealousy of those who worked for him. Turing's failing was not jealousy, but merely a lack of interest in administration.

When Turing returned from the U.S. he became a first-class marathon runner. Unfortunately, he developed some leg complaint that prevented his getting into the Olympic Games.

Hugh sometimes seemed sorry that he'd played too much chess at Cambridge and had thus failed to become a fellow of a Cambridge or Oxford College. I told Hugh that I'd once made a blunder against a weak player in Cambridge and was put on too low a board for the next two years, although I played 31 consecutive games without loss. Hence I never became a chess master. Hugh's reply was, "Lucky for you!" He was gratified to learn that most dons have the same human failings as most people.

Alexander and I were not the only chess players in Hut 8: there was also the chess master Harry Golombek, who still writes the chess column for the *Observer*, and who was one of the authors of the "Alexander Memorial Volume," which contained Alexander's best games of chess (Golombek and Hartson, 1976). There was also an expert player, Tony Perkins. Milner-Barry was another chess master who, after the war, joined the Treasury and was awarded a knighthood. He wrote a fine obituary for Hugh Alexander, which was reprinted in Golombek *et al.* (1976). The authorities, and Hugh Alexander himself, presumably believed that chess players were likely to be good cryptanalysts (see Fig. 2.) Perhaps a better rule is to choose people who are skillful in two distinct areas.

The BOMBE was essentially an electromagnetic relay machine, more than electronic, and it was extremely special purpose. After the first BOMBES were produced the Americans were informed about them, and they eventually produced faster and better ones. Winterbotham describes the BOMBE as a "bronze goddess." It was about 8 ft high and had wheels corresponding to the rotors of the ENIGMA, together with other complicated circuits. It was presumably the world's first large fast cryptanalytic machine, but I do not know what the Russians had.

When Max Newman started his section, which dealt with another problem, I was transferred from Hut 8 to Hut F, the Newmanry. In my opinion Max Newman has a gestalt mind, that is, the ability to see matters as a whole. Of course, like any mathematician he could attend to details also, when necessary.

A few months after I was transferred to Hut F, Shaun Wylie followed and, later still, two other members of Hut 8 arrived (Michael Ashcroft and Arthur Chamberlain). Shaun Wylie had a very exact logical mind. When he understood anything he seemed to understand it completely. He was a human embodiment of Wittgenstein's saying that if anything can be said at all it can be said clearly. Also, Shaun was president of the "Bletchley Park" Dramatic Club, an international hockey player, a first-class teacher, and a winner of the unarmed combat competition of the local battalion of the

(a)

(b)

Figure 2 (a) Chess players on the steps of Balliol College Hall during a match between Bletchley Park and Oxford University on 2 December 1944. The match, which B.P. won by 8 to 4, was reported in the *British Chess Magazine* of February 1945. (b) Legend: 1, T. H. Tyler (later Sir Theodore) (Ox); 2, C. H. O'D. Alexander (B.P.); 4, J. W. Cornforth (Ox); 5, Art Levensen (B.P.); 6, Harry Golombek (B.P.); 8, H. G. Schenck (Ox); 9, I. J. Good (B.P.); 10, Walter W. Jacobs (B.P.); 11, Sir Robert Robinson (Ox); 13, J. M. Aitken (B.P.); 14, David Rees (B.P.); 16, Peter J. Hilton (B.P.); 17, Tony Perkins (B.P.); 18, Mac Chamberlain (B.P.). [Others not remembered.]

Home Guard. He never mentioned any of his successes. I once noticed an acknowledgement to him in Hardy and Wright's "Theory of Numbers" and the next morning I called him "Dr. Wylie." He said, "You must have been reading Hardy and Wright." Shaun was a perfect gentleman who never lost his temper except on purpose, and was an extremely good listener. I used to believe that he wouldn't interrupt a conversation even to mention that the war was over. Among other cryptanalysts who later joined the Newmanry was J. H. C. Whitehead, the famous topologist. He had a low opinion of the theological speculations of his uncle, the famous philosopher A. N. White-head. Also, he once remarked that "Bertrand Russell would have been a better philosopher if he had been a better mathematician," and that Russell had used up too much of his mathematical energy on "Principia Mathematica" (written jointly with A. N. Whitehead). In spite of these caustic remarks, Henry Whitehead was genial and enthusiastic.

Another member of the Newmanry was Michael Crum, a son of a Deacon of Canterbury. He was another first-class intellect, with very high ethical standards both for himself and others. I should rather tell a risqué story to a lady than to Michael.

Peter J. Hilton, now a professor at Seattle, and who later wrote a joint book on homology with Shaun Wylie, was in an allied section called Major Tester's Section, or the Testery. Hilton had previously worked in Hut 8 for a short time. In the Testery he was a tower of strength and my impression is that his production was about equal to that of the whole of the rest of that section. He had a very quick mind. He was also very good at telling dirty jokes. Roy Jenkins, now a Cabinet Minister, was also in the Testery, as was Peter Benenson, who later became prominent in Amnesty International.

When I arrived in Hut F, which I believe was the autumn of 1942, Donald Michie was the only other cryptanalytic assistant to Newman. I think Michie had been in the Newmanry for a week or so. He was the only cryptanalyst in the Newmanry who was not a mathematician; in fact he had won a major scholarship at Balliol College in classics. His wartime experiences inveigled him into scientific work and he is now a professor of machine intelligence at Edinburgh. A few years ago he invited me to talk about computer chess at Syracuse, New York, when he was a visiting professor there. When introducing me he said my first words to him were, "I'm Good," and he said I'd been getting better ever since.

When I arrived in the Newmanry there were several Wrens,* one of whom, Odette, later married Shaun Wylie. They were the thinnest healthy couple I've met. An electronic machine called HEATH ROBINSON had just started working when I arrived, although it had many teething troubles

---

* WRNS: Women's Royal Naval Service.

that were never eliminated.* Its vertical cross section was about the size of a couple of doors. Its input was from two five-hole paper tapes, which it read at 2000 characters/sec. It surprised me that the paper tape was strong enough not to tear as soon as the machine was switched on. The tapes were driven by their sprocket holes as well as by pulleys, and analysis was carried out by means of photoelectric readers and electronic circuits. My present impression is that HEATH ROBINSON had between 30 and 80 valves. The main designer was Wynn-Williams of TRE† with important help from E. A. Speight, Arnold C. Lynch, D. A. Campbell, and F. O. Morrell, all at the Post Office Research Station at Dollis Hill. Incidentally, I had known Arnold Lynch in the chess world but never knew until much later that we had both worked on the same problem. Speight and Lynch designed the photoelectric reader. The output of HEATH ROBINSON was a primitive printer. As you may guess from its name, this machine had been put together with emphasis on speed of completion more than on reliability. In fact, so many things could go wrong, with the machine and tape preparation, that the success rate was extremely low and discouraging for some weeks, and the future of the Newmanry was perhaps in the balance. (Max Newman knows more about that.) By introducing more checks into the entire system and also by other research carried out by Michie and myself, the success rate was improved enough to show the reasonableness of Newman's faith in a machine attack on the problem in hand. Thus, funds were made available for a more powerful machine, namely, the COLOSSUS. The main specification of this machine was also Newman's and the main engineering design was by T. H. Flowers of the Post Office Research Station at Dollis Hill. Among other highly important engineers who worked on this machine were S. W. Broadhurst, W. W. Chandler, and A. W. M. Coombs. I believe that Michie and I had a small influence on the design of the first COLOSSUS and very important influence on MARK II.

I was often able to recognize that HEATH ROBINSON had gone wrong and to diagnose the fault from the kind of noises that it made. The COLOSSUS was much more carefully engineered so that its faults could not usually be diagnosed by sound. This is a disadvantage of a well-built machine! In one sense HEATH ROBINSON was almost human since one of its ailments could be diagnosed by smell! This was when it became overheated and tried to catch fire. But as Randell says in his report, "Although the ROBINSONS produced only a small amount of output which was of value in itself, they played an enormously important role in preparing the way for the successful use of the COLOSSI" (Randell, 1976).

The COLOSSUS had only one input tape because the function of the

---

* The cartoonist Heath Robinson was the British counterpart of Rube Goldberg. They both specialized in cartoons of crazy machines.

† TRE: Telecommunications Research Establishment.

other input tape was represented in the internal electronics of the machine. One important advantage of this was that it avoided the need for a great deal of additional tape preparation. Another advantage was that the driving of the tape could be entirely by pulleys without the need to synchronize two tapes by any sprockethole driving. The machine was programmed largely by means of plugboards and it was capable of flexible Boolean operations. It read the tape at 5000 characters/sec and, at least in MARK II, the circuits were in quintuplicate so that in a sense the reading speed was 25,000 bits/sec. This compares well with the speed of the electronic computers of the early 1950s. The later COLOSSI were capable of carrying out more than 10^{11} consecutive elementary Boolean (and/or) operations without error, which is a tribute both to the engineering design and to the level of maintenance. The first COLOSSUS had 1500 valves, which was probably far more than for any electronic machine previously used for any purpose. This was one reason why many people did not expect COLOSSUS to work. But it was installed in December 1943 and began producing results almost immediately. Most of the failures of valves were caused by switching the machine on and off.

According to Randell's report, in about March 1944 the Post Office was told that more machines were required by 1 June (Randell, 1976). This was an impossible request, but by dint of an enormous effort in Dollis Hill and at Bletchley, the first MARK II COLOSSUS started work exactly on 1 June, five days before D day. Half the facilities at the Post Office Research Station were devoted to the project, according to Brian Randell's report.

One of the main uses of a COLOSSUS involved a synergy between man and machine that has been achieved with ordinary computers only during the last few years. ("Symbiosis" is a wrong term since COLOSSUS was not biological.) The analyst would sit at the typewriter output and call out instructions to a Wren to make changes in the programs. Some of the other uses were eventually reduced to decision trees and were handed over to the machine operators (Wrens).

The organization of the department was fairly democratic. If anyone had an idea concerning operations or research he would write on the blackboard in the Research Room an item for the agenda of a "Tea Party." These Tea Parties were free-for-all informal meetings where many decisions were made.

The flexibility of COLOSSUS was such that in principle one could almost do ordinary radix 10 multiplication on it. This was demonstrated at the end of the war by Geoffrey Timms. I say "almost" because the circuits for this job became so complicated that the pulses were delayed to the succeeding clock pulse. The clock pulses were generated by the photoelectric reader of the sprocket holes, thus automatically achieving synchronization of the electronics with the mechanical part of the input.

Although there was no point in doing radix 10 multiplication, the capability shows that the machine was in principle more general purpose than its designer intended. Basically this is because ordinary calculations can be expressed in Boolean terms. Another feature of the COLOSSUS that made it resemble to some extent a general-purpose electronic computer was the feature of conditional branching. I cannot give the explanation of this because it might involve some information that is still classified.

Part of the program could be changed quickly by means of toggle switches, which were connected to produce circuits in series or in parallel as required.

The COLOSSI produced quite a bit of heat, and it was once proposed that the operators should be topless.

A brief description of COLOSSUS is given in the Public Record Office, which I quote here, with slight modifications. I shall here repeat some of what I said before.

Colossus had the following facilities:

(a) five-hole punched paper tape input, read at 5000 characters/sec;
(b) photoelectric tape readers;
(c) clock pulses produced from reading the sprocket holes;
(d) bistable valve circuits performing counting, binary arithmetic, and Boolean logical operations;
(e) conditional (branching) logic;
(f) logic functions preset by a plugboard and toggle switches, or conditionally selected by telephone relays*;
(g) fully automatic operation;
(h) electric typewriter output (about 15 characters/sec);
(i) about 1500 valves (MARK II had about 2500, I believe);
(j) parallel (quintupled) circuitry for additional speed, at least for the MARK II version.

Photographs of Colossus are available at the Public Record Office and are on display at the Science Museum in London.†

At the end of the war Newman left almost immediately to take up his new post as a professor at Manchester University, and he asked me to edit the history of his department. This history was written in conjunction with Donald Michie and Geoffrey Timms. I was able to write my part very quickly because I had the work more at my fingertips than anything else I've known, and, when I left, Donald Michie was in charge of the editing for a short time.

---

* There were two kinds of plugboard. One was quick to use and was on the front of the machine, whereas the other was slower, plugged less frequently, and was on the back.

† They are reproduced in the paper by Randell in this volume.

We decided in advance to limit the history to 500 pages: it would have been easier to write 1500 pages. Meanwhile Newman appointed me as a lecturer in mathematics at Manchester university with some responsibility for the electronic computer, and David Rees had a similar appointment as an assistant lecturer. I left Bletchley on 28 September 1945. I have preserved most of the notes I made on electronic computers during the $2\frac{1}{2}$ years that I was in Manchester, but that's another story, although it does form a small part of the early history of electronic computers.

Addendum

I am writing this addendum primarily to make a correction that depends on information released since I delivered my NPL lecture in September 1976. The correction refers to the sinking of the Bismarck (sunk at 10:36 a.m., 27 May 1941). The statement I made on this topic seemed to agree well enough with Winterbotham (1974, pp. 82–84) but seems to be contradicted by the new declassified information. There is a fascinating chapter on the topic in the book by Beesly (1977). Beesly says that cryptanalysis played only a small part in this battle. In case this should give the wrong impression about the effects of cryptanalysis as a whole he goes on to say that "B.P.'s [Bletchley Park's] enormous contribution to the war at sea was still to be made." This large contribution started in June 1941. For example, Beesly says that cryptanalysis "certainly enabled the Admiralty to deliver a shattering blow against her [the Bismarck's] supply ship organization, which virtually ruled out any further long distance cruises by the remaining heavy units . . . ." At Bletchley some of us thought one of our decryptions made a critical difference to the sinking of the Bismarck because we did not know it had already been located. In a conversation with me in February 1977, the military historian Ronald Lewin suggested this explanation of our apparent misconception.

Beesly says (1977, p. 61) that B.P.'s work constituted for years the Operational Intelligence Centre's "most priceless source of intelligence." To mention just one example, the sinking of the Scharnhorst on 26 December 1942 was greatly helped by "Special Intelligence" according to Beesly's account. One of the messages was in Offizier cipher (Beesly, 1977, p. 210), which meant encipherment of the encipherment. (This reminds me incidentally of an occasion on which we were unable to decipher an Offizier message owing to a mistake made by the German encipherer. The next night I dreamt that he had done the two encipherments in the wrong order and this turned out to be correct. It will never be known whether this particular message was important.)

Beesly says (1977, p. 160) that the only way to control the battle of the Atlantic was as if it were a game of chess (in spite of the loss of lives). If it hadn't been that both sides were reading some of the other's ciphers it would have been like a game of Kriegspiel. (Kriegspiel is a form of chess in which the positions of the opponent's men are unknown, but the umpire informs a player when his own pieces are taken.) As it was, the battle was intermediate between Kriegspiel and chess in so far as it could be regarded as a "game."

Beesly also mentions (1977, p. 162) that both sides had suspicions about the security of their own cryptographic systems, but the Germans thought "treason" (i.e., loyalty to humanity) was the more likely source of our uncanny information.

Historians are naturally interested in the effects of cryptanalysis on World War II, and in December 1976 there was a session on "cryptanalysis and intelligence in the European theater" in the annual meetings of the American Historical Association in Washington, D.C. Two of the speakers were David Kahn and Jürgen Rohwer. Rohwer is a German historian who served on a mine-sweeper and who has an extensive knowledge of the battle of the Atlantic. Some of this knowledge was obtained by him from the British government (see Rohwer, 1977). His help was acknowledged in Beesly (1977). Ronald Lewin is also working on a book on a similar subject (Lewin, 1978). He has already published books on Rommel, Montgomery, Churchill's war administration, and Field Marshall Slim. Lewin was head of the BBC Home Service for many years and has contacts in high places. Incidentally, the BBC has published a book "The Secret War" (Johnson, 1978) which is based on a series of broadcasts with the same title one of which was concerned with cryptanalysis. Another relevant work has been written by R. V. Jones, who was Assistant Director of Research at the Air Ministry (see Jones, 1978).

In November 1978, a conference on Ultra was held in Germany and has been reported by Kahn (1979).

The official history of wartime intelligence is being prepared by Harry Hinsley and I hope it will be available to the public.

REFERENCES

Beesly, P. (1977). "Very Special Intelligence: The Story of the Admiralty's Operational Intelligence Centre, 1939–1945." Hamish Hamilton, London.

Brown, A. C. (1975). "Bodyguard of Lies." Harper, New York.

Golombek, H., and Hartson, W. (1976). "The Best Games of C. H. O'D. Alexander" (with a memoir by Sir Stuart Milner-Barry). Oxford Univ. Press, London and New York.

Johnson, B. (1978). "The Secret War." British Broadcasting Corporation, London.

Jones, R. V. (1978). "Most Secret War." Hamish Hamilton, London. American edition: "The Wizard War." Coward, McCann, and Geoghegen, New York.

Kahn, D. (1967). "The Code Breakers." Macmillan, New York.

Kahn, D. (1979). The Ultra Conference, *Cryptologia* **3**, 1–8.

Lewin, R. (1978). "Ultra Goes to War." Hutchinson, London. [Also McGraw-Hill, New York, 1979.]

Randell, B. (1976). The Colossus, this volume.
Rohwer, J. (1977). "The Critical Convoy Battles of March 1943." Naval Institute Press, Annapolis, Maryland.
Stevenson, W. (1976). "A Man Called Intrepid." Harcourt, New York.
Winterbotham, F. W. (1974). "The Ultra Secret." Harper, New York.

DEPARTMENT OF STATISTICS
VIRGINIA POLYTECHNIC INSTITUTE AND STATE UNIVERSITY
BLACKSBURG, VIRGINIA

The COLOSSUS

B. RANDELL

In October 1975, after an official silence lasting 32 years, the British Government made a set of captioned photographs of COLOSSUS available at the Public Record Office. These confirm the fact that a series of programmable electronic digital computers was built in Britain during World War II, the first being operational in 1943. It is stated that COLOSSUS incorporated 1500 valves, and operated in parallel arithmetic mode at 5000 pulses/sec. A number of its features are disclosed, including that it had 5000 character/sec punched paper tape inputs, electronic circuits for counting, binary arithmetic and Boolean logic operations, "electronic storage registers changeable by an automatically controlled sequence of operations," "conditional (branching) logic," "logic functions pre-set by patch-panels or switches, or conditionally selected by telephone relays," and typewriter output.

Professor M. H. A. Newman is named as being responsible for formulating the requirements for COLOSSUS, and Mr. T. H. Flowers as leading the team which developed the machine. An indication is given that the design of COLOSSUS was influenced by the prewar work on computability by Alan Turing, who was employed in the same department of the British Government as Newman.

The partial relaxation of the official secrecy surrounding COLOSSUS has made it possible to obtain interviews with a number of people involved in the project. This paper is in the main based on these interviews, and is supplemented by material already in the public domain. It attempts to document as fully as is now permissible the story of the development of CO-LOSSUS. Particular attention is paid to interactions between the COLOSSUS project and other work carried out elsewhere on digital techniques and computers, and to the role that those involved with COLOSSUS played in postwar computer developments in Britain.

Details are given of the careers of the people involved, of how the basic concept of CO-LOSSUS was arrived at, of how the first machine was designed and built, and of the subsequent design and construction of a MARK II version. The paper also attempts to assess Turing's role in the COLOSSUS story, and to relate the work to contemporary work in the U.S., particularly that on ENIAC. The official photographs and the accompanying explanatory captions are reproduced in the paper.

47

1. Introduction

Babbage's work in 1837 first established the logical principles of digital computers. His ideas were developed further in Turing's classical paper in 1936. The COLOSSUS machine produced by the Department of Communications of the British Foreign Office, and put into operation in December 1943, was probably the first system to implement these principles successfully in terms of contemporary technology . . . . The requirement for the machine was formulated by Professor M. H. A. Newman, and the development was undertaken by a small team led by T. H. Flowers. A. Turing was working in the same department at that time, and his earlier work had its full influence on the design concept.

These statements are quoted from the explanatory caption accompanying a set of photographs of COLOSSUS that were made available at the Public Record Office in London on 20 October 1975. (The explanatory caption is reproduced in its entirety in the Appendix, and the photographs as Figs. 1–5). Thus 32 years later, the British Government has at last declassified, at least partially, the electronic computers developed secretly in Britain during

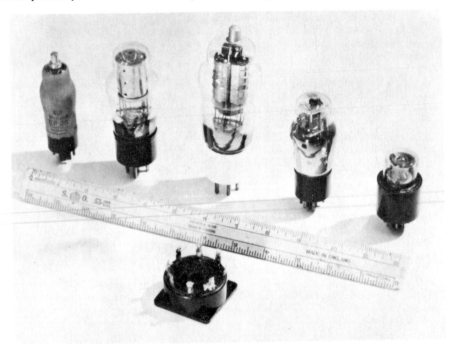

Figure 1   The valves used in COLOSSUS, showing the four valves and the photoelectric cell that were most commonly used throughout COLOSSUS. They are (left to right) EF 36, GTIC, 807, L63, and photocell RCA. In the foreground is the surface mounting octal valve holder used extensively throughout this machine.

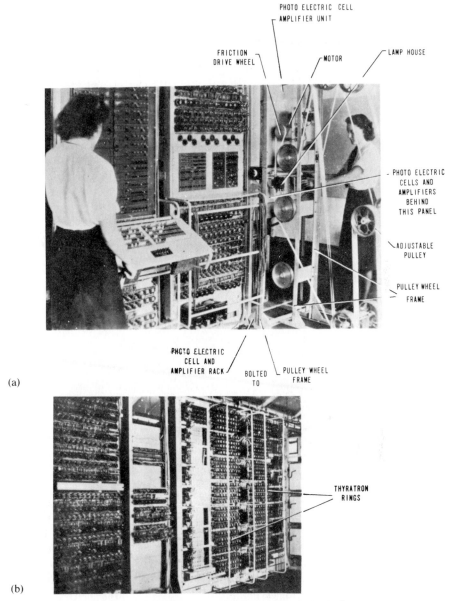

PHOTO ELECTRIC CELL
AMPLIFIER UNIT

FRICTION
DRIVE WHEEL

MOTOR

LAMP HOUSE

PHOTO ELECTRIC
CELLS AND
AMPLIFIERS
BEHIND
THIS PANEL

ADJUSTABLE
PULLEY

PULLEY WHEEL
FRAME

(a)

PHOTO ELECTRIC
CELL AND
AMPLIFIER RACK

BOLTED
TO

PULLEY WHEEL
FRAME

THYRATRON
RINGS

(b)

Figure 2   COLOSSUS, (a) front view and (b) back view.

Figure 3   COLOSSUS, view of front racks and bedsteads.

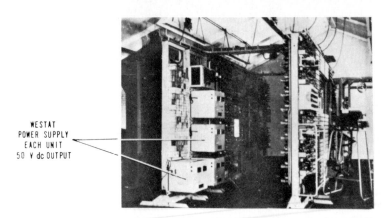

Figure 4   COLOSSUS, side view.

World War II. Over the years a number of requests had been made to the Government to declassify the COLOSSI. I myself made one such request in 1972, which although unsuccessful did lead to my receiving an assurance from the Prime Minister's Office that an official history would be prepared, although this history would have to remain classified [61]. During recent years a few details about the COLOSSI have been disclosed by some of the people involved—these details were summarized in a two-page article by Michie [63]. The present release provides welcome official confirmation of the overall accuracy of this summary and indeed provides some further technical details. However, the release makes it clear by implication that the Government still regards the detailed logical design, and the use made of the

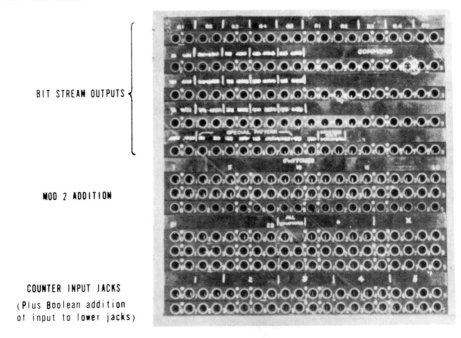

BIT STREAM OUTPUTS

MOD 2 ADDITION

COUNTER INPUT JACKS
(Plus Boolean addition
of input to lower jacks)

JACK FIELD

Figure 5   COLOSSUS, view of jack field.

COLOSSI, as classified. My understanding is that the promised history has been completed, but remains secret—fortunately the security relaxation has been sufficient for me to obtain assistance in interviewing a number of the people who were most closely involved in the design and use of the CO-LOSSI. The aim has been to attempt to clarify the relationship of the CO-LOSSUS work to other better-known work on electronic computers and devices, and thus provide an appropriate perspective on COLOSSUS with respect to the history of digital computers, both American and British. The present paper is in the main based on these interviews, but is supplemented by material already in the public domain. To the best of my knowledge I have managed to collate all the releasable and verifiable information on CO-LOSSUS and its significance in the history of electronic digital computers.

However, a word of warning is in order at this point. The people I interviewed were being asked to recall happenings of 30 or so years ago, and to do so without any opportunity to inspect original files and documents. Many of them had made conscious efforts to forget about their Foreign Office work as soon as they returned to their normal professions in 1945. During the war, secrecy considerations were paramount and gave rise to a rigid compartmentalization of activities so that few would have any detailed knowledge of the work outside their own small group. I have therefore tried where possible to obtain confirmation of what I learned from each person by asking similar questions of his colleagues, and have tried to document the exact source (or sources) of each item reported. However, it is to be expected that if and when the files documenting the wartime work of the Foreign Office's Department of Communications are declassified the present account will be seen to be fragmentary and far from exact. Moreover, only then will it be possible to see COLOSSUS in its true perspective as a tool developed for a particularly urgent wartime need—the present account has perforce to concentrate on COLOSSUS itself, and so runs the risk of providing a rather distorted view of the events that it attempts to chronicle.

2. Turing and Babbage

The work that Alan Turing documented in his famous paper, On Computable Numbers with an Application to the Entscheidungsproblem (published in 1937), was done while he was at King's College, Cambridge. He had gone to King's as a mathematical scholar in 1931, at the age of 19, and was elected to a Fellowship in 1935 [79]. M. H. A. Newman (Fig. 6) had been a University Lecturer in Mathematics at Cambridge since 1924, and it is believed that Turing's work was sparked off by one of Newman's lectures. This was a lecture in which Newman discussed Hilbert's view that any mathematical problem can be solved by a fixed and definite process [69]. Turing seized on Newman's phraseology, "a purely mechanical process," and interpreted it as "something that could be done by an automatic machine." He introduced a simple abstract machine in order to prove Hilbert was wrong, and in fact showed that there is a "universal automaton" that can perform any calculation that any special automaton can, if first provided with the appropriate instructions as input.

Turing thus was the first to arrive at an understanding of the universal nature of a (conceptual) digital computer that matches and indeed surpasses

Figure 6   Professor M. H. A. Newman.

the philosophic understanding that I believe Babbage had attained, a century earlier, of the universality of his planned (mechanical) Analytical Engine. Babbage's phrasing was "that the whole of the conditions which enable a *finite* machine to make calculations of *unlimited* extent are fulfilled in the Analytical Engine" [2 p. 128], where the term "extent" encompassed both the amount and accuracy of the data to be processed, and the length and logical complexity of the algorithm to be performed. Central to the Universal Turing Machine is the idea of having data, and input data in particular, represent a program (called a "table" in Turing's paper). A hitherto little-known manuscript by Babbage [1], which has recently been published for the first time, makes it clear that Babbage had reached an almost similar level of understanding. In the manuscript he points out that a fully detailed sequence of "formula cards" might be prepared by the Analytical Engine from a more abstract sequence. However, this is not to say that Turing's work was in any way derived from Babbage's—indeed there is no evidence that Turing even knew of Babbage at this time, but this topic will be returned to later.

In September 1936, Turing left Cambridge to spend a year in the Mathematics Department of Princeton University [79], where the staff included Church, Courant, Hardy, Einstein, and von Neumann. He spent the summer of 1937 back in Britain, and returned to Princeton on a Procter Fellowship, receiving his Ph.D. in 1938. Von Neumann "was enormously intrigued with" [40] his idea of a universal automaton, and offered Turing a post as his assistant. This offer was refused and Turing returned in the summer of 1938 to King's College, Cambridge, where his fellowship had been renewed [39, 79]. According to the biography written by his mother, Turing was taken on as a temporary Civil Servant in the Foreign Office in the Department of Communications immediately following the declaration of war. At first his whereabouts were kept secret, though it was divulged later that he was working at Bletchley Park [80].

3. Bletchley Park

The nature of the work undertaken at Bletchley Park (Fig. 7) during World War II is still secret, but statements have been appearing in published works in recent years that strongly suggest that it included an important part of the British Government's cryptologic effort. It was referred to somewhat briefly in Kahn's massive survey [50] published in 1967, and in various later books. Muggeridge described it as "a manor house . . . [where] the staff were a curious mixture of mathematicians, dons of various kinds, chess and crossword maestros [and] an odd musician or two . . ." [68, p. 128]. Seale and McConville state that during the war it housed the Government Code and Cypher School ("known to its inmates as the Golf Club and Chess Society" [75, p. 144]).

Figure 7   Bletchley Park as it is now. Two original wartime huts can be seen on the right.

Bletchley is also referred to in Winterbotham's book [88]. The book's one reference to computers comes in the statement, "It is no longer a secret that the backroom boys of Bletchley used the new science of electronics to help them . . . . I am not of the computer age nor do I attempt to understand them, but early in 1940 I was ushered with great solemnity into the shrine where stood a bronze-coloured face, like some Eastern Goddess who was destined to become the oracle of Bletchley" [88, p. 15].* (The book also made the surprising statement that Babbage worked at Bletchley Park: but this turns out to be Dr. D. W. Babbage, who is now President of Magdalene College, Cambridge. Dr. Babbage is in fact a distant relative, though not a direct descendant, of Charles Babbage [3].) Subsequently, in a lengthy newspaper article prompted by Winterbotham's book, Calvocoressi referred to the use at Bletchley of "machines called bombs which were prototype computers" [8]. The book also spurred Kozaczuk to write an article containing the claim that the Bletchley Park work was in part based on work done in Poland before the war that had involved the construction of "bombs" that were "complex electronic units with tens of thousands of subassemblies and details" [53, p. 33]. However, the brief description that he provides gives the impression that these were similar in concept to Lehmer's "photo-electric number sieve" [55], a basically electromechanical device used to tackle problems in number theory, in particular, to search for primes.

The recently published book by Cave Brown [13] also refers to a machine called "The Bomb," which was designed by Turing [13]. Quoting Cave Brown,

> Specifications were soon ready, and they were with the engineers during the last quarter of 1938. The contract went to the British Tabulating Machine Company at Letchworth, not far from Bletchley, and BTM assigned the task of building 'The Bomb'—as the Turing Engine came to be called—to its Chief Engineer, Harold Keen, and a team of twelve

---

* Quoted by permission of F. W. Winterbotham and of Weidenfeld and Nicolson.

men . . . . It was a copper-coloured cabinet some 8 feet tall and perhaps 8 feet wide at its base, shaped like an old-fashioned keyhole. And inside the cabinet was a piece of engineering which defied description. As Keen said, it was not a computer, and 'There was no other machine like it. It was unique, built especially for [its] purpose. Neither was it a complex tabulating machine.' . . . Its initial performance was uncertain, and its sound was strange; it made a noise like a battery of knitting needles as it worked . . . [13, pp. 22–23].*

I can in no way vouch for Cave Brown's statements, impressively detailed though they are. Indeed, the dates he gives for Turing's involvement are not consistent with the statement quoted earlier from Turing's biography implying that he joined the Foreign Office in September 1939. Furthermore, the description of the Turing Engine does not seem to match the implication that it was related to the concept of the Universal Turing Machine.

My investigation has concentrated on COLOSSUS, and there seems no doubt that the work on COLOSSUS postdates by a couple of years the work on "The Bomb" referred to by Brown and Winterbotham. I have learned from Mr. T. H. Flowers and Professor M. H. A. Newman that their involvement with the Foreign Office work dates from February 1941 and September 1942, respectively [28, 70]. This adds credence to Kahn's statement in a review of Winterbotham's book that it was in order to solve other problems that "the Bletchley geniuses evolved perhaps the first modern electronic computer which they nicknamed 'COLOSSUS' " [52]. However, questions concerning the use made of COLOSSUS are outside the scope of this paper.

4.   T. H. Flowers

In 1941, Mr. T. H. Flowers (Fig. 8) was in charge of the switching group at the Post Office Research Station, which was situated at Dollis Hill in northwest London [29]. The group at this time contained about ten graduate engineers and 50 persons in all, and was the biggest group in the Research Station. Flowers had joined the Research Station as a probationary engineer in 1930 after serving his apprenticeship at Woolwich Arsenal [5, 28]. His major research interest over the years had been long-distance signalling, and in particular the problem of transmitting control signals, enabling human operators to be replaced by automatic switching equipment. Even at this early date he had considerable experience with electronics, having started research on the use of electronic valves for telephone switching in 1931. This work had resulted in an experimental toll dialing circuit that was certainly operational in 1935, as he recalls using it to telephone his fiancée, whom he married in that

---

* Quoted by permission of Antony Cave Brown and W. H. Allen Ltd.

Figure 8   Mr. T. H. Flowers.

year. The first production system is believed to have been installed by 1939 [29, 30].

However, Flowers and his switching group had worked on a great variety of research topics—as he has put it "work was fired at us from all directions" [29, p. 3]. He had used thyratrons for counting purposes, and he had some contact with C. A. Beevers, an x-ray crystallographer who was working on a special-purpose digital calculator made from electromechanical telephone switching components [4]. This was perhaps Flowers's earliest direct contact with digital computation, although he did know Comrie and his work. On the analog side, he had some knowledge of the differential analyzer at Manchester University, having seen it there at an exhibition in 1937 [28], and later having Alan Fairweather, one of the graduates who had worked on it, as a member of his staff.

As war approached Flowers became involved with various special projects. One involved an electromechanical digital device for anti-aircraft ranging, originated by Dr. Hart of the Royal Aircraft Establishment, Farnborough [29]. However, this project, being based on sound detection, was a cause of some embarrassment to Flowers, who had since 1937 been cleared to receive information about what later came to be known as radar. He thus knew that Hart's project was likely to be obsolete before completion, but was not able to tell the others of this fact.

In February 1941, Flowers was approached by Dr. W. G. (later Sir W. Gordon) Radley, Director of the Post Office Research Station, to work on a problem for Bletchley Park [29]. Until this time he had reported to Radley through a division head. However, even the division head was not told of the Bletchley Park request, for security reasons, and from then on Flowers reported directly to Radley. Apparently Flowers and Radley were the first Post Office people to be initiated into the work at Bletchley Park [30]. Flowers had the impression that he had been approached at the suggestion of Dr. C. E. Wynn-Williams, and that Wynn-Williams was, with Turing, among the first people he met at Bletchley [28, 29]. However, Dr. Wynn-Williams has stated that he did not get involved with Foreign Office work until November 1941 [94]. It was Dr. Wynn-Williams who pioneered the use of electronics for high-speed counters used in nuclear physics research. At the Cavendish Laboratory in 1931 he built the first electronic binary counter, using thyratrons [92]. By 1935 such a counter had been incorporated into a device which, by means of electromagnetic relays and uniselectors, provided binary–decimal conversion and automatic printing. Wynn-Williams moved from the Cavendish Laboratory to Imperial College in 1935 and by 1939 he had built a second version of this apparatus incorporating "a programme device . . . which could control experimental conditions and carry out cycles of pre-arranged runs by remote control of the equipment" [93].

Wynn-Williams was released by Imperial College, when war broke out in 1939, to join the radar program at TRE (Telecommunications Research Establishment) as it later became known after its move to Malvern in May 1942. (Wynn-Williams was first stationed at Dundee and then from May 1940 at Swanage [96].)

Flowers's next six months were spent building a special-purpose electromechanical device for Bletchley Park [29]. The work was done mainly at Dollis Hill, but Flowers spent a lot of time at Bletchley Park, where he worked with Turing and Mr. W. Gordon Welchman [29]. (Welchman was a Fellow of Sidney Sussex College, Cambridge, and at Bletchley Park became Assistant Director for Mechanization [70]. After the war he spent three years as Director of Research for the John Lewis Partnership and then went to the U.S. and entered, or perhaps one should say re-entered, the computer field. He headed the applications research phase of the Whirlwind computer project at MIT for a few years, and then worked for various American and British computer companies—ERA, Remington Rand, and Ferranti. Welchman in fact gave the first course on digital computers in the Electrical Engineering Department at MIT [84, 85].) Turing paid several visits to Dollis Hill at this time for discussions with Flowers, but for security reasons the majority of their meetings were held at Bletchley Park [5, 29].

During this period one of Flowers's colleagues at Dollis Hill, Mr. S. W. Broadhurst (Fig. 9), was brought in to help with the project as soon as he received security clearance [5, 28, 29]. Broadhurst's forte was electromechanical equipment. He had, in his own words, "come up the hard way, but it was quite enjoyable"—having joined the Post Office as a workman. He had taken this job to tide him over while he continued to look for an engineering job after finishing his apprenticeship with the South–East and Chatham Railway in 1923 [5, 6]. He was soon upgraded and served for a period on commissioning and maintaining one of the early automatic exchanges before being transferred to the newly formed Circuit Laboratory at Post Office Headquarters. From there he went to the P. O. Engineering Training School and later to Dollis Hill. Here he taught courses on automatic telephony,

Figure 9 Mr. S. W. Broadhurst.

which was then a fairly new subject within the Post Office. Eventually he
was promoted into the Research Branch, joining Flowers's group, in which
he spent the first 18 months of the war working on various projects associated with radar.

The device that Flowers and Broadhurst built for Turing involved the use
of high-speed rotary switches [29]. It could be described as a type of computer, with much of the data and logic on banks of switches [28]. However, it
was straightforward engineering work with nothing in the way of arithmetic
or programming facilities. In fact the whole project turned out to have been a
mistake, as the speed requirement that was initially specified turned out to
have been grossly underestimated [29]. Flowers has the impression that one
of the reasons they were then introduced to some of the other problems at
Bletchley Park was that the people there felt somewhat guilty at having
wasted his and Broadhurst's time [29].

At this stage another of Flowers's staff, Mr. W. W. Chandler (Fig. 10),
joined in the work for Bletchley Park. Chandler was the youngest of the three,

Figure 10 Mr. W. W. Chandler.

having joined Dollis Hill as a trainee in 1936. His main work since then had been on voice frequency signalling for trunk lines, with a Mr. Hadfield. This he believes was the first use of thermionic valves for switching purposes in Post Office communications [15]. In fact Flowers has described Chandler as the most "mathematical and computer-minded and electronic-minded" [28] of the three of them.

They became involved in various aspects of a very different project that both Wynn-Williams of TRE and H. M. Keen of the British Tabulating Machine Company (BTM) were working on. Again Flowers and his colleagues found themselves getting much of their direction from Turing. The basic problem was to provide a much faster version of an earlier electrome-chanical device that BTM had built [29]. Chandler spent from January to May 1942 at Swanage, where Wynn-Williams was experimenting with a device that was to use high-speed commutators [15, 16]. Flowers and his people were brought in, because of their prior experience, to provide the electronic relays that would be needed with such commutators. There were considerable difficulties with the commutators, and it was discovered and demonstrated that the problem was due to a potential drop occurring across a contact being made with a moving surface [29]. (The actual demonstration was made possible by a precision test instrument, involving a 3-in. cathode-ray tube, which had been built before the war at Dollis Hill by Hadfield.)

A different approach to the problem was taken by Keen at BTM [29]. Flowers and Chandler spent some time at Letchworth with Keen, who had been trying to speed up the earlier electromechanical device and was having problems getting fast enough relays. The Flowers team proposed and demonstrated the use of hot cathode gas discharge tubes in place of relays, on grounds of increased speed and reliability, but for various reasons their solution was not adopted [28]. However, through these various activities they had established themselves as the leading exponents of electronics at Bletchley, in time for the beginning of the project that led to the COLOSSUS [29].

5. Newmanry and Testery

The staff at Bletchley Park was divided into different sections, each housed in different huts on the grounds [8, 45]. One such section was headed by Major (later Colonel) Tester and was working on yet another problem using pencil-and-paper rather than mechanized procedures and techniques. The section, and its type of work, were sometimes known as the Testery, and it was this section that Donald Michie joined initially on his arrival at Bletchley Park in the autumn of 1942 [64].

In the Testery, Michie was taught by P. J. Hilton to carry out a particular procedure. In the process he was referred back to Turing, who acted as an informal consultant to the section, having developed the procedure from earlier work done by W. T. Tutte [64]. Tutte had reached Bletchley Park in mid-1941 from Cambridge University, where he had abandoned his studies for a Ph.D. in chemistry after becoming interested in combinatorial mathematics. At Bletchley he was a member of a small central research section, under Major G. W. Morgan. As Tutte himself has put it, "I think it was at Bletchley Park that I first acquired some standing as a mathematician. In 1942 I found myself elected as a Fellow of Trinity, though only one or two of the electors can have known what it was for" [80].

M. H. A. Newman reached Bletchley Park in September 1942, where he also joined the central research section [70]. Newman on arrival at Bletchley Park had, like Michie, been assigned to the Testery. The work there required an extraordinary type of ingenuity, rather akin to solving crossword puzzles, and Newman soon realized that he was no good at it and considered resigning and returning to Cambridge. (He had gone in voluntarily, as a civilian, and could have left if he had so chosen [69].) But then he had an idea whereby Tutte's original procedure could be assisted by mechanical means. (Tutte himself had no direct concern with the development of machinery [80].) Newman went to Commander (later Sir Edward) Travis, the head of Bletchley Park, and obtained authorization to set up a new section for this purpose [69], housed in what was known as Hut F [45]. By this time he had made the acquaintance of Wynn-Williams, who undertook to develop the required machine [69]. This was the machine that became known as the HEATH ROBINSON, after a cartoonist famous for his fanciful machines intended for all sorts of extraordinary tasks [30].

The techniques used in Newman's section, the Newmanry, even with the hoped-for mechanical aid, would still involve a great deal of mathematical skill, and he started to assemble a team of mathematicians [69]. The first to arrive were Michie and I. J. Good [47, 48, 64]. Michie had only recently left school and knew little mathematics at the start. Despite this he played an important role, and learned enough mathematics at Bletchley to continue to play a valuable role even as the work gradually become more technical [70]. Good had joined Bletchley Park in May 1941 from Jesus College, Cambridge. He had been doing research in pure mathematics, having obtained his Ph.D. about a year earlier and also having won the Cambridgeshire chess championship [45]. At Bletchley his first 18 months were spent in a section headed by Turing, for whom he acted as a statistical assistant. Thus by the time he joined Newman he was already a strong mathematician and statistician who also had both a taste and a talent for troubleshooting of every kind. He and Michie with some thirty Wrens* as machine operators and a few electronic engineers formed Newman's entire staff during the early part of the ROBINSON era [70].

---

*WRNS: Women's Royal Naval Service.

6. HEATH ROBINSON

The summary published by Michie included the following details of the HEATH ROBINSON:

> The machine incorporated two synchronised photo-electric paper tape readers, capable of reading 2000 char/sec. Two loops of 5-hole tape, typically more than 1000 characters in length, would be mounted on these readers. . . . Counts were made of any desired Boolean function of the two inputs. Fast counting was performed electronically, and slow operations, [such as the later stages of the counters* and] control of peripheral equipment, by relays. The machine and all its successors were entirely automatic in operation, once started, and incorporated an on-line output teleprinter or typewriter [63].

In fact I have been informed that output did not use a typewriter-like device, but rather a primitive line printer known as the Gifford printer after its designer, Mr. Tom Gifford of TRE [37]. The HEATH ROBINSON used two counters alternately so that results of one counter could be printed while the next count was continuing. The printer used a set of circular decimal print wheels that were rotated by a common drive when a number was to be set up. Each wheel had ten contacts fixed to its side, to which the output of the appropriate decade of a counter would be fed. These contacts were used to determine how far each wheel should be allowed to rotate. The printing of a line of digits occurred after all the wheels had stopped rotating.

HEATH ROBINSON and a number of similar machines, which went by such names as "PETER ROBINSON" and "ROBINSON AND CLEAVER" (the names of two London stores), were built through the combined efforts of teams at TRE and Dollis Hill [16, 63]. At TRE Wynn-Williams had assembled a small group of carefully selected people, all of whom first had to be approved by Bletchley [94]. This group and the Superintendent (A. P. Rowe) and Assistant Superintendent (W. B. Lewis) were the only people in TRE who knew what was going on, and why. Dr. Wynn-Williams undertook to produce the electronic counters and necessary circuitry but recommended that a Post Office telegraph engineer be given the tape driving and reading problem [31]. It was thus that Mr. F. O. Morrell, head of the telegraph group at Dollis Hill, became involved during the summer of 1942 [28, 61, 68]. He commissioned Dr. E. A. Speight and Mr. (now Dr.) A. C. Lynch of the physics group at Dollis Hill to produce a photoelectric reader. (Dr. Speight, incidentally, had designed much of the Post Office's Speaking Clock [59].)

Speight and Lynch were not told [32] of the intended purpose of the photoelectric reader, which they knew as the Mark I Telegraph Transmitter, or

---

* See [37].

more exactly, the "Transmitter, Telegraph, Mark I." Since some of the components that they used had originally been intended for apparatus at RAF Fighter Command at Bentley Priory, when it was found that the reader was for "B.P." many people assumed that this stood for Bentley Priory. Their first design was a prototype constructed hurriedly from whatever components could be found, and was followed by a more considered design. Both designs used double-crescent masks in order to produce a nearly rectangular pulse of light as a circular hole crossed the mask. One of the photographic masks from the second design of the reader has survived, although broken, as is shown in Fig. 11. This was used to read two successive rows of five hole tape simultaneously, and to detect the sprocket hole in order to produce a timing pulse. Each reader incorporated a number of lenses, and much of the optical work was done by Dr. Speight's assistant, Mr. D. A. Campbell. The prototype used Type CMG 25 photocells (gas-filled) and the second design vacuum photocells [58]. It seems probable that the second design was used for HEATH ROBINSON as well as CO-LOSSUS, although there is some uncertainty as to the speed at which the reader was operated on the HEATH ROBINSON. Some accounts of the speed of HEATH ROBINSON give it either directly, or via comparisons with COLOSSUS, as being about 200 rather than 2000 characters/sec [15, 29, 62, 69], while Dr. Lynch has stated that the specification of the first reader called for a speed of 1000 characters/sec [58]. This confusion seems to

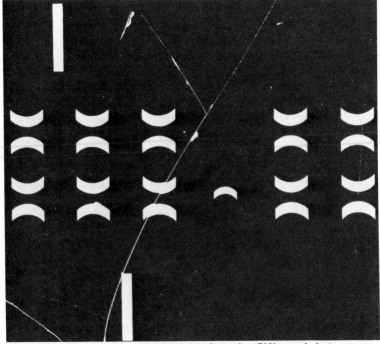

Figure 11   Mask used in photoelectric reader (70% actual size).

have arisen due to the fact that although the electronics of ROBINSON were capable of operating at 2000 characters/sec, in practice the operating speed was limited by several factors:

(a) the deionization time of the initial stages of the thyratron counters. By selecting suitable valves 2000 characters/sec could be achieved for a time.

(b) the length of the tape. A finite time was needed for the printing operation and with a short tape the machine had to be run more slowly to provide this.

(c) the length and strength of the tape. Long tapes, even with the friction drive assistance, placed more strain on the paper at the sprocket drive and were usually run more slowly [16, 31].

Morrell took Speight and Lynch's reader, and used the output from the sprocket holes as a carrier which he phase modulated with the character hole outputs to derive pulses that were counted [31]. He also produced an auxiliary machine, which was used to produce the tapes that formed one of the two inputs to the HEATH ROBINSON [33, 67]. This machine was a straightforward piece of electromechanical engineering, incorporating plugboards and sets of keys. Input data could be set up on the plugboards and the keys were used to control the choice and sequencing of the data [67].

The TRE and Dollis Hill halves of the HEATH ROBINSON, which was not in fact a particularly large machine, were put together, it is believed, at Bletchley Park in about April 1943 [94]. By this time a third skilled mathematician, Dr. Shaun Wylie, had arrived, and others soon followed. From this time on the work benefited from numerous discussions, usually chaired by Newman, which later became more like formal meetings, although they always remained free and easy, and produced a great flow of good ideas [70].

Once the machine was considered operational Professor Newman and his staff took it over, although people from TRE and Dollis Hill remained available to deal with teething troubles [94]. There were at the start very considerable reliability problems, mostly concerned with the paper tape reading mechanism [29, 45, 64]. This mechanism involved a rigid shaft with two sprocket wheels which engaged the sprocket holes of the two tapes, keeping the two in alignment [62]. The paper-tape loops could not withstand the wear and tear caused by the sprocket wheels, and would break. This would mean that the job would have to be started over again from the beginning [29]. Eventually, this problem was solved by Morrell, who designed a system for driving the tapes by pulley, that is, by friction, and using the sprockets for tape alignment only [33]. However, even then it was still the case that the machine would often produce slightly different results from repeated runs of the same tapes, something Newman was very put out about [29]. This problem was probably due to the method of obtaining pulses for counting. Another problem was that things could get out of phase due to tape shrinkage, which mattered because there was a 2-in. gap between the sprocket drive and the point at which the sprocket hole was read [15, 37]. In addition, according to Newman the machine even had a tendency to seize up and catch fire [69]!

Over and above all this it took quite some time to develop an effective methodology, and to gather the logical data that would enable the HEATH ROBINSON to be at all effective. Thus Newman, who had done the enormous amount of work and persuasion necessary to get the project authorized and the machine built, came under tremendous pressure to produce results, though he remained exceedingly determined and confident. Somewhat premature attempts were made to use it operationally, but in the evenings Good and Michie, with the aid of a few volunteer Wrens and electronic engineers, undertook the research that was first needed [64]. (The Wrens served as machine operators, and the engineers did maintenance work and very minor machine modifications as required.)

All of this activity paid off handsomely in that it proved completely the correctness of Newman's intentions. Thus, although the ROBINSONs produced only a small amount of output that was of value in itself, they played an important role in preparing the way for COLOSSUS [64, 71].

7. The First COLOSSUS

Some time after the start of the HEATH ROBINSON project Flowers and Broadhurst, who up to that time were unaware of the work, were brought into the project [31]; Newman has the impression that this was at Turing's suggestion [69]. Flowers's original task was to redesign the electronic counter, which had proved to be unreliable. However, he soon formed the view that the sprocket wheel problem was unlikely to be solved mechanically, so he proposed a much different solution, one involving considerable electronic complexity [29]. This approach was very much in contrast to that of Wynn-Williams, who preferred to use as few valves as possible, favoring electromagnetic relays instead. Flowers, on the other hand, was confident that switching circuit networks involving even large numbers of valves could be made to work reliably. As one of his colleagues has put it, "The basic thing about Flowers was that he didn't care about how many valves he used" [15, p. 5], although of course efforts were made to keep the number of valves within reasonable bounds [37]. He knew from his prewar experience that most valve failures occurred when, or shortly after, power was switched on. He realized that, given appropriate design practices, electronic equipment that could be left on permanently could be expected to achieve a high level of reliability, although this remained to be proven in a large machine [28]. Wynn-Williams though, being at TRE, was probably influenced by the experience of radar sets that were used intermittently, and in adverse environments.

Flowers proposed that he and his colleagues design and build a machine that was to have no fewer than 1500 valves. This is, as far as I can ascertain, considerably in excess of anything else that had been tried to that time in Britain or the U.S., for radar or for purposes of logical or numerical calculation. (Indeed this is nearly twice the number of valves that were used in the Pilot ACE computer, built at NPL after the war [97].) It is thus hardly surprising that many people were unconvinced by these proposals, although Newman was on Flowers's side. Failing to get official support from Bletchley Park, Flowers instead got the project authorized by Radley, the director of the Dollis Hill Research Station [15, 29].

In the incredibly short space of 11 months the machine that the Bletchley Park people were to christen the COLOSSUS was built [5, 28, 29]. The construction was carried out at Dollis Hill by technicians in Flowers's group [15]. The electronic design was done mainly by Flowers and Chandler with Broadhurst concentrating on the auxiliary electromechanical equipment [5]. The photoelectric reader was a redesigned version of the one used on HEATH ROBINSON, working at 5000 characters/sec [33, 63]. The electronic counters were biquinary [34], based on those developed before the war by W. B. Lewis, who had been at the Cavendish Laboratory with Wynn-Williams [56]. Lewis played an important, though perhaps unwitting, role in the CO-LOSSUS story through his book on counting circuits. Flowers credits this book [57] as an important landmark in his own understanding of electronics: "When he produced this work a lot of things I had learnt in the past suddenly clicked. I knew about Eccles–Jordan and trigger circuits but it never occurred to me very clearly how to use them to substitute relays and stores" [28, p. 15]. When Flowers tried out Lewis's original circuit he found it didn't work properly for him, so he produced a redesigned circuit [15, 24] that didn't require such accurate components, which was later patented [26]. Apparently the key change in this redesigned circuit was the use of the EF 36 valve with its short grid base, which made the potential dividers in the circuits less critical [37]. Flowers's counter circuits were much more sophisticated than Lewis's, using, for example, the screen and suppressor grid connections for various purposes, such as reset to zero. Cathode follower drive and readoff circuits were also employed.

A small team of junior technicians who also helped in the electronic design of COLOSSUS were mainly responsible for commissioning the machine, which became operational at Bletchley Park in December 1943 [28, 29]. The machine was assembled and tested at Dollis Hill using short loops of tape on which repetitive patterns had been punched [17]. This turned out to be an advantage because these patterns facilitated the synchronization of an oscilloscope. The machine was then partially unwired prior to transportation to Bletchley Park, where it was reassembled [15]. As luck would have it, the first job that was run on the COLOSSUS at Bletchley Park happened to take only ten minutes—jobs could equally well take several hours. Moreover, when the job was repeated it produced the same results again. No wonder that, as Flowers puts it: "They just couldn't believe it when we brought this string and sealing wax sort of thing in and it actually did a job. They were on their beam ends at the time, ROBINSON just hadn't got enough output, they wouldn't go fast enough and suddenly this bit of string and sealing wax, in about ten minutes . . . and then they started to take notice!" [29, p. 12]. (This reference to string and sealing wax is of course too modest— the prototype must have been well engineered, since with 1500 valve circuits that had to operate consistently there was no room for ad hoc construction methods.)

What Flowers had done was to generate some of the required data electronically within the machine, so that only one input data tape was required. The problem of keeping two tapes synchronized vanished. Furthermore, by using the pulses obtained from reading the sprocket holes to generate timing signals, the sprocket wheel itself could be dispensed with [29]. It therefore became necessary to provide means for setting up the machine before a run so as to have it generate the required sets of data from parameters stored in thyratron rings. For this purpose plugboards and sets of keys, based on those incorporated in the auxiliary tape preparation machine used with the ROBINSONs, were built into COLOSSUS. Therefore the bother and time needed to produce a second tape were eliminated [33]. More important, after the first COLOSSUS was made available to the mathematicians they began to make use of it to do processes that were not possible on ROBINSONs, by making the dynamically generated data dependent on the result of instantaneous processing [28, 69].

Turning to the question of electronic design, the prototype COLOSSUS included the following historically significant features:

(a) It used a clock pulse to synchronize and time operations throughout the machine. It was this feature that made the size of the machine possible by eliminating cumulative timing errors.

(b) It used binary hard valve electronic circuitry on a large scale. It was this that contributed to its reliability because there were no valves (other than in the tape reader photocell amplifiers) that were not either cut off or conducting representing the 0 or 1 condition.

(c) It had a shift register (five step).

(d) It used two-state circuits and clock control, meaning that the machine could operate at any speed down to zero. (The photocell amplifiers were the exception.) This meant that the machine could be "hand stepped" for test purposes.

(e) It used cathode followers to isolate the operation of the switching circuits from the output.

Reconstructed diagrams of the basic circuits Flowers designed for the prototype COLOSSUS are given in Figs. 12–16 [37].

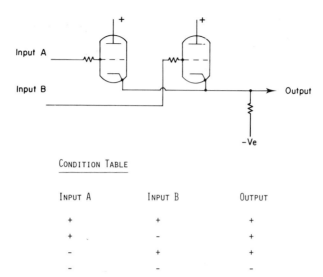

Condition Table

Input A	Input B	Output
+	+	+
+	–	+
–	+	+
–	–	–

Figure 12 Boolean addition circuit in COLOSSUS.

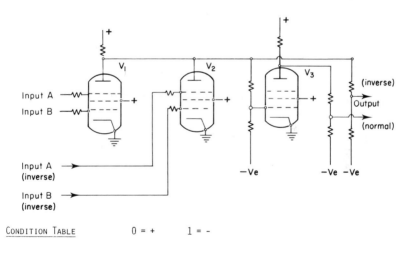

Condition Table   0 = +   1 = –

Input A	Input A (Inverse)	Input B	Input B (Inverse)	V_1	V_2	Output (Normal	Inverse)
+	–	+	–	C	NC	+	–
–	+	–	+	NC	C	+	–
+	–	–	+	NC	NC	–	+
–	+	+	–	NC	NC	–	+

Figure 13 Binary addition circuit as used in COLOSSUS. All valves are Mullard EF 36. Input and output voltages typically +20 (= 0) or −30 (= 1). Valve conditions: C, conducting; NC, non-conducting.

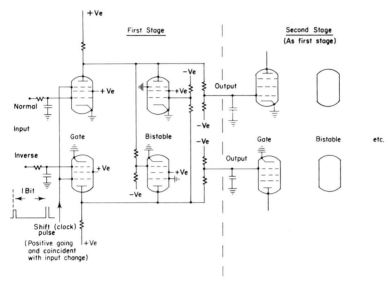

Figure 14   Shift register as used in COLOSSUS—circuit element.

8.   The MARK II COLOSSUS

The last major figure in the COLOSSUS story, Dr. A. W. M. Coombs (Fig. 17), joined in at about the time the first machine was commissioned [5]. After leaving university and joining the Post Office in 1936, he had been almost wholly involved in various items of war work and became experienced with a great variety of electromechanical equipment and electronics, but not electronic switching. He had been brought into the Foreign Office work in Octo-

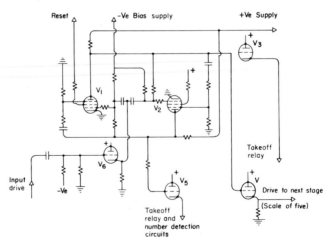

Figure 15   Biquinary counter as used in COLOSSUS—scale of two circuit elements. Valves V_1 and V_2 are EF 36: V_3–V_6 are L63.

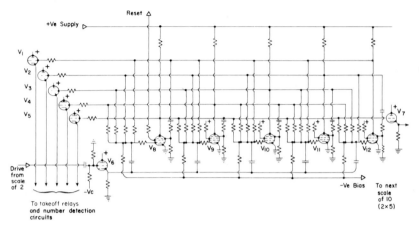

Figure 16 Biquinary counter as used in COLOSSUS—scale of five circuit elements. Valves V_1–V_7 are L63: V_8–V_{12} are EF 36.

ber 1943. He was to have undertaken further work related to HEATH ROB-INSON at Dollis Hill but the advent of COLOSSUS changed all that [15, 29].

As soon as the first COLOSSUS, the string and sealing wax prototype as he called it, was working Flowers asked for advance warning of any require-ments for further machines [29]. This was not forthcoming at first, but he took the precaution of arranging for the manufacture of some of the more time-consuming components. Then in March 1944 the group was told that more machines were required by 1 June. There was no conceivable way of meeting this requirement, but Flowers undertook to get the production of an initial set of three machines started, and to try and get one machine working by the deadline [15, 30].

Michie's summary of published statements about the COLOSSI indi-cates that the production or MARK II machines were five times faster than

Figure 17 Dr. A. W. M. Coombs.

the prototype [63]—"an effective speed of 25,000 characters/sec was obtained by a combination of parallel operations and short term memory." Five-stage shift registers were used to give access to five sequential characters simultaneously, even though the basic clock rate remained unchanged at 5000 characters/sec [37]. In addition, although testimony is not entirely clear on this point, it seems probable that starting with the first production COLOSSUS extra facilities were provided that had not been available on the ROBINSON or the prototype COLOSSUS [64]. These facilities included wired logic processes and a "logic switching panel" comprising rows of key switches on which Boolean functions could be set up to control the logical operations performed by the machine [35].

Although the basic logic and Flowers's original circuit technology remained virtually unchanged, the MARK II COLOSSUS involved extensive redesign of the prototype. For example, an additional counter was provided, more use was made of shift registers, and a number of detailed modifications were made to the original circuitry [37]. The design work was divided up between Flowers, Broadhurst, Chandler, and Coombs, who remembers Flowers literally tearing his basic logic diagram into pieces and handing out one each to be redesigned [15, 29]. Their designs were then handed over to various less senior engineers, including Oswald Belcher, Freddy Wraight, and Stan Willis, who laid out the circuits on standard panels and supervised the actual construction. This was done in what was essentially a factory, set up for the purpose in the Dollis Hill Research Station.

To save time the first MARK II machine was assembled on site at Bletchley Park, rather than at Dollis Hill [17]. The commissioning of the machine was the responsibility of Chandler and a colleague, Wilfred Saville. By 31 May it was nearly complete. Flowers, Broadhurst, Chandler, Coombs, and Saville were all at Bletchley Park, but they could not get the machine to work. Eventually, in the early hours of 1 June, the others went home to get some sleep, leaving Chandler to work on, since the trouble was in the part he had redesigned. In his words, "The whole system was in a state of violent parasitic oscillation at a frequency outside the range of our oscilloscopes [and then] by way of diversion, at about 3:00 a.m. a nearby radiator started leaking, sending a pool of warm water towards the equipment!" [16]. He eventually found a means of curing the problem and at nearly 4:00 a.m. left Norman Thurlow, one of the maintenance engineers, to finish the required rewiring. The others arrived back at 8:30 a.m. to find that the machine was working. The deadline had been beaten—and it was just five days to D-day, 6 June 1944!

Several more MARK II COLOSSI were soon installed, but during all of this time Newman and his mathematicians were having frequent discussions to explore the possibilities that had been opened up by the COLOSSI, and their requirements for further facilities [70]. One such request arose from some successful experiments on one of the machines. These were carried out by Good and Michie, and involved making manual connections and re-connections while the machine was actually operating, and observing the effects on its outputs [64, 66]. Apparently hard-wired facilities were later provided for doing these manipulations automatically, internally and at high speed. Professor Newman's recollection is that several production machines had been delivered before these facilities were provided, and so greatly speeded up a particular task that the COLOSSI were being used for—however, it was not possible to obtain confirmation of these points from the machine designers [46, 70]. It is not clear how much additional electronics was involved in the various new facilities incorporated in some of the MARK II machines. Even the earliest of these, it is believed, incorporated about 2400 valves, as well as much relay and other electromechanical equipment for data input and output [15, 30, 36]. The MARK II COLOSSI were apparently still fairly similar in appearance to the prototype, though Chandler and Coombs decided after close inspection that the recently released photographs are of one of the MARK II machines rather than the prototype [15].

Production of the COLOSSI took up about half the total workshop and production capability at the Dollis Hill Research Station [28]. Construction of the panels for the first two or three machines was undertaken by a staff of wiremen there, but subsequently the panels were built at the Post Office factory in Birmingham under Dollis Hill supervision. The racks on which the panels were installed were standard ones from Post Office stores, but the frames on which the tape pulleys were mounted (called the "bedsteads") were built by the Dollis Hill workshops. The racks were wired together for the first time at Bletchley Park, an operation that took two or three weeks, since there was a lot of inter-rack wiring [15]. In 1944, Coombs was placed in charge of the work at Dollis Hill when Flowers was promoted [62]. Published claims have been made that in all a total of about ten COLOSSI were manufactured [63], but the official explanatory caption merely states that after the first machine "a considerable number of further machines was built and gave reliable and effective service until the end of the war." What happened to them afterward has not been revealed.

Design work continued right up to the end of the war, since no two CO-LOSSI were the same [5, 15]. Apparently a whole series of smaller specialized machines and attachments (with various intriguing names) was built by Coombs's group for Bletchley Park [15, 29]. Flowers also designed at least one other machine after the COLOSSUS, the SUPER ROBINSON [37, 62]. This involved four data tapes, and to some extent went back to the use of sprocket wheels in order to keep the tapes synchronized. The problem that it addressed could have been solved electronically, but Flowers and his people did not have the time, and the problems of tape wear caused by the sprocket wheels had been largely solved by Morrell [29]. The SUPER ROBINSON was a hybrid, which used COLOSSUS circuit technology to a very large extent, its multiple tape inputs being roughly synchronized by the sprocket drive, and then electronically synchronized to the clock pulse derived from one tape [37]. However, I am told that neither SUPER ROBINSON nor any of the other specialized machines could be regarded as a further major step toward the modern computer, either by virtue of the amount of electronics it involved, or its logical power [5, 15, 28, 29, 64]. All were special-purpose machines for which, in effect, the program was wired in or set up with keys. They were nearly all mixed relay/electronic machines, without as much electronics as COLOSSUS. They therefore can be presumed to be of little significance with respect to the development of the modern digital computer.

9. An Assessment

A proper assessment of the COLOSSI as precursors to the modern general-purpose computer is hampered by the lack of detailed information concerning the functions they performed, and the facilities that were provided for controlling their operation. As it is we must rely mainly on the official explanatory caption (Appendix 1), where we find among the list of features:

> Electronic storage registers changeable by an automatically controlled sequence of operations,
> Conditional (branching) logic,
> Logic functions preset by patch panels or switches, or conditionally selected by telephone relays,
> Fully automatic operation.

To these we can also add, from previously published sources,

> variable programming by means of lever keys which controlled gates which could be connected in series or parallel as required [27],
> calculated complicated Boolean functions involving up to about 100 symbols [43],

although it is possible that these apply only to the MARK II COLOSSI.

Certainly it seems fair to classify the COLOSSUS as a special-purpose program-controlled electronic digital computer. It was, however, externally programmed and there is no question of its having been a stored-program computer. This final step in the invention of the modern computer had to await the development of a practical high-speed store, capable of holding a large number of binary digits. The only variable stores on the COLOSSUS were gas tubes and hard valve trigger circuits [33].

There were other programmable computers in existence in 1944, but as far as is known none were electronic [74]. The use of electronics permitted a thousandfold increase in internal speed over contemporary relay or electro-mechanical devices. The first of Zuse's computers to work successfully, the

Z3, had been completed in 1941, but this was built with telephone relays, as were the Bell Laboratories Relay Interpolator and Ballistic Computer (completed in September 1943 and May 1944, respectively). The Harvard MARK I, which was entirely electromechanical, had been demonstrated at Endicott in January 1943, but became operational at Harvard in May 1944. All these machines were tape controlled, and so could have programs of considerable length and complexity, but none had conditional branching facilities, an omission that would have surprised Babbage. On the other hand, digital electronics had, as far as we know, been used only for single-purpose devices. The most complex of these was Atanasoff's linear equation solver, although both Zuse and Vannevar Bush had investigated the idea of a program-controlled electronic digital computer. (More details of Bush's work are given in Section 13.)

Program control by means of plugboards was available on punched card machines, and was well known to Flowers and his team. In fact Flowers has assessed the prototype COLOSSUS as probably being less programmable than some contemporary IBM machines [33]. However, because of its additional logic switching panel, the MARK II COLOSSUS was much more flexible than the prototype. Although a special-purpose device, it turned out to have considerable generality within its own subject area, more in fact than Newman and his team had asked for [69], although Newman himself was a strong believer in the importance of having flexibility in the design of the machine [45]. This flexibility was exploited fully once it was appreciated, and the COLOSSUS ended up being used for several types of jobs that had not been anticipated when the machine was first designed. For example, early in 1945 Wylie showed that without any modifications or additions the MARK II COLOSSUS could perform a task which had hitherto been the responsibility of the Testery, and was thought of as one that could not be mechanized [70]. (An account I received early in my investigations had implied that this task was made possible by the hardware that simulated the manual connections and reconnections described in Section 8, but it now seems that this was not the case [64].) A number of other diverse tasks were performed by the machine, but all were related to the particular work with which the Newmanry and the Testery were concerned [29, 45].

Clearly, the machine with which the COLOSSI are most aptly compared is the ENIAC.* The ENIAC project was started in May 1943, and the machine was first used in late 1945 or early 1946. It was a much larger and faster machine than the COLOSSUS, having about 18,000 valves, and being able to store 20 ten-digit decimal variables. It had conditional branching facilities, and was programmed using pluggable cables, a process that could take a day or so, although later a method or programming that involved manually setting values into a function table was introduced [74]. Like COLOSSUS, it

* See the papers in this volume by Burks, Eckert, and Mauchly.

was built for a very special purpose, the solution of differential equations such as those occurring in ballistics problems—it was first known as the Electronic Difference Analyzer [95]—but it was in fact also used for a variety of other numerical calculations [83]

The distinction between special-purpose and general-purpose digital computers is of course very blurred, unless one equates "general purpose" to some sort of finite approximation of a Universal Turing Machine. Neither COLOSSUS nor ENIAC is general purpose in this sense, so the opening sentences of the explanatory caption might perhaps be somewhat misleading with respect to the capabilities of COLOSSUS.

This leaves the question of the relative extent to which ENIAC and CO-LOSSUS were "special purpose." ENIAC had facilities for addition, subtraction, multiplication, division, the extraction of square roots, and could test the sign of a number and whether two numbers were equal. It used punched-card input and output. According to Weik [83] it was used not only for ballistics calculations but also for weather prediction, atomic energy calculations, thermal ignition, random number studies, wind tunnel design, and other specific applications.

At present our assessment of the extent to which COLOSSUS was a special-purpose computer must depend mainly on the remembered knowledge of people who were closely involved, particularly Chandler, Good, and Michie. Quoting Chandler, "We could say that if a count exceeded a certain value you would do one thing, if it was less than a certain value you would do another thing, so this was conditional branching logic" [15, p. 21]. Good recollects that Geoffrey Timms showed that COLOSSUS could be plugged up to do multiplication: "It took a great deal of plugging and it wasn't worthwhile . . . but the flexibility was such as to let it be used for something for which it was not designed . . . it was a Boolean calculating machine . . . it was rather general just because it dealt with binary symbols, but it wasn't designed to be an ordinary number cruncher" [45, pp. 14–15]. Finally, Michie's summing up of the situation is

> The use of COLOSSUS to do other things unconnected with the purpose for which it was built, although possible, would have been strained and artificial . . . we could fake up some of the properties of branching on a condition, essentially through manipulations of the data tape, but that sort of thing stopped a long way short of a Turing Machine or any of its linguistic or hardware embodiments . . . my impression is that CO-LOSSUS would not be very far away on the scale of ascent [towards a general purpose computer] from the ENIAC [64, p. 12].

It seems that a reasonable summing up would be as follows: ENIAC and COLOSSUS (which preceded it by nearly two years) were both program-controlled electronic digital computers, the one specialized toward numerical calculations, the other somewhat more specialized, in this case toward

Boolean calculations of a particular type. Each was a splendid achievement of great importance. But it was among the ENIAC group that the final step toward the modern computer was first taken, namely, the design of a practical stored-program computer, the EDVAC. The apportionment of credit for this work among Eckert, Mauchly, von Neumann, and Goldstine is a matter of some controversy, not appropriate to enter into here. There is a possibility that Turing also had some direct influence in this matter, but this is unproven (see Sections 12 and 14).

10.   The COLOSSI in Operation

Newman's section had expanded rapidly, even before the first CO-LOSSUS was completed. Its hut was replaced by a brick building, still referred to as Hut F for convenience, and later another building, Hut H, was added to house some of the COLOSSI [45]. The next mathematicians to join the section included, in approximate order of arrival, J. H. C. Whitehead, Oliver Atkin, Michael Ashcroft, Gordon Preston, Geoffrey Timms, and Joe Gillis, followed after a pause by others [64]. As Newman has put it, his section had a lot of outstanding people in it, including some who were or were to become the best mathematicians in Britain [69].

In addition to their mathematical duties, these people all manned a duty officer roster [64]. The duty officer served as an operations manager, directing the flow of jobs on and off the machines. In the early days it was typical for a mathematician to sit at a machine, interact with it while it operated, and be closely concerned with deciding what tasks should be run. This involved a form of analysis and decision making that has been characterized as somewhat similar to that involved in playing chess [45]. Some of the procedures that evolved later became codified into decision trees that could be followed independently by the operators. These were Wrens, with a Senior Wren as Chief Operator responsible for several machines, as well as the scheduling of their job queues [45, 69]. It was a long time before those involved were to see again a room whose pattern of activity so closely matched that of a modern large computer installation [64].

The COLOSSI were maintained by Post Office personnel. The maintenance engineers were chosen from among those working on the COLOSSI at Dollis Hill, and typically would have prior experience of maintaining telephone exchanges. Chandler was placed in charge of the general installation, but did not move to the Bletchley area. Instead he traveled daily from Dollis Hill so as to keep in close touch with the work going on there [15].

The COLOSSI achieved very high levels of reliability. Such problems as did occur were in general not due to valves but to such things as the typewriter and photoelectric reader [15, 29, 45]. This must have been largely due to the care that was taken to design the machines so that standard components could be incorporated. This was done using safety factors to allow for components having characteristics that were some way from, and would drift even further away from, their nominal values [15, 28]. It was difficult to get good resistors since the normal source of prewar supply was Germany! A scheme was devised that involved classifying resistors acording to their closeness to the intended value [16]. Thus Group A might be 15–20% above nominal value, Group B 10–15%, etc. Care would be taken to use resistors from just a single group in a given trigger network or perhaps on a particular rack—this technique was introduced by Coombs.

The first week or so of operation served to weed out poor valves—a calculation of the number of valves involved in the various machines indicated that this totalled between 20,000 and 30,000 [15]—and the valve holders were more of a problem than the valves themselves, so some critical valves were wired in directly [5, 28]. The photoelectric cells gave a certain amount of trouble because sensitivity could decrease after a long series of consecutive tape "holes" [37]. The paper tape itself caused problems—the edges of the tape would saw their way through the hardened steel pins that served as tape guides [15]. During one test a machine was run successfully at 9700 characters/sec, but then the tapes kept breaking—in Dr. Coombs's words, "If you got a very long tape which broke, by the time you could do something about it there was tape everywhere, all over the place, festoons of it!" [15, p. 13].

11. Secrecy and Priority

One cannot attempt to picture the environments within which the COLOSSI were built and used without some appreciation of the circumstances under which the work at Bletchley Park and Dollis Hill was undertaken. Wartime conditions must have given a great sense of urgency [49]—Broadhurst can remember occasions driving back toward London and seeing the city ablaze from high ground. Dollis Hill itself suffered minor bomb damage, but none is recalled at Bletchley Park [5, 15].

Within Bletchley Park itself, as at all wartime defense establishments, security precautions were applied. People in one section normally knew little or nothing about the work of other sections, although there was active liaison between the Testery and the Newmanry. Discussion of work would be avoided outside the particular hut. At lunchtime Newman and a group of his staff might lunch together, but even in an otherwise empty cafeteria there would be no thought of discussing their work. Instead the conversation would usually be about mathematics and brainteasers of all kinds [28, 64].

At Dollis Hill very few people had any knowledge of Bletchley Park or the tasks undertaken on the machines. Paperwork was kept to a minimum. Flowers's team was initially not allowed to use the drawing office, so circuit diagrams were drawn freehand. The individual panels from which the machines were made were small enough that it was impossible for the wiremen who were assembling them (either at Dollis Hill or Birmingham) to figure out what the circuits were for [5, 15, 29].

The workmen therefore had to take on trust the importance of their task, which was such that unusual amounts of overtime were called for. On one occasion it was arranged that Flowers invite Newman and a uniformed high-ranking officer to Dollis Hill so that the people there could have evidence that their work was fully appreciated. Flowers remembers that the visitors "were absolutely flabbergasted because as far as they were concerned nothing had happened for months yet they found [the] men working like hell—great forms of wiring being done and panels going through—they just couldn't believe it, and it had a good effect on both sides" [28, p. 21].

The Dollis Hill people had priority on stores and in the Post Office factories, and did not have to account for anything [5, 28]. When they asked for automatic typewriters instead of teleprinters these were flown from the U.S. with reserved places, no questions asked. Perhaps the best anecdote is Chandler's, who remembers telephoning an official in the Ministry of Supply yet again to ask for another couple of thousand EF 36 valves and being asked, "What the bloody hell are you doing with these things, shooting them at the Jerries?"[15, p. 15].

12. Turing's Role

The explanatory caption states that Turing's "earlier work had its full influence on the design concept" of the COLOSSUS. This is one of the points I have concentrated on trying to elucidate during the interviews with people who took part in the design and use of the COLOSSI.

Questions of influence are always difficult to assess. In the case of work at Bletchley Park this is especially true, not just because of the unavailability of original records, but also because of the atmosphere in which the work was carried out. The sense of urgency, the spirit of cooperation, and the lack of an audience combined to make people much less conscious of the attribution of individual credit than would, understandably, have been the case in more normal times [64].

Turing, clearly, was viewed with considerable awe by most of his colleagues at Bletchley because of his evident intellect and the great originality and importance of his contributions, and also with considerable discomfort by many because his personality was so outlandish. Many people found him incomprehensible, perhaps being intimidated by his reputation but more likely being put off by his character and mannerisms [15, 64]. But all of the Post Office engineers who worked with him say that they found him very easy to understand. Broadhurst characterized him as "a born teacher—he could put any obscure point very well" [5, p. 7]. Their respect for him was immense, although, as Chandler said, "The least said about him as an engineer the better" [15, p. 8]. This point is echoed by Michie, who said, "He was intrigued by devices of every kind, whether abstract or concrete—his friends thought it would be better if he kept to the abstract devices but that didn't deter him" [64, p. 7].

Turing had a strange obsession with self-sufficiency, both in everyday life and in mathematics, where he could not forbear to discover all the well-known subsidiary results as well as the main theorem, causing great waste of time for himself and extra trouble for his readers, who had to learn his nonstandard notations and proofs. Yet embedded in this were deep and profoundly original ideas [64, 71].

He seems to have worked on a wide variety of mathematical topics during this period. Good's postwar book [42] indicates that during the war Turing developed a technique for facilitating Bayesian probability calculations. Good has since written that Turing "anticipated, in classified work, a number of statistical techniques which are usually attributed to other people" [44]. In fact his very important statistical method [46, 65, 70, 71], was rediscovered and developed further by Wald and called "sequential analysis" [82].

As described in Section 4, the early projects that the Dollis Hill people carried out for Bletchley Park were done in close cooperation with Turing, and Flowers recollects that during the period they were involved with the HEATH ROBINSON they were seeing him every day [29]. Apparently he did not have any direct involvement in, or influence on, the design or use of COLOSSUS [33, 69]. His visits to Dollis Hill occurred prior to the start of the COLOSSUS work, and Newman does not remember his presence at any of the meetings that Newman and Flowers held at Bletchley Park [69]. Turing's prewar work on computability was well known, and virtually all of the people I have interviewed recollect wartime discussions of his idea of a universal automaton [5, 15]. (Flowers, incidentally, also recalls lunchtime conversations with Newman and Turing about Babbage and his work [28].) Good has written that "Newman was perhaps inspired by his knowledge of Turing's 1936 paper" [43, 46]. However, Newman's view now is that although he and his people all knew that the planned COLOSSUS was theoretically related to a Turing Machine, they were not conscious of their work having any dependence on either these ideas or those of Babbage [69].

The Turing Machine did provide a conceptual background for Turing's extracurricular work on, and discussions of, the idea of "thinking machines" [64]. In the main these discussions were with some of the younger scientists at Bletchley Park—the more senior ones tended to disapprove of such science-fiction-like topics. He concentrated on game playing as an arena in which to test out his ideas, and on chess in particular. It was through a common interest in chess that Michie got to know Turing, and to become involved in the idea of "machine chess." Because of the methods of recruitment to Bletchley Park, those of Turing's circle there who played chess at all tended to be Masters or at least experts. By their standards Turing was a beginner, as was Michie. They were in fact evenly matched and used to meet for regular games at a pub in Wolverton. Turing developed his ideas on thinking machines quite extensively during the war. According to Michie the fundamental notions that were discussed then, and which originated with Turing, included the idea of look ahead, of backing up by the minimax rule, of using an evaluation function to assign strategic values to the terminal nodes of the look-ahead tree, and the notion of quiescence as it would now be called (Turing called them dead positions) as a criterion for cutoff of the look-ahead process. His first paper on the topic of thinking machines was prepared a year or so after the end of the war, but not published until many years later [78].

The one other aspect of Turing's role that I would dearly like to clarify is his reputed wartime meeting with von Neumann [48, 75]. The story, or rather legend, is that the meeting was of critical importance to the development of the modern computer. Regretfully, my further investigations have not thrown much further light on this matter. Turing is known to have made at least one wartime visit to the States. According to Cave Brown he visited the States sometime before May 1942, to describe how the "Turing Engine" worked, and again in 1943, but his biography described just one visit, in November 1942 [13, 79]. I. J. Good believes that the visit had some connection with the atomic bomb project, as he recollects Turing posing him a problem concerning the probability of the explosion of one barrel of gunpowder, set among others on a two-dimensional grid, causing the other barrels to explode [45]. It is known that Turing visited Bell Labs, where he met Claude Shannon, but apparently they did not talk about programmable computers [51]. He saw one or two of the early Bell Labs Relay Computers but showed very little interest in them [76]. Von Neumann visited Bell Labs in about 1942, and saw the nearly completed Ballistic Computer. He also visited Britain during the war, and Newman reports that he met him during this visit, but that von Neumann did not visit Bletchley Park [74].

This then is where the investigation must rest. For my part I am now disinclined to believe the legend, although I think that the situation was probably summarized well by Frankel when he wrote [38]

> Many people have acclaimed von Neumann as the 'father of the computer' (in a modern sense of the term) but I am sure that he would never have made that mistake himself. He might well be called the midwife, perhaps, but he firmly emphasized to me, and to others I am sure, that the fundamental conception is owing to Turing—insofar as not anticipated by Babbage, Lovelace and others. In my view von Neumann's essential role was in making the world aware of these fundamental con-

cepts introduced by Turing and of the development work carried out in the Moore School and elsewhere. Certainly I am indebted to him for my introduction to these ideas and actions. Both von Neumann and Turing, of course, also made substantial contributions to the 'reduction to practice' of these concepts but I would not regard these as comparable in importance with the introduction and explication of the concept of a computer able to store in its memory its program of activities and of modifying that program in the course of these activities.

13.   The American Scene

Flowers and his colleagues did not learn about any of the American work on electronic or electromagnetic digital calculators and computers, such as those at Bell Labs, Harvard, Iowa State, IBM, MIT, or the Moore School, until close to or after the end of the war [5, 15, 28, 69]. The ENIAC project had only just started by the time the first COLOSSUS was operational, but such was the secrecy surrounding COLOSSUS that it is very unlikely that any knowledge of it could have reached the Moore School. When Flowers and Chandler visited there in 1945 they were unable to reveal anything at all about their wartime work for Bletchley Park. As far as I can determine the immense amount of testimony and documentary evidence about the ENIAC project in the litigation concerning the validity of Eckert and Mauchly's patents contains no mention of Bletchley Park or the COLOSSUS [69].

It is unclear to what extent scientists and engineers working on similar problems at Bell Labs, IBM, and elsewhere in the States were in touch with the work of Flowers and his team, but there is no evidence at all of any American involvement in the design of COLOSSUS [5, 15, 69]. Although special-purpose machines were being developed in the States during the war, as is the case with COLOSSUS, they are not yet fully declassified. However, my correspondents were able to provide me with some details of the American work—enough, I believe, to put the COLOSSUS in a proper perspective.

One large relay machine was built by S. B. Williams at Bell Labs. The machine was quite flexible but had no arithmetic [9–11]. Williams built most of the Bell Labs series of relay computers, and the existence of his machine had at least a small influence on the decision to develop the early Ballistic Computers [76].

An American machine which in concept was similar to the HEATH ROBINSON, and which preceded it, was developed by Vannevar Bush starting in 1936 [9, 25]. Bush is of course famous for, among other things, his invention in 1930 of the differential analyzer, but he also worked on digital devices. In a set of memoranda written in 1937 and 1938 he proposed and investigated some of the design problems of a program-controlled electronic digital computer. This work led to a research project at MIT, the Rapid Arithmetical Machine Project, sponsored by the National Cash Register Company (NCR), in which various basic electronic circuits, such as registers and counters, were developed [72]. Another project at MIT, sponsored by Eastman Kodak and NCR, grew out of a device, the Rapid Selector, that Bush had invented in 1936 [7, 87]. This device was intended for the automatic retrieval and photographic copying of information held on reels of 35-mm microfilm, using photoelectric scanning of coded identifiers. Both research groups were disbanded in 1942 because their staff were required for military projects elsewhere. The Rapid Selector group, which was led by John Howard and included Lawrence R. Steinhardt, had been working on Bush's HEATH ROBINSON–like machine from late 1940.

This machine incorporated electronic counters and two photoelectric tape readers. The tape was apparently backing tape from 70-mm photographic film, rather than ordinary telegraph tape. (Such backing tape has sprocket holes cut in it with the same care as in the film itself.) Each character was represented by a single hole placed at one of 40 positions across the tape. Apparently the machine was linked to more or less standard tabulating machines where plugboards could of course be plugged to do a variety of functions [10, 23].

Bush's machine was completed by John Howard and Lawrence Steinhardt and it functioned in a desultory fashion for many years [9]. After the war, John Howard, Howard T. Engstrom, and Charles Tompkins were part of the group that founded Engineering Research Associates Inc. (ERA) [23]. All three had been in a Navy communications operation and had close contacts in Britain, and close acquaintance with Turing [18]. It has been claimed, though without supporting evidence, "that ERA, under contract to the Navy, produced one of the world's first three computers, a powerful top-secret intelligence computer known as Machine 13" [22]. In fact, this was an electronic computer called ATLAS, developed under a multiproject Navy contract, delivered in 1950. It was a single-address machine, with 24-bit parallel arithmetic and word organization, and magnetic drum storage [19, 24]. An earlier relay version, named ABEL, with the same order code, was later handed over to George Washington University [89]. A commercial version of the electronic computer was produced under the designation ERA 1101 (this of course being binary for 13) [19].*

My information is that there were no earlier or contemporary electronic machines in the American communications operations that matched the size or complexity of COLOSSUS [9]. A group of sophisticated American devices, operating in about 1942, was based on the use of counting and optical matching techniques, rather than complex electronic circuits [12, 23–25]. One machine used glass plates because of a concern for dimensional stabil-

---

* See paper on ERA in this volume by Tomash.

ity, later found to be exaggerated, and other machines used 35- or 70-mm film instead. One device enabled 20,000 bits to be represented on each frame of film. Both Flowers and Coombs vaguely recollect learning about some such machine [15, 29].

Various other machines were developed in the U.S. during the war for related purposes, including ones whose electronic complexity matched, and in fact exceeded, that of COLOSSUS [24]. However, American special-purpose electronic devices that predated COLOSSUS were much simpler. For example, one device that involved the use of electronics for calculation purposes was invented by Arnold I. Dumey. Two versions of this machine, which involved perhaps 300 valves, and which probably postdated HEATH ROBINSON, were completed. They calculated in real time the expected value of the number of successes in a set of trials plus and minus a certain fixed number of standard deviations. Only if the observed number fell outside the calculated limits was printing of the result permitted [23]. Dumey later had responsibility for a larger device, involving approximately 4000 valves, which became operational a year after the end of the war. There were devices incorporating even more valves. The largest operational device that Dumey had any involvement with had no less than 10,000 valves. As he himself puts it, "The most interesting thing about life at this time was the way every new electrical invention was tried out as soon as possible in some new device. Yet the only early improvement on COLOSSUS was in a more compact way of holding and running the tapes" [25].

The above meagre details undoubtedly give a totally inadequate impression of the quantity and variety of machines that were developed, and of the importance of the work that was done in the U.S. in this field during the war. They are given here merely to buttress the statements I have received from both sides of the Atlantic concerning the COLOSSUS, namely, that it had no rivals or precedents as a programmable electronic computer, and that there were no links between it and the ENIAC project [15, 24, 64, 69].

14. The Aftermath

Official awards were made to a number of people involved in the Bletchley Park work, after the war, but of a quite inadequate nature in my opinion. Newman considered the O.B.E. awarded to Turing, which apparently he accepted somewhat as a joke, quite ludicrous in relation to his achievements [69]. Flowers was awarded an M.B.E. and a £1000 Award to Inventors, but as Coombs has said, "If it had been £10,000 or £100,000 it still wouldn't have been too much" [15, p. 33]. Broadhurst and Coombs received £100 awards, but Chandler, being on a more lowly engineering grade, received nothing at all [5]. These matters are perhaps of little importance, and certainly all of the Dollis Hill group are unanimous in describing their work for Bletchley Park as the most satisfying thing they have ever done.

Most of the group continued full-time work for Bletchley Park until the end of the war, but Flowers ceased his full-time involvement after his promotion in 1944, when he handed the responsibility for the work over to Coombs, although Coombs continued to report to him [28]. Instead Flowers started to become involved in the Post Office planning for work to be carried out on the telephone system after the war had ended. He did take part in a visit of inspection to Germany on behalf of Bletchley Park two months after the cessation of hostilities [29]. The party included Alan Turing and the man who was in charge of work on radio reception for Bletchley Park. They went in order to see what communications research the Germans had been doing during the war. The visit started on 15 July 1945 and was due to last six weeks, but Flowers returned after ten days, having visited Frankfurt and Eberbach.

This visit caused a postponement of a visit by Flowers and Chandler to the States, which had originally been planned for early 1945. This was in connection with a project concerning radar, the Data Recorder Project [15, 29]. The Ministry of Supply needed a means for testing auto-following radar. This was to involve recording data from radar and from a kine-theodolite, which were both tracking an aircraft, and then using these data to compare the two. Stibitz had been involved in some such work on data recording, and the plan was to learn about this and about American work on digital computers.

According to Goldstine, John Womersley, the Superintendent of the newly created Mathematics Division of NPL, was the first person from Britain to visit the ENIAC project [40]. He was in the U.S. from February to April 1945. The fact that Womersley had come back with information about American developments nearly caused Flowers's and Chandler's trip to be cancelled, but it turned out that he did not have the level of knowledge about the engineering aspects of the American machines that they needed [29]. After their visit was fixed Flowers invited Professor Hartree, who had also recently returned from a trip to the Moore School, to come to Dollis Hill to brief them [15].

The two traveled to the States at the beginning of September 1945, and stayed for approximately six weeks. During this time they visited the Aberdeen Proving Ground, Bell Labs, Harvard, MIT, the Moore School, and the University of Vermont. At Bell Labs they met S. B. Williams, and saw the Relay Interpolator. They attended a series of lectures by Williams and his team on the Model V relay computer, which was then nearing completion. They were most impressed by the way the work was organized, and in particular by the fact that the maintenance manuals were already being written — they have no recollection of any maintenance manuals ever being written for the COLOSSI! They found that Stibitz had already left Bell Labs for the University of Vermont, so they traveled to Burlington by rail, and spent a weekend with him [15, 28].

At MIT they met Sam Caldwell, who was then making a differential analyzer that was in part digital. Their visit to Harvard University enabled them to meet Howard Aiken and Grace Hooper and to see the Harvard MARK I. In all these visits they had to avoid any mention of COLOSSUS, and be very discreet about their own expertise in digital electronics. This applied even to S. B. Williams, although from one or two comments he made they realized that he must have had some involvement with the sort of work that they had been doing [15].

At the Moore School they met von Neumann, Eckert, and Mauchly, saw the ENIAC, and learned about the plans for EDVAC. Flowers was surprised to find that Lewis's original biquinary counter circuit had been used in the ENIAC without any trouble, perhaps because the Moore School people had had access to more uniform components than he had. One other recollection he has of the visit is of being told by Eckert of the problems of making the first delay line work. Flowers and Chandler were impressed by ENIAC but a bit appalled at the amount of electronics—of course, by this time the plans for EDVAC had already made the design of ENIAC obsolete [15, 28–30]. Yet again their visit must have been a discreet one—Goldstine, who gives considerable detail about the sequences of early visitors to the ENIAC, mentions only that in addition to Comrie, Hartree, and Womersley, "two others connected with the British Post Office Research Station also came" [41, p. 21].

Shortly after his return to Britain, Flowers was taken off the Data Recorder Project by Radley, who wanted him to resume work on the telephone network. Coombs replaced him, and for the next few years he and Chandler worked together, first on the data recorder itself, and then on digital computer design, since a means of analyzing the recorded data was required. For a time they worked closely with NPL and thus Chandler resumed close collaboration with Turing, although it was Coombs's first encounter with him [15]. Turing had been invited to join NPL at Newman's suggestion [41]. However, he apparently spent some time after leaving Bletchley Park on further classified work at a different establishment involving the actual construction of electronic equipment. No details of this work have been revealed [79].

Within a short time of joining NPL, Turing had produced a set of proposals for an "Automatic Computing Engine" [77]. This report postdated and referenced von Neumann's famous draft report on EDVAC [81], but went considerably further, being much more detailed, and containing the full concept of a stored-program computer. In fact it has been said that "Turing's proposal is one of the first complete designs for a stored-program computer (possibly the first)," and that "what we now regard as one of the fundamental characteristics of the von Neumann machine was as far as we know suggested independently, if not originally by Turing" [12]. (In von Neumann's report data and instruction words were differentiated, and only the address field of an instruction could be modified.)

Turing's report seems to have marked the real start of the ACE project. It was formally presented to the NPL Executive Committee on 19 March 1946 by Womersley and Turing. Womersley's accompanying memorandum summarizes Turing's proposal, which he states is based on the plans for EDVAC although he claims that von Neumann's EDVAC report "contains a number of ideas which are Dr. Turing's own" [90]. No mention is made of Turing's wartime work, but it is surely significant that one of the points listed in the argument for building the ACE is that "Commander Sir Edward Travis, of the Foreign Office, will give his support." The Executive Committee's formal decision was one of unanimous support [91], but the project went through many changes and vicissitudes. For a while the plan was, in accordance with Turing's wishes, that the machine be built for NPL by Chandler and Coombs at Dollis Hill [28]. This fell through, and they went on and designed and built the MOSAIC [20], which was largely based on an early version of the ACE design [14, 15, 28]. Turing grew disenchanted with the lack of progress at NPL and after a sabbatical at Cambridge joined Newman at Manchester University in late 1948 [54].

Newman had gone from Bletchley Park to Manchester, where he took the Chair of Pure Mathematics in October 1945 [69]. Two members of his section, I. J. Good and David Rees, went with him [54]. Newman was very interested in Turing's work, and in the impact that computers might have on mathematics. P. M. S. Blackett, who had been Director of Naval Operational Research during the war and so was conversant with the Bletchley Park work, as well as radar and the various other scientific contributions to the war effort, was already at Manchester [15]. He encouraged Newman to apply to the Royal Society for a grant "for a projected calculating machine laboratory at Manchester University" [54]. Professor Hartree, who is often credited with having played a very important role in promoting and obtaining support for the first postwar computer developments in Britain, particularly those at Cambridge, was closely involved in these matters. Apparently he visited Bletchley Park shortly after the end of the war to see the COLOSSI, the invitation having been made expressly to gain his support for the proposed project [45]. Support was forthcoming, and the Royal Society grant was awarded in July 1946. This enabled Newman to send Rees to the States that summer to attend the Moore School lectures at which the plans for EDVAC were presented. Later that year he himself visited the Moore School and saw ENIAC while spending a period at the Institute for Advanced Study, Princeton [15, 40].

Blackett had a hand also in getting F. C. Williams to Manchester from TRE in late 1946. Williams in turn arranged that Tom Kilburn should join him from TRE shortly afterward [69]. They learned from Newman the basic principles of von Neumann's stored-program computer, which was then fully designed but not yet operative [70, 86]. Within 18 months they had designed and built an experimental prototype stored-program electronic computer, believed to be the world's first. The work at Manchester was therefore at a very advanced stage when Turing arrived in September 1948, taking the nominal title of Deputy Director of the Computing Machine Laboratory, although he was actually in Newman's Mathematics Department [54]. Newman's belief is that Turing appreciated that the computer project was a more professional piece of engineering than anything he could compete with and so turned his attention to work on morphogenesis [15]. He did take some part in the work of the computer project, his most important contribution being the specification of input–output facilities [86]. He also did some programming, and wrote the first Manchester programming manual. Newman had some involvement with programming but his one notable claim to fame with respect to computer design is that of being an inventor of the index register [54, 69].

These, then, are the known links from the Bletchley Park work to postwar British computer development. Flowers and Broadhurst did not have any such involvement—their postwar careers were spent in telecommunications research and development. Flowers remained as Head of the Switching Division in the Post Office Research Department until 1964. During this time he was mainly concerned with electronic exchanges of various types—initially with cold-cathode switching and later with solid-state-time-division multiplex switching. He and his group were centrally involved in the first work in Britain on electronic exchanges, and completed the basic design of an all-electronic exchange by 1950. In 1964 he took the post of Head of the Advanced Development Group in Standard Telephones and Cables Ltd., from which he retired in 1970 [29, 35, 60]. Similarly, Broadhurst continued to work in the Switching Division, where he was responsible for the design of register-translators for telephone exchanges. He did design one special-purpose computer, but this was an analog computer, a "traffic machine," used for calculating the expected traffic through an exchange. Later, he led the team that developed the original ERNIE, a machine using a random-number source to select the numbers of winning Premium Bonds. He retired from the Post Office in 1963 and served as a consultant to the Telephone Equipment Manufacturers' Association for some years following [5, 60].

Chandler and Coombs separated after their work on MOSAIC. Coombs designed an early speech interpolation system for use in transatlantic cables, but not in fact the one that was eventually employed. In 1961, he began working on problems of pattern recognition, and in particular the problem of recognizing typescript multifont postcodes (ZIP codes). Chandler went back to work for the Foreign Office, but in 1968 joined Coombs in the work on pattern recognition machines [15, 60]. It was this work that led to their meeting Donald Michie again, who was by this time Professor of Machine

Intelligence at Edinburgh University. The influence of his wartime discussions with Turing had been great, and he had maintained contact with I. J. Good and Turing until the latter's tragic death in 1954, although it was not until 1960 that he first started to use computers for his researches into machine intelligence [64].

15. Conclusions

Goldstine has expressed surprise that, despite the ravages of war, "Great Britain had such vitality that it could immediately after the war embark on so many well-conceived and well-executed projects in the computer field" [40, p. 321]. It is my opinion that the COLOSSUS project was an important source of this vitality, one that has been largely unappreciated, as has the significance of its place in the chronology of the invention of the digital computer. It is unfortunate that the continuing secrecy surrounding many aspects of the project makes its proper evaluation so difficult. For this reason I choose to let some quotations from those associated directly with the machine serve as a conclusion to this account.

> The basic picture—a few mathematicians of high repute in their own field accidentally encounter a group of telephone engineers, of all people . . . and they found the one really enthusiastic expert in the form of Flowers, who had a good team with him, and made these jobs possible, with I think a lot of mutual respect on both sides. And the Post Office was able to supply the men, the material, and the maintenance, without any trouble, which is a great tribute to the men and the organization (Broadhurst [5]).

> The value of the work I am sure to engineers like myself and possibly to mathematicians like Alan Turing, was that we acquired a new understanding of and familiarity with logical switching and processing because of the enhanced possibilities brought about by electronic technologies which we ourselves developed. Thus when stored program computers became known to us we were able to go right ahead with their development (Flowers [27]).

> It was a great time in my life—it spoilt me for when I came back to mundane things with ordinary people (Flowers [28]).

Appendix*

Babbage's work in 1837 first established the logical principles of digital computers. His ideas were developed further in Turing's classical paper in 1936. The COLOSSUS machine produced by the Department of Com-

---

* Explanatory caption accompanying a set of photographs of COLOSSUS that were made available at the Public Record Office in London on 20 October 1975.

munications of the British Foreign Office, and put into operation in December 1943, was probably the first system to implement these principles successfully in terms of contemporary electronic technology. COLOSSUS was distinguished by the following features:

> punched paper tape inputs operating at 5000 characters per second;
> photo-electric tape readers;
> bistable hard-valve circuits performing counting, binary arithmetic and Boolean logic operations;
> electronic storage registers changeable by an automatically controlled sequence of operations;
> conditional (branching) logic;
> logic functions pre-set by patch-panels or switches, or conditionally selected by telephone relays;
> fully-automatic operation;
> solenoid operated electric typewriter output.

COLOSSUS used approximately 1000 hard valves and 500 gas-filled ones. It operated in parallel arithmetic mode at 5000 pulses per second. The requirement for the machine was formulated by Professor M. H. A. Newman, and the development was undertaken by a small team led by T. H. Flowers. A. Turing was working in the same department at that time, and his earlier work had its full influence on the design concept.

The attached World War II photographs* depict various aspects of COLOSSUS and a set of reproductions has been annotated to show some of its major features. A considerable number of further machines was built and gave reliable and effective service until the end of the war.

Addendum

Since this paper was prepared the British Government has for the first time made available at the Public Record Office a substantial number of the messages that were deciphered at Bletchley Park during World War II. This release of information has enabled much more substantial and authoritative accounts to be produced of the role of Bletchley Park, and of its impact on the war, than have been available hitherto. Particularly noteworthy are those by R. Lewin, "Ultra Goes to War: The Secret Story" (Hutchinson, London, 1978), and by P. Beesly, "Very Special Intelligence" (Hamish Hamilton, London, 1977). A three-volume history of British Intelligence in World War II, which deals with the activities of Bletchley Park, has been approved for publication. The first volume will be published by Her Majesty's Stationery Office in 1979. Also since the paper was written, the author has had further correspondence with Professor Good, Professor Michie, and

* Public Record Office Number FO 854/234 (Crown Copyright Reserved).

Professor Newman concerning the various uses made of COLOSSUS. It is now apparent that it was the technique, developed by Good and Michie, involving manual connections and reconnections while the machine was running (described in Section 8) that led to the COLOSSI being used to mechanize very important tasks that had hitherto been carried out manually in the Testery. The work by Wylie referred to in Section 9 concerned some quite different aspect of the set of problems on which the COLOSSI were employed.

ACKNOWLEDGMENTS

The preparation of this paper has been a very pleasant experience, particularly because of the opportunity it afforded me to meet, in most cases for the first time, and have lengthy discussions and extensive correspondence with Mr. S. W. Broadhurst, Mr. W. W. Chandler, Dr. A. W. M. Coombs, Mr. T. H. Flowers, Professor D. Michie, and Professor M. H. A. Newman. They have all been very hospitable and helpful. One other person closely involved with CO-LOSSUS, Professor I. J. Good, was interviewed and provided valuable assistance, but in this case David Kahn kindly visited him in Virginia to record an interview for me. A number of other people provided helpful replies to my letters, including Dr. D. W. Babbage, Professor H. Campaigne, Professor A. A. Cohen, Dr. D. W. Davies, Mr. A. I. Dumey, Dr. A. C. Lynch, Mr. C. A. May, Mr. F. O. Morrell, Dr. W. T. Tutte, Mr. W. G. Welchman, Professor K. L. Wildes, Mr. M. W. Woodger, and Dr. C. E. Wynn-Williams. Each person who provided me with material especially for this paper has had the opportunity to check the relevant sections of a draft version. However, ultimate responsibility for all errors, particularly those of analysis and interpretation, must rest with the author. I should also like to express my gratitude to the British Government for releasing material on the COLOSSUS. Finally I should like to thank Miss J. A. Lennox and Mrs. E. M. Smith, who coped splendidly with the typing of numerous versions of this paper, the transcriptions of many hours of recorded interviews, and a large volume of correspondence.

REFERENCES

1. Babbage, C., On the Mathematical Powers of the Calculating Engine, Manuscript dated 26 December 1837. (Printed in Randell [74].)
2. Babbage, C., "Passages from the Life of a Philosopher." Longman, Green, London, 1864. (Reprinted by Augustus M. Kelley, New York, 1969).
3. Babbage, D. W., Letter to the author (19 September 1975).
4. Beevers, C. A., A machine for the rapid summation of Fourier series, *Proc. Phys. Soc. London* **51**(4), 660–663 (1939).
5. Broadhurst, S. W., Transcript of interview (11 November 1975).
6. Broadhurst, S. W., Letter to the author (20 January 1976).
7. Bush, V., "Pieces of the Action." Morrow, New York, 1970.
8. Calvocoressi, P., The Ultra Secrets of Station X. *Sunday Times*, pp. 33–34 (24 November 1974).
9. Campaigne, H., Letter to the author (8 July 1975).
10. Campaigne, H., Letter to the author (11 October 1975).
11. Campaigne, H., Letter to the author (28 January 1976).
12. Carpenter, B. E., and Doran, R. W., The other Turing machine, *Comput. J.* **20**(3), 269–279 (1977).

13. Cave Brown, A., "Bodyguard of Lies." Allen, London, 1976.
14. Chandler, W. W., Gates and trigger circuits, "Automatic Digital Computation," pp. 181–186. HM Stationery Office, London, 1954.
15. Chandler, W. W., and Coombs, A. W. M., Transcript of interview (10 November 1975).
16. Chandler, W. W., Letter to the author (24 January 1976).
17. Chandler, W. W., Letter to the author (30 January 1976).
18. Cohen, A. A., Letter to the author (30 May 1975).
19. Cohen, A. A., Letter to the author (21 January 1976).
20. Coombs, A. W. M., MOSAIC: The "Ministry of Supply Automatic Computer." "Automatic Digital Computation," pp. 38–42. HM Stationery Office, London, 1954.
21. Coombs, A. W. M., Letter to the author (20 January 1976).
22. Charles B. Tomkins dies in Los Angeles, *Datamation* **17**(4), 54, 61 (1971).
23. Dumey, A. I., Letter to the author (25 August 1975).
24. Dumey, A. I., Letter to the author (13 November 1975).
25. Dumey, A. I., Letter to the author (29 February 1976).
26. Flowers, T. H., Pulse counting circuits, U.K. Patent No. 584, 704 (17 November 1944).
27. Flowers, T. H., Letter to the author (15 February 1972). (Quoted in Randell [73].)
28. Flowers, T. H., Transcript of interview (31 October 1975).
29. Flowers, T. H., Transcript of interview (17 December 1975).
30. Flowers, T. H., Letter to the author (21 January 1976).
31. Flowers, T. H., Letter to the author (23 January 1976).
32. Flowers, T. H., Letter to the author (31 January 1976).
33. Flowers, T. H., Letter to the author (16 February 1976).
34. Flowers, T. H., Letter to the author (25 March 1976).
35. Flowers, T. H., Letter to the author (2 April 1976).
36. Flowers, T. H., Letter to the author (4 April 1976).
37. Flowers, T. H., Letter to the author (26 May 1976).
38. Frankel, S., Letter to the author (11 February 1972). (Quoted in Randell [73].)
39. Goldstine, H. H., Letter to the author (15 October 1971). (Quoted in Randell [73].)
40. Goldstine, H. H., "The Computer from Pascal to von Neumann." Princeton Univ. Press, Princeton, New Jersey 1972.
41. Goodwin, E. T., Letter to the author (13 March 1972). (Quoted in Randell [73].)
42. Good, I. J., "Probability and the Weighing of Evidence." Griffin, London, 1950.
43. Good, I. J., Some future social repercussions of computers, *Internat. J. Environm. Stud.* **1**, 67–79 (1970).
44. Good, I. J., Letter to the author (27 January 1972). (Quoted in Randell [73].)
45. Good, I. J., Transcript of interview (29 January 1976).
46. Good, I. J., Letter to the author (9 April 1976).
47. Good, I. J., Letter to the author (12 April 1976).
48. Halsbury, Earl of, Ten years of computer development, *Comput. J.* **1**, 153–159 (1969).
49. Hay, I., "The Post Office Went to War." HM Stationery Office, London, 1946.
50. Kahn, D., "The Code-Breakers." Macmillan, New York, 1967.
51. Kahn, D., Letter to the author (6 June 1972).
52. Kahn, D., The Ultra Secret, *New York Times Book Review,* p. 5 (29 December 1974).
53. Kozaczuk, W., The war of wits, *Poland* **6**, 10–11, 34–35 (1975); **7**, 32–34 (1975).
54. Lavington, S. H., A History of Manchester Computers. National Computing Centre, Manchester, 1975.
55. Lehmer, D. H., A photo-electric number sieve, *Amer. Math. Monthly* **40**(7), 401–406 (1933).
56. Lewis, W. B., A "Scale of Two" high-speed counter using hard vacuum triodes, *Proc. Cambridge Philos. Soc.* **33**, 549–558 (1937).
57. Lewis, W. B., "Electrical Counting: With Special Reference to Alpha and Beta Particles." Cambridge Univ. Press, London and New York, 1942.
58. Lynch, A. C., The "Transmitter, Telegraph, Mark 1". Unpublished memorandum (1976).

59. Lynch, A. C., Letter to the author (26 March 1976).
60. May, C. A., Letter to the author (20 January 1976).
61. Meltzer, B., and Michie, D., Introduction, "Machine Intelligence" (B. Meltzer and D. Michie, eds.), Vol. 7, pp. xiii–xiv. Edinburgh Univ. Press, Edinburgh, 1972.
62. Michie, D., Letter to the author (18 March 1972). (Quoted in Randell [73].)
63. Michie, D., The Bletchley machines, "Origins of Digital Computers" (B. Randell, ed.), pp. 327–328. Springer-Verlag, Berlin, 1973.
64. Michie, D., Transcript of interview (6 December 1975).
65. Michie, D., Letter to the author (10 December 1975).
66. Michie, D., Letter to the author (5 February 1976).
67. Morrell, F. O., Letter to the author (3 February 1976).
68. Muggeridge, M., "Chronicles of Wasted Time. Part 2: The Infernal Grove." Collins, London, 1973.
69. Newman, M. H. A., Transcript of interview (1 November 1975).
70. Newman, M. H. A., Letter to the author (20 March 1976).
71. Newman, M. H. A., Letter to the author (2 April 1976).
72. Radford, W. H., Report on an Investigation of the Practicability of Developing a Rapid Computing Machine. MIT, Cambridge, Massachusetts (15 October 1939).
73. Randell, B., On Alan Turing and the origins of digital computers, "Machine Intelligence" (B. Meltzer and D. Michie, eds.), Vol. 7., pp. 3–20. Edinburgh Univ. Press, Edinburgh, 1972.
74. Randell, B. (ed.), "The Origins of Digital Computers: Selected Papers." Springer-Verlag, Berlin and New York, 1973.
75. Seale, P., and McConville, M., "Philby: The Long Road to Moscow." Hamish Hamilton, London, 1973.
76. Stibitz, G. R., Letter to the author (6 June 1972).
77. Turing, A., Proposals for Development in the Mathematics Division of an Automatic Computing Engine (A.C.E.), Rep. E.882. Executive Committee, National Physical Laboratory, Teddington, Middlesex (1945).
78. Turing, A., Intelligent Machinery. (September 1947). [Reprinted in "Machine Intelligence" (B. Meltzer and D. Michie, eds.), Vol. 5, pp. 3–23. Edinburgh Univ. Press, Edinburgh, 1969.]
79. Turing, S., "Alan M. Turing." Heffer, Cambridge, 1959.
80. Tutte, W. T., Letter to the author (28 January 1976).
81. von Neumann, J., First Draft of a Report on the EDVAC, Contract No. W-670-ORD-4926. Moore School of Electrical Engineering, Univ. of Pennsylvania, Philadelphia, Pennsylvania (30 June 1945).
82. Wald, A., "Sequential Analysis." Wiley, New York, 1947.
83. Weik, M. H., The ENIAC story, Amer. Ordnance Assoc. 3–7 (January–February 1961).
84. Welchman, W. G., Letter to the author (9 January 1975).
85. Welchman, W. G., Letter to the author (8 March 1976).
86. Williams, F. C., Letter to the author (3 February 1972). (Quoted in Randell [73].)
87. Wildes, K. L., The Digital Computer—Whirlwind (unpublished).
88. Winterbotham, F. W., "The Ultra Secret." Weidenfeld and Nicolson, London, 1974.
89. Wolf, J. J., The ONR Relay Computer, Math Tables Other Aids Comput 6(40), 207–212.
90. Womersley, J. R., "ACE" Machine Project. Executive Committee, National Physical Laboratory, Teddington, Middlesex (13 February 1946).
91. Woodger M., Summary of Minutes Relating to "Large Electronic Calculating Machine ACE," National Physical Laboratory, Executive Committee Meeting of 19 March 1946 (1976) (unpublished).
92. Wynn-Williams, C. E., A Thyratron "Scale of Two" automatic counter, Proc. Roy. Soc. London Ser. A 136, 312–324 (1932).
93. Wynn-Williams, C. E., The scale-of-two counter, Year Book Phys. Soc. 53–60 (1957).

94. Wynn-Williams, C. E., Letter to the author (16 March 1976).
95. Report on an Electronic Difference Analyzer. Moore School of Electrical Engineering, Univ. of Pennsylvania, Philadelphia, Pennsylvania (8 April 1943).
96. Honeywell Inc., Plaintiff vs. Sperry Rand Corporation and Illinois Scientific Developments, Inc., Defendants File No. 4-67. Civ. 138. United States District Court, District of Minnesota, Fourth Division, Minneapolis, Minnesota (1973).
97. Automatic Computation at the N.P.L., *Engineering* **171,** 6–8 (1951).

COMPUTING LABORATORY
UNIVERSITY OF NEWCASTLE UPON TYNE
NEWCASTLE UPON TYNE, ENGLAND

Von Neumann: The Interaction of Mathematics and Computing

S. M. ULAM

I shall be writing primarily about von Neumann. My title is: Von Neumann, the interaction of mathematics and computing, but it is very hard to separate sharply mathematics from physics in this connection. I'd go further and stress the very great possibilities that the same set of ideas, the same set of technological developments, can have in other natural sciences—primarily biology, for example, and that soon. One could call this the "music of the future," and I think this aspect of the future is something that should not be neglected, even in a meeting devoted to the past.

It must have been in 1938 that I first had discussions with von Neumann about problems in mathematical physics, and the first I remember were when he was very curious about the problem of mathematical treatment of turbulence in hydrodynamics. I think he discussed this with Norbert Wiener also shortly before. He was fascinated by the role of the Reynolds number, a dimensionless number, a pure number because it is the ratio of two forces, the inertial one and the viscous, and has the following importance: When its value surpasses a critical size, about 2000, the regular laminar flow, as it is called, becomes highly irregular and turbulent. Both Wiener in a general way and von Neumann, who I think knew more practical physics than Norbert, wanted to find an explanation or at least a way to understand this very puzzling large number. Small numbers like π and e, are of course very frequent in physics, but here is a number of the order of thousands and yet it is a pure number with no dimensions: it does whet our curiosity.

93

I remember that in our discussions von Neumann realized that the known analytical methods, the methods of mathematical analysis, even in their most advanced forms, were not powerful enough to give any hope of obtaining solutions in closed form. This was perhaps one of the origins of his desire to try to devise methods of very fast numerical computations, a more humble way of proceeding. Proceeding by "brute force" is considered by some to be more lowbrow. I was not present at the discussions between Norbert Wiener and Johnny von Neumann—he just told me about them. A little later these two men had apparently developed different philosophies. Wiener thought that the computers (if you could use the word at that time) would be more in the nature of analog machines than digital. Von Neumann maintained the opposite view. Wiener thought of the hormonal activity of the human brain— obviously there is no mechanical relay system in our brain—so he though that the big developments would go in the direction of some kind of system of fluids, whereas von Neumann from the start was thinking of developing a digital or binary or purely discrete system.

I remember also discussions about the possibilities of calculating the weather at first only locally, and soon after that, about how to calculate the circulation of meteorological phenomena around the globe. There is of course already available from the last century some marvelous theoretical work, Laplace's and others' but it is not detailed enough to enable meteorologists to predict the motion of air locally, very little but on the largest scale round the globe. Some progress has been made since that time, but not nearly as much as in some other fields that I shall mention.

I can mention two cases in other fields of mathematical physics in which computers have played a decisive role and in which progress has been more obvious: the study of the equilibrium or even of the evolution of a star, and the calculations without which it would be impossible to predict the behavior of star clusters or gravitating masses of gas. In some ways the original intention or motivation is not what was immediately followed with rapid success. I think this is typical of many developments in technology. The original application of a new fact or tool is not what ultimately turns out to be its greatest application or achievement. In this connection I remember that when a release of nuclear energy was discovered in Chicago and developed in Los Alamos, with all its terrifying consequences, von Neumann remarked that the first use of naphtha or petroleum as we now call it was as a laxative. Look what happened in the following centuries! This is merely to point out that nuclear energy will have more interesting and certainly more beneficial effects and applications than its original one, the bombs.

The first papers that von Neumann wrote as a young man around 1924– 1925 were in mathematical logic and the study of formal systems. It is perhaps a matter of chance, that computer development became possible only by a confluence of at least two entirely different streams. One is the purely theoretical study of formal systems. The study of how to formalize a descrip-

tion of natural phenomena or even of mathematical facts. Professor May*
has spoken felicitously of "genetic development": we call it axioms and
rules of procedure. The whole idea of proceeding by a given set of rules from
a given set of axioms was studied successfully in this connection. The second
stream is the technological development in electronics, which came at just
the right time. Of course, the war had greatly accelerated the availability of
funds and effort just a few years later.

Remember that for many years von Neumann was very much a pure
mathematician. It was only, to my knowledge, just before World War II that
he became interested not only in mathematical physics but also in more concrete physical problems. His book on quantum theory is very abstract and
is, so to say, about the grammar of the subject. Now it is extremely important to attempt even only tentatively to put a rigorous foundation to a new
part of physics, and it is a valuable and important work. But it did not, it seems
to me, contribute directly to any truly new insights or new experiments—
there are probably some physicists who might dispute this point of view, but
in the large it seems to me that it is so.

Already some years before the war von Neumann expected a catastrophe.
He thought there would come a great conflict involving also the United
States. Living here and having come from Europe he was in a good position
to see further. On the whole people who lived only in Europe or here in the
States probably did not sense the currents as well as he did.

My own involvement with problems of a more practical physical nature
started when I came to Los Alamos. I arrived during the last few days of
1943 and learned right away what the project was working on, was introduced
to a number of physicists, and, when I came into one of the offices, found to
my surprise, von Neumann (who came frequently for periods of a week or
two), Teller, who was with him, and some others. The blackboard was filled
with very complicated equations that you could encounter in other forms in
other offices. This sight scared me out of my wits: looking at these I felt
that I should never be able to contribute even an epsilon to the solution of
any of them. But during the following days, to my relief, I saw that the same
equations remained on the blackboards. I noticed that one did not have to
produce immediate solutions.

Even though I was not an applied mathematician, I knew some physics in
a sort of platonic way, having always been interested in quantum theory and
ideas of relativity and in astrophysics especially. Little as I already knew
about partial differential equations or integral equations, I could feel at once
that there was no hope of solution by analytical work that could yield practical answers to the problems that appeared.

One of the first problems that was crucial to the success of the whole
project was the behavior of an implosion of a spherical system. The word

* See his paper in this volume.

itself was highly classified during the war. It would have been a terrible breach of security even to utter it, and this was true even for a couple of years after the war. But then it became a *"secret de polichinelle"*; everybody at least had heard of the word. The idea was to compress a mass of material into higher density by surrounding it with explosives and try to figure out what pressures and densities would be achievable, and how the material could get to such configurations. It was not enough to know the answers within a factor of two or three. One had to have a more precise numerical value, an estimate of the pressure, say, within 10%. This was really impossible to guess, or to derive from an analysis of theoretical dimensional reasonings alone. We had a long discussion about using a purely "brute force" approach.

Being so erudite in many fields of mathematics in addition to his own, he tried to work out with some of his collaborators at least partway analytical methods, to find out what would happen when the material was pushed together. However, the accuracy or reliability was quite unsatisfactory. I was trying to press him at least to try some step-by-step numerical procedures assuming, of course, knowledge of the equations of state and so on—these were known with some accuracy. Von Neumann was at that time a consultant to the Aberdeen Ballistics Laboratory, and he knew the computing machines there. I did convince him; we received administrative support for getting all possible means to enable one to calculate implosions more exactly. He did a lot of this work around 1948–1949 on the ENIAC at Aberdeen.

The study of the implosion problem gave one of the great impulses to the development of fast computers. There were many others of the same sort of equal importance to Los Alamos, such as the equations of state themselves. And because it had to solve these problems Los Alamos, consciously or not, made a great and fundamental contribution to the development of computing.

So far I have been speaking of mathematical physics, in which such great developments took place. But in mathematics itself these were slower. It was more of a luxury, since machine time was expensive, to try to compute things of only pure mathematical interest. The calculations and experiments were at first in the nature of fillers: There was sometimes a free period of time on the machine, and one could amuse oneself by trying to work on problems in pure mathematics. So I am saying that the interaction of computers and mathematics started almost playfully. But remember the theory of probability, which is now so fundamental in many areas of theoretical physics, statistical mechanics, quantum theory, etc., and pervades all kinds of very theoretical and of course also more mundane kinds of mathematics. The natural material to play with in those early days was in combinatorial problems and in number theory. As far as number theory goes, the use of computers has an older history. I was still a student in Poland in the late 1920s when I first heard from my professor Hugo Steinhaus of a mathematician in California who had devised a mechanical way to find primes and to study some of their properties using a system of cylinders with holes. That was D. N. Lehmer, the father; his son, Professor D. H. Lehmer, has worked with this machine and is one of the pioneers of the use of electronic computers in number theory.

Of course, when it comes to operations in prime numbers or other questions in number theory, and to the consideration of very large numbers, this becomes possible only with very fast machines. From the outset the most impressive thing about electronic computers has been their speed. One of the fears expressed by mathematicians about the use of computers was that the interesting numbers in combinatorial mathematics are so large, even in relatively simple problems, that even the biggest computers could not begin to touch the general cases so as to give us confidence in the asymptotic behavior. This is less and less true. There are now examples of situations in which many billions of alternatives have been sieved through in a few hours. One such example is the famous four-color problem: if you have a map on a plane or a sphere and want to color the countries so that countries with a common boundary always have different colors, how many colors do you need? The conjecture is that this can always be done with four colors, but nobody was able to prove this until very recently. Strangely enough this problem can be studied on a computer. I studied it in a multilated form and a former student of mine in Colorado managed to prove the conjecture for an infinite band seven countries wide—for which millions of cases had to be examined. Very recently the full problem has been solved, by a method that would not have been possible without a fast computer.*

The reason I mention all this is that mathematicians, all of whom tend perhaps to be a little snobbish, are not satisfied with the purely finite: they need at least an inkling of infinity! So in order to "hook" mathematicians in my own modest attempts to interest them in some problems of mathematical biology, I always try to formulate the problems in such a way that they have a sense not only for finite assemblies but for cases with true infinity. This is merely a sort of psychological stratagem, but it will cease to be so in the future when some "elements" of true infinity may be, by use of so-called quantifiers in algebra, *mirrored* in operations on finite computers.

When I talked to von Neumann about this I learned that it was also his hope and belief. I use the word quantifier; perhaps I should explain its meaning.

The machines can express well the Boolean–Aristotelian expression in logic, which consists of the words *and* or *not*, Mathematicians however, greatly love expressions like "there exists an X such that . . . ." Now this "exists" is a quantifier. The other quantifier is "for all," as in "for all X such

---

* See K. Appel and W. Haken, The solution of the four-color problem, *Sci. Amer.* **237**(4), 108–121 (1977).

and such is true." There are just these two quantifiers, which seems so very innocent, but they have a character different from the purely Aristotelian operations. Somehow they have not yet been incorporated, even by approximation, on the computers, except in the most primitive and too literally finite way. So this is one of the possibilities for the future, beyond the merely continuously improving way of surveying larger and larger numbers of cases, which ultimately might give insights into the true nature of physical laws by natural induction.

It seems to me that the great advances we now see, great as they are interesting are still only in their infancy. I feel that the future holds much more. The present machines can execute only instructions given in advance, and as far as the logical operations or the arithmetical operations go, they are limited to Boolean operations, Aristotelian logic, and the four arithmetic operations or else ensuing evaluations of integrals, derivatives, etc. There is no doubt that a more general abstract way of following and studying the development of mathematical symbols will be rendered possible to a much larger extent by new machines.

I should like to propagandize, if that is needed, some work to develop the use of machines operating in parallel, on many channels at the same time. Up to now our computers essentially follow the course of making one step, one deduction at a time, this of course with some reservations and caveats. I hope that in the future, perhaps even the near future, there will be machines built to imitate more closely certain features of a brain and of the nervous system, which certainly works simultaneously on very many channels.

This is another story. After the war, von Neumann was interested—starting with the analogies between the computer and some of the mental processes—in the mysteries of the workings of the nervous system and the brain itself. He published several papers on this. We are not yet at the stage where one can say anything very meaningful even only about the physiological nature of human memory. There are fundamental controversies among physiologists: Does the memory reside in molecules or is it maintained as a system of currents between the neurons of the brain? That simple dichotomy is not resolved. Some partial understanding of how the memory works will probably come in a not too distant future, and with it more effective means of creating work in parallel on computers that will be so superior to even the best we have now. Von Neumann realized that the search mechanism used by the brain must be very different from the ones we use on our computers, and this, when we understand it, must be the one we shall then use.

Our conscious reasoning, the things we write down, appears to be linear. But the real search in our memory and the process of thought certainly proceed simultaneously on very many channels. I remember in discussions with von Neumann the great marvel was that there are many billions of neurons in the brain and, as he told me at that time, there were perhaps as many as 50 or 100 connections between some of them. Today this number turns out to be perhaps several thousand instead of 50; in the central region it may be 100,000. So complications grow not only in the foundations of physics or in astrophysics but even in anatomy. Everything in science seems to become much more complicated than we once thought.

NOTES

1.   A full biography of von Neumann by the present author, with a complete list of his publications, and seven papers by other authors on different fields of his work, appears in the special issue of *Bull. Amer. Math. Soc.* **64**(3, Part 2) (1958).

2.   A. H. Taub, ed., "Von Neumann: Collected Works, 1903–1957." Pergamon, Oxford, 1961.

3.   For John von Neumann's thoughts on the brain see his last book, "The Computer and the Brain." Yale Univ. Press, New Haven, Connecticut, 1958.

DEPARTMENT OF MATHEMATICS
UNIVERSITY OF FLORIDA
GAINESVILLE, FLORIDA

Turing's Work at the National Physical Laboratory and the Construction of Pilot ACE, DEUCE, and ACE

J. H. WILKINSON

1. Introduction

The ACE project at the National Physical Laboratory is of particular interest in the history of computing machines because of its connection with the work of A. M. Turing. He and J. von Neumann are now universally acknowledged to be the two outstanding men of genius of the computer revolution, and it is a severe misfortune that neither survived to attend the Los Alamos conference. In this paper I shall not attempt to give a review of Turing's work as a whole but shall content myself with an account of the ACE project at NPL from a personal standpoint.

The Mathematics Division of the National Physical Laboratory was set up in 1945 in response to a need to coordinate the various scientific computing activities that had developed in an ad hoc way at a number of government establishments during the war. Chief among these was the Admiralty Computing Service organized and supervised by John Todd; this was attached to HM Nautical Almanac Office, which was under the direction of D. H. Sadler. In addition to work in the general field of numerical mathematics, the terms of reference of the Division specifically included research on new computing equipment.

J. R. Womersley was appointed the first Superintendent and the Division included a desk computing section under E. T. Goodwin, a statistics section under E. C. Fieller, a punched-card section under T. B. Boss, a differential analyzer section under J. G. L. Michel, and an electronics section under A. M. Turing. It was the desk computing section that was effectively the "numerical analysis" section at that time; the nucleus of its staff was drawn from the Admiralty Computing Service and included E. T. Goodwin, L. Fox, F. W. J. Olver, and H. H. Robertson.

Turing's early research, first at Cambridge and then at Princeton, had been in mathematical logic and had led him to introduce the concepts of "computable numbers" and what are now known as "Turing machines." During the war his work at the Foreign Office provided him with a knowledge of pulse techniques, and it was this that led to an interest in the construction of an electronic computer. Turing joined Mathematics Division in the autumn of 1945, and for the first few months he worked on this project entirely on his own, producing a comparatively detailed proposal for the Executive Committee of the NPL which was duly accepted. At that stage the member of the Executive Committee with special responsibility for Mathematics Division was D. R. Hartree, and he played an important role in supporting the electronic computer project at NPL.

Turing was in no sense an "empire builder," and he assembled his team with extreme caution. I joined NPL in May 1946, having worked for the duration of the war at the Ministry of Supply on internal and external ballistics and the thermodynamics of explosives, using numerical techniques. I was assigned to Turing for half time only; the other half was to be spent in the desk computing section acquiring a knowledge of numerical analysis. I shall never know whether Turing was undecided whether he required my services at all, or whether he thought I should be so effective that half my time would be adequate for his purposes.

2. Version V of ACE

When I arrived Turing was working on what he called Version V of his Automatic Computing Engine (ACE), the use of the word "engine" being in recognition of the pioneering work of Babbage on his Analytic Engine. Documentation was not a strong point of Turing's work, and I never saw anything of Versions I to IV. By the standards of that time ACE was to be a very large computer with a delay line storage of some 6400 words of 32 binary digits each, held in 200 long mercury delay lines. Turing was confident that a megacycle pulse rate would be perfectly practical, and since each delay line stored 32 words the circulation time was 1024 μsec, i.e., about 1 msec.

The machine had a highly original code, although since at that time I had no other experience of digital computers this was not evident to me, and I only gradually appreciated how far out of step were projects elsewhere. Turing was obsessed with speed of operation; if consecutive instructions were to be stored in consecutive positions in a long delay line it would be possible to execute only one instruction per msec. To avoid this, insofar as was possible consecutive instructions were stored in such relative positions that each emerged from a delay line just as it was required. This subsequently came to be known as "optimum coding" although Turing never used this expression; he thought of it just as coding. The use of optimum coding made it necessary to indicate in each instruction the storage position of the next.

In order to increase the speed further, the operation of the computer was not based on the use of a central accumulator. Each instruction represented the transfer of information from a "source" to a "destination." Included in the sources and destinations were, of course, the 200 long delay lines, but there were also a number of short delay lines storing one or two words each. These were provided not only with the usual source and destination gates but were also associated with a number of functional sources and destinations. One of the one-word delay lines had an additive destination and a subtractive destination; this was also true of one of the two-word delay lines. In addition to the natural arithmetic operations, all versions of the ACE included a very full set of logical operations. In Version V these were provided by functional sources associated with pairs of short delay lines. Thus, for example, associated with short delay lines A and B (say) there would be functional sources giving A and B, A V B, and A $\neq$ B, respectively. The machine had one other very unusual feature but this is perhaps best described in connection with Version VII.

3. Version VII

Later in 1946, M. Woodger joined the ACE section, and the three of us worked together. Our main effort was devoted to modifying the logical design of ACE in the light of experience gained in trying to program the basic procedures of numerical analysis. Version V was quickly abandoned and replaced by Versions VI and VII, which were essentially four-address code machines in which each instruction was of the form

A FUNCTION B $\rightarrow$ C, NEXT INSTRUCTION D.

This code was adopted partly in order to give a closer relationship between a mathematical algorithm and its coded version and partly to give greater speed. From Turing's point of view the latter was at least as important as the former. In some instructions it virtually replaced three single-address instructions of the form

A $\rightarrow$ ACCUMULATOR: B $\rightarrow$ ACCUMULATOR, ADDING:

ACCUMULATOR $\rightarrow$ C,

although this much exaggerates its overall efficiency.

The extra speed was attained at the cost of extra equipment; each delay line had to be fitted with two independent source gates leading into two different highways; these highways fed into a "function box" from which emerged the required function of the two sources; the result was then fed directly to the required destination. An operation of the type $A + B \rightarrow C$ took only one word time. In version VII this had become 40 μsec (a minor cycle) since the word length had been increased to 40 binary digits to accommodate the more comprehensive instruction, although by that time we were more than willing to increase the word length for purely computational reasons. The maximum rate at which instructions could be executed was one every two minor cycles, one minor cycle being required for setting up the instruction and one for executing it. Turing was constantly fretting to reduce this to one minor cycle by a further duplication of equipment.

An intriguing feature is that the transfer of information from A and B to C could take place for a prolonged period of up to 32 minor cycles (the period of circulation in a long delay line) the period being essentially determined by the position of the next instruction D. (This feature was also included in Version V.) This made coding excessively untidy but in some situations it was a very powerful feature. One could, for example, by means of an instruction

```
A + B → C continued 32 minor cycles
```

add all 32 numbers in delay line A to the corresponding numbers in delay line B and send the resulting vector sum to delay line C. By having the carry suppression at the end of every minor cycle, every other minor cycle, or omitting it altogether one could deal automatically with one-word numbers, two-word numbers, or multilength numbers. By means of an instruction of the form

```
A + B → B,
```

where A was a long delay line and B a one-word delay line, one could add up to 32 consecutive entries in A to the contents of B. The possibilities of this feature should now be obvious. In this way the fullest advantage was taken of the fact that ACE was a serial machine. ACE may be said to have had some of the features of modern vector machines!

In 1947, D. W. Davies, G. G. Alway, B. Curtis, and H. J. Norton joined the ACE section, and altogether from 1946–1948 a great deal of quite detailed coding was done. It included basic subroutines for such things as multilength arithmetic (including multiplication, division, and square roots), floating-point arithmetic (both single-precision and double-precision), and interval arithmetic. Turing was originally very enthusiastic about interval arithmetic, but this enthusiasm waned after we had discovered the weakness in Hotelling's analysis of the buildup of rounding errors in Gaussian elimination. We realized that interval arithmetic would frequently give severe overestimates of the effect of rounding errors in matrix processes. The subroutines for floating-point arithmetic were particularly detailed. They were produced by Alway and myself in 1947 for both Versions V and VII, but all members of the group contributed to the final codes. They were almost certainly the earliest floating-point subroutines. Those for Version V were essentially the same as the subroutines that were subsequently used on the Pilot ACE. At a time when the arithmetic provided on modern computers is often so disappointing, it is salutary to recall that the subroutines included provision for accumulating inner products in double-precision floating-point arithmetic and all rounding was immaculate!

During this period Turing introduced some of the earliest automatic computing procedures, and he and M. Woodger did a fair amount of work in this area. The rather complicated nature of the code perhaps provided an inducement to develop such techniques, though at the same time making it much more difficult to do so.

A considerable effort was made on numerical linear algebra, and some of this work is included in a Progress Report on the Automatic Computing Engine published in 1948 [3]. The solution of linear systems by the Gauss–Seidel method and by Gaussian elimination with partial pivoting plus iterative refinement are included in this report. An interesting feature of these codes is that they make a very intensive use of subroutines; the addition of two vectors, multiplication of a vector by a scalar, inner products, etc, are all coded in this way. It is a pity from a historical standpoint that we did not take this opportunity to provide a detailed and comprehensive review of the coding effort in the years 1946–1948 since many of the codes that were produced must have been the first of their kind. In view of its subsequent wide use on automatic computers perhaps it is worth mentioning that the Runge–Kutta method was coded, but not with Gill's refinements. In 1947, the Runge–Kutta method was not widely known and was out of the mainstream of methods used in the desk computing section at NPL. However, at the time I produced that report I was more concerned with the lack of progress in the construction of the computer than in providing an historical document.

4. Huskey at NPL

The decision was taken quite early not to set up a hardware section at NPL but to subcontract this side of the work to some other government department, preferably where there had been previous experience with pulse techniques. Some decisions are seen to have been incorrect only in retrospect; this appeared to me to be a deplorable decision even at the time. Either the chosen department would prove not to be interested in the project, in which case it would obviously be a bad decision, or it *would* prove to be interested, in which case NPL would inevitably have lost control of an exciting project. For the first year or so at NPL, Turing continued his association with two former wartime colleagues who were by then working at the Post Office Station at Dollis Hill. Unfortunately, in spite of the enthusiasm of Flowers, it was not possible to provide sufficient manpower at Dollis Hill to pursue such an ambitious project.

In 1947, the policy of trying to get the computer built outside was finally abandoned and an Electronics Section was set up at NPL with responsibility to R. L. Smith-Rose, Superintendent of the Radio Division. The head of the section was H. A. Thomas, an energetic man, but unfortunately his chief interest was in industrial electronics rather than in the construction of an electronic computer. I found it difficult to feel as critical of this preference on the part of Thomas as did others associated with the computer project. Although wholly committed to the construction of a digital computer myself and therefore disappointed by Thomas's views it did not seem unreasonable at that stage in history for somebody to take the view that industrial electronics was the more important field. The new Electronics Section was recruited mainly from members of other divisions of NPL who had some previous interest in electronics but, by and large, they had to acquire the detailed expertise in pulse techniques by working on the project itself. However, they did bring to the team a great deal of experience, which was to prove invaluable when the construction of a computer was finally under way. In addition to the NPL contingent, two persons, E. A. Newman and D. O. Clayden, were recruited from EMI, and they certainly had previous experience that was wholly appropriate to the ACE project. Turing and Thomas had virtually nothing in common, and it was evident from the start that collaboration between the two men was unlikely to be satisfactory.

In January 1947, H. D. Huskey, on the advice of D. R. Hartree, came to the ACE section of Mathematics Division for a sabbatical year. Huskey had worked on the ENIAC and had considerable experience in the electronic field. Unfortunately Turing did not cooperate well with Huskey, although Huskey's relations with other members of the ACE section were very cordial. He made no secret of his views that the idea of getting the computer built elsewhere was a mistake, and almost from the start pressed for a more active policy on the hardware side in Mathematics Division. Turing did not oppose the idea but never fully associated himself with it, possibly because he was becoming increasingly disillusioned with progress at NPL and had decided to take a Sabbatical at King's College, Cambridge, where he was still a Fellow. Huskey finally persuaded the rest of the group to work with him on the construction of a pilot machine which for simplicity was based on version V. The machine was christened the "Test Assembly." The objective was to build the smallest computer that could successfully demonstrate the feasibility of Turing's grand project. I remember taking as our objective in the design the ability to solve a system of some eight simultaneous linear equations by Gaussian elimination. Since it was not thought of as a permanent computer the full weight was thrown on the programmer and in deciding whether or not a feature should be included, the question we asked ourselves was, "Could we possibly make do without it?"

By the time the Test Assembly was under way, Huskey was more than half way through his year at NPL. He was eager to have the computer working before he left, and, viewed in retrospect, this was clearly an impractical objective since he was depending so much on members of the ACE section of Mathematics Division. Of these, only Davies had any relevant background experience; Alway, Woodger, and myself were "just learning on the job."

It is not surprising that this project was unwelcome to Thomas since its success (however improbable) would obviously have threatened his Electronics Section. Nevertheless, considerable progress was made with the construction of the Test Assembly before it was ruled by Director NPL that the work should cease and the electronics side should be left entirely to Thomas's team. In spite of the failure of this venture, it did play quite an important part in the ultimate success of the Pilot ACE. It stimulated the interest of the Mathematics group in the construction side, and we learned a good deal about pulse techniques, which was to stand us in good stead later on.

However, for the time being the collapse of the Huskey project found morale in the Mathematics group at its lowest ebb, with Huskey disillusioned and Turing away at Cambridge. For the next few months the group worked on the production of the progress report on ACE, but our hearts were not in it. Had it been produced in more promising circumstances, it could have been an invaluable contribution to the history of early programming efforts. Turing returned briefly to NPL in May 1948, but was so dissatisfied with progress that he decided to join F. C. Williams and T. Kilburn on the Manchester project.

5.   The Pilot ACE

In 1948, Thomas decided to leave NPL for Unilever, which was in line with his natural preference for industrial electronics, and F. M. Colebrook of Radio Division replaced him as head of the section. It was soon obvious to Colebrook that the ACE project was in a state of complete disarray, and he came to the conclusion that the lack of communication between Mathematics Division and the Electronics Section was a severe handicap to progress. He had heard of the abortive Test Assembly project and was therefore aware that we were interested in the hardware side. Shortly after his appointment he came to see me and told me that it was his opinion that the enterprise was likely to founder unless something fairly decisive was done. He then made the remarkable proposal that the four of us who had been mainly concerned with the Test Assembly, Alway, Davies, Woodger, and myself, should join his team temporarily and that we should all work together on the construction of some pilot machine.

I was a little taken aback by the suggestion, but on reflection decided there was a lot to be said for it. It was clearly unsatisfactory to remain in Mathematics Division coding for a series of hypothetical machines, and I was too fascinated by the idea of an automatic digital computer to contemplate giving it up and joining the desk computing section. I was delighted to find that this view was shared by the other three. There remained the problem of squaring this with Womersley, but fortunately I persuaded Goodwin (for whom in theory I was still working half time!) to back the proposal, and this virtually ensured its acceptance. It was a risky venture since if it failed our position in our own division would have been unenviable.

That Colebrook should make the suggestion, the four of us should be so enthusiastic in our acceptance, and Mathematics Division should agree to our going was a remarkably improbable combination of events. There can be no doubt that it was an extremely successful experiment. The two groups were soon collaborating very well indeed in spite of the previous unpromising history. Together we formed a well-balanced team, and the experience of those members drawn from other divisions of NPL proved to be a great asset. A difficulty for most people working in the electronics area in the United Kingdom at that time was the problem of supplies; the wide experience of W. Wilson helped us over what might otherwise have been insuperable difficulties. The comparative absence of friction owed a great deal to the tactful administration of F. M. Colebrook. He took the decision that he was unlikely to make a substantial contribution on the technical side and concentrated all his efforts on making things run as smoothly as possible. It paid handsome dividends.

Early in 1949, we started on the detailed design of the Pilot ACE. In concept this owed more to the abortive Test Assembly than it was wise to emphasize. Again it was based essentially on Turing's version V and the equipment was kept as simple as possible, consistent with the objective of being able to carry significant computations. We had had time for reflection since the design of the Test Assembly, however, and wherever it differed the Pilot ACE was markedly superior. The original design included no multiplier since optimum coding made it possible to perform a programmed multiplication in about 10 msec. A very compact form of construction was decided upon with interchangeable plug-in chassis. The circuit design of the individual chassis was undertaken by members of both groups though the basic circuits such as the gates were mainly based on the recommendations of Newman and Clayden.

We were well served by the NPL workshops; and by the autumn of 1949 completed chassis were being delivered and assembly was under way. The first chassis to arrive were those designed by Alway and myself, and consequently we installed them on the main frame. The next to be completed were designed by Newman, and he collaborated with us in installing them; from that time onward the three of us worked together until the computer was in operation. The first half of the machine was assembled very rapidly, but in December 1949, the main control chassis were added and progress was somewhat slower. By February 1950, a sufficient number of chassis had been assembled for it to be capable of storing and carrying out a simple program, but it was not until May that it actually did so. In 1950, E. C. (now Sir Edward) Bullard had succeeded Sir Charles Darwin as Director NPL, and on his tour of inspection of the Laboratory he paid us a visit. He had obviously heard of the earlier trouble with the ACE project and was more than skeptical when he said that we would have something working "almost any day." We promised to let him know when we had, and it was fortunate that we did not keep him waiting for too long.

Toward the end of the day on May 10, 1950, we had working all the basic pulse circuits, the control unit, one long delay line, and a short delay line fitted with an additive and a subtractive input. The punched-card input and output had not yet been added, and the only method of inserting instructions was via a set of 32 switches on which we could set up one instruction at a time in binary; our only method of output was via a set of 32 lights to which a binary number could be sent. Unfortunately, the amplifier on the delay line was barely adequate, and the probability of remembering a pulse pattern for as long as a minute was not very high. This was particularly true in the late hours of the afternoon since the mains voltage tended to drop because of the national overload, and this affected the marginal circuits adversely.

We concocted a very elementary program consisting of a few instructions only; this took the number on the input switches, added it to the short delay once per msec. and put on the next of the set of 32 output lights when the accumulator overflowed. The lights therefore came on at a speed directly proportional to the size of the number on the input switches. We laboriously fed this program into the computer again and again, but each time the memory would fail before we could complete the input. We decided to wait until the mains voltage recovered somewhat and then to try again. Finally we succeeded in inserting the whole program, and immediately all the lights flashed on. This could, of course, have happened to anybody. We reduced the input number, and the lights came up slowly one by one; we doubled it and the rate doubled; finally we trebled it and the rate trebled. What could be more conclusive than that on a binary machine? We switched off for the day knowing that the computer was working. It was a little while before we reached this high peak again and could convince the Director that it was indeed working. He conceded our point but remarked that the program was "scarcely epoch making." From our point of view he was quite wrong, and history proved us to be correct. The little program was christened "Successive Digits"; it persisted throughout the life of Pilot ACE and DEUCE and was known affectionately as "Suck Digs." The next day the

Director was with us again, bringing a problem associated with his research on the origin of the earth's magnetic field. It involved the solution of a system of simultaneous partial differential equations. We were not quite ready for it, but that problem too was to play an important role in the history of digital computing at NPL.

From that point onward we were under constant pressure to have a demonstration for the press, but there was a good deal to do before this was possible. Most early computer builders have a "hard luck story" for their first public demonstration. Ours was a "good luck story." The demonstration was to last for three days; the first day was for the popular press, the second for the technical press, and the third for VIPs, including our competitors F. C. Williams and T. Kilburn from Manchester and M. V. Wilkes from Cambridge. For the demonstrations we had three main programs, two popular and one serious. Of the popular programs the first took in a date in decimal from input keys and gave out the corresponding day of the week on a cathode-ray tube, while the second took in a six-figure decimal number and gave its highest factor. A bottle of beer was offered to any member of the press who could give a six-figure prime. Popular programs provide a merciless test since the slightest error is readily apparent; it is particularly inadvisable to play such games with the popular press; the technical press is slightly more understanding. The serious program traced the paths of rays through a complex set of lenses; it was virtually impossible for anybody not intimately connected with the computer to know for certain whether this was really working. Up to within a few days of the demonstration period the computer had never performed the serious program correctly, and we were not even certain that the program was free from errors. We discovered a rather subtle machine fault only a day or two before the demonstration, and this cleared up the problem. In the event the Pilot ACE worked virtually perfectly for the whole three days, a level of performance that it had not been within striking distance of achieving before and did not attain again for some considerable time.

6. Pilot ACE in Action

At the time when we had decided to build the Pilot ACE, the atmosphere had been one of crisis. In the circumstances it was not surprising that no plans for the long-term future had actually been spelled out. For my own part I had regarded the Pilot ACE purely as an experimental machine built with the object of demonstrating the competence of the team as computer engineers. I had imagined that when it was successfully completed, a full-scale computer would be built. No doubt most of the others had shared this view, but it did not work out like that. At the time when it was successfully demonstrated it was the only computer in a United Kingdom Government Department, and indeed the only other working stored program computers were EDSAC at Cambridge, SEAC at the National Bureau of Standards, and an early version of the Manchester machine. The very success of the public demonstrations ensured that we came under very heavy pressure to use the Pilot ACE for serious computing. We accordingly embarked on a small set of modifications, which included the addition of an automatic multiplier and improvements to the control unit that made programming a little less arduous. The computer was then moved to Mathematics Division, where it did yeoman service for a number of years. Fortunately the compact form of construction made it, unlike EDSAC and SEAC, eminently transportable. (Indeed the Pilot ACE was moved a week or two before the press demonstration in order to make it accessible and the move was achieved without mishap.)

Initially the only storage on the Pilot ACE consisted of mercury delay lines, which altogether held some 300 words of 32 binary digits each. This had to cover both instructions and numbers, and the code was, of course, fairly inefficient in terms of storage space required for a given program. My initial reaction when contemplating its use on a wide range of research and day-to-day problems was one of dismay. However, for a number of reasons the Pilot ACE proved to be a far more powerful computer than we had expected. Oddly enough much of its effectiveness sprang from what appeared to be weaknesses resulting from the economy in equipment that dictated its design.

Optimum coding was a controversial matter at the time, but much of what was said about it, both for and against, appears in retrospect to have been irrelevant. Of course, nobody would use optimum coding if he were offered an immediate access store giving the same effective speed of operation. However, faced again with the same choice as we had then, I would certainly use it. (I did not make the choice; Turing did!) An illustration of its effectiveness is provided by the floating-point subroutines on Pilot ACE. Programmed floating-point arithmetic involved a considerable number of instructions, and on a conventional computer such as EDSAC, which performed only one instruction per circulation time of a long delay line, it was too slow to be used for any extensive computation. On Pilot ACE it was only marginally slower than fixed-point computation, thanks to optimum coding. Paradoxically, the speed was further increased by the rudimentary nature of the multiplier. Although this did not even deal with signed numbers, it was an entirely autonomous unit. Both the sign correction and the manipulation of the exponents could be carried out in independent adders and subtractors while multiplication was proceeding, and hence this effectively took no extra time. Even double-precision and triple-precision floating-point routines were reasonably fast, and we gained extensive experience with such computation long before it was mechanized elsewhere.

During the experimental programming years 1947–1948 we came to the conclusion that it would be quite convenient to perform most computations involving large arrays (such as matrix algorithms) in fixed-point arithmetic so that floating-point arithmetic would mainly be used in situations in which storage problems were not paramount. Accordingly we used one word for the exponent and one word for the mantissa, thereby saving the time needed for unpacking. (Packed floating routines were also coded but were little used.) We also used floating binary rather than floating decimal, again primarily in the interests of speed. The conversion to decimal for output was not regarded as an obstacle and time considerations at the output stage were not important. It is interesting that at Cambridge, where the floating-point routines were in any case too slow to be of practical value, the alternative decisions were taken in each case. I think it is no exaggeration to claim that the development of floating-point error analysis at NPL, which was well in advance of that elsewhere, was an indirect consequence of our use of optimum coding. As remarked above all of our early experience was with floating-point arithmetic in which a full word was available for the exponent. As a result of this I became accustomed to regarding floating-point computation as essentially free from all problems of overflow and underflow except in such algorithms as successive root squaring, where naturally one expects it to be a preoccupation. I was to have a rude awakening when I started to use floating-point hardware with its comparatively limited exponent range.

Turing had planned in terms of punched-card input and output right from the start, and we followed his lead on Pilot ACE. It was only recently that I discovered that paper tape had been used by Turing and his colleagues during the war, and I am intrigued that he never at any time suggested using it on ACE. Again the very elementary way in which input and output were organized played a decisive role in our use of punched cards. A great deal of linear algebra with matrices of comparatively high order was done on the Pilot ACE using storage in binary on cards. For example, the multiplication of a vector held in the store by a matrix stored on cards was performed by running cards at full speed through the reader, all the computation and red-tape instructions being done in the intervals between rows of cards. This was faster than would have been possible on EDSAC and SEAC even if they had had adequate delay line store to hold the matrix. By putting two numbers on each row of a card we could have doubled the speed, and it would have then rivaled what could have been achieved on Pilot ACE itself with unlimited delay line store!

Since the use of the punched-card equipment required the use of an operator, it encouraged user participation generally, and this was a distinctive feature of Pilot ACE operation. For example, various methods of accelerating the convergence of matrix iterative processes were left under the control of operators, and the skill with which these stratagems were used by young women with no more than high school mathematics qualifications was most impressive. Speaking for myself I gained a great deal of experience from user participation, and it was this that led to my own conversion to backward error analysis. Present-day developments are again moving in this direction, but they rarely provide participation as satisfactory as that which we took for granted on the Pilot ACE. The whole philosophy of computer operation at NPL on Pilot ACE was poles apart from that adopted at Cambridge on EDSAC, but no doubt each was appropriate to the circumstances. I have often wondered whether it was the machines that determined the philosophy or whether it was the natural characteristics of the personnel involved that led to the development of such different computers.

7. The DEUCE Computer

During the period when the Pilot ACE was being built, the English Electric Company became interested in electronic computers, and a small group from the company joined us at NPL and gave valuable assistance in the later stages, although all the construction was done in NPL workshops. After the success of Pilot ACE, English Electric decided to gain experience by building engineered versions of it. I was not in favor of this decision since it perpetuated something that had originally been designed merely for experimental purposes, and it removed any sense of urgency from the development of the full-scale ACE. However, before these engineered versions were produced a magnetic drum store was added to the Pilot ACE and with this addition it was, in spite of its obvious shortcomings, a very powerful computer. In the event the engineered version, marketed under the name DEUCE, was undoubtedly a success. Perhaps the mistake was the decision taken considerably later to build the full-scale ACE. By the time it was completed core store machines were working well and it was difficult for a delay line machine to shine against such competition.

8. Numerical Analysis and Pilot ACE

In this article I have concentrated on the design and construction of the Pilot ACE. However, during the years 1946–1948 the ACE group spent an appreciable time working on problems in numerical analysis, often in collaboration with desk computing, this being interspersed with design work. It is not possible to convey the full flavor of that period without including a description of both activities. I attempted to cover both aspects of the work in the first two of the inaugural series of Forsythe Lectures given at Stanford University in the fall quarter of 1977. In them I also traced the influence of the Pilot ACE on the subsequent development of error analysis at NPL. These lectures are to be published by the Computer Science Department of Stanford.

REFERENCES

1. Turing, A. M., On computable numbers, with an application to the Entscheidungsproblem, *Proc. London Mth. Soc. Ser. 2* **42**, 230 (1937).
2. Turing, A. M., Proposal for the Development of an Electronic Computer, National Physical Laboratory Rep. Com. Sci. 57 (1972) (Reprinted from the original with a foreword by D. W. Davies).
3. Wilkinson, J. H., Progress Report on the Automatic Computing Engine, Mathematics Division Rep. MA/17/1024 (1948).
4. Wilkinson, J. H., Report on the Pilot Model of the Automatic Computing Engine, Part II, The Logical Design, Report of the Mathematics Division and the Electronics Section, NPL (1951).

NATIONAL PHYSICAL LABORATORY
TEDDINGTON, ENGLAND

The Smithsonian Computer History Project and Some Personal Recollections

HENRY S. TROPP

The problem of doing research in contemporary history and of making use of oral history interviews is a rather difficult one. A recent issue of *Saturday Review* (Note 1) had as its central theme the problems connected with the writing of contemporary history. In one of the articles (Note 2) there was a paraphrase of a very famous quotation: ". . . we ought not to leave history to the professional historians . . ." (Note 3).

When I was asked to be a part of the Los Alamos conference, I really wondered where I belonged, what I could have to add in relation to the pioneers and the actual creators of that period we now call the computer revolution, who would be in attendance and able to speak for themselves on their roles, accomplishments, difficulties, environment, motivations, etc. I came to realize that the Computer History Project is itself a historical object. Like the early generations of computers, the first dinosaurs, the Computer History Project itself has been relegated to museum status. Perhaps, like these same dinosaurs, it will become an exhibit, or it may evolve into a somewhat different form.

The project at the Smithsonian originated with a contract signed by American Federation of Information Processing Societies (AFIPS) and the Smithsonian's National Museum of History and Technology (NMHT) in 1967. The origins and specifics are much too complicated to go into in detail here: Cuthbert Hurd, Isaac Auerbach, and Walter Carlson were three of the individuals who conceived the importance of what they called "Preserving

115

the History of Computing" (Note 4). They felt that we had a golden opportunity to preserve the history with the members of the original cast and that it would be tragic if we let this golden opportunity pass by. The advisory committee at the time I joined the project (spring of 1971) consisted of Isaac Auerbach, Cuthbert Hurd, Walter Carlson, Rudy Winnacker (the Chief Historian of the Office of the Secretary of Defense), Robert Multhauf (a senior historian of the Smithsonian), and Barney Finn (the chairman of NMHT's division of physical science).

I had thought long and hard about how one structures a project of this nature. I was faced with what Ken May spoke about at the opening session of the conference, the problem of structuring a historiographic model for a contemporary period in which I was going to be dealing with the problem of recording information with the individuals who had been part of the process and at the same time collecting the documentation, trying to locate things that had been lost or misplaced, and trying to identify ideas and events that perhaps people had forgotten. The problem of structure alone promised to be a major obstacle. I thought about the history of mathematics, which I knew best, and how histories of mathematics were written. I knew there were a variety of ways in which the project could be structured. Finally, I took two extremely diverse historical approaches, the "strict chronology" method and the "great man" approach, and I tried to find a linear combination of them in order to come up with some form of structure that would work for me both philosophically and practically.

As I look back on the model upon which I ultimately decided, I realize that I was doing something that Philip Davis identified at a talk at the American Mathematical Society winter meeting held at San Antonio (10 January 1976), seeking a Jamesian approach to history (Note 5). In an essay entitled "Great men in their environment," the American philosopher William James said: "The Community stagnates without the impulse of the individual. The impulse dies away without the sympathy of the community" (Note 6). His thesis is that ". . . social evolution is a resultant of the interaction of two wholly distinct factors: the individual, deriving his peculiar gifts from the play of physiological and infrasocial forces, but bearing all the power and initiative and origination in his hands; and second, the social environment, with its power of adopting or rejecting both him and his gifts. Both factors are essential to change" (Note 7).

When I got into the research and began talking to individuals, I realized that James's 19th-century concept of a social environment was an extremely broad term encompassing a complexity of ideas. For me it involved not only the working atmosphere in the individual projects, but such things as project needs, internal and external pressures, group and individual motivations, the backgrounds which individuals brought to these projects, and, as they moved on to other endeavors, what kinds of attitudes and new concepts they took along with them and the forces of government, war, and economics which prevailed in 1935–1955, the era of my research concentration. It also included asking questions, such as: What was the prevailing technology and what were the attitudes toward that technology at various times? What kinds of ideas were in the air? What form of management existed and what role did it play? Etc., etc., etc.

I said earlier that I had a lot of help in trying to design this project. Perry Crawford (IBM Corp.) gave me an important starting point by preparing a large chart that had a basic time scale beginning at about 1900 and running roughly to 1960. There were "events" on this; that is, machines, projects, inventions, publications, etc. This chart was a beginning skeleton, and from there I began to put some skin, meat, and muscle on it. First, I needed to identify the individuals who were associated with these "events." One "event," for example, was Project Whirlwind (Note 8).

Another factor that people like Cuthbert Hurd and Isaac Auerbach impressed on me was that priorities had to be carefully selected and established and that I had to keep these in mind. Some of the individuals were getting on in years, and these priorities had to be established not so much by dates of key events, but by the state of the health and age of the individuals. A classic example is the late Howard Aiken.

I can remember being given two top priorities at my very first meeting with the advisory committee: Vannevar Bush and Howard Aiken. I did not succeed in obtaining an interview with Vannevar Bush before he died. We did have a number of appointments, each of which was canceled because of the state of his health. Howard Aiken was another story. He was an extremely active person, and one found his tracks everywhere, including a patent issued as recently as 1972. Everytime I called him, he kept saying, "I'm too busy." In the meantime, I interviewed everybody with whom he had been associated during the years at Harvard and later in Florida (Note 9). I kept calling Aiken and trying to arrange an interview; and, as he continued to reject me, I kept being a bit more insistent and less polite. In one of my more persistent phone calls, he finally said, "Sure, you can come down." I said, "When?" He said, "Tomorrow."

So I set up the earliest possible date (Note 10), and our visit was an incredible experience. Professor I. Bernard Cohen from Harvard joined me, and we spent three or four days, from early morning till late evening, working with him in both informal discussions and taped interviews. His health during this period appeared to be fantastic. He was very active intellectually and extremely busy doing consulting work for Monsanto Chemical on aspects related to their research developments on magnetic bubbles (Note 11).

Both Professor Cohen and I felt that this first set of interviews ought to be like a fairly broad brush stroke. We decided not to worry too much about a lot of specific details, because obviously here was a man in excellent health, extremely cooperative, and planning to devote considerable time to us. Unfortunately, on 14 March 1973, about three weeks after these talks,

Howard Aiken, on a consulting trip to Monsanto in St. Louis, had a heart attack and died. A golden opportunity had arrived, and we had not taken full advantage of it. This potentially critical firsthand source of information is now lost forever (Note 12).

It had been said that Aiken dragged his feet about going from electromechanical computers to electronic devices. I asked him specifically about this. Anyone who knew Howard Aiken knew that the best way to relate to him was to be direct and not to beat around the bush. You did not circle personally sensitive subjects in Aiken's case. The best approach was to be open, blunt, and direct. I said, "Howard, you've been accused of a lot of things, and one of the things is dragging your feet about going electronic."

He said, "No, I knew that was the way to go. I didn't want to bother with technology. I didn't want to have to worry about the reliability of components that were unfamiliar and untried in this new application. As soon as I saw the other projects going and running and I saw that the engineers had learned how to adapt the available technology, then I went electronic too"(Note 13). I think the record bears that out in the form of Aiken's design and construction of the Harvard MARK III and the MARK IV (Note 14).

The best way to illustrate at least a small piece of the historiographic model I used in the project is to take one specific instance. I have chosen for this purpose a gentleman and a series of machines that did not figure explicitly at the Los Alamos conference*: George Stibitz and the early Bell Laboratories Relay machines.

Let me start then with the Bell MOD K relay machine. The data are from approximately 1937. To begin with, I set up my interview with Professor Stibitz at Dartmouth College, and, for those who do not know him, he is extremely delightful and cooperative. I arranged first for him to work out a large time-oriented chart centering around MOD K, MOD I, . . ., up to MOD VI (Note 15). These computers were put on an approximate time scale, which could be checked later for more accurate dating. Then, we added to this chart, which was drawn on a long, narrow sheet torn out of a computer terminal, things like needs, motivation, pressures, available technology, events that may or may not have affected his thinking (such as Alan Turing's paper, Claude Shannon's paper), events that we now recognize as important intellectual milestones.

As Stibitz told me, it all began one night sitting around his kitchen, which is where the K comes from: the Kitchen Computer. He had been doing research on relays, and it suddenly struck him that one ought to be able to do binary arithmetic with relays. So he took some relays he had at home and went out to his shop in his garage. He got a small, approximately 1-ft-square piece of plywood, put a few relays on it, and discovered he could indeed represent one-digit binary addition in this manner. The next morning, he

* See the paper by Stibitz in this volume.

took this to the laboratory and showed it to a few people there, and they said, "You know, that is really interesting."

At this point, I interjected and said, "Let's stop a minute. What made you think about binary addition?"

"Oh, I just had always known about it, because I learned my algebra from Chrystal, and Chrystal has a section on binary algebra (Note 16). So I thought about this and I thought about some problems we have at the Laboratories. One of them is the use of our computers doing calculations involving complex numbers. They have to add, subtract, multiply, and divide numbers of the form $a + bi$ in order to do problems related to circuit design."

A computer at that time (in fact, even in the pre-1956 dictionary sense) was a human being and not an object. Computers were a group of young women, each of whom had a "programmed" set of operations to perform which were checked, passed along for more computations, more checks, etc., until at the end of the chain a set of results appeared. So, Stibitz and his colleagues considered the possibility of mechanizing this sequential series of calculations, checks, and procedures in a binary mode. The Complex Calculator, later renamed the Bell Labs MODEL I, was the end result of that collaboration. This was a calculator designed to meet a specific need that the Laboratories was concerned about.

Another bit of information that came out of this discussion is Professor Stibitz's comment that when the design was completed for the Complex Calculator and they were far enough along to feel confidence in its working ability, he went to the powers that be at Bell Laboratories and said (and this is pre-1940), "Gentlemen, for $50,000 I think I can build you a general-purpose relay calculator."

The general response was, "Gee, who wants to spend $50,000 just to be able to calculate?"

As is now realized, we had the technical capability to build relay, electromechanical, and even electronic calculating devices long before they came into being. I think one can conjecture when looking through Babbage's papers, or even at the Jacquard loom, that we had the technical capability to do calculation with some motive power like steam. The realization of this capability was not dependent on technology as much as it was on the existing pressures (or lack of them), and an environment in which these needs could sympathetically be brought to some level of realization.

The Complex Calculator has some interesting stories connected with it. The people at the Labs were so pleased with it that they wanted to demonstrate it. There was a mathematical meeting scheduled for Dartmouth College in the summer of 1940. The original plan was to take the Complex Calculator from New York City to Hanover, New Hampshire, and have Stibitz give a paper and use the machine for a demonstration.

He was scheduled to give this talk at Dartmouth when, in early summer, it was decided not to move the Calculator to Dartmouth. It was planned instead to set up a Teletype terminal in the hallway outside of a lecture hall in Dartmouth and make it possible for any of the mathematicians to use the calculator in New York after they had heard Stibitz's talk and explanation of how to perform these arithmetic operations from the remote terminal. This is what was done, and John Mauchly told me a story about that meeting, which I will repeat. John attended that meeting, and he remembers wandering through the hall and seeing a man playing with the Teletype input and output and becoming very angry. He finally went up to the gentleman and asked whether the machine had something wrong with it. "No problem with the machine," was the response. He was trying to find a way to get the thing to divide by zero, and it just wouldn't do it. Stibitz, of course, was too good a mathematician not to have taken care of this possibility. John later learned that the man at the machine was none other than Norbert Wiener (Note 17).

To conclude, I should like to emphasize one aspect of the environment during the early computer development: the enthusiasm and sharing of ideas by the original creators. Maurice Wilkes touched on it during his talk at the Los Alamos conference when he discussed the summer course he was invited to in 1946 at the Moore School (when he was introduced to ENIAC and the proposed EDVAC), and later. the bimonthly colloquia that he organized at Cambridge after the completion of EDSAC. Howard Aiken's open environment at Harvard and his early symposia and the DCA (predecessor of SHARE) on the west coast of the U.S. are but a few examples of the exciting and open intellectual environment that characterized that early era. In a recent editorial, (Note 18), Jim C. Warren, Jr., the editor of *Dr. Dobb's Journal of Computer Calisthenics and Orthodontia,* a journal for computer hobbyists, referring to a talk I gave to the ACM chapter in Menlo Park, California, in December 1975, commented on my attempt to reconstruct this aspect of the early era.

> It is this open sharing that particularly delights me. . . . The sharing of ideas is useful in that it allows us to stand on one another's shoulders, instead of standing on one another's feet. But, there is something else being shared that is of at least equal value: the enthusiasm and intellectual excitement. There is no doubt in my mind that the sharing of such enthusiasm, as well as information, was a significant factor in the prodigious creativity of these original researchers.

NOTES

1. *Saturday Review,* 29 May 1976.
2. Lerner, M., "The writing of 'hot history,'" *Saturday Review* (29 May 1976), pp. 16–19.
3. "We can parallel Clemenceau's remark about not leaving war to the generals by saying that we ought not to leave history to the professional historians, who are in danger of stifling it. The craft of history is always in need of barbarizing by the energy of talented amateurs lest it come under the dictatorship of mandarins," *Saturday Review* (29 May 1976), p. 19.

4. In 1972, a pamphlet entitled "Preserving the History of Computers" was prepared by me with the editorial assistance of Tom White and his staff at AFIPS headquarters in Montvale, New Jersey. This pamphlet describes the initial purpose and primary goals of the Computer History Project.

5. Davis, P. J., "On the elitist theory of the history of mathematics."

6. This essay originally appeared under the title "Great men, great thoughts and the environment," *Atlantic Monthly* **46**, 441–449 (1880). It was later reprinted in "The Will to Believe and Other Essays in Popular Philosophy," Longmans, New York, 1897; and in "Selected Papers on Philosophy," Everyman's Library, Dutton, New York, 1917, under the title Great men and their environment.

7. *Atlantic Monthly* **46**, 448. (1880).

8. In the chronology involving WHIRLWIND, for example, one chain leads from Vannevar Bush's Network Analyzer, to his Differential Analyzer, the early work of Sam Caldwell, Harold Hazen, Harold Black, Fred Taylor, and Perry Crawford's M. S. thesis, etc. Another chain comes from Link Trainers into the Special Devices Division and MIT's Aeronautics Division. Then there is another set of developments coming out of the work of Gordon Brown and Harold Hazen and MIT's Servomechanism Laboratory and leading into various types of training and design simulations. Also, not to be ignored were various developments in MIT's Radiation Laboratory, MIT's administrative aspects, the cold war and the needs of the Defense Department, etc. The Smithsonian archive included 16 linear feet of indexed files containing the complete documentation of Project WHIRLWIND: quarterly reports, engineering notebooks, bimonthly reports, photographs, etc. We were also provided with an administrative history of WHIRLWIND prepared by Professors Redmond and Smith. WHIRLWIND now is on exhibit in the Smithsonian's National Museum of History and Technology, thanks to the efforts of Robert Everett, the president of MITRE Corporation.

9. People like Grace Hopper, Bob Campbell, Dick Bloch, Robert Burks, and Bernie Howard.

10. 26 February 1973, in Fort Lauderdale, Florida.

11. For an early exposition of this area of research into what may be the technology of the 1980s, see: Bobeck, A. H. and Scovil, H. E. D., Magnetic bubbles, *Sci. Amer.* **224**(6), 78–90 (1971).

12. This series of taped interviews, beginning on 26 February 1973 and extending through 1 March 1973, is in the Smithonian archive. It is supposed to be sealed from general use except with the permission of Howard Aiken's widow, Mary. The tapes have also been transcribed. The transcription, 220 pages long, is supposed to have the same restriction as the actual tapes. That was the state of the material when I left Washington in August 1973, so I cannot be sure of its current status.

13. Because I do not have the tapes available for consultation, this quotation and others that appear in this text are paraphrased from my memories of the conversations. I can vouch for their essence, but not for the precise wording.

14. A Harvard Computational Laboratory document entitled Description of a Magnetic Drum Calculator is dated January 1948. This was a description of what eventually became the electronic MARK III. Its design was actually begun before the electromechanical MARK II was completed. There was a time overlap for these two machine projects, and this fact should put to rest the prevailing myth about Aiken's "dragging his feet" about going electronic. It is my personal feeling that, when the research is completed surrounding Howard Aiken, he will be seen as one of the major visionaries of the early computer era. His strong personality and opinionated viewpoint of what was the correct way to go had a strong impact on many of the key personalities who came in contact with him during the 1940s and 1950s.

15. For a brief expository article on early Bell Labs Relay computers, including photographs of MOD I; see Stevenson, M. G., Bell Labs: A pioneer in computing technology, *Bell Lab. Record* **51** (11), 344–351 (1973). For articles covering later developments, see: *ibid.* **52** (1), 13–20 (1974); **52** (2), 55–63 (1974). Also see the paper by Stibitz in this volume.

16. Chrystal, G., "Textbook of Algebra," Vol. 1 (7th ed.), pp. 169–170, Chelsea Pub. Co., New York, 1964.

17. A joint project between myself (representing the Smithonian Institution/AFIPS Computer History Project) and the Dartmouth College Library resulted in the organization of Professor Stibitz's papers and the publication of "An Inventory of the Papers of George Robert Stibitz Concerning the Invention and Development of the Digital Computer," Dartmouth College, Hanover, New Hampshire, 1973. The work was done by Mrs. Ingrid Vignos, with the assistance of Professor Stibitz and the Dartmouth College Library staff. It is 128 pages in length and includes a brief biography of Stibitz. This collection is available to interested researchers and includes reports, memoranda, notes, lectures, correspondence, and patents encompassing the period 1937–1962.

18. Editorial, *Dr. Dobb's J. Comput. Calisthenics Orthodontia* **1** (4), 3 (1976).

19. For the sake of brevity, many facets of the procedures and results of the Smithsonian project have been omitted. For example, each taped interview was transcribed, smoothed, edited, and sent to the interviewee for correction, addition, smoothing, release, etc. The transcripts returned were then retyped, indexed, and bound in multiple copies, one of which was sent to the interviewee. The tapes were also preserved in originals and copies. By mid-1973, approximately 200 interviews had been conducted, of which 30–50 had reached the final level of editing and indexing. In addition, a large file of documents was collected. These included correspondence, patents, engineering notebooks, manuals, blueprints, progress reports, and copies of early programs and problems run. One major goal was to establish a comprehensive research archive that would be available to anyone with a serious interest. During my brief period at the Smithsonian, many individuals availed themselves of the facilities. As far as I know the collection has not been made available to anyone since September 1973. It is still my hope that sometime in the future, officials at the Smithsonian will recognize their responsibility and again make this material accessible to scholars and interested practitioners. I was told when I joined the Smithsonian Institution staff that it was a National Museum and that its contents belonged to the American people in the spirit in which James Smithson's original 1826 bequest was made: ". . . to found at Washington, under the name of the Smithsonian Institution, an establishment for the increase and diffusion of knowledge among men." (Since writing the above, and beginning sometime in the latter part of 1977, officials of the Smithsonian informed me that an effort is being made to complete editing and clearing the available interview transcriptions. By this date (April 1978) a number of additional interviews are available to interested scholars. Interested individuals should contact Dr. Uta Merzbach, NMHT, Smithsonian Institution, Washington, D.C. 20560.)

DEPARTMENT OF MATHEMATICS
HUMBOLDT STATE UNIVERSITY
ARCATA, CALIFORNIA

Part III

The Languages

Programming in America in the 1950s— Some Personal Impressions

JOHN BACKUS

1. Introduction

The subject of software history is a complex one in which authoritative information is scarce. Furthermore, it is difficult for anyone who has been an active participant to give an unbiased assessment of his area of interest. Thus, one can find accounts of early software development that strive to appear objective, and yet the importance and priority claims of the author's own work emerge rather favorably while rival efforts fare less well.

Therefore, rather than do an injustice to much important work in an attempt to cover the whole field, I offer some definitely biased impressions and observations from my own experience in the 1950s.

2. Programmers versus "Automatic Calculators"

Programming in the early 1950s was really fun. Much of its pleasure resulted from the absurd difficulties that "automatic calculators" created for their would-be users and the challenge this presented. The programmer had to be a resourceful inventor to adapt his problem to the idiosyncrasies of the computer: He had to fit his program and data into a tiny store, and overcome bizarre difficulties in getting information in and out of it, all while using a limited and often peculiar set of instructions. He had to employ every trick

125

he could think of to make a program run at a speed that would justify the large cost of running it. And he had to do all of this by his own ingenuity, for the only information he had was a problem and a machine manual. Virtually the only knowledge about general techniques was the notion of a subroutine and its calling sequence[1].

Some idea of the machine difficulties facing early programmers can be had by a brief survey of a few of the bizzare characteristics of the Selective Sequence Electronic Calculator (SSEC). This vast machine (circa 1948–1952) had a store of 150 words; instructions, constants, and tables of data were read from punched tapes the width of a punched card; the ends of an instruction tape were glued together to form a paper loop, which was then placed on one of 66 tape-reading stations. The SSEC could also punch intermediate data into tapes that could subsequently be read by a tape-reading station. One early problem strained the SSEC's capacity to the limit. The computation was divided into three phases; in the first phase a tape of many yards of intermediate results was punched out; during the second phase this tape was glued into a loop and mounted on a tape-reading station so that in the third phase it could be read many times. The problem ran successfully through many cycles of these three phases, but then a mysterious error began to appear and disappear regularly in the third phase. For a long time no one could account for it. Finally, the large pile of intermediate data tape was pulled from the bin below its reading station and a careful inspection revealed that it had been glued to form a Möbius strip rather than a simple loop. The result was that on every second revolution of the tape each number would be read in reverse order.

Today a programmer is often under great pressure from superiors who know just how and how long he should take to write a program; his work is no longer regarded as a mysterious art, and much of his productive capacity depends on his ability to find what he needs in a 6-in.-thick manual of some baroque programming or operating system. In contrast, programming in the early 1950s was a black art, a private arcane matter involving only a programmer, a problem, a computer, and perhaps a small library of subroutines and a primitive assembly program. Existing programs for similar problems were unreadable and hence could not be adapted to new uses. General programming principles were largely nonexistent. Thus each problem required a unique beginning at square one, and the success of a program depended primarily on the programmer's private techniques and invention.

3. The Freewheeling Fifties

Programming in the America of the 1950s had a vital frontier enthusiasm virtually untainted by either the scholarship or the stuffiness of academia. The programmer–inventors of the early 1950s were too impatient to hoard an idea until it could be fully developed and a paper written. They wanted to convince others. Action, progress, and outdoing one's rivals were more important than mere authorship of a paper. Recognition in the small programming fraternity was more likely to be accorded for a colorful personality, an extraordinary feat of coding, or the ability to hold a lot of liquor well than it was for an intellectual insight. Ideas flowed freely along with the liquor at innumerable meetings, as well as in sober private discussions and informally distributed papers. An idea was the property of anyone who could use it, and the scholarly practice of noting references to sources and related work was almost universally unknown or unpracticed. Thus, of 15 papers presented at an Office of Naval Research (ONR) symposium on automatic programming for digital computers in May 1954 [2], only two have separate acknowledgements and none refers to other papers.

As in any frontier group, the programming community had its purveyors of snake oil. Sometimes the snake oil worked and sometimes it did not. Thus some early programming concepts and systems enjoyed a chimerical fame as a result of the energy with which they were publicized. Numerous talks about some system might suggest it had mysterious, almost human abilities to understand the language and needs of the user; closer inspection was likely to reveal a complex, exception-ridden performer of tedious clerical tasks that substituted its own idiosyncrasies for those of the computer. Other systems achieved good reputations by providing clear and accurate descriptions to their users, since clear descriptions were even scarcer than elegant designs.

The success of some programming systems depended on the number of machines they would run on. Thus, an elegant system for a one-of-a-kind machine might remain obscure while a less-than-elegant one for a production computer achieved popularity. This point is illustrated by two papers at the 1954 ONR symposium [2]. One, by David E. Muller, describes a floating-point interpretive system for the ILLIAC designed by D. J. Wheeler. The other, by Harlan Herrick and myself, describes a similar kind of system for the IBM 701 called Speedcoding. Even today Wheeler's 1954 design looks spare, elegant, and powerful, whereas the design of Speedcoding now appears to be a curious jumble of compromises. Nevertheless, Wheeler's elegant system remained relatively obscure (since only ILLIAC users could use it) while Speedcoding provided enough conveniences, however clumsily, to achieve rather widespread use in many of the eighteen 701 installations.

4.   The Priesthood

Just as freewheeling westeners developed a chauvinistic pride in their frontiersmanship and a corresponding conservatism, so many programmers of the freewheeling 1950s began to regard themselves as members of a priesthood guarding skills and mysteries far too complex for ordinary mortals.

This feeling is noted in an article by J. H. Brown and John W. Carr, III, in the 1954 ONR symposium: ". . . many 'professional' machine users strongly opposed the use of decimal numbers . . . to this group, the process of machine instruction was one that could not be turned over to the uninitiated." This attitude cooled the impetus for sophisticated programming aids. The priesthood wanted and got simple mechanical aids for the clerical drudgery which burdened them, but they regarded with hostility and derision more ambitious plans to make programming accessible to a larger population. To them, it was obviously a foolish and arrogant dream to imagine that any mechanical process could possibly perform the mysterious feats of invention required to write an efficient program. Only the priests could do that. They were thus unalterably opposed to those mad revolutionaries who wanted to make programming so easy that anyone could to it.

There was little awareness even as late as 1955 and 1956 that programming methods of that era were the most time-consuming and costly roadblock to the growth of computing. Thus, of 21 articles in the *Journal of the ACM* for all of 1955, only three concern general-purpose programming aids: one by H. Rutishauser discusses his astonishingly early plans for an algebraic compiler; another describes an interesting floatingpoint system at the University of Toronto; and the third gives a punched-card method for alleviating some programming drudgery.

It was a time in which recognition of a basic need was often the key insight leading to a significant development. But due to the resistance of the priesthood even the announcement of an important insight or invention was likely to be ignored unless it was accompanied by a widely distributed system that proved the practicality of the idea beyond a doubt. A good example of the resistance of the priesthood to revolutionary ideas is the reception it gave to the world's first algebraic compiler, produced by Laning and Zierler at MIT.

5. The Priesthood versus the Laning and Zierler Algebraic Compiler

Very early in the 1950s, J. Halcombe Laning, Jr., recognized that programming using algebraic expressions would be an important improvement. As a result of that insight he and Neal Zierler had the first algebraic compiler running on WHIRLWIND at MIT in January 1954 [3]. (A private communication from the Charles Stark Draper Laboratory indicates that they had demonstrated algebraic compiling sometime in 1952!) The priesthood ignored Laning's insight for a long time. A 1954 article by Charles W. Adams and Laning (presented by Adams at the ONR symposium) devotes less than 3 out of 28 pages to Laning's algebraic system; the rest are devoted to other MIT systems. The complete description of the system's method of operation as given there is the following [2, p. 64]:

The system is mechanized by a compilation of closed subroutines entered from blocks of words, each block representing one equation. The sequence of equations is stored on the drum, and each is called in separately every time it is used. The compiled routine is then performed interpretively using the CS [MIT Comprehensive System] routines.

The article points out that the system yields a 10-to-1 reduction in speed, but that such a large reduction is due in part to the fact that the system was begun when the WHIRLWIND had a store of only 1024 registers. The elegant source code is described: single-letter variables with single subscripts, expressions and assignment statements involving variables, constants, functions, and arithmetic operators, plus some simple input, output, and control commands.

After the 1954 ONR article the Laning and Zierler system seems to be virtually unmentioned in the literature until much later when its historical significance was recognized. The extensively reported uses of the WHIRLWIND in the *ONR Digital Computer Newsletter* from October 1954 through January 1956 do not once mention the Laning and Zierler system or its use. The only early references to it I have found are (1) the Adams and Laning 1954 ONR article [2]; (2) the *ONR Digital Computer Newsletter* for April 1954, which mentions a December 1953 seminar by Laning: An Interpretive Program for Mathematical Equations; and (3) an Instrumentation Laboratory Report of 1954, E-364, by Laning and Zierler [3]. It boggles the mind to realize that this obscurity and neglect was the reaction of the priesthood to an elegant concept elegantly realized.

6. An Historical Footnote

The purpose of recounting the following historical detail is to point out that one cannot rely even on participants' accounts of an event given not too long after the event. In this case I am the culprit. I have up to now believed the following account of the origin of the FORTRAN project and have for a long time responded to questions about it accordingly: work on FORTRAN began in the summer of 1954 after some friends and I had earlier seen a demonstration of the Laning and Zierler algebraic system, and it was this demonstration which gave us the idea to use algebraic expressions as an important part of the FORTRAN language.

I have recently learned the facts of the matter from discussions with Irving Ziller, from a copy of the letter I wrote to Laning in 1954 asking for the demonstration (which Dr. Laning has kindly sent me), and from the 1954 Speedcoding article [2] mentioned earlier. The facts are these: work on FORTRAN began about January 1954 by Ziller and myself. By about April we had been joined by Harlan Herrick, who coauthored with me the paper "IBM 701 Speedcoding and other Automatic Programming systems" for the

ONR symposium on 13 and 14 of May. In that paper [2, pp. 111–112] we
observe that a programmer "would like to write '$X + Y$' instead of (the
machine code)" and that

> he would like to write $\Sigma a_{ij} \cdot b_{jk}$ instead of the fairly involved set of in-
> structions corresponding to this expression. In fact a programmer might
> not be considered too unreasonable if he were willing only to produce
> the formulas for the numerical solution of his problem and perhaps a
> plan showing how the data was to be moved from one storage hierarchy
> to another and then demand that the machine produce the results for his
> problem.

The article goes on to raise the following questions:

> The question is, can a machine translate a sufficiently rich mathematical
> language into a sufficiently economical program at a sufficiently low
> cost to make the whole affair feasible?

> consider the advantages of being able to state the calculations . . . for
> a problem solution in a concise, fairly natural mathematical language.

I had long assumed that this article was written *after* the Laning and Zierler
demonstration. It turns out, however, that my letter to Laning requesting it
is dated 21 May, 1954 and the demonstration evidently took place on 2 June,
1954. The letter shows that (1) our article was written *before* we first heard of
Laning's work at the ONR symposium and before the demonstration, and (2)
by 21 May the FORTRAN group comprised four people: Herrick, Robert A.
Nelson, Ziller, and myself. The letter states that after his talk about their
work Adams had given me a copy of the Laning and Zierler report [3]. It
says "our formulation of the problem is very similar to yours: however, we
have done no programming or even detailed planning." It goes on to ask for
a meeting on 2 June at MIT among Laning and Herrick, Ziller and myself.

The article and the letter therefore show that, much to my surprise, the
FORTRAN effort was well under way before the ONR symposium and that,
independently of Laning (but later), we had already formulated more ambi-
tious plans for algebraic notation (e.g., $\Sigma a_{ij} \cdot b_{jk}$) than we were later to find
in Laning and Zierler's report and see demonstrated at MIT. It is therefore
unclear what we learned from seeing their pioneering work, despite my mistaken assumption over the years that we had gotten our basic ideas from
them.

7.   The Origins of FORTRAN

FORTRAN did not really grow out of some brainstorm about the beauty of
programming in mathematical notation; instead it began with the recognition

of a basic problem of economics: programming and debugging costs already exceeded the cost of running a program, and as computers became faster and cheaper this imbalance would become more and more intolerable. This prosaic economic insight, plus experience with the drudgery of coding, plus an unusually lazy nature led to my continuing interest in making programming easier. This interest led directly to work on Speedcoding for the 701 and to efforts to have floating point as well as indexing built into the 704.

The viability of most compilers and interpreters prior to FORTRAN had rested on the fact that most source operations were not machine operations. Thus even large inefficiencies in compiling or interpreting looping and testing operations and in computing addresses were masked by the fact that most operating time was spent in floating-point subroutines. But the advent of the 704 with built-in floating-point and indexing radically altered the situation. The 704 presented a double challenge to those who wanted to simplify programming; first it removed the raison d'être of earlier systems by providing in hardware the operations they existed to provide, and second, it increased the problem of generating efficient programs by an order of magnitude by speeding up floating-point operations by a factor of ten and thereby leaving inefficiencies nowhere to hide. So what could be done now to ease the programmer's job? Once asked, the answer to this question had to be: Let him use mathematical notation. But behind that answer (in the new 704 environment) there was the really new and hard question: Can a machine translate a sufficiently rich mathematical language into a sufficiently economical machine program to make the whole affair feasible? Having asked the question and having got Cuthbert Hurd, my boss, to approve the effort, a few friends and associates of mine finally did answer it after three years of pioneering invention and hard work.

The initial external design for FORTRAN was completed in November 1954, a paper describing it was circulated, and a number of talks about it were given to prospective 704 users. All of this was met with the usual indifference and skepticism of the priesthood, with a few notable exceptions. Walter Ramshaw at United Aircraft agreed to let Roy Nutt work with us; he eventually designed and implemented most of the I/O features of the system plus its special assembly program. Charles W. Adams at MIT agreed that Sheldon Best could go on leave to work with us. Sidney Fernback at the Livermore Radiation Laboratory lent us the help of Bob Hughes for a short time. Harry Cantrell at G.E. in Schenectady was an enthusiastic supporter of our effort from the beginning. And my successive bosses at IBM, Hurd, Charles DeCarlo, and John McPherson, cheerfully endured our requests for more help and more time and our many missed deadlines. But, with a few other exceptions, our plans and efforts were regarded with a mixture of indifference and scorn until the final checking out of the compiler, at which time some other groups became more interested.

8. Optimization Techniques in FORTRAN

A large number of difficult problems had to be solved by the nine persons* who were the principal planners and programmers of the six sections of the 704 FORTRAN I compiler. It was their collective efforts that proved for the first time that efficient object programs could be compiled for a machine with built-in floating point and indexing. Without belittling the important contributions of the whole group, I should like to comment especially on the work of the three principal architects of the key optimization techniques which made it possible for FORTRAN-coded programs to compete with and often exceed the efficiency of hand-coded ones.

Robert A. Nelson and Irving Ziller devised general methods for analyzing and optimizing loops and references to arrays which were truly remarkable in the number of situations they could treat optimally. Their methods could move computations from the object program to the compiler and from inner to outer loops when the situation permitted. They could identify special circumstances in which even a single, usually required instruction in the exit path of a loop could be eliminated.

Sheldon Best invented methods for optimizing the use of index registers based on the expected frequency of execution of various parts of the program. As of 1970 there were no known provably optimal algorithms for the problem he dealt with; his methods were the basis of many subsequent storage-allocation algorithms and produced code that is very difficult to improve. (For more details of Best's methods see [4, pp. 510–515].)

The result of the optimization efforts of the FORTRAN group and particularly of the pioneering work of Best, Nelson, and Ziller was a level of optimization of object programs which was not to be found again in subsequent compilers until the late 1960s.

9. Emil Post and Syntax Description

The notation for syntax description known as BNF offers another example of a development which began with a prosaic recognition of a need. After involvement with two language design efforts—FORTRAN and IAL (ALGOL 58)—it became clear, as I was trying to describe IAL in 1959, that difficulties were occurring due to the absence of precise language definitions. In a recent course on computability given by Martin Davis, I had been exposed to the work of the logician Emil Post and his notion of a "production." As soon as the need for precise description was noted, it became obvious that Post's productions were well suited for that purpose. I hastily adapted them for use in describing the syntax of IAL. The resulting paper [5] was received

---

* These were S. Best, R. Goldberg, L. M. Haibt, H. L. Herrick, R. A. Nelson, D. Sayre, P. B. Sheridan, I. Ziller (IBM), and R. Nutt (United Aircraft).

with a silence that made it seem that precise syntax description was an idea whose time had not yet come. As far as I know that paper had only one reader, Peter Naur. Fortunately, he had independently recognized the need for precision; he improved the notation (replacing $\overline{or}$ by | and := by :=), improved its readability by not abbreviating the names of metavariables, and then used it to describe the syntax of ALGOL 60 in the definitive paper on that language. He thus proved the usefulness of the idea in a widely read paper and it was accepted.

10. What Is a Compiler?

There is an obstacle to understanding, now, developments in programming in the early 1950s. There was a rapid change in the meaning of some important terms during the 1950s. We tend to assume that the modern meaning of a word is the same one it had in an early paper, but this is sometimes not the case. Let me illustrate this point with examples concerning the word "compiler."

In the proceedings of the 1954 ONR symposium there are a number of articles about "compilers." Three use the word in their title, and at least one other contains a description of a program called a compiler. (The articles are: "Compiler method of automatic programming" by Nora B. Moser; "New York University compiler system" by Roy Goldfinger; "The LMO edit compiler" by Merritt Elmore; and "Automatic programming on the Burroughs Laboratory computer" by Hubert M. Livingston.) As noted earlier there is also a brief description of the Laning and Zierler algebraic compiler, although it is never called a compiler but rather a "system." The most elaborate system called a compiler is the A-2 compiler described in the article by Nora Moser [6]. The NYU and Burroughs "compilers" were essentially assembly programs of a primitive type; the LMO edit "compiler" produced "editing" routines for formatting and printing output by inserting parameters from simple specifications into skeleton programs.

The Moser article on A-2 is somewhat difficult for an outsider to understand fully, but the following points emerge with reasonable certainty. (Quotes are from the Moser article [6]. Keep in mind that the A-2 compiler Moser describes in May 1954 is apparently quite different from the A-2 compiler described in material available in 1955.)

(a) ". . . The compiler method of automatic programming consists of assembling and organizing a program from . . . routines or . . . sequences of computer code which have been made up previously."

(b) There appears to be no standard "pseudocode" for this compiler; rather the problem input to the compiler is a sequence of "compiling instructions" as indicated below.

(c) "The compiling instructions for one operation include the call word of the subroutine, the serial number, the working storage location of each argument and result of the particular subroutine. . . . A generator may require all these and in addition one or more words of specifications. . . . Hand-tailored coding begins with a sentinel and the number of lines in the sequence, followed by the coding itself.''

(d) A routine, ''the Translator, permits many compiling instructions to be written in abbreviated form, where one word replaces up to seven words.''

(e) Apparently the user had to assign absolute working storage locations manually to all symbolic and ''relative'' addresses he used.

(f) The ''abbreviated (compiling) instructions'' are apparent forerunners of ''pseudocode'' (a term nowhere used in the article); however, the article suggests that they are a recent and less-than-major item in the system.

(g) In addition to inserting addresses and parameters into coding, replacing relative and symbolic addresses by programmer-assigned values and translation of ''abbreviated instructions'' into their ''complete form,'' the compiler ''segmented'' the object program to fit into the available storage space and arranged to call in the next segment, performed various checks, and searched and updated library tapes.

The above items give some idea of what the word ''compiler'' meant to one group in early 1954. It may amuse us today to find ''compiler'' used for such a system, but it is difficult for us to imagine the constraints and difficulties under which its authors worked. After studying the seven pages of the A-2 article, it is startling to find in the same volume three scant pages devoted to Laning's algebraic system with its elegant source language and its use of combined compilation and interpretation. Oddly enough, Laning and Zierler's abstract for their report calls their system ''an interpretive program,'' and ''compilation of closed subroutines'' is the closest they come to using the word ''compiler.''

By 1955, the A-2 compiler had acquired a definite set of fixed format ''pseudo-instructions'' not unlike those of earlier interpretive systems in form but with more sophisticated operations added, such as ''repeat.''

I have tried to assess the A-2 compiler of early 1954 on the basis of a single, not-too-clear article. I realize it is possible to have misjudged it. Much of the difficulty appears to come from changes in the system between early 1954 and 1955.

REFERENCES

1. Wilkes, M. V., Wheeler, D. J., and Gill, S., ''The Preparation of Programs for an Electronic Digital Computer.'' Addison-Wesley, Reading, Massachusetts, 1957. (First edition published in 1951.)
2. *Proc. Symp. Automatic Programming Digital Comput., Office of Naval Research, Washington, D.C.* 13–14 May 1954).

3. Laning, J. H., and Zierler, N., A Program for Translation of Mathematical Equations for Whirlwind I. Engineering Memorandum E-364, Instrumentation Lab., MIT, Cambridge, Massachusetts (January 1954).
4. Cocke, J., and Schwartz, J. T., "Programming Languages and Their Compilers," Preliminary notes, second revised version. Courant Inst. of Math. Sci., New York Univ. (April 1970).
5. Backus, J. W., "The Syntax and Semantics of the Proposed International Algebraic Language of the Zurich ACM-GAMM Conference, *Proc. Internat. Conf. Inf. Proc., UNESCO, Paris* (June 1959).
6. Moser, N. B., Compiler method of automatic programming, *Proc. Symp. Automatic Programming Digital Comput.* Office of Naval Research, Washington, D.C. (May 13–14, 1954).

IBM RESEARCH LABORATORY
SAN JOSE, CALIFORNIA

The Early Development of Programming in the USSR*,†

ANDREI P. ERSHOV

and

MIKHAIL R. SHURA-BURA

This historical paper attempts to analyze, based on publications, personal reminiscences and the authors' own archives, the first 15 years of the formation and development of computer programming in the USSR, considered both as a human practice and a scientific discipline. After a brief description of the context in which this development took place and an analysis of the initial base of knowledge, the authors argue that many important components of programming (especially general theory and methodology and compilation techniques) were strongly influenced in the USSR by internal creative impulses. The account traces Soviet development through the release of the first ALGOL compliers in 1963.

Translator's Preface

When I began editing this paper, I decided to make the English as natural as I could so that there would be nothing to distract the reader from the contents of this fascinating account. In conforming to standard practice for English-language publications, I made several systematic changes, which, al-

---

* English text edited by Ken Kennedy, Department of Mathematical Sciences, Rice University, Houston, Texas.

† This research was carried out for the International Research Conference on the History of Computing held at Los Alamos, New Mexico, 10–15 June 1976.

137

though minor, are nevertheless deviations from the strict translation. I wish to take full responsibility for these changes, so I briefly detail them here:

(1)   The authors referred to themselves throughout the paper by their initials. The reason is given in the following excerpt which I have deleted from the introduction:

> During the presentation we must refer occasionally to our own work. As usualy in such cases, a problem of self-identification arises. On one hand, we wish to be free of over personalization but, on the other, we want to avoid the curious habit of referring to ourselves as strangers. As a compromise, we shall use the identifiers as AE and ShB.

I felt this convention would have an effect opposite to the one intended — it would draw excessive attention to the authors' names — so in keeping with the more common practice, I have substituted the last names of the authors wherever these initials appeared.

(2)   The authors frequently used the title "Professor," particularly with the names of American and English computer scientists. I systematically eliminated all such titles except "Academician," which seemed to be of substantial importance, particularly within the Soviet Union.

(3)   A number of minor issues involving capitialization in titles of papers, books, and conferences were resolved in favor of standard English practice.

(4)   On many occasions I was faced with fairly tricky sentence and paragraph rearrangements in order to make the language flow more easily. I tried to be very careful, but it is possible that some subtle changes in meaning resulted. It is my hope that these are few and insubstantial.

(5)   I frequently consolidated several short paragraphs into one longer one if these paragraphs contained a common theme.

I sincerely hope that I have succeeded in making the language comfortable enough so that you can enjoy reading this fresh and exciting paper as much as I have enjoyed working on it.

Ken Kennedy
Houston, January 1978

Introduction

A history of the formation and development of programming in the USSR is not easily separated from a history of other fields of computing. The closer a scientific discipline is to its sources, the stronger are its connections to and dependencies on the general context and closely related fields. To trace the formation of a scientific discipline or human professional activity is to notice watersheds and to observe those moments when an inner structure forms; such moments are almost always tied to events occurring in the background. Understanding this inseparability, we must express some reservations about the completeness of this work.

First, the development of related fields, specifically hardware and numerical methods, is discussed only briefly. We make no effort to expose the internal structure of their development and their histories must wait for other authors. We describe only a few features of these disciplines and only to the extent to which they were essential for the development of programming.

Second, we have worked primarily from publications, relying less heavily on archival materials. However, we have used our personal archives and our own recollections when it seemed appropriate. Some original publications, especially foreign ones, were unavailable to us, so references to them may contain inaccuracies; we apologize for these in advance.

Third, we have deliberately restricted ourselves to the first fifteen years of the development of programming, ending the narration with the release of the first ALGOL compliers in 1963. Although programming in the Soviet Union attained its modern form and current degree of completeness during the years subsequent to 1963, its development during this period had less of a unique character and became tightly connected with established world scientific and technological trends. During the first 15 years, as the reader will see, programming was primarily influenced by impulses internal to the Soviet Union as the intuition and broad-mindedness of mature mathematicians were multiplied by the energy and enthusiasm of a young generation of newly educated programmers.

Although we do not wish to spend a great deal of time detailing our reasons for presenting this research, we feel that two are worth mentioning. The history of a scientific discipline is a part of its self-determination and, having devoted our lives to programming, we are unable to resist the temptation to chronicle those events with which we have been so closely involved. But more important, undertaking this work provides us the opportunity to remember those scientists, engineers, and ordinary workers who, by their creative efforts, have created the house in which we, as programmers, now live. We regret that some of them have left us forever and will never hear these words of appreciation.

We cite original papers throughout the work, but our aim is not merely to recreate the past. Wherever feasible, scientific ideas and technical results are formulated in modern terms and interpreted in retrospect. Though such an approach can bring some subjectivity into the discussion, we nevertheless find it interesting to analyze the connections between different times during the development.

We realize that there may be inaccuracies and omissions in the narrative, and we shall be grateful to anyone who will assist us by pointing these out.

1. Prehistory (1946–1949)

In the USSR, World War II interrupted a series of scientific research and technical projects in the field of mathematical machinery (as it was called). A continuous tradition, tracing its roots to P. L. Tschebyscheff, of interest in applied mathematics and calculation methods, had existed in the USSR; this tradition was strongly reinforced by the scientific and public activity of Academician A. N. Krylov in the formative years of Soviet science. On the other hand, demands of the war resulted in new applied research in numerical methods and automation of calculations mainly for control of artillery fire. Radiolocation and radiocommunication requirements led to an accumulation of experience in uhf circuitry and the associated technology.

This contradictory situation was expressively demonstrated in a subject-oriented issue of the journal *Uspekhi Mathematicheskikh Nauk* (UMN) [*Advances in Mathematical Sciences*] 1(5–6) (1946), which had resumed regular publication immediately after the war. The issue contained two original review papers that had been prepared well before the war and two translated papers, one of which (on Bush's differential analyzer) was rather influential. There were no hints in these papers of electronic computing machinery or the concept of a program-controlled calculator. On the other hand, the introductory paper by N. E. Kobrinsky and L. A. Lusternik began with such a remarkable prediction of the role of computing machinery that it could, as a problem statement, easily open any modern computer conference. It seems appropriate to include some excerpts from this paper [1, pp. 4–6]:

> Modern computational practice is extremely varied and, accordingly, we can see many different types of technical aids to computation.
> First of all we must focus our attention on the "everyday" computational practices of finance and accounting, statistics and engineering. Mathematically, the computations are simple, requiring no more than arithmetic operations. On the other hand, the number of people involved in such computations is enormous . . . Manufacture of calculating instruments to serve this mass practice is now in some countries a recognizable branch of industry.
> . . . Computations . . . which have to be carried out in a combat environment form a special class of mass computational practice. Obviously, the speed of the computations, which are sometimes quite nonelementary, is of critical importance. Similar computational methods play a significant role in nonmilitary technology, for example, in navigation and in automated control of complex machines.
> Finally we have the field of "scientific computations" connected with the solution of scientific and complex technological problems. Such computations require a large amount of very specialized work.

Here we face a variety of problems which are sometimes quite new in their mathematical formulations (systems of linear and/or differential equations, boundary and initial value problems for equations from mathematical physics).

Progress in science and technology gives rise to new problems for computational mathematics. Quite recently, solution of integral equations was a refined field of theoretical analysis but now they are solved by a routine computational technique. Increasing speeds in aviation . . . require the solution of boundary problems for equations of the mixed elliptic–hyperbolic type. Progress in rocket engines has made the computation of trajectories for variable-mass bodies very important. Concepts from modern theoretical physics stress the importance of finding proper values and functions for different kinds of operators.

Thus we may conclude that urgent needs of science and engineering have led to the formation of a new branch of technology which could be called the design and production of "calculating devices," that is, instruments and machines for the solution of mathematical problems. Existence of these machines has caused the revision of problem statements in computational mathematics. A problem solution algorithm which is oriented to some machine is not necessarily a replica of a "manual" algorithm. Technical aids to modern computational mathematics allow direct solutions of problems previously considered practically unsolvable . . . Modern "computer mathematics" becomes a powerful tool of the natural sciences and technological disciplines and is a very attractive complex field requiring the joint efforts of mathematicians, physicists, and engineers of many specialties—mechanical, electrical, optical, etc.

. . . Recent advances in "computer mathematics" are closely connected to the progress in automation. In modern large-scale machines we can see automated control of a complex aggregate with sequencing of given operations performed by different components, with complicated flow of data from one component to another, with synchronization of concurrent processes and so forth. It is appropriate to say that "mathematical machinery" is an experimental basis for automation in general. Thus its achievements play a great role for all technology.

This farsighted view of computing machinery was developed at the Mathematical Institute of the Soviet Academy of Sciences (MIAN). At that time, the institute was not only a place for first-class research in pure mathematics but was also supporting the attack on a broad range of applied mathematical problems, due primarily to a charge to the Academy of Sciences from the government to undertake important applied research and computations related to the development of new fields of technology. In charge of this activity in MIAN was Academician M. V. Keldysh, an associate director of the institute under its director, Academician I. M. Vinogradov. The computational aspects of applied mathematics were studied by the department of approximate calculations headed by Lusternik, who was then a corresponding member of the USSR Academy of Sciences. In that department some important applied computations were prepared under the leadership of K. A. Semendyaev.

The idea of a program-controlled automatic digital computer came to the Soviet Union in 1947, when M. L. Bykhovsky, practically the only translator of English literature on computing at that time, published a short note [2] in UMN (based on publications [3–5]) announcing the MARK I and ENIAC computers. A similar but later paper by Hartree [6] and a more detailed description of the MARK I [7] appeared in Russian translation in UMN in 1948 [8, 9]. The note [2] contained no speculative comments on the material and its title seemingly indicated an analogy with punch-card equipment (a literal translation of the Russian term used in the title would be "calculating and analytical machines") instead of stressing the birth of a new concept in automatic computation.

The principal source materials on the concepts and logical structure of program-stored electronic digital computers [10–13] were then (and even now in the original form) unavailable in the USSR. (The authors of reviews [16] and [20] also complained that these historical documents were difficult to acquire.) However, during 1947 and 1948 a number of "secondhand" papers containing a reasonable amount of scientific information appeared in various journals such as *Review of Scientific Instruments, Electronics, Proc. of the IRE, Mathematical Tables and Other Aids to Computation, Journal of the Franklin Institute,* and some others. The proceedings of the well-known 1947 symposium at Harvard University [14] became available in the USSR a bit later. On the basis of these materials, Bykhovsky published a long review paper under the title Principles of electronic mathematical machines for discrete computations [15]. Because it was prepared in great haste and because of size limitations, the paper contained neither references nor specifications for particular computers; nevertheless, it was written in a businesslike style and included a very useful description of the engineering and design principles of various units of an electronic computer. In this sense, it was similar to the first monograph describing computers [16] edited by W. Stiffler and published in the U.S. in 1950 and available in the USSR in a Russian translation by 1952 [17].

That monograph, together with a small part of a book by F. Murray, "The Theory of Mathematical Machines" [18, Chap. V] (Russian translation, 1949 [19]) and a well-known European review paper by H. Rutishauser, *et al.* [20] (Russian translation, 1952 [21]), roughly encompasses the knowledge available to and used by Soviet specialists who began work in the field of electronic computing machinery during the first postwar five-year period.

Returning to Bykhovsky's paper [15], it seems appropriate to include here the discussion of principles of program control as it appeared in that early Russian paper [15, pp. 110–111]:

> Solving a problem by machine requires a decomposition of the problem into a sequence of arithmetic and logical operations, written as a long series of "commands" to be read into the machine in some form. In general, each such command must contain the following information: (1) where to find the numbers upon which the operation is to be performed, (2) which operation is to be performed, (3) where to put the result, and (4) where to get the next command. . . . Commands are written in coded form as ordinary digits usually in the binary number system. These binary number commands are read into the machine on paper (or magnetic) tape. From such tapes they are transmitted to other storage units, particularly electronic memory, where they are operated on as ordinary numbers. A given command is transmitted from electronic memory to the control unit where it is decoded into a sequence of signals which select the units to perform the command. Moreover, the given command indicates the place where the next command is to be found. That indication is decoded and, during the next time cycle, the subsequent command is switched to the control unit. Thus the machine automatically executes any prescribed sequence. It should be noted that the sequence of commands necessary for the solution of a certain problem can be simplified considerably if new commands are constructed from old ones by applying logical operations to the commands; such operations can be viewed as arithmetic operations over numbers representing commands. To achieve this, number and commands may be transmitted from memory not only to the control unit, but also to the calculation circuits. Simplification and rational construction of series of commands for the solution of various problems is the most urgent task arising from modern universal machines for discrete computation.

The actual start of work on electronic computing machinery dates from 1947, when S. A. Lebedev, director of the Electrotechnical Institute of the Ukranian Academy of Sciences in Kiev, initiated research on computer design. His first experiments were along the same lines as ENIAC but from the very beginning he was especially interested in high-speed digital elements and computer circuitry. Lebedev's initiative was energetically supported by Academician M. A. Lavrentyev, who also worked at Kiev. At that time it was difficult to find working space in the half-destroyed city, so Lavrentyev, who was conducting experiments which would lead to a theory of cumulative explosion, allotted several rooms in an old building of the former Feofania Monastery to Lebedev's team. There in 1951 the first electronic computer in the USSR and continental Europe began operation [22]; this machine was later named MESM, an acronym for Malaya Electronnaya Schetnaya Mashina (Small Electronic Computing Machine).

2. Formation of Initial Knowledge

From the beginning, experiments on the MESM computer demonstrated that the preparation of a problem for computer solution was a separate task to be specially considered. This task became the subject of systematic treatment at a seminar on programming initiated by Lusternik in 1950 at the Institute of Precise Mechanics and Computing Machinery of the USSR Academy of Sciences. The seminar, conducted in parallel with work on the BESM computer, resulted in the writing of one of the world's first monographs devoted entirely to programming [23] (by Lusternik, A. A. Abramov, V. I. Shestakov, and Shura-Bura). Since the first generation of Soviet programmers grew up with this book it is appropriate to present its contents in more detail.

The primary references for the book were the translation of Murray's book [19], the monograph edited by Stiffler [16], and the review paper by Rutishauser, *et al.* [20]. Murray's book was devoted mostly to older machinery but a small chapter on electronic computers contained an expressive example—a cyclic process programmed as an interative loop based upon the "current difference," with an index to count the prescribed number of repetitions. Stiffler's book provided a detailed account of the fundamentals of electronic computer arithmetic, a general description of the principle of program control, and an example of a one-address instruction code (with reference to [12]). The review [20] repeated many topics from Stiffler's book but contained an account of the work by Goldstine and von Neumann [24] on three important concepts: the flow diagram as an explicit representation of program branches and loops, the loop control variable, and address dependence on a control variable. The review also considered different instruction codes (from one- to four-address) and mentioned for the first time the index register concept (i-register in MARK III). No less important was an attempt by the authors to systematize programming and to attract attention to the use of the computer itself as an aid to programming. They wrote [20, Section 4.1]:

> Preparation of a problem to be solved by a program-controlled computer consists of the following stages:
>
> (a)   The problem, usually submitted to a computing department in physical or engineering terms, must be reformulated mathematically.
>
> (b)   An adequate numerical method for solution of the new mathematical problem must be chosen (numerical formulation).
>
> (c)   Every numerical method chosen for use in the solution must have its formulas decomposed into individual arithmetic operations. In addition, transition operations which specify the work of the computer must be determined.
>
> Arithmetic and logical operations can be called computing instruc-

tions; together, they compose the program for the computation. Actually, this is nothing more than a detailed description of a numerical solution, prepared for an unskilled human calculator for whom a computing machine is substituted.

(d)   Finally, the computing program must be translated into computer "language." In this process, each instruction is written in coded form as the corresponding control signal (or "command") on the paper or magnetic tape.

It is easier to distinguish the concept of "computing program" from that of "sequence of control signals" if one understands that a computing program, expressed as formulas and instructions, represents a rather general numerical solution of the problem and as such is suitable for any computing machine, while a sequence of control signals is suited only to a specific machine.

From the introduction [20, Sections 1.3 and 1.4]:

The preparation of a program can be partially performed by another computing machine which expands a general control signal prepared by a human being into a whole series of separate control signals. An example of such a general control signal might be: "Compute the indefinite integral of a function which is allocated in locations 1 – 100 of the store." A first step in this direction has been taken on the MARK III computer where a program is written on tape by an encoding machine which can process computational operations prescribed by mathematicians in ordinary mathematical notation. Thus it is inappropriate to think that progress in computers consists only of increasing their speed.

The preparation of a computational problem for a computer (coding or programming) can be considered a special branch of logic. To this end, the structure of a mathematical process and the course of its transformation into machine language must be studied.

One other paper [25] on the use of subroutines in EDSAC was an important source of material.

We now return to survey the contents of the book "Programming for High-Speed Electronic Computers" [23]:

Chapter 1. Digital Computers and Automation of Computations (21 pages).

Concept of a digital computer, number systems, logical structure of algorithms (sequence, loop, branching), punch-card machines, automatic computers, principle of program control, operative and external memories.

Chapter 2. Operations on Numbers in Digital Computers (94 pages).

Number representation, fixed and floating point, operations on numbers and binary words, singularities in operations on numbers of bounded length, multiplication, division and square root computational schemes.

The material of this chapter was treated very thoroughly and was broader in scope than necessary for the specific purposes of the BESM design.

Chapter 3. Some Standard Processes in Automatic Computations (24 pages).

Brief description of computational schemes and arithmetization rules for some frequently-used algorithms: sum of products, number conversion, double-precision arithmetic, polynomial evaluation, serial sums and differences, solution of equations by nested intervals, function evaluation by means of series, continuous fractions and iteration methods, logical methods of computation checking including parity and Hamming checks.

Chapter 4. Programming Solutions of Mathematical Problems (86 pages).

This chapter begins with a discussion of principles of program control and the properties of machine instructions: memory location, operation codes and addressing. One- and three-address codes are described as preferable and their equivalence (in principle) is stated. Three-address code is characterized as more convenient while one-address code is said to be informationally more economical. The well-known rule of thumb that a one-address program is twice as long as an equivalent three-address program is formulated for the first time. A simple example program (complex division) is given in three- and one-address EDSAC code. Conditional and unconditional jumps in various instruction formats are treated thoroughly and illustrated in programs to solve quadratic and cubic equations. Also discussed are digital encoding of instructions and ways to transform instructions as a whole or in part; instruction initialization, additive address advancing, address formation, and "restoration" of an instruction to its initial form are given special emphasis. A sample instruction set for an abstract three-address machine, along with symbolic coding techniques and discipline for memory allocation, is then given, establishing a tradition for stylistic arrangement of programming texts in which an abstract machine is used to illustrate programming principles. Loop control by a comparison instruction and by a counter are demonstrated through examples. Then for the first time a general principle of loop programming with a non zero number of repetitions is formulated [23, p. 189]:

If a problem solution consists of the periodic repetition of a basic sequence of operations then this sequence will be called a cycle and processes which consist of repetitions of cycles will be called cyclic . . . Let $A_1, A_2, \ldots, A_n$ be a sequence of operations such that A_{i+1} can be systematically obtained from A_i if initial data are properly allocated to memory. Then it is appropriate to construct the program according to one of the following plans:

    I. A_1
   II. Transformation of A_i into A_{i+1} $(A_i \rightarrow A_{i+1})$
  III. Control comparison

or

    I. $A_i \rightarrow A_{i+1}$
   II. A_0
  III. Control comparison

A special paragraph in the chapter is devoted to the methods for constructing complex programs from simpler ones. Subroutine calls are discussed briefly with only two aspects considered: formation of the return to the main program before the jump to a subroutine and the use of two instruction counters, central control for the main program and local control for the subroutine. It is recommended that a problem be decomposed into meaningful subproblems and that a flow chart relating the subproblems be constructed. A systematic, but not automatic, procedure for allocating a program to a prescribed location is introduced. Then a method for use of common pieces of code in different branches of a computation is presented, a method which would now be called "proceduring." The chapter closes with examples: a numerical solution of ballistic equations and sixteen programs implementing the standard algorithms from the previous chapter.

Chapter V. Programs for the Solution of Some Mathematical Problems (85 pages).

This chapter contains seventeen programs for solution of the following problems: $\log_2 x$, $\sin x$, $\Gamma(1 + z)$, algebraic polynomial conversions, Runge–Kutta method for solution of ordinary differential equations, solution of systems of linear algebraic equations, Adams' method for integrating the equations of ballistics, tabulation of Bessel functions.

An important feature of the book was many detailed comments to the program text whenever complicated technical rules or program tricks were used (representation of permutations, interaction of control instructions in nested loops, techniques to check the number of repetitions, standardization of a computation to more effectively use looping in a program, speed–memory tradeoffs, etc.).

In the same year (1952), the well-known book by M. Wilkes *et al.* , [26] first appeared in the USSR and was published in a Russian translation the following year [27]. This book significantly extended the programming material presented in [23] and remains so widely known that it makes no sense to repeat its contents here. From today's perspective it is worthwhile to view the book not only as a treasury of real programming experience, so rare at that time, and not only as an excellent contribution to programming technology (libraries of routines and program check-out methods), but also as a demonstration of how much more effective a computer can be when it has proper program support. Actually, this book contained the first description of an integrated software system that was, at the same time, "closed" in the sense of completeness (it included hardware testing programs, pseudoinstructions, a mathematical library, input–output subroutines, debugging modules, loader and assembly modules, and small application packages) and "open" to growth. All this was tailored to the specific style of work on the computer and balanced with the modest capabilities of the hardware.

Because of these source materials, programmers in the USSR were reasonably well prepared when the first Soviet computers went into intensive use.

It should be noted that, although the importance of computing machinery was not disputed, it was not easy to make a decisive turn to universal electronic digital computers. The problem lay not only in the insufficient technological base and related postwar difficulties; there was also a serious split over universal versus specialized computing devices. The standard bearers of specialization were backed not only by the inertia of the old school but also by a methodological principle: "A specific problem can be more effectively solved by special means." Universal machines were also opposed by some dogmatic philosophers who were quite suspicious of "cybernetic speculations about electronic brains." Both authority and will were needed to establish and protect the development of computer technology and the associated methodology.

Much of that authority and will were contributed by Academicians M. V. Keldysh, A. A. Dorodnitsyn, S. L. Sobolev, and M. A. Lavrentyev, who worked in different fields of applied mathematics. These academicians not only properly oriented their own departments but together they succeeded in convincing the appropriate agencies and industries that universal electronic computers should be the central focus in the development of computing machinery.

In 1948, the Institute of Precise Mechanics and Computing Machinery (ITMiVT) was established at the Academy of Sciences. It was originally directed by Academician N. G. Bruyevich, a well-known specialist in the field of machines and mechanical devices. This institute consolidated a number of groups, already extant within the academy, which dealt with mechanical computations and the design of mathematical instruments. In the beginning ITMiVT was a conglomerate of different scientific and technical directions, among which electronic computers was hardly the leader. Much of the credit for reorienting ITMiVT to a more modern goal-oriented direction belongs to Lavrentyev, who came to Moscow in 1950 to assume directorship. He began by organizing a new department of digital computers, which he invited S. A. Lebedev to head. This department was charged with initiating the design of a large-scale electronic computer immediately, without waiting for completion of work on MESM. Initially, the design group consisted primarily of graduate students at the Moscow Institute of Energy. Among those students were V. S. Burtsev, the current director of ITMiVT, and V. A. Melnikov, a principal designer of the famous BESM 6 computer. V. M. Kurochkin participated in the design of the instruction set from the mathematical side.

Design of the new computer was completed in 1951, and production runs began in 1952; it was given the acronym BESM for Bystrodeystvuyushchaya Elektronnaya Schotnaya Mashina (High-Speed Electronic Computing Machine). BESM was designed for a memory implemented by Williams tubes, but because these tubes were unavailable, mercury delay lines were used until 1955. Part of the high-speed memory was read-only and was manufactured as a matrix of sockets with spring contacts pressing on the lid, much like a wafer iron. Each wafer iron contained a single 45-column punch card with each row representing a single instruction. All the equipment except the Williams tubes and other electronic components was "homemade," including a papertape input device, a two-head magnetic tape drive, a magnetic drum, and mercury memory. For that time, the BESM was rather high speed (see Table I in Section 3) but many obstacles had to be overcome during its implementation—some of them were quite unexpected. Burtsev tells the story that when the computer went into the integration period, it required (naturally) a few thousand electronic tubes of a new type. This was an unimaginable quantity for the time; distribution (by quota) of these tubes to academic institutions was by tens, not hundreds or thousands. In seeking a solution to this problem, engineers noticed that the tube factory had a test bed where thousands of tubes were subjected to operational voltages for a reasonably long period. In typical pragmatic fashion they forged an agreement to let the computer serve as test bed for the tubes—a function it performed until a sufficient stock could be accumulated.

The BESM computer had a three-address instruction set with one curious feature, seemingly inspired by the MARK I and II computers: two program counters, one central and one local. One-level subroutine call was implemented by an unconditional jump combined with a switch to the local program counter; return simply consisted of switching back to the central counter. The local counter was also used for transput operations.

During the same period, design of another electronic computer had begun at the design bureau of the Ministry of Instrumentation and Automation Means of USSR, headed by M. A. Lesechko. This computer, tailored especially for industrial manufacturing at the Moscow SAM (Schetno-Analyticheskaya Mashina—Calculating and Analytical Machine) plant, was called STRELA (arrow). The chief designer was Y. Y. Bazilevsky and one of his closest co-workers was B. I. Rameev, later the chief designer of the Ural computers. Serial production requirements predetermined several properties of the design: less speed, potential rather than impulse circuitry, loose assembly, etc. STRELA had no drum; instead it used a specially designed 45-head tape. It also had a rather convenient instruction repertoire; for example, every arithmetic and logical instruction produced a Boolean value (omega-tag) which could be used for subsequent conditional branching. Another feature was the inclusion of "grouped operations," which performed component-by-component operations on vector arrays. Half of the fast memory was read-only, having its own control counter; this was used for storing a small built-in subroutine library. The first STRELA was delivered in 1953 to the Division of Applied Mathematics at MIAN. By the end of 1953 it had passed all its field tests and production runs had begun.

Another pioneer in Soviet computing machinery was Corresponding Member of the Academy of Sciences I. S. Bruk, director of the Laboratory of Electrical Systems at the Institute of Energy of the USSR Academy of Sciences. He began work in 1951 with the design of a small prototype computer known as the M-1. After an initial accumulation of experience, he formed a group and directed the design of a successor, the M-2, in 1952. A leading designer in Bruk's group was M. A. Kartsev, who was to make substantial contributions to the theory and design of arithmetic units. The M-2 originated a methodology for the design of medium-scale computers that emphasized economy as the fundamental principle. To this end, the M-2 design was quite successful, and its architecture established a lengthy tradition among Bruk's disciples leading to the production of several series of inexpensive computers for widespread use. One of these disciples was G. P. Lopato, who became chief designer for the Minsk computers.

3. Early Experience and the First Conference (1954–1956)

Delivery of the first computers in the USSR was regarded as a very important scientific and technological event. S. A. Lebedev, director of the MESM project, was elected to full membership in the Academy of Science, filling a special vacancy in "computer technology"; Y. Y. Bazilevsky, designer of STRELA, was given the highest state award: the title "Hero of Socialist Labor" with the Golden Star and Lenin Order. The Academy of Science and the Ministry of Higher Education undertook the formation and support of organizations involved in the design and use of computing machinery.

Work on applied mathematics was concentrated at MIAN's Division of Applied Mathematics (OPM MIAN) which, under the management of M. V. Keldysh, would eventually become the separate Institute of Applied Mathematics. In that division the first programming department in the USSR was organized in 1953, headed by A. A. Lyapunov for the first year and by Shura-Bura from 1954 to the present.

A year earlier the Department of Computational Mathematics of Moscow University had been reorganized and a new curriculum, intended to prepare applied mathematicians for work on computers, had been introduced. S. L. Sobolev was asked to chair that department.

The Computing Center of the USSR Academy of Sciences was established in 1955 to conduct fundamental research in the field of computer mathematics and to provide an openshop computer service. The director was A. A. Dorodnitsyn, who had been elected to full membership in the Academy in 1953.

In the Department of Approximate Computations of the Leningrad Branch of MIAN (LOMI), work on programming began in 1952 under the guidance of L. V. Kantorovich, previously known for his work in functional analysis and his pioneering research in linear programming.

When Lebedev left Kiev for Moscow, the director of the Mathematical Institute of the Ukrainian Academy of Sciences, B. V. Gnedenko, invited the team of MESM designers to his institute to form the kernel of a computing laboratory. Within a few years the laboratory was headed by V. M. Glushkov, a recent Doctor of Sciences in theoretical algebra. In addition to his mathematical background, Glushkov had a professional education in electrical engineering, and to him the field of computing machinery presented an ideal opportunity to combine successfully both specialties. At the end of the 1950s, the computing laboratory was to form the nucleus for the Computing Center of the Ukrainian Academy of Sciences, which would eventually become the well-known Institute of Cybernetics.

In 1953, Lavrentyev turned over the directorship of ITMiVT to Lebedev. Later when the Computing Center of the Academy of Sciences was being formed, a considerable number of mathematicians were transferred there from ITMiVT (these included Ershov who began work at ITMiVT in 1953 while he was still a student at Moscow University).

In 1955, a computing center was established at Moscow University in which an M-2 was used for both research and instruction.

Bruk's group left the Institute of Energy of the Academy of Sciences to form the Laboratory of Control Computers and Systems of the Academy in 1956; this group was to become the Institute for Control Machines (INEUM).

In these organizations early research and experimentation laid the foundation for development and application of the first generation of Soviet computers. This work was fully described at the first all-Union scientific meeting solely devoted to computing machinery. The conference was entitled Prospects for the Development of Soviet Mathematical Machinery and Instrumentation and was held at Moscow University, 12–17 March 1956.

For the time, it was an extremely representative conference with a large audience; over 1000 participants were present and 75 talks were presented [29]. The conference took place amid the political and moral enthusiasm of the historic Twentieth Congress of the Communist Party of the Soviet Union. At the Party Congress, in the program for development of the national economy in the sixth five-year period, the following goals had been set forth [30, pp. 447–448]:

> To develop in every possible way the radio and instrumentation industries, . . . To increase by four and one half times the production of computing and punch-card machines, . . . To enhance the work on design and manufacturing of high-speed machines for solution of mathematical problems and automation of process control . . . To expand and intensify research and development on semiconductor instruments and to broaden their practical applications.

In general, the period was marked by a reversal of the dogmatically negative approach to the ideas of cybernetics on unity of the laws of control and information processing, and by the first experiments with computer simulation of intellectual activity. In the previous year, at the 1955 Darmstadt Conference, the Soviet delegation headed by Lebedev had made Soviet work on computing machinery public for the first time, receiving a favorable response from other specialists at the conference.

This general background, coupled with a comprehensive and businesslike program, explains the fundamental role this conference played in the development of computer research in the USSR and in shaping and illuminating the new reality created by electronic computers.

The conference was opened by Professor D. Y. Panov's talk, History and development of electronic computers, which stressed the first Soviet achievements in electronic computing machinery and characterized the serious historical tradition of computation in the USSR, while nevertheless objectively presenting the decisive contributions of American and English scientists toward development of program-controlled automatic computing machines, tracing back as far as Babbage. Panov specifically emphasized the broad scope and comprehensive nature of industrial design and production of computers in the U.S. [28, Plenary Sessions, 5–30].

Although the main stress was on problems related to the universal electronic computer, the conference organizers nevertheless sought to emphasize the variety of existing computing equipment and to present a well-balanced technical program. Three of the six plenary talks were devoted to the following problems [28, Plenary Sessions, 31–43, 61–132]:

> "High speed universal computers," S. A. Lebedev (the general characteristics of early Soviet computers are shown in Table I);
> "Special purpose computers and prospects for their development," Y. Y. Bazilevsky;
> "Modeling devices and trends in their development," V. B. Ushakov.

TABLE I[a]

FIRST SOVIET COMPUTERS

Name	MESM	BESM	M-2	STRELA	URAL	M-3
Project leader	S. A. Lebedev	S. A. Lebedev	I. S. Bruk	Y. Y. Bazilevsky	B. I. Rameev	I. S. Bruk
Pilot model	1951	1952	1952	1953	1955	1956
Production model	—	1956 (BESM 2)	—	1953	1956	1957
No. of addresses	3	3	3	3	1	2
Clock interval (μsec)		2.5	12.5	—		6
Basic cycle (μsec)		77	220	220	10000	60+
Average speed (op/sec)		8000	2000	2000	100	30000
Access time (μsec)		12	25	30	10000	30
Memory type	trigger register	CRT	CRT	CRT	drum	drum
Memory size (words)	31 numb. 63 instr. + 100 read-only	1024+ 376 read-only	512	1024+ 496 read-only	1023	2048
Word length (bit)	21	39	34	43	35	30
Arithmetics (point)	fix	float	fix float	float	fix	fix
No. of tubes	3800	4000	1879	8000	870	805
Drum (words)	2500	5120	512	—	1023	2048
Tape (words)	—	4 × 30K	50K	2 × 100K	40K	—
Input	manual	p/t	p/t	p/c	p/t	p/t
Output	tab print	tab print	t/t	p/c	tab print	tab print
Source	[28]	[28]	[28, 31]	[28]	[28]	[28, 32]

[a] Legend: CRT, cathode-ray tube; p/t, paper tape; p/c, punch card; tab, tabular; t/t, teletype; —, absent feature; , no information.

In his talk, Lebedev identified the main directions in the development of universal mathematical machines:

(1)   increasing speed,
(2)   enlarging the memory,
(3)   increasing reliability,
(4)   simplification of mathematical and technical maintenance.

Simplification of mathematical maintenance was accomplished, according to Lebedev, by "simplification of computer logic and the development of machines better suited to the logic of programming and to solving mathematical problems." As examples of developments in this direction, he mentioned automatic address modification and loop control.

The plenary talk by Dorodnitsyn, Solving mathematical and logical problems on high-speed electronic computing machines [28, Plenary Sessions, 44–52], which was devoted primarily to the solution of partial differential equations, contained some problem statements and prognoses concerned with the development and use of computers. In that talk, Dorodnitsyn noted:

> An analysis of problems from different fields of technology shows that an increase in computation speed to the order of a million operations per second and an enlargement of the operative memory to ten thousand numbers and beyond are well-justified and even modest goals.

This was the first statement of the goals which would lead to the delivery of the BESM 6 computer eight years later. Dorodnitsyn also remarked:

> The advent of high-speed computing machinery drastically changes the role of numerical methods. When solving many technological problems, it is now possible to require from a numerical method a complete account of factors influencing the process under study. Computations can provide a precision greater than that provided by an experiment be-cause the latter is carried out under conditions which may not conform exactly to natural ones and its accuracy is restricted by the accuracy of measurements.

Following the main line of presentation, we now review the scientific results in programming which were reported at the conference.

Lyapunov's Operator Method

A. A. Lyapunov began his work in the Programming Department of OPM MIAN after wartime service as an artillery officer. He had received a Doctor of Sciences degree in descriptive set theory and had taught mathematics at a military academy. Lyapunov's scientific style was marked by a broad natural-science background and an interest in discovering general laws and broad analogies. Formation of the view of programming as a scientific discipline in the USSR is, in large part, to his credit.

Lyapunov analyzed programming as a whole and identified several of its fundamental concepts. He considered the process of program execution as a discrete sequence of actions (operators) extracted from the program text according to control rules. A rather important part of the theory was his classification of operators: He introduced arithmetic operators (assignment statements) acting on data, logical operators (including both evaluation of Boolean relations and transfer of control), and modification operators acting on other operators. Modification operators are based upon the idea of dependence of an operator on some parameter (usually an integer variable); they consist of formation operators (initialization), readdressing operators (modification by a stepwise advancement of the parameter), and restoration operators (which restore a statement to its original form). Program text is viewed as being composed of two parts: a program scheme, in which symbolic denotations of operators, classification of operators, and control jumps are presented, and an operator specification, in which the functioning of operators is defined. This partition of the program text reflects the two stages of a programming process: the general planning of an algorithm, which results in the program scheme and an external specification of the operators (creative part), and then the systematic implementation of the operators in machine language (routine formalizable part). The possibility of systematic program transformations to aid the programming process was also emphasized.

This methodology, called the "operator method" of programming by A. I. Kitov, was described by Lyapunov in the first university course on programming in the USSR. The course was presented at Moscow State University during the 1952–1953 academic year under the title "Principles of Programming." The method was also briefly described in a talk at the conference given jointly with Y. I. Yanov [28, Part II, 5–8]. The Lyapunov-operator method led to the formation of program schemata theory and to the first Soviet compilers. It also originated a long-standing style for publication of algorithms, which is sometimes seen now [34].

The First Compilers

The problem of automation of programming was first described by Lyapunov, in the framework of his operator method, as a search for systematic procedures that implement program scheme operators by producing machine instructions from some formal specification of the functioning of these operators. [*Editor's Note:* From here on we will depart from the literal translation of the Russian оператор and use the native English term "statement."]

The idea of an integrated program that fully implements all statements constituting a program scheme was expressed by S. S. Kamynin and E. Z. Lubimsky in the summer of 1954 when they began work on a design for such a program in the Programming Department at OPM MIAN. During the following months they experimented on the STRELA computer with compilation algorithms containing arithmetic, logical, and readdressing statements. The resulting prototype compiler was called a "programming program" (PP-1). Its promising performance stimulated Shura-Bura to gather a larger team of young programmers for the task of designing a system that would serve not only as a test bed for compilation algorithms but also as a tool for production programming. The compiler was finished in 1955 and was called PP-2. The PP-2 source language preserved Lyapunov's partition of program text into scheme and statement specification. "Circulation" statements, which allowed a reduction in the number of occurrences of subscripted variables and restoration statements in a program, were added to Lyapunov's original set. The parsing of expressions ignored the priorities of infix operators and was performed by a reduction method in which a programmed term was replaced in the source string at each of (possibly) multiple occurrences by the symbol of the working cell containing the value of the term.

A parallel compiler project, to produce a compiler for the BESM (PP-BESM) was undertaken by Ershov, L. N. Korolev, V. M. Kurochkin, and a group of ITMiVT staff members. The project was directly stimulated by Lubimsky's seminar on PP-1 delivered at Moscow University in the fall of 1954, by an experiment conducted by Korolev on programming arithmetic expressions using operation priorities, and by Ershov's own thoughts on the nature of cyclic processes in programs. The PP-BESM source language contained arithmetic statements and a logical statement resembling the modern case statement. The most important novelties in PP-BESM were loop statements and subscripted variables (only loop counters were allowed as subscripts). Finally, the program text was not divided into scheme and statement specifications but looked like a formatless sequence of statements separated by semicolons.

These two compilers were discussed at the conference in talks by Kamynin and Lubimsky and by Ershov [28, Part III, 9–29]. Table II contains examples of program text expressed in Lyapunov's operator notation, the source languages of these two compilers, and the source languages of two later compilers (discussed in the next chapter). Seidel's iterative algorithm for solving a system of nth-order linear equations is taken as the sample problem. The computational scheme of this algorithm given by F. Murray in his book [19] was the first Russian-language publication of an algorithm designed for implementation on a program-controlled automatic computer and, seemingly, is modeled after the early work by Goldstine and von Neumann.

It is interesting to compare Lyapunov's notational system with Murray's symbolic representation of the abovementioned computational scheme. Seemingly used by Murray "on the fly" without generalizing comments, it provides a sound example of scientific prophecy in what was effectively the "Old Testament period" of programming.

TABLE II

PROGRAM TEXTS OF FIRST COMPILERS: MATHEMATICAL FORMULA
(SEIDEL ITERATIONS)

$$x_t^{(k+1)} = \frac{1}{a_{tt}} \left(b_t - \sum_{\substack{j=1 \\ j \neq t}}^{n} a_{tj} \cdot x_j \right)$$

I. Informal computational scheme by F. Murray [19, p. 275]

   A. Start iteration count from $k = 1$.

   B. Start the current iteration, set nonzero increment tag $\omega = 0$, start substitution count from $t = 1$.

   C. Start the current substitution into the tth equation, start count of equation members from $j = 1$, set sum s equal zero.

   D. If $j = t$, then skip the jth member and continue from F. Otherwise,

   E. Add the current member $a_{tj} \cdot x_j$ to the sum.

   F. If $j = n$, then continue from G. Otherwise advance j by 1, repeat the loop from D.

   G. Compute a new approximation

$$x = \frac{b_t - s}{a_{tt}}$$

   H. Form a difference $\delta = x - x_t$.

   I. If $\delta = 0$, then continue from K. Otherwise,

   J. Add δ to x_t, set $\omega = 1$.

   K. If $t = n$, then continue from L. Otherwise advance t by 1, repeat loop from C.

   L. If $\omega = 0$, then terminate the iterations. Otherwise repeat the loop from B.

II. Schematic representation of the computational process by F. Murray [19, p. 276]

$$A\{B[C(D(?)EF)_{j=1}^{n}GHI(?)JK]_{t=1}^{n} L\}_k$$

III. Computational scheme by A. A. Lyapunov

$$A \prod_k \left\{ B \prod_{t=1}^{n} \left[C \prod_{j=1}^{n} (p(j \neq t)E_{tj})G_t H_t\, p(\delta \neq 0)J_t \right] p(\omega \neq 0) \right\}$$

IV. Program scheme by A. A. Lyapunov:

$$(1 \rightarrow k) \downarrow^{1} (1 \rightarrow t)(0 \rightarrow \omega) \downarrow^{2} (1 \rightarrow j)(0 \rightarrow s) \downarrow^{3} p(j \neq t)E_{tj}$$

$$\underline{F}(j)\, p(j \leq n)\, \uparrow^{3} \underline{F}^{-n}(j)G_t H_t\, p(\delta \neq J_t\, \underline{F}(t)$$

$$p(t \leq n)\, \uparrow^{2} \underline{F}^{-n}(t)\, p(\omega \neq 0) \uparrow^{1} \underline{Stop}$$

(continued)

V. Source text for PP-2 compiler

$$A_1 \underset{17}{\rfloor} A_2 \underset{14}{\rfloor} A_3 \rfloor P_4 \overset{6}{\lceil} A_5 \overset{4}{\rceil} A_6 F_7 P_8 \underset{4}{\lfloor} A_9 P_{10} \overset{12}{\lceil} A_{11} \overset{10}{\rceil} A_{12} F_{13} P_{14} \underset{3}{\lfloor} O_{15} A_{16} P_{17} \underset{2}{\lfloor}$$

A_1: $l=k$	F_7: A_5 is readdressed by j
A_2: $l=t$	F_{13}: A_5 is readdressed by t
$\quad 0=\omega$	$\quad A_9$ is readdressed by t
	$\quad A_{11}$ is readdressed by t
A_3: $l=j$	
$\quad 0=s$	
A_5: $a_{tj}\cdot x_j+s = s$	O_{15}: restores A_5, A_9, A_{11}
A_6: $1+j = j$	a_{tj} depends on j by 1
A_9: $(b_t-s)a_{tt}^{-1}-x_t = \delta$	x_j depends on j by 1, on t by $-n$
	b_t depends on t by 1
A_{11}: $x_t+\delta = x_t$	a_{tt} depends on t by $n+1$
$\quad 1=\omega$	x_t depends on t by 1
A_{12}: $1+t = t$	
A_{16}: $1+k = k$	
P_4: p_1	p_1: $j \neq t$
P_8: p_2	p_2: $j > n$
P_{10}: p_3	p_3: $\delta \neq 0$
P_{14}: p_4	p_4: $t > n$
P_{17}: p_5	p_5: $\omega = 0$

VI. Source text for PP-BESM compiler

$$\left[0 \Rightarrow \omega \underset{k}{} \left[0 \Rightarrow s \underset{t}{} \left[P\ (j,\ 0101,\ \overset{0102}{\llbracket t,t \rrbracket}); \underset{0101}{\lfloor\_\_} s + a_{tj} \times x_j \Rightarrow s \underset{0102}{\lfloor\_\_} \right]; \right. \right.$$

$$(b_t - s): a_{tt} - x_t \Rightarrow \delta;\ P\ (\delta,\ 0103,\ \overset{0104}{\llbracket 0,0 \rrbracket});$$

$$\underset{0103}{\lfloor\_\_} x_t + \delta \Rightarrow x_t;\ 1 \Rightarrow \omega \underset{0104}{\lfloor\_\_} \left. \left. \right]\right];\ \text{Stop}$$

```
k:    from 1 to ω = 0
t:    from 0 to k
j:    from 0 to n
Array a — n² locations
```

$\langle a_{tj} \rangle = n.t + 1.j$
$\langle a_{tt} \rangle = (n + 1).t$

```
Array b — n locations
```

$\langle b_t \rangle = 1.t$

```
Array x — n locations
```

$\langle x_j \rangle = 1.j$
$\langle x_t \rangle = 1.t$

Table II (continued)

VII. Source text for PP STRELA compiler

$$\Phi(k, 1) \overset{4}{\ulcorner} \ 0 \Rightarrow s \ \ \Phi(t, 1) \ \ 0_1(t, \ 0_2, \ A_2) \overset{3}{\ulcorner} \ \Phi(j, 1) 0_2(j, \ A_1)$$

$$\overset{1}{\ulcorner} \ A_1 \left(P \ (j \ = \ t) \overset{0}{\ulcorner} s \ + \ a_{tj} x_j \Rightarrow s \overset{0}{\urcorner} \right) F \ (j, \ A_1) p(j > n) \overset{1}{\urcorner}$$

$$A_2 \left((b_t - s) : \ a_{tt} \ - \ x_t \Rightarrow \delta \ P \ \ (\delta = 0) \ \overset{2}{\ulcorner} x_t \ + \ \delta \Rightarrow x_t, \ 1 \Rightarrow w \ \overset{2}{\urcorner} \right)$$

$$F \ (t, \ A_1, \ A_2) \ p(t > n) \overset{3}{\urcorner} \ p(\omega \ \neq \ 0) \overset{4}{\urcorner}$$

Parameter dependencies

j: a_{tj} by 1, x_j by 1
t: a_{tj} by n, a_{tt} by $n + 1$, x_t by 1

VIII. Source text for PPS compiler

$$\left\{ \ 0 \Rightarrow \omega \overset{n}{\underset{k=1}{\left\{}} \ 0 \Rightarrow s \overset{n}{\underset{t=1}{\left\{}} \ \underset{j=1}{\text{л}} \ (j{=}t \ \overset{7001}{\boxed{}} \ ) ; \ s \ + \ a_{tj} \ \times \ x_j \Rightarrow s \underset{7001}{\rule{1em}{0.4pt}} \right] ;$$

$$(b_t - s) : \ a_{tt} - \ x_t \Rightarrow \delta ; \ \text{л} \left(\delta \ = \ 0 \ \overset{7002}{\boxed{}} \right) ; \ x_t \ + \ \delta \ \Rightarrow x_t \ ;$$

$$1 \Rightarrow \omega \underset{7002}{\rule{1em}{0.4pt}} \left. \Big\} \Big\} \right\}^{\omega \neq 0} ; \ \text{Stop}$$

Array 1, n^2 locations

$$a_{ij} = H \ - \ (1 \ + \ n) \ + \ r.t \ + \ 1.j$$

Array 2, n locations

$$x_j = H \ - \ 1 \ + \ 1.j$$

IX. Address program after V. S. Korolyuk and Y. L. Yusshchenko

```
        1 ⇒ k
1...    0 ⇒ t
        0 ⇒ ω
        A ⇒ a
        A ⇒ aa
2...    0 ⇒ j
        0 ⇒ s
3...    P ('j = 't) ↑ 4
        's + ''a × '(X + 'j) ⇒ s
```

(continued)

Table II (continued)

4... $'a + 1 \Rightarrow a$	
$'j + 1 \Rightarrow j$	
$P('j > n) \uparrow 3$	
$('(B + 't) - 's):\quad ''aa \Rightarrow Nx$	
$X + 't \Rightarrow Nx$	
$Nx - adx \Rightarrow \delta$	
$P('\delta = 0) \uparrow 5$	
$''adx + '\delta \Rightarrow 'adx$	
$1 \Rightarrow \omega$	
5... $adx + n + 1 \Rightarrow aa$	$\|a_{ij}\|$ starts from A
$'t + 1 \Rightarrow t$	$\|b_t\|$ starts from B
$P('t < n) \uparrow 2$	$\|x_j\|$ starts from X
$P('\omega \neq 0) \uparrow 1$	$'x$ means ref x
Stop	n is a constant

Large Block Programming.

L. V. Kantorovich, in discussions of programming problems with a group of 1953 and 1954 graduates of Leningrad University who made up the core of programmers at LOMI, had developed several deep ideas concerning the role of information connections in a program representation. In particular, he introduced a tree representation of arithmetic expressions (Kantorovich's tree). He also introduced composite data structures as program objects and developed the concept of a descriptor. The rules for composition of complex objects from primitive ones were called "geometrical operations." Elaboration of a program considered as an information network (scheme) of separate modules was treated by Kantorovich as an activity of some superprogram that supervised the execution of modules based on an analysis of the information and control flow in the scheme. Many of these concepts of large-block programming were later to be rediscovered at a higher level in the development of structured file systems and in what is now called "modular programming."

It seems interesting to quote from the original talk by Kantorovich, L. T. Petrova, and M. A. Yakovleva at the conference [28, Part III, 30–36]:

The essence of this system is a computational plan of the task expressed in large elements which are encoded and executed by a special prewritten "Prorab" program (прораб—abbreviated from производитель работ—work superintendant). This program also deals with the allocation of data to the operative and secondary memories, readdressing, etc. Thus a complete program for the task is never compiled nor is its construction a goal—the goal is finding the results of the computation. If you like, this is programless programming, however paradoxical that might sound.

When transmitting a mathematical task to a machine, the notation used is of great importance. Obviously, the closer the human mathematical language to the language perceptible by machine, the easier the transmission process . . . In the past, mathematical notation was changed and developed following the development of new fields in mathematics. Naturally, the use of computers must similarly influence contemporary symbolics. On the other hand, the machine itself may be thought "to understand" not only the simplest operations but also more complicated ones such as matrix computations, etc.

It is convenient when writing schemes to work not with single members but with large objects which might be termed quantities. Examples of such quantities are a vector, a matrix, and a three-dimensional matrix. The numerical contents of a given quantity are supplemented by a descriptor which contains a description of the form and allocation of the quantity . . . Such a descriptor for a $k \times n$ matrix M has the form

$$\begin{pmatrix} P & n & h_1 \\ & k & h_2 \end{pmatrix},$$

where P is a location number which addresses the first element of the quantity, n is the number of columns, k is the number of rows, h_1 is a distance between adjacent elements of each row, and h_2 is the distance between the first (or, more generally, the ith) elements of two adjacent rows.

Note that the descriptor of the transposed matrix M^* has the form

$$\begin{pmatrix} P & k & h_2 \\ & n & h_1 \end{pmatrix},$$

The separation of a descriptor from its numerical content is justified by the fact that several quantities may use common numerical material.

. . . A computational plan for a machine can be specified as a general scheme (represented by a tree defining a partial ordering of the results) of which elements may be:

(1) numerical quantities, programs, matrices of programs, schemes, and

(2) operations over these quantities . . . such as simplification of a scheme, for a given scheme (formula) construction of the corresponding program, or recursive repetition of a scheme until some condition is satisfied.

Organization of Programming and of Computer Runs

At the conference, these problems were discussed primarily in the talk by Shura-Bura [28, Plenary Sessions, 53–60]. The first year of production runs showed that "the real performance of a computer has to be measured by the number of problems actually solved, by the time necessary to get the solution of each problem, and by the number of people involved in preparation of problems, running of jobs and engineering maintenance."

The nature of the interaction between "mathematician" and "programmer" in the process of solving a problem by computer was also discussed in the talk. A formula for "equal rights" cooperation along with a definite partition of responsibilities was stated:

> Successful work on the development of new computational methods is possible only under conditions of close cooperation between researchers dealing with mathematical problem formulation and programmers. This close cooperation does not imply, however, mixing their functions. Proper choice of an "extended algorithm" [*Authors' Note:* That is, one where numerical operations are properly supplemented by control operations which organize the computation in space and time] not only is just as important as the right choice of an initial algorithm but also has some unique aspects requiring the specific skills of the programmer.

By 1956, the technological principles of running computer jobs had gradually taken shape. The operator had attained a position of central importance at the computer. He made up and ran the batch of jobs in the absence of their originators, who provided him with formal written instructions. (The "banishment" of programmers from the machine room had not been an easy transition.) A distinction had arisen between production and check-out runs and between urgent and background jobs. The first control and check-out programs appeared in 1955: interpretive trace programs with dynamic printouts, memory dumps, programs to print end points of linear components of a program, etc. At the same time, a paradoxical situation, from today's point of view, arose when compilation techniques were ahead of other programming techniques such as symbolic coding or subroutine libraries. In his talk, Shura-Bura stated the goals of a more harmonious union of techniques and an expansion of "automation of programming."

It is appropriate to conclude the review of the 1956 conference with a list of the talks devoted to computer applications. The inclusions as well as the omissions speak for themselves [28, Part III, 62–180].

Three talks were devoted to mechanical translation (one from French to Russian and two from English to Russian). The remaining talks covered the following topics: calculation of elementary functions, computation of mathematical tables, general application of the M-2 computer at the educational computing center of Moscow University, Monte Carlo methods, computation of level curves of a function of two variables, and determination of stability of electrical systems.

It is worth noting that 1956, on the whole, was a year of widespread publicity for computing in the USSR. In June, the first textbook devoted to the computer, "Electronic Digital Computers," by A. I. Kitov, appeared [33].

In June and July at the Third All-Union Mathematical Congress, programmers for the first time presented reports of their work to a mathematical audience [35]. These were mainly repetitions of talks from the March conference. A special session of the Academy of Sciences held in October 1956 became a culminating event in the public emergence of computer science and practice [36]. All of the leading scientists involved in the birth and first years of development of computing in the USSR delivered speeches at the session. It was a unique meeting in which the austere style of an academic session was spiced by elements of a show: the talk on the BESM computer was accompanied by a demonstration of a giant electrified dynamic display that illustrated the principle of program control and, during the presentation of a talk on mechanical translation, a direct connection was established between a teleprinter and computer for a demonstration of on-line input of text and output of its translation.

It was a period of unbounded optimism as a kind of "computer euphoria" came over scientists in every country that had begun to produce and use electronic computing machinery.

4. Experience Accumulation and Knowledge Development (1956–1959)

We have seen that in 1956 practicing programmers and students had in their possessions five methods for programming concrete problems:

   (1)   the "operator method" and "programming programs" [28];
   (2)   the method of program libraries [27];
   (3)   symbolic coding as presented by Kitov [33] with a reference to work carried out for the IBM 701 [37];
   (4)   "large block" programming after Kantorovich [28];
   (5)   "manual" programming in octal or hexadecimal machine code using flowcharts or logical schemes as informal tools.

The pioneering work by authors and proponents of each of these methods needed not only time for further improvement and development but also a period of coexistence so that balanced production programming procedures could have a chance to emerge—procedures that would satisfy not only the ambitions of their proponents but also more objective demands of general efficiency and convenience.

To this end, it was rather important to extend the scope of activity and, in particular, to accumulate experience with development and use of standard subroutine libraries. This approach to programming was specifically developed in the Computing Center for Moscow University where, after two years of intensive work, an extensive program library was developed, the major part of which was published in 1958 as a monograph [38]. This is how the authors explained their goals:

One of the ways to programming automation is through the use of *libraries of standard subroutines*. The essence of the method is to carefully prepare special subroutines for the most frequent algorithms—this would be done once for all users. These subroutines may then be used as ready program parts whenever a need for the corresponding algorithms arises. This method saves a great deal of programmer effort.

To be more efficient, the library should be implemented as part of a *system* which automates to a maximal degree the process of incorporating subroutines into a main program, provides a convenient way to use subroutines in various problems, and, finally, contains a rich and well-organized library whose subroutines satisfy some standard requirements of the given system.

It is natural that this book closely resembled the book by Wilkes *et al.* [27] since they shared similar aims. A useful feature of the Russian monograph was a special chapter on basic programming concepts and techniques in which most of the pertinent technical terms were collected and explained. It was also the first book to broadly use Lyapunov's program schemata to describe the logical structure of programs.

1958 was indeed a fruitful year for publications on programming. A description of the PP-BESM compiler was published by the Academy of Sciences [39]. It contained a general account of the operator method, descriptions of the source language and main compilation algorithms, and detailed flowcharts of the compiler. In the same year, the first issue of the well-known "red series" founded by Lyapunov under the title *Cybernetics Problems* was published. It contained, in particular, a full description of the PP-2 compiler [40.2–40.6] and also an original Lyapunov paper which reported on work done in 1952–1953 which led him to the operator method [40.1].

Compiler writing based on the operator method became at that time a rather fashionable activity. Almost every programming team to receive a STRELA computer developed its own version of a compiler. We shall here mention two such projects that contributed to the development of compilation methods.

A group of Computing Center staff members (at the Academy of Sciences) developed the PPS compiler for the STRELA-3 computer [41, 42]. This compiler was a direct outgrowth of the PP-BESM compiler (see Table II, VIII). It allowed, in particular, more natural notations for loops and for conditions in logical statements. Unary procedures could be declared but in a restricted form requiring the procedure body to be an arithmetic expression or a piece of machine code.

When the STRELA-4 computer appeared at the Moscow University Computing Center, an established programming technique (for the M-2 computer) already existed there—the method of subroutine libraries discussed earlier. This technique was expanded in a natural way into an integrated automatic programming system of which a compiler was only one component. Thus, beside the compiler developed by N. P. Trifonov, the system contained a standard subroutine library, an assembling program (combination of a loader and a simple assembler) developed by Y. A. Zhogolev, and a series of debugging routines. This automatic programming system was thoroughly described in a collection of papers published in 1961 [43]. The assembling program was rather general for that time. The load blocks had a relocatable form, there was a linkage editor, overlays were possible, and the memory allocation could be either prescribed or automatic. The compiler output was a standard load block. Source language was similar to that of PP-2 although it did not require a strict separation of the program scheme from the specification part. To some extent, macrofacilities were implemented, where a macrodefinition was a "subscheme" that was substituted by a preprocessor for an abbreviated symbolic notation of the subscheme. DO statements were treated in this mechanism as "superstatements," i.e., reducible to basic statements.

In parallel with the above project, Shura-Bura began thinking about another approach to automation of the use of standard subroutines—one that would not require static assembling. The idea was to take a subroutine from the library and allocate it a dynamically prescribed place in memory during the first call to that subroutine. This approach required that an "administrative system" be kept in memory while the program was being run. The small memory sizes then available required an economical solution to the problem of memory allocation and some tactics for throwing subroutines out of memory during a working field overflow. Solutions were found, and the second version of the interpretive system (IS-2) became the exclusive method of subroutine use in a new M-20 computer delivered in 1958 (see the next section) [44, 45].

Elements of symbolic coding were included in the early PP-2 and PP-BESM compilers. Source text could contain so-called "nonstandard operators," i.e., pieces of machine code in which symbolic names could appear in the address parts of instructions. But a symbolic coding system in its, so to say, pure form appeared relatively late—in 1957 for the STRELA computers and 1959 for the M-20 [44.4, 46].

There was an interesting development in symbolic coding at the Computing Center of the Ukrainian Academy of Science, which had been organized at the end of 1958 from several departments of the Kiev Institute of Mathematics, including the team of MESM designers. In 1958 V. S. Koroluk [47] introduced referencing and dereferencing functions, which, on an abstract algorithms level, allow the use of operations such as getting a value via an address, considering a value as the address of another value, and sending a value to a address. These functions were called address functions. Using them, Koroluk was able to give a precise description of such control actions as program modification based on a given memory location, jumps to computed labels, index arithmetic, readdressing and address formation, and parameter passing [48]. These techniques resulted in the design of an original programming language containing only assignment statements for scalar expressions and conditional jumps controlled by predicates (Table II, IX). With some extensions, this so-called "address language" became the basis for a whole family of compilers developed over a number of years in the programming departments first of the Computing Center (at the Ukrainian Academy) and then of the Institute of Cybernetics, under the direction of Y. L. Yushchenko [49]. Stylistically these compilers slightly resembled R. A. Brooker's autocodes [50]. One of the first was developed for the "Kiev" computer (the first large-scale computer designed after MESM by the staff of the Ukranian Computing Center—between 1956 and 1958). A one-pass compilation scheme was considered a distinctive feature of this compiler; another was the use of reverse Polish notation for expressions [51].

In the framework of "large-block programming" a series of experimental application programs was developed primarily at the Laboratory of Approximate Computations at LOMI. In the systems used for these programs there were several improvements: the use of "slices" in operations over arrays [52.1], "geometrical" operations for composition of arrays and a class of settheoretic array operations [52.2], and some analytical manipulation rules [52.3, 52.4], in particular, a rather extensive system for handling polynomials [52.5].

In discussing various programming systems in terms of the first four programming methods from the beginning of the section, we must admit frankly that these methods were far from overwhelming in their influence on everyday programming. First, the concept of a program product did not really exist at that time and, except for a few standard subroutine libraries, the first programming systems were exclusively associated with their authors. Second, since the BESM-2 and STRELA computers had no alphanumeric I/O devices, the harsh necessity of numeric coding of source programs led some experienced programmers to the opinion that octal coding of a machine language program from a carefully constructed flowchart is just as efficient as numerical encoding of any symbolic program scheme. This "old guard" of production programmers represented the prevailing opinion up to the mid-1960s. Another of their arguments for machine language programming was that full control over the object program was required, and machine language was the only way to achieve it. Essentially these same views, in modern dress, were later adopted by the new generation of unbending assembly language programmers who, even in our time, are both bearers of a conservative tradition in programming and a source of problems for advocates of programming automation.

Nevertheless, despite internal deficiencies and external obstacles, these first-generation programming systems should be credited with three achievements. First, they worked. Second, they shaped an advance ideology for such systems that influenced both enthusiasts and opponents. Finally, they introduced concrete methods and findings into programming practice. Let us mention a few of the more significant techniques that were developed. First, we survey the methods related to compilation and general information processing.

In 1953, Shura-Bura proposed the use of a tracing technique for debugging programs; this method was implemented the same year by E. Z. Lubimsky.

V. S. Shtarkman invented and implemented in PP-2 a method for minimizing working locations based on a backward pass through basic block instructions [40.6]. This method is still in use.

Also implemented in PP-2 was a method for evaluation of Boolean expressions, which made a sequence of binary checks and took an immediate jump when the value of the expression became known [40.3].

PP-BESM incorporated a technique for decomposition of arithmetic expressions invented by L. N. Korolev. The method used operation priorities and a stack (called a "semiprogram") to produce the decomposed expression structured as a list in which an intermediate result was represented by a pointer to the instruction computing it rather than by a symbol [39].

PP-BESM used a universal compilation scheme for DO statements, which included some optimizations—loop control by a variable instruction, combining restoration of the inner loop parameter with readdressing by the outer one, etc. [39].

DO statements in PP-BESM were implemented by a method that was later called "decision tables." There were 12 ways to implement a dependence of a variable address on a parameter. These were arranged in a table entry to which was controlled by four binary tags [39, pp. 49–50].

In PP-2 common subexpressions were eliminated within formulas and in PP-BESM they were eliminated within basic blocks (linear components).

The Moscow University compiler eliminated common subexpressions in source language basic blocks by an algorithm that analyzed alternative branches in conditional expressions and took associativity of operations and expression sign changes into account [43].

The PPS compiler used a compatibility matrix for pairs of basic source program symbols to achieve partial syntactic control [41].

Ershov treated the expression decomposition problem as one of finding an optimal ordering of the expression tree preserving the given partial order. He introduced the notion of the "width" of a particular decomposition as the maximum number of coexisting information connections from results to arguments and found an ordering algorithm that yielded the minimal width for expressions without common subexpressions [53].

Next we survey the results related to problems of representation, search, and retrieval of information.

In 1952, Shura-Bura proposed a universal method for machine representation of sets that are subsets of some general enumerated set $\{m_1, \ldots, m_n\}$. Each such subset $\{m_{i_1}, \ldots, m_{i_k}\}$ is represented by a binary vector $|\beta_1, \ldots, \beta_n|$, where $\beta_{i_1} = \beta_{i_2} = \ldots = \beta_{i_k} = 1$, whereas the other elements are all equal to zero. Such a vector is called a "logical scale." Computing the cardinality of such sets and other set theoretic operations are rather conveniently reduced to machine instructions such as shift, normalization, and bitwise logical operations [33].

In PP-BESM, Ershov used a general rule for "address encoding" of various objects that must be manipulated during compilation. In this method, an object is encoded by the address of a location where information about this object is stored. This encoding substantially reduces search time and corresponds nicely to the structure of random access memory. The codes are now called "qualified pointers."

We have already mentioned Kantorovich's descriptor, a fixedformat object that contains specifications used in access to components of a dynamically structured object [28.4].

In 1957, Ershov reinvented hashing (independently, but after a group at IBM) as a way to reduce the time required for information search on a key, experimentally investigated its statistical properties, and applied it to a linear time algorithm for common subexpression elimination.

In 1957, in the framework of experiments at ITMiVT on mechanical translation, Korolev developed a way to speed up the associative search in dictionary files and a method for isomorphic keyword compression [54, 55].

At the end of the 1950s, a group of mathematicians in Moscow began a study of computerized chess. Sixteen years later, these studies would lead to victory in the first world chess tournament for computer programs held in Stockholm during the 1974 IFIP Congress. An important component of this success was a deep study of the problems of information organization in computer memory and of various search heuristics. G. M. Adelson-Velsky and E. M. Landis invented the binary search tree ("dichotomic inquiry") [56] and A. L. Brudno, independent of J. McCarthy, discovered the (α, β)-heuristic for reducing search times on a game tree [57].

During the period under discussion, work that was to lead to the theory of program schemata was undertaken in the Soviet Union. Program schemata became an important part of theoretical programming or, in the English terminology, the mathematical theory of computation. The first essential results were due to Y. I. Yanov, who began work in 1953 as a postgraduate student of Lyapunov. Using concepts of the operator method and abstracting the logical structure of programs in a separate construction, Yanov arrived at a formulation of the notion of a program scheme, known in the literature as "Yanov's scheme." For that class of schemata, he developed a complete theory including an algorithmic decision of the equivalence problem and a complete system of equivalent transformations. The results were announced in a joint report by Lyapunov and Yanov to the 1956 conference [28.1] and a complete account of the results was published in the first issue of *Cybernetics Problems* [58].

Yanov's results gave rise to a whole series of investigations that attempted to develop a more concrete theory either in the framework of Yanov's formalisms or its direct generalizations or through more general Lyapunov symbolics. Some classes of concrete transformations in Lyapunov's schemata were studied by R. I. Podlovchenko, who also became a postgraduate student of Lyapunov in 1953 [59]. A. N. Krinitsky, in his thesis written under Lyapunov's supervision [60], introduced variable and function symbols into Yanov's schemata, producing a formalism equivalent to the modern standard ALGOLlike schemata. Within this formalism, he developed a complete theory of loop-free schemata with an algorithmic decision of the functional equivalence problem and a complete system of transformations [61].

A note, On algorithmization of mathematical problems, written in 1957 by Kiev mathematician L. A. Kaluzhnin [62], proved to be rather useful. In a sense, it rehabilitated the flowchart concept by showing that the logical structure of a program presented in graphical form not only gives an illuminating picture of the program but can also be the object of fruitful mathematical study.

A metalanguage called "operator algorithms," proposed by Ershov [63], allowed the formal description of various classes of programs with respect to the signatures of basic operations and the properties of the storing medium. In this formalism, a fragment of an algorithmic language and a model mahine language were described along with invariants that permitted the introduction of an equivalence relation between programs expressed in these two languages of different levels.

Lubimsky, in his search for a higher-level source language free of "overdeterminacy" of algorithmic prescriptions, introduced the idea of a "parametric record" of mathematical problems, an unordered collection of computational formulas (assignments). Each formula contained some "parameters" as free variables that represented either quantified elements of those sets over which the formula was to be repeatedly applied or arguments of a special "trigger" predicate. This predicate, which was "continuously" evaluated, signaled with its truth value that the formula it "guarded" was ready to be computed. Except for a few publications [64, 65], this idea was not immediately elaborated, but it was later reincarnated in the "trigger function" concept in parallel programming [66] and Dijkstra's "guarded commands" [67].

In 1958, the first contacts between Soviet programmers and their American and British counterparts took place. In June of that year, a delegation from the USSR headed by Academician A. A. Dorodnitsyn visited the U.S. It had been invited by John W. Carr III to participate in a Michigan University summer school. One member of the delegation, Korolev, gave a lecture with a brief review of Soviet work on translators [68].

In November 1958, Ershov, as a member of a Soviet delegation on automation, visited England and participated in the wellknown conference on mechanization of thought processes at the National Physical Laboratory, Teddington. There he met John Backus and Grace M. Hopper. His talk was a review of the compilers developed at the Computing Center of the Academy of Sciences [69] and some results in theoretical programming. A shortened version of this talk appeared in *Datamation* [70].

In August 1958, a reciprocal American delegation of four members headed by Carr visited the Soviet Union. Carr delivered a talk on the new American computer STRETCH, and Alan Perlis brought and presented a "freshly brewed" preliminary report on product of a joint German–American committee, the algorithmic language ALGOL [71], later known as ALGOL 58.

As a result of these contacts, Soviet programmers became acquainted with a series of the first American programming systems, descriptions of which were published in a Russian translation in 1961 [72]. As to ALGOL 58, it was fated to play a rather important role in the development of programming in the USSR. It became a kind of crystalization center for a new atmosphere in programming which was maturing in the USSR at the threshold of the second generation of computers.

5. The New Frontiers (1959–1963)

During the sixth five-year period, intensive work on computer design, within the limits of available resources, was carried out. During that time, at least eight new computers appeared. Except for the URAL-2 and M-20, these projects all played an intermediate role. Some were individual projects of a do-it-yourself kind (GIFTI, CEM-1), another was really the intermediate stage of a search for an ultimate direction (KIEV), still others were primarily experimental (SETUN). On the whole (besides the introduction of ferrite-core memory) they were vacuum tube prototypes of future transistorized computers (Table III).

In November 1959, an All-Union Meeting on Numerical Mathematics and Computing Machinery was held at Moscow University. In contrast to the modest title, it was a grandiose scientific congress with almost 2000 participants and 217 talks delivered in four parallel sections [44]. Unfortunately, the meeting organizers did not collect the texts and publish proceedings.

Shura-Bura and Ershov were invited to deliver a joint talk on The current state of automatic programming to a plenary session. The talk was delivered but, frankly, the authors must admit that they failed to develop a unified view of the subject. At the end of the 1950s, each of them had his own idea of

TABLE III[a]

The Second Line of First Generation Computers

Name	GIFTI	KIEV	CEM-1	SETUN	URAL 2	MINSK	RAZDAN	M-20
First delivery	1957	1959	1953	1959	1959	1959	1959	1959
Place of production	Gorky	Kiev	Moscow	Moscow	Penza	Minsk	Erevan	Moscow
Number of addresses	1(3)	3	2	1	1	2	2	3
Arithmetics (point)	fix	fix	fix	float	float	fix	float	float
Word length (bit)	32	40	31	18(ternary) 9 for instr.	40 20 for instr.	31	36	45
Memory type	drum/register	core	mercury line	core	core	core	core	core
Memory size (words)	1800/32	1024/ 512 read only	496	81	2048	2024	2048	4096
Basic cycle (μsec)	5000/80	10/4	600	90	30	20	20	6
No. of index-registers	4	—	—	—	—	—	—	1
Average speed (op/sec)	100	10000	350	4500	5000	2500	5000	20000
Drum (words)	1800	3 × 3K	4K	4K	8 × 8K	2K	—	3 × 4K
Tape (words)	—	—	—	—	100K	—	120K	4 × 75K
Input	p/t	p/t	p/t	p/t	p/t	p/t	p/t	p/c
Output	p/t, t/t	p/t, tab print	p/t, t/t	p/t, t/t	p/t, tab print	p/t, t/t, tab print	p/t, tab print	p/c, tab print
No. of tubes		2300	1700	40	2100	1200	1200	3500
Source	[28], [74]	[51]	[75]	[76]	[76]	[77]	[61]	[61]

[a] Legend: p/t, paper tape; p/c, punch card; tab, tabular; t/t, teletype; —, absent feature; , no information.

171

what the next direction in programming development should be. These two views were partially presented in a series of papers, some of which were delivered at the same meeting [45, 73]. The difference was not so much reflected in the papers themselves as in the background that dominated the authors at the time.

Shura-Bura had participated in the logical design of the M-20 computer. The M-20 was an unusual case—its design had been a joint effort of designers, engineers, and mathematicians represented, respectively, by ITMiVT, the industrial design bureau where the STRELA was designed, and MIAN. This design team took on a heavy responsibility because the architecture was to be embodied in several important series of computer (M-20, BESM-3, BESM-3M, BESM-4, M-220, M-220M, M-222). In turn, this was to affect programming by substantially increasing the scale of use; as a result, precedents of the accumulation of "natural" programming economy, suitable for individual scientific computation centers, was absolutely unsuitable for the future computers. Gradually, the concept of a software system (or "mathematical support" in a literal translation) emerged. This was understood to mean an integrated and convenient system of different programming support mechanisms (libraries, compilers, debugging tools) properly interfaced with a discipline for running jobs on the computer. Experimental systems projects at the Moscow University Computing Center [38, 43] and the everyday computations at MIAN, which required a high degree of accuracy and reliability of both computers and programs, were strong influences on the formation of Shura-Bura's programming philosophy.

There were many obstacles on the way to a complete understanding of the software problem. They were organizational as well as scientific and technical in nature—and one of them was the rather weak elaboration of the concept of program product. Experience with the STRELA computers reassuringly showed that programming tools diverge if there is no common inviolable software base constructed directly on the "naked machine." At that time, the standard subroutine library provided such a base for the M-20. The idea of converting that library into a portable program product for general use turned into a major task for Shura-Bura, one that led to the formation of a more general view of software. The result of that project, IS-2, became a kind of mini-operating system that provided, at a low level, some uniformity in the organization of executed programs.

Ershov's interests, on the other hand, were of quite another character. Continuing his work on compilers and their source languages, he was in a state of permanent "scientific sublimation," proceeding from one compiler to another in search of new ideas and becoming more deeply engrossed in the technical problems of compilers and languages. As he was busy forming a systems programming team for the newly organized Siberian Branch of the Academy of Sciences, and as he had been involved in reading and translating new (mainly American) works on automatic programming [72] and in mastering the information so obtained, he tried to interest his new co-workers in the rather ambitious project of design and implementation of a "Siberian programming language" [73].

Clearly, these two views lay in different planes, so to speak, and this became obvious during discussions of the Moscow meeting. There was a clear need for an object of research and development that could, in equal parts, solve the problem of software unification, be an effective programming aid, and put forward new scientific problems. ALGOL 60 was to become that object.

As we have mentioned, the Russian acquaintance with the German–American project dated from August 1958, when Perlis brought a preliminary draft of the ALGOL report to the USSR. Its first readers were staff members of the Computing Center of the Academy of Sciences who were working on the PPS compiler and the initial group of staff members of the Computing Center of the soon-to-be-formed Siberian Branch of the Academy of Sciences. It was obvious from the very beginning that the document was of great general scientific value, thus deserving wide dissemination. Without waiting for publication of the whole collection of papers [72], the Computing Center published Ershov's translation of the ALGOL draft report and distributed it at the November 1959 meeting [80].

Meanwhile, an international group of scientists produced a final specification of the new algorithmic language. Peter Naur, editor of the final Report on the algorithmic language ALGOL 60 [81], kept in close contact with Soviet colleagues. This contact made it possible, by March 1960, to have G. I. Kozhukhin's Russian translation of the report ready for publication. The translation was published in May 1960 by the Computing Center of the Academy of Sciences and, within a year, by the new *Journal of Numerical Mathematics and Mathematical Physics* [82].

The spring of 1960 happened to be a very appropriate time for the adoption of ALGOL 60 as a single universal language for programming scientific and engineering computations. We have already discussed the general premises to a language unification. ALGOL 60 not only possessed its own obvious merits together with substantial scientific content but, because it was produced by an international committee that took into equal consideration the individual opinions on the language, it was effectively protected from criticisms based on matter-of-taste arguments. Another favorable factor was the absence of inertia because the small number of existing STRELA and BESM computers was relatively insignificant when compared to the number of M-20s being produced.

In June 1960, a coordinating meeting on ALGOL 60 implementation was held at the Computing Center of the Academy of Sciences. Three projects won out over a somewhat chaotic variety of proposals. These were the TA-1, TA-2, and ALPHA compilers, all to be implemented on the M-20 series under direction of S. S. Lavrov, Shura-Bura, and Ershov, respectively. Although started as independent, even competing, efforts, as work proceeded they became mutually complementary and, finally, provided a satisfactory, coordinated set of solutions to the problem of providing ALGOL on the M-20.

Shura-Bura tried to unify the machine representation of ALGOL 60 source text to provide compatibility between compilers with respect to source strings. Unfortunately, technical differences of opinion prevented a complete solution. One serious obstacle was the lack of standard alphanumeric I/O equipment for the M-20 at that time, which forced users and compiler designers to make do with individual, temporary solutions. Also, Ershov was already too far along in his development of the "Siberian language" to stay within the limits of ALGOL 60. That language had been adapted to a superset of ALGOL 60 and, as much, it was named "INPUT language" and "ALPHA language" in its machine representation [83]. The most significant extensions in the language allowed complex and multidimensional values as arguments and results of basic operations, and provided formation and partitioning operations for those values. It is worth noting that all three systems were also based on the IS-2 system as a monitor of standard subroutine calls.

On 22–24 December 1960, a working conference, Development of Programming Programs Based on the ALGOL Language, was held at Moscow University. By that time a general approach to language implementation and compilation had taken shape in each of the implementation projects. TA-1 achieved a fast, compact compilation scheme without optimization by elimination of recursive procedures and by other language restrictions. The main goal of the TA-2 project was to implement an almost complete version of the language without heavy losses in efficiency. The ALPHA system implementors, on the other hand, aimed to produce high-quality object programs while maintaining reasonable compilation speed [92, p 24]. The talk by ALPHA system implementors established the classic precedent of a two-fold or threefold miscalculation of the requirements and other quantitative characteristics of large programming efforts, a miscalculation that would be repeated in many other projects. The authors planned to develop a system of 15,000 instructions at the expense of 15 man-years, but they eventually spent 30 man-years to develop a system of 45,000 instructions [92, p. 64].

Further development was influenced by the scientific results from a conference on compilation methods for ALGOL 60 held in the U.S. at about the same time. Many talks from this conference were later published in an issue of the *Communications of the ACM* [84], which became a standard reference for systems programmers.

One indication of the public recognition of ALGOL 60 was an invitation to Shura-Bura and Ershov to deliver a talk to a plenary session of the Fourth All-Union Mathematical Congress held at Leningrad in June 1961.We take the liberty to cite some excerpts from that talk, which was entitled Machine languages and automatic programming [85].

When we look for a numerical solution to a mathematical problem we must take into account the commonly used language of mathematical description which, though not fully formalized . . . is nevertheless sufficiently expressive and, importantly, is commonly understood. Therefore . . . it is highly desirable to make the source language as close to the conventional language of mathematics as possible.

. . . Use of a universal programming language eliminates the problem of translating programs from one machine to another, avoids multiple efforts when writing a program for different machines and greatly facilitates the exchange of information between programming groups.

. . . We have to admit that current work on the design of a universal language (especially for numerical analysis algorithms) has progressed mainly through the initiative and activity of a group of West German and American scientists which, after a year and a half of work and discussions, produced the specification of an internatonal programming language known as ALGOL 60.

. . . All these ALGOL 60 features . . . the possibility of a stepwise partitioning of the algorithm, establishment of contexts for understanding of the notations used, an ability to introduce arbitrary functional notations . . . bring ALGOL close to the mathematical language for description of computational processes.

In parallel with the work on ALGOL, events were developing that would lead to the formation of an M-20 users' association. At the June ALGOL 60 meeting, representatives of organizations using M-20 computers were invited to represent the opinions of users in deliberations about implementation. At the December 1960 conference on ALGOL 60 implementaion, a prospective assembly of user association members was announced. The assembly was held at the beginning of 1961 and Shura-Bura was elected chairman of the association council. In July 1961, the association was conferred legal status by a decree of the Presidium of the Academy of Sciences of the USSR. It was officially named the "Commission of the Use of M-20 Computers." Here are some excerpts from the charter of that commission:

To serve this purpose, the Commission shall:

(a)   organize a regular exchange of information between Commission members on use and maintenance of computers, elaborate recommendations on use and maintenance, organize consultations on pertinent problems;

(b)   encourage common programming and organize an exchange of programs and algorithms;

(c)   organize development of standard programs, coordinating projects undertaken by Commission members;

(d)   conduct research on programming automation for the M-20;

(e) organize conferences devoted to problems arising from the use of M-20 computers.

The Commission was of great importance not only because it set a precedent for similar associations for the BESM-2, the Ural series, and later the Minsk series, but because it facilitated development of the concept of "mathematical support" (software). This word came into common use in 1963. Looking ahead a bit, we note that the IS-2 library and the TA-1 and TA-2 compilers were to become the first program products delivered by manufacturers along with the hardware to form an interated programming system.

By late 1963, the ALGOL compilers were approaching the end of their development cycle. The reports for the TA-1 and TA-2 compilers were published at the beginning of 1964 [86, 87], and the ALPHA system report appeared a year later [88, 89]. Let us briefly review the technical achievements of these projects.

In the TA-1 compiler, G. M. Zaikina an S. S. Lavrov implemented a general scheme for compiling expressions that used a stack and treated operation symbols as generalized paired delimiters and separators [86].

As we have said, a practially complete ALGOL 60 was implemented by the TA-2 compiler. That compiler used, for the first time, a systematic method of table driven generation, a new method of compiling recursive procedures that did not require copying "thunks" [90], and a directly addressed field of "mathematical memory" that included both the operative and external memories of the M-20 [91].

In the ALPHA compiler, hash functions were systematically used to speed up compilation [92, p. 35] and, in particular, for the elimination of common subexpressions [92, p. 187]. A multivariant system for compiling procedures and loops based on an analysis of program structure was applied [92, pp. 92, 153] as was a global memory optimization method [92, p. 201] based on a theory developed by Lavrov [93] and Ershov [94]. ALPHA also used a number of other optimizing transformations on the intermediate language level; in particular, union of loops with similar headings [92, p. 112] and loop "cleaning" [92, p. 153].

Scientific achievements of the compiler development projects were summarized at the Second Regional Conference of Socialist Countries held in Kiev in the summer of 1963 and at an M-20 users' association conference at Novosibirsk in January 1964. The latter was specifically remembered by participants for its hot discussions and a severe freeze, below −40°C. Some premises to continued coordination of programming work on the level of international cooperation (GAMS Committee) were stated at the Kiev conference. Later a GAMS working group (ALGAMS [95]), to define an international standard ALGOL 60 subset, was formed.

In 1963, in the Computation Center of the Siberian Division of the USSR Academy of Sciences, S. P. Surzhikov began experiments with the automation of processing of programs from a punched-card "batch." For his purpose, an M-20 computer was slightly modified by the addition of an interrupt system and a small I/O processor. Surzhikov's system was one of the few prototypes of a monoprogram batch processing operating system implemented on first-generation computers. Later, this work would form the basis for a modernization of the M-20, which resulted in the M-222 [96].

On the whole, the second-generation computers (MINSK 2, RAZDAN 2, BESM-3, M-220, BESM-6, DNEPR) appeared too early for a proper maturing of the software concept or an identification of systems programming. On the other hand, in the period 1959–1963, premises to an improvement of the situation took shape. Starting in 1964, software development became a component of the state technological policy. The State Committee for Science and Technology became both the coordinator of work on software for manufactured software and the general contractor to the industry for sotware for newly designed computers. Users' associations were rather active as representatives of the scientific and technological public opinion and played an important role in the dissemination of new programs. Approval of new programming systems and, later, operating systems was undertaken by the Interagency Commission on Software headed by Academician A. A. Dorodnitsyn as well as by ad hoc acceptance commissions.

The activities of ALGAMS and other working groups established the precedent of international cooperation on the science and technology of computers, which was to later reemerge in the ES EVM ("Ryad") joint project.

The intensive work on ALGOL compilers led to the gradual disappearance of the profession of "assistant programmer involved in machine coding" and its replacement by "systems programmer." Having provided programming automation for users, systems programmers found themselves in the position of a shoemaker without shoes—all the first compilers were written in octal code with a minimum of automated assistance. As a result, the first systems programming languages were developed [97, 98] and later the first compiler writing system, based on the universal machine-oriented intermediate language ALMO, was produced [99]. In 1964, the design of multiprogramming batch processing operating systems, complete with loaders, assemblers, and job control languages, was begun. The 1965 IFIP Congress played an important role in forming the modern view of software and computer architecture by focusing the interest of Soviet specialists on concepts like compatible computer series, time-sharing, and minicomputers. The spectrum of Soviet work on systems programming in the 1960s can be represented by the subject breakdown of the 99 talks reported to the First All-Union Conference on Programming in Kiev, October 1968 [100]:

general reviews   3
procedural languages and compilers   14

languages for commercial applications and their compilers   9
operating systems   14
time sharing systems   2
systems architecture   12
software engineering   12
applications programs   11
theoretical programming   22

6. Evolution of Programming Education

In the USSR there exists one level of graduation in higher education (''diploma'd specialist'') and two levels of academic degrees (Candidate of Sciences and Doctor of Sciences). A diploma'd specialist is a graduate of a five-year course, without intermediate graduation, at a university or a specialized polytechnical institute, like a technical university or technological school. Thus he is roughly equivalent of a Master of Science in the U.S. The Candidate of Sciences degree corresponds roughly to the Doctor of Philosophy, and the Doctor of Sciences, which has no direct analog in western universities, approximately corresponds in qualifications to a full professor.

Diplomas and academic degrees also certify the competence of the holder in some specialty, i.e., some science, technical discipline, or professional activity. The Ministry of Higher Education (for diplomas) and the Higher Qualification Commission of the USSR (for academic degrees) keep and update formal lists of such specialties, each list containing about 100 entries. These lists play an important role in the system of education and qualification in the USSR since they serve as a means for identification and formal recognition of various components of scientific and technological progress. In particular, each educational specialty has the right to have its own curriculum from the first year of higher education to graduation. Most of the courses of a curriculum are compulsory and the curriculum as a whole is approved for each university by the Ministry of Higher Education. However, there are a number of optional courses and seminars that can be used to achieve a narrower specialization within the framework of a given specialty.

In 1952 several universities started a new specialty in ''computing mathematics'' in addition to the existing specialty in mathematics. This new area was designed to produce specialists in the use of the new computing machinery. A curriculum for the computing mathematics specialty as it was taught at Moscow State University in the early 1950s (rewritten from Ershov's 1954 diploma) was:

Foundations of Marxism–Leninism   Electrical Engineering
Political Economy   Theory of Machines and Mechanisms

Dialectical Materialism
Historical Materialism
Foreign Language (English)
Physical Culture and Sports
Mathematical Analysis
Analytic Geometry
Modern Algebra
Astronomy
Physics
Theoretical Mechanics
Differential Geometry
Equations of Mathematical Physics
Theory of Functions of Complex Variables
Variational Calculus
Probability Theory with Theory of Errors
History of Mathematics
Calculating Machines and Instruments
Radioelectronics

Approximate Computations
Practice in Approximate Computations
Nomography
  Technical Drawing
  Course Project
  Practice
Special Courses (electives):
  Programming Principles
  Computing and Analytical Engines (Punch-Card Machines)
  Mathematical Logic
Special Seminars:
  Theory of Switching Circuits
  Computational Methods of Linear Algebra
Diploma Thesis
State Examinations:
  Foundations of Marxism–Leninism
  Computing Mathematics

In retrospect, the curriculum demonstrates the dominance of general mathematics and natural science, on one hand, and the conglomerate character of specialized disciplines on the other.

The first course on programming in the USSR was taught by Lyapunov at Moscow University in the 1952–1953 academic year under the title Principles of Programming. In a sense, that course took shape right before the students' eyes. The first part followed the book "Programming for High-Speed Electronic Computers" [23], but between semesters, Lyapunov discovered some approaches to the "operator method." Thus the second half of the course was actually devoted to joint work by professor and students on creation and improvement of a symbolic system for writing program schemata. The course was taught with enthusiasm and was well received by the students—it was no accident that almost half of the students, all previously specializing in mathematics, became professional programmers after graduation.

In 1955, Shura-Bura took over the teaching of the programming course. In two years the syllabus had stabilized to contain the following topics:

Computer Architecture
Arithmetic Foundations
Machine Instructions

Program Synthesis in the Framework of the Operator Method
Programming Techniques (style,

Programming of Linear Instruc-
tion Sequences
Programming of Branches
Programming of Loops

comments, flow charts, program
schemata, debugging).
Software Components (libraries,
translators, debugging methods)

For teaching purposes, either the STRELA or an abstract three-address machine was studied.

The first Russian textbook on computers for the mass audience was A. I. Kitov's "Electronic Computers" [33], published in mid-1956. That book was criticized by some for inaccuracies and for its superficial treatment of the subject. However, having reread the book almost 20 years after its publication, we believe that it was an honest and especially well-timed account of the knowledge on computers at the time. A particularly good quality of the book was its fresh and exciting description of the various innovations brought by computers into practical human activity.

An extension of this book and of lecture notes published in 1956 for students of the Artillery Engineering Academy [101] resulted in a book by Kitov and N. A. Krinitsky, "Electronic Computers and Programming" [102]. It was the first book formally approved by the Ministry of Higher Education as a textbook on computers. Twenty-five thousand copies of this rather long (572 pages) text were printed. The book suffered from a somewhat incoherent style varying from an elementary treatment of foundations to the business-like language of compilers users' manuals. The presentation of programming principles followed the established scheme (as above) but contained an additional two chapters with a thorough account of program schemata theory (essentially following Yanov) and a description of the source language of the PP-S compiler for the STRELA. A curious generalization, which could be of interest to ALGOL 68 authors, was the ability to use assignment statements as operands in a logical condition. For example [102, p. 502] the text

```
1.  x = t > 0     7002, 4005
2.  x² + y² = r  < 5∧ x-z>3     4012, 4015
```

was permissible, and in ALGOL 68 notation, means

```
if (t:= x) > 0 then goto L5
else if (r:= x↑2 + y↑2) <5∧x-z > 3
     then goto L12
     else goto L15 fi fi
```

The first text solely devoted to programming was a book by Kiev authors B. V. Gnedenko, *et al.* entitled "Elements of Programming" [103]. It used an abstract machine and followed Lyapunov's didactics. A special chapter was devoted to symbolic address programming.

The first attempt to create a solid university course on programming ''based on modern scientific and methodological principles'' [104, p. 2] was a book by E. A. Zhogolev and N. P. Trifonov, ''The Programming Course'' [104], arising from experience with the regular lecture course at Moscow University. It was also the first course based on ALGOL 60. The attempt was very successful indeed, and this book was a primary textbook for higher education on programming until the appearance of third-generation machines. It was published several times with the total number of copies approaching 300,000. Here is the table of contents for the first edition:

1. The Subject of the Course.
2. Positional Number Systems.
3. Physical Principles of Computer Design.
4. Description of the Abstract Machine.
5. Algorithms and the Algorithmic Language.
6. Programming of Simple Arithmetic Expressions.
7. Elements of Mathematical Logic and Conditions (*if*-Clauses).
8. Programming of *if*-Clauses and Boolean Expressions.
9. Assignment Statements and Their Programming.
10. Composite Statements in the ALGOL Language.
11. Programming of *for*-Statements.
12. Procedures and Their Implementation.
13. Automatic Instruction Modification.
14. Methods of Number Scaling.
15. Computation of Elementary Functions.
16. Input and Output of Information.
17. Computer Console. Program Check-Out.
18. Advanced Features of ALGOL.
19. Overview of Computers and their Classification.
20. Programming with Subroutine Libraries.
21. Compiling and Interpreting Programs.

A modernized version of this text is still widely used in introductory courses on programming.

The ''computational mathematics'' specialty continued the predominance of courses in general mathematics and numerical methods. The demand for systems programming specialists with a background in software engineering, particularly in general software, applications packages, and management information systems, led to the formation in 1969 of a new specialty in ''applied mathematics'' with specializations in ''mathematical support'' (general software) and in ''computer applications,'' primarily for universities and polytechnical institutes, and a specialty in ''automated management and control systems'' for industrial institutes. These specialities have much in common with ''informatics'' in European universities and ''computer science'' in American universities. In 1975, 54 departments of applied mathematics and 43 departments of automated management and control systems offered these specialties to about 5000 graduating students each year (not counting evening courses) [105].

The 1974 curriculum for applied mathematics as taught by the Faculty of Computational Mathematics and Cybernetics at Moscow University (which graduates 350 students a year—12 times more than in 1954) was

Marxist–Leninist Philosophy
Political Economy
Scientific Communism
Fundamentals of Scientific Athe-
  ism
Soviet Law
Foreign Language
Physical Education
Introduction to Specialty
Mathematical Analysis
Algebra and Analytic Geometry
Differential Equations
Physics
Equations of Mathematical Phys-
  ics
Probability Theory and Mathe-
  matical Statistics
Discrete Mathematics
Computers and Programming
Numerical Methods
Theory of Games and Operations
  Research

Methods for Solving Extremal
  Problems
Mathematical Models in Natural
  Science and Control Theory
Mathematical Models in Econom-
  ics
Computer Practice
Foundations of Automated Con-
  trol Systems
Methodology and History of Ap-
  plied Mathematics
Advanced Problems in Program-
  ming
Mathematical Logic
Elements of Cybernetics
Special Courses
Special Seminars
Educational Practice
Working Practice
Course Project
Diploma Thesis
State Examinations:
  Scientific Communism
  Mathematics

The standard duration of the programming course for this specialty is two years (four semesters, two hours weekly, not counting computer practice). The first part, devoted to an introduction to programming, resembles the previously described course of Zhogolev and Trifonov. The second part, devoted to computer software, consists of modular programming, assemblers, loaders, macroassemblers and macrogenerators, basic data structures and their use, modern computer architecture, hardware and software integration, programming systems, application packages, operating systems, and general organization of computational processes.

The first dissertation on electronic computers known to the authors was a candidate thesis written by I. S. Mukhin who was for many years a deputy director of ITMiVT. The thesis was devoted to a computation of equistable soil slopes and was defended in 1953 [106]. The computations, which were performed on the BESM in 1952, involved the solution of a system of hyperbolic equations on a plane. This work was the first of many application dissertations that demonstrated the power and extraordinary potential of the computer. The situation with programming itself was much more complicated, and it was several years before it overcame its inferiority complex and outsiders recognized its scientific content.

Seemingly, the first academic treatment of programming proper was a chapter of Shura-Bura's doctoral thesis, defended in 1953, which was devoted as a whole to round-off errors. In the chapter in question, a systematic procedure for automatic repetition of computations to provide more reliable results was presented. Despite the practical importance of the problem and the usefulness of the proposed scheme, this part of the dissertation has been ignored by some people and disputed by others.

In 1954, Ershov, in his diploma work on matrix inversion, wrote a chapter that described a general scheme for programming and presented an algorithm for relocation of program coding. A reviewer, while commenting favorably on the paper as a whole, nevertheless recommended that the chapter on programming be removed. Although Ershov wrote a book on PP-BESM [39],he felt that it was inappropriate to submit it as a candidate dissertation and switched to a thesis on operator algorithms [63] because it was more "mathematical" by nature.

Gradually, more sensible views emerged. At the MIAN scientific council there was spirited "metadiscussion" during the public defense of the first dissertation solely devoted to programming—E. Z. Lubimsky, On programming automation and the programming programs method [64]. Having devoted the main portion of the thesis to a description of the PP-2 compiler, the author supplemented the text with a theoretical chapter including a "parametric record" of problems for computer solution. Professor A. S. Kronrod criticized Lubimsky for his "opportunism" and defended the right to offer operational, well-described, complex systems programs as dissertations, where the existance and use of a program product itself is certification of the creative capabilities of the author.

In the same year (1957), Yanov defended his candidate thesis [107]. This work, which became a classic of theoretical programming, also met a cool reception from some mathematicians.

During the next two years, two more dissertations, based on the first experiments in mechanical translation, were defended. The authors were O. S. Kulagina, who designed a specialized language for programming mechanical translation algorithms [108], and L. N. Korolev, who studied problems of optimal organization of dictionary files and their use [109]. In 1965, Korolev became the first university full professor who had been a programmer from the start of his career.

The first programming dissertation for the Doctor of Science degree was publicly defended by Y. L. Yushchenko in 1965. Its subject was the development of a series of compilers for the address language [49].

In the beginning, all these dissertations were classified in the specialties extant at the time, such as computational mathematics and calculating devices. In the mid-1960s, the work on theoretical programming led to the creation of a new specialty, "mathematical logic and programming." The use of "programming" in the specialty name caused mathematically minded scientific councils to be faced with an outpouring of systems programming work that was methodologically pretty far from mathematical logic. Recently, in 1971, programmers dissociated from logicians and formed their own specialty, "software for computer, automated control, and management systems."

The authors would like to conclude this chapter by mentioning two permanent all-Moscow seminars that contributed in an essential way to the development of programming in the USSR. In 1955, the Chair of Computational Mathematics at Moscow University announced a seminar on topics related to cybernetics and physiology, which, in 1956, took the name Seminar on Cybernetics. Ershov happened to be the first speaker at that seminar, reviewing a paper on simulation of conditional relfexes on the EDSAC computer [110]. This seminar was interdisciplinary in character and paid substantial attention to the nonarithmetic applications of computers. Discussions at that seminar helped the programmers who attended to develop a broader view of computer applications and a better understanding of their place in that process. This seminar, in a modified form, is still held at Moscow University under the direction of Corresponding Members of the Academy of Sciences S. V. Yablonsky and O. B. Lupanov.

In 1956, also at Moscow University, Trifonov and Shura-Bura started a scientific seminar on programming, which has continued to the present. Although it began as a seminar for staff members of the University Computing Center and professors of the Computational Mathematics Department, it gradually gained all-Moscow status, sometimes drawing several hundred participants. Its representative character permitted fast and effective dissemination of information during those "hot days" of new ideas and directions in programming. Among the many active and fruitful discussions at that seminar, we remember the development of a programming system for the university STRELA computer in 1957–1958, the ALGOL familiarization period in 1960–1961, and, later, the period of work on the BESM 6 and the development of operating systems concepts.

7. Conclusion

In this paper, we have attempted to provide an integrated overview of the development of programming in the USSR, based primarily on facts documented in publications. Since this is the work of participants, not merely witnesses, our concluding remarks may be particularly vulnerable to criticism. Instead of claiming objectivity, we emphasize the personal nature of some of these concluding observations.

Some specific circumstances contributed to the fact that, until almost the middle of the 1960s, programming in the USSR developed somewhat autonomously. These circumstances include the late start of work on electronic computers (about five years late); fewer available resources, reducing the scope of development by comparison with the U.S. or England*; the lack of practically any imported computing machinery or technology; the language barrier and comparatively fewer close personal contacts with researchers in other countries; and some general differences in organization and the style of research. For the specialist, this acknowledgment provides both a justification and a greater responsibility. On one hand, there is no need to apologize for a lack within the USSR of all components of world scientific and technological progress. On the other hand, Soviet specialists cannot expect to rely on outside assistance to help them satisfy the specific needs of the society in which they work.

In view of this autonomy, a question arises as to the degree of independence of the Soviet development and its contribution to the vocabulary of science. To this end, it is probably accurate to say that only Yanov's work on program schemata and perhaps some of the work on compiler optimization and general information processing processes directly influenced the international development of programming theory. An indirect but seemingly important contribution to world trends was the widespread use of ALGOL 60 in the USSR. As to the other results described in this paper, most were independent discoveries or rediscoveries of results usually credited to workers outside the Soviet Union; however, without this research a healthy development of programming theory and practice would have been impossible.

Some idea of the degree of independence of Soviet development can be conveyed by an analysis of terminology. In undertaking this study, we have chosen about 150 programming terms from the literature. We tend to think of these terms as "having always existed," but every one has its origin. For each of the terms, we have found the publication in Russian in which it was first used. A term used in an original work is considered to be original only if the work does not contain a direct acknowledgment of a previous source. A term appearing in a translated work is considered borrowed and is marked by an asterisk in the list below. The list consists of modern English equivalents of Russian versions; whenever appropriate, a literal translation of the

---

* Annual production of computing machinery in the USSR is given by the following figures, in millions of rubles [111, p. 90]: 1940—0.3; 1945—0.5; 1950—2.0; 1955—15.0; 1960—79.9; 1965—245; 1970—710; 1975—2917.

original Russian term is given between slashes. The source is indicated by the bracketed bibliography number followed by the year of appearance.

Basic Programming Terms

computer mathematics [1] 1946
*electronic calculating machine [8] 1948
*memory [8] 1948
*instruction [15] 1949
*arithmetic unit [19] 1949
*storage (unit) [19] 1949
*program control [19] 1949
*register [19] 1949
*loop [19] 1949
*loop parameter [19] 1949
*control unit [17] 1952
*internal memory [17] 1952
*external memory [17] 1952
*program [17] 1952
*input [17] 1952
*output [17] 1952
*accumulator [17] 1952
*operation code [17] 1952
*address [17] 1952
*address part [17] 1952
*conditional jump [17] 1952
*unconditional jump [17] 1952
*floating point [17] 1952
*fixed point [17] 1952
*high-speed computer [17] 1952
*electronic computer [17] 1952
*(memory) location [17] 1952
*arithmetic operation [17] 1952
*logical operation [17] 1952
*programming [21] 1952
*scale factor [21] 1952
*index register [21] 1952
*subroutine [23] 1952
*main program [23] 1952
*branching [23] 1952
*flow chart [23] 1952
working location [23] 1952
instruction initialization (formation) [23] 1952

standard subroutine [23] 1952
word/code/ [23] 1952
*closed subroutine [27] 1953
*open subroutine [27] 1953
*parameter (of a subroutine) [27] 1953
*return [27] 1953
*subroutine library [27] 1953
*library subroutine [27] 1953
*compiler [28, Panov] 1956
*interpreter [28, Panov] 1956
programmer [28, Shura-Bura] 1956
program documentation [28, Shura-Bura] 1956
program scheme [28.1] 1956
logical scheme [28.1] 1956
computation scheme [28.1] 1956
statement/operator/ [28.1] 1956
readdressing statement [28.1] 1956
restoration statement [28.1] 1956
initialization/formation/statement [28.1] 1956
automation of programming [28.2] 1956
/programming program/translator, compiler [28.2] 1956
/arithmetical/assignment statement [28.2] 1956
/logical/control statement [28.2] 1956
working location economy [28.2] 1956
debugging [28.2] 1956
macrodefinition/standard sub-scheme/ [28.2] 1956
DO statement [28.3] 1956
variable instruction [28.3] 1956
array [28.3] 1956

relative address [28.3] 1956
memory allocation [28.3] 1956
descriptor [28.4] 1956
monitor/prorab/ [28.4] 1956
external devices [33] 1956
instruction set [33] 1956
bit string/logical scale/ [33] 1956
*symbolic coding [33] 1956
*symbolic address [33] 1956
*absolute address [33] 1956
modular/large block/programming
   [35] 1956
stack/semiprogram array/ [39]
   1958
common expression elimination
   [39] 1958
(global) program analysis [39]
   1958
indirect address [47] 1958
graph scheme [62] 1959
program relocation [44] 1959
*algorithmic language [80] 1959
*user [80] 1959
*reference language [80] 1959
*hardware representation [80]
   1959
*publication language [80] 1959
*delimiter [80] 1959
*separator [80] 1959
*identifier [80] 1959
*declaration [80] 1959
*switch [80] 1959
*type [80] 1959
*expression [80] 1959
*procedure [80] 1959
*label [80] 1959
*formal, actual parameter [80]
   1959
*metalinguistic variable [82] 1960

*string [82] 1960
*local, global values [82] 1960
*conditional statement [82] 1960
*procedure call [82] 1960
*array dimensionality [82] 1960
*subscripted variable [82] 1960
*bound pair [82] 1960
*recursive procedure [82] 1960
*pseudoinstruction [82] 1961
load module/standard module/
   [43] 1961
assembler/assembling program/
   [43] 1961
external address [43] 1961
internal address [43] 1961
linkage table [43] 1961
tracing [43] 1961
*input/output statement [72] 1961
*overflow [72] 1961
*format [72] 1961
*object computer [72] 1961
*exit (from a block) [72] 1961
*relocatable program [72] 1961
inconsistency graph [93] 1961
memory economy [93] 1961
live zone/route/ [93] 1961
control flow graph [93] 1961
file descriptor [56] 1962
search tree [56] 1962
software/mathematical support/ †
   1963
internal language [88] 1965
multiinstruction [88] 1965
hash function [88] 1965
heap/common list/ [88] 1965
loop cleaning [88] 1965
regular loop [88] 1965
*dynamic array [88] 1965

It turns out that 78 of the 135 terms on the list are borrowed and 57 are original to the Russian sources.

† The first use of this term known to the authors occurs in the working documents of the State Committee for Science and Technology.

In spite of our generally positive view of the initial period of programming development in the USSR, we nevertheless feel obligated to mention some difficulties and gaps. The development and widespread application of programming automation techniques were hampered by the lack of alphanumeric I/O devices, which became available only with second-generation computers. This not only caused difficulties with the encoding of source information but also slowed the development and application of debugging aids and symbolic coding techniques. A more indirect but deeper consequence was a lack of attention to textual presentation of source programs for the first compilers. It might even be said that phrase structure of programming languages completely slipped away from the attention of pre-ALGOL compiler designers.

Another negative influence of hardware arose from the prevailing requirement that it be possible to generate any machine program from some source text. This led to the inclusion in source languages of so-called "nonstandard" statements, ugly logical statements patterned after machine instructions, and many other anomalies. Sometimes the syntax of source languages was artificially tailored to favor optimization algorithms. It seems paradoxical, but the three-address instruction system reinforced machine dependencies; quite often, a specific three-address instruction, being a logically self-contained unit, was squeezed into a source language under thin syntactic cloth. A second problem with three-address instructions was the restricted length permitted for addresses, which made an expansion of the operative memory more difficult.

Returning to I/O devices, another early design error should be mentioned. In an effort to make the format of punch cards as compact as possible, the bits of machine words were laid out along rows rather than columns, so that cards were transported through the devices broad side first, making it more difficult to introduce alphanumeric codes and to achieve faster card processing. The situation was changed only in the second half of the 1960s.

A factor that narrowed the front of programming work was the dominance of scientific applications during the period under consideration. There existed no "mass user" concept in the practice of computing, although there was no such deficiency in the view of programmers' labor. It was not an accident that Kitov, in his 1956 book, estimated the number of mathematicians needed to prepare programs for a single computer installation as between 50 and 150 [33, p. 26].

Programmers with a university education in mathematics constituted the majority in the USSR. However positive this factor, it has been long understood that the mathematical aspects of a programmer's education must be balanced by the engineering approach so necessary in systems programming.

One more factor was both a reason for and a consequence of the relatively narrow scope of work in programming. The problem was that the leading programmers were altogether too busy. For almost 15 years, the same people conducted research, taught students, developed software, and organized production runs in computing centers. It is difficult to find someone who can completely harmonize all these jobs. Almost every successful experimental system was somehow converted into a program product, often to the detriment of both the experiment and the product.

The authors hope that these sincere criticisms will not keep the reader from drawing a positive conclusion about the achievements of the formative period of programming in the USSR. Now, as we enter the 25th year since the neon indicators on computer consoles in the Soviet Union began their permanent run, "seven days a week, twenty-four hours a day," a hundredfold-larger new generation of young men and women will experience anew that unique moment when a programmer brings a machine to life by transferring to it a particle of his intelligence, in the form of a program. The authors dedicate this paper to that new generation.

REFERENCES

UMN   Uspekhi Matematicheskikh Nauk (journal)
IL   Inostrannaya Literatura (publishing house)
VINITI   Vsesoyuznyi Institut Nauchnoi i Tekhnicheskoi Informatsii (publishing house)
GITTL   Gosudarstvennoye Izdatelstvo Tekhniko-Teoreticheskoi Literatury (publishing house)
GIFML   Gosudarstvennoye Izdatelstvo Fiziko-Matematicheskoi Literatury (publishing house)
TsBTI   Tsentralnoye Buro Tekhnicheskoi Informatsii (publishing house)
GITL USSR   Gosudarstvennoye Izdatelstvo Tekhnicheskoi Literatury (of Ukrainian SSR) (publishing house)
ZVMiMF   Zhurnal Vychislitelnoi Matematiki i Matematicheskoi Fiziki (journal)

1. Tsykl statei po matematicheskoi tekhnike [A cycle of papers on mathematical machinery] UMN **1** (5–6), 3–174 (1946).
    N. E. Kobrinski, L. A. Lusternik, Matematicheskaya tekhnika (Vvedenie v tsykl) [Mathematical machinery (An introduction to the cycle)].
    I. N. Yanzhul, Schetnye avtomaty i ikh primenenie k astronomicheskim vychisleniyam [Calculating automata and their use in astronomical computation].
    V. M. Proshko, Pribory dlya opredeleniya kornei sistem lineinykh uravenenii [Instruments for finding roots of systems of linear equations].
    V. Bush and S. Caldwell, Novyi differentsialnyi analizator [translation of A new type of differential analyzer, Franklin Inst. **240**(4) (1945)].
    M. Born, R. Furts, and R. B. Princhl, Fotoelektricheskii pribor dlya funktsionalnogo preobrazovaniya Furye [translation of A photoelectric Fourier transformer, *Nature,* (*London*) (22 December), 756–757 (1945)].
2. M. L. Bykhovski, Novye amerikanskiye schetno-analiticheskiye mashiny [New American calculating and analytical machines], UMN **2** (2), 231–234 (1947).

3. Popular Science (October 1944), p. 86.
4. Popular Science (April 1946), p. 83.
5. D. R. Hartree, The Eniac. An electronic calculating machine, *Nature (London)* **157**(3990), 527.
6. D. R. Hartree, The ENIAC, an electronic computing machine. *Nature (London)* **158** (4015) (12 October) (1946).
7. H. H. Aiken and Grace M. Hopper, The automatic sequence controlled calculator. *Electr. Eng.* 8–10 (1946).
8. D. R. Hartree, "Eniak"-electronnaya schetnaya mashina (translated from [6]) UMN **3**(5), 146–158 (1948).
9. H. H. Aiken and G. M. Hopper, Avtomaticheski upravlyaemaya vychislitelnaya mashina (translated from [7]), UMN **3** (4), 119–142 (1948).
10. Theory and techniques for design of electronic digital computers (Lectures given at the Moore School, 8 July–31 August, 1946), Vols. 1–4. University of Pennsylvania, Moore School of Electrical Engineering, Philadelphia, Pennsylvania, 1946.
11. A. W. Burks, H. H. Goldstine, and J. von Neumann, Preliminary discussion of the logical design of an electronic computing instrument. Institute for Advanced Study, Princeton, New Jersey, July 1946.
12. A. W. Burks, H. H. Goldstine, and J. von Neumann, Report on the mathematical and logical aspects of an electronic computing instrument, 2nd ed., Part I. Institute for Advanced Study, Princeton, New Jersey, 1947.
13. A. W. Burks, H. H. Goldstine, and J. von Neumann, Preliminary discussion of the logical design of an electronic computing instrument. 2nd. ed. The Institute for Advanced Study, Princeton, New Jersey, 1947.
14. *Proc. Symp. Large-Scale Digital Comput. Machin. Harvard Comput. Lab.* 1947, *Ann. Comput. Lab. Harvard Univ.* Vol. 16. Cambridge, Massachusetts, 1948.
15. M. L. Bykhovski, Osnovy elektronnykh matematicheskikh mashin diskretnogo scheta [Principles of electronic mathematical machines for discrete computation], UMN **4** (3), 69–124 (1949).
16. W. W. Stiffler, ed., High-speed computing devices, 1st ed. By the staff of Engineering Research Associates, Inc., supervised by C. B. Tompkins and J. N. Wakelin, 1950.
17. Bystrodeistvuyushchiye Vychislitelnye Mashiny [translated from [16] edited by D. Yu. Panov]. IL, Moscow, 1952.
18. F. J. Murray, "The Theory of Mathematical Machines," Rev. ed. 1948.
19. F. J. Murray, "Teoriya Matematicheskikh Mashin" [translated from [18]]. IL, Moscow, 1949.
20 H. Rutishauser, A. Speiser, and E. Stiefel, Programmgesteuerte digital Rechengeräte (elektronische Rechenmaschinen), *Angew. Math. Phys.* (ZAMP).
    I.   **1**, (5), 277–297;
    II. 1(6), 339–362;
    III. 2(1), 1–25;
    Schluss, **2** (2), 63–91.
21. H. Rutishauser, A. Speiser, and E. Stiefel, Elektronnye tsifrovye schetnye mashiny s programmnym upravleniem [translated from [20]]. Voprosy raketnoi tekhniki, **2,** 134–163; **3,** 132–151; 140–151; 161–174.
22. "'MESM'. Entsiklopedia Kibernetiki," Vol. 2, p. 36. Naukova Dumka, Kiev, 1974.
23. L. A. Lusternik, A. A. Abramov, V. I. Shestakov, and M. R. Shura-Bura, "Reshenie Matematicheskikh Zadach na Avtomaticheskikh Tsyfrovykh Mashinakh. Programmirovanie dlya Bystrodeistvuyushchikh Elektronnykh Schetnykh Mashin. ["Solution of Mathematical Problems on Automatic Digital Machines. Programming for High-Speed Electronic Computers."] Izdatelstvo Akademii Nauk SSSR, 1952.
24. H. H. Goldstine, and J. von Neumann, Planning and coding for an electronic computing instrument, Vols. 1–3. Institute for Advanced Study, Princeton, New Jersey, 1947/1948.

25. M. V. Wilkes, Programme design for a high-speed automatic calculating machine. *J. Sci. Instrum.*, **26**, 217–220 (1949).
26. M. V. Wilkes, D. J. Wheeler, and S. Gill, "The Preparation of Programs for an Electronic Digital Computer" Cambridge Univ. Press, Cambridge, England, 1951.
27. M. V. Wilkes, D. J. Wheeler, and S. Gill, "Sostavlenie programm dlya electronnykh schetnykh mashin" (translated from [26]). IL, Moscow, 1953.
28. Konferentsia "Puti razvitiya sovetskogo matematicheskogo mashinostroyeniya i priborostroyeniya" Plenarnye zasedaniya (132 str.). Sektsia universalnykh tsifrovykh mashin, chast I (230 str.), chast II (259 str.), chast III (180 str.), Moskva, 12–17 marta, 1956. Napechatano VINITI po resheniyu orgkomiteta konferentsii ["Prospects of development of the Soviet industry for mathematical machines and instruments," Plenary sessions, Section of universal digital machines, Parts I–III, Moscow, 12–17 March 1956. Printed by VINITI according the decision of the organizing committee of the conference.]
   28.1. A. A. Lyapunov, and Yu. I. Yanov, O logicheskikh skhemakh programm [On logical program schemata], Part III, pp. 5–8.
   28.2 S. S. Kamynin and E. Z. Lubimskii, Avtomatizatsiya programmirovaniya [Automation of programming], Part III, pp. 9–17.
   28.3. A. P. Ershov, Programmiruyushchaya programma dlya BESM AN SSSR [The programming program for the USSR Academy of Sciences BESM computer], Part III, pp. 18–29.
   28.4. L. V. Kantorovich, L. T. Petrova, and M. A. Yakovleva, Ob odnoi sisteme programmirovaniya [On one programming system], Part III, pp. 30–36.
29. Konferentsia "Puti razvitiya sovetskogo matematicheskogo mashinostroeniya i priborostroyeniya" (programma) ["Prospects of development of the Soviet industry for mathematical machines and instruments" (Program)]. Moscow, 12–17 March 1956.
30. XX syezd Kommunisticheskoi partii Sovetskogo Soyuza. Stenograficheskii otchet. Tom II [Twentieth Congress of the Communist Party of the Soviet Union, Stenographical report]. Politizdat, Moscow, 1956.
31. I. S. Bruk, ed., "Bystrodeistvuyushchaya Vychislitelnaya Mashina M-2" ["The M-2 high-speed computer"]. GITTL, Moscow, 1957.
32. V. V. Belynskii, V. M. Dolkart, B. M. Kagan, G. P. Lopato, and I. Ya. Matyukhin, "Malogabaritnaya Elektronnaya Vychislitelnaya Mashina M-3" ["The M-3 Compact Electronic Computer"]. Filial VINITI, Moscow, 1957.
33. A. I. Kitov, "Elektronnye Vychislitelnye Mashiny" ["Electronic Computers"]. Sovetskoye Radio, Moscow, 1956.
34. S. D. Pogorelyi and L. I. Pshenichnyi, Organizatsiya upravleniya obmenom v mini-EVM [The organization of I/O control in a minicomputer] *Programmirovaniye* **1**, 48–52 (1976).
35. Trudy tretyego vsesoyuznogo matematicheskogo syezda. Moskva, iyun-iyul 1956. Tom II. Kratkoye soderzhaniye obzornykh i sektsionnykh dokladov [*Works of the Third All-Union Mathematical Congress*, Moscow, June–July 1956, Vol. II. Abstracts of plenary and sectional talks]. USSR Academy of Sciences, Moscow, 1956.
36. Sessiya Akademii nauk SSSR po nauchnym problemam avtomatizatsii proizvodstva. 1956. Plenarnye zasedaniya [Session of the USSR Academy of Sciences on scientific problems of production automation, 1956, Plenary sessions]. USSR Academy of Sciences, Moscow, 1957.
37. N. Rochester, Symbolic programming. *IRE Electron. Comput. Trans.* **2**(1), 10–15 (1953).
38. E. A. Zhogolev, G. S. Roslyakov, N. P. Trifonov, and M. R. Shura-Bura, "Sistema Standartnykh Podprogramm" ["A System of Standard Subroutines]. GIFML, Moscow, 1958.
39. A. P. Ershov, "Programmiruyushchaya Programma dlya Bystrodeistvuyushchei Electronnoi Schetnoi Mashiny" ["A Programming Program for the BESM Computer"]. Izdatelstvo Akademii Nauk SSSR, Moscow, 1958.
40. 1. A. A. Lyapunov, O logicheskikh skhemakh programm [On logical program schemata].

2. S. S. Kamynin, E. Z. Lyubimskii, and M. R. Shura-Bura, Ob avtomatizatsii pro-
    grammirovaniya pri pomoshchi programmiruyushchei programmy [On programming
    automation by means of programming programs].
3. E. S. Lukhovitskaya, Blok obrabotki logicheskikh uslovii v PP-2 [The block for
    processing logical conditions in PP-2].
4. E. Z. Lyubimskii, Arifmeticheskii blok v PP-2 [The arithmetical block in PP-2].
5. S. S. Kamynin, Blok pereadresatsii v PP-2 [The readdressing block in PP-2].
6. V. S. Shtarkman, Blok ekonomii rabochikh yacheek v PP-2 [The block of economiza-
    tion of working locations in PP-2], *Problemy Kibernet.* **1,** 46–74 (1958); **1,** 135–189
    (1958).
41. T. M. Velikanova, A. P. Ershov, K. V. Kim, V. M. Kurochkin, Yu. A. Oleinik-Ovod,
    and V. D. Podderyugin, Programmiruyushchaya programma dlya mashiny "Strela." Te-
    zisy dokladov soveshchaniya po vychislitelnoi matematike i primeneniyu sredstv vychis-
    litelnoi tekhniki [A programming program for the "Strela" computer. Abstracts of talks
    to a meeting on computational mathematics and computer applications]. Izdatelstvo AN
    Azerbaidjan SSR, Baku, 1958.
42. A. P. Ershov, and K. V. Kim. Programmiruyushchaya programma dlya vychislitelnoi
    mashiny STRELA-3 (PPS) [The PPS programming program for the STRELA-3 com-
    puter]. Vychislitelnyi Tsentr AN SSSR, Moscow, 1961.
43. N. P. Trifonov, and M. R. Shura-Bura, eds., "Sistema Avtomatizatsii Programmirovan-
    iya" ["A System of Programming Automation"]. GIFML, Moscow, 1961.
    Razdel I. Sistema programmirovaniya s ispolzovaniyem biblioteki podprogramm [Sec-
    tion I. A programming system based on a subroutine library], pp. 15–70.
    Razdel II. Programmiruyushchaya programma [Section II. A programming program],
    pp. 71–148.
    Razdel III. Avtomatizatsiya otladki programm i kontrolya vychislenii [Section III. Au-
    tomation of program debugging and computation check-out], pp. 149–187.
44. 1. M. R. Shura-Bura, Interpretiruyushchaya sistema na EVM. [An interpretive system
        for a computer].
    2. S. S. Kamynin. Sistema standartnykh podprogramm dlya metoda interpretatsii [A
        system of standard subroutines based on the method of interpretation].
    3. V. I. Sobelman. Vspomogatelnye programmy IS-2 [Auxiliary programs for IS-2].
    4. V. V. Martynyuk. Programma avtomaticheskogo prisvoyeniya adresov [A program
        for automatic address allocation].
        Vsesoyuznoye soveshchanie po vychislitelnoi matematike i vychislitelnoi tekhnike
        (Programma). Moskva, 16–21 noyabrya 1959 g. [An All-Union meeting on compu-
        tational mathematics and computing machinery (Program). Moscow, 16–21 Novem-
        ber 1959]. Izdatelstvo Moskovskogo Universiteta, Moscow, 1959.
45. M. R. Shura-Bura, Sistema interpretatsii IS-2. V sbornike "Biblioteka standartnykh pro-
    gramm" [The IS-2 interpretive system. *From* "A library of standard routines"]. TsBTI,
    Moscow, 1961.
46. V. V. Martynyuk, O metode simvolicheskikh adresov [On the method of symbolic ad-
    dresses], *Problemy Kibernet.,* **6,** 45–58 (1961).
47. V. S. Korolyuk. Ob odnom sposobe programmirovaniya (Ukrainian) [On one program-
    ming method], *Dokl. Akad. Nauk Ukr. SSR* **12,** 1292–1295 (1958).
48. V. S. Korolyuk. O ponyatii adresnogo algoritma [On the address algorithm concept],
    Problemy Kibernet. **4,** 95–110 (1960).
49. E. L. Yushchenko, "Adresnoye Programmirovanie" ["Address programming"]. GITL
    USSR, Kiev, 1963.
50. R. A. Brooker, The autocode programs developed for the Manchester University com-
    puters. Reprint from *Comput. J.* (1958).
51. V. M. Glushkov and E. L. Yushchenko "Vychislitelnaya mashina 'Kiev'" ["The 'Kiev'
    computer"]. GITL USSR, Kiev, 1962.

52. 1. M. A. Yakovleva, Krupnoblochnaya sistema programmirovaniya [A large-block programming system].
    2. L. T. Petrova and I. A. Platunova, Realizatsiya na mashine vychislenii v ishkodnom klasse spiskov [The computer implementation of computation in the initial class of lists].
    3. T. N. Pervozvanskaya, Provedeniye analiticheskikh vykladok na EVM pri reshenii nekotorykh tipov differentsialnykh uravnenii [Conducting analytical manipulations on a computer for solution of some types of differential equations].
    4. K. V. Shakhbazyan, Ischisleniye programm funktsionalnykh operatsii [A calculus of programs for functional operations].
    5. T. N. Smirnova, Polinomialnyi prorab i provedeniye analiticheskikh vykladok na EVM [The polinomial executive and conducting analytical manipulation at a computer].
    Trudy Matematicheskogo instituta imeni V. A. Steklova. LXVI. Raboty po avtomaticheskomu programmirovaniyu, chislennym metodam i funktsionalnomu analizu [Transactions of V. A. Steklov Mathematical Institute. LXVI. Works on automatic programming, numerical methods and functional analysis], pp. 4–112. Izdatelstvo AN SSSR, Moscow and Leningrad, 1962.

53. A. P. Ershov, O programmirovanii arifmeticheskikh operatorov [On programming of arithmetical operators], Dokl. Akad. Nauk SSSR 118 (3), 427–430 (1958).

54. L. N. Korolev, Kodirovanie i svertyvanie kodov [Coding and code compression], Dokl. Akad. Nauk SSSR 113(4), 746–747 (1957).

55. L. N. Korolev, Metody vyborki nuzhnogo slova iz slovarya. V sbornike "Vychislitelnaya Tekhnika" [Methods of finding words in a dictionary. From "Computing Machinery"], pp. 116–118. Izdatelstvo AN SSSR, Moscow, 1958.

56. G. M. Adelson-Velskii and E. M. Landis, Odin algoritm organizatsii informatsii [An algorithm for organizing information], Dokl. Akad. Nauk SSSR 146(2), 263–266 (1962).

57. A. L. Brudno, Grani i otsenki dlya sokrashcheniya perebora variantov. [Bounds and estimates for reduction of variant search], Problemy Kibernet. 10, 141–150 (1963).

58. Yu. I. Yanov, O logicheskikh skhemakh algoritmov. [On logical algorithm schemata], Problemy Kibernet. 1, 75–127. (1958).

59. R. I. Podlovchenko, Ob osnovnykh ponyatiyakh programmirovaniya [On the basic programming notions], Problemy Kibernet. 1, 128–134 (1958); 2, 123–138 (1960).

60. N. A. Krinitskii, Ravnosilnye preobrazovaniya logicheskikh skhem. Avtoreferat dissertatsii [Equivalent transformations of logical schemata. Thesis abstract]. Moscow State University, Moscow, 1959.

61. N. A. Krinitskii, G. A. Mironov, and G. D. Frolov, "Programmirovanie" ["Programming"]. Nauka, Moscow, 1966.

62. L. A. Kaluzhnin, Ob algoritmizatsii matematicheskikh zadach [On algorithmization of mathematical problems], Problemy Kibernet. 2, 51–68 (1959).

63. A. P. Ershov, Operatornye algoritmy. I (Osnovnye ponyatia) [Operator algorithms. I (The basic concepts)] Problemy Kibernet. 3, 5–48 (1960). Operatornye algoritmy. II (Opisanie osnovnych konstruktsii programmirovaniya) [Operator algorithms. II (A description of the basic programming concepts)], Problemy Kibernet. 8, 211–233 (1962).

64. E. Z. Lyubimskii, Ob avtomatizatsii programmirovaniya i metode programmiruyushchikh programm. Avtoreferat dissertatsii [On programming automation and the programming program method. Thesis abstract.]. Matematicheskii Institut AN SSSR, Moscow, 1958.

65. I. B. Zadykhailo, Organizatsiya tsiklicheskogo protsessa scheta po parametricheskoi zapisi spetsialnogo vida [Organization of cyclic computation by a special kind of parametric record] ZVMiMF 3(2), 337–357 (1963).

66. V. E. Kotov and A. S. Narinyani, Asinkhronnye vychislitelnye protsessy nad pamyatyu [Asynchronous computing processes over memory], Kibernetika 3, 64–71 (1966).

67. E. Dijkstra, Guarded commands, nondeterminacy and formal derivation of programs. *Comm. ACM* **18** (8), 453–457 (1975).

68. L. N. Korolev, Some methods of automatic coding for BESM and STRELA computers. Computer programming and artificial intelligence. (Lectures given at the University of Michigan, Summer 1958.) (John W. Carr III, ed.), pp. 489–510, College of Engineering, University of Michigan, Ann Arbor, 1958.

69. A. P. Ershov, Works of the Computing Center of the Academy of Sciences of the USSR in the field of automatic programming. *Proc. Symp. Mechaniz. Thought Processes,* NPL, Teddington, 24–27 November 1958.

70. A. P. Ershov, Automatic programming in the Soviet Union, *Datamation* **5** (4), 14–20 (1959).

71. A. J. Perlis and K. Samelson, eds., Report on the algorithmic language ALGOL, *Comm. ACM* **1** (12) (1958).

72. A. P. Ershov (ed.), "Avtomatizatsiya programmirovaniya. Sbornik perevodov." "Programming automation. Collection of translated papers." (FORTRAN, UNICODE, SOAP2, IT, FORTRANSIT, ALGOL). GIFML, Moscow, 1961.

73. A. P. Ershov, Kakoi dolzhna byt sleduyushchaya programmiruyushchaya programma? Vsesoyuznoe soveshchanie po vychislitelnoi matematike i vychislitelnoi tekhnike (Programma). Moskva, 16–21 noyabrya 1959 [Which should be the next programming program? All-Union meeting on computational mathematics and computing machinery (Program). Moscow, 16–21 November 1959]. Moskovskii Universitet, Moscow, 1959. [The text of the talk is published in [79]].

74. A. M. Gilman, O nekotorykh priemakh programmirovaniya v kode komand EVM GIFTI [A technique of programming for the GIFTI computer], *Problemy Kibernet.* **3**, 139–148 (1960).

75. G. A. Mikhailov, B. N. Shitikov, and N. A. Yavlinskii, Tsifrovaya elekronnaya schetnaya mashina CEM-1 [The CEM-1 electronic digital computer] *Problemy Kibernet.* **1**, 190–202 (1958).

76. N. A. Krinitskii, G. A. Mironov, and G. D. Frolov, "Programmirovanie" ["Programming"]. GIFML, Moscow, 1963.

77. I. G. Ilzynya, "Programmirovanie dyla Dvukhadresnykh Tsifrovykh Vychislitelnykh Mashin" [Programming for Two-Address Digital Computers]. Izdatelstvo AN Latviiskoi SSR, Riga, 1962.

78. M. R. Shura-Bura, Programmirovanie. Matematika v SSSR za 40 let. Tom 1 [Programming. *In* "40 Years of Mathematics in the USSR," Vol. 1], pp. 879–886 GIFML, Moscow, 1959.

79. A. P. Ershov, Osnovnye printsipy postroyeniya programmiruyushchei programmy Instituta matematiki SOAN SSSR. [The main principles of development of the programming program of the Institute of Mathematics of the Siberian Division of the USSR Ac. Sci.], *Sibirski Mate. Z.* **2**(6) 835–852 (1961).

80. Soobshcheniye ob algoritmicheskom yazyke ALGOL. Pod redaktsiei Perlisa A. Dzh, Zamelzona K. [Translated by A. P. Ershov from [71]]. Vychislitelnyi Tsentr AN SSSR, Moscow, 1959.

81. J. W. Backus, F. L. Bauer, J. Green, C. Katz, J. McCarthy, P. Naur, A. J. Perlis, H. Rutishauser, K. Samelson, B. Vauquois, J. H. Wegstein, A. van Winjngaarden, and M. Woodger. Report on the algorithmic language ALGOL 60 (Peter Naur, ed.) ALGOL Bulletine. Suppl. 2 (1 March). Regnecentralen, Valby, Denmark, 1960.

82. J. W. Backus *et al.,* Soobshchenie ob algoritmicheskom yazyke ALGOL 60. [Translated by G. I. Kozhukhin from [81] and edited by A. P. Ershov.] Vychislitelnyi Tsentr An SSSR, Moscow, 1960. ZVMiMF **1**(2), 308–342 (1961).

83. A. P. Ershov, G. I. Kozhukhin, and Yu. M. Voloshin, Vkhodnoi yazyk sistemy avtomaticheskogo programmirovaniya (predvaritelnoe soobshchenie [The input language of an

automatic programming system (a preliminary report)]. Vychislitelnyi Tsentr AN SSSR, Moscow, 1961.

84. Comm. *ACM* **4**(1) (1961).

85. M. R. Shura-Bura and A. P. Ershov, Mashinnye yazyki i avtomaticheskoye programmirovanie. Trudy 4-go Vsesoyuznogo matematicheskogo syezda. Leningrad, 3–12 iyulya 1961. Tom 1. Plenarnye doklady [Machine languages and automatic programming. *Proc. 4th All-Union Math. Cong. Leningrad, 3–12 July 1961*, Vol. 1 Plenary talks], pp. 243–250. Izdatelstvo Academii Nauk SSSR, Leningrad, 1963.

86. V. N. Popov, V. A. Stepanov, A. G. Stisheva, and N. A. Travnikova, Programmiruyushchaya programma [A programming program], ZVMiMF **4**(1), 78–95 (1964).

87. M. R. Shura-Bura and E. Z. Lyubimskii, Translyator ALGOL-60 [An ALGOL 60 translator], ZVMiMF **4**(1), 96–112 (1964).

88. G. I. Babetskii, M. M. Bezhanova, Yu. M. Voloshin, A. P. Ershov, B. A. Zagatskii, L. L. Zmievskaya, G. I. Kozhukhin, S. K. Kozhukhina, R. D. Mishkovich, Yu. I. Mikhalevich, I. V. Pottosin, and L. K. Trokhan, Sistema avtomatizatsii programmirovaniya ALFA [The ALPHA automatic programming system], ZVMiMF **5**(2), 317–325 (1965).

89. A. P. Ershov, G. I. Kozhukhin, and Yu. M. Voloshin, "Vkhodnoi Yazyk dlya Sistem Avtomaticheskogo Programmirovaniya" ["An Input Language for Automatic Programming Systems"]. Sibirskoe otdelenie AN SSR, Novosibirsk, 1964.

90. V. I. Sobelman and M. R. Shura-Bura, Realizatsiya rekursivnych protsedur v yazyke ALGOL-60 [Implementation of recursive procedures in the ALGOL 60 language] ZVMiMF **2**(2), 303–316 (1962).

91. M. R. Shura-Bura and V. V. Martynyuk, Ob effektivnoi organizatsii dinamicheskogo ispolzovaniya pamyati [On an efficient organization of dynamic memory allocation], ZVMiMF **4**(5) 963–967 (1962).

92. G. I. Babetskii *et al.* [see [88]]. "ALFA—sistema avtomatizatsii programmirovaniya." Pod redaktsiei A. P. Ershova ["ALPHA—an Automatic Programming System." Edited by A. P. Ershov]. Nauka, Sibirskoe otdelenie, Novosibirsk, 1967.

93. S. S. Lavrov, Ob ekonomii pamyati v zamknutykh operatornykh skhemakh [On memory economization in closed operator schemata], ZVMiMF **1**(4), 687–701 (1961).

94. A. P. Ershov, Svedenie zadachi raspredeleniya pamyati pri sostavlenii programm k zadache raskraski vershin grafov [The reduction of the problem of memory allocation during programming to the problem of graph vertex coloring]. *Dokl. Akad. Nauk SSSR* **142**(4), 785–787 (1962).

95. Opisanie yazyka ALGAMS [A description of the ALGAMS language], *Algoritmy i Algoritm. Jazyki* **3**, 3–56 (1968).

96. S. P. Surzhikov, Avtomatizatsiya polzovaniya mashinoi srednego klassa tipa M-20 (Avtooperator-2). 1-aya Vsesoyuznaya konferentsiya po programmirovaniyu. Oktyabr 1968 [Automatic operation of M-20 type medium-class computers (Autooperator-2). The first All-Union conference on programming, October 1968]. Institut Kibernetiki AN USSR, Kiev, 1968.

97. V. L. Katkov, V. P. Morozov, I. V. Pottosin, A. F. Rar, L. Ya. Semenova, and A. E. Khoperskov, EPSILON—sistema avtomatizatsii programmirovaniya zadach simvolnoi obrabotki [EPSILON—a system of automatic programming for symbol manipulation]. Nauka, Sibirskoe otdelenie, Novosibirsk, 1972.

98. V. L. Katkov and A. F. Rar, Programmirovanie na yazyke EPSILON [Programming on the EPSILON language]. Nauka, Sibirskoe otdelenie, Novosibirsk, 1972.

99. S. S. Kamynin and E. Z. Lyubimskii, Algoritmicheskii mashinnoorientirovannyi yazyk — ALMO [ALMO—an algorithmic machine-oriented language], *Algoritmy i Algoritm. Jazyki* **1**, 5–58 (1967).

100. A. P. Ershov, Programmirovanie-68 (Vstupitelnyi doklad na 1-i Vsesoyuznoi konferentsii po programmirovaniyu. Kiev, oktyabr 1968). Trudy seminara "Avtomatizatsiya pro-

grammirovaniya" [Programming-68 (Opening talk at the first All-Union conference on programming. Kiev, October 1968). Proceedings of the Seminar on programming automation], pp. 3–26. Akademiya Nauk USSR, Kiev, 1969.

101. A. I. Kitov, N. A. Krinitskii, and P. N. Komolov, "Elementy Programmirovaniya" ["Elements of Programming"]. Izdatelstvo Artilleriiskoi Akademii imeni Dzerzhinskogo, Moscow, 1956.

102. A. I. Kitov and N. A. Krinitskii, "Elektronnye Tsifrovye Mashiny i Programmirovanie" ["Electronic Digital Computers and Programming"]. GIFML, Moscow, 1959.

103. B. V. Gnedenko, V. S. Koroluk, and E. L. Yushchenko, "Elementy Programmirovaniya" ["Elements of programming"]. GIFML, Moscow, 1961.

104. E. A. Zhogolev and N. P. Trifonov. "Kurs Programmirovaniya" ["A Programming Course"]. Nauka, Moscow, 1964.

105. "Spravochnik dlya Postupayushchikh v Vysshie Uchebnye Zavedeniya v 1975 Godu" ["A Guide for Applicants to Higher Educational Institutions in 1975"]. Vysshaya shkola, Moscow, 1975.

106. I. S. Mukhin and A. I. Sragovich, Forma konturov ravnoustoichivykh otkosov [Shaping equistable side-slopes]. Inzhenernyi sbornik **23,** 121–131 (1956).

107. Yu. I. Yanov, O ravnosilnosti i preobrazovaniyakh skhem programm. Avtoreferat dissertatsii [On program equivalence and transformations. Thesis abstract]. Matematicheskii Institut AN SSSR, Moscow, 1957.

108. O. S. Kulagina, Nekotorye teoreticheskie voprosy mashinnogo perevoda. Avtoreferat dissertatsii [Some theoretical problems of machine translation. Thesis abstract]. Matematicheskii Institut AN SSSR, Moscow, 1958.

109. L. N. Korolev, Nekotorye voprosy teorii mashinnogo slovarya. Avtoreferat dissertatsii [Some problems of the machine dictionary theory. Thesis abstract]. Institut Tochnoi Mekhaniki i Vychislitelnoi Tekhniki, Moscow, 1959.

110. Seminary po kibernetike v Moskovskom universitete [Seminars on cybernetics in the Moscow University]. *Problemy Kibernet* **1,** 263 (1958).

111. TSU SSSR. SSSR v tsifrakh v 1975 godu [USSR Census Bureau. The USSR in digits in 1975]. Statistika, Moscow, 1976.

Andrei P. Ershov
COMPUTING CENTER
SIBERIAN BRANCH
 OF THE USSR ACADEMY OF SCIENCES
NOVOSIBIRSK, USSR

Mikhail R. Shura-Bura
INSTITUTE FOR APPLIED MATHEMATICS
THE USSR ACADEMY OF SCIENCES
MOSCOW, USSR

The Early Development of Programming Languages*†

DONALD E. KNUTH

and

LUIS TRABB PARDO

This paper surveys the evolution of "high-level" programming languages during the first decade of computer programming activity. We discuss the contributions of Zuse in 1945 (the "Plankalkül"), Goldstine and von Neumann in 1946 ("Flow Diagrams"), Curry in 1948 ("Composition"), Mauchly *et al.* in 1949 ("Short Code"), Burks in 1950 ("Intermediate PL"), Rutishauser in 1951 ("Klammerausdrücke"), Böhm in 1951 ("Formules"), Glennie in 1952 ("AUTOCODE"), Hopper *et al.* in 1953 ("A-2"), Laning and Zierler in 1953 ("Algebraic Interpreter"), Backus *et al.* in 1954–1957 ("FORTRAN"), Brooker in 1954 ("Mark I AUTOCODE"), Kamynin and Lîubimskiĭ in 1954 ("ПП-2"), Ershov in 1955 ("ПП"), Grems and Porter in 1955 ("BACAIC"), Elsworth *et al.* in 1955 ("Kompiler 2"), Blum in 1956 ("ADES"), Perlis *et al.* in 1956 ("IT"), Katz *et al.* in 1956–1958 ("MATH-MATIC"), Bauer and Samelson in 1956–1958 (U.S. Patent 3,047,228). The principal features of each contribution are illustrated and discussed. For purposes of comparison, a particular fixed algorithm has been encoded (as far as possible) in each of the languages. This research is based primarily on unpublished source materials, and the authors hope that they have been able to compile a fairly complete picture of the early developments in this area.

* The preparation of this paper has been supported in part by National Science Foundation Grant No. MCS 72-03752 A03, by the Office of Naval Research contract N00014-76-C-0330, and by IBM Corporation. The authors wish to thank the originators of the languages cited for their many helpful comments on early drafts of this paper.

† Reprinted from J. Belzer, A. G. Holzman, and A. Kent (eds.), "Encyclopedia of Computer Science and Technology," Vol. 6, pp. 419–493. Dekker, New York, 1977. Courtesy of Marcel Dekker, Inc.

Introduction

It is interesting and instructive to study the history of a subject not only because it helps us to understand how the important ideas were born—and to see how the "human element" entered into each development—but also because it helps us to appreciate the amount of progress that has been made. This is especially striking in the case of programming languages, a subject that has long been undervalued by computer scientists. After learning a high-level language, a person often tends to think mostly of improvements he or she would like to see (since all languages can be improved), and it is very easy to underestimate the difficulty of creating that language in the first place. In order to perceive the real depth of this subject properly, we need to realize how long it took to develop the important concepts that we now regard as self-evident. These ideas were by no means obvious a priori, and many years of work by brilliant and dedicated people were necessary before our current state of knowledge was reached.

The goal of this paper is to give an adequate account of the early history of high-level programming languages, covering roughly the first decade of their development. Our story will take us up to 1957, when the practical importance of algebraic compilers was first being demonstrated, and when computers were just beginning to be available in large numbers. We will see how people's fundamental conceptions of algorithms and of the programming process evolved during the years—not always in a forward direction —culminating in languages such as FORTRAN I. The best languages we shall encounter are, of course, very primitive by today's standards, but they were good enough to touch off an explosive growth in language development; the ensuing decade of intense activity has been detailed in Jean Sammet's 785-page book [SA 69]. We shall be concerned with the more relaxed atmosphere of the "pre-Babel" days, when people who worked with computers foresaw the need for important aids to programming that did not yet exist. In many cases these developments were so far ahead of their time that they remained unpublished, and they are still largely unknown today.

Altogether we shall be considering about 20 different languages, and it follows that we shall have neither the space nor the time to characterize any one of them completely; besides, it would be rather boring to recite so many technical rules. The best way to grasp the spirit of a programming language is to read example programs, so we shall adopt the following strategy: A certain fixed algorithm—which we shall call the "TPK algorithm" for want of a better name*—will be expressed as a program in each language we discuss. Informal explanations of this program should then suffice to capture the essence of the corresponding language, although the TPK algorithm will not, of course, exhaust that language's capabilities; once we have understood a

---

* Cf. "Grimm's law" in comparative linguistics, and/or the word "typical," and/or the names of the authors of this article.

program for TPK, we shall be able to discuss the most important language features that it does not reveal.

Note that the same algorithm will be expressed in each language, in order to provide a simple means of comparison. A serious attempt has been made to write each program in the style originally used by the author of the corresponding language. If comments appear next to the program text, they attempt to match the terminology used at that time by the original authors. Our treatment will therefore be something like "a recital of 'Chopsticks' as it would have been played by Bach, Beethoven, Brahms, and Brubeck." The resulting programs are not truly authentic excerpts from the historic record, but they will serve as fairly close replicas; the interested reader can pursue each language further by consulting the bibliographic references to be given.

The exemplary TPK algorithm which we shall be using so frequently can be written as follows in a dialect of ALGOL 60:

```
1    TPK: begin integer i; real y; real array a[0:10];
2              real procedure f(t); real t; value t;
3                f := sqrt(abs(t)) + 5 × t ↑ 3;
4              for i := 0 step 1 until 10 do read(a[i]);
5              for i := 10 step − 1 until 0 do
6                begin y := f(a[i]);
7                if y > 400 then write(i, "TOO LARGE")
8                            else write(i, y);
9                end
10       end.
```

[Actually ALGOL 60 is not one of the languages we shall be discussing, since it was a later development, but the reader ought to know enough about it to understand TPK. If not, here is a brief run-down on what the above program means: Line 1 says that i is an integer-valued variable, whereas y takes on floating point approximations to real values; and $a_0, a_1, \ldots, a_{10}$ are also real-valued. Lines 2 and 3 define the function $f(t) = \sqrt{|t|} + 5t^3$ for use in the algorithm proper, which starts on line 4. Line 4 reads in the values $a_0, a_1, \ldots, a_{10}$, in this order; then line 5 says to do lines $6, 7, 8, 9$ (delimited by **begin** and **end**) for $i = 10, 9, \ldots, 0$, in *that* order. The latter lines cause y to be set to $f(a_i)$, and then one of two messages is written out. The message is either the current value of i followed by the words "TOO LARGE", or the current values of i and y, according as $y > 400$ or not.]

Of course this algorithm is quite useless; but for our purposes it will be helpful to imagine ourselves vitally interested in the process. Let us pretend that the function $f(t) = \sqrt{|t|} + 5t^3$ has a tremendous practical significance, and that it is extremely important to print out the function values $f(a_i)$ in the opposite order from which the a_i are received. This will put us in the right frame of mind to be reading the programs. (If a truly useful algorithm were being considered here, it would need to be much longer in order to illustrate as many different programming language features.)

Many of the programs we shall discuss will have italicized line numbers in the left-hand margin, as in the ALGOL code above. Such numbers are not really part of the programs, they appear only so that the accompanying text can refer easily to any particular line.

It turns out that most of the early high-level languages were incapable of handling the TPK algorithm exactly as presented above; so we must make some modifications. In the first place, when a language deals only with integer variables, we shall assume that all inputs and outputs are integer valued, and that "sqrt(x)" denotes the largest integer not exceeding $\sqrt{x}$. Second, if the language does not provide for alphabetic output, the string "TOO LARGE" will be replaced by the number 999. Third, some languages do not provide for input and output at all; in such a case, we shall assume that the input values $a_0, a_1, \ldots, a_{10}$ have somehow been supplied by an external process, and that our job is to compute 22 output values $b_0, b_1, \ldots, b_{21}$. Here $b_0, b_2, \ldots, b_{20}$ will be the respective "i values" 10, 9, ..., 0, and the alternate positions $b_1, b_3, \ldots, b_{21}$ will contain the corresponding $f(a_i)$ values and/or 999 codes. Finally, if a language does not allow the programmer to define his own functions, the statement "$y := f(a[i])$" will essentially be replaced by its expanded form "$y := \text{sqrt}(\text{abs}(a[i])) + 5 \times a[i] \uparrow 3$."

Prior Developments

Before getting into real programming languages, let us try to set the scene by reviewing the background very quickly. How were algorithms described prior to 1945?

The earliest known written algorithms come from ancient Mesopotamia, about 2000 B.C. In this case the written descriptions contained only sequences of calculations on particular sets of data, not an abstract statement of the procedure; it is clear that strict procedures were being followed (since, for example, multiplications by 1 were explicitly performed), but they never seem to have been written down. Iterations like "**for** $i := 0$ **step** 1 **until** 10" were rare, but when present they would consist of a fully expanded sequence of calculations. (See [KN 72] for survey of Babylonian algorithms.)

By the time of Greek civilization, several nontrivial abstract algorithms had been studied rather thoroughly; for example, see [KN 69, p. 295] for a paraphrase of Euclid's presentation of "Euclid's algorithm." The description of algorithms was always informal, however, that is, rendered in natural language.

During the ensuing centuries, mathematicians never did invent a good notation for dynamic processes, although of course notations for (static) functional relations became highly developed. When a procedure involved nontrivial sequences of decisions, the available methods for precise description remained informal and rather cumbersome.

Example programs written for early computing devices, such as those for

Babbage's calculating engine, were naturally presented in "machine language" rather than in a true programming language. For example, the three-address code for Babbage's machine was to consist of instructions such as "$V_4 \times V_0 = V_{10}$", where operation signs like "$\times$" would appear on an operation card and subscript numbers like (4, 0, 10) would appear on a separate variable card. The most elaborate program developed by Babbage and Lady Lovelace for this machine was a routine for calculating Bernoulli numbers; see [BA 61, pp. 68, 286–297]. An example MARK I program given in 1946 by Howard Aiken and Grace Hopper [see RA 73, pp. 216–218] shows that its machine language was considerably more complicated.

Although all of these early programs were in a machine language, it is interesting to note that Babbage had noticed already on 9 July 1836 that machines as well as people could produce programs as output [RA 73, p. 349]:

> This day I had for the first time a general but very indistinct conception of the possibility of making an engine work out *algebraic* developments. I mean without *any* reference to the *value* of the letters. My notion is that as the cards (Jacquards) of the Calc. engine direct a series of operations and then recommence with the first so it might perhaps be possible to cause the same cards to punch others equivalent to any given number of repetitions. But there hole [*sic*] might perhaps be small pieces of formulae previously made by the first cards.

In 1914, Leonardo Torres y Quevedo used natural language to describe the steps of a short program for his hypothetical automaton. Helmut Schreyer gave an analogous description in 1939 for the machine he had helped Konrad Zuse to build [see RA 73, pp. 95–98, 167].

To conclude this survey of prior developments, let us take a look at A. M. Turing's famous mathematical paper of 1936 [TU 36], where the concept of a universal computing machine was introduced for theoretical purposes. Turing's machine language was more primitive, not having a built-in arithmetic capability, and he defined a complex program by giving what amounts to macroexpansions or open subroutines. For example, here was his program for making the machine move to the leftmost "a" on its working tape:

m-config.	symbol	behavior	final m-config.
$\mathfrak{f}(\mathfrak{C}, \mathfrak{B}, a)$	ә	L	$\mathfrak{f}_1(\mathfrak{C}, \mathfrak{B}, a)$
	not ә	L	$\mathfrak{f}(\mathfrak{C}, \mathfrak{B}, a)$
$\mathfrak{f}_1(\mathfrak{C}, \mathfrak{B}, a)$	a		$\mathfrak{C}$
	not a	R	$\mathfrak{f}_1(\mathfrak{C}, \mathfrak{B}, a)$
	None	R	$\mathfrak{f}_2(\mathfrak{C}, \mathfrak{B}, a)$
$\mathfrak{f}_2(\mathfrak{C}, \mathfrak{B}, a)$	a		$\mathfrak{C}$
	not a	R	$\mathfrak{f}_1(\mathfrak{C}, \mathfrak{B}, a)$
	None	R	$\mathfrak{B}$

[In order to carry out this operation, one sends the machine to state $\mathfrak{f}(\mathfrak{C}, \mathfrak{B}, a)$; it will immediately begin to scan left (L) until first passing the symbol ə. Then it moves right until either encountering the symbol a or two consecutive blanks; in the first case it enters into state $\mathfrak{C}$ while still scanning the a, and in the second case it enters state $\mathfrak{B}$ after moving to the right of the second blank. Turing used the term "m-configuration" for state.]

Such "skeleton tables," as presented by Turing, represented the highest-level notations for precise algorithm description that were developed before our story begins—except, perhaps, for Alonzo Church's "λ-notation" [CH 36], which represents an entirely different approach to calculation. Mathematicians would traditionally present the control mechanisms of algorithms informally, and the computations involved would be expressed by means of equations. There was no concept of assignment (i.e., of replacing the value of some variable by a new value); instead of writing $s \leftarrow -s$ one would write $s_{n+1} = -s_n$, giving a new name to each quantity that would arise during a sequence of calculations.

Zuse's "Plancalculus"

Near the end of World War II, Allied bombs destroyed nearly all of the sophisticated relay computers that Konrad Zuse had been building in Germany since 1936. Only his Z4 machine could be rescued, in what Zuse describes as a fantastic [*abenteuerlich*] way; and he moved the Z4 to a little shed in a small Alpine village called Hinterstein.

> It was unthinkable to continue practical work on the equipment; my small group of twelve co-workers disbanded. But it was now a satisfactory time to pursue theoretical studies. The Z4 Computer which had been rescued could barely be made to run, and no especially algorithmic language was really necessary to program it anyway. [Conditional commands had consciously been omitted; see [RA 73, p. 181].] Thus the PK [*Plankalkül*] arose purely as a piece of desk-work, without regard to whether or not machines suitable for PK's programs would be available in the foreseeable future. [ZU 72, p. 6].

Zuse had previously come to grips with the lack of formal notations for algorithms while working on his planned doctoral dissertation [ZU 44]. Here he had independently developed a three-address notation remarkably like that of Babbage; for example, to compute the roots x_1 and x_2 of $x^2 + ax + b = 0$, given $a = V_1$ and $b = V_2$, he prepared the following *Rechenplan* [p. 26]:

$$V_1 : 2 = V_3$$
$$V_3 \cdot V_3 = V_4$$
$$V_4 - V_2 = V_5$$
$$\sqrt{V_5} = V_6$$

$$V_3(-1) = V_7$$
$$V_7 + V_6 = V_8 = x_1$$
$$V_7 - V_6 = V_9 = x_2$$

He realized that this notation was limited to straight line programs [so-called *starre Pläne*], and he had concluded his previous manuscript with the following remark [ZU 44, p. 31]:

Unstarre Rechenpläne constitute the true discipline of higher combinatorial computing; however, they cannot yet be treated in this place.

The completion of this work was the theoretical task Zuse set himself in 1945, and he pursued it very energetically. The result was an amazingly comprehensive language which he called the *Plankalkül* [program calculus], an extension of Hilbert's *Aussagenkalkül* [propositional calculus] and *Prädikatenkalkül* [predicate calculus]. Before laying this project aside, Zuse had completed an extensive manuscript containing programs far more complex than anything written before. Among other things, there were algorithms for sorting; for testing the connectivity of a graph represented as a list of edges; for integer arithmetic (including square roots) in binary notation; and for floating-point arithmetic. He even developed algorithms to test whether or not a given logical formula is syntactically well formed, and whether or not such a formula contains redundant parentheses—assuming six levels of precedence between the operators. To top things off, he also included 49 pages of algorithms for playing chess. (Who would have believed that such pioneering developments could emerge from the solitary village of Hinterstein? His plans to include algorithms for matrix calculations, series expansions, etc., had to be dropped since the necessary contacts were lacking in that place; furthermore, his chess playing program treated "en passant captures" incorrectly, because he could find nobody who knew chess any better than he did [ZU 72, pp. 32, 35]!)

Zuse's 1945 manuscript unfortunately lay unpublished until 1972, although brief excerpts appeared in 1948 and 1959 [ZU 48, ZU 59]; see also [BW 72], where his work was brought to the attention of English speaking readers for the first time. It is interesting to speculate about what would have happened if he had published everything at once; would many people have been able to understand such radical new ideas?

The monograph [ZU 45] on Plankalkül begins with the following statement of motivation:

Aufgabe des Plankalküls ist es, beliebige Rechenvorschriften rein formal darzustellen. [The mission of the Plancalculus is to provide a purely formal description of any computational procedure.]

So, in particular, the Plankalkül should be able to describe the TPK algorithm; and we had better turn now to this program, before we forget what

TPK is all about. Zuse's notation may appear somewhat frightening at first, but we will soon see that it is really not difficult to understand.

```
 1      A2 = (A9,AΔ1)
 2      P1      |R(V) ⇒ R
 3           V  | 0      0
 4           A  | Δ1     Δ1

 5                  √|V| + 5 × V³ ⇒ R
 6           V  | 0              0    0
 7           A  | Δ1             Δ1   Δ1

 8      P2      | R(V) ⇒ R
 9           V  |  0      0
10           A  | 11 × Δ1   11 × 2

11      W2(11) ⌐R1(V) ⇒ Z
12           V      | 0  0    0
13           K      |      i
14           A      | Δ1   Δ1

15                  | Z > 400 ⇢ (i,+∞) ⇒ R ⌐(10-i)
16           V      | 0                    0
17           K      |
18           A      | Δ1        9      2        9

19                  | Z̄ > 400 ⇢ (i, Z) ⇒ R ⌐(10-i)
20           V      | 0              0    0
21           K      |
22           A      | Δ1        9 Δ1    2        9
```

Line *1* of this code is the declaration of a compound data type, and before we discuss the remainder of the program we should stress the richness of data structures provided by Zuse's language (even in its early form [ZU 44]). This is, in fact, one of the greatest strengths of the Plankalkül; none of the other languages we shall discuss had such a perceptive notion of data, yet Zuse's proposal was simple and elegant. He started with data of type S0, a single bit [*Ja-Nein-Wert*] whose value is either "−" or "+". From any given data types $\sigma_0, \ldots, \sigma_{k-1}$, a programmer could define the compound data type $(\sigma_0, \ldots, \sigma_{k-1})$, and individual components of this compound type could be referred to by applying the subscripts $0, \ldots, k-1$ to any variable of that type. Arrays could also be defined by writing $m \times \sigma$, meaning m identical components of type σ; this idea could be repeated, in order to obtain arrays of any desired dimension. Furthermore m could be "□", meaning a list of *variable* length, and Zuse made good use of such list structures in his algorithms dealing with graphs, algebraic formulas, and chess play.

Thus the Plankalkül included the important concept of hierarchically structured data, going all the way down to the bit level. Such advanced data structures did not enter again into programming languages until the late 1950s in IBM's Commercial Translator. The idea eventually appeared in many other languages, such as FACT, COBOL, PL/I, and extensions of ALGOL 60; cf. [CL 61] and [SA 69, p. 325].

Integer variables in the Plankalkül were represented by type A9. Another special type was used for *floating-binary numbers,* namely,

$$A \Delta 1 = (3 \times S0, 7 \times S0, 22 \times S0).$$

The first three-bit component here was for signs and special markers—indicating, for example, whether the number was real or imaginary or zero; the second was for a seven-bit exponent in two's complement notation; and the final 22 bits represented the 23-bit fraction part of a normalized number, with the redundant leading "1" bit suppressed. Thus, for example, the floating point number $+400.0$ would have appeared as

$$(-+-, ---+---, ------------------+--+),$$

and it also could be written

$$(LO, LOOO, LOOLOOOOOOOOOOOOOOOOOOOO).$$

[The + and − notation has its bits numbered 0, 1, . . . , from left to right, while the L and O notation corresponds to binary numbers as we now know them, having their most significant bits at the left.] There was a special representation for "infinite" and "very small" and "undefined" quantities; for example,

$$+\infty = (LLO, LOOOO, O).$$

Note that the TPK program uses $+\infty$ instead of 999 on line *15*, since such a value seems an appropriate way to render the concept "TOO LARGE."

Let us return now to the program itself. Line *1* introduces the data type A2, namely, an ordered pair whose first component is an integer (type A9) and whose second component is floating point (type $A\Delta 1$). This data type will be used later for the 11 outputs of the TPK algorithm. Lines *2–7* define the function $f(t)$, and lines *8–22* define the main TPK program.

The hardest thing to get used to about Zuse's notation is the fact that each operation spans several lines; for example, lines *11–14* must be read as a unit. The second line of each group (labeled "V") is used to identify the subscripts for quantities named on the top line; thus

R, V, Z   stands for the variables R_0, V_0, Z_0.
0 0 0

Operations are done primarily on output variables [*Resultatwerte*] R_k, input variables [*Variablen*] V_k, and intermediate variables [*Zwischenwerte*] Z_k.

The "K" line is used to denote components of a variable, so that, in our example,

$$V \qquad \text{means component } i \text{ of the input variable } V_0.$$
$$0$$
$$i$$

(A completely blank "K" line is normally omitted.) Complicated subscripts can be handled by making a zigzag bar from the K line up to the top line, as in line *17* of the above program where the notation indicates component $10 - i$ of R_0. The bottom line of each group is labeled A or S, and it is used to specify the type of each variable. Thus the "2" in line *18* of our example means that R_0 is of type A2; the "$\Delta 1$" means that Z_0 is floating point (type A$\Delta 1$); and the "9" means that i is an integer. Each "A" in the left margin is implicitly attached to all types in its line.

Zuse remarked [ZU 45, p. 10] that the number of possible data types was so large that it would be impossible to indicate a variable's type simply by using typographical conventions as in classical mathematics; thus he realized the importance of apprehending the type of each variable at each point of a program, although such information is usually redundant. This is probably one of the main reasons he introduced the peculiar multiline format. Incidentally, a somewhat similar multiline notation has been used in recent years to describe musical notes [SM 73]; it is interesting to speculate whether this notation will evolve in the same way that programming languages have.

We are now ready to penetrate further into the meaning of the above code. Each plan begins with a specification part [*Randauszug*], stating the types of all inputs and outputs. Thus, lines *2–4* mean that P1 is a procedure that takes an input V_0 of type A$\Delta 1$ (floating point) and produces R_0 of the same type. Lines *8–10* say that P2 maps V_0 of type $11 \times$ A$\Delta 1$ (namely, a vector of 11 floating-point numbers, the array a_i of our TPK algorithm) into a result R_0 of type $11 \times$ A2 (namely, a vector of 11 ordered pairs as described earlier).

The double arrow $\Rightarrow$, which Zuse called the *Ergibt-Zeichen* (yields sign), was introduced for the assignment operation; thus the meaning of lines *5–7* should be clear. As we have remarked, mathematicians had never used such an operator before; in fact, the systematic use of assignments constitutes a distinct break between computer-science thinking and mathematical thinking. Zuse consciously introduced a new symbol for the new operation, remarking [ZU 45, p. 15] that

$$Z + 1 \Rightarrow Z$$
$$3 \qquad\quad 3$$

was analogous to the more traditional equation

$$Z \quad + 1 = Z$$
$$3.i \qquad\quad 3.i + 1 \cdot$$

(Incidentally, the publishers of [ZU 48] used the sign $\succcurlyeq$ instead of $\Rightarrow$, but Zuse never actually wrote $\succcurlyeq$ himself.) Note that the variable receiving a new value appears on the right, while most present-day languages have it on the left. We shall see that there was a gradual "leftist" trend as languages developed.

It remains to understand lines *11–22* of the example. The notation "W2(n)" represents an iteration, for $i = n - 1$ down to 0, inclusive; hence W2(11) stands for the second **for** loop in the TPK algorithm. (The index of such an iteration was always denoted by i, or $i.0$; if another iteration were nested inside, its index would be called $i.1$, etc.) The notation

$$R1(x)$$
$$0$$

on line *11* stands for the result R_0 of applying procedure P1 to input x. Lines *15–18* of the program mean "**if** $Z_0 > 400$ **then** $R_0[10 - i] := (i, +\infty)$"; note Zuse's new notation $\rightarrow$ for conditionals. Lines *19–22* are similar, the bar over "$Z_0 > 400$" indicating the negation of that relation. There was no equivalent of "**else**" in the Plankalkül, nor were there **go to** statements. Zuse did, however, have the notation "Fin" with superscripts, to indicate a jump out of a given number of iteration levels and/or to the beginning of a new iteration cycle [cf. ZU 72, p. 28; ZU 45, p. 32]; this idea has recently been revived in the BLISS language [WR 71].

The reader should now be able to understand the above code completely. In the text accompanying his programs in Plankalkül notation, Zuse made it a point to state also the mathematical relations between the variables that appeared. He called such a relation an *impliciter Ansatz;* we would now call it an "invariant." This was yet another fundamental idea about programming, and, like Zuse's data structures, it disappeared from programming languages during the 1950s, waiting to be enthusiastically received when the time was ripe [HO 71].

Zuse had visions of using the Plankalkül someday as the basis of a programming language that could be translated by machine (cf. [ZU 72, pp. 5, 18, 33, 34]), but in 1945, he was considering first things first—namely, he needed to decide what concepts should be embodied in a notation for programming. We can summarize his accomplishments by saying that the Plankalkül incorporated many extremely important ideas, but it lacked the "syntactic sugar" for expressing programs in a readable and easily writable format.

Zuse says he made modest attempts in later years to have the Plankalkül implemented within his own company, "but this project necessarily foundered because the expense of implementing and designing compilers outstripped the resources of my small firm." He also mentions his disappointment that more of the ideas of the Plankalkül were not incorporated into ALGOL 58, since some of ALGOL's original designers knew of his work [ZU

72, p. 7]. Such an outcome was probably inevitable, because the Plankalkül was far ahead of its time from the standpoint of available hardware and software development. Most of the other languages we shall discuss started at the other end, by asking what was possible to implement rather than what was possible to write; it naturally took many years for these two approaches to come together and to achieve a suitable synthesis.

Flow Diagrams

On the other side of the Atlantic, Herman H. Goldstine and John von Neumann were wrestling with the same sort of problem that Zuse had faced: How should algorithms be represented in a precise way, at a higher level than the machine's language? Their answer, which was due in large measure to Goldstine's analysis of the problem together with suggestions by von Neumann, Adele Goldstine, and Arthur W. Burks [GO 72, pp. 266–268], was quite different from the Plankalkül: They proposed a pictorial representation involving boxes joined by arrows, and they called it a "flow diagram." During 1946 and 1947 they prepared an extensive and carefully worked out treatise on programming based on the idea of flow diagrams [GV 47], and it is interesting to compare this work to that of Zuse. There are striking differences, such as an emphasis on numerical calculation rather than on data structures; and there are also striking parallels, such as the use of the term "Plan" in the titles of both documents. Although neither work was published in contemporary journals, perhaps the most significant difference was that the treatise of Goldstine and von Neumann was beautifully "varityped" and distributed in quantity to the vast majority of people involved with computers at that time. This fact, coupled with the high quality of presentation and von Neumann's prestige, meant that their report had an enormous impact, forming the foundation for computer programming techniques all over the world. The term "flow diagram" became shortened to "flow chart" and eventually it even became "flowchart"—a word that has entered our language as both noun and verb.

We all know what flowcharts are, but comparatively few people have seen an authentic original flow diagram. In fact, it is very instructive to go back to the original style of Goldstine and von Neumann, since their inaugural flow diagrams represent a transition point between the mathematical "equality" notation and the computer-science "assignment" operation. Figure 1 shows how the TPK algorithm would probably have looked if Goldstine and von Neumann had been asked to deal with it in 1947.

Several things need to be explained about this original notation, and probably the most important consideration is the fact that the boxes containing "$10 \rightarrow i$" and "$i - 1 \rightarrow i$" were *not* intended to specify any computation. This amounts to a viewpoint significantly different from what we are now accustomed to, and the reader will find it worthwhile to ponder this concep-

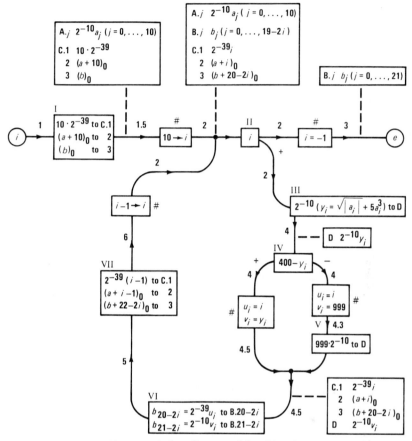

Figure 1 A flow diagram of the old style.

tual difference until he or she understands it. The box "$i - 1 \to i$" represents merely a change in *notation*, as the flow of control passes that point, rather than an action to be performed by the computer. For example, box VII has done the computation necessary to place $2^{-39}(i - 1)$ into storage position C.1; so after we pass the box "$i - 1 \to i$" and go through the subsequent junction point to box II, location C.1 now contains $2^{-39}i$. The external notation has changed but location C.1 has not! This distinction between external and internal notations occurs throughout, the external notation being problem-oriented while the actual contents of memory are machine-oriented. The numbers attached to each arrow in the diagram indicate so-called "constancy intervals," where all memory locations have constant contents and all bound variables of the external notation have constant meaning. A "storage table" is attached by a dashed line to the constancy intervals, to show the relevant relations between external and internal values at that point. Thus, for example, we note that the box "$10 \to i$" does not specify any computation, but it provides the appropriate transition from constancy interval 1.5 to constancy interval 2 (cf. [GV 47, sections 7.6 and 7.7]).

There were four kinds of boxes in a flow diagram: (a) Operation boxes, marked with a Roman numeral; this is where the computer program was supposed to make appropriate transitions in storage. (b) Alternative boxes, also marked with a Roman numeral, and having two exits marked $+$ and $-$; this is where the computer control was to branch, depending on the sign of the named quantity. (c) Substitution boxes, marked with a # and using the "$\rightarrow$" symbol; this is where the external notation for a bound variable changed, as explained above. (d) Assertion boxes, also marked with a #; this is where important relations between external notations and the current state of the control were specified. The example shows three assertion boxes, one that says "$i = -1$", and two asserting that the outputs u_i and v_i (in a problem-oriented notation) now have certain values. Like substitution boxes, assertion boxes did not indicate any action by the computer; they merely stated relationships that helped to prove the validity of the program and that might help the programmer to write code for the operation boxes.

The next most prominent feature about original flow diagrams is the fact that a programmer was required to be conscious of the *scaling* (i.e., the binary point location) of all numbers in the computer memory. A computer word was 40 bits long and its contents was to be regarded as a binary fraction x in the range $-1 \le x < 1$. Thus, for example, the above flowchart assumes that $2^{-10} a_j$ is initially present in storage position A.j, rather than the value a_j itself; the outputs b_j are similarly scaled.

The final mystery that needs to be revealed is the meaning of notations such as $(a + i)_0$, $(b)_0$, etc. In general, "x_0" was used when x was an integer machine address; it represented the number $2^{-19}x + 2^{-39}x$, namely, a binary word with x appearing twice, in bit positions 9 to 20 and 29 to 40 (counting from the left). Such a number could be used in their machine to modify the addresses of 20-bit instructions that appeared in either half of a 40-bit word.

Once a flow diagram such as this had been drawn up, the remaining task was to prepare so-called "static coding" for boxes marked with Roman numerals. In this task a programmer would use his problem-solving ability, together with his knowledge of machine language and the information from storage tables and assertion boxes, to make the required transitions. For example, in box VI one should use the facts that $u_i = i$, that storage D contains $2^{-10}v_i$, that storage C.1 contains $2^{-39}i$, and that storage C.3 contains $(b + 20 - 2i)_0$ (a word corresponding to the location of variable B.20−2i) to carry out the specified assignments. The job of box VII is slightly trickier: One of the tasks, for example, is to store $(b + 22 - 2i)_0$ in location C.3; the programmer was supposed to resolve this by adding $2 \cdot (2^{-19} + 2^{-39})$ to the previous contents of C.3. In general, the job of static coding required a fairly high level of artificial intelligence, and it was far beyond the state of the art in those days to get a computer to do such a thing. As with the Plankalkül, the notation needed to be simplified if it was to be suitable for machine implementation.

Let us make one final note about flow diagrams in their original form: Goldstine and von Neumann did not suggest any notation for subroutine calls, hence the function $f(t)$ in the TPK algorithm has been written in-line. In [GV 47, section 12] there is a flow diagram for the algorithm that a loading routine must follow in order to relocate subroutines from a library, but there is no example of a flow diagram for a driver program that calls a subroutine. An appropriate extension of flow diagrams to subroutine calls could surely be made, but it would have made our example less "authentic."

A Logician's Approach

Let us now turn to the proposals made by Haskell B. Curry, who was working at the Naval Ordnance Laboratory in Silver Spring, Maryland; his activity was partly contemporaneous with that of Goldstine and von Neumann, since the last portion of [GV 47] was not distributed until 1948.

Curry wrote two lengthy memoranda [CU 48, CU 50] that have never been published; the only appearance of his work in the open literature has been the brief and somewhat cryptic summary in [CU 50']. He had prepared a rather complex program for ENIAC in 1946, and this experience led him to suggest a notation for program construction that is more compact than flowcharts.

His aims, which correspond to important aspects of what we now call "structured programming," were quite laudable [CU 50, paragraph 34]:

> The first step in planning the program is to analyze the computation into certain main parts, called here divisions, such that the program can be synthesized from them. Those main parts must be such that they, or at any rate some of them, are independent computations in their own right, or are modifications of such computations.

But in practice his proposal was not especially successful, because the way he factored a problem was not very natural; his components tended to have several entrances and several exits, and perhaps his mathematical abilities tempted him too strongly to pursue the complexities of fitting such pieces together. As a result, the notation he developed was somewhat eccentric; and the work was left unfinished. Here is how he might have represented the TPK algorithm:

$$F(t) = \{\sqrt{|t|} + 5t^3 : A\}$$
$$I = \{10 : i\} \to \{t = L(a + i)\} \to F(t) \to \{A : y\}$$
$$\to II \to It_7(0, i) \to O_1 \& I_2$$
$$II = \{x = L(b + 20 - 2i)\} \to \{i : x\} \to III$$
$$\to \{w = L(b + 21 - 2i)\} \to \{y : w\}$$
$$III = \{y > 400\} \to \{999 : y\} \& O_1$$

The following explanations should suffice to make the example clear, although they do not reveal the full generality of his language:

$\{E : x\}$ means "compute the value of expression E and store it in location x."

A denotes the accumulator of the machine.

$\{x = L(E)\}$ means "compute the value of expression E as a machine location and substitute it for all appearances of 'x' in the following instruction groups."

$X \rightarrow Y$ means "substitute instruction group Y for the first exit of instruction group X."

I_j denotes the jth entrance of this routine, namely, the beginning of its jth instruction group.

O_j denotes the jth exit of this routine (he used the words "input" and "output" for entrance and exit).

$\{x > y\} \rightarrow O_1 \& O_2$ means "if $x > y$, go to O_1, otherwise to O_2."

$It_7(m, i) \rightarrow O_1 \& O_2$ means "decrease i by 1, then if $i \geq m$ go to O_2, otherwise to O_1."

Actually the main feature of interest in Curry's early work is not this programming language, but rather the algorithms he discussed for converting parts of it into machine language. He gave a recursive description of a procedure to convert fairly general arithmetic expressions into code for a one-address computer, thereby being the first person to describe the code-generation phase of a compiler. (Syntactic analysis was not specified; he gave recursive reduction rules analogous to well-known constructions in mathematical logic, assuming that any formula could be parsed properly.) His motivation for doing this was stated in [CU 50', p. 100]:

Now von Neumann and Goldstine have pointed out that, as programs are made up at present, we should not use the technique of program composition [i.e., subroutines] to make the simpler sorts of programs—these would be programmed directly—but only to avoid repetitions in forming programs of some complexity. Nevertheless, there are three reasons for pushing clear back to formation of the simplest programs from the basic programs [i.e., machine language instructions], viz.: (1) Experience in logic and in mathematics shows that an insight into principles is often best obtained by a consideration of cases too simple for practical use—e.g., one gets an insight into the nature of a group by considering the permutations of three letters, etc. . . . . (2) It is quite possible that the technique of program composition can completely replace the elaborate methods of Goldstine and von Neumann; while this may not work out, the possibility is at least worth considering. (3) The technique of program composition can be mechanized; if it should prove desirable to set up programs, or at any rate certain kinds of them, by machinery, presumably this may be done by analyzing them clear down to the basic programs.

The program that his algorithm would have constructed for $F(t)$, if t^3 were replaced by $t \cdot t \cdot t$, is

$$\{|t| : A\} \to \{\sqrt{A} : A\} \to \{A : w\} \to \{t : R\} \to \{tR : A\} \to \{A : R\} \to \{tR : A\}$$
$$\to \{A : R\} \to \{5R : A\} \to \{A+w : A\}.$$

Here w is a temporary storage location, and R is a register used in multiplication.

An Algebraic Interpreter

The three languages we have seen so far were never implemented; they served purely as conceptual aids during the programming process. Such conceptual aids were obviously important, but they still left the programmer with a lot of mechanical things to do, and there were many chances for errors to creep in.

The first "high-level" programming language actually to be implemented was the Short Code, originally suggested by John W. Mauchly in 1949. William F. Schmitt coded it for the BINAC at that time. Late in 1950, Schmitt recoded Short Code for the UNIVAC, with the assistance of Albert B. Tonik, and J. Robert Logan revised the program in January 1952. Details of the system have never been published, and the earliest extant programmer's manual [RR 55] seems to have been written originally in 1952.

The absence of data about the early Short Code indicates that it was not an instant success, in spite of its eventual historic significance. This lack of popularity is not surprising when we consider the small number of scientific users of UNIVAC equipment in those days; in fact, the most surprising thing is that an algebraic language such as this was not developed first at the mathematically oriented centers of computer activity. Perhaps the reason is that mathematicians were so conscious of efficiency considerations that they could not imagine wasting any extra computer time for something a programmer could do by himself. Mauchly had greater foresight in this regard; and J. R. Logan put it this way [RR 55]:

> By means of the Short Code, any mathematical equations may be evaluated by the mere expedient of writing them down. There is a simple symbological transformation of the equations into code as explained by the accompanying write-up. The need for special programming has been eliminated.
>
> In our comparisons of computer time with respect to time consumed by manual methods, we have found so far a speed ratio of at least fifty to one. We expect better results from future operations.

. . . It is expected that future use of the Short Code will demonstrate its power as a tool in mathematical research and as a checking device for some large-scale problems.

We cannot be certain how UNIVAC Short Code looked in 1950, but it probably was closely approximated by the 1952 version, when TPK could have been coded in the following way:

Memory equivalents: i = W0, t = T0, y = Y0.

Eleven inputs go respectively into words U0, T9, T8, . . . , T0.

Constants: Z0 = 000000000000
  Z1 = 010000000051 [1.0 floating-decimal form]
  Z2 = 010000000052 [10.0]
  Z3 = 040000000053 [400.0]
  Z4 = ΔΔΔTOOΔLARGE
  Z5 = 050000000051 [5.0]

Equation number recall information [labels]:

$$0 = \text{line } 01, \quad 1 = \text{line } 06, \quad 2 = \text{line } 07$$

Short code:

	Equations				Coded representation		
00	i = 10	00	00	00	W0	03	Z2
01	0: $y = (\sqrt{\text{abs } t}) + 5$ cube t	T0	02	07	Z5	11	T0
02		00	Y0	03	09	20	06
03	y 400 if ≤ to 1	00	00	00	Y0	Z3	41
04	i print, 'TOO LARGE' print-and-return	00	00	Z4	59	W0	58
05	0 0 if = to 2	00	00	00	Z0	Z0	72
06	1: i print, y print-and-return	00	00	Y0	59	W0	58
07	2: T0 U0 shift	00	00	00	T0	U0	99
08	$i = i - 1$	00	W0	03	W0	01	Z1
09	0 i if ≤ to 0	00	00	00	Z0	W0	40
10	stop	00	00	00	00	ZZ	08

Each UNIVAC word consisted of twelve 6-bit bytes, and the Short Code equations were "symbologically" transliterated into groups of six 2-byte packets using the following equivalents (among others):

01 −	06 abs value	1n $(n + 2)$nd power	59 print and return carriage
02)	07 +	2n $(n + 2)$nd root	7n if = to n
03 =	08 pause	4n if ≤ to n	99 cyclic shift of memory
04 /	09 (	58 print and tab	Sn, Tn, . . . , Zn quantities

Thus, "i = 10" would actually be coded as the word "00 00 00 W0 03 Z2" as shown; packets of 00s could be used at the left to fill a word. Multiplication was indicated simply by juxtaposition (see line *01*).

The system was an *algebraic interpreter*, namely, an interpretive routine that continuously scanned the coded representation and performed the appropriate operations. The interpreter processed each word from right to left, so that it would see the "=" sign last. This fact needed to be understood by the programmer, who had to break long equations appropriately into several words (cf. lines *01* and *02*); see also the print instructions on lines *04* and *06*, where the codes run from right to left.

This explanation should suffice to explain the TPK program above, except for the "shift" on line *07*. Short Code had no provision for subscripted variables, but it did have a 99 order, which performed a cyclic shift in a specified block of memory. For example, line *07* of the above program means "*temp* = T0, T0 = T1, ..., T9 = U0, U0 = *temp*"; and fortunately this facility is all that the TPK algorithm needs.

The following press release from Remington Rand appeared in the *Journal of the ACM*, 1955, p. 291:

> Automatic programming, tried and tested since 1950, eliminates communication with the computer in special code or language. . . . The Short-Order Code is in effect an engineering "electronic dictionary" . . . an interpretive routine designed for the solution of one-shot mathematical and engineering problems.

(Several other automatic programming systems, including "B-zero"—which we shall discuss later—were also announced at that time.) This is one of the few places where Short Code has been mentioned in the open literature; Grace Hopper referred to it briefly in [HO 52, p. 243] (calling it "short-order code"), [HO 53, p. 142] ("short-code"), and [HO 58, p. 165] ("Short Code"). In [HM 53, p. 1252] it is stated that the "short code" system was "only a first approximation to the complete plan as originally conceived." This is probably true, but several discrepancies between [HM 53] and [RR 55] indicate that the authors of [HM 53] were not fully familiar with UNIVAC Short Code as it actually existed.

The Intermediate PL of Burks

Independent efforts to simplify the job of coding were being made at this time by Arthur W. Burks and his colleagues at the University of Michigan. The overall goal of their activities was to investigate the process of going from the vague "ordinary business English" description of some data-processing problem to the "internal program language" description of a machine-language program for that problem; and, in particular, to break this process up into a sequence of smaller steps [BU 51, p. 12]:

This has two principal advantages. First, smaller steps can more easily be mechanized than larger ones. Second, different kinds of work can be allocated to different stages of the process and to different specialists.

In 1950, Burks sketched a so-called "intermediate programming language" that was to be the step one notch above the internal program language. Instead of spelling out complete rules for this intermediate programming language, he took portions of two machine programs previously published in [BU 50] and showed how they could be expressed at a higher level of abstraction. From these two examples it is possible to make a reasonable guess at how he might have written the TPK algorithm at that time:

1.	$10 \to i$	
To 10		

From 1,35

10.	$A + i \to 11$	Compute location of a_i
11.	$[A + i] \to t$	Look up a_i and transfer to storage
12.	$|t|^{\frac{1}{2}} \to 5t^3 \to y$	$y_i = \sqrt{|a_i|} + 5a_i^3$
13.	$400, y; 20, 30$	Determine if $v_i = y_i$
To 20	if $y > 400$	
To 30	if $y \le 400$	

From 13

20.	$999 \to y$	$v_i = 999$
To 30		

From 13,20

30.	$(B + 20 - 2i)' \to 31$	Compute location of b_{20-2i}
31.	$i \to [B + 20 - 2i]$	$b_{20-2i} = i$
32.	$(B + 20 - 2i) + 1 \to 33$	Compute location of b_{21-2i}
33.	$y \to [(B + 20 - 2i) + 1]$	$b_{21-2i} = v_i$
34.	$i - 1 \to i$	$i \to i + 1$
35.	$i, 0; 40, 10$	Repeat cycle until i negative
To 40	if $i < 0$	
To 10	if $i \ge 0$	

From 35

40.	F	Stop execution

Comments at the right of this program attempt to indicate Burks's style of writing comments at that time; they succeed in making the program almost completely self-explanatory. Note that the assignment operation is well established by now; Burks used it also in the somewhat unusual form "$i \to i + 1$" shown in the comment to instruction 34 [BU 50, p. 41].

The prime symbol that appears within instruction 30 meant that the computer was to save this intermediate result, as it was a common subexpression that could be used without recomputation. Burks mentioned that several of the ideas embodied in this language were due to Janet Wahr, Don Warren, and Jesse Wright. He also made some comments about the feasibility of automating the process [BU 51, p. 13]:

> Methods of assigning addresses and of expanding abbreviated commands into sequences of commands can be worked out in advance. Hence the computer could be instructed to do this work. . . . It should be emphasized, however, that even if it were not efficient to use a computer to make the translation, the Intermediate PL would nevertheless be useful to the human programmer in planning and constructing programs.

At the other end of the spectrum, nearer to ordinary business language, Burks and his colleagues later proposed an abstract form of description that may be of independent interest, even though it does not relate to the rest of our story. The accompanying example suffices to give the flavor of their "first abstraction language," proposed in 1954.

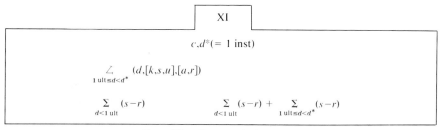

Form XI: Customer's Statement

On the first line, c denotes the customer's name and address, and d^* is "1 inst," the first of the current month. The symbol $\angle_i(x_i, \ldots, x_n)$ was used to denote a list of all n-tuples $(x_1, \ldots, x_n)$ of category i, in order by the first component x_1, and the meaning of the second line is "a listing, in order of date d, of all invoices and all remittances for the past month." Here $[k, s, u]$ was an invoice, characterized by its number k, its dollar amount s, and its discount u; $[a, r]$ was a remittance of r dollars, identified by number a; and "1 ult" means the first of the previous month. The bottom gives the customer's old balance from the previous statement, and the new balance on the right. "The notation is so designed as to leave unprejudiced the method of the statement's preparation" [BC 54]. Such notations have not won over the business community, however, perhaps for reasons explained by Grace Hopper in [HO 58, p. 198]:

> I used to be a mathematics professor. At that time I found there were a certain number of students who could not learn mathematics. I then was charged with the job of making it easy for businessmen to use our com-

puters. I found it was not a question of whether they could learn mathematics or not, but whether they would. . . . They said, "Throw those symbols out—I do not know what they mean, I have not time to learn symbols." I suggest a reply to those who would like data processing people to use mathematical symbols that they make them first attempt to teach those symbols to vice-presidents or a colonel or admiral. I assure you that I tried it.

Rutishauser's Contribution

Now let us shift our attention once again to Europe, where the first published report on methods for machine code generation was about to appear. Heinz Rutishauser was working with the Z4 computer, which by then had been rebuilt and moved to the Swiss Federal Institute of Technology [Eidgenössische Technische Hochschule (ETH)] in Zürich; and plans were afoot to build a brand new machine there. The background of Rutishauser's contribution can best be explained by quoting from a letter he wrote some years later [RU 63]:

> I am proud that you are taking the trouble to dig into my 1952 paper. On the other hand it makes me sad, because it reminds me of the premature death of an activity that I had started hopefully in 1949, but could not continue after 1951 because I had to do other work—to run practically singlehanded a fortunately slow computer as mathematical analyst, programmer, operator and even troubleshooter (but not as an engineer). This activity forced me also to develop new numerical methods, simply because the ones then known did not work in larger problems. Afterwards when I would have had more time, I did not come back to automatic programming but found more taste in numerical analysis. Only much later I was invited—more for historical reasons, as a living fossil so to speak, than for actual capacity—to join the ALGOL venture. The 1952 paper simply reflects the stage where I had to give up automatic programming, and I was even glad that I was able to put out that interim report (although I knew that it was final).

Rutishauser's comprehensive treatise [RU 52] described a hypothetical computer and a simple algebraic language, together with complete flowcharts for two compilers for that language. One compiler expanded all loops completely, while the other produced compact code using index registers. His source language was somewhat restrictive, since there was only one nonsequential control structure (the **for** statement); but that control structure was in itself an important contribution to the later development of programming languages. Here is how he might have written the TPK algorithm:

1   Für $i = 10(-1)0$
2 $a_i \not\Rightarrow t$
3 $(\text{Sqrt Abs } t) + (5 \times t \times t \times t) \not\Rightarrow y$
4 $\text{Max}(\text{Sgn}(y - 400), 0) \not\Rightarrow h$
5 $Z\ 0_i \not\Rightarrow b_{20 \times 2i}$
6 $(h \times 999) + ((1 - h) \times y) \not\Rightarrow b_{21-2i}$
7   Ende Index i
8   Schluss

Since no "**if** . . . **then**" construction—much less **go to**—was present in his language, the computation of

$$\begin{array}{ll} y & \text{if} \quad y \le 400 \\ 999 & \text{if} \quad y > 400, \end{array}$$

has been done here in terms of the Max and Sgn functions he did have, plus appropriate arithmetic; see lines *4* and *6*. (The function $\text{Sgn}(x)$ is 0 if $x = 0$, or $+1$ if $x > 0$, or -1 if $x < 0$.) Another problem was that he gave no easy mechanism for converting between indices and other variables; indices (i.e., subscripts) were completely tied to Für–Ende loops. The above program therefore invokes a trick to get i into the main formula on line *4*; "$Z\ 0_i$," is intended to use the Z instruction, which transferred an indexed address to the accumulator in Rutishauser's machine [RU 52, p. 10], and it is possible to write this in such a way that his compiler would produce the correct code. It is not clear whether or not he would have approved of this trick; if not, we could have introduced another variable, maintaining its value equal to i. But since he later wrote a paper entitled "Interference with an ALGOL procedure," [RU 61], there is some reason to believe he would have enjoyed the trick very much.

As with Short Code, the algebraic source code symbols had to be transliterated before the program was amenable to computer input, and the programmer had to allocate storage locations for the variables and constants. Here is how our TPK program would have been converted to a sequence of (floating-point) numbers on punched paper tape, using the memory assignments $a_i = 100 + i$, $b_i = 200 + i$, $0 = 300$, $1 = 301$, $5 = 302$, $400 = 303$, $999 = 304$, $y = 305$, $h = 306$, $t = 307$:

	Für	i	= 10	(-1)	0			
1	10^{12}	, 50	, 10	, -1	, 0	, Q ,		
	begin stmt	a	sub i	$\not\Rightarrow$		t		
2	010000	, 100	, .001	, 200000	, 307	, Q ,		
	begin stmt	(	t	Abs	dummy	Sqrt		
3	010000	, 010000	, 307	, 110000	, 0	, 350800 ,		
	dummy	)	+	(	5	×	t	×
	0	, 2000000	, 020000	, 010000	, 302	, 060000	, 307	, 060000 ,

	t	$\times$	t	)	$\rightrightarrows$	y			
	307 ,	060000 ,	307 ,	200000 ,	200000 ,	305 ,	Q ,		

	begin stmt	(		(	y	$-$	400	)	Sgn
4	010000	, 010000 ,	010000 ,	305 ,	030000 ,	303 ,	200000 ,	100000 ,	

	dummy	)	Max	0	$\rightrightarrows$	h	
	0	, 200000 ,	080000 ,	300 ,	2000000 ,	306 ,	Q ,

	begin stmt		Z	0	sub i	$\rightrightarrows$	b_{20}	sub $-2i$
5	010000	, 0 ,	230000 ,	0 ,	.001 ,	200000 ,	220 ,	$-.002$, Q ,

	begin stmt	(	h	$\times$	999	)	+	(
6	0100000	, 010000 ,	306 ,	060000 ,	304 ,	200000 ,	020000 ,	010000 ,

	(	1	$-$	h	)	$\times$	y	)	$\rightrightarrows$
	010000 ,	301 ,	030000 ,	306 ,	200000 ,	060000 ,	305 ,	200000 ,	200000 ,

b_{21} sub $-2i$
221 , $-.002$, Q ,

	Ende
7	Q , Q ,

	Schluss
8	Q . Q .

Here Q represents a special flag that was distinguishable from all numbers. The transliteration is straightforward, except that unary operators such as "Abs x" have to be converted to binary operators "x Abs 0". An extra left parenthesis is inserted before each formula, to match the $\rightrightarrows$ (which has the same code as right parenthesis). Subscripted variables whose address is $\alpha + \Sigma c_j i_j$ are specified by writing the base address α followed by a sequence of values $c_j 10^{-3j}$; this scheme allows multiple subscripts to be treated in a simple way. The operator codes were chosen to make life easy for the compiler; for example, 020000 was the machine operation "add" as well as the input code for $+$, so the compiler could treat almost all operations alike. The codes for left and right parentheses were the same as the machine operations to load and store the accumulator, respectively.

Since his compilation algorithm is published and reasonably simple, we can exhibit exactly the object code that would be generated from the above source input. The output is fairly long, but we shall consider it in its entirety in view of its importance from the standpoint of compiler history. Each word in Rutishauser's machine held two instructions, and there were 12 decimal digits per instruction word. The machine's accumulator was called Op.

Machine instruction		Symbolic form
230010	200050	$10 \to$ Op, Op $\to i$,
230001	120000	$1 \to$ Op, $-$Op $\to$ Op,
200051	230000	Op $\to i'$, $0 \to$ Op

200052	220009	$Op \rightarrow i''$, $* + 1 \rightarrow IR_9$
239001	200081	$1 + IR_9 \rightarrow Op$, $Op \rightarrow L_1$
000000	230100	no$-$op, loc $a \rightarrow Op$
200099	010050	$Op \rightarrow T$, $i \rightarrow Op$
020099	210001	$Op + T \rightarrow Op$, $Op \rightarrow IR_1$
011000	200307	$a_i \rightarrow Op$, $Op \rightarrow t$
010307	110000	$t \rightarrow Op$, $|Op| \rightarrow Op$
220009	350800	$* + 1 \rightarrow IR_9$, go to Sqrt
000000	000000	no-op, no-op
200999	010302	$Op \rightarrow P_1$, $5 \rightarrow Op$
060307	060307	$Op \times t \rightarrow Op$, $Op \times t \rightarrow Op$
060307	200998	$Op \times t \rightarrow Op$, $Op \rightarrow P_2$
010999	020998	$P_1 \rightarrow Op$, $Op + P_2 \rightarrow Op$
200305	010305	$Op \rightarrow y$, $y \rightarrow Op$
030303	200999	$Op - 400 \rightarrow Op$, $Op \rightarrow P_1$
010999	100000	$P_1 \rightarrow Op$, Sgn $Op \rightarrow Op$
200998	010998	$Op \rightarrow P_2$, $P_2 \rightarrow Op$
080300	200306	Max$(Op,0) \rightarrow Op$, $Op \rightarrow h$,
230000	200099	$0 \rightarrow Op$, $Op \rightarrow T$
010050	020099	$i \rightarrow Op$, $Op + T \rightarrow Op$
210001	230220	$Op \rightarrow IR_1$, loc $b_{20} \rightarrow Op$
200099	230002	$Op \rightarrow T$, $2 \rightarrow Op$
120000	060050	$- Op \rightarrow Op$, $Op \times i \rightarrow Op$
020099	210002	$Op + T \rightarrow Op$, $Op \rightarrow IR_2$
010000	231000	$(0) \rightarrow Op$, $IR_1 \rightarrow Op$
202000	230221	$Op \rightarrow b_{20-2i}$, loc $b_{21} \rightarrow Op$
200099	230002	$Op \rightarrow T$, $2 \rightarrow Op$
120000	060050	$- Op \rightarrow Op$, $Op \times i \rightarrow Op$
020099	210001	$Op + T \rightarrow Op$, $Op \rightarrow IR_1$
010301	030306	$1 \rightarrow Op$, $Op - h \rightarrow Op$
200999	010306	$Op \rightarrow P_1$, $h \rightarrow Op$
060304	200998	$Op \times 999 \rightarrow Op$, $Op \rightarrow P_2$
010999	060305	$P_1 \rightarrow Op$, $Op \times y \rightarrow Op$
200997	010998	$Op \rightarrow P_3$, $P_2 \rightarrow Op$
020997	201000	$Op + P_3 \rightarrow Op$, $Op \rightarrow b_{21-2i}$
010081	210009	$L_1 \rightarrow Op$, $Op \rightarrow IR_9$
010050	220008	$i \rightarrow Op$, $* + 1 \rightarrow IR_8$
030052	388003	$Op - i'' \rightarrow Op$, to $(IR_8 + 3)$ if $Op = 0$
010050	020051	$i \rightarrow Op$, $Op + i' \rightarrow Op$
200050	359000	$Op \rightarrow i$, to (IR_9)
000000	999999	no-op, stop
999999		stop

(Several bugs on pp. 39–40 of [RU 52] needed to be corrected in order to produce this code, but Rutishauser's original intent was reasonably clear.

The most common error made by a person who first tries to write a compiler is to confuse compilation time with object-code time, and Rutishauser gets the honor of being first to make this error!)

The above code has the interesting property that it is completely relocatable—even if we move all instructions up or down by half a word. Careful study of the output shows that index registers were treated rather awkwardly; but after all, this was 1951, and many compilers even nowadays produce far more disgraceful code than this.

Rutishauser published slight extensions of his source language notation in [RU 55] and [RU 55'].

Böhm's Compiler

An Italian graduate student, Corrado Böhm, developed a compiler at the same time and in the same place as Rutishauser, so it is natural to assume—as many people have—that they worked together. But in fact, their methods had essentially nothing in common. Böhm (who was a student of Eduard Stiefel) developed a language, a machine, and a translation method of his own, during the latter part of 1950, knowing only of [GV 47] and [ZU 48]; he learned of Rutishauser's similar interests only after he had submitted his doctoral dissertation in 1951, and he amended the dissertation at that time in order to clarify the differences between their approaches.

Böhm's dissertation [BO 52] was especially remarkable because he not only described a complete compiler, he also defined that compiler in its own language! And the language was interesting in itself, because *every* statement (including input statements, output statements, and control statements) was a special case of an assignment statement. Here is how TPK looks in Böhm's language:

A. Set $i = 0$ (plus the base address 100 for the input array a).

$$\pi' \to A$$
$$100 \to i$$
$$B \to \pi$$

B. Let a new input a_i be given. Increase i by unity, and proceed to C if $i > 10$, otherwise repeat B.

$$\pi' \to B$$
$$? \to \downarrow i$$
$$i + 1 \to i$$
$$[(l \cap (i \div 110)) \cdot C] + [(l \div (i \div 110)) \cdot B] \to \pi$$

C. Set $i = 10$.

$$\pi' \to C$$
$$110 \to i$$

D. Call x the number a_i, and prepare to calculate its square root r (using subroutine R), returning to E.

$$\pi' \to D$$
$$\downarrow i \to x$$
$$E \to X$$
$$R \to \pi$$

E. Calculate $f(a_i)$ and
   attribute it to y.
   If $y > 400$, continue
   at F, otherwise at G.

$$\pi' \to E$$
$$r + 5 \cdot \downarrow i \cdot \downarrow i \cdot \downarrow i \to y$$
$$[(I \cap (y \mathbin{\dot-} 400)) \cdot F] + [(I \mathbin{\dot-} (y - 400)) \cdot G] \to \pi$$

F. Output the actual value
   of i, then the value
   999 ("too large").
   Proceed to H.

$$\pi' \to F$$
$$i \mathbin{\dot-} 100 \to ?$$
$$999 \to ?$$
$$H \to \pi$$

G. Output the actual
   values of i and y.

$$\pi' \to G$$
$$i \mathbin{\dot-} 100 \to ?$$
$$y \to ?$$
$$H \to \pi$$

H. Decrease i by unity,
   and return to D if
   $i \geq 0$. Otherwise stop.

$$\pi' \to H$$
$$i \mathbin{\dot-} 1 \to i$$
$$[(I \mathbin{\dot-} (100 \mathbin{\dot-} i)) \cdot D] + [(I \cap (100 \mathbin{\dot-} i)) \cdot \Omega] \to \pi$$

Here comments in an approximation to Böhm's style appear on the left, while the program itself is on the right. As remarked earlier, everything in Böhm's language appears as an assignment. The statement "$B \to \pi$" means "go to B," i.e., set the program counter π to the value of variable B. The statement "$\pi' \to B$" means "this is label B"; a loading routine preprocesses the object code, using such statements to set the initial value of variables like B rather than to store an instruction in memory. The symbol "?" stands for the external world, hence the statement "$? \to x$" means "input a value and assign it to x"; the statement "$x \to ?$" means "output the current value of x." An arrow "$\downarrow$" is used to indicate indirect addressing (restricted to one level); thus, "$? \to \downarrow i$" in part B means "read one input into the location whose value is i," namely, into a_i.

Böhm's machine operated only on *nonnegative integers* of 14 decimal digits. As a consequence, his operation $x \mathbin{\dot-} y$ was the logician's subtraction operator,

$$x \mathbin{\dot-} y = \begin{cases} x - y & \text{if } x > y \\ 0 & \text{if } x \leq y. \end{cases}$$

He also used the notation $x \cap y$ for $\min(x, y)$. Thus it can be verified that

$$I \cap (i \mathbin{\dot-} j) = \begin{cases} 1 & \text{if } i > j \\ 0 & \text{if } i \leq j; \end{cases}$$

$$I \mathbin{\dot-} (i \mathbin{\dot-} j) = \begin{cases} 0 & \text{if } i > j \\ 1 & \text{if } i \leq j. \end{cases}$$

Because of these identities, the complicated formula at the end of part B is equivalent to a conditional branch,

$$C \to \pi \quad \text{if} \quad i > 110$$
$$B \to \pi \quad \text{if} \quad i \le 110.$$

It is easy to read Böhm's program with these notational conventions in mind. Note that part C doesn't end with "$D \to \pi$", although it could have; similarly we could have deleted "$B \to \pi$" after part A. (Böhm omitted a redundant go-to statement only once, out of six chances he had in [BO 52].)

Part D shows how subroutines are readily handled in his language, although he did not explicitly mention them. The integer square root subroutine can be programmed as follows, given the input x and the exit location X:

R.   Set $r = 0$ and $t = 2^{46}$. $\pi' \to R$
$$0 \to r$$
$$70368744177664 \to t$$
$$S \to \pi$$

S.   If $r + t \le x$, go to T, $\pi' \to S$
     otherwise go to U. $r + t \doteq x \to u$
$$[(l \doteq u) \cdot T] \, a \, [(l \cap u) \cdot U] \to \pi$$

T.   Decrease x by $r + t$, $\pi' \to T$
     divide r by 2, increase $x \doteq r \doteq t \to x$
     r by t, and go to V. $r : 2 + t \to r$
$$V \to \pi$$

U.   Divide r by 2. $\pi' \to U$
$$r : 2 \to r$$
$$V \to \pi$$

V.   Divide t by 4. If $t = 0$, $\pi' \to U$
     exit, otherwise return to S. $t : 4 \to t$
$$[(l \doteq t) \cdot X] + [(l \cap t) \cdot S] \to \pi$$

(This algorithm is equivalent to the classical pencil-and-paper method for square roots, adapted to binary notation. It was given in hardware-oriented form as example P9.18 by Zuse in [ZU 45, pp. 143–159]. To prove its validity, one can verify that the following invariant relations hold when we reach step S:

> t is a power of 4;
> r is a multiple of $4t$;
> $r^2/4t + x = $ initial value of x;
> $0 \le x < 2r + 4t$.

At the conclusion of the algorithm these conditions hold with $t = \frac{1}{4}$; so r is the integer square root and x is the remainder.)

Böhm's one-pass compiler was capable of generating instructions rapidly, as the input was being read from paper tape. Unlike Rutishauser, Böhm recognized operator precedence in his language; for example, $r : 2 + t$ was interpreted as $(r : 2) + t$, the division operator ":" taking precedence over addition. However, Böhm did not allow parentheses to be mixed with precedence relations: If an expression began with a left parenthesis, the expression had to be *fully* parenthesized even when associative operators were present; on the other hand, if an expression did *not* begin with a left parenthesis, precedence was considered but no parentheses were allowed within it. The complete program for his compiler consisted of 114 assignments, broken down as follows:

- (i)   59 statements to handle formulas with parentheses:
- (ii) 51 statements to handle formulas with operator precedence;
- (iii) 4 statements to decide between (i) and (ii).

There was also a loading routine, described by 16 assignment statements; so the compiler amounted to only 130 statements in all, including 33 statements that were merely labels ($\pi' \to \cdots$). Such brevity is especially surprising when we realize that a good deal of the program was devoted solely to checking the input for correct syntax; this check was not complete, however. (It appears to be necessary to add one more statement in order to fix a bug in his program, caused by overlaying information when a left parenthesis follows an operator symbol; but even with this "patch" the compiler is quite elegant.)

Rutishauser's parsing technique often required order n^2 steps to process a formula of length n. His idea, which we have seen illustrated above, was to find the leftmost pair of parentheses that has the highest level, so that they enclose a parenthesis-free formula α, and to compile the code for "$\alpha \to P_q$"; then the subformula "(α)" was simply replaced by "P_q," q was increased by 1, and the process was iterated until no parentheses remained. Böhm's parsing technique, on the other hand, was of order n, generating instructions in what amounts to a linked binary tree while the formula was being read in; to some extent, his algorithm anticipated modern list-processing techniques, which were first made explicit by Newell, Shaw, and Simon about 1956 (cf. [KN 68, p. 457]). The table on the following page indicates briefly how Böhm's algorithm would have translated the statement $((a : (b \cdot c)) a ((d \cap e) \div f)) \to g$, assuming that the bug referred to above had been removed. After the operations shown in the table, the contents of the tree would be punched out, in reverse preorder:

$$d \cap e \to ⑤$$
$$⑤ \div f \to ④$$
$$b \cdot c \to ③$$
$$a : ③ \to ②$$
$$② + ④ \to ①$$

Contents of tree (instructions and stack pointers)

Input	Current partial instruction	Current position in tree	1	2	3	4	5
⌣		①	⓪				
⌣		②	⓪	①			
a	a	②	⓪	①			
:	a :	②	⓪	①			
⌣		③	⓪	a : ③ , ①			
b	b	③	⓪	a : ③ , ①	②		
.	b ·	③	⓪	a : ③ , ①	②		
c	b · c	②	⓪	a : ③ , ②	②		
⌢		①	⓪	a : ③ → ②	②		
⌢		①	⓪	a : ③ → ②	b · c → ③		
+	② +	④	② / + ④	a : ③ → ②	b · c → ③	①	
⌣		⑤	② / + ④	a : ③ → ②	b · c → ③	①	④
d	d	⑤	② / + ④	a : ③ → ②	b · c → ③	①	④
⊂	d ∩	⑤	② / + ④	a : ③ → ②	b · c → ③	①	④
e	d ∩ e	⑤	② / + ④	a : ③ → ②	b · c → ③	①	④
⌢		④	② / + ④	a : ③ → ②	b · c → ③	①	d ∩ e → ⑤
÷	⑤ ÷	④	② / + ④	a : ③ → ②	b · c → ③	⑤ / ÷ f → ④	d ∩ e → ⑤
f	⑤ ÷ f	④	② / + ④	a : ③ → ②	b · c → ③	⑤ / ÷ f → ④	d ∩ e → ⑤
⌢		①	② / + ④	a : ③ → ②	b · c → ③	⑤ / ÷ f → ④	d ∩ e → ⑤
⌢		⓪	② / + ④ → ⓪	a : ③ → ②	b · c → ③	⑤ / ÷ f → ④	d ∩ e → ⑤
↑	①	⓪	② / + ④ → ⓪	a : ③ → ②	b · c → ③	⑤ / ÷ f → ④	d ∩ e → ⑤

and the following symbol "g" would evoke the final instruction "$\textcircled{1} \rightarrow g$."

Böhm's compiler assumed that the source code input would be transliterated into numeric form, but in an Italian patent filed in 1952 he proposed that it should actually be punched on tape using a typewriter with the keyboard [BO 52', Fig. 9] shown in Fig. 2. Constants in the source program were to be assigned a variable name and input separately.

Of all the authors we shall consider, Böhm was the only one who gave an argument that his language was *universal*, i.e., capable of computing any computable function.

Meanwhile, in England

Our story so far has introduced us to many firsts, such as the first algebraic interpreter, the first algorithms for parsing and code generation, the first compiler in its own language. Now we come to the first *real* compiler, in the sense that it was really implemented and used; it really took algebraic statements and translated them into machine language.

The unsung hero of this development was Alick E. Glennie of Fort Halstead, the Royal Armaments Research Establishment. We may justly say "unsung" because it is very difficult to deduce from the published literature that Glennie introduced this system. When Christopher Strachey referred favorably to it in [ST 52, pp. 46–47], he did not mention Glennie's name, and it was inappropriate for Glennie to single out his own contributions when he coauthored an article with J.M. Bennett at the time [BG 53, pp. 112–113]. In fact, there are apparently only two published references to Glennie's authorship of this early compiler; one of these was a somewhat cryptic remark inserted by an anonymous referee into a review of Böhm's paper [TA 56] while the other appeared in a comparatively inaccessible publication [MG 53].

Glennie called his system AUTOCODE; and it may well have helped to inspire many other "AUTOCODE" routines, of increasing sophistication, developed during the late 1950s. Strachey said that AUTOCODE was beginning to come into use in September 1952. The Manchester MARK I machine lan-

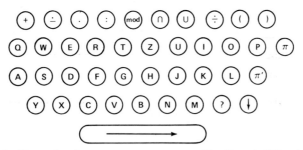

Figure 2 Typewriter for program entry, proposed by Corrado Böhm in 1952.

guage was particularly abstruse—see [WO 51] for an introduction to its complexities, including the intricacies of teleprinter code (used for base-32 arithmetic, backwards)—and its opaqueness may have been why this particular computer witnessed the world's first compiler. Glennie stated his motivations this way, at the beginning of a lecture he delivered at Cambridge University in February 1953 [GL 52]:

> The difficulty of programming has become the main difficulty in the use of machines. Aiken has expressed the opinion that the solution of this difficulty may be sought by building a coding machine, and indeed he has constructed one. However it has been remarked that there is no need to build a special machine for coding, since the computer itself, being general purpose, should be used. . . . *To make it easy, one must make coding comprehensible.* This may be done only by improving the notation of programming. Present notations have many disadvantages: all are incomprehensible to the novice, they are all different (one for each machine) and they are never easy to read. It is quite difficult to decipher coded programmes even with notes, and even if you yourself made the programme several months ago.
>
> Assuming that the difficulties may be overcome, it is obvious that the best notation for programmes is the usual mathematical notation, because it is already known. . . .
>
> Using a familiar notation for programming has very great advantages, in the elimination of errors in programmes, and the simplicity it brings.

His reference to Aiken should be clarified here, especially because Glennie stated several years later [GL 65] that "I got the concept from a reported idea of Professor Aiken of Harvard, who proposed that a machine be built to make code for the Harvard relay machines." Aiken's coding machine for the Harvard MARK III was cited also by Böhm [BO 52, p. 176]; it is described in [HA 52, pp. 36–38, 229–263, illustrated on pp. 20, 37, 230]. By pushing appropriate buttons on the console of this machine, one or more appropriate machine codes would be punched on tape for the equivalent of three-address instructions such as " $-b3 \times |ci| \rightarrow ai$ " or " $1/\sqrt{x9} \rightarrow r0$ "; there was a column of keys for selecting the first operand's sign, its letter name, and its (single) subscript digit, then another column of keys for selecting the function name, etc. (Incidentally, Heinz Rutishauser is listed as one of the 56 authors of the Harvard report [HA 52]; his visit to America in 1950 is one of the reasons he and Böhm did not get together.)

Our TPK algorithm can be expressed in Glennie's AUTOCODE as follows:

```
1      c@VA t@IC x@½C y@RC z@NC
2      INTEGERS +5 → c
3            → t
```

4	$+t$ TESTA Z
5	$-t$
6	ENTRY Z
7	SUBROUTINE $6 \to z$
8	$+tt \to y \to x$
9	$+tx \to y \to x$
10	$+z+cx$ CLOSE WRITE 1
11	$a@/\frac{1}{2}$ $b@$MA $c@$GA $d@$OA $e@$PA $f@$HA $i@$VE $x@$ME
12	INTEGERS $+20 \to b$ $+10 \to c$ $+400 \to d$ $+999 \to e$ $+1 \to f$
13	LOOP $10n$
14	$n \to x$
15	$+b-x \to x$
16	$x \to q$
17	SUBROUTINE $5 \to aq$
18	REPEAT n
19	$+c \to i$
20	LOOP $10n$
21	$+an$ SUBROUTINE $1 \to y$
22	$+d-y$ TESTA Z
23	$+i$ SUBROUTINE 3
24	$+e$ SUBROUTINE 4
25	CONTROL X
26	ENTRY Z
27	$+i$ SUBROUTINE 3
28	$+y$ SUBROUTINE 4
29	ENTRY X
30	$+i-f \to i$
31	REPEAT n
32	ENTRY A CONTROL A WRITE 2 START 2

Although this language was much simpler than the MARK I machine code, it was still very machine oriented, as we shall see. (Rutishauser and Böhm had had a considerable advantage over Glennie in that they had designed their own machine code!) Lines *1–10* of this program represent a subroutine for calculating $f(t)$; "CLOSE WRITE 1" on line *10* says that the preceding lines constitute subroutine number 1. The remaining lines yield the main program; "WRITE 2 START 2" on line *32* says that the preceding lines constitute subroutine number 2, and that execution starts with number 2.

Let's begin at the beginning of this program and try to give a play-by-play account of what it means. Line *1* is a storage assignment for variables c, t, x, Y, and z, in terms of absolute machine locations represented in the beloved teleprinter code. Line *2* assigns the value 5 to c; like all early compiler writers, Glennie shied away from including constants in formulas. Actually his language has been extended here: he had only the statement

"FRACTIONS" for producing constants between $-\frac{1}{2}$ and $\frac{1}{2}$, assuming that a certain radix point convention was being used on the Manchester machine. Since scaling operations were so complicated on that computer, it would be inappropriate for our purposes to let such considerations mess up or distort the TPK algorithm; thus the INTEGERS statement (which is quite in keeping with the spirit of his language) has been introduced to simplify our exposition.

Upon entry to subroutine 1, the subroutine's argument was in the machine's lower accumulator; line 3 assigns it to variable t. Line 4 means "go to label Z if t is positive"; line 5 puts $-t$ in the accumulator; and line 6 defines label Z. Thus the net effect of lines 4–6 is to put $|t|$ into the lower accumulator. Line 7 applies subroutine 6 (integer square root) to this value, and stores it in z. On line 8 we compute the product of t by itself; this fills both upper and lower accumulators, and the upper half (assumed zero) is stored in y, the lower half in x. Line 9 is similar; now x contains t^3. Finally line 10 completes the calculation of $f(t)$ by leaving $z + 5x$ in the accumulator. The "CLOSE" operator causes the compiler to forget the meaning of label Z, but the machine addresses of variables c, x, y, and z remain in force.

Line 11 introduces new storage assignments, and in particular it reassigns the addresses of c and x. New constant values are defined on line 12. Lines 13–18 constitute the input loop, enclosed by LOOP $10n$ . . . REPEAT n; here n denotes one of the index registers (the famous Manchester B-lines), the letters k, l, n, o, q, r being reserved for this purpose. Loops in Glennie's language were always done for *decreasing* values of the index, down to and including 0; and in our case the loop was performed for $n = 20, 18, 16, \ldots , 2, 0$. These values are twice what might be expected, because the MARK I addresses were for half-words. Lines 14–16 set index q equal to $20 - n$; this needs to be done in stages (first moving from n to a normal variable, then doing the arithmetic, and finally moving the result to the index variable). The compiler recognized conversions between index variables and normal variables by insisting that all other algebraic statements begin with a $+$ or $-$ sign. Line 17 says to store the result of subroutine 5 (an integer input subroutine) into variable a_q.

Lines 20–31 constitute the output loop. Again n has the value $2i$, so the true value of i has been maintained in parallel with n (see lines 19 and 30). Line 21 applies subroutine 1 [namely, our subroutine for calculating $f(t)$] to a_n and stores the result in y. Line 22 branches to label Z if $400 \geq y$; line 25 is an unconditional jump to label X. Line 23 outputs the integer i using subroutine 3, and subroutine 4 in line 24 is assumed to be similar except that a carriage return and line feed are also output. Thus the output is correctly performed by lines 22–29.

The operations "ENTRY A CONTROL A" on line 32 define an infinite loop "A: **go to** A"; this was the so-called *dynamic stop* used to terminate a computation in those good old days.

Our analysis of the sample program is now complete. Glennie's language was an important step forward, but of course it still remained very close to the machine itself. And it was intended for the use of experienced programmers. As he said at the beginning of the user's manual [GL 52'], "The left hand side of the equation represents the passage of information to the accumulator through the adder, subtractor, or multiplier, while the right hand side represents a transfer of the accumulated result to the store." The existence of two accumulators complicated matters; for example, after the multiplication in lines 8 and 9 the upper accumulator was considered relevant (in the $\rightarrow y$), while elsewhere only the lower accumulator was used. The expression "$+ a + bc$" meant "load the *lower* accumulator with a, then add it to the double length product bc," whereas "$+ bc + a$" meant "form the double-length product bc, then add a into the *upper* half of the accumulator." Expressions like $+ ab + cd + ef$ were allowed, but not products of three or more quantities; and there was no provision for parentheses. The language was designed to be used with the 32-character teleprinter code, where $\rightarrow$ was substituted for the double-quote mark.

We have remarked that Glennie's papers have never been published; this may be due to the fact that his employers in the British atomic weapons project were in the habit of keeping documents classified. Glennie's work was, however, full of choice quotes, so it is interesting to repeat several more remarks he made at the time [GL 52]:

> There are certain other rules for punching that are merely a matter of common sense, such as not leaving spaces in the middle of words or misspelling them. I have arranged that such accidents will cause the input programme to exhibit symptoms of distress. . . . This consists of the programme coming to a stop and the machine making no further moves.

> [The programme] is quite long but not excessively long, about 750 orders. . . . The part that deals with the translation of the algebraic notation is the most intricate programme that I have ever devised . . . [but the number of orders required] is a small fraction of the total, about 140.

> My experience of the use of this method of programming has been rather limited so far, but I have been much impressed by the speed at which it is possible to make up programmes and the certainty of gaining correct programmes. . . . The most important feature, I think, is the ease with which it is possible to read back and mentally check the programme. And of course on such features as these will the usefulness of this type of programming be judged.

At the beginning of the user's manual [GL 52'], he mentioned that "the loss of efficiency (in the sense of the additional space taken by routines made with AUTOCODE) is no more than about 10%." This remark appeared also in

[BG 53, p. 113], and it may well be the source of the oft-heard opinion that compilers are "90% efficient."

On the other hand, Glennie's compiler actually had very little tangible impact on other users of the Manchester machine. For this reason, Brooker did not even mention it in his 1958 paper entitled "The Autocode programs developed for the Manchester University computers" [BR 58]. This lack of influence may be due in part to the fact that Glennie was not resident at Manchester, but the primary reason was probably that his system did little to solve the really severe problems that programmers had to face, in those days of small and unreliable machines. An improvement in the coding process was not regarded then as a breakthrough of any importance, since coding was often the simplest part of a programmer's task. When one had to wrestle with problems of numerical analysis, scaling, and two-level storage, meanwhile adapting one's program to the machine's current state of malfunction, coding itself was quite insignificant.

Thus when Glennie mentioned his system in the discussion following [MG 53], it met with a very cool reception. For example, Stanley Gill's comment reflected the prevailing mood [MG 53, p. 79]:

> It seems advisable to concentrate less on the ability to write, say
>
> $$+ a + b + ab \rightarrow c$$
>
> as it is relatively easy for the programmer to write
>
> A a
> A b
> H a
> V b
> T c.

Nowadays we would say that Gill had missed a vital point, but in 1953 his remark was perfectly valid.

Some 13 years later, Glennie had the following reflections [GL 65]:

> [The compiler] was a successful but premature experiment. Two things I believe were wrong: (a) Floating-point hardware had not appeared. This meant that most of a programmer's effort was in scaling his calculation, not in coding. (b) The climate of thought was not right. Machines were too slow and too small. It was a programmer's delight to squeeze problems into the smallest space. . . .
>
> I recall that automatic coding as a concept was not a novel concept in the early fifties. Most knowledgeable programmers knew of it, I think. It was a well known possibility, like the possibility of computers playing chess or checkers. . . . [Writing the compiler] was a hobby that I undertook in addition to my employers' business: they learned

about it afterwards. The compiler . . . took about three months of spare time activity to complete.

Early American "Compilers"

None of the authors we have mentioned so far actually used the word "compiler" in connection with what they were doing; the terms were *automatic coding, codification automatique, Rechenplanfertigung*. In fact it is not especially obvious to programmers today why a compiler should be so called. We can understand this best by considering briefly the other types of programming aids that were in use during those early days.

The first important programming tools to be developed were, of course, general-purpose subroutines for such commonly needed processes as input–output conversions, floating-point arithmetic, and transcendental functions. Once a library of such subroutines had been constructed, there was time to think of further ways to simplify programming, and two principal ideas emerged: (a) Coding in machine language could be made less rigid, by using blocks of relocatable addresses [WH 50]. This idea was extended by M. V. Wilkes to the notion of an "assembly routine," able to combine a number of subroutines and to allocate storage [WW 51, pp. 27–32]; and Wilkes later [WI 52, WI 53] extended the concept further to include general symbolic addresses (i.e., not simply relative to a small number of origins). For many years these were called "floating addresses." Similar developments in assembly systems occurred in America and elsewhere (cf. [RO 52]). (b) An artificial machine language or *pseudocode* was devised, usually providing easy facilities for floating-point arithmetic as if it had been built into the hardware. An "interpretive routine" (sometimes called "interpretative" in those days) would process these instructions, emulating the hypothetical computer. The first interpretive routines appeared in programming's first textbook, by Wilkes, Wheeler, and Gill [WW 51, pp. 34–37, 74–77, 162–164]; the primary aim of this book was to present a library of subroutines and the methodology of their use. Shortly afterward a refined interpretive routine for floating-point calculation was described by Brooker and Wheeler [BW 53], including the ability for subroutines nested to any depth. Interpretive routines in their more familiar compact form were introduced by J. M. Bennett (cf. [WW 51, Preface and pp. 162–164], [BP 52]); the most influential was perhaps John Backus's IBM 701 Speedcoding System [BA 54, BH 54]. As we have already remarked, Short Code was a different sort of interpretive routine. The early history of library subroutines, assembly routines, and interpretive routines remains to be written; we have just reviewed it briefly here in order to put the programming language developments into context.

During the latter part of 1951, Grace Murray Hopper developed the idea that pseudocodes need not be interpreted; they could also be expanded out into direct machine language instructions. She and her associates at UNIVAC proceeded to construct an experimental program that would do such a translation, and they called it a *compiling routine* [MO 54, p. 15].

> To compile means to compose out of materials from other documents. Therefore, the compiler method of automatic programming consists of assembling and organizing a program from programs or routines or in general from sequences of computer code which have been made up previously.

(See also [HO 55, p. 22].) The first "compiler" in this sense, named A-0, was in operation in the spring of 1952, when Dr. Hopper spoke on the subject at the first ACM National Conference [HO 52]. Incidentally, M. V. Wilkes came up with a very similar idea, and called it the method of "synthetic orders" [WI 52]; we would now call this a macroexpansion.

The A-0 "compiler" was improved to A-1 (January 1953) and then to A-2 (August 1953); the original implementors were Richard K. Ridgway and Margaret H. Harper. Quite a few references to A-2 have appeared in the literature of those days [HM 53, HO 53, HO 53', MO 54, WA 54], but these authors gave no examples of the language itself. Therefore it will be helpful to discuss here the state of A-2 as it existed late in 1953, when it was first released to UNIVAC customers for testing [RR 53]. As we shall see, the language was quite primitive by comparison with those we have been studying, hence we choose to credit Glennie with the first compiler although A-0 was completed first; yet it is important to understand what was called a "compiler" in 1954, in order to appreciate the historical development of programming languages.

Here is how TPK would have looked in A-2 at the end of 1953:

```
Use of working storage
00  02   04    06   08   10   12   14  to  34  36    38        40        42–58
10   5  400   −1    ∞    4    3   a₀  to  a₁₀  i    y,y′,y″   t,t′,t″   temp storage
```

Program

0.	GMI000	000002	Read input and necessary constants from T_2
	ITEM01	WS.000	
	SERV02	BLOCKA	
	1RG000	000000	

1.	GMM000	000001	
	000180	020216	$10.0 = i$
	1RG000	001000	

2.	AM0034	034040	$a_{10}^2 = t$
3.	RNA040	010040	$\sqrt[4]{t} = t'$
4.	APN034	012038	$a_{10}^3 = y$
5.	AM0002	038038	$5y = y'$
6.	AA0040	038038	$t' + y' = y''$
7.	AS0004	038040	$400 - y'' = t''$

```
 8.   OWNΔCO   DEΔ003
      K00000   K00000
      F00912   E001RG      if t" ≥ 0, go on to Op. 10
      000000   Q001CN
      1RG000   008040
      1CN000   000010

 9.   GMM000   000001
      000188   020238      'ΔΔΔTOO ΔLARGE ΔΔΔΔΔΔ ΔΔΔΔΔΔ' = y"
      1RG000   009000

10.   YTO036   038000      Print i,y"

11.   GMM000   000001
      000194   200220      Move 20 words from WS14 to WS40
      1RG000   011000

12.   GMM000   000001
      000222   200196      Move 20 words from WS40 to WS16
      1RG000   012000

13.   ALL012   F000Tɏ
      1RG000   013036      Replace i by i+(-1) and go to Op. 2
      2RG000   000037      if i ≠ -1, otherwise go to Op. 14
      3RG000   000006
      4RG000   000007
      5RG000   000006
      6RG000   000007
      1CN000   000002
      2CN000   000014
      1RS000   000036
      2RS000   000037

14.   OWNΔCO   DEΔ002
      810000   820000      Rewind tapes 1 and 2, and halt.
      900000   900000
      1RG000   014000

      ʁØENDΔ   INFO.ʁ
```

There were 60 words of working storage, and each floating-point number used two words. These working storages were usually addressed by numbers $00, 02, \ldots, 58$, except in the GMM instruction (move generator) when they were addressed by $180, 182, \ldots, 238$, respectively; see operations 1, 9, 11, and 12. Since there was no provision for absolute value, operations 2 and 3 of this program find $\sqrt{|a_{10}|}$ by computing $\sqrt[4]{a_{10}^2}$. (The A-2 compiler would replace most operators by a fully expanded subroutine, in line; this subroutine would be copied anew each time it was requested, unless it was one of the four basic floating-point arithmetic operations.) Since there was no provision for subscripted variables, operations 11 and 12 shift the array elements after each iteration.

Most arithmetic instructions were specified with a three-address code, as shown in operations 2–7. But at this point in the development of A-2 there was no way to test the relation "≥" without resorting to machine language —only a test for equality was built in—so operation 8 specifies the necessary UNIVAC instructions. (The first word in operation 8 says that the following 003 lines contain UNIVAC code. Those three lines extract (E) the sign of the first numeric argument (1RG) using a system constant in location 912, and if it was positive they instruct the machine to go to program operator 1CN. The next two lines say that 1RG is to be t'' (working storage 40), and that 1CN is to be the address of operation 10. The "008" in the 1RG specification tells the compiler that this is operation 8; such redundant information was checked at compile time. Note that the compiler would substitute appropriate addresses for 1RG and 1CN in the machine language instructions. Since there was no notation for "1RG + 1", the programmer had to supply ten different parameter lines in operation 13.)

By 1955, A-2 had become more streamlined, and the necessity for OWN CODE in the above program had disappeared; see [PR 55] for a description of A-2 coding, vintage 1955. (Another paper [TH 55] also appeared at that time, presenting the same example program.) Operations 7–14 of the above program could now be replaced by

```
7.    QT0038  004000     To Op. 9 if y" > 400
      1CN000  000009
8.    QU0038  038000     Go to Op. 10
      1CN000  000010
9.    MV0008  001038
10.   YT0036  038000
11.   MV0014  010040
12.   MV0040  010016
13.   AAL036  006006     Same meaning as before, but new syntax.
      1CN000  000002
      2CN000  000014
14.   RWS120  000000
      ENDΔCO  DINGΔΔ
```

Laning and Zierler

Grace Hopper was particularly active as a spokesperson for automatic programming during the 1950s; she went barnstorming throughout the country, significantly helping to accelerate the rate of progress. One of the most important things she accomplished was to help organize two key symposia on the topic, in 1954 and 1956, under the sponsorship of the Office of Naval Research. These symposia brought together many people and ideas at an important time. (On the other hand, it must be remarked that the contributions of Zuse, Curry, Burks, Mauchly, Böhm, and Glennie were not mentioned at either symposium, and Rutishauser's work was cited only once — not quite accurately [GO 54, p. 76]. Communication was not rampant!)

In retrospect, the biggest event of the 1954 symposium on automatic programming was the announcement of a system that J. Halcombe Laning, Jr., and Niel Zierler had recently implemented for the WHIRLWIND computer at MIT. However, the significance of that announcement is not especially evident from the published proceedings [NA 54], 97% of which are devoted to enthusiastic descriptions of assemblers, interpreters, and 1954-style "compilers." We know of the impact mainly from Grace Hopper's introductory remarks at the 1956 symposium, discussing the past two years of progress [HO 56]:

> A description of Laning and Zierler's system of algebraic pseudocoding for the Whirlwind computer led to the development of Boeing's BACAIC for the 701, FORTRAN for the 704, AT-3 for the UNIVAC, and the Purdue System for the Datatron and indicated the need for far more effort in the area of algebraic translators.

A clue to the importance of Laning and Zierler's contribution can also be found in the closing pages of a paper by John Backus and Harlan Herrick at the 1954 symposium. After describing IBM 701 Speedcoding and the tradeoffs between interpreters and "compilers," they concluded by speculating about the future of automatic programming [BH 54]:

> A programmer might not be considered too unreasonable if he were willing only to produce the formulas for the numerical solution of his problem, and perhaps a plan showing how the data was to be moved from one storage hierarchy to another, and then demand that the machine produce the results for his problem. No doubt if he were too insistent next week about this sort of thing he would be subject to psychiatric observation. However, next year he might be taken more seriously.

After listing numerous advantages of high-level languages, they said: "Whether such an elaborate automatic-programming system is possible or feasible has yet to be determined." As we shall soon see, the system of Laning and Zierler proved that such a system is indeed possible.

Brief mention of their system was made by Charles Adams at the symposium [AL 54]; but the full user's manual [LZ 54] ought to be reprinted someday because their language went so far beyond what had been implemented before. The programmer no longer needed to know much about the computer at all, and the user's manual was (for the first time) addressed to a complete novice. Here is how TPK would look in their system:

1 $v|N = \quad \langle \text{input} \rangle,$
2 $i = 0,$

3	1	$j = i + 1$,
4		$a\lvert i = v\lvert j$,
5		$i = j$,
6		$e = i - 10.5$,
7		CP 1,
8		$i = 10$,
9	2	$y = F^1(F^{11}(a\lvert i)) + 5(a\lvert i)^3$,
10		$e = y - 400$,
11		CP 3,
12		$z = 999$,
13		PRINT i,z.
14		SP 4,
15	3	PRINT i,y.
16	4	$i = i - 1$,
17		$e = -0.5 - i$,
18		CP 2,
19		STOP

The program was typed on a Flexowriter, which punched paper tape and had a fairly large character set (including both upper and lower case letters); at MIT they also had superscript digits ^{0}, ^{1}, ..., ^{9} and a vertical line $\lvert$. The language used the vertical line to indicate *subscripts;* thus the "$5(a\lvert i)^3$" on line 9 means $5a_i^3$.

A programmer would insert his 11 input values for the TPK algorithm into the place shown on line *1*; then they would be converted to binary notation and stored on the magnetic drum as variables v_1, v_2, ..., v_{11}. If the numbers had a simple arithmetic pattern, an abbreviation could also be used; e.g.,

$$v\lvert N = 1(.5)\,2\,(.25)\,3.5\,(1)\,5.5$$

would set $(v_1, \ldots, v_{11}) \leftarrow 1$, 1.5, 2, 2.25, 2.5, 2.75, 3, 3.25, 3.5, 4.5, 5.5). If desired, a special code could be punched on the Flexowriter tape in line *1*, allowing the operator to substitute a data tape at that point before reading in the rest of the source program.

Lines *2–7* are a loop that moves the variables v_1, ..., v_{11} from the drum to variables a_0, ..., a_{10} in core. (All variables were in core unless specifically assigned to the drum by an ASSIGN or $\lvert$N instruction. This was an advanced feature of the system not needed in small problems.) The only thing that isn't self-explanatory about lines *2–7* is line *7*; "CP k," means "if the last expression computed was negative, go to the instruction labeled k."

In line *9*, F^1 denotes square root and F^{11} denotes absolute value. In line *14*, "SP" denotes an unconditional jump. (CP and SP were the standard mnemonics for jumps in WHIRLWIND machine language.) Thus, except for control statements—for which there was no existing mathematical convention—Laning and Zierler's notation was quite easy to read.

Their expressions featured normal operator precedence, as well as implied multiplication and exponentiation; and they even included a built-in Runge–Kutta mechanism for integrating a system of differential equations if the programmer wrote formulas such as

$$Dx = y + 1,$$
$$Dy = -x,$$

where D stands for d/dt! Another innovation, designed to help debugging, was to execute statement number 100 after any arithmetic error message, if 100 was a PRINT statement.

According to [LM 70], Laning first wrote a prototype algebraic translator in the summer of 1952. He and Zierler had extended it to a usable system by May 1953, when the WHIRLWIND had only 1024 16-bit words of core memory in addition to its drum. The version described in [LZ 54] utilized 2048 words and drum, but earlier compromises due to such extreme core limitations caused it to be quite slow. The source code was translated into blocks of subroutine calls, stored on the drum, and after being transferred to core storage (one equation's worth at a time) these subroutines invoked the standard floating-point interpretive routines on the WHIRLWIND [AL 54, p. 64].

> The use of a small number of standard closed subroutines has certain advantages of logical simplicity; however, it also often results in the execution of numerous unnecessary operations. This fact, plus the frequent reference to the drum required in calling in equations, results in a reduction of computing speed of the order of magnitude of ten to one from an efficient computer program.

From a practical standpoint, those were damning words. Laning recalled, eleven years later, that [LA 65]

> This was in the days when machine time was king, and people-time was worthless (particularly since I was not even on the Whirlwind staff). . . . [The program] did perhaps pay for itself a few times when a complex problem required solutions with a twenty-four hour deadline.

In a recent search of his files, Laning found a listing of the WHIRLWIND compiler's first substantial application [LA 76]:

> The problem addressed is that of a three-dimensional lead pursuit course flown by one aircraft attacking another, including the fire control equations. What makes this personally interesting to me is tied in with the fact that for roughly five years previous to this time the [MIT Instrumentation] Lab had managed and operated the MIT Rockefeller Differential Analyzer with the principal purpose of solving this general class of problem. Unfortunately, the full three dimensional problem required more integrators than the RDA possessed.

My colleagues who formulated the problem were very skeptical that it could be solved in any reasonable fashion. As a challenge, Zierler and I sat down with them in a 2½ hour coding session, at least half of which was spent in defining notation. The tape was punched, and with the usual beginner's luck it ran successfully the first time! Although we never seriously capitalized on this capability, for reasons of cost and computer availability, my own ego probably never before or since received such a boost.

The lead-pursuit source program consisted of 79 statements, including 29 that merely assigned initial data values. These statements also included seven uses of the differential equation feature.

Laning describes his original parsing technique as follows [LA 76]:

Nested parentheses were handled by a sequence of generated branch instructions (sp). In a one-pass operation the symbols were read and code generated a symbol at a time; the actual execution sequence used in-line sp orders to hop about from one point to another. The code used some rudimentary stacks, but was sufficiently intricate that I didn't understand it without extreme concentration even when I wrote it. . . . Structured programs were not known in 1953!

The notion of operator precedence as a formal concept did not occur to me at the time; I lived in fear that someone would write a perfectly reasonable algebraic expression that my system would not analyze correctly.

Plans for a much expanded WHIRLWIND compiler were dropped when the MIT Instrumentation Lab acquired its own computer, an IBM 650. Laning and his colleagues Philip C. Hankins and Charles P. Werner developed a compiler called MAC for this machine in 1957 and 1958. Although MAC falls out of the time period covered by our story, it deserves brief mention here because of its unusual three-line format proposed by R. H. Battin circa 1956, somewhat like Zuse's original language. For example, the statement

$$
\begin{array}{l|l}
\text{E} & \hspace{5.5cm} 3 \\
\text{M} & \quad Y = SQRT(ABS(A \hspace{1.2cm})) = 5\ A \\
\text{S} & \hspace{3cm} I + 1 \hspace{1.5cm} I + 1
\end{array}
$$

would be punched on three cards. Although this language has not become widely known, it was very successful locally: MAC compilers were later developed for use with IBM 704, 709, 7090, and 360 computers, as well as the Honeywell H800 and H1800 and the CDC 3600. (See [LM 70].) "At the present time [1976], MAC and FORTRAN have about equal use at CSDL," according to [LA 76]; here CSDL means C. S. Draper Laboratory, the successor to MIT Instrumentation Lab.

But we had better get back to our story of the early days.

FORTRAN **0**

During the first part of 1954, John Backus began to assemble a group of people within IBM to work on improved systems of automatic programming (see [BA 76]). Shortly after learning of the Laning and Zierler system at the ONR meeting in May, Backus wrote to Laning that "our formulation of the problem is very similar to yours: however, we have done no programming or even detailed planning." Within two weeks, Backus and his co-workers Harlan Herrick and Irving Ziller visited MIT in order to see the Laning–Zierler system in operation. The big problem facing them was to implement such a language with suitable efficiency [BH 64, p. 382]:

> At that time, most programmers wrote symbolic machine instructions exclusively (some even used absolute octal or decimal machine instructions). Almost to a man, they firmly believed that any mechanical coding method would fail to apply that versatile ingenuity which each programmer felt he possessed and constantly needed in his work. Therefore, it was agreed, compilers could only turn out code which would be intolerably less efficient than human coding (intolerable, that is, unless that inefficiency could be buried under larger, but desirable, inefficiencies such as the programmed floating-point arithmetic usually required then). . . .
>
> [Our development group] had one primary fear. After working long and hard to produce a good translator program, an important application might promptly turn up which would confirm the views of the sceptics: . . . its object program would run at half the speed of a hand-coded version. It was felt that such an occurrence, or several of them, would almost completely block acceptance of the system.

By November 1954, Backus's group had specified "The IBM Mathematical FORmula TRANslating system, FORTRAN". (Almost all the languages we shall discuss from now on had acronyms.) The first paragraph of their report [IB 54] emphasizes that previous systems had offered the choice of easy coding and slow execution or laborious coding and fast execution, but FORTRAN would provide the best of both worlds. It also places specific emphasis on the IBM 704; machine independence was not a primary goal, although a concise mathematical notation that "does not resemble a machine language" was definitely considered important. Furthermore they stated that "each future IBM calculator should have a system similar to FORTRAN accompanying it" [IB 54].

> It is felt that FORTRAN offers as convenient a language for stating problems for machine solution as is now known. . . . After an hour course in FORTRAN notation, the average programmer can fully understand the steps of a procedure stated in FORTRAN language without any additional comments.

They went on to describe the considerable economic advantages of programming in such a language.

Perhaps the reader thinks he knows FORTRAN already; it is certainly the earliest high-level language that is still in use. However, few people have seen the original 1954 version of FORTRAN, so it is instructive to study TPK as it might have been expressed in "FORTRAN 0":

```
 1          DIMENSION A(11)
 2          READ A
 3      2   DO 3,8,11 J=1,11
 4      3   I=11-J
 5          Y=SQRT(ABS(A(I+1)))+5*A(I+1)**3
 6          IF (400 >= Y) 8,4
 7      4   PRINT I,999.
 8            GO TO 2
 9      8   PRINT I,Y
10     11   STOP
```

The READ and PRINT statements do not mention any FORMATs, although an extension to format specification was contemplated [p. 26]; programmer-defined functions were also under consideration [p. 27]. The DO statement in line 3 means, "Do statements 3 thru 8 and then go to 11"; the abbreviation "DO 8 J = 1,11" was also allowed at that time, but the original general form is shown here for fun. Note that the IF statement was originally only a two-way branch (line 6); the relation could be =, >, or > =. On line 5 we note that function names need not end in F; they were required to be at least three characters long, and there was no maximum limit (except that expressions could not be longer than 750 characters). Conversely, the names of variables were restricted to be at most *two* characters long at this time; but this in itself was an innovation, FORTRAN being the first language in which a variable's name could be longer than one letter, contrary to established mathematical conventions. Note that mixed mode arithmetic was allowed; the compiler was going to convert "5" to "5.0" in line 5. A final curiosity about this program is the GO TO statement on line 8; this did not begin the DO loop all over again, it merely initiated the next iteration.

Several things besides mixed mode arithmetic were allowed in FORTRAN 0 but withdrawn during implementation, notably: (a) subscripted subscripts to one level, such as A(M(I, J),N(K, L)) were allowed; (b) subscripts of the form N*I + J were allowed, provided that at least two of the variables N, I, J were declared to be "relatively constant" (i.e., infrequently changing); (c) a RELABEL statement was intended to permute array indices cyclically without physically moving the array in storage. For example, "RELABEL A(3)" was to be like setting (A(1), A(2), A(3), ..., A(n)) ← (A(3), ..., A(n), A(1), A(2)).

Incidentally, statements were called *formulas* throughout the 1954 document; there were arithmetic formulas, DO formulas, GO TO formulas, etc. Similar terminology had been used by Böhm, while Laning and Zierler and Glennie spoke of "equations"; Grace Hopper called them "operations." Furthermore, the word "compiler" is never used in [IB 54]; there is a FORTRAN language and a FORTRAN system, but not a FORTRAN compiler.

The FORTRAN 0 document represents the first attempt to define the syntax of a programming language rigorously; Backus's important notation [BA 59], which eventually became "BNF" [KN 64], can be seen in embryonic form here.

With the FORTRAN language defined, it "only" remained to implement the system. It is clear from reading [IB 54] that considerable plans had already been made toward the implementation during 1954; however, the full job took 2.5 more years (18 man-years), so we shall leave the IBM group at work while we consider other developments.

Brooker's AUTOCODE

Back in Manchester, R. A. Brooker introduced a new type of AUTOCODE for the MARK I machine. This language was much "cleaner" than Glennie's, being nearly machine-independent and using programmed floating-point arithmetic; but it allowed only one operation per line, there were few mnemonic names, and there was no way for a user to define subroutines. The first plans for this language, as of March 1954, appeared in [BR 55], and the language eventually implemented [BR 56, pp. 155–157] was almost the same. Brooker's emphasis on economy of description was especially noteworthy: "What the author aimed at was two sides of a foolscap sheet with possibly a third side to describe an example" [BR 55].

The floating point variables in Brooker's MARK I AUTOCODE are called $v1, v2, \ldots$, and the integer variables—which may be used also as indices (subscripts)—are called $n1, n2, \ldots$. The AUTOCODE for TPK is easily readable with only a few auxiliary comments, given the memory assignments $a_i = v_{1+i}$, $y = v_{12}$, $i = n_2$:

6	$n1 = 1$	sets $n_1 = 1$
1	$vn1 = I$	reads input into v_{n_1}
	$n1 = n1 + 1$	
	$j1, 11 \geq n1$	jumps to 1 if $n_1 \leq 11$
	$n1 = 11$	
2	$*n2 = n1 - 1$	prints $i = n_1 - 1$
	$v12 = vn1$	
	$j3, v12 \geq 0{\cdot}0$	
	$v12 = 0{\cdot}0 - v12$	sets $v_{12} = |v_{12}|$
3	$v12 = F1(v12)$	$(v_{12} = \sqrt{|a_i|})$
	$v13 = 5{\cdot}0 \otimes vn1$	

$$v13 = vn1 \otimes v13$$
$$v13 = vn1 \otimes v13 \qquad (v_{13} = 5a_i^3)$$
$$v12 = v12 + v13 \qquad (y = f(a_i))$$
$$j4, \; v12 > 400 \cdot 0$$

	$^*v12 = v12$	prints y
	j5	
4	$^*v12 = 999 \cdot 0$	prints 999
5	$n1 = n1 - 1$	
	$j2, \; n1 > 0$	tests for last cycle
	H	halt
	$(j6)$	starts programme

The final instruction illustrates an interesting innovation: An instruction or group of instructions in parentheses was obeyed immediately, rather than added to the program. Thus "$(j6)$" jumps to statement 6.

This language is not at a very high level, but Brooker's main concern was simplicity and a desire to keep information flowing smoothly to and from the electrostatic high-speed memory. MARK I's electrostatic memory consisted of only 512 20-bit words, and it was necessary to make frequent transfers from and to the 32K-word drum; floating-point subroutines could compute while the next block of program was being read in. Thus two of the principal difficulties facing a programmer—scaling and coping with the two-level store—were removed by his AUTOCODE system, and it was heavily used. For example [BR 58, p. 16]:

> Since its completion in 1955 the MARK I AUTOCODE has been used extensively for about 12 hours a week as the basis of a computing service for which customers write their own programs and post them to us.

George E. Felton, who developed the first AUTOCODE for the Ferranti PEGASUS, says in [FE 60] that its specification "clearly owes much to Mr. R. A. Brooker." Incidentally, Brooker's next AUTOCODE (for the MARK II or "Mercury" computer, first delivered in 1957) was considerably more ambitious; see [BR 58, BR 58', BR 60].

Russian Programming Programs

Work on automatic programming began in Russia at the Mathematical Institute of the Soviet Academy of Sciences, and at the Academy's computation center, which originally was part of the Institute of Exact Mechanics and Computing Technique. The early Russian systems were appropriately called programming programs [Programmiruĭoshchye Programmy]—or ПП for short. An experimental program ПП-1 for the STRELA computer was constructed by E. Z. Lĭubimskiĭ and S. S. Kamynin during the summer of 1954; and these two authors, together with M.R. Shura-Bura, E. L. Lukhovitskaĩa, and V. S. Shtarkman, completed a production compiler called ПП-2 in February 1955. This compiler is described in [KL 58]. Meanwhile, A. P. Ershov began in December 1954 to design another programming program, for the BESM computer, with the help of L.N. Korolev, L. D. Panova, V. D. Poderñugin and V. M. Kurochkin; this compiler, called simply ПП, was completed in March 1956, and it is described in Ershov's book [ER 58]. A review of these developments appears in [KO 58].

In both of these cases, and in the later system ПП-C completed in 1957 (see [ER 58′]), the language was based on a notation for expressing programs developed by A. A. Lïapunov in 1953. Lïapunov's operator schemata [LJ 58] provide a concise way to represent program structure in a linear manner; in some ways this approach is analogous to the ideas of Curry we have already considered, but it is somewhat more elegant and it became widely used in Russia.

Let us consider first how the TPK algorithm (exclusive of input–output) can be described in ПП-2. The overall operator scheme for the program would be written

$$A_1 \underset{13}{\lrcorner} Z_2 A_3 R_4 \overset{6}{\ulcorner} A_5 \overset{4}{\urcorner} A_6 R_7 \underset{10}{\llcorner} A_8 N_9 \overset{11}{\ulcorner} \lrcorner A_{10} \overset{9}{\urcorner} A_{11} F_{12} R_{13} \underset{2}{\llcorner} N_{14} .$$

Here the operators are numbered 1 through 14;

$$\overset{n}{\ulcorner} \quad \text{and} \quad \underset{m}{\llcorner}$$

mean "go to operator n if true, go to operator m if false," respectively, while

$$\overset{i}{\urcorner} \quad \text{and} \quad \underset{i}{\lrcorner}$$

are the corresponding notations for "coming from operator i." This operator scheme was not itself input to the programming program explicitly, it would be kept by the programmer in lieu of a flowchart. The details of operators would be written separately and input to ПП-2 after dividing them into operators of types R (relational), A (arithmetic), Z (dispatch), F (address modification), O (restoration), and N (nonstandard, i.e., machine language). In the above case, the details are essentially this:

R_4.	$p_1; 6, 5$	[if p_1 is true go to 6 else to 5]
R_7.	$p_2; 8, 10$	[if p_2 is true go to 8 else to 10]
R_{13}.	$p_3; 14, 2$	[if p_3 is true go to 14 else to 2]
p_1.	$c_3 < v_2$	[$0 < x$]
p_2.	$c_4 < v_3$	[$400 < y$]
p_3.	$v_6 < c_3$	[$i < 0$]
A_1.	$c_6 = v_6$	[$10 = i$, i.e., set i equal to 10]
A_3.	$v_1 = v_2$	[$a_i = x$]
A_5.	$c_3 - v_2 = v_2$	[$0 - x = x$]

A_6.	$(\sqrt{v_2}) + (c_5 \cdot v_1 \cdot v_1 \cdot v_1) = v_3$	$[(\sqrt{x}) + (5 \cdot a_i \cdot a_i \cdot a_i) = y]$
A_8.	$v_6 = v_4, c_2 = v_5$	$[i = b_i, 999 = c_i]$
A_{10}.	$v_6 = v_4, v_3 = v_5$	$[i = b_i, y = c_i]$
A_{11}.	$v_6 - c_1 = v_6$	$[i - 1 = i]$
Z_2.	$v_1; 3, 6$	[dispatch a_i to special cell, in operators 3 thru 6]
F_{12}.	$v_6; 2, 10$	[modify addresses depending on parameter i, in operators 2 thru 10]
N_9.	BP 11	[go to operator 11]
N_{14}.	OST	[stop]
Dependence on parameter v_6.	$v_1, v_1, -1; v_4, v_5, +2$	[when i changes, v_1 goes down by 1, v_4 through v_5 go up 2]
c_1.	$.1 \cdot 10^1$	[1]
c_2.	$.999 \cdot 10^3$	[999]
c_3.	0	
c_4.	$.4 \cdot 10^3$	[400]
c_5.	$.5 \cdot 10^1$	[5]
Working cells: 100,119		[compiled program can use locations 100–119 for temp storage]
v_1.	130	[initial address of a_i]
v_2.	131	[address of x]
v_3.	132	[address of y]
v_4.	133	[initial address of b_i]
v_5.	134	[initial address of c_i]
v_6.	154	[address of i]

Operator 1 initializes i, then operators 2–13 are the loop on i. Operator 2 moves a_i to a fixed cell, and makes sure that operators 3–6 use this fixed cell; this programmer-supplied optimization means that fewer addresses in instructions have to be modified when i changes. Operators 3–5 set $x = |a_i|$, and operator 6 sets $y = f(a_i)$. (Note the parentheses in operator 6; precedence was not recognized.) Operators 7–10 store the desired outputs in memory; operators 11 and 12 decrease i and appropriately adjust the addresses of quantities that depend on i. Operators 13 and 14 control looping and stopping.

The algorithms used in ПП-2 are quite interesting from the standpoint of compiler history; for example, they avoided the recomputation of common subexpressions within a single formula, and they carefully optimized the use of working storage. They also produced efficient code for relational operators compounded from a series of elementary relations, so that, for example,

$$(p_1 \vee (p_2 \cdot p_3) \vee \overline{p_4}) \cdot p_5 \vee p_6$$

would be compiled as shown in Fig. 3.

Ershov's ПП language improved on ПП-2 in several respects, notably: (a) the individual operators need not be numbered, and they may be intermixed in the natural sequence; (b) no address modification need be specified, and there was a special notation for loops; (c) the storage for variables was allocated semiautomatically; (d) operator precedence could be used to reduce

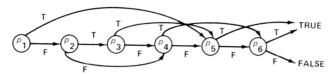

Figure 3 Optimization of Boolean expressions in an early Russian compiler.

the number of parentheses within expressions. The TPK algorithm looks like this in ПП:

1	Massiv a (11 íacheek)	[declares an array of 11 cells]
2	$a_0 = 0$	[address in array a]
3	$a_j = -1 \cdot j + 10$	[address in array a depending on j]
4	$j: j_{\text{nach}} = 0, j_{\text{kon}} = 11$	[information on loop indexes]
5	$0, 11, 10, 5, y, 400, 999, i$	[list of remaining constants and variables]
6	$(\text{Ma}, 080, 0, a_0); (\text{Mb}, 0, 0\bar{1}, 0);$	
7	$[10 - j \Rightarrow i; \sqrt{\underset{0101}{\;}} \bmod a_j + 5 \times a_j^3 \Rightarrow y;$	
8	$\text{R}(y, 0102; \ulcorner (400, \infty));$	

After declarations on lines *1–5*, the program appears here on lines *6–10*. In ПП each loop was associated with a different index name, and the linear dependence of array variables on loop indices was specified as in line *3*; note that a_j does not mean the jth element of a; it means an element of a that *depends* on j. The commands in line *6* are BESM machine language instructions that read 11 words into memory starting at a_0. Line *7* shows the beginning of the loop on j, which ends at the "]" on line *10*; all loop indices must step by $+1$. (The initial and final-plus-one values for the j loop are specified on line *4*.) Line *8* is a relational operator that means, "If y is in the interval $(400, \infty)$, i.e., if $y > 400$, go to label 0101; otherwise go to 0102." Labels were given as hexadecimal numbers, and the notation

9	$\underset{0101}{\llcorner} \text{Vyd } i, \Rightarrow 0; \text{Vyd } 999, \Rightarrow 0; \overset{0103}{\ulcorner};$
10	$\underset{0102}{\llcorner} \text{Vyd } i, \Rightarrow 0; \text{Vyd } y, \Rightarrow 0; \underset{0103}{\llcorner}]; \text{STOP}$

indicates the program location of label n. The "Vyd" instruction in lines *9* and *10* means convert to decimal, and ", $\Rightarrow 0$" means print. Everything else should be self-explanatory.

The Russian computers had no alphabetic input or output, so the programs written in ПП-2 and ПП were converted into numeric codes. This was a rather tedious and intricate process, usually performed by two specialists who would compare their independent hand transliterations in order to prevent errors. As an example of this encoding process, here is how the above program would actually have been converted into BESM words in the form required by ΠΠ. [The hexadecimal digits were written 0, 1, ..., 9, $\bar{0}$, $\bar{1}$, ..., $\bar{5}$. A 39-bit word in BESM could be represented either in instruction format,

$$bbh\ bqhh\ bqhh\ bqhh,$$

where b denotes a binary digit (0 or 1), q a quaternary digit (0, 1, 2, or 3), and h a hexadecimal digit; or in floating-binary numeric format,

$$\pm 2^k, hh\ hh\ hh\ hh,$$

where k is a decimal number between -32 and $+31$ inclusive. Both of these representations were used at various times in the encoding of a ΠΠ program as shown below.]

Location	Contents	Meaning
07	000 0000 0000 0000	no space needed for special subroutines
08	000 0000 0000 0013	last entry in array descriptor table
09	000 0000 0000 0015	first entry for constants and variables
$0\bar{0}$	000 0000 0000 001$\bar{2}$	last entry for constants and variables
$0\bar{1}$	000 0000 0000 002$\bar{5}$	base address for encoded program scheme
$0\bar{2}$	000 0000 0000 0042	last entry of encoded program
$0\bar{3}$	000 0000 0000 029$\bar{5}$	base address for "block γ"
$0\bar{4}$	000 0000 0000 02$\bar{1}\bar{5}$	base address for "block α"
$0\bar{5}$	000 0000 0000 023$\bar{5}$	base address for "block β"
10	01$\bar{5}$ 0000 000$\bar{1}$ 0000	a = array of size 11
11	000 1001 0000 0000	coefficient of -1 for linear dependency
12	2^1, 00 00 00 00	$a_0 = 0$ relative to a
13	2^2, 14 00 00 0$\bar{0}$	$a_j = -1 \cdot j + 10$ relative to a
14	000 0015 0016 0000	j = loop index from 0 to 11
15	2^{-32}, 00 00 00 00	0
16	2^4, $\bar{1}$0 00 00 00	11
17	2^4, $\bar{0}$0 00 00 00	10
18	2^3, $\bar{0}$0 00 00 00	5
19	2^9, $\bar{2}$8 00 00 00	400
$1\bar{0}$	2^{10}, $\bar{5}$9 $\bar{2}$0 00 00	999
$1\bar{1}$	000 0000 0000 0000	i
$1\bar{2}$	000 0000 0000 0000	y
30	016 0080 0000 0012	(Ma, 080, 0, a_0)
31	017 0000 000$\bar{1}$ 0000	(Mb, 0, 0$\bar{1}$, 0)

Location	Contents	Meaning
32	018 0014 0000 0000	$[_j$
33	2^0, 17 04 14 08	$10 \times j \Rightarrow$
34	2^0, $1\overline{1}$ $\overline{53}$ $\overline{52}$ 13	$i \sqrt{}$ mod a_j
35	2^0, 03 18 09 13	$+ 5 \times a_j$
36	2^0, $0\overline{2}$ 08 $1\overline{2}$ 00	$^3 \Rightarrow y$
37	018 0000 $001\overline{2}$ 0102	$R(y, 0102;$
38	008 0019 0000 0101	$\ulcorner$ (400, $\propto$))
39	018 0101 0000 0000	$\llcorner$
$3\overline{0}$	2^0, $\overline{54}$ $1\overline{1}$ 07 00	Vyd $i, \Rightarrow 0$
$3\overline{1}$	2^0, $\overline{54}$ $1\overline{0}$ 07 00	Vyd 999, $\Rightarrow 0$
$3\overline{2}$	$01\overline{1}$ 0000 0000 0103	$\ulcorner$
$3\overline{3}$	018 0102 0000 0000	$\llcorner$
$3\overline{4}$	2^0, $\overline{54}$ $1\overline{1}$ 07 00	Vyd $i, \Rightarrow 0$
$3\overline{5}$	2^0, $\overline{54}$ $1\overline{2}$ 07 00	Vyd $y, \Rightarrow 0$
40	018 0103 0000 0000	$\llcorner$
41	$01\overline{5}$ $13\overline{55}$ $13\overline{55}$ $13\overline{55}$	$]$
42	$01\overline{5}$ 0000 0000 0000	STOP

The BESM had 1024 words of core memory, plus some high-speed read-only memory, and a magnetic drum holding 5×1024 words. The ПП compiler worked in three passes (formulas and relations, loops, final assembly), and it contained a total of 1200 instructions plus 150 constants. Ershov published detailed specifications of its structure and all its algorithms in [ER 58], a book that was extremely influential at the time—for example, a Chinese translation was published in Peking in 1959. The book shows that Ershov was aware of Rutishauser's work [p. 9], but he gave no other references to non-Russian sources.

A Western Development

Computer professionals at the Boeing Airplane Company in Seattle, Washington, felt that "in this jet age, it is vital to shorten the time from the definition of a problem to its solution." So they introduced BACAIC, the Boe-

ing Airplane Company Algebraic Interpretive Computing system for the
IBM 701 computer.

BACAIC was an interesting language and compiler developed by Manda-
lay Grems and R. E. Porter, who began work on the system in the latter part
of 1954; they presented it at the Western Joint Computer Conference held in
San Francisco, in February 1956 [GP 56]. Although the "I" in BACAIC stands
for "interpretive," their system actually translated algebraic expressions
into machine-language calls on subroutines, with due regard for parentheses
and precedence, so we would now call it a compiler.

The BACAIC language was unusual in several respects, especially in its
control structure, which assumed one-level iterations over the entire program; a program was considered to be a nearly straight-line computation to
be applied to various "cases" of data. There were no subscripted variables;
however, the TPK algorithm could be performed by inputting the data in reverse order using the following program:

1. $I - K1*I$
2. X
3. WHN X GRT $K2$ USE 5
4. $K2 - X*2$
5. SRT $2 + K3 . X$ PWR $K4$
6. WHN 5 GRT $K5$ USE 8
7. TRN 9
8. $K6*5$
9. TAB I 5

Here "$*$" is used for assignment, and ".'' for multiplication; variables are
given single-letter names (except K), and constants are denoted by $K1$
through $K99$. The above program is to be used with the following input data:

Case 1. $K1 = 1.0$ $K2 = 0.0$ $K3 = 5.0$ $K4 = 3.0$
$K5 = 400.0$ $K6 = 999.0$ $I = 11.0$ $X = a_{10}$

Case 2. $X = a_9$

Case 3. $X = a_8$

.

.

.

Case 11. $X = a_0$

Data values are identified by name when input; all variables are zero initially, and values carry over from one case to the next unless changed. For
example, expression 1 means "$I - 1 \rightarrow I$," so the initial value $I = 11$ needs
to be input only in case 1.

Expressions 2–4 ensure that the value of expression 2 is the absolute
value of X when we get to expression 5. (The "2" in expression 4 means
expression 2, not the constant 2.) Expression 5 therefore has the value $f(X)$.

A typical way to use BACAIC was to print the values associated with all expressions 1, 2, . . . ; this was a good way to locate errors. Expression 7 in the above program is an unconditional jump; expression 9 says that the values of I and of expression 5 should be printed.

The BACAIC system was easy to learn and to use, but the language was too restrictive for general-purpose computing. One novel feature was its "check-out mode," in which the user furnished hand-calculated data and the machine would print out only the discrepancies it found.

According to [BE 57], BACAIC became operational also on the IBM 650 computer, in August 1956.

Kompilers

Another independent development was taking place almost simultaneously at the University of California Radiation Laboratory in Livermore, California; this work has apparently never been published, except as an internal report [EK 55]. In 1954, A. Kenton Elsworth began to experiment with the translation of algebraic equations into IBM 701 machine language, and called his program Kompiler 1; at that time he dealt with only individual formulas, without control statements or constants or input–output. Elsworth and his associates Robert Kuhn, Leona Schloss, and Kenneth Tiede went on to implement a working system named Kompiler 2 during the following year. This system is somewhat similar in flavor to ПП-2, except that it is based on flow diagrams instead of operator schemata. They characterized its status in the following way [EK 55, p. 4]:

> In many ways Kompiler is an experimental model; it is therefore somewhat limited in applications. For example it is designed to handle only full-word data and is restricted to fixed-point arithmetic. At the same time every effort was made to design a workable and worthwhile routine: the compiled code should approach very closely the efficiency of a hand-tailored code; learning to use it should be relatively easy; compilation itself is very fast.

In order to compensate for the fixed-point arithmetic, special features were included to facilitate scaling. As we shall see, this is perhaps Kompiler 2's most noteworthy aspect.

To solve the TPK problem, let us first agree to scale the numbers by writing

$$A_i = 2^{-10}a_i, \qquad Y = 2^{-10}y, \qquad I = 2^{-35}i.$$

Furthermore we will need to use the scaled constants

$$V = 5{\cdot}2^{-3}, \qquad F = 400{\cdot}2^{-10}, \qquad N = 999{\cdot}2^{-10}, \qquad W = 1{\cdot}2^{-35}.$$

The next step is to draw a special kind of flow diagram for the program, as shown in Fig. 4.

The third step is to assign the data storage, for example as follows:

$$61 \equiv I, \quad 63 \equiv Y, \quad 65 \equiv V, \quad 67 \equiv F, \quad 69 \equiv N, \quad 71 \equiv W;$$
$$81 \equiv A_0, \quad 83 \equiv A_1, \quad \ldots, \quad 101 \equiv A_{10}.$$

(Addresses in the IBM 701 go by half-words, but variables in Kompiler 2 occupy full words. Address 61 denotes half-words 60 and 61 in the "second frame" of the memory.)

The final step is to transcribe the flow-diagram information into a fixed format designated for keypunching. The source input to Kompiler 2 has two parts: the so-called "flow-diagram cards," one card per box in the flow diagram, and the "algebraic cards," one per complex equation. In our case the flow-diagram cards are

1CARD	61	2		235	0	103	310	310	135	0	61
2CARD	81	2		310	310	310	310	310	310	310	95	14
3CALC	101	8		65		101	8	63		
4TRPL	67	63	6							
5PLUS	69		63							
6PRNT	61	63	2	1	35	10				
7MINS	71	61	61							
8DECR	2									
9TRPL	61	Z	3							
10STOP										

and the algebraic cards are

1*ΔCARD
2*ΔPRNT
3ΔSRTΔABSA.−05+VA3.+13=Y

Here is a free translation of the meaning of the flow diagram cards:

1. Read data cards into locations beginning with 61 in steps of 2. The words of data are to be converted using respective scale codes 235, 0, 103, ..., 0; stop reading cards after the beginning location has become 61, i.e., immediately. [The scale code ddbb means to take the 10-digit data as a decimal fraction, multiply by 10^{dd}, convert to binary, and divide by 2^{bb}. In our case the first input datum will be punched as 1000000000, and the scale code 235 means that this is regarded first as $(10.00000000)_{10}$ and eventually converted to $(.00\ldots01010)_2 = 10 \cdot 2^{-35}$, the initial value of I. The initial value of N, with its scale code 310, would therefore be punched 9990000000. Up to seven words of data are punched per data card.]

2. Read data cards into locations beginning with 81 in steps of 2. The words of data are to be converted using respective scale codes 310, 310,

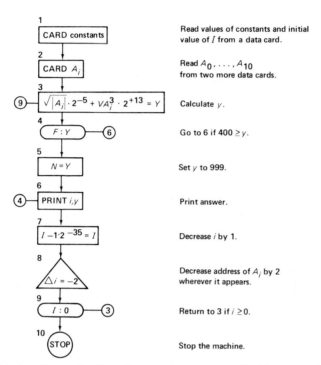

1

CARD constants — Read values of constants and initial value of I from a data card.

2

CARD A_i — Read $A_0, \ldots, A_{10}$ from two more data cards.

3

(9) $\sqrt{|A_i| \cdot 2^{-5} + VA_i^3 \cdot 2^{+13}} = Y$ — Calculate y.

4

$F : Y$ —(6) — Go to 6 if $400 \geq y$.

5

$N = Y$ — Set y to 999.

6

(4)— PRINT i, y — Print answer.

7

$I - 1 \cdot 2^{-35} = I$ — Decrease i by 1.

8

$\triangle i = -2$ — Decrease address of A_i by 2 wherever it appears.

9

$I : 0$ —(3) — Return to 3 if $i \geq 0$.

10

STOP — Stop the machine.

Figure 4 This flow diagram for Kompiler input is to be transcribed into numeric format and punched onto cards.

$\ldots$, 310; stop reading cards after the beginning location has become 95. The beginning location should advance by 14 between data cards (hence exactly two cards are to be read).

3. Calculate a formula using the variables in the respective locations 101 (which changes at step 8); 65; 101 (which changes at step 8); and 63.

4. If the contents of location 67 minus the contents of location 63 is nonnegative, go to step 6.

5. Store the contents of location 69 in location 63.

6. Print locations 61 through 63, with 2 words per line and 1 line per block. The respective scale factors are 35 and 10.

7. Subtract the contents of location 71 from the contents of location 61 and store the result in location 61.

8. Decrease all locations referring to step 8 (cf. step 3) by 2.

9. If the contents of location 61 is nonnegative (Z stands for zero), go to step 3.

10. Stop the machine.

The first two algebraic cards in the above example simply cause the library subroutines for card reading and line printing to be loaded with the object program. The third card is used to encode

$$\sqrt{|A_i|} \cdot 2^{-5} + VA_i^3 \cdot 2^{13} = Y.$$

The variable names on an algebraic card are actually nothing but dummy placeholders, since the storage locations must be specified on the corresponding CALC card. Thus, the third algebraic card could also have been punched as

$$3\Delta SRT\Delta ABSX. -05 + XX3. + 13 = X$$

without any effect on the result.

Kompiler 2 was used for several important production programs at Livermore. By 1959 it had been replaced by Kompiler 3, a rather highly developed system for the IBM 704 that used three-line format analogous to the notation of MAC (but apparently designed independently).

A Declarative Language

During 1955 and 1956, E. K. Blum at the U.S. Naval Ordnance Laboratory developed a language of a completely different type. This language ADES (Automatic Digital Encoding System) was presented at the ACM national meetings in 1955 (of which no proceedings were published) and in 1956 [BL 56''], and at the ONR symposium in 1956 [BL 56']. He described it as follows:

> The ADES language is essentially mathematical in structure. It is based on the theory of the recursive functions and the schemata for such functions, as given by Kleene [BL 56', p. 72].

> The ADES approach to automatic programming is believed to be entirely new. Mathematically, it has its foundations in the bedrock of the theory of recursive functions. The proposal to apply this theory to automatic programming was first made by C. C. Elgot, a former colleague of the author's. While at the Naval Ordnance Laboratory, Elgot did some research on a language for automatic programming. Some of his ideas were adapted to ADES [BL 56, p. iii].

A full description of the language was given in a lengthy report [BL 56]; it is rather difficult to understand several aspects of ADES, and we will content ourselves with a brief glimpse into its structure by considering the following ADES program for TPK. (The conventions of [BL 57'] are followed here since they are slightly simpler than the original proposals in [BL 56].)

1 $a_0 11 : q_0 11,$
2 $f_{50} = a \sqrt{\text{abs }} c_1 \cdots 5\, c_1\, c_1\, c_1,$
3 $d_{12} b_1 = r_0,$

4 $d_{22}b_2 = \leq b_3 \; 400, \; b_3, \; 999,$
5 $b_3 = f_{50} \, a_0 \, r_0,$
6 $r_0 = -10 \, q_0,$
7 $-0 \, q_0 \; 10 \, b_0 = f_0 \, b_1 \, b_2,$

Here is a rough translation: Line *1* is the so-called "computer table," meaning that input array a_0 has 11 positions, and that the "independent index symbol" q_0 takes 11 values. Line 2 defines the auxiliary function f_{50}, our $f(t)$; arithmetic expressions were defined in Łukasiewicz's parentheses-free notation, now commonly known as "left Polish." Variable c_1 here denotes the first parameter of the function. (Incidentally, "right Polish" notation seems to have been first proposed shortly afterwards by C. L. Hamblin in Australia; cf. [HA 57].)

Line *3* states that the dependent variable b_1 is equal to the dependent index r_0; the "d_{12}" here means that this is to be output as component 1 of a pair. Line *4* similarly defines b_2, which is to be component 2. This line is a "branch equation" meaning "**if** $b_3 \leq 400$ **then** b_3 **else** 999." (Such branch equations are an embryonic form of the conditional expressions introduced later by McCarthy into LISP and ALGOL. Blum remarked that the equation "$\leq x \, a, f, \; g$," could be replaced by $\varphi f + (1 - \varphi)g$, where φ is a function that takes the value 1 or 0 according as $x \leq a$ or $x > a$ [BL 56, p. 16].

The function φ is a primitive recursive function, and could be incorporated into the library as one of the given functions of the system. Nevertheless, the branch equation is included in the language for practical reasons. Many mathematicians are accustomed to that terminology, and it leads to more efficient programs.

In spite of these statements, Blum may well have intended that f or g not be evaluated or even defined when $\varphi = 0$ or 1, respectively.)

Line *5* says that b_3 is the result of applying f_{50} to the r_0th element of a_0. Line *6* explains that r_0 is $10 - q_0$. Finally, line *7* is a so-called "phase equation" that specifies the overall program flow, by saying that b_1 and b_2 are to be evaluated for $q_0 = 0, 1, \ldots, 10$.

The ADES language is "declarative" in the sense that the programmer states relationships between variable quantities without explicitly specifying the order of evaluation. John McCarthy put it this way, in 1958 [ER 58', p. 275]:

Mathematical notation as it presently exists was developed to facilitate stating mathematical facts, i.e., making declarative sentences. A program gives a machine orders and hence is usually constructed out of imperative sentences. This suggests that it will be necessary to invent new notations for describing complicated procedures, and we will not merely be able to take over intact the notations that mathematicians have used for making declarative sentences.

The transcript of a 1965 discussion of declarative versus imperative languages, with comments by P. Abrahams, P. Z. Ingerman, E. T. Irons, P. Naur, B. Raphael, R. V. Smith, C. Strachey, and J. W. Young, appears in *Comm. ACM* **9** (1966), 155–156, 165–166.

Although ADES was based on recursive function theory, it did not really include recursive procedures in the sense of ALGOL 60; it dealt primarily with special types of recursive equations over the integers, and the emphasis was on studying the memory requirements for evaluating such recurrences.

An experimental version of ADES was implemented on the IBM 650, and described in [BL 57, BL 57']. Blum's translation scheme was what we now recognize as a recursive approach to the problem, but the recursion was not explicitly stated; he essentially moved things on and off various stacks during the course of the algorithm. This implementation points up the severe problems people had to face in those days: The ADES encoder took 3500 instructions while the Type 650 calculator had room for only 2000, so it was necessary to insert the program card decks into the machine repeatedly, once for each equation! Because of further machine limitations, the above program would have been entered into the computer by punching the following information onto six cards:

```
A00  011  P02  Q00  011  P01  F50  E00  F02  F20
F06  C01  F04  F04  F04  005  C01  C01  C01  P01
D12  B01  E00  R00  P01  D22  B02  E00  F11  B03
400  P01  B03  P01  999  P01  B03  E00  F50  A00
R00  P01  R00  E00  F03  010  Q00  P01  P03  000
Q00  010  B00  E00  F00  B01  B02  P01   –    –
```

Here Pnn was a punctuation mark, Fnn a function code, etc. Actually the implemented version of ADES was a subset that did not allow auxiliary *f*-equations to be defined, so the definition of b_3 in line 5 would have been written out explicitly.

The IT

> In September, 1955, four members of the Purdue University Computing Laboratory—Mark Koschman, Sylvia Orgel, Alan Perlis, and Joseph W. Smith—began a series of conferences to discuss methods of automatic coding. Joanne Chipps joined the group in March, 1956. A compiler, programmed to be used on the Datatron, was the goal and result [OR 58, p. 1].

Purdue received one of the first DATATRON computers, manufactured by Electrodata Corporation (cf. *J. ACM* **2** (1955), 122, and [PE 55]); this machine was later known as the Burroughs 205. By the summer of 1956, the Purdue group had completed an outline of the basic logic and language of its compiler, and they presented some of their ideas at the ACM national meeting [CK 56]. Note that their 1956 paper used both the words "compiler" and "statement" in the modern sense; a comparison of the ONR 1954 and 1956 symposium proceedings makes it clear that the word "compiler" had by now acquired its new meaning. Furthermore the contemporary FORTRAN manuals [IB 56, IB 57] also used the term "statement" where [IB 54] had said "formula." Terminology was crystallizing.

At this time Perlis and Smith moved to the Carnegie Institute of Technology, taking copies of the flowcharts with them, and they adapted their language to the IBM 650 (a smaller machine) with the help of Harold Van Zoeren. The compiler was put into use in October 1956 (cf. [PS 57, p. 102]), and it became known as IT, the Internal Translator.

> Compilation proceeds in two phases: 1) translation from an IT program into a symbolic program, PIT and 2) assembly from a PIT program into a specific machine coded program, SPIT [PS 57', p. 1.23].

The intermediate "PIT" program was actually a program in SOAP language [PM 55], the source code for an excellent symbolic assembly program for the IBM 650. Perlis has stated that the existence of SOAP was an important simplifying factor in their implementation of IT, which was completed about three months after its authors had learned the 650 machine language.

This was the first really *useful* compiler; IT and IT's derivatives were used frequently and successfully in hundreds of computer installations until the 650 became obsolete. (Indeed, R. B. Wise stated in October 1958 that "the IT language is about the closest thing we have today to the universal language among computers" [WA 58, p. 131].) The previous systems we have discussed were important steps along the way, but none of them had the combination of powerful language and adequate implementation and documentation needed to make a significant impact in the use of machines. Furthermore, IT proved that useful compilers could be constructed for small computers without enormous investments of manpower.

Here is an IT program for TPK:

```
1:   READ
2:   3, I1, 10, −1, 0,
5:   Y1 ← "20E, ACI1 + 1)"
            + (5 × (C(I1 + 1) * 3))
6:   G3 IF 400.0 ≥ Y1
7:   Y1 ← 999
3:   TI1 TY1
10:  H
```

Each statement has an identifying number, but the numbers do not have to be in order. The READ statement does not specify the names of variables being input, since such information appears on the data cards themselves.

Floating-point variables are called Y1, Y2, . . . , or C1, C2, . . . , the above program assumes that the input data will specify 11 values for C1 through C11.

Statement number 2 designates an iteration of the following program through statement number 3 inclusive; variable I1 runs from 10 in steps of -1 down to 0. Statement 5 sets Y1 to $f(C_{I1+1})$; the notation "20E, x" is used for "language extension 20 applied to x," where extension 20 happens to be the floating-point square root subroutine. Note the use of mixed integer and floating-point arithmetic here. The redundant parentheses emphasize that IT did not deal with operator precedence, although in this case the parentheses need not have been written since IT evaluated expressions from right to left.

The letter A is used to denote absolute value, and $*$ means exponentiation. Statement 6 goes to 3 if $Y1 \le 400$; and statement 3 outputs $I1$ and $Y1$. Statement 10 means "halt."

Since the IBM 650 did not have such a rich character set at the time, the above program would actually be punched onto cards in the following form —using K for comma, M for minus, Q for quote, L and R for parentheses, etc.:

```
0001  READ                              F
0002  3K I1K 10K M1K 0K                 F
0005  Y1 Z Q 20EK ACLI1S1R Q            F
0005      S L5 X LCLI1S1R P 3RR         F
0006  G3 IF 400J0 W Y1                  F
0006  Y1 Z 999                          F
0003  TI1 TY1                           F
0010  H                                FF
```

The programmer also supplied a "header card," stating the limits on array subscripts actually used; in this case the header card would specify one I variable, one Y variable, 11 C variables, 10 statements. (It was possible to "go to" statement number n, where n was the value of any integer expression, so an array of statement locations was kept in the running program.)

The Purdue compiler language discussed in [CK 56] was in some respects richer than this; it included the ability to type out alphabetic information and to define new extensions (functions) in source language. On the other hand, [CK 56] did not mention iteration statements or data input. Joanne Chipps and Sylvia Orgel completed the DATATRON implementation in the summer of 1957; the language had lost the richer features in [CK 56], however, probably since they were unexpectedly difficult to implement. Our program in the Purdue compiler language [OR 58] would look like this:

```
input   i0   y0   c10   s10   f      [maximum subscripts used]
   1   e   "800e"   f                 [read input]
```

2	s	$i0 = 10$ f	[set $i_0 = 10$]
5	s	$y0 = $ ``$200e, aci0$'' $+ (5 \times (ci0p3))$ f	
6	r	$g8, r\ y0 \le 400.0$ f	[go to 8 if $y_0 \le 400.0$]
7	s	$y0 = 999$ f	
8	o	$i0$ f	[output i_0]
9	o	$y0$ f	[output y_0]
4	s	$i0 = i0 - 1$ f	
3	r	$g5, r\ 0 \le i0$ f	[go to 5 if $i_0 \ge 0$]
10	h	f	[halt]

Note that subscripts now may start with 0, and that each statement begins with a letter identifying its type. There are enough differences between this language and IT to make mechanical translation nontrivial.

The Arrival of FORTRAN

During all this time the ongoing work on FORTRAN was widely publicized. Max Goldstein may have summed up the feelings of many people when he made the following remark in June 1956: "As far as automatic programming goes, we have given it some thought and in the scientific spirit we intend to try out FORTRAN when it is available. However . . ." [GO 56, p. 40].

The day was coming. October 1956 witnessed another "first" in the history of programming languages, namely, a language description that was carefully written and beautifully typeset, neatly bound with a glossy cover. It began thus [IB 56]:

> This manual supersedes all earlier information about the FORTRAN system. It describes the system which will be made available during late 1956, and is intended to permit planning and FORTRAN coding in advance of that time [p. 1].

> Object programs produced by FORTRAN will be nearly as efficient as those written by good programmers [p. 2].

"Late 1956" was, of course, a euphemism for April 1957. Here is how Saul Rosen described FORTRAN's debut [RO 64, p. 4]:

> Like most of the early hardware and software systems, FORTRAN was late in delivery, and didn't really work when it was delivered. At first people thought it would never be done. Then when it was in field test, with many bugs, and with some of the most important parts unfinished, many thought it would never work. It gradually got to the point where a program in FORTRAN had a reasonable expectancy of compiling all the way through and maybe even of running.

In spite of these difficulties, it is clear that FORTRAN I was worth waiting for; it soon was accepted even more enthusiastically than its proponents had dreamed [BA 58, p. 246]:

> A survey in April of this year [1958] of twenty-six 704 installations indicates that over half of them use FORTRAN for more than half of their problems. Many use it for 80% or more of their work (particularly the newer installations) and almost all use it for some of their work. The latest records of the 704 users' organization, SHARE, show that there are some sixty installations equipped to use FORTRAN (representing 66 machines) and recent reports of usage indicate that more than half the machine instructions for these machines are being produced by FORTRAN.

On the other hand, not everyone had been converted. The second edition of programming's first textbook, by Wilkes, Wheeler, and Gill, was published in 1957, and the authors concluded their newly added chapter on "automatic programming" with the following cautionary remarks [WW 57, pp. 136–137]:

> The machine might accept formulas written in ordinary mathematical notation, and punched on a specially designed keyboard perforator. This would appear at first sight to be a very significant development, promising to reduce greatly the labor of programming. A number of schemes of formula recognition have been described or proposed, but on examination they are found to be of more limited utility than might have been hoped. . . . The best that one could expect a general purpose formula-recognition routine to do, would be to accept a statement of the problem after it had been examined, and if necessary transformed, by a numerical analyst. . . . Even in more favorable cases, experienced programmers will be able to obtain greater efficiency by using more conventional methods of programming.

An excellent paper by the authors of FORTRAN I, describing both the language and the organization of the compiler, was presented at the Western Joint Computer Conference in 1957 [BB 57]. The new techniques for global program flow analysis and optimization, due to Robert A. Nelson, Irving Ziller, Lois M. Haibt, and Sheldon Best, were particularly important. By expressing TPK in FORTRAN I we can see most of the language changes that had occurred:

```
C   THE TPK ALGORITHM, FORTRAN STYLE
    FUNF(T) = SQRTF(ABSF(T))+5.0*T**3
    DIMENSION A(11)
1   FORMAT(6F12.4)
    READ 1, A
```

```
     DO 10 J = 1, 11
     I = 11 - J
     Y = FUNF(A(I+1))
     IF (400.0-Y) 4, 8, 8
   4 PRINT 5, I
   5 FORMAT(I10, 10H TOO LARGE)
     GO TO 10
   8 PRINT 9, I, Y
   9 FORMAT(I10, F12.7)
  10 CONTINUE
     STOP 52525
```

The chief innovations were

(1)   Provision for comments: No programming language designer had thought to do this before! (Assembly languages had comment cards, but programs in higher-level languages were generally felt to be self-explanatory.)
(2)   Arithmetic statement functions were introduced. These were not mentioned in [IB 56], but they appeared in [BB 57] and (in detail) in the Programmer's Primer [IB 57, pp. 25, 30–31].
(3)   Formats are provided for input and output. This feature, due to Roy Nutt, was a major innovation in programming languages; it probably had a significant effect in making FORTRAN popular since input–output conversions were otherwise very awkward to express on the 704.
(4)   Lesser features not present in [IB 54] are the CONTINUE statement, and the ability to display a five-digit *octal* number when the machine halted at a STOP statement.

MATH-MATIC and FLOW-MATIC

Meanwhile, Grace Hopper's programming group at UNIVAC had also been busy. They had begun to develop an algebraic language in 1955, a project that was headed by Charles Katz, and the compiler was released to two installations for experimental tests in 1956 (cf. [BE 57, p. 112]). The language was originally called AT-3; but it received the catchier name MATH-MATIC in April 1957, when its preliminary manual [AB 57] was released. The following program for TPK gives MATH-MATIC's flavor:

```
(1)   READ-ITEM A(11)  .
(2)   VARY I 10(-1)0 SENTENCE 3 THRU 10  .
(3)   J = I+1  .
(4)   Y = SQR |A(J)| + 5*A(J)³  .
(5)   IF Y > 400, JUMP TO SENTENCE 8  .
(6)   PRINT-OUT I, Y  .
```

```
(7)   JUMP TO SENTENCE 10 .
(8)   Z = 999 .
(9)   PRINT-OUT I, Z .
(10)  IGNORE .
(11)  STOP .
```

The language was quite readable; note the vertical bar and the superscript 3 in sentence (4), indicating an extended character set that could be used with some peripherals. But the MATH-MATIC programmers did not share the FORTRAN group's enthusiasm for efficient machine code; they translated MATH-MATIC source language into A-3 (an extension of A-2), and this produced extremely inefficient programs, especially considering the fact that arithmetic was all done by floating point subroutines. The UNIVAC computer was no match for an IBM 704 even when it was expertly programmed, so MATH-MATIC was of limited utility.

The other product of Grace Hopper's programming staff was far more influential and successful, since it broke important new ground. This was what she originally called the data processing compiler in January, 1955; it was soon to be known as "B-0," later as the "Procedure Translator" [KM 57], and finally as FLOW-MATIC [HO 58, TA 60]. This language used English words, somewhat as MATH-MATIC did but more so, and its operations concentrated on business applications. The following examples are typical of FLOW-MATIC operations:

```
(1)   COMPARE PART-NUMBER (A) TO PART-NUMBER (B); IF
      GREATER GO TO OPERATION 13; IF EQUAL GO TO
      OPERATION 4; OTHERWISE GO TO OPERATION 2 .
(2)   READ-ITEM B; IF END OF DATA GO TO OPERATION 10 .
```

The allowable English templates are shown in [SA 69, pp. 317–322].

The first experimental B-0 compiler was operating in 1956 [HO 58, p. 171], and it was released to UNIVAC customers in 1958 [SA 69, p. 316]. FLOW-MATIC had a significant effect on the design of COBOL in 1959.

A Formula-Controlled Computer

At the international computing colloquium in Dresden, 1955, Klaus Samelson presented the rudiments of a particularly elegant approach to algebraic formula recognition [SA 55], improving on Böhm's technique. Samelson and his colleague F. L. Bauer developed this method during the ensuing years, and their subsequent paper [SB 59] describing it became well known.

One of the first things they did with their approach was to design a computer in which algebraic formulas *themselves* were the machine language. This computer design was submitted to the German patent office in the spring of 1957 [BS 57], and to the U.S. patent office (with the addition of wiring diagrams) a year later. Although the German patent was never granted, and the machines were never actually constructed, Bauer and Samelson eventually received U.S. Patent 3,047,228 for this work [BS 62].

Their patent describes four possible levels of language and machine. At the lowest level they introduced something like the language used on today's pocket calculators, allowing formulas consisting only of operators, parentheses, and numbers, while their highest level includes provision for a full-fledged programming language incorporating such features as variables with multiple subscripts and decimal arithmetic with arbitrary precision.

The language of Bauer and Samelson's highest-level machine is of principal concern to us here. A program for TPK could be entered on its keyboard by typing the following:

```
 1   ◇     0000.00000000 ⇒ a ↓ 11 ↑
 2          2.27 ⇒ a ↓ 1 ↑
 3          3.328 ⇒ a ↓ 2 ↑
        . . .
12          5.28764 ⇒ a ↓ 11 ↑
13          10 ⇒ i
14   44*    a ↓ i + 1 ↑ ⇒ t
15          √Bt + 5 × t × t t ⇒ y
16          i = □□ ⇒ i
17          y > 400 → 77*
18          y = □□□.□□□ ⇒ y
19          → 88*
20   77*    999 = □□□ ⇒ y
21   88*    i − 1 ⇒ i
22          i > −1 → 44*
```

(This is the American version; the German version would be the same if all the decimal points were replaced by commas.)

The "◇" at the beginning of this program is optional; it means that the ensuing statements up to the next label (44*) will not enter the machine's "formula storage," they will simply be performed and forgotten. The remainder of line *1* specifies storage allocation; it says that a is an 11-element array whose entries will contain at most 12 digits.

Lines *2–12* enter the data into array a. The machine also included a paper-tape reader in addition to its keyboard input; and if the data were to be entered from paper tape, lines *2–12* could be replaced by the code

```
              1 ⇒ i
       33*    •••••• ⇒ a ↓ i ↑
              i + 1 ⇒ i
              i < 12 → 33*
```

Actually this input convention was not specifically mentioned in the patent, but Bauer [BA 76'] recalls that such a format was intended.

The symbols ↓ and ↑ for subscripts would be entered on the keyboard but they would not actually appear on the printed page; instead, the printing mechanism was intended to shift up and down. The equal signs followed by square boxes on lines *16*, *18*, and *20* indicate output of a specified number of digits, showing the desired decimal point location. The rest of the above program should be self-explanatory, except perhaps for the B in line *15*, which denotes absolute value (*Betrag*).

Summary

We have now reached the end of our story, having covered essentially every high-level language whose design began before 1957. It is impossible to summarize all of the languages we have discussed by preparing a neat little chart; but everybody likes to see a neat little chart, so here is an attempt at a rough but perhaps meaningful comparison (see Table I).

Table I shows the principal mathematically oriented languages we have discussed, together with their chief authors and approximate year of greatest research or development activity. The "arithmetic" column shows X for languages that deal with integers, F for languages that deal with floating-point numbers, and S for languages that deal with scaled numbers. The remaining columns of Table I are filled with very subjective "ratings" of the languages and associated programming systems according to various criteria.

Implementation: Was the language implemented on a real computer? If so, how efficient and/or easy was it to use?

Readability: How easy is it to read programs in the language? (This includes such things as the variety of symbols usable for variables, the closeness to familiar notations.)

Control structures: At how high a level are the control structures? Are the existing control structures sufficiently powerful? (By "high level" we mean a level of abstraction; something the language has that the machine does not.)

Data structures: At how high a level are the data structures? (For example, can variables be subscripted?)

Machine independence: How much does a programmer need to keep in mind about the underlying machine?

Impact: How many people are known to have been directly influenced by this work at the time?

Finally there is a column of "firsts," which states some new thing(s) that this particular language or system introduced.

TABLE I

Language	Principal author(s)	Year	Arithmetic	Implementation	Readability	Control structures	Data structures	Machine independence	Impact	First
Plankalkül	Zuse	1945	X, S, F	F	D	A	A	B	C	Programming language, hierarchic data
Flow diagrams	Goldstine and von Neumann	1946	X, S	F	A	D	C	B	A	Accepted programming methodology
Composition	Curry	1948	X	F	D	C	D	C	F	Code generation algorithm
Short Code	Mauchly	1950	F	C	C	F	F	B	D	High-level language implemented
Intermediate PL	Burks	1950	?	F	A	D	C	A	F	Common subexpression notation
Klammerausdrücke	Rutishauser	1951	F	F	B	F	C	B	B	Simple code generation, loop expansion
Formules	Böhm	1951	X	F	B	D	C	B	D	Compiler in own language
AUTOCODE	Glennie	1952	X	C	C	C	C	D	D	Useful compiler
A-2	Hopper	1953	F	C	D	F	F	C	B	Macroexpander
Algebraic interpreter	Laning and Zierler	1953	F	B	A	D	C	A	B	Constants in formulas, manual for novices
AUTOCODE	Brooker	1954	X, F	A	B	D	C	A	C	Clean two-level storage
IIII-2	Kamynin and Liubimskiĭ	1954	F	B	C	D	C	B	D	Code optimization
IIII	Ershov	1955	F	B	B	C	C	B	C	Book about a compiler
BACAIC	Grems and Porter	1955	F	A	A	D	F	A	D	Use on two machines
Kompiler 2	Elsworth and Kuhn	1955	S	C	C	D	C	C	F	Scaling aids
ADES	Blum	1956	X, F	D	D	B	C	A	F	Declarative language
IT	Perlis	1956	X, F	A	B	C	C	A	B	Successful compiler
FORTRAN I	Backus	1956	X, F	A	A	C	C	A	A	I/O formats, global optimization
MATH-MATIC	Katz	1956	F	B	A	C	C	A	D	Heavy use of English
Patent 3,047,228	Bauer and Samelson	1957	F	D	B	D	C	B	C	Formula-controlled computer

The Sequel

What have we not seen, among all these languages? The most significant gaps are the lack of high-level *data structures* other than arrays (except in Zuse's unpublished language), the lack of high-level *control structures* other than iteration controlled by an index variable, and the lack of *recursion*. These three concepts, which now are considered absolutely fundamental in computer science, did not find their way into high-level languages until the 1960s. Our languages today probably have too many features, but the languages up to FORTRAN I had too few.

At the time our story leaves off, explosive growth in language development was about to take place, since the successful compilers touched off a language boom. Programming languages had reached a stage when people began to write translators from IT to FORTRAN [GR 58] and from FORTRAN to IT (cf. [BO 58], who describes the FOR TRANSIT compiler which was developed by a group of programmers at IBM under the direction of R. W. Bemer and D. Hemmes). An excellent survey of the state of automatic programming at the time was prepared by R. W. Bemer [BE 57].

Perhaps the most significant development then in the wind was the international project attempting to define a "standard" algorithmic language. Just after the 1955 meeting in Darmstadt, a group of European computer scientists began to plan a new language (cf. [LE 55]), under the auspices of the Gesellschaft für Angewandte Mathematik und Mechanik (GAMM, the Association for Applied Mathematics and Mechanics). They later invited American participation, and an ad hoc ACM committee chaired by Alan Perlis met several times beginning in January 1958. During the summer of that year, Zürich was the site of a meeting attended by representatives of the American and European committees: J. W. Backus, F. L. Bauer, H. Bottenbruch, C. Katz, A. J. Perlis, H. Rutishauser, K. Samelson, and J. H. Wegstein. (See [BB 58] for the language proposed by the European delegates.)

It seems fitting to bring our story to a close by stating the TPK algorithm in the "international algebraic language" (IAL, later called ALGOL) developed at that historic Zürich meeting [PS 58]:

```
procedure TPK(a[ ]) =: b[ ];
array (a[0:10], b[0:21]);
comment Given 11 input values a[0], ..., a[10], this procedure
                produces 22 output values b[0], ..., b[21], according to
                the classical TPK algorithm;
begin for i := 10(-1)0;
  begin y := f(a[i]);
        f(t) := sqrt(abs(t)) + 5 × t ↑ 3 ↓ ;
        if (y > 400); y := 999;
        b[20 - 20 × i] := i;
        b[21 - 2 × i] := y
```

end;
return;
integer (*i*)
end *TPK*

REFERENCES

[AB 57] R. Ash, E. Broadwin, V. Della Valle, C. Katz, M. Greene, A. Jenny, and L. Yu, "Preliminary Manual for MATH-MATIC and ARITH-MATIC systems (for Algebraic Translation and Compilation for UNIVAC I and II)." Remington Rand Univac, Philadelphia, Pennsylvania, 1957. ii + 125 pp.

[AL 54] C. W. Adams and J. H. Laning, Jr., The M.I.T. systems of automatic coding: Comprehensive, Summer Session, and Algebraic, *Symp. Automat. Programm. Digital Comput.* Office of Naval Research, Dept. of the Navy, Washington, D.C., 1954, pp. 40–68. [Although Laning is listed as co-author, he did not write the paper or attend the conference; in fact, he states that he learned of his "co-authorship" only 10 or 15 years later!]

[BA 54] J. W. Backus, The IBM 701 Speedcoding system, *J. ACM* **1**, 4–6 (1954).

[BA 58] J. W. Backus, Automatic programming: Properties and performance of FORTRAN systems I and II, *Mechanisation of Thought Processes, Nat. Phys. Lab. Symp. 10, 1958*, pp. 231–255. HM Stationery Office, London, 1959.

[BA 59] J. W. Backus, The syntax and semantics of the proposed International Algebraic Language of the Zürich ACM-GAMM conference, *Proc. Int. Conf. Inf. Processing*, pp. 125–131. UNESCO, Paris, 1959.

[BA 61] Philip Morrison and Emily Morrison (eds.), "Charles Babbage and his Calculating Engines," Dover, New York, 1961. xxxviii +400 pp.

[BA 76] J. W. Backus, Programming in America in the 1950s—some personal impressions, this volume.

[BA 76'] F. L. Bauer, letter to D. E. Knuth dated 7 July 1976. 2 pp.

[BA 79] J. W. Backus, The history of FORTRAN I, II, and III, *Ann. Hist. Comput.* **1**, 21–37 (1979).

[BB 57] J. W. Backus, R. J. Beeber, S. Best, R. Goldberg, L. Mitchell Haibt, H. L. Herrick, R. A. Nelson, D. Sayre, P. B. Sheridan, H. Stern, I. Ziller, R. A. Hughes, and R. Nutt, The FORTRAN automatic coding system, *Proc. Western Joint Comp. Conf., 1957*, pp. 188–197.

[BB 58] F. L. Bauer, H. Bottenbruch, H. Rutishauser, and K. Samelson, Proposal for a universal language for the description of computing processes, *in* "Computer Programming and Artificial Intelligence" (John W. Carr, III, ed.), pp. 353–373. University of Michigan, College of Engineering, Ann Arbor, 1958. [Translation of original German draft dated 9 May 1958, in Zürich.]

[BC 54] Arthur W. Burks, Irving M. Copi, and Don W. Warren, Languages for analysis of clerical problems, Engineering Research Institute, Informal Memorandum 5 (Univ. of Michigan, Ann Arbor, 1954). iii + 24 pp.

[BE 57] R. W. Bemer, The status of automatic programming for scientific problems, *Proc. 4th Ann. Comput. Appl. Symp., Armour Res. Found., 1957*, pp. 107–117.

[BG 53] J. M. Bennett and A. E. Glennie, Programming for high-speed digital calculating machines, *in* "Faster Than Thought" (B. V. Bowden, ed.), pp. 101–113. Pitman, London, 1953.

[BH 54] J. W. Backus and H. Herrick, IBM 701 Speedcoding and other automatic-programming systems, *Symp. Automat. Programm. Digital Comput.*, pp. 106–113. Office of Naval Research, Dept. of the Navy, Washington, D.C., 1954.

[BH 64] J. W. Backus and W. P. Heising, FORTRAN, *IEEE Trans. Electron. Comp.* **EC-13**, 382–385 (1964).

[BL 56] E. K. Blum, Automatic Digital Encoding System, II (ADES II), NAVORD Rep. 4209, Aeroballistic Research Report 326, U.S. Naval Ordnance Laboratory (8 February 1956).

[BL 56'] E. K. Blum, Automatic Digital Encoding System, II, *Symp. Adv. Programm. Methods Digital Comput., Washington, D.C.* ONR Symp. Report ACR-15, pp. 71–76 (1956). v + 45 pp. + appendices.

[BL 56''] E. K. Blum, Automatic Digital Encoding System, II (ADES II), *Proc. ACM Nat. Conf. 6,* paper 29 (1956). 4 pp.

[BL 57] E. K. Blum, Automatic Digital Encoding System II (ADES II), Part 2: The Encoder, NAVORD Rep. 4411, U.S. Naval Ordnance Laboratory (29 November 1956). 82 pp. + appendix.

[BL 57'] E. K. Blum and S. Stern, "An ADES Encoder for the IBM 650 calculator, " NAVORD Rep. 4412, U.S. Naval Ordnance Laboratory (19 December 1956), 15 pp.

[BO 52] C. Böhm, Calculatrices digitales: Du déchiffrage de formules logico-mathématiques par la machine même dans la conception du programme [Digital computers: On the deciphering of logical-mathematical formulae by the machine itself during the conception of the program], *An. Mat. Pura Appl.* **37**, (4) 175–217 (1954).

[BO 52'] C. Böhm, Macchina calcolatrice digitale con programma preordinato fisso con tastiera algebrica ridotta atta a comporre formule mediante la combinazione dei singoli elementi simbolici [Programmable digital computer with a fixed preset program and with an algebraic keyboard able to compose formulae by means of the combination of single symbolic elements], Patent application No. 13567, filed in Milan on 1 October 1952. 26 pp. + 2 tables.

[BO 54] C. Böhm, Sulla programmazione mediante formule [On programming by means of formulas], Atti 4° Sessione Giornate della Scienza, suppl. de "La ricerca scientifica" (Rome, 1954), 1008–1014.

[BO 58] B. C. Borden, FORTRANSIT, a universal automatic coding system, *Proc. Canadian Conf. Computing Data Process., Univ. of Toronto, 1958,* pp. 349–359.

[BP 52] J. M. Bennett, D. G. Prinz, and M. L. Woods, Interpretative sub-routines, *Proc. ACM Nat. Conf. 2, Toronto, 1952,* 81–87.

[BR 55] R. A. Brooker, An attempt to simplify coding for the Manchester electronic computer, *Brit. J. Appl. Phys.* **6**, 307–311 (1955). [This paper was received in March 1954.]

[BR 56] R. A. Brooker, The programming strategy used with the Manchester University Mark 1 computer, *Proc. Inst. Electr. Engrs. Part B, Suppl.,* **103**, 151–157 (1956).

[BR 58] R. A. Brooker, The Autocode programs developed for the Manchester University computers, *Comp. J.* **1**, 15–21 (1958).

[BR 58'] R. A. Brooker, Some technical features of the Manchester Mercury AUTOCODE programme, *Mechanisation of Thought Processes, Nat. Phys. Lab. Symp. 10, 1958,* pp. 201–229.

[BR 60] R. A. Brooker, MERCURY Autocode: Principles of the Program Library, *Ann. Rev. Automat. Prog.* **1**, 93–110 (1960).

[BS 57] F. L. Bauer and K. Samelson, Verfahren zur automatischen Verarbeitung von kodierten Daten und Rechenmaschine zur Ausübung des Verfahrens, Deutsches Patentamt, Auslegeschrift 1094019 (30 March 1957), published December 1960. 26 cols. plus 6 Figs.

[BS 62] F. L. Bauer and K. Samelson, Automatic computing machines and method of operation, U.S. Patent Office, Patent No. 3,047,228 (31 July 1962). 32 cols. plus 17 Figs.

[BU 50]   A. W. Burks, The logic of programming electronic digital computers, *Indust. Math.* **1**, 36–52 (1950).

[BU 51]   A. W. Burks, An intermediate program language as an aid in program synthesis, Engineering Research Institute, Report for Burroughs Adding Machine Company (Univ. of Michigan, Ann Arbor, 1951). ii + 15 pp.

[BW 53]   R. A. Brooker and D. J. Wheeler, Floating operations on the EDSAC, *Math. Tables Other Aids Comput.* **7**, 37–47 (1953).

[BW 72]   F. L. Bauer and H. Wössner, The "Plankalkül" of Konrad Zuse: A forerunner of today's programming languages, *Comm. ACM* **15**, 678–685 (1972).

[CH 36]   A. Church, An unsolvable problem of elementary number theory, *Amer. J. Math.* **58**, 345–363 (1936).

[CK 56]   J. Chipps, M. Koschmann, S. Orgel, A. Perlis, and J. Smith. A mathematical language compiler, *Proc. ACM Nat. Conf. 6*, paper 30 (1956). 4 pp.

[CL 61]   R. F. Clippinger, FACT—A Business Compiler: Description and comparison with COBOL and Commercial Translator, *Ann. Rev. Automat. Prog.* **2**, 231–292 (1961).

[CU 48]   H. B. Curry, On the composition of programs for automatic computing, Naval Ordnance Laboratory Memorandum 9806 (Silver Spring, Maryland, 1949). [Written in July, 1948.] 52 pp.

[CU 50]   H. B. Curry, A program composition technique as applied to inverse interpolation, Naval Ordnance Laboratory Memorandum 10337 (Silver Spring, Maryland, 1950). 98 pp. + 3 figs.

[CU 50'] H. B. Curry, The logic of program composition, *Appl. Sci. Logique Math., Actes 2e Colloque Internat. Logique Math., 1952*, pp. 97–102. [Paper written in March 1950.]

[EK 55]   A. K. Elsworth, R. Kuhn, L. Schloss, and K. Tiede, "Manual for KOMPILER 2," Univ. of California Radiation Lab., Livermore, Calif., Report UCRL-4585 (7 November 1955). 66 pp.

[ER 58]   A. P. Ershov, "Programmiruĭoshchaĭa Programma dlĭa Bystrodeĭstvuĭoshchei Elektronnoĭ Schetnoĭ Mashiny" (Akad. Nauk SSSR, Moscow, 1958). 116 pp. [English translation: "Programming Programme for the BESM Computer" (Pergamon, London, 1959). v + 158 pp.]

[ER 58'] A. P. Ershov, The work of the Computing Centre of the Academy of Sciences of the USSR in the field of automatic programming, *Mechanisation of Thought Processes, Nat. Phys. Lab. Symp. 10, 1958*, pp. 257–278.

[FE 60]   G. E. Felton, Assembly, interpretive and conversion programs for PEGASUS, *Ann. Rev. Automat. Prog.* **1**, 32–57 (1960).

[GL 52]   A. E. Glennie, The automatic coding of an electronic computer (unpublished lecture notes dated 14 December 1952). [This lecture was delivered at Cambridge University in February 1953.] 15 pp.

[GL 52'] A. E. Glennie, Automatic Coding, unpublished manuscript (undated, probably 1952). [This appears to be a draft of a user's manual to be entitled "The Routine AUTOCODE and Its Use."] 18 pp.

[GL 65]   A. E. Glennie, letter to D. E. Knuth dated 15 September 1965. 6 pp.

[GO 54]   S. Gorn, Planning universal semi-automatic coding, *Symp. Automat. Programm. Digital Comput.*, pp. 74–83. Office of Naval Research, Dept. of the Navy, Washington, D.C., 1954.

[GO 56]   M. Goldstein, Computing at Los Alamos, Group T-1, *Symp. Adv. Programm. Meth. Digital Comput., Washington, D.C.* ONR Symp. Report ACR-15, pp. 39–43 (1956).

[GO 57]   S. Gorn, Standardized programming methods and universal coding, *J. ACM* **4**, 254–273 (1957).

[GO 72]   H. H. Goldstine, "The Computer from Pascal to von Neumann" (Princeton Univ. Press, Princeton, New Jersey, 1972). xi + 378 pp.

[GP 56] M. Grems and R. E. Porter, A truly automatic computing system, *Proc. Western Joint Comp. Conf. 1956,* pp. 10–21.

[GR 58] R. M. Graham, Translation between algebraic coding languages, *Proc. ACM Nat. Conf. 8,* paper 29 (1958). 2 pp.

[GV 47] H. H. Goldstine and J. von Neumann, "Planning and Coding of Problems for an Electronic Computing Instrument: Report on the Mathematical and Logical Aspects of an Electronic Computing Instrument." Vol. 1, iv + 69 pp.; Vol. 2, iv + 68 pp.; Vol. 3, iii + 23 pp. (Institute for Advanced Study, Princeton, New Jersey, 1947–1948). Reprinted in von Neumann's "Collected Works" (A. H. Taub, ed.), Vol. 5, pp. 80–235. (Pergamon, London, 1963).

[HA 52] Staff of the Computation Laboratory [Howard H. Aiken and 55 others], "Description of a Magnetic Drum Calculator," The Annals of the Computation Laboratory of Harvard University, Vol. 25 (Harvard Univ. Press, Cambridge, Massachusetts, 1952). xi + 318 pp.

[HA 57] C. L. Hamblin, Computer languages, *Austr. J. Sci.* **20** (6), 135–139 (1957).

[HM 53] G. M. Hopper and J. W. Mauchly, Influence of programming techniques on the design of computers, *Proc. IRE* **41,** 1250–1254 (1953).

[HO 52] G. M. Hopper, The education of a computer, *Proc. ACM Nat. Conf. 1, Pittsburgh, 1952,* pp. 243–250.

[HO 53] G. M. Hopper, The education of a computer, *Symp. Indust. Appl. Automat. Comput. Equip., Kansas City, Missouri, 1953,* pp. 139–144.

[HO 53'] G. M. Hopper, Compiling routines. *Comput. Automat.* **2** (4), 1–5 (1953).

[HO 55] G. M. Hopper, Automatic coding for digital computers, *Comput. Automat.* **4** (9), 21–24 (1955).

[HO 56] G. M. Hopper, The interlude 1954–1956, *Symp. Adv. Programm. Meth. Digital Comput., Washington, D.C.* ONR Symp. Report ACR-15, pp. 1–2 (1956).

[HO 57] G. M. Hopper, Automatic programming for business applications, *Proc. 4th Ann. Comput. Appl. Symp., Armour Research Foundation, 1957,* pp. 45–50.

[HO 58] G. M. Hopper, Automatic programming: Present status and future trends, *Mechanisation of Thought Processes, Nat. Phys. Lab. Symp. 10, 1958,* pp. 155–200.

[HO 71] C. A. R. Hoare, Proof of a program: FIND, *Comm. ACM* **14,** 39–45 (1971).

[IB 54] Programming Research Group, IBM Applied Science Div., Specifications for The IBM Mathematical FORmula TRANslating System, FORTRAN, Preliminary report (IBM, New York, 1954). i + 29 pp.

[IB 56] J. W. Backus, R. J. Beeber, S. Best, R. Goldberg, H. L. Herrick, R. A. Hughes, L. B. Mitchell, R. A. Nelson, R. Nutt, D. Sayre, P. B. Sheridan, H. Stern, and I. Ziller, "Progammer's Reference Manual: The FORTRAN Automatic Coding System for the IBM 704 EDPM." (Applied Science Div. and Programming Research Dept., IBM, 15 October 1956.) 51 pp.

[IB 57] IBM Corporation, "Programmer's Primer for FORTRAN Automatic Coding System for the IBM 704" (IBM, New York, 1957). iii + 64 pp.

[KA 57] C. Katz, Systems of debugging automatic coding, *in* "Automatic Coding," Franklin Institute Monograph No. 3, pp. 17–27 (1957).

[KL 58] S. S. Kamynin, E. Z. Liubimskiĭ, and M. R. Shura-Bura, Ob avtomatizatsii programmirovaniĭa pri pomoshchi programmiruĭoshcheĭ programmy, *Problemy Kibernet.* **1,** 135–171 (1958). [English translation: Automatic programming with a programming programme, *Prob. Cybernet.* **1,** 149–191 (1960).]

[KM 57] H. Kinzler and P. M. Moskowitz, The Procedure Translator—a system of automatic programming, *in* "Automatic Coding," Franklin Institute Monograph No. 3, pp. 39–55 (1957).

[KN 64] D. E. Knuth, Backus Normal Form vs. Backus Naur Form, *Comm. ACM* **7,** 735–736 (1964).

[KN 68]   D. E. Knuth, "Fundamental Algorithms," The Art of Computer Programming, Vol. 1 (Addison-Wesley, Reading, Massachusetts, 1968). xxi + 634 pp.

[KN 69]   D. E. Knuth, "Seminumerical Algorithms," The Art of Computer Programming, Vol. 2 (Addison-Wesley, Reading, Massachusetts, 1969). xi + 624 pp.

[KN 72]   D. E. Knuth, Ancient Babylonian algorithms, *Comm. ACM* **15**, 671–677 (1972); Errata, *Comm. ACM* **19**, 108 (1976).

[KO 58]   L. N. Korolev, Some methods of automatic coding for BESM and STRELA computers, Inst. of Exact Mechanics and Computing Technique, Acad. Sci. USSR, Moscow, 1958. 32 pp. Reprinted in "Computer Programming and Artificial Intelligence" (John W. Carr, III, ed.), pp. 489–507 (Univ. of Michigan, College of Engineering, Ann Arbor, 1958).

[LA 65]   J. H. Laning, letter to D. E. Knuth dated 13 January 1965. 1 p.

[LA 76]   J. H. Laning, letter to D. E. Knuth dated 2 July 1976. 11 pp.

[LE 55]   N. J. Lehmann, Bemerkungen zur Automatisierung der Programmfertigung für Rechenautomaten, "Elektronische Rechenmaschinen und Informationsverarbeitung —Electronic Digital Computers and Information Processing," (proceedings of October 1955 conference at Darmstadt) *Nachrichtentech. Fachber.* **4**, 143 (1956) (including discussion).

[LJ 58]   A. A. Liapunov, O logicheskikh skhemakh programm, *Problemy Kibernet.* **1**, 46–74 (1958). [English translation: The logical structure [sic] of programs, *Prob. Cybernet.* **1**, 48–81 (1960).]

[LM 70]   J. H. Laning and J. S. Miller, The MAC algebraic language, MIT Instrumentation Lab. Rep. R-681 (November 1970). 23 pp.

[LZ 54]   J. H. Laning, Jr., and N. Zierler, A program for translation of mathematical equations for Whirlwind I, Engineering Memorandum E-364, MIT Instrumentation Lab. (January 1954).

[MG 53]   E. N. Mutch and S. Gill, Conversion routines, *Proc. Symp. Automat. Digital Comput., Nat. Phys. Lab., 25–28 March 1953*, pp. 74–80.

[MO 54]   N. B. Moser, Compiler method of automatic programming, *Proc. Symp. Automat. Programm. Digital Comput.*, pp. 15–21. (Office of Naval Research, Dept. of the Navy, Washington, D.C., 1954.)

[NA 54]   Navy Mathematical Computing Advisory Panel, *Proc. Symp. Automat. Programm. Digital Comput., Washington, D.C., 1954*. (Office of Naval Research, Dept. of the Navy, Washington, D.C., 1954.) v + 152 pp.

[OR 58]   S. Orgel, "Purdue Compiler: General Description" (Purdue Research Foundation, West Lafayette, Indiana, 1958). iv + 33 pp.

[PE 55]   A. J. Perlis, DATATRON (transcript of lecture given 11 August 1955), *in* "Digital Computers and Data Processors" (J. W. Carr, III, and N. R. Scott, eds.), section VII.20.1 (Univ. Michigan, College of Engineering, Ann Arbor, 1956).

[PE 57]   R. M. Petersen, Automatic coding at G.E., *in* "Automatic Coding," Franklin Institute Monograph No. 3, pp. 3–16 (1957).

[PM 55]   S. Poley and G. Mitchell, Symbolic Optimum Assembly Programming (SOAP), 650 Programming Bull. 1, Form 22-6285-1 (IBM, New York, November, 1955). 4 pp.

[PR 55]   Programming Research Section, Eckert Mauchly Division, Remington Rand, Automatic programming: The A-2 Compiler System, *Comput. Automat.* **4**(9), 25–29 (1955); **4**(10), 15–27 (1955).

[PS 57]   A. J. Perlis and J. W. Smith, A mathematical language compiler, *in* "Automatic Coding," Franklin Institute Monograph No. 3, pp. 87–102 (1957).

[PS 57'] A. J. Perlis, J. W. Smith, and H. R. Van Zoeren, Internal Translator (IT): A compiler for the 650. Computation Center, Carnegie Institute of Technology. (March, 1957). Part I, Programmer's Guide; Part II, Program Analysis; Addenda (flow charts were promised on p. 3.12). Reprinted in "Applications of Logic to Advanced Digital

Computer Programming'' (Univ. of Michigan, College of Engineering, Ann Arbor, 1957). This report was also available from IBM Corp. as a 650 Library Program; File Number 2.1.001. [Autobiographical note: D. E. Knuth learned about system programming by reading the program listings of part II in the summer of 1957; this changed his life.]

[PS 58]   A. J. Perlis and K. Samelson, Preliminary report, International Algebraic Language, *Comm. ACM* **1**(12), 8–22 (1958). Report on the Algorithmic Language ALGOL by the ACM Committee on Programming Languages and the GAMM Committee on Programming, *Numer. Math.* **1**, 41–60 (1959). Reprinted in *Ann. Rev. Automat. Prog.* **1**, 269–290 (1960).

[RA 73]   B. Randell, "The Origins of Digital Computers: Selected Papers" (Springer, Berlin, 1973). xvi + 464 pp.

[RO 52]   N. Rochester, Symbolic programming, *IRE Trans. Electron. Comput.* **EC-2**, 10–15 (1952).

[RO 64]   S. Rosen, Programming systems and languages, a historical survey, *Proc. Spring Joint Computer Conf., 1964*, pp. 1–16.

[RR 53]   Remington Rand, Inc., "The A-2 Compiler System Operations Manual" (15 November 1953). Prepared by R. K. Ridgway and M. H. Harper under the direction of G. M. Hopper. iii + 54 pp.

[RR 55]   Remington Rand UNIVAC, UNIVAC Short Code, unpublished collection of dittoed notes. Preface by A. B. Tonik, dated 25 October 1955, 1 p.; preface by J. R. Logan, undated but apparently from 1952, 1 p.; Preliminary Exposition (1952?), 22 pp., where pp. 20–22 appear to be a later replacement; Short Code Supplementary Information, Topic One, 7 pp.; Addenda # 1–4, 9 pp.

[RU 52]   H. Rutishauser, Automatische Rechenplanfertigung bei programmgesteuerten Rechenmaschinen [Automatic machine-code generation on program-directed computers], *Mitteilungen aus dem Inst. für angew. Math. an der ETH Zürich*, No. 3 (Birkhäuser, Basel, 1952). ii + 45 pp.

[RU 55]   H. Rutishauser, Some programming techniques for the ERMETH, *J. ACM* **2**, 1–4 (1955).

[RU 55']   H. Rutishauser, Massnahmen zur Vereinfachung des Programmierens (Bericht über die in fünfjähriger Programmierungsarbeit mit der Z4 gewonnenen Erfahrungen), Elektronische Rechenmaschinen und Informationsverarbeitung—Electronic Digital Computers and Information Processing (proceedings of October 1955 conference at Darmstadt) *Nachrichtentech. Fachber.* **4**, 26–30 (1956). [English summary: Methods to simplify programming, experiences based on five years of programming work with the Z4 computer, p. 225.]

[RU 61]   H. Rutishauser, Interference with an ALGOL procedure, *Ann. Rev. Automat. Prog.* **2**, 67–76 (1961).

[RU 63]   H. Rutishauser, letter to D. E. Knuth (dated 11 October 1963). 2 pp.

[SA 55]   K. Samelson, Probleme der Programmierungstechnik, *Aktuelle Probleme der Rechentechnik, Ber. über das Int. Mathematiker-Kolloquium, Dresden, 1955*, pp. 61–68.

[SA 69]   J. E. Sammet, "Programming Languages: History and Fundamentals" (Prentice-Hall, Englewood Cliffs, New Jersey, 1969). xxx + 785 pp.

[SB 59]   K. Samelson and F. L. Bauer, Sequentielle Formelübersetzung, *Elektron. Rechenanlagen* **1**, 176–182 (1959); Sequential formula translation, *Comm. ACM* **3**, 76–83 (1960); **3**, 351 (1960).

[SM 73]   Leland Smith, Editing and printing music by computer, *J. Music Theory* **17**, 292–309 (1973).

[ST 52]   C. S. Strachey, Logical or non-mathematical programmes, *Proc. ACM Nat. Conf. 2, Toronto, 1952*, pp. 46–49.

[TA 56]   D. Tamari, review of [BO 52], *Zentralbl. Math.* **57**, 107–108 (1956).

[TA 60]   A. E. Taylor, The FLOW-MATIC and MATH-MATIC Automatic Programming Systems, *Ann. Rev. Automat. Prog.* **1**, 196–206 (1960).

[TH 55]   B. Thüring, Die UNIVAC A-2 Compiler Methode der automatischen Programmierung, Elektronische Rechenmaschinen und Informationsverarbeitung—Electronic Digital Computers and Information Processing (proceedings of October 1955 conference at Darmstadt) *Nachrichtentech. Fachber.* **4**, 154–156 (1956). [English summary: p. 226.]

[TU 36]   A. M. Turing, On computable numbers, with an application to the Entscheidungsproblem, *Proc. London Math. Soc.* (2) **42**, 230–265 (1936); correction **43**, 544–546 (1937).

[WA 54]   J. Waite, Editing generators, *Proc. Symp. Automat. Programm. Digital Comput.* pp. 22–29. Office of Naval Research, Dept. of the Navy, Washington, D.C., 1954.

[WA 58]   F. Way III, Current developments in computer programming techniques, *Proc. 5th Ann. Comp. Appl. Symp., Armour Research Foundation, 1958,* pp. 125–132.

[WH 50]   D. J. Wheeler, Programme organization and initial orders for the EDSAC, *Proc. Roy. Soc. A* **202**, 573–589 (1950).

[WI 52]   M. V. Wilkes, Pure and applied programming, *Proc. ACM Nat. Conf. 2, Toronto, 1952,* pp. 121–124.

[WI 53]   M. V. Wilkes, The use of a "floating address" system for orders in an automatic digital computer, *Proc. Cambridge Philos. Soc.* **49**, 84–89 (1953).

[WO 51]   M. Woodger, "A comparison of one and three address codes," *Proc. Manchester Univ. Comput. Inaugural Conf., Manchester, 1951,* pp. 19–23.

[WR 71]   W. A. Wulf, D. B. Russell, and A. N. Habermann, BLISS, a language for systems programming, *Comm. ACM* **14**, 780–790 (1971).

[WW 51]   M. V. Wilkes, D. J. Wheeler, and S. Gill, "The Preparation of Programs for an Electronic Digital Computer: With special reference to the EDSAC and the use of a library of subroutines." (Addison-Wesley, Cambridge, Massachusetts, 1951). xi + 170 pp.

[WW 57]   M. V. Wilkes, D. J. Wheeler, and S. Gill, "The Preparation of Programs for an Electronic Digital Computer," 2nd ed. (Addison-Wesley, Reading, Massachusetts, 1957). xii + 238 pp.

[ZU 44]   K. Zuse, Ansätze einer Theorie des allgemeinen Rechnens unter besonderer Berücksichtigung des Aussagenkalküls und dessen Anwendung auf Relaisschaltungen [Beginnings of a theory of calculation in general, considering in particular the propositional calculus and its application to relay circuits], Manuscript dated 1944; Chapter 1 has been published in *Ber. Ges. Math. Datenverarbeitung,* **63**, Part 1 (1972). 32 pp. [English translation: **106**, 7–20 (1976).]

[ZU 45]   K. Zuse, Der Plankalkül, manuscript prepared in 1945. Published in *Ber. Ges. Math. Datenverarbeitung,* **63**, Part 3, (1972). 285 pp. [English translation of all but pp. 176–196, **106**, 42–244 (1976).]

[ZU 48]   K. Zuse, Uber den allgemeinen Plankalkül als Mittel zur Formulierung schematisch kombinativer Aufgaben, *Arch. Math.* **1**, 441–449 (1948/49).

[ZU 59]   K. Zuse, Uber den Plankalkül, *Elektron. Rechenanl.* **1**, 68–71 (1959).

[ZU 72]   K. Zuse, Kommentar zum Plankalkül, *Ber. Ges. Math. Datenverarbeitung* **63**, Part 2, (1972). 36 pp. [English translation, **106**, 21–41 (1976).]

COMPUTER SCIENCE DEPARTMENT
SCHOOL OF HUMANITIES AND SCIENCES
STANFORD UNIVERSITY
STANFORD, CALIFORNIA

Reflections on the Evolution of Algorithmic Language

MARK B. WELLS

1. Introduction

This paper is concerned less with the recording of historical fact and more with an interpretation of existing history. Also, it is concerned primarily with the period after 1960. This is not history in the sense of this volume. Nevertheless, perhaps it is not inappropriate here to consider where we seem to have been headed with respect to programming language design.

My goal is to present a view of how the language of man-machine communication is evolving with respect to its technical characteristics. Evolution of language is a slow process, to us in the language design business painfully so. However, I think we would agree that certain patterns are emerging. For instance, recursive procedures have withstood the test of time while the COMMON statement seems to be going the way of the dinosaur. A designer of a general-purpose scientific programming language today would think twice before *omitting* recursive procedures, or on the other hand, before *including* the COMMON statement at least in the form first introduced by FORTRAN [1]. It is my conclusion that, in spite of the seeming proliferation of programming languages today, the various features are being sorted out, and in fact general-purpose languages are converging toward "everyday" algorithmic language.

My experience with language design has been with various versions of the MADCAP programming language developed at the Los Alamos Scientific

275

Laboratory (LASL) beginning in about 1956. MADCAP compilers have historically existed on the unique MANIAC II computer at LASL; hence the language is not well known. I mention it here because my interpretation of language is of course significantly colored by that experience. The basic goal of MADCAP development has been to make the computer more accessible to the scientist. The development took place in a limited but active scientific research environment. This has been a favorable atmosphere for technical evolution as we have been somewhat protected from the effects of many nontechnical concerns that have inhibited evolution in the real world. In any event, please bear with my repeated references to MADCAP and use of it as a standard of comparison.

Algorithmic language before computers was essentially textual with a liberal sprinkling of examples and three dots. Figure 1 shows the Euclidean algorithm written essentially in the algorithmic language of Euclid [2] and written in a more modern language, namely, MADCAP. The purpose of this figure is not to compare differences in languages, which of course is always unfair in one specific example, but to suggest the ways in which language has been influenced by use of the computer. Foremost in this respect is the question of *precision* of language. Use of the computer has certainly taught us the importance of taking care to be precise in the statement of our algorithms. Also, we are learning that *structure* and *abstraction* are important if we are to understand our creations. I think you will agree that the modern version does have more structure. With respect to abstraction, a little reflection will show that the only reference to the form of the data in the modern version is in the declaration of the input parameters. Thus the same algorithm could be applied to polynomials or other data that have the basic operations defined on them. Structure and abstraction are two important threads of algorithmic language evolution to which I will often refer in this paper.

Beside the need for precision of specification, the chief motivations for language mutations, hence fundamental to language evolution, are the need for efficiency and economy, and the desire for algorithmic understanding. There are three types of efficiency considerations: real computer time, problem-solution time, and algorithmic complexity. These considerations are not

EUCLID

. . . the less of the numbers AB, CD being continually subtracted from the greater, some number will be left which will measure the one before it . . .

MODERN

```
(a, b):  @ INTEGER
if b > a:   a ↔ b
while b > 0:
          a ← a mod b
          a ↔ b
```

Figure 1   How the computer has changed the Euclidean algorithm.

independent, of course. Efficiency of actual computer time was the strongest motivation in the early days. More recently, the total problem solution time and the complexity of the algorithm have played an increasingly prominent role.

With regard to understanding our creations, it seems to me there are three important aspects of language: expressiveness, program readability, and algorithm provability. First, the ability to express algorithmic ideas easily and conveniently is essential. Second, having created an algorithm, it is important that we can discuss and communicate it with our colleagues, and in fact with ourselves at a later date. Third, we must be able to convince ourselves that the algorithm is correct. Actually, as has been so many times pointed out by Professor Dijkstra (e.g., [3]) the question of provability is not independent of other aspects of understanding. It is desirable that construction of correct and readable programs be a unified process.

2.   Evolution of Particular Features

I have selected six modern language characteristics whose evolution I wish briefly to trace. Concern is not with their precise history but more with their role in the evolution of general-purpose algorithmic language.

2.1.   Block Structuring

The first concept is that of block structuring, that is, the ability to isolate variable names in program blocks that are organized into a hierarchical structure. A chronology of certain facets of the use and evolution of block structuring appears in Fig 2. FORTRAN of course allows such isolation to only one sublevel, and hence does not qualify; this is indicated by the brackets on the chart. The concept appeared first in a language in ALGOL 58–60 [4] although it is related of course to the idea of bound and free variables of logic, which existed before computers. (Incidentally, the dates at which a langauge or author appears on a chart generally corresponds to a publication; the work likely was performed earlier.) Prominent in the ALGOL 60 implementation of block structure is the concept of an "activation record," an interval of storage added to the stack when a block is entered for use in storing the local variables. This activation record and its variables disappeared when exit from the block was made.

We had a block structure based on procedures in MADCAP 4, but the declaration properties were reversed. That is, a variable was automatically local unless specifically declared to be global.

I have put PL/1 [5] and PASCAL [6] on the chart to indicate the continuance of the concept of block structuring. Both these languages adopted the idea from ALGOL 60.

The contribution of SIMULA 67 [7] was that certain activation records were retained, that is, in certain contexts it is possible to access local vari-

1952 -

-

1954 -

-

1956 -

- [FORTRAN]

1958 -

-

1960 - ALGOL 60

1962 -

-

- MADCAP 4

1964 -

-

1966 - PL/1

- SIMULA 67

1968 - [APL]; ALGOL 68 (Function data type)

-

1970 -

- Johnston/Berry (Contour model)

1972 - PASCAL; MADCAP 6 (Filing system)

-

1974 - [CLU (Restricted external access)]

-

1976 -

Figure 2 Block structuring.

ables from a previously exited module. This concept of activation record retention was formalized in 1971 papers by Johnston [8] and Berry [9] discussing Johnston's contour model.

I put APL on the chart to show that not all modern languages are block structured. There *is* a nested isolation of names in APL [10], but like LISP [11] it is created by the dynamic linking of procedure calls rather than by the static structure of the program.

Recently many language designers have been questioning the global variable accessing rules of the basic block-structuring concept [12]. This is exemplified in MIT's CLU language [13] in which global access is restricted only to procedure names and "cluster" names. A cluster is a data abstraction module; I shall say more about this concept later.

Our own work on MADCAP has merged block structuring with the filing system [14] and has made use of activation record retention in the implementation of a powerful function data type [15]. The concept of a function data type appeared in LISP [11], PL/1 [5], and ALGOL 68 [16], yet its usefulness does not seem to be generally recognized.

2.2. Structured Control

Figure 3 reviews the evolution of structured control. As Knuth and Pardo have indicated [17], before 1960, control structures were mostly various unconditional and conditional jump commands and simple repetitive statements. A major contribution came around 1960 with ALGOL introduction of recursive procedures. We did not have recursive procedures in MADCAP until 1971. I was a victim of misapprehensions concerning efficiencies, and put an efficiently implementable nested iteration statement into MADCAP in 1962 [18]. This was useful for many special kinds of recursion.

It was interesting to learn at this conference that Zuse's Plankalkül language [19], though never implemented, had restricted GOTO's in the form of exits from iterations. The MADCAP 5 language [20] had one-level exits from loops and procedures, and the language BLISS [21] has multilevel exits. In the mid-1960s people began to question the classical control structures. I heard Dijkstra's 1965 talk in New York [22]; he discussed the quality, or lack thereof, of spaghettilike programs using many GOTO's. I had noticed myself, using MADCAP's powerful set-theoretic structures and *while* statement, that a jump was almost never required. In a 1966 paper [23], Hoare and Wirth introduced the *case* statement and pushed use of the *while* statement as the most general and understandable form of iterative statement. Then there was Böhm and Jacopini's theoretical paper [24], which showed that conditional and iterative statements are sufficient, and Dijkstra's famous GOTO Statements Considered Harmful letter in 1968 [25]. We had entered the structured-programming craze of the past decade.

```
1952 -
     -
1954 -
     -
1956 -
     -                    Golden era of the GOTO
1958 -
     -
1960 - ALGOL 60 (Recursive procedures)
     -
1962 -
     -
1964 - MADCAP 5 (Exits)
     - Dijkstra "Programming . . . activity"
1966 - Hoare/Wirth (Case statement)
     - Böhm/Jacopini ". . . Two formation rules"
1968 - Dijkstra "GOTO's . . . harmful"
     -
1970 - BLISS (No GOTO's)
     - PASCAL
1972 - MADCAP 6 (No jumps)
     - FORTRAN Preprocessors
1974 - CLU (No jumps)
     - Dijkstra (Guarded commands)
1976 -
```

FIGURE 3   Structured control.

Some of the more prominent authors of this period were Dijkstra [26], Naur [27], Wirth [28], and Mills [29]. Some of the language developments appear on the chart in Fig 3. The language BLISS, developed at Carnegie-Mellon University, has no GOTO's but does have exits [21]. PASCAL has GOTO's but they are almost never used [30]. MADCAP 6 was originally designed with only exits [31], but the exits never were implemented and we haven't missed them. MIT's CLU language also has no jumps [13]. We have also seen many FORTRAN preprocessors that allow structure control surface in the last few years [32, 33]. I should say that real progress has been made in the general area of structured control.

It is still much too early to judge the impact, if any, of Dijkstra's "guarded commands" [34].

2.3. Data Structuring

Figure 4 gives the highlights of the evolution of the concept of data structuring, that is, the construction and use of hierarchical and recursive data structures. In the late 1950s, several languages were developed to handle "linked lists," the two most prominent being IPL [35] and LISP [11]. The need for hierarchical structures in business-oriented computing was met with the

```
1952 -
     -
1954 -
     -
1956 -
     -
1958 -
     -
1960 - IPL-V; LISP
     -
1962 - COBOL

1964 -
     - AED
1966 - PL/1; Hoare/Wirth "A contribution . . ."
     - SIMULA 67
1968 - ALGOL 68
     - Knuth—Volume 1
1970 -
     - PASCAL
1972 - MADCAP 6; Hoare "Notes on data structuring"
     -
1974 -
     -
1976 -
```

Figure 4   Data structuring: hierarchical and recursive data.

COBOL language in the early 1960s [36]. Notable in the mid-1960s was the work of Ross at MIT on the AED language [37] with his development of hierarchical records and that of Hoare and Wirth again [23], which eventually culminated in the *records* of the PASCAL language in 1971. Also PL/1 adopted and extended the hierarchical structures of COBOL, and SIMULA 67 introduced its "sets" [7], a convenient means of linking data. ALGOL 68 introduced a reference (i.e., pointer) variable mechanism [16], which provides a very general way to structure data but is too undisciplined for some of us. I have listed Knuth [38] since it contains an influential formalization of many data structuring questions.

The data structures of MADCAP are interesting in that by using a "by-reference" computation model [39] hierarchical and recursive structures exist without the need for pointer variables, much as in SNOBOL 4 [40].

The reference to Hoare's paper [41], is included to make the point, often overlooked, that many people view "structured programming" in a much more general light than just as structured control.

A simple conclusion from this history might be that the need for general data structuring has been recognized.

2.4. Data Abstraction

The next concept has even a shorter documented history than those previously discussed. However, its, importance warrants its inclusion here.

Relative to algorithmic language, data abstraction (Fig. 5) has to do with mechanisms for suppressing irrelevant details of data representation from the algorithms themselves that process the data. We wish to be able to separate off definitions of data representation, isolating them into easily modifiable and protected modules.

SIMULA 67 uses activation record retention to isolate the data definitions in modules called "classes" [7]. The extensible system ECL, developed at Harvard, allows redefinition of a restricted class of operators onto new data types [42]. ALGOL 68, SNOBOL 4, and PASCAL perhaps do not have abstract data types in the modern sense, but the powerful type definitional facilities of ALGOL 68 [16], those of SNOBOL 4 [40], and the important compiler-time type checking of PASCAL [6] prompted me to list them here. CLU is the MIT language briefly mentioned before. Its contribution is a much more protected version of SIMULA-like classes [13].

Data abstraction is definitely an idea whose time has come. A host of languages—ALPHARD [43], MESA [44], MADCAP [45], MODEL [46]—now have an abstract data type facility.

The final two language characteristics I wish to discuss are more notational and perhaps not as important as the others. However, I do know something about the history of both features and, in my opinion, their importance is yet to be fully recognized.

1952 -
       -
1954 -
       -
1956 -
       -
1958 -
       -
1960 -
       -
1962 -
       -
1964 -
       -
1966 -
       - SIMULA 67
1968 - [ALGOL 68 (modes), SNOBOL 4 (User-defined types)]
       - ECL
1970 -
       - [PASCAL (strong typing)]
1972 -
       -
1974 - CLU; ALPHARD
       - MESA
1976 - . . . , MADCAP; MODEL, . . .

Figure 5   Data abstraction.

2.5. Two-Dimensional Notation

Figure 6 sketches a chronology of two-dimensional notation in programming languages, that is, notation such as

$$A_i^2 \quad \Sigma_{0 \le i < I} \; B_i \quad \frac{a + b}{a - b} \quad ,$$

which resembles textbook mathematics. This symbolism has not received widespread attention in the first quarter-century of programming language development because of the need for special hardware. While the early work at MIT [47, 48] was based on a 3 card/line approach, the work on MADCAP [49], COLASL [50], MIRFAC [51], and the Klerer–May system [52] made use of specially designed typewriters. With the arrival of scope display terminals in the late 1960s, several languages [53–55] adopted two-dimensional output. Making use of storage-tube electronics, which easily allows half-line spacing, MADCAP has retained two-dimensional input as well as output [56].

A more detailed overview of two-dimensional notation in programming languages has been given elsewhere [57]. I wish here to point out that the goal is to allow the previously evolved form of mathematical expressions in the algorithmic language. Such two-dimensional forms are no less precise

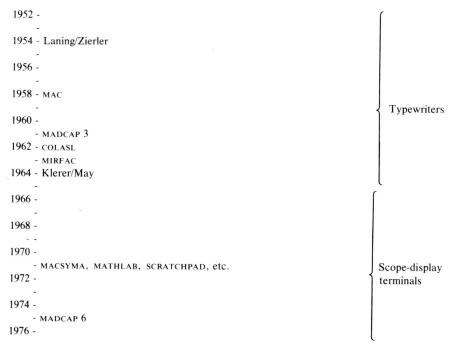

Figure 6   Two-dimensional (textbook) notations.

than the linearized versions found in the common languages of today, but because of their natural *structure* are a lot more readable.

2.6.   Set-Theoretic Concepts

A similar comment applies to set-theoretic notations such as

$$\text{for } i \in S \quad \text{do} \quad A \cup B \qquad \{2x : 3 \leq x \leq 10\}.$$

They are an important part of mathematics, and hence should find their way into algorithmic language; indeed, a quick look at modern textbooks on algorithms (e.g., [58, 59]) shows this to be the case. The importance of set-theoretic symbolism is that its use allows a natural first level of abstraction in algorithm construction. Unfortunately, as indicated in Fig. 7, programming language development lags in this area [6, 60, 61].

3.   Conclusion

There are four areas of language in which structure plays a prominent role: (1) program organization; (2) program control; (3) data; and (4) expression notation. Progress toward common algorithmic language has

```
1952 -
      -
1954 -
      -
1956 -
      -
1958 -
      -
1960 -
      -
1962 -
      -
1964 - MADCAP (Natural numbers)
      -
1966 -
      -
1968 -
      -
1970 -
      - PASCAL (Small universe)
1972 - SETL (General sets)
      -
1974 -
      -
1976 -
```

Figure 7 Set-theoretic notations and concepts.

been made in all four areas, with particular signs of convergence relative to program control and, to a lesser extent, to data. With respect to abstraction, there are three areas mentioned in this paper: (1) subroutines and procedures; (2) set-theoretic symbolism; and (3) algorithm–data-representation independence. We certainly have made progress relative to the design and use of procedures, while set-theoretic notation and data abstraction are just beginning to come into prominence.

So much for the evolution of programming languages with respect to their design; in my opinion, good progress has been made in 20 years. However, with respect to their use, progress has been less dramatic. The impact of algorithmic language evolution on general computer use remains in the future. Some people might say that for general scientific computer use, languages have already converged—to FORTRAN. And, indeed, there is evidence to support this view. On the other hand, while we would probably all agree on the tremendous impact that FORTRAN has had on computer usage in the 1960s, there definitely are signs that it is "over the hill." I close on this optimistic note.

REFERENCES

1. Programmer's Primer for FORTRAN Automatic Coding System for the IBM 704, IBM Corporation 32-0306-1 (1957).

2. Sir T. L. Heath, "Euclid's Elements," Vol. 3. Dover, New York, 1956.
3. E. W. Dijkstra, Correctness concerns and among other things, why they are resented, *SIGPLAN Notices* **10**, No. 6, 546–550 (1975).
4. P. Naur (ed.), Report on the algorithmic language ALGOL 60, *Comm. ACM* **3**, No. 5, 299–314 (1960).
5. G. M. Weinberg, "PL/1 Programming Primer." McGraw-Hill, New York, 1966.
6. N. Wirth, The programming language PASCAL, *Acta Informat.* **1**, 35–63 (1971).
7. O. J. Dahl, Myhrhaug, and K. Nygaard. "The Simula 67 Common Base Language." Norwegian Computing Center, Oslo, Norway (1968).
8. J. B. Johnston, The contour model of block structured process, *SIGPLAN Notices* **6**, No. 2, 55–82 (1971).
9. D. Berry, Introduction to oregano, *SIGPLAN Notices* **6**, No. 2, 171–190 (1971).
10. W. Prager, "An Introduction to APL." Bacon, Boston, Massachusetts, 1971.
11. J. McCarthy *et al.*, Lisp 1 Programmer's Manual, MIT Computation Center and Research Lab. of Electronics, Cambridge, Massachusetts (1960).
12. M. Shaw, and W. Wulf, Global variables considered harmful, *SIGPLAN Notices* **8**, No. 2, 28–34 (1973).
13. B. Liskov and S. Zilles, Programming with abstract data types, *SIGPLAN Notices* **9**, No. 4, 50–59 (1974).
14. M. J. Devaney and J. Hudgins, The terminal control language for the MADCAP programming system, *SIGPLAN Notices* **7**, No. 10, 130–136 (1972).
15. M. B. Wells, Implementation and application of a function data type. *AFIPS Conf. Proc. Nat. Comput. Conf.* **46**, 389–395 (1977).
16. A. Van Wijngaarden *et al.*, Report on the algorithmic language Algol 68, *Numer. Math.* **14**, 79–218 (1969).
17. D. E. Knuth and L. T. Pardo, this volume.
18. M. B. Wells, Recent improvements in MADCAP, *Comm. ACM* **6**, No. 11, 674–678 (1963).
19. C. Zuse, this volume.
20. J. E. Sammet "Programming Languages: History and Fundamentals," Section IV.7.3 Madcap, pp. 271–281. Prentice-Hall, Englewood Cliffs, New Jersey, 1969.
21. W. A. Wulf, D. B. Russell, and A. N. Habermann, Bliss: A language for systems programming, *Comm. ACM,* **14**, No. 12, 780–790 (1971).
22. E. W. Dijkstra, Programming considered as a human activity, *Proc. IFIP Congr. 65, New York* 213–218 (1965).
23. C. A. R. Hoare and N. Wirth, A contribution to the development of Algol, *Comm. ACM,* **9**, No. 6, 413–432 (1966).
24. C. Böhm, and G. Jacopini, Flow Diagrams, turing machines, and languages with only two formation rules, *Comm. ACM,* **9**, No. 5, 366–371 (1966).
25. E. W. Dijkstra, GOTO statement considered harmful (letter to editor), *Comm. ACM* **11**, No. 3, 147–148 (1968).
26. E. W. Dijkstra, Notes on Structured Programming, EWD 249. Technical V. Eindhoven, The Netherlands (1969).
27. P. Naur, Programming by action clusters, *BIT* **9**, 250–258 (1969).
28. N. Wirth, Program development by stepwise refinement, *Comm. ACM* **0**, 221–227 (1971).
29. H. Mills, Top-down programming in large systems, "Debugging Techniques in Large Systems" (R. Rustin, ed.), pp. 41–55. Prentice-Hall, Englewood Cliffs, New Jersey, 1971.
30. N. Wirth, "Systematic Programming: An Introduction," Prentice-Hall, Englewood Cliffs, New Jersey, 1973.
31. J. B. Morris Jr. and M. B. Wells, The specification of program flow in MADCAP 6, *Proc. ACM Nat. Conf. Boston, Massachusetts* **2**, 755–762 (1972).
32. A. J. Cook and L. J. Shustek, Mortan 2, a Macro-based Structured Fortran Extension, COMPCON Spring 1975, pp. 245–248. IEEE Computer Society, New York (1975).
33. B. W. Kernighan, RATFOR—A Rational FORTRAN, Workshop on FORTRAN preprocessors for Numerical Software, SIGNUM (1974).

34. E. W. Dijkstra, Guarded commands, non-determinacy, and formal derivation of programs, *Comm. ACM* **18**, No. 8, 453–457 (1975).
35. A. Newell and F. M. Tonge, An introduction to information processing language V, *Comm. ACM* **3**, No. 4, 205–211 (1960).
36. J. E. Sammet, Basic elements of COBOL 61, *Comm. ACM* **5**, No. 5, 237–253 (1962).
37. R. B. Lapin, D. T. Ross, and R. B. Wise, Some Experiments with an Algorithmic Graphical Language, MIT ESL-TM-220. Electronic Systems Lab., Cambridge, Massachusetts (August 1965).
38. D. E. Knuth, "The Art of Computer Programming, Volume 1: Fundamental Algorithms." Addison-Wesley, Reading, Massachusetts, 1969 (2nd printing).
39. M. B. Wells and J. B. Morris, Jr., The unified data structure capability in Madcap VI, *Int. J. Comput. Informat. Sci.* **1**, No. 3, 193–208 (1972).
40. R. E. Griswold, J. F. Poage, and I. P. Polansky, "The SNOBOL 4 Programming Language." Prentice-Hall, Englewood Cliffs, New Jersey, 1968.
41. C. A. R. Hoare, Notes on data structuring, "Structured Programming," Chapter II. Academic Press, New York, 1972.
42. B. Wegbreit, The treatment of data types in EL 1, *Comm. ACM* **17**, No. 5, 251–264 (1974).
43. M. Shaw, W. A. Wulf, and R. L. London, Abstraction and verification in ALPHARD: Defining and specifying iteration and generators, *Comm. ACM* **20**, No. 8, 553–564 (1977).
44. C. M. Geschke, J. H. Morris, Jr., and E. H. Satterwrite, Early experience with MESA, *Comm. ACM* **20**, No. 8, 540–552 (1977).
45. M. B. Wells and F. Cornwell, A data type encapsulation scheme utilizing base language operators, *SIGPLAN Notices* **11**, No. 3, 170–178 (1976).
46. R. T. Johnson and J. B. Morris, Abstract data types in the MODEL programming language, *SIGPLAN Notices* **11**, No. 3, 36–46 (1976).
47. J. H. Laning and N. Zierler, A Program for Translation of Mathematical Equations for Whirlwind I, Eng. Memo. E-364, C. S. Draper Lab., MIT, Cambridge, Massachusetts (1954).
48. J. H. Laning and J. S. Miller, The MAC Algebraic Language System, Rep. R-681. C. S. Draper Lab., MIT, Cambridge, Massachusetts (1970).
49. M. B. Wells, MADCAP: A scientific compiler for a displayed formula textbook language, *Comm. ACM* **4**, No. 1, 31–36 (1961).
50. K. G. Balke and G. Carter, The COLASL Automatic Coding System, *Proc. 1962 ACM National Conf.,* Lewis Winner, NY, pp. 44–45.
51. H. J. Gawlik, MIRFAC: A compiler based on standard mathematical notation and plain english, *Comm. ACM* **6**, No. 9, 545–547 (1963).
52. M. Klerer and J. May, An experiment in a user-oriented computer system, *Comm. ACM* **7**, No. 5, 290–294 (1964).
53. W. A. Martin and R. J. Fateman. The MACSYMA system, *Proc. Symp. Symbolic Algebraic Manipulation, 2nd* ACM, New York, pp. 59–75 (March 1971).
54. C. Engelman, MATHLAB: A program for on-line assistance in symbolic computations, *Proc. FJCC, AFIPS* **27**, Part 2, 117–126 (1965).
55. J. H. Griesmer and R. D. Jenks, SCRATCHPAD: A capsule view, *SIGPLAN Notices* **7**, No. 10, 93–102 (October 1972).
56. M. B. Wells, An Algorithm for the Recognition of Typed Two-Dimensional Mathematical Expressions, LA 6138 MS, Los Alamos, New Mexico (November 1975).
57. M. B. Wells, A review of two-dimensional programming langauges, *SIGPLAN Notices* **7**, No. 10, 1–10 (October 1972).
58. A. V. Aho, J. E. Hopcroft, and J. D. Ullman, "The Design and Analysis of Computer Algorithms." Addison-Wesley, Reading, Massachusetts, 1974.
59. E. Reingold, J. Nievergelt, and N. Deo, "Combinatorial Algorithms: Theory and Practice." Prentice-Hall, Englewood Cliffs, New Jersey, 1977.

60. M. B. Wells, Aspects of language design for combinatorial computing, *IEEE Trans. EC* **13,** No. 4 431–438 (1964).
61. J. T. Schwartz, On Programming-An Interim Report on the SETL Project, Installment I: Generalities. Courant Inst. Publ. New York Univ. (February 1973).

LOS ALAMOS SCIENTIFIC LABORATORY
LOS ALAMOS, NEW MEXICO

Part IV

The Machines

Computer Development at the Institute for Advanced Study

JULIAN BIGELOW

Writing about computer development some 30 years ago at the Institute for Advanced Study (IAS) is a bit like returning to the scene of an early love affair. It revives deep feelings of involvement still for me, and I am sure also for all who took part. A long chain of improbable chance events led to our involvement; people ordinarily of modest aspirations, we all worked so hard and selflessly because we believed—we knew—it was happening here and at a few other places right then, and we were lucky to be in on it. We were sure because von Neumann cleared the cobwebs from our minds as nobody else could have done. A tidal wave of computational power was about to break and innundate everything in science and much elsewhere, and things would never be the same afterward. It would cleanse and solve areas of obscurity and debate that had piled up for decades. Those who really understood what they were trying to do would be able to express their ideas as coded instructions, calculate with powerful machines, and find answers and demonstrate explicitly by numerical experiments. The process would advance and solidify knowledge and tend to keep men honest.

The circumstances in which the Institute's computer project was started were improbable in several ways. Originally von Neumann intended that the development of the new computer would be done by a team under the leadership of J. P. Eckert from Moore School, but some sort of conflict or disagreement about the arrangements occurred, and the outcome was that he decided to find his own team leader and to assemble a new engineering group

291

at the Institute. It so happened that von Neumann knew Norbert Wiener of MIT quite well, and I had been associated with Wiener on a war research project, so by this string of accidents the task landed in my lap. When I got to Princeton in June 1946, three engineers had already been employed without any knowledge or contact on my part, and two more were on the way. In fact, they turned out to be excellent choices, and I should particularly like to mention James Pomerene, who is now an IBM Fellow, Ralph Slutz, who had recently finished his Ph.D. in physics at Princeton and is now with the Bureau of Standards at Boulder, and Willis Ware, who is now with the Rand Corporation at Santa Monica. Both Ware and Pomerene had valuable earlier experience in electronics — not in the electronic computer field, because no such field then existed, but in pulse coded devices developed during World War II for airborne usage known as IFF (Interrogator Friend or Foe), in which one sends a radar inquiry beam up to scan an aircraft and if same is equipped with a properly coded IFF transponder device, it sends back an encoded message, "We are friends, don't shoot at us." Experience of this sort was the best available at that time.

At the Institute, Burks, Goldstine, and von Neumann had drafted the first version of Preliminary Discussions of the Logical Design of an Electronic Computing Instrument and had obtained contractual support from military agencies and the Atomic Energy Commission, which fortunately were free of any security complications. Employment arrangements at IAS were set up for the engineering team, made attractive by an agreement that patents would be sought by the Institute on behalf of those engineers who might invent various features of the forthcoming computer, such patents to be property of said engineers modulo provision for royalty-free use by the U.S. Government. (This patent agreement was in fact never carried out.)

Another feature of the arrangement for financial support provided that, as sections of the computer were successfully developed, working drawings would be sent out by our engineering group to five other development centers supported by similar government contracts, notably to Los Alamos Laboratory, the University of Illinois, Oak Ridge National Laboratory, Argonne National Laboratory, and the Rand Corporation. For the first year or so this requirement that what we produced was in effect going to be duplicated at five distinguished laboratories elsewhere added to the anxieties of the IAS team, especially since these correspondents were mostly well established and supported by facilities and resources wholly lacking *chez nous*. We anticipated that any mistakes we might make in sending out piecewise the fruits of our efforts would thereby be exposed to possibly hostile or competitive criticism, leaving us no place to hide, but in fact problems of this sort never arose, and communication with all people at these laboratories was entirely friendly and stimulating. Another anxiety about the arrangements also proved groundless; this was that since it was obvious to all of us that von Neumann was more clever than anybody and often twice as impatient, he might want to design and build the actual machine, or if not, to approve or disapprove techniques of its realization. In fact, although he liked to receive verbal progress reports in his office from the engineers—most often myself —about once a week, he came into the laboratory areas to see things only once every few months. He asked searching questions, penetrating to the core of each development problem, but made few, if any, suggestions.

One aspect of the arrangements, tacitly agreed to by all, was that we would obtain help from outside our own group for the development of as many portions of the proposed computer as we possibly could. Thus an agreement was made with RCA for the development of the fast-access memory, which was to be composed of RCA "Selectron" storage tubes, then under development at their Princeton Laboratories, and with the National Bureau of Standards in Washington for controllers for serial type input–output media such as punched and/or magnetically inscribed tapes. About these, more later.

At the Institute in 1946 there were no tangible assets relevant to computer development except books, brains, prestige, and high hopes—and von Neumann and Goldstine in person. (Arthur Burks returned to the University of Michigan about September 1946.) Equipment shortages of all sorts prevailed, due to the aftermath of World War II. We read through Preliminary Discussions . . .* often and discussed with each other and with Johnny and Herman, who were already trying out exploratory coding procedures on paper.

Early on, we came to understand how the "preliminary discussion" report had reduced the concept of a general-purpose computer to simple essentials without sacrificing flexibility, and what the magic of stored coded programs enabled to be done. Moreover, we understood the massive binary data flow and transformations required by this prescription, with tapestries of interdependent gating activities, including chains of conditional switching sequences often of great length. Since an item of data was to consist of 40 binary digits handled in parallel, most of the arithmetical circuitry involved 40-fold replication throughout, working concurrently at microsecond time intervals or even faster. It was abundantly clear to us that the occurrence of a single undetected chance error anywhere in such 40-fold circuitry would produce numerical hash at unprecedented rates. Various reputable experts outside the engineering group at IAS made gloomy predictions, moreover, that the attempt to produce a 40-place parallel computer was ill advised and would certainly require many times more electron tubes, gating elements, etc., than a serial machine and be cumbersome and unreliable. We kept our own counsel and went ahead heedlessly.

Johnny often emphasized that the big performance payoff would be in

---

* Preliminary Discussions of the Logical Design of an Electronic Computing Instrument, by Burks, von Neumann, and Goldstine.

multiplication speed, and asked how fast we thought we could make this instruction function. If one made a thoughtless estimate, crises would arise at lightning speed, for the estimate would be used by him as a basis for a vast structure of deductions about what sorts of calculations would or would not be feasible in consequence of such speeds. We soon learned that such questions required replies of utmost caution, with wide upper and lower bounds on the estimate. But it was easy to get carried away to an inadvertence, Johnny was so personable and relationship with him so easy and pleasant, often laced with good humor, anecdotes, limericks, and friendly insights that removed all social defenses.

The period from June 1946 through June 1947 can fairly be described as one of engineering and organization rather than actual design. We knew that the package we must achieve would need to have unprecedented speed of action and sustained reliability incorporated everywhere throughout extensive structures consisting of thousands of electron tubes, resistors, and circuit elements, necessitating tens of thousands of soldered connections. We knew that the development time for improving a circuit element such as a vacuum tube or resistor, when one included the time to get it into production, could not be less than one or two years at best, and that no avenues of this sort should be considered unless no other way could be devised, using existing parts, to reach our goals. So we decided to use standard available parts as best we could—or find out why we could not.

Accordingly, we divided our half-dozen engineers into several task-area subgroups, having responsibility in such areas as

(a)   test equipment for operating and evaluating digital circuits, etc.— that is, pulse sequence generators, interval timers, power sources, etc.;

(b)   recording media—mostly magnetic—for in/out and mass backup memories such as drums, coated wires, tapes, etc.;

(c)   circuit elements for digital use (electron tubes, etc.), their availability, reliability, uniformity, compactness, power requirements, etc.;

(d)   bistable circuits and logical gating elements: speed, reliability, simplicity.

Pending progress in these areas, we felt that it was premature (to say the least) to attempt a design of large sections of the computer because we simply did not have enough technical facts with which to proceed. Progress in areas (a) and (c) were prerequisites for the study of areas (b) and (d). In the 1970s it might seem incredible, but no instrumentation was commerically available that was suitable for the study of electronic events in the microsecond time range and to observe what was happening. The only thing we had at the start was an A–R radar range oscilloscope borrowed from a military agency and later returned to them. Tektronic scopes did not yet exist. By various ingenious approaches, pulse sequence generators with adjustable intervals in the right range were built using tapped delay lines, etc., by talent within our group and served well to get us started in the study of time resolution problems in areas (b) and (d) above.

By early 1947 our new laboratory building had been completed, and progress in areas (a), (b), (c), and (d) to provide us with facts about what could be expected of available parts was proceeding rapidly. A survey of digital recording on magnetic materials showed that special electroplated surfaces on metallic base would accept at least 50 bits/in. and spray coatings of ferric oxide promised even better densities; however, it must be remembered that coated plastic tape such as mylar was not on the market until a few years later.

With regard to fast arithmetical and gating circuitry, we knew that for shifting registers, binary counters, control logic, and much else we would need bistable electronic subunits in great abundance. As everybody knows today, a bistable circuit (or "binary cell") is a device that has two stable states, changeable at will, to which may be assigned representation of the digit 0 or 1. As the digits are moved about, and transformed by arithmetic, it must be possible to change the bistable state very quickly when needed, but at all other times the last state into which it is put must faithfully be retained. Circuits for doing this have been in the electrotechnical literature since 1919 when Eccles and Jordan first published such an arrangement consisting of two amplifying electron tubes cross connected so that either one makes the other go "off" when it itself is "on." A common use of such bistable circuits has been to form stages of electronic counters, either scale-of-2 or scale-of-10 or the like. In most applications the bistable circuit is arranged to "remember" which state it is in by virtue of an active current flowing in the "on" side, this current being of course smoothed and "upper frequency limited" by the capacitance inherent in the electrode structure of the tubes. Typically the cross connections of the tube pair (we called it "transpose" connection) was provided with an $R-C$ time constant so that an agnostic command pulse applied to both tubes "symmetrically" (i.e., on a common voltage bus) would cause a change of state (from 0 to 1 or from 1 to 0) in the circuit. The agnostic command pulse would have to have a steep front and the right duration, so that information about the previous state preserved during change by the $R-C$ transpose would not be lost during "flipover." These circuits are called "flip-flops" in much of the literature; our group preferred the term "toggle."

The typical circuit of this type usually served as a binary counter stage, but it can serve as a cell of a binary register if the gating is arranged to command, not simply "change state," but "change state to become 1" or "to become 0." Since our prospective computer was obviously going to need arrays of hundreds of such devices so operated, we made a very careful analytical and experimental investigation of what determined the long-time stability, quickness of change, safe operating regime under all variations in operating parameters, and general reliability in use. We also studied the interdependence of these on the methods used to "gate in" and "gate out" information to the toggles. We found out what we should have known beforehand, that rate of digit flow among such binary cells depends on the gating techniques, and that with enough gating power commanding the cell to assume the desired state, that is to say, with directed gating, changeover delay can be made as brief as you please. In this mode, information exchange rates among binary cells depended on the gain in both the tubes in the cells and the tubes in the gates.

By mid-1947 progress had been made in understanding bistable circuitry and gating techniques, and these were on so sound a basis that we were in a position to proceed with exploratory design of larger sections of the arithmetic unit, such as 40-stage shifting registers and adders, and various binary counters. In fact, we worked out several versions of each of these without fixing upon a final design, and this progress toward increasingly exciting stages of the work marked an upswing in spirit and confidence within the engineering team and kept everybody fascinated and busy. I was able to turn my attention to restudy "Preliminary Discussions . . ." to understand better the sequences of internal control commands needed to carry out automatically the sequences of data manipulations in the arithmetic unit as specified by the instruction repertoire. About this time I became aware that the 40-stage adder need be nothing more that a 40-fold array of logical gates that proceeds automatically to form a binary sum C as soon as addends A and B are offered to it; that is, the adder needs no further exterior commands and no interior state-preserving memory devices to do its job, since its output C is uniquely determined by its inputs A and B. However, as soon as the sum C is formed, the script says it is supposed to replace one of the addends, say B, by being deposited in that addend register Rb. So it became obvious that if the adder is fast—as it ought to be—then transit through it would be fast, and a potentially risky race condition could result, for as soon as one starts to deposit C in Rb, then addend B starts to change, so then C starts to change, etc., leading to a train wreck. Simple, even trivial; anyone would have recognized it, quickest of all von Neumann, had his attention been centered upon engineering aspects of the machine.

Detail such as this is boring, but we recount this instance because it clarified and crystallized our thinking and influenced the whole computer design thereafter. We recognized that either *all* information flow routes through the adder would have to be made slower than the time required to replace addepend B by sum C in register Rb, or else an extra ready register row would be required in Rb to receive adder outputs. Since adder response time determines the speed of the arithmetic unit and hence of the whole computer, the slowup alternative was intolerable; hence was born the double-row shift register finally used for Ra and Rb.

Once this medicine had been swallowed, we recognized that the decision to avoid race conditions by providing extra rows of toggle cells to receive advancing information rather than relying upon transit delays would make several other problems we were required to solve simpler and more straightforward. For example, the multiplication and division instructions required chains of adds/subtracts, at each step followed immediately by single right/left shifts, and these shifts could now be done efficiently by providing a choice of "diagonal down" gates G_r and G_l that accomplished the R/L shift automatically while advancing the partial results from the temporary row of the double register to the main register row. The gate-command sequences to accomplish $\times$ and $\div$ (also ShR, ShL, etc.) thus became simple and regular operations applied in proper sequence to selected busses common to all 40 digits, and the path of the data flow became quite immediate for these orders. In case of interruption of the gate-command sequence, partial results would be preserved. Indeed, step-by-step proof testing of gating-command sequences and of their safety margin at each step for each of the 40 stages became possible at manual speeds by manipulating limit checking rheostats, without special pulsing and observing equipment.

Systematic use of such direct gating procedures to advance binary data locked in "sending" cells to "receiving" cells became the preferred technique used throughout the arithmetic unit, also in most of the logical control and in much elsewhere. Information was first locked in the sending toggle; then gating made it common to both sender and receiver, and then when securely in both, the sender could be cleared. Information was never "volatile" in transit; it was as secure as an acrophobic inchworm on the crest of a sequoia. We were amused to realize that the functioning was like a ship canal lock system and that the information advancing processes of the whole arithmetic unit resembled a complex clock escapement. We enjoyed some interesting speculative discussions with von Neumann at this time about information propagation and switching among hypothetical arrays of cells, possibly responsive to alternating waves of (say) blue and red light, and I believe that some germs of his later celluar automata studies may have originated here.

By the summer of 1947 our confidence in our ability satisfactorily to design the arithmetic unit and its control logic was very high, but also we had done a great amount of work on digital recording on magnetic media for input–output purposes and also for outer "mass memory" to back up the inner fast memory that was immediately associated with the arithmetic unit. A fair estimate would be that I/O and magnetic recording studies had absorbed half of our effort to that date. It seemed to us that the most promising material available at that date was Brush Development electroplated bronze wire, which had become available in 1947 in experimental batches. In the spring of 1947 we built a comical piece of test apparatus consisting of two bicycle wheels operated on the same shaft, with a simple differential motor between them, and arranged so that the Brush wire came off one wheel, passing over a head, and back onto the other wheel, the loop size being adjusted by action of the differential. Though primitive, this rig seemed to work promisingly well, and since a young mechanical engineer, Peter Panagos, had recently joined our team, he and I decided to initiate a crash program to design a production version of this wiredrive rig, with all the features it ought to have to work at both high speeds to reload the fast inner memory, and at low speeds to exchange information with punched Teletype tape.

I want to devote a few paragraphs to this effort, not because the resulting apparatus played an important role in the IAS computer—which it did not—but because I feel that what occurred may be fully as educational and historically interesting as if the outcome had proved to be of great use. The design of the wire drive unit was started on 1 July 1947 and finished on 2 August 1947—one month of intensive work. It combined in one package paired wire reel assemblies with quick removal and replacement design similar to a modern "disk pack." The magnetic wire came off one reel and went back onto the other at speeds up to 100 ft/sec, and passed over a pivoted head support that provided for "level winding" and loop follow-up motions, the latter being reported to the differential servo amplifier by Selsyn. The follow-up differential motor was fully enclosed and positioned the reels by concentric shafts with quick detach teeth engaging the reels. The main drive was by V-pulley, the interior of which was cut away to receive an electrically actuated friction brake, normally "on" when the main drive motor was off, so that the wire would not creep when the drive was off. The anchor plate for this brake was rotatable by worm gearing, so as to provide the slow speed range, Teletype-compatible drive mode. An electric tachometer provided feedback of actual wire scan speed. A 45° mirror below the reel housing permitted viewing the wire tracking over the head, and the level wind and loop follower action.

It was a thing of beauty in the eyes of its creator, and perhaps even in the eyes of other knowledgeable observers, but in the end it was doomed to be of little use. The wire wore deep grooves in the face of the heads, especially at high speeds; the wear released dust and powder, which produced errors in the information. Whereas the wire was quite strong, it also was unyielding and occasionally broke; it could be knotted and run, but this caused new complications. Finally, by about 1949 plastic tapes of nylon and mylar became available, and were clearly superior. In retrospect, the high-speed wire drive effort proved to be a mistake, not because of incompetence in its execution but because advancing technology made it obsolete before it played any important role. Moreover, we had not estimated realistically the number of skilled man-years needed adequately to perfect such an apparatus. We had succeeded in producing an elegant and compact design in two man-months and hoped that one machinist and one engineer could finish the construction and perfect operation of the apparatus in perhaps another six months. However, in the light of industrywide experience in the middle

1950s developing magnetic tape drives, we all know today that something like 5 to 10 man-years would have been a more realistic estimate for the IAS high-speed drive. Nevertheless, the wire drive was actually built and test run—not entirely satisfactorily—by early 1948, at which juncture we realized that the main goal aimed at by that effort (a capacity on the order of a million 40-bit words) was less urgently needed than other parts of the computer system, such as the fast inner memory to work with the arithmetic unit.

In the fall of 1947 our engineering group had to go through another phase of maturation in connection with the circuitry of the adder portion of the arithmetic unit. As indicated above, we had developed various 10-stage assemblies such as shifting registers and counters, and achieved test results that were reassuring, but the experimental adders, of which several versions were evolved, typically gave promising results with encouraging speeds, etc., in test units of two or three stages, but when built and tested in prototypes of 10 stages, malfunction was quite apparent. Repeated readjustment and "trimming" of the circuit elements on the test bench were tried by the team who had undertaken this design task without decisive correction of the

Figure 1 The I.A.S. Computer—Register Side.

Figure 2   Interior of Reels chamber—door open.

trouble. As chief engineer, I was hesitant to probe too aggressively into what was occurring because the task team included persons very experienced in television circuitry and the like, but finally I asked Jim Pomerene (not a member of that team) to investigate what was happening and whether it was a matter that parameter adjustment would cure or not. He made a table of digital input states, and of voltage ranges, and reported that for no set of adjustments would the thing work in all 10 stages for all digital inputs. I then understood that this prototype adder had not been analyzed and designed adequately on paper at the engineer's desk with regard to circuit element tolerances, gating levels, worst-case combinations, etc. In effect, an attempt was being made to "patch up" the design on the lab test bench, without full appreciation of the combinatorial problem involved in such digital circuitry.

Regretfully, I realized that complete democracy in circuit design was a luxury we could not afford. An engineering meeting was called, and for almost an entire day we analyzed aspects of the adder circuitry, calculating on the blackboard what would happen for various tolerances of resistors, gate tube conductances, voltage bus levels, etc., and out of this work session we

Figure 3 High-speed mechanical wire drive.

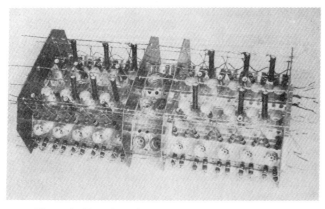

Figure 4 Top view of production model shifting register.

evolved a set of circuit-design rules and procedures, which was dubbed "the new look." It included complete tolerance specifications, such as "all circuits shall be designed to gate correctly with the worst combination of resistors deviating by $\pm 10\%$ from specified values" and also "with the tube conductance varying in worst combination from half nominal to twice nominal." All circuit parts used were to be acceptance tested to tolerances twice as severe, etc. At the end of this "new look" session we had redesigned the adder on the blackboard so that everybody in the group knew it would work correctly the first time it was so built regardless of input digit combinations or of how many parallel stages one chose to employ.

By late 1947 we had thus completed our circuit design of the arithmetic unit and built and tested 10-stage prototypes of the required subassemblies. We began to pay attention to the physical design and layout of the first 40-stage arithmetic unit. It had been decided that we would use almost exclusively "minature double triode" electron tubes, mostly type 6J6, which were about the size of one's thumb and were then in mass production. In the arithmetic unit there would be needed about 2000 of these, and we gave careful attention to problems of chassis design, to provide for the shortest and most direct connections of all parallel digital-information wires and for longitudinal gate-command sequencing buses. To get heater and other non-information-bearing wiring out of the way, we developed a built-up copper strip sandwich that lay flat along the rows of tube sockets, much in the spirit of modern "printed circuitry." The individual tube-row chassis were channel shaped and designed so that the resistors and wire connections could be put in as directly as possible without bending and so that all soldered joints could be visually inspected. The chassis channels were assembled so that the tube envelopes, resistors, and other heat-generating elements faced inward in the main frame, where they were cooled by forced air. The entire arithmetic unit was assembled, wired, and tested by June 1948. Everything worked the first time tested, as designed, and properly.

During the period of assembly and test of the arithmetic unit in the spring of 1948, von Neumann came over several times to see various tests, and when 10 stages were completed we inserted trial addends and caused their addition to occur. Both addends and sum were visible on neon indicator lamps provided for marginal test purposes, and Johnny enjoyed doing the additions in his head and calling out the answer. The first few times he was right, but then we put in more complicated addends with also a "left end" carry, and it eventually happened that what he called out as the answer disagreed with the result shown by the adder. Upon rechecking, Johnny found he had made an error, and acknowledged the victory of matter over mind.

As the construction of the final version of the arithmetic unit progressed toward completion in the spring of 1948, and as each section performed in tests as prescribed, the weekly engineering progress reports in von Neumann's office underwent a gradual shift of emphasis. It was clear that the arithmetic organ of the computer was no longer in doubt, and reports on it became perfunctory. What von Neumann was becoming increasingly concerned about was the possibility that we would be stuck without a fast parallel memory to operate with the arithmetic unit. The Selectron tube, under development by a talented team at RCA, was reported to be progressing well each time we made quarterly inquiry; however, not one wholly operative tube had been produced after about two years of effort. No one in the IAS team was sufficiently expert in electron tube design and manufacture to be able to estimate what the outcome of this effort would be, to say nothing of being able to assist it, but in conference with von Neumann I made an attempt to list all the variables which would have to be kept under control to produce a 50% yield of successful Selectron tubes, covering a range of digital capacities from the original goal of 4096 digits per tube, down through 2048, 1024, 512, etc. It appeared to us that the prevailing RCA goal of 4096 per Selectron was probably far too ambitious, and that acceptable production yields might be far sooner attained if the goal had been reduced to (say) 128 digits per tube. In any event, although the Selectron effort continued to hold our intellectual respect and admiration, we had increasing doubts that it would provide something we could use in the near future. (The Selectron actually became available in capacities of 256 digits per tube in the early 1950s and was used by the Rand group.)

Accordingly, to give ourselves some guarantee against being left without any fast parallel memory to run the machine, we initiated (in the spring of 1948) a crash program to see what could be done to develop a quick-access parallel-track magnetic drum. Our goal was to achieve an access time of about 1 msec, which, although about 100-fold slower than the originally planned electronic memories, would still permit the computer to do interim calculations and to be used in perfecting programming techniques, etc. Such an access time would require 30,000 rpm if two diametrical head positions per track were to be used, and 15,000 rpm if four heads per track. Either speed of revolution would be a formidable challenge, and we gave considerable care to the design, which involved a sort of expanding mandrel capable of supporting a 5-in.-diam high-tensile bronze tube, which was machined on its own bearings to very close tolerance. Each of the 44 tracks provided space for 2048 digits, and accordingly the heads would have to read and write microsecond pulses. It was obvious from the beginning of this exploratory effort that any ordinary recording head with wound magnetic core would be hopeless for this purpose, and we produced an interesting development in the form of a head consisting of a single strand of 1-mil wire spaced at about 1-mil clearance from the surface and excited by microsecond pulses of several amperes, which gave promising results at the required speeds. This apparatus was built by the summer of 1948, and was undergoing tests at that time.

However, in the spring of 1948, we explored other schemes for the achievement of high-speed memory, including an idea for coupling a cathode-ray tube (CRT) and an iconoscope "back-to-back" to produce a memory stage, which I discussed with von Neumann. It looked feasible but very elaborate and expensive if attempted in 40 parallel stages. Then we heard of work being done by F. C. Williams of Manchester, England, in which an ordinary cathode-ray tube was used by picking up beam displacement currents via an external metallic screen. In June we received a preprint copy of a report by Williams and Kilburn from Manchester, and it was read quickly by everybody in our group. The consensus was that this looked like the most promising scheme yet, and arrangements were made for me to go to Manchester for a few weeks to visit Williams, while at IAS Jim Pomerene would start an effort to see whether the Williams scheme could be made to work in an experimental rig at our laboratory. My visit to Manchester (also to Cambridge and London) was a delightful experience; F. C. Williams was a true example of the British "string and sealing wax" inventive genius, who had built a primitive electronic computer from surplus World War II radar parts strictly on his own inspiration—in the middle of which were two cathode-ray tubes storing digits in serial access mode—the "Williams memory." I can remember him explaining it to me, when there was a flash and a puff of smoke and everything went dead, but Williams was unperturbed, turned off the power, and with a handy soldering iron, replaced a few dangling wires and resistors so that everything was working again in a few minutes. When I phoned Princeton from Manchester after being away about three weeks, Pomerene reported to me that an experimental Williams memory tube was already working there and storing some 16 digits. So I came home.

In the fall of 1948, we all worked exhaustively to understand the peculiarities, strengths, and weaknesses of the Williams technique. It is not fitting to go into great detail here, but as everybody now knows, the whole technique depends upon clever exploitation of the fortuitous secondary electron emission properties of cathode-ray-tube phosphor screens—phosphors that had been chosen and incorporated purely to give good visual response without regard for secondary electron emission. In this sense it was a lucky accident that the scheme worked at all. It required delicate and sophisticated circuitry to get one or two Williams CRTs working reliably as memories, and the project of doing this with 40 CRTs en masse taxed our circuit skills and ingenuity to the extreme. Spots on the CRT phosphors that had inoperable secondary electron emission characteristics would show up without apparent cause; also the arrangement was inherently one of mankind's most sensitive detectors of electromagnetic environmental disturbances. But, on the other hand, it was possible to do it with standard commerical CRTs bought off the shelf; nothing inside had to be modified, and it promised fast access (about 10 μsec) and a capacity of about 1024 digits per tube.

We set up a test bench in our laboratory to scan CRTs for Williams store capability, in which the Williams performance of the tube undergoing test was visually displayed on another CRT slaved to it, and we sorted through literally hundreds of candidate CRTs. At first these were obtained from surplus; later an agreement was made with a manufacturer to let us scan his productive output for good specimens, returning those not wanted but paying their reinspection and handling costs. We designed and tested special shielding using exotic sheet metals to protect the Williams tubes, including a fully enclosed video amplifier for each stage. We designed and tested a powerful direct coupled beam deflection and raster generating system capable of driving all 40 CRT stages in parallel through 1024 digit locations. We designed special counters to step the beam through the raster while "restoring" in standby mode, and circuits for interrupting when random access was required to exchange information with the arithmetic unit, and for resuming "restoring" at the same point after interruption. By the summer of 1949, the circuitry for the entire 40-tube Williams memory (plus a 41st monitor stage) had been designed along with shielding, frame and chassis, etc., and a prototype stage built and tested. The arrangement chosen looked more or less like a "V-40" engine and was designed to go under the arithmetic unit, thus permitting short parallel information connections therewith. The whole computer thus was to be relatively compact; about 6 ft high, 8 ft long, and 2 ft wide. In retrospect, it seems fair to say that especially in regard to the Williams unit and the space allowed for control circuits, it was too compact for convenient maintenance.

During the fall of 1949, our small shop team, ably led by Richard Melville, who was in charge of all production aspects, constructed and assembled the 40-stage Williams memory with all its complicated design features, while the circuit and logical control people including myself were busy with the interactive control to make the marriage between memory and arithmetic units work under the command of the coded instructions. This was a mixed marriage, in that the arithmetic unit had been designed to operate "asynchronously," that is, without explicit use of a "clock" to advance the progression of gating acts, which were to be timed by feedback "completion" signals, whereas in the Williams memory the stored digits were not in stably locked cells but rather in volatile charge patterns that needed frequently to be read and restored at clocked intervals, else all would be lost. Thus the interruptability and time insensitivity and locked information aspects we had already incorporated in the design of the arithmetic unit could not be used throughout the Williams design, and a restore cycle clock of 10-μsec intervals played an essential role. The Williams memory had two distinct modes of operation: while not being consulted, it busily stepped through each memory address in sequence, reading what was there and then restoring same to full strength, but while being "consulted" by the main arithmetic processes, it had to interrupt the restore mode, go to the address of inquiry and do the equivalent of a restore at that address, and then resume the restore mode where it had left off. This mode-interaction requirement

between memory and arithmetic organs was met by the design of logical in-
terlock circuitry permitting the Williams to complete the cycle it was doing
before any interrupt by the arithmetic organ; also by the design of certain
complex address counters capable of remembering where it was restoring
during a read/write consultation, etc.

In the course of finding the required solutions of these concrete problems
to make the rig work, we became aware that our solutions consisted in
making the stronger parts of our design (arithmetic unit, etc.) wait upon the
weaker, less technologically secure part, and that this principle is of general
importance in the "systems design" field. In any event, once the nose of a
camel is in your tent, the whole animal is sure to follow, and the successful
operation of the Williams memory became thereby sensitive to several spe-
cies of time parameters that we should have liked—and originally planned—
to avoid but now could not. For example, each Williams restore cycle took
10 μsec, but many of the simpler arithmetic operations ($+$, $-$, etc.) took not
much more, so if your program consisted mostly of "short" operations, the
Williams restore did not progress far between intervals. If, however, longer
arithmetic operations (say$\times$, $\div$) were common in the program, restore sequences progressed well. Actually, this potential difficulty rarely caused
trouble in practice, but it was one more requirement that needed safe-
guarding and was the first recognized of a consequent chain of program-de-
pendent machine usage precautions of a type we had vowed to avoid but
were now obliged to observe.

By January 1950, the "V-40" Williams memory had been constructed
and assembled, and the essential interaction control counters, etc., were
built so that shortly thereafter the main frames could be joined and primitive
full-scale tests initiated. To get information into and out of the computer, the
Bureau of Standards "Inscribe" and "Outscribe" control units were put
into operation, using Teletype tape perforated on Teletype machines that we
had modified so that performances were in proper binary arrangement. To
get reliability, the key-in procedure had to be done twice independently,
using a special verifier that would not advance the final tape unless every key
stroke agreed. The resulting verified tape was then "end-shifted" into the
arithmetic unit in groups of 40 binary digits, each such "word" then being
stored in the Williams memory in parallel by means of the standard "store"
instruction. This procedure was slow and cumbersome even after the verified Teletype tape had been finished, and required almost half an hour to fill
the Williams memory, but it was used until late 1951, when it was replaced
by IBM punched cards modified to read in and punch out 40 digits in parallel
from every card row, and this could load and unload the Williams memory in
about 5 min. Also, the punched cards gave another very important advantage: the machine user could, with practice, learn to interpret the perfora-
tions visually and so diagnose what was happening to his computation while
away from the machine. In fact, this was recognized early as a most urgently

needed in–out function, and would have been included in the original specification instead of Teletype were it not for the fact that IBM was reluctant, prior to about 1952 to allow any customer to attach any non-IBM apparatus to their card-handling equipment.

1950 was a year of extreme pressure for the IAS engineering group; our laboratory building was overflowing with applied scientists of various sorts, especially fluid dynamicists, meteorologists, nuclear physicists, and the like. Words like "geostrophic," "Hartree–Fock", "WKB" were echoing up and down the hallways, and people with actual programs in their hands were going to and from Herman Goldstine's office, and on the way peeking into the machine room. We ran tests; most of the machine orders worked as specified, and a few minor specifications (such as the 2° behavior during shifts) had at this point to be changed in the light of programming experience to date. We made various shortcuts such as foregoing various logical-completion feedback signals originally aspired to in the arithmetic control, i.e., logical carry completion signals, and substituted appropriate dummy delays to span the subprocesses involved, and then made long tests of the memory under conditions of simulated use. The memory worked rather well by the summer of 1950 but required about an hour of test runs and tune-up after being turned on to become stable and operative with 1024 words of 40 bits, and with the increased logical flexibility of addressing fully operational, another time-dependent program-interactive effect called "read-around" came under scrutiny. This effect was caused by contamination of the neighborhood of a given address due to excessive density of programmed consultation in that vicinity. This proved to be a particularly distressing kind of interference, and required that programmers limit the number of references to any given address during short iteration loops to something like 10 or 15 events, unless between these occurred "long" orders.

As minor details of logical control and Williams memory adjustment were made in the fall of 1950, every shortcut we could think of was put into effect to bring the machine to early operation. To provide stable and noise-free dc power supplies, a back room full of lead storage batteries was used, which served for several years until we had time to build the required regulated sources. The arithmetic control, which had been planned to utilize a primitive form of "microprogramming" to facilitate possible control-sequence error diagnosis, was hooked up without full utilization of these ideas and features, although factoring of the instruction digits and of the machine clear-gate command sequences so as to synthesize the "long orders" from standard elementary processes was done.

The entire computer was completed with about 2600 electron tube envelopes—a number believed to set economy records for that time, and which seemed to surprise the "serial mode" advocates. Of course, the rig can be viewed as a big tube test rack, and despite our most careful tube acceptance-test procedures, we found that the most frequent fault in the machine, exclusive of Williams memory, was due to structural failure—open or short—of electron tube elements, heaters, etc. Such failures tended to occur early in the usage cycle of the tube; the longer a tube remained in use, the more reliable it proved to be, up to lifetimes of several years. Moreover, heater failures proved to be due to thermal stress when the machine was turned on and off, and early on we learned to leave heaters on if possible and to cycle very gradually when making a shutdown. Also we learned that tube types sold at premium prices, because claimed to be especially made for long life, were often less reliable in regard to structural failures than ordinary tube types manufactured in larger production lots (e.g., 2c51 versus 6J6).

By the end of 1950, extensive tests and many trial or test problems had been done, and although some details of the machine were still incomplete and some features enabling it to function were still considered temporary expedients, it was now possible to put a program into the machine and get results out. During the spring of 1951, the machine became increasingly available for use, and programmers were putting their programs on for exploratory runs, debugging, etc., and the machine error rate had become low enough so that most of the errors found were in their own work. Meanwhile, tune-up and adjustment procedures for the machine had become standardized, and included systematic limit checking and the running of programmed test routines for memory reliability, read-around safety, etc.

During the summer of 1951, a team of scientists from Los Alamos came and put a large thermonuclear calculation on the IAS machine; it ran for 24 hours without interruption for a period of about 60 days, many of the intermediate results being checked by duplicate runs, and throughout this period only about half a dozen errors were disclosed. The engineering group split up into teams and was in full-time attendance and ran diagnostic and test routines a few times per day, but had little else to do. So it had come alive.

In the decades since this work was done, several people have asked questions about what we were thinking at the time, when we got our ideas, and in particular how much we knew about—and possibly gained from—developments taking place at other places such as project WHIRLWIND at MIT and the ex–Moore School team in Philadelphia. The answer is that we had no communication contact except rumors, and as far as I know each of these groups proceeded along its own avenues, directed toward its own goals and developing its own criteria of what constituted excellence. In some ways our group developed and achieved a certain kind of computer realization technique that to us seemed simpler and more direct than various alternatives, and some aspects of this could be argued to have anticipated techniques used in solid-state technology 10 and 20 years later; but we recognize that this view is subjective and that a rich variety of technical approaches were available on this new frontier. Other groups could likely have done what we did, but probably would have done it quite differently; perhaps the greatest historical interest may lie in seeing and comparing the different realizations that sprouted under initial conditions that entailed common objectives.

However this may be, it is certainly important to put on record a clear refutation of the notion that groups like ours had any need to borrow ideas from one another. As soon as some elementary successes were achieved, ideas on how next to proceed came in torrents to all of us; the difficult thing was to eliminate those that were perhaps attractive but less essential to the main course of progress. Many of our ideas were simply inventions to overcome obstacles encountered; targets of opportunity, so to speak. Others were simple insights that gave intellectual pleasure, such as the insight that a binary counter is simply a pair of bistable cells communicating by gates having the connectivity of a Möbius strip. Many specific technical problems solved gave pleasure when viewed as examples in a larger frame of interpretation, such as why the human memory organ has no erase capability, and why computations are characteristically irreversible processes.

There were many surprises, such as the discovery that circuit element tolerances, which required design safety rules which we called the "new look," were more important in limiting speed than the actual gain of the tubes used, and after the computer was built we examined the effect of miniaturization by various scale factors. Slutz and I one evening, after the thing was designed and built, wondered why we had Kirchhoff in our Kirchhoff adder, and by competing with each other to see if it could be done, designed a purely logical gating adder with the same number of tubes. Ideas and surprises abounded, many of which were set on the back burner with the hope that there would later be a second version of the machine with opportunity to follow them through to realization. We were in constant danger of being captured by the seeming elegance of ideas that occurred to us, and it was hard to sort the byways from the highways among them.

Finally, a few words about some aspects of the machine itself that may have been forgotten in the intervening years in which so much progress has been made. At least up to 1950, von Neumann thought of fast powerful computers as tools for applied scientists—quite exclusively. The IAS machine was programmed directly in machine order code, and one had to know what state the machine was left in by every order used—what registers the product of a multiplication would remain in, etc. There was no floating point or significance arithmetic; although double precision (80-bit) could be programmed on it, the programmer had to estimate where the most significant digit had wandered to and test for the program corrections to bring it back into focus before proceeding. Due to the limitations of the Williams memory behavior, the programmer had also to do certain bookkeeping tests on the programmed order statistics. None of this seemed a serious concern to von Neumann, and indeed much valuable computation was done even with the requirement for such juggling. But it is still a bit surprising that so little heed was given to matters of programming convenience; in fact, one of the early users of the IAS machine came up with some ideas containing the germs of assembly techniques and other aspects of higher languages, but received a cool reception. The "popular use" desiderata for such a machine seemed quite far from the prevailing thought at IAS at that time.

Finally, the IAS computer ran productively until about 1960, when it was given to the Smithsonian Institution for an exhibit. The great hopes many of us had for a permanent center for applied mathematics at the Institute had begun to unravel early in the 1950s, when there was a period of tension and discord among the faculty at IAS indirectly related to the Oppenheimer security clearance problem and other prickly issues, and the computer utilization people drifted elsewhere; von Neumann became increasingly involved with the AEC, and it became clear that the Institute faculty would not welcome further contract support.

During the period of development of the IAS computer, many noted scientists visited our laboratory for periods ranging from several weeks to many months. These included:

C. E. Froeberg (Sweden)	K. Booth (England)
E. Stemme (Sweden)	M. Wilkes (England)
A. Speiser (Switzerland)	A. van Wijngarden (Netherlands)
D. Booth (England)	C. V. L. Smith (ONR)

Other outstanding engineering people employed by our laboratory for varying lengths of time included

R. Melville	G. Estrin
W. Ware	P. Panagos
J. Pomerene	H. Crane
T. E. Hildebrandt	L. Harmon
M. Rubinoff	R. Shaw
R. L. Snyder	J. Davis
S. Y. Wong	J. Sims
A. Bliss	D. Slotnick
J. Rosenberg	D. Gillies
G. Kent	R. Slutz

INSTITUTE FOR ADVANCED STUDY
PRINCETON, NEW JERSEY

From ENIAC to the Stored-Program Computer:
Two Revolutions in Computers*

ARTHUR W. BURKS

1. Introduction

There has been a long controversy over "who invented the stored-program computer?" Unfortunately, this question is over simplistic. The development of the stored-program computer took place in many steps and involved many people. I shall trace this development through its main stages, starting with the antecedents of the ENIAC and ending with the first generation of stored program computers: EDVAC, IAS, WHIRLWIND, EDSAC, UNIVAC I, and many others.

This period saw two important revolutions in computers. The first was the employment of vacuum tubes to make a fast, reliable, powerful, general-purpose computer. This development began with John Atanasoff's† slow, special-purpose electronic computer. It culminated in ENIAC, shown in Fig. 1. ENIAC was developed, designed, and built by a group of engineers, including myself, under the direction of Pres Eckert and John Mauchly. ENIAC was revolutionary: it was the first electronic, digital, general-pur-

---

* This is a revised and expanded version of my paper at the International Research Conference on the History of Computing, Los Alamos Scientific Laboratory, Los Alamos, New Mexico. The paper was written under NSF Grant No. MCS76-04297. I wish to thank Brian Randell and Cuthbert Hurd for helpful comments.
† Reference in Randell bibliography.

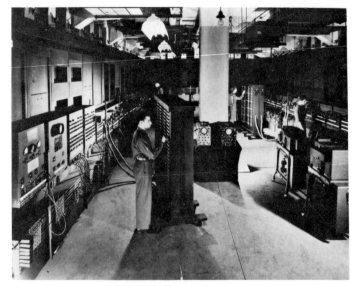

Figure 1   ENIAC, overall view.

pose scientific computer, and it computed 1000 times as fast as its electromechanical competitors.

The second revolution was the stored-program computer. It too had
important antecedents, which I shall explain in due course. There were two
main steps. Pres and John invented the circulating mercury delay line store,
with enough capacity to store program information as well as data. Von
Neumann created the first modern order code and worked out the logical
design of an electronic computer to execute it.

This early work on electronic computers arose out of the background of
modern electronics and out of a well-established technology of mechanical
and electromechanical computing (see Fig. 2). Many of the circuits of
ENIAC were electronic versions of mechanical and electromechanical digital computing devices, and the architecture of ENIAC derived from the mechanical differential analyzer. Thus ENIAC established electronic technology as the way to do computing hitherto done mechanically and
electromechanically.

ENIAC necessarily used electromechanical equipment for input and output, and thereby tested the relative merits of the two technologies for computing. Not surprisingly, some of the older and more experienced engineers
at the Moore school were sceptical about ENIAC. 18,000 vacuum tubes? No
one had ever operated a system of more than 100 tubes or so. At any moment at least one tube will be inoperative, and that may spoil the answer!
But the electromechanical I/O of ENIAC and EDVAC gave at least as much
trouble as the electronics. And so it has remained to this day.

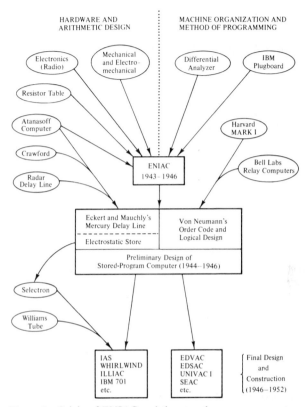

Figure 2 Origin of ENIAC and the stored program computer.

In my discussion I shall largely ignore input–output equipment, for the hardware revolutions of ENIAC and the first stored-program computers concerned the size, speed, and cost of internal components. The computing part of ENIAC dominated its I/O equipment, both in size and cost. Today the situation is reversed. The logical equivalent of internal ENIAC can be put on the end of your finger, and it costs much less than ENIAC equivalent I/O.

2. ENIAC Hardware and Arithmetic Design

Vacuum tubes had been developed for radio and telephone communication. In the mid-1930s they were still used mostly in analog or continuous fashion, though flip-flops, counters, and small vacuum-tube switching circuits had been invented and were used occasionally.

John Atanasoff pioneered in using vacuum-tube circuits for computing. Starting about 1935 he designed and partially built a special-purpose digital electronic computer for solving simultaneous equations by Gaussian elimination. He was assisted by Clifford Berry. They stored binary numbers on capacitors embedded in rotating drums, and did arithmetic and logic with vacuum-tube circuits. These circuits were slow, operating at 60 pulses/sec, which was about the speed of relay circuits.

In the spring of 1941, Atanasoff conceived of a digital electronic version of the differential analyzer. He communicated his idea to John Mauchly, who joined the faculty of the Moore School of Electrical Engineering in the fall of 1941. The Moore School had a differential analyzer, which was used some but often stood idle.

After we entered World War II, the Moore School became a center for calculating firing tables. The differential analyzer was soon used full time for trajectories. A group of young women calculated trajectories on electrically powered mechanical calculators: Friedens, Monroes, Marchants. Herman Goldstine was the Army Lieutenant in charge of this activity.

One day John suggested to Herman that trajectories could be calculated much faster with vacuum tubes. Herman thought John's suggestion a good one, and asked for a proposal. John, Pres Eckert, and J. G. Brainerd then wrote Report on an Electronic Diff.* [sic] Analyzer (2 April 1943). This was submitted to the Ballistic Research Laboratory, Aberdeen Proving Grounds, on behalf of the Moore School of Electrical Engineering, University of Pennsylvania.

In this proposal the Moore School offered a machine that could compute ballistic trajectories at least 10 times as fast as the differential analyzer, and at least 100 times as fast as a human computer with a desk calculator. Herman persuaded the Ballistic Research Laboratory to fund the proposal. The electronic diff.* analyzer later became the Electronic Numerical Integrator and Computer, or ENIAC for short.

John and Pres proposed to achieve this very high computing speed by operating vacuum-tube circuits at 100,000 pulses/sec. Physicists had used fast electronic circuits for counting cosmic rays, but these did not need to be, and were not, very reliable. The first development task on the ENIAC project was to design reliable counters that worked at 100,000 pulses/sec and to show by test that switching circuits could work at a comparable speed. The final ENIAC operated at 100,000 pulses/sec and thus became the first computer to exploit fully the vacuum-tube technology of the time.

We shall discuss some of ENIAC's arithmetic circuits in a moment, but to put this discussion in perspective we must first make a few general remarks about the machine's organization. ENIAC was composed of a large number of semiautonomous computer units, arranged as in Fig. 3. There were 25 computing units proper: 20 accumulators, one high-speed multiplier, three function table units, and a divider and square rooter. There was a constant transmitter for input and a printer unit for output. Each of these units had its own local program circuits, and there was also a central program control, called the master programmer. All these units were timed by signals from a central clock, the cycling unit.

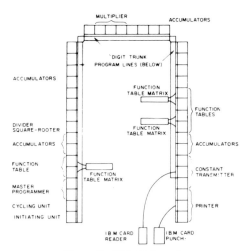

Figure 3 ENIAC layout.

The programming circuits of ENIAC were very important and occupied a large part of the machine. In the computing units proper the control circuits were about equivalent in size to the arithmetic circuits and more complex. We shall discuss ENIAC programming in detail later (Section 4). For the moment it suffices to say that subroutines were set up mechanically on local program controls. These subroutines were connected to the master programmer, which operated them in proper sequence, each subroutine being employed a fixed number of times or until a branch occurred.

One last point needs to be made before we return to ENIAC arithmetic. The units of ENIAC were not fully autonomous, because computing always required the cooperation of two or more of them. For example, addition was accomplished by transmitting from one accumulator to another. Correspondingly, local program controls on these accumulators had to be stimulated simultaneously.

The arithmetic design of ENIAC was influenced mainly by two kinds of calculators: mechanical desk calculators, electrically powered and hand operated; and electromechanical cardoperated IBM machines. We knew of the relay computers built and being built at the Bell Telephone Laboratories by George Stibitz, Sam Williams, and others. We also knew of the Harvard MARK I, a general-purpose electromechanical calculator designed by Howard Aiken and several IBM engineers. We did not know of the work of Konrad Zuse or of the British COLOSSI machines.

In mechanical technology, arithmetic registers were formed of toothed wheels, and carrying was done with cams and ratchets. Numbers were transmitted by shafts with gears, or the linear equivalent, toothed racks. In electromechanical technology, relays were used for switching, and stepping switches were used for counting. Relays could be "locked" to form flipflops. Numbers were transmitted as electrical pulses on wires. IBM ma-

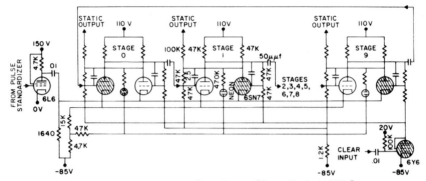

Figure 4 ENIAC decade ring counter. [From Burks (1947).]

chines and the Harvard MARK I combined mechanical and electromechanical technology.

In ENIAC, the toothed wheel and stepping switch became the electronic counter. A decade ring counter is shown in Fig. 4. Switching was done with vacuum tubes. The 6SA7 (tube 9) of Fig. 5 functions as a "gate" or switch. The program control is activated when a program pulse (from another program control or the master programmer) sets the flip-flop (tubes 1, 2, 3, and 4). When the flip-flop is set, it activates one input of the 6SA7 gate. The next program pulse from the cycling unit is then passed by the 6SA7. This pulse resets the flip-flop, closing the 6SA7 gate, and via tubes 10 and 11 drives a program line to start the program controls used in the next operation.

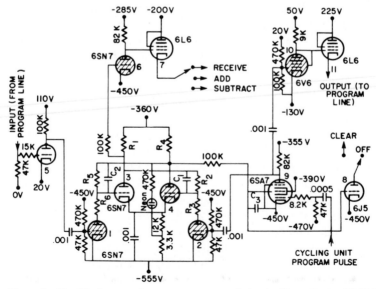

Figure 5 Simplified accumulator program control circuit. [From Burks (1947).]

Both numbers and control signals were transmitted as voltage pulses. We called these "pulses" when they lasted about 3 μsec, and "gates" when they lasted much longer. The basic pulses and gates came ultimately from the cycling unit (see Fig. 13 below).

We have listed the main electronic building blocks of ENIAC: counters, flip-flops, and vacuum-tube switches. Let us now move up a full level in the hierarchy of ENIAC structure and consider how the high-speed multiplier worked. For brevity I'll call it the "multiplier," and the two numbers to be multiplied the *"ier"* and the *"icand."*

Since the multiplier could not multiply by itself, we need to consider it and four associated accumulators: *ier* accumulator, *icand* accumulator, and two partial products accumulators. The three uncovered panels in the center of Fig. 6 constitute the multiplier, and the associated accumulators are to the left and right.

The time required for an ENIAC multiplication depended only on the number of *ier* digits called for in programming a multiplication. After a preparatory addition time, ENIAC multiplied one digit of the *ier* by the whole *icand* in a single addition time, dividing the partial product into left-hand (LH) and right-hand (RH) components. It did this by means of a prewired multiplication table. Two final addition times were used for combining the LH and RH partial products and making complement connections.

For the reader interested in the task of an ENIAC design engineer, I'll

Figure 6 ENIAC high-speed multiplier and associated accumulators.

explain how the multiplication circuits worked. Figures 7 and 8 show a sample of these circuits. The figures cover a two-digit *ier,* a two-digit *icand,* and that part of the multiplication table and its output tubes needed for the *icand* digits of 0, 1, 2, and 3.

The *ier* selector in the upper left-hand corner of Fig. 7 consists of and-gates with two inputs (tubes A0–A9 and B0–B9). Each selector gate is connected on one input to the *ier* accumulator and on its other input to a control wire. These control wires select the digit positions in turn; line 1 for the units

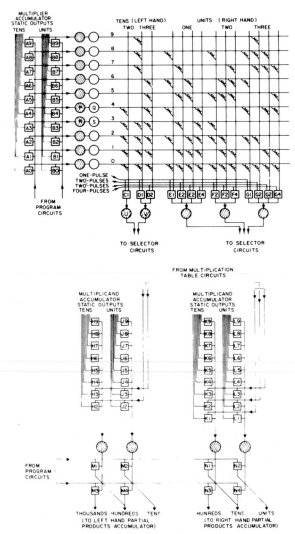

Figure 7 Simplified block diagram of ENIAC multiplier selector and multiplication table circuits (top) and multiplicand selector and shifter circuits (bottom). [From Burks (1947).]

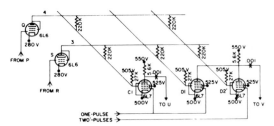

Figure 8   Cross section of ENIAC multiplication table. [From Burks (1947).]

digit, then line 2 for the tens digit. The selected *ier* selector gate activates the multiplication table through a driver (P, Q, R, S, etc.).

The multiplication table proper is a resistor matrix, each resistor establishing a direct electrical connection from an input digit wire (0–9) to a table output gate below (tubes C1, D1, D2′, E1–E4, F2–F4, and G1–G4).* A multiplication table input wire that is activated drops its voltage, thereby closing those output gates to which it is directly connected via a resistor.

The table output gates also receive groups of pulses from the cycling unit (see Fig. 13). Each gate left on by the multiplication table passes these pulses, which go through tubes U, V, etc., to the *icand* selectors below. Thus the table output gates produce, on separate wires, pulses that represent the product of the selected *ier* digit by all the digits 1–9, divided into LH and RH components. The LH components go to the LH *icand* selector (H2–H9, J2–J9), then to the LH shifter (M1–M4), and finally to the LH partial products accumulator. The RH components go to the RH *ier* selector (K1–K9, L1–L9), RH shifter (N1–N4), and RH partial products accumulator.

We shall trace the logical behavior of these circuits for a specific example. Let the *ier* be 40 and the *icand* 30, so the desired product is 1200, consisting of a LH component of 1000 and a RH component of 200. Consider the action of the multiplier while it processes the tens *ier* digit, which is 4.

The program circuits hold line 2 active while the tens digit of the *ier* is being processed. Hence the *ier* selector gates A0–A9 are activated from the right. (The shifter gates M3, M4, and N3, N4 are also activated by control line 2.) Tube A4 is also activated on the left by the *ier* accumulator, so it goes on, turning P off and Q on, thereby lowering the voltage on input line 4. This line turns off all the table output gates to which it is directly connected through resistors, leaving the remaining gates on. As far as the *icand* digit 3 is concerned, the LH gate D1 is on and D2′ is off, while the RH gate G2 is on and gates G1, G2′, G4 are off. Gate D1 sends one pulse to row 3 of the LH *icand* selector (H3, J3) and gate G2 sends two pulses to row 3 of the RH *ier* selector.

---

* Those table output tubes that are fed with two′–pulses should have primes on their numerals (D2′, E2′, F2′, and G2′).

These streams of pulses are gated by the *icand* selectors and then shifted by the shifters before being transmitted to the partial products accumulators. Since the *icand* is 30, a pulse representation of 100 comes from the LH selector and a pulse representation of 20 from the RH selector. Because line 2 is activated by the program circuits these are shifted one position to the left, so 1000 goes to the LH partial products accumulator and 200 to the RH partial products accumulator. At the end of the multiplication process these would be combined to give 1200, which is the product of 40 times 30.

This completes our expanation of how the ENIAC multiplier and its associated accumulators performed high-speed multiplication. The multiplication table was invented for mechanical calculators about 100 years ago. It was used in the IBM 601 crossfooting multiplier of 1931, which could be programmed to compute things like $A \times B + C + D$, $A + C - D$, and $A \times B - C$. This machine will be described below in connection with ENIAC programming (See Section 4 and Figs. 14 and 15).

Was this particular adaptation from mechanical technology wise for ENIAC? Fast multiplication made mechanical and electromechanical calculators superior to their predecessors. But ENIAC did many more operations, solved much more complicated problems, and had to be slowly programmed for each of these. Did fast multiplication in ENIAC provide a sufficient gain in speed over the method of repeated addition, or the faster method of repeated addition-or-subtraction, to justify it? Would the binary system have been a better choice than the decimal system? These are interesting questions that I cannot go into here.

I'll tell a story about the IBM 601 and ENIAC, which illustrates a general point about invention. An inventive IBM engineer wrote me a few years ago concerning the ENIAC multiplier: "I felt you were doing electronically almost exactly what we had had in general use for 12 years in the 600 and 601." I am reminded of the following story. In 1904 John Fleming invented the diode. Two years later Lee de Forest invented the triode. Someone is supposed to have said of de Forest's vacuum tube: That is not invention; all de Forest did was add a third wire to Fleming's valve!

Actually Fleming's tube was "only" a rectifier, whereas de Forest's triode was an amplifier, and amplification is what made the radio and electronics industry possible. Likewise, the computer industry became truly important when it moved from mechanical and electromechanical technology to electronics. This technological shift produced the transition from the industrial revolution to our current computer-control revolution.

Besides Atanasoff, we knew of two others who had worked on special-purpose electronic computers, in both cases for fire control. Perry Crawford wrote his master's thesis at MIT on controlling antiaircraft guns electronically, and Jan Rajchman did preliminary development work on an electronic fire-control calculator at RCA. Both developed electronic computing circuits and both invented a hardware constituent used in ENIAC, the resistor matrix function table. I described the fixed resistor table of the multiplier a moment ago. In it, a given input line drove a fixed set of output lines through resistors. One could make a variable table by installing a 10-position switch for each digit entry of the table. The resistor from the input line could then be manually switched to any one of ten output wires, representing the digits 0–9. ENIAC had three function table units for storing arbitrary functions, and each of these was based on a variable resistor matrix table set by switches.

The straightforward way to build a switching network, such as a multiplication table or function table, is to connect a diode between an input wire and each output wire it is to drive. The ratio of the backward resistance to the forward resistance of the diode is very high. But solid-state diodes did not exist then, and a vacuum diode was about as "expensive" as a triode, so in many applications this method of switching was not practical.

The resistor matrix function table was a way of using linear resistors as switching devices in read-only memories. When Jan Rajchman told von Neumann of his invention, Johnny replied: "That can't work, Jan, its just one big short circuit!" His point was that resistors are not rectifiers, and hence every output is connected to every input. This is clear from Figs. 7 and 8. But with careful design* the desired paths had much less resistance than undesired paths, and output gates could safely sense the difference. thus Fig. 8, tube Q (line 4) does not directly drive the input to gate D1, but only through highly resistant back circuits.

The ENIAC project was funded to facilitate the preparation of firing tables. The calculation of trajectories was a good problem for computing machines, because the calculation depends critically on the drag function $G(v^2)$, which gives the resistance of the air to the movement of the shell as a function of the velocity squared. This function is an ill-behaved function of the shell's velocity, especially as the shell passes through the sound barrier. In hand calculation the resistance was read from printed tables, and on the differential analyzer the resistance was fed in from an input table. Such a table is shown on the right in Fig. 9. Originally it was operated by hand. Later it was operated automatically by means of a photocell which read a black–white boundary and signaled a servomechanism feedback circuit.

All of these table-input methods were too slow for ENIAC. Hence we used variable resistor matrices set by hand switches. There were three function table units. Each had two panels of electronic equipment and a portable function table matrix box (see Fig. 3). One portable matrix appears in the foreground of Fig. 1 and the other two in the right rear, with operators setting switches.

A function table stored 104 entries, each with 12 decimal digits and two signs. Two signs were provided so that two numerical functions of six-digit

---

* See the paper by Rajchman in this volume.

Figure 9   Aberdeen differential analyzer. [From Eames (1973).]

accuracy could be stored in one table. Two decimal digits were used to select a function value in the range 0–99; the extra four entries (−2, −1, 100,
101) were there to facilitate interpolation. Note that the total digit capacity of
the three read-only tables was about 4000 decimal digits, or 20 times that of
the 20 READ–WRITE accumulators!

When ENIAC computed a trajectory the ballistic drag function was
stored in one of these function tables. Without the resistor matrix the values
of this function would have had to be brought in from the outside as needed,
a much slower process. At its dedication the ENIAC computed a trajectory
in 20 sec, faster than the shell itself, which took 30 sec to reach its target!
Thus the read-only resistor matrix played an essential role in the success of
ENIAC.

3.   ENIAC Organization and the Differential Analyzer

I have already mentioned that ENIAC was composed of 25 computing
units (accumulators, multipliers, function tables, and divider and square
rooter), an input unit, and an output unit. To program ENIAC to solve a particular problem one had to interconnect the digit circuits of these units and
also their programming circuits. In addition, the programming circuits had to
be connected to the master programmer.

ENIAC's organization came from, and closely paralleled, that of the differential analyzer. The 1943 ENIAC proposal by Mauchly, Eckert, and
Brainerd, on which Ordnance staked about $100,000, was titled Report on an
Electronic Diff.* Analyzer, with a footnote explanation that "diff.*" would
represent "differential" for the analyzer and "difference" for the proposed
electronic machine.

The differential analyzer was a mechanical analog computer for solving differential equations. It had been invented by Vannevar Bush at MIT. The Moore School had built one for itself and a similar one for Aberdeen Proving Ground. Figure 9 shows the Aberdeen machine. The differential analyzer could solve a variety of differential and integral equations, and hence was to some degree a general-purpose machine.

There were three fundamental types of calculating units in the differential analyzer: integrators for integration of functions, differential gears for addition–subtraction, and fixed gears for multiplication–division by a constant. There was no primitive unit for multiplication. Multiplication was accomplished through integration by parts; this required two integrators and one differential gear.

Inputs were inserted as initial conditions, or supplied continuously from an input table. The outputs were plotted on output tables or printed. In Fig. 9 the integrators are on the left, the input–output plotting tables on the right, and the printing mechanism is in the foreground. The main bay holds the shafts used for interconnections. Differential and fixed gears were mounted on these shafts.

An integrator consisted of a metal wheel riding on a rotating glass disk at a variable distance $f(y)$ from the disk's center. For each increment dy of rotation of the glass disk, the metal wheel rotated the amount $f(y)\, dy$. The wheel output was thus $\int f(y)\, dy$. This rotational output went to a torque amplifier and thence to a shaft in the bay. Originally the torque amplifiers were mechanical, but during the war they were replaced by an arrangement of two polaroid disks, a light beam, a photocell, and a servomotor.

To set up the differential analyzer to solve a particular system of differential equations, the operator interconnected the units by shafts and gears into a pattern corresponding to the equations. The whole system was driven by a shaft representing the independent variable. This shaft was rotated by an electrical motor.

Figure 10 is a diagram from Douglas Hartree's book (1947) showing the setup for the integral equation,

$$\frac{dy}{dx} = -\int \frac{dy}{dx}\, dy + \int y \cos(x + y)\, dx,$$

where x is the independent variable and y the dependent variable. Scale factors and signs are omitted from the diagram. The independent variable shaft x is driven by a motor. The output was recorded from the dependent variable shaft y.

With this information about the differential analyzer as background, let us look at the structure of ENIAC. Figure 11 is from the 1943 ENIAC proposal, and shows how the units of the machine were to be interconnected and controlled so as to solve the differential equation

$$\frac{d^2y}{dt^2} = ky.$$

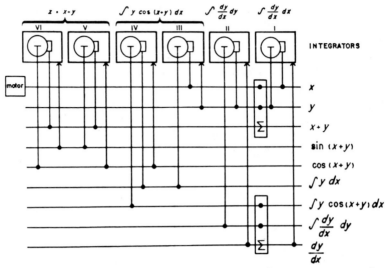

Figure 10   Setup diagram for a differential analyzer. [From Hartree (1947).]

The solution for y is, of course, an exponential, sine, or cosine, with suitable constants.

The corresponding difference equation is $\Delta^2 y = k(\Delta t)^2 y$. For the nth step of the integration the "electronic diff. analyzer" needs to compute

$$(\Delta^2 y)_n = [k(\Delta t)^2] \times y_{n-1},$$
$$(\Delta y)_n = (\Delta y)_{n-1} + (\Delta^2 y)_n,$$
$$y_n = y_{n-1} + (\Delta y)_n.$$

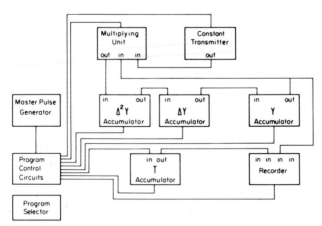

Figure 11   Block diagram illustrating method of solution of $d^2y/dt^2 = ky$ or $\Delta^2 y = k(\Delta t)^2 y$. [From Mauchly *et al.* (1943).]

The constant transmitter holds $k(\Delta t)^2$ and the accumulators hold the quantities indicated in Fig. 11.

I shall trace one step of the integration. The constant transmitter sends $k(\Delta t)^2$ to the multiplier and the y accumulator sends y_{n-1}. The multiplier computes $[k(\Delta t)^2] \times y_{n-1}$, which is $(\Delta^2 y)_n$, and sends it to the $\Delta^2 y$ accumulator for temporary storage. It is added from there into the Δy accumulator to give the new value of Δy. That is then added into the y accumulator to give the new value of y.

Note that the $\Delta^2 y$ accumulator was used only for temporary storage. Moreover, if k and Δt are chosen so that $k(\Delta t)^2$ is a power of ten, the electronic multiplier can be replaced by a mechanical shifter of wires. The difference equations then reduce to

$$(\Delta y)_n = (\Delta y)_{n-1} + 10^{-d} y_{n-1},$$
$$y_n = y_{n-1} + (\Delta y)_n.$$

These can be solved with just two accumulators, one for $(\Delta y)_n$ and one for y_n. The second transmits to the first through a wire shifter which shifts the transmitted number d positions to the right, and the first then transmits to the second, the quantities received being accumulated in both cases.

This method was used to test two ENIAC accumulators in the summer of 1944. The number in each accumulator was displayed with neon lights, and it was interesting to see the contents of the accumulators going up and down, one displaying the sine and the other displaying the cosine.

These two accumulators were connected in a pattern very similar to the interconnection pattern of integrators V and VI of Fig. 10. Each of these integrators feeds the other, just as each ENIAC accumulator augmented the other. In Fig. 10 both integrator V and integrator VI are fed $x + y$ as the independent variable. The output from the metal wheel of each controls the distance between the metal wheel and the center of the rotating glass disk of the other. Hence one integrator produces $\sin(x + y)$ and the other produces $\cos(x + y)$.

The shift from the analog differential analyzer to the digital ENIAC required a shift in the representation of data.

In the differential analyzer, the values of variables were represented by the positions of integrator wheels and disks, and the positions of the shafts driving and driven by the integrators. In ENIAC, numbers were held in the counters of accumulators, and transmitted in pulse form over groups of wires called digit trunks. Sometimes a digit trunk was an 11-wire cable, but usually it was composed physically of digit "trays" connected to each other and to program panels by 11-wire cables. A "tray" was 8 ft long, 1 in. thick, and wide enough to carry 11 wires shielded from each other by metal partitions. Ten wires were used for decimal digits, each digit being transmitted as a pulse sequence, and one wire was used for the sign.

In Fig. 12 the program panels are in the middle, and the digit trays are

Figure 12   ENIAC programming panels and cables.

above them. The trays below are used for program lines in a similar way; they will be discussed in the next section.

A caveat should be entered here. I am describing the general way in which ENIAC did things and am not attempting to be complete. For example, some numbers were transmitted as slow signals over cables. The contents of the *ier* and *icand* accumulators were transmitted to the *ier* and *icand* selectors of the multiplier in this manner.

The differential analyzer had a unique shaft, the independent variable shaft. It was driven by a motor, the speed of the motor controlling the speed of computation. In ENIAC this shaft became a 10-wire truck carrying clock signals to ENIAC units, and the motor was replaced by a complicated clock used to synchronize ENIAC operations. This clock was called "the master pulse generator" in the proposal and "cycling unit" in the final ENIAC. Its ten outputs are shown in Fig. 13. There are nine distinct groups of pulses, the individual pulses lasting about 3 μsec. There is one long pulse of 70 μsec, called the "carry-clear gate" and used mainly in the accumulators.

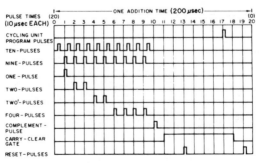

Figure 13   ENIAC cycling-unit pulses.

Some earlier digital machines were clocked. IBM punched-cards calculators were timed from the rotating mechanism that pulled the cards through the machine. Thus the significance of an electric pulse from a hole depended on the position of the hole in the card.

The shift from analog differential analyzer to digital ENIAC also required the addition of programming circuits. In the differential analyzer all computing units operated simultaneously. In ENIAC two or more units were required for an arithmetic operation, but they played different roles. For example, if the contents of accumulator 7 were to be added to those of accumulator 9, accumulator 7 transmitted and accumulator 9 received. Hence programming circuits were needed to operate the arithmetic circuits in proper parallelism and sequence. These circuits will be discussed in the next section.

4. Programming ENIAC

The differential analyzer was programmed manually, with a wrench in one hand and a gear in the other. ENIAC programming was also manual, but one plugged cables and wires, and set switches. The method of programming by plugging wires was derived from the IBM plugboard. I'll explain this in connection with the IBM 601 crossfooting multiplier (see Figs. 14 and 15).

The plugboard of Fig. 15 is wired to calculate $A \times B + C + D$. We mentioned earlier that the IBM 601 multiplied one digit of A (the *ier*) by all of B

Figure 14   IBM 601 crossfooting multiplier.

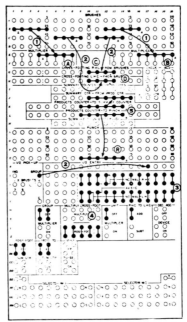

Figure 15   Wiring diagram for IBM 601 plugboard. [From IBM (1947).]

(the *icand*) in one addition time. The partial products were placed in two counters, a left-hand counter (LHC) and a right-hand counter (RHC). The numbers C and D were placed in these counters initially, and thus appeared in the final sum. The addition of C and D to the product was called "crossfooting," from an accounting term meaning to add across rather than up and down a column of numbers, Note that the LHC and RHC accumulated sums; in ENIAC we called them "accumulators."

I shall explain the wiring of Fig. 15 in terms of a payroll calculation. There is a punched card for each employee, with A being the number of hours, B the hourly rate, and C and D fixed amounts to be added to the paycheck. Point 1 shows that the brushes that pick up A and B are wired to the *ier* and *icand* counters, respectively. At point 2 the factors C and D are transferred from the brushes to RHC and LHC; the position of these wires depends on the locations of the decimal points. In the middle of the plugboard another occurrence of 2 shows that a $\frac{1}{2}$ entry is wired into one of the partial product counters. This $\frac{1}{2}$ produces a rounded digit in the position to the left; the contents of its position and the positions to the right are deleted from the answer. ENIAC used the same method of roundoff.

At point 3 the stepwise multiplication results are wired into RHC and LHC. Point 4 shows how some control wires are to be plugged in. I'll explain two of the connections. The multiply crossfoot switch is wired to accomplish crossfooting (the addition of C and D to $A \times B$) rather than for mere multiplication ($A \times B$ alone). Also, RHC and LHC are wired so their contents, the right- and left-hand components, will be combined at the end. Point 5 is located near the middle of the diagram. It shows wiring that carries the result $A \times B + C + D$ to the brushes and to a summary counter which accumulates $A \times B + C + D$ for each employee, and hence registers the total payroll.

The wiring of Fig. 15 is deceptively simple, because groups of digit wires are represented by single lines. For example, at upper left the brushes B21–B25 are joined by a straight line, an arrow from B23 goes to the multipler counter digit position E6, and positions E4–E8 are connected by a horizontal line. This symbolism means that brush B21 (reading column 21 of the card) is to be connected to multiplier counter digit position E4, and similarly for the other five digits of the *ier*. Thus a single arrow represents a bundle of six digit wires. A typical IBM plugboard was somewhat of a mess, as was an ENIAC problem setup.

Let us now see how ENIAC was set up or programmed to solve a specific problem. This was a dual task: digital communication paths were established among the numerical circuits of the units, and a program proper was set up on the program controls. To avoid ambiguity we will call the first part "numerical programming" and the second part "programming proper." Except for the branch operation, these two parts of a program were separate. I shall now discuss them in turn.

Each of the ENIAC computing units had input and output sockets for 10-digit signed numbers. These inputs and outputs were connected to digit trays by jumper cables. The cables are prominent in Fig. 12, where they go from the top of the accumulator program panels to the trays above. They are on the left in Fig. 6. The jumper cables and trunk lines are shown schematically at the top of Figs. 16 and 17.

Interconnecting the numerical circuits of ENIAC was analogous to setting up the differential analyzer. Both operations established data communication channels between computing units. But there was an important difference. In the differential analyzer, all shafts rotated simultaneously. In

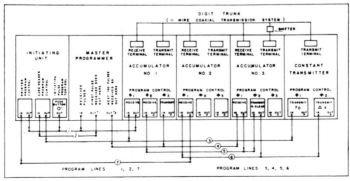

Figure 16 Simplified ENIAC program diagram. [From Burks (1946).]

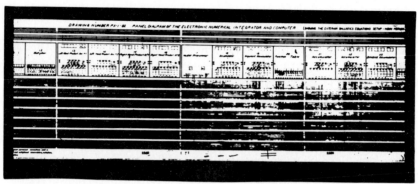

Figure 17 ENIAC program for Heun method trajectory. [From Eames (1973).]

ENIAC, the digital channels were used as needed, according to instructions set on local program controls. An accumulator, for example, had five input sockets (labeled α, β, γ, δ, and ϵ) and two output sockets (one for "add" and one for "subtract"). When setting up an accumulator program control the operator set a switch to one of the eight positions α, β, γ, δ, ϵ, A, S, AS. The AS position caused the accumulator to transmit simultaneously over both its add output and its subtract output, so it could add into one accumulator and subtract into another at the same time.

The main function of a numerical program of an ENIAC was to establish digital communication channels among the units. An auxiliary function was to arrange for some simple numerical transformations. Mechanical "shifters" and "deleters" could be inserted into digital sockets. A shifter was a plug–socket combination in which the wires were shifted to effect a multiplication or division by a power of ten. It was the digital equivalent of the fixed gear of the differential analyzer. To round-off the number in an accumulator, the operator did two things. She set a switch to clear the accumulator to "five" in one decade position. And she inserted deleters in the outputs to delete the unwanted digits.

Two adjacent accumulators could be interconnected for double precision (20 decimal digits).

This concludes our explanation of the numerical part of an ENIAC program. This part determined the precise effect of the instructions set on local program controls, so it is analogous to microprogramming. We turn next to the second part of an ENIAC setup, the programming proper. This involved interconnecting ENIAC control circuits and setting switches so that these circuits would direct the numerical circuits to perform the desired computation.

Each of the ENIAC computing units had several program controls. I shall describe first how the programmer used them and then how they controlled the numerical circuits. The reader should refer to the lower parts of Figs. 16 and 17 for schematic representations of ENIAC programs. Figure 17 pictures part of a chart showing how to set up ENIAC to integrate a trajectory by the Heun second-order method. This was a program that I had drawn up in the spring of 1944, while ENIAC was still being designed.

A typical program control had an input socket, some switches on which the instruction was set, and an output socket. When stimulated with a program pulse the program control carried out the instruction set on its switches, and then emitted a program pulse. These program pulses were transmitted around the machine on a system of trays and cables running below the program panels. A subroutine was established by interconnecting local program controls in parallel and in series and setting the switches to specify the operations wanted.

I shall illustrate this process by showing how ENIAC solved the very simple differential equation

$$\frac{dy}{dx} = y,$$

using the first-order difference equations

$$\Delta y_i = y_{i-1} \Delta x,$$
$$y_i = y_{i-1} + y_i.$$

The program calculates 100 values of y_i ($i = 1, 2, \ldots, 100$) starting from the initial value y_0. The interval of integration Δx is chosen to be a power of ten (e.g., 0.01) so the multiplication $y_{i-1} \Delta x$ can be done with a mechanical shifter.

The program has two subroutines, one for input (lines 2 and 3) (Fig. 16) and one for calculating and printing (lines 4–7). Each subroutine is started by a pulse from the master programmer, and when each is finished it returns a pulse to the master programmer (on line 1). The operator starts the program by pushing a button on the initiating unit. The pulse produced goes to the master programmer on line 1. From there it goes to line 2 to start the input subroutine.

The input subroutine has two substeps. The pulse on line 2 goes to the card reader program control, which causes the card reader to read a card containing y_0 and Δx. The output pulse on line 3 then goes to instruct the constant transmitter to transmit y_0 and also to instruct accumulator no. 1 (or program control #1) to receive y_0. The output from the latter on line 1 goes back to the master programmer.

The master programmer then executes the calculation and print subroutine 100 times, for steps $i = 1, 2, \ldots, 100$. At the beginning of step i the contents of the accumulators are

No. 1 holds y_{i-1}
No. 2 holds x_{i-1}
No. 3 is clear.

This subroutine has four substeps, which I shall identify by their program input lines.

4   y_{i-1} is transmitted from accumulator no. 1 (control #3) and received by accumulator no. 3 (control #1).

5   Accumulator no. 3 (control #2) transmits y_{i-1}, which becomes $y_{i-1} \Delta x$ (i.e., Δy_i) after being shifted two positions to the right by a mechanical shifter. Accumulator no. 1 receives Δy_i (control #2) and adds it to y_{i-1}, to make the new value y_i.

6   The constant transmitter sends Δx and accumulator no. 2 (control #1) adds it to x_{i-1} to obtain x_i.

7   The printer now punches the values of y_i (accumulator no. 1) and x_i (accumulator no. 2) on a card.

The output pulse goes on 1 to the master programmer, which stops the computation after the step $i = 100$ is completed.

The role of the master programmer in an ENIAC program should be clear from this example. The master programmer had input and output sockets for program pulses, six-stage counters for controlling subroutines in sequence, and banks of decade counters for counting the number of times a subroutine has been executed. The desired numbers were set on switches. By these means it could operate a set of subroutines in sequence, causing each to be executed a fixed number of times (as preset on switches) or until a branch occurred. Overall, the master programmer had electronic facilities for managing a large and rather complicated structure of subroutines.

For the branch operation the sign digit of a number was converted into a program signal by an otherwise unused (dummy) program control and then fed into a program channel. A negative sign resulted in a program pulse, which caused the master programmer to shift to another subroutine. A positive sign produced no program pulse, so on this alternative the master programmer continued to execute the same subroutine.

This completes our description of ENIAC programming proper. I shall next make a few remarks on the control circuits of a typical ENIAC unit. These circuits were of two kinds: the local program controls and the common control circuits. Through its program switches, each local control of a unit operated the common control circuits of the unit, and the common circuits in turn operated the numerical circuits.

A simplified accumulator program control circuit is shown in Fig. 5. A pulse on its input set the flip-flop, which remained on during the execution of the instruction, in this case for one addition time. Tubes 3 and 4 are the flip-flop proper, and tubes 1 and 2 are used to set and reset it. When it is set the flip-flop performs the following switching actions. Through tubes 6 and 7 it activates the common control circuits for receiving a number, transmitting a number (for adding), or transmitting the complement of a number (for subtracting), according to the switch setting. Through tube 8 it operates common circuits for clearing or not clearing the accumulator after transmission, according to the switch setting. The flip-flop also turns on gate 9, which then passes a program pulse from the cycling unit at the end of the addition period. This pulse resets the flip-flop. It may also go through tubes 10 and 11 to a program line, where it will initiate the next step of the program.

Let us summarize our discussion of ENIAC programming. It had two parts: numerical programming and programming proper. The method for each was mechanical: plugging in cables and wires and setting switches by hand. This method was derived from the IBM plugboard.

Numerical programming was analogous to and derived from the process of setting up the differential analyzer to solve a problem. Programming proper involved interconnecting ENIAC control circuits and setting switches so that these circuits would direct the numerical circuits to perform the desired computation. Subroutines were established on the local program controls of the computing, input, and output units of ENIAC. The master programmer was then set up to orchestrate these subroutines into a single master routine for solving the problem.

5 Evaluation of ENIAC

We have covered the antecedents and nature of ENIAC, its hardware, arithmetic design, organization, and method of programming. After summarizing the results I'll take stock and see what ENIAC added to the history of computers. I'll conclude that its main contribution was a hardware revolution: the successful employment of vacuum tubes to make a fast, reliable, powerful, general-purpose scientific, digital computer.

We saw in Section 3 that ENIAC's organization derived from the differential analyzer. To a person familiar with modern computers, this organization does not seem natural or simple. Let me illustrate this point with a story.

Once I gave a lecture on ENIAC and wanted to display a program tray, a heavy metal object 8 ft long. A computer science student was nearby and I asked him to help me carry it to the lecture hall. He looked very puzzled and uninterested, and I could see him thinking: "That piece of junk! What's that for?" So I said: "That's a communication channel of ENIAC." He continued to stare at me, so I added: "ENIAC was the first general-purpose electronic computer." He remained unimpressed. Finally I said: "That's part of the ENIAC, the first multiprocessor." His face lit up, and he rushed to help me!

However, ENIAC was not really a multiprocessor in the modern sense. No ENIAC unit could compute by itself, just as no unit of the differential analyzer could compute by itself. A single fully electronic arithmetic unit did not come until the first stored-program computers.

The original aim of the ENIAC project was to build a digital electronic version of the differential analyzer. Later, it was realized that this would be a general-purpose scientific computer. The following question was not asked at the time, but it is relevant here. Various electronic computing organs were available: counters, flip-flops, switches, and resistor matrices. How could these organs best be organized to make a large, powerful, general-purpose computer? ENIAC's organization was not a simple and efficient answer to this question. A logical organization more like that of the first stored-program computers would have produced a smaller and better machine. But even with ideal designs ENIAC would have been a very large machine, perhaps 50 times as large as any known electronic system.

We saw in Section 4 that ENIAC was programmed by a mechanical technique derived from the IBM plugboard. For comparable problems, ENIAC was easier to program than the differential analyzer, because wires and switches were easier to manipulate then shafts and gears. However, an electromechanical method of programming would have been superior. For example, programs could have been set up on a central bank of stepping switches and relays. For a specific problem these could have been positioned by electrical signals from a paper tape or deck of punched cards.

In their 1943 ENIAC proposal, Mauchly, Eckert, and Brainerd mentioned the possibility of centralized control by punched cards. Referring to Fig. 11, they said that the Program Selector could be controlled by punched cards, and could be used to change the sequence of operations as well as the initial conditions. This was not achieved in ENIAC.

In evaluating ENIAC, one should keep in mind that it was developed during World War II. The immediate goal was to calculate firing tables. The long-range goal was a general-purpose computer. ENIAC's organization and method of programming served this purpose without being novel. Moreover, because of the emergency character of the war, ENIAC was developed very rapidly. The proposal was written in April 1943. Work on electronic counters began in June. The prototype accumulators were working and the basic logical design of the whole machine completed by the summer of 1944. ENIAC began to solve its first problem in December 1945. This was an important problem from Los Alamos, still classified. By February 1946, ENIAC completed this problem, and had been demonstrated publicly. The whole period was less than three years.

The engineering of ENIAC was most excellent. This was due primarily to Pres Eckert. He led in the design of fast circuits and saw the importance of reliability for such a large and novel system.

Rigid safety factors were imposed on all electronic designs; for example, a factor of three on voltage swings, a factor of two on switching times. The whole system was constructed from a few basic circuit types. Circuits were mounted on removable plug-in units whenever the number of inputs and outputs were sufficiently small. Components were carefully selected, pretested, and operated below their standard ratings. We always gated short pulses (about 3 μsec) against long pulses (which we called gates), never short pulses against short pulses.

Several diagnostic modes of operation were incorporated in the system. Just as the independent variable motor of the differential analyzer could be slowed down to improve the accuracy of the computation, so the cycling unit of ENIAC could be slowed down to insure correct operation or for diagnostic purposes. In addition, the operator could set the cycling unit to operate in a control mode. When it was in this mode she could call for clock pulses as she wanted them, either in cycles of one addition time, or pulse by pulse. All ENIAC circuits were designed to hold their information in static form whenever the cycling unit stopped. Also, all flip-flops and counters had neon lights attached to each stage, so their states were easily ascertained.

The master programmer could be rearranged so that the program was divided into small segments operable independently. By all these means, the operator could step the computation along, program segment by program segment, addition by addition, pulse by pulse, until she located the error. Also, the parallel programming facilities of ENIAC allowed her to have test routines on the machine to be run periodically.

These design precautions were sufficient. ENIAC needed to be carefully maintained and operated with suitable precautions. It turned out, for example, that whenever the heaters of the vacuum tubes were turned on several tubes would fail, so it was necessary to always keep the heaters on. After it was completely debugged and when it was properly maintained, ENIAC operated with good reliability.

The 18,000-vacuum-tube ENIAC proved that electronic technology could be used to make fast, powerful, reliable, general-purpose computers. Its speed of computation was three orders of magnitude greater than the speed obtainable with electromechanical technology, and it solved problems hitherto beyond the reach of man. The electronic design of ENIAC was optimal, and led naturally to the stored program computer.

ENIAC constituted a hardware revolution in computers. It took them from the electromechanical to the electronic. It began our modern age of electronic computers.

6. High-Speed READ–WRITE Electronic Stores

ENIAC had fast electronic circuits for storage, arithmetic, and control, and executed complicated programs rapidly. However, its storage capacity was small and its programming procedures mechanical. The technology was available for programming it electromechanically, but even then its programming equipment would have been one full level of technology below its electronic computing circuits.

Both the storage and programming deficiencies of ENIAC were eliminated by its successors, the first generation of stored-program computers.

These machines put programming on a par with arithmetic and control, and thereby began a second revolution in computing.

I shall divide the development of the stored program computer into two historical stages, the preliminary design stage (1944–1946) and the final design and construction stage (1946–1952). The preliminary design stage had two related parts, the development of hardware for storing information, and the design of an order code and suitable organization for the stored-program computer. The final design and construction stage saw the development and completion of many stored program computers, those of the EDVAC family (EDVAC, EDSAC, UNIVAC I, SEAC, SWAC, etc.) and those if the IAS family (IAS, WHIRLWIND, ILLIAC, JOHNNIAC, IBM 701, etc.). I shall not have time to discuss this stage.

From the beginning, designers of electronic computers were aware of the need for a storage device superior to the vaccum-tube register or counter. Atanasoff invented his rotating drum with capacitors as a solution to this problem. Both Crawford and Rajchman invented the resistor matrix function table store, but this was only a partial solution, since it was a read-only memory. Perry Crawford made an important contribution when he proposed a cyclic magnetic disk memory. Pres Eckert realized that a computer based on such a memory would be superior to ENIAC. Early in 1944, he proposed a numerical calculating machine based on rotating magnetic disks or drums.

The next step in the development of electronic memories occurred when Pres and John combined the cyclic idea of drum and disk memories with the supersonic delay line being used to time radar signals. To measure the elapsed time of a radar pulse from the antenna to the airplane and back to the antenna, another pulse was sent down a delay line and reflected back. Pres had earlier worked on these lines at the Moore School for the MIT Radiation Laboratory.

Figure 18 shows the delay lines of Maurice Wilkes's Cambridge EDSAC, the first stored program computer to operate. I'll explain how the delay line memory worked, using the schematic diagram of Fig. 19.

Electronic circuits were connected in a cycle with a tube of mercury which had a quartz crystal at each end. A quartz crystal is a piezoelectric device that will convert electrical pulses into physical or acoustic vibrations, and vice versa. An electrical pulse from the circuits caused the input crystal to vibrate, producing an acoustic pulse in the mercury. This acoustic pulse traveled down the tube and caused the output crystal to vibrate, so it produced an electrical pulse. The electrical pulse returned to the electronic circuits, where it was retimed by reference to a clock pulse and reshaped. The absence of a pulse would cycle similarly.

Preliminary design work was done by Pres Eckert and Kite Sharpless. Measurments indicated that 1000 pulse positions (bits), spaced 1 μsec apart, could be stored in a single delay line. About 10 vacuum tubes (envelopes) were needed to reshape and retime pulses and to switch pulse streams in and

Figure 18   EDSAC delay lines. [From Eames (1973).]

out of memory, so that 1000 bits could be stored at the cost of about 10 envelopes. Moreover, because of the serial nature of the delay memory, fewer switching tubes were required for entering and recovering information than in flip-flop or counter memories. Thus the new memory was better by more than a factor of 100 to 1! It was now possible to store program information, as well as data, electronically and at high speed.

In the late summer of 1944, not long after Pres and John invented the mercury delay line store, von Neumann conceived of using an electron-

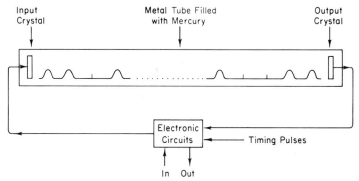

Figure 19   Diagram of acoustic delay line memory. The sequence of acoustic pulses and blanks traveling down the mercury from left to right is depicted schematically.

beam oscilloscope for computer storage. Information is placed on the surface of an iconoscope tube by means of light coming from the outside; this information is then sensed by an electron beam. Johnny thought that information could also be placed on the inside surface of such a tube by having an electron beam either deposit a charge in a small area or not. The recorded information would later be read by means of the same beam. Charge would leak from one area to the next, so the information would need to be periodically refreshed, as in Atanasoff's drum memory.

This idea was not worked out at the time. It turned out to be more difficult to reduce to practice than the mercury delay line, but electrostatic stores were later developed by Jan Rajchman and, independently, by F. C. Williams in England.*

Thus two forms of high-speed, READ–WRITE memory of sizable capacity were conceived in 1944: the cyclic mercury delay line store and the randon access electrostatic store.

7. Code and Organization for the Stored-Program Computer

At the Moore School we then planned to build a stored-program computer, the EDVAC (for Electronic Discrete Variable Arithmetic Computer). It would have a large mercury delay line memory, at least 1024 words of 32 bits. In comparison, ENIAC had 20 words of variable storage, about 400 words of read-only store, and the equivalent of perhaps 200 instructions, mechanically set.

Pres and John had devised ways of operating circuits at a megacycle pulse rate, matching pulse against pulse for switching at this rate. Serial addition could be done in 32 μsec, as fast as the numbers circulated. Multiplication by repeated addition would be several times faster than "high-speed" ENIAC multiplication, and would match well with the waiting time for the circulating delay memory.

Because EDVAC would be so much faster, smaller, and simpler than ENIAC, there was no longer the need for parallelism to gain speed, and it was decided to store numbers serially and process them serially. The guiding principle of EDVAC design was: One thing at a time, down to the last bit!

The delay line store was to be used for both numbers and orders. In his earlier proposal for a numerical calculating machine based on magnetic disks or drums, Pres had proposed storing program information on some disks or drums. Since the storage of instructions and data in the same device is unique to the stored program computer, it is important to be clear on our concept of a "program" at that time.

The Harvard MARK I and the Bell Laboratories' machines used electro-

---

* See relevant papers in this volume[Ed.].

magnetic components for storage and computation. They, like ENIAC, were limited in their READ–WRITE storage capacity. Orders for these machines were expressed in binary coded form and punched into paper tape. Paper tape is a read-only memory, and the orders punched into it referred to storage bins by means of fixed addresses. Thus these machines used fixed or constant address order codes.

In March 1945, von Neumann spent two days at the Moore School having extended conversations with Pres, John, Herman, and me about EDVAC. These meetings were devoted mostly to the hardware design and local organization of the memory and the arithmetic equipment. EDVAC was to have a memory unit of mercury tanks, arithmetic equipment, magnetic tapes for input and output, and control equipment. There were to be one or two switches to transfer instructions and numbers from memory tanks to the computing equipment. There were to be serial adding, multiplying, and dividing circuits, fed by short delay lines.

After these meetings Johnny went off and wrote a draft report on the design of EDVAC. Without his knowledge, this was issued as First Draft of a Report on the EDVAC (von Neumann, 1945). Undoubtedly he would have given credits to others. In my personal opinion these would have gone primarily to Pres Eckert and John Mauchly, and secondarily to Herman Goldstine and myself.

I'll give a brief description of von Neumann's EDVAC organization and order code. For this description I'll draw on my introduction to his "Theory of Self-Reproduction Automata" (von Neumann, 1966).

The basic internal units of EDVAC were a high-speed memory M, a central arithmetic unit CA, and a central control CC. For communication there was an outside recording medium R, an input organ I, and an output organ O.

The memory M was to be composed of possibly as many as 256 delay lines each capable of storing 32 words of 32 bits each, together with the switching equipment for connecting a position of M to the rest of the machine. The memory was to store initial conditions and boundary conditions for partial differential equations, arbitrary numerical functions, partial results obtained during a computation, etc., as well as the program (sequence of orders) directing the computation.

The outside recording medium R could be composed of punched cards, paper tape, magnetic wire or tape, photographic film, or combinations thereof. It was to be used for input and output, as well as for auxiliary low-speed storage. The input organ I transferred information from R to M; the output organ O transferred information from M to R. The notation of M was binary; that of R was decimal.

The central arithmetic unit CA was to contain some auxiliary registers (one-word delay lines) for holding numbers. Under the direction of the central control CC it was to add, subtract, multiply, divide, compute square roots, perform binary–decimal and decimal–binary conversions, transfer numbers among its registers and between its registers and M, and choose one of two numbers according to the sign of a third number. The last operation was to be used for transfer of control (jumping conditionally) from one order in the program to another.

The first bit of each word was zero for a number, one for an order. There was a single switch connecting the memory to the rest of the machine. This switch sensed the first bit of a word coming from memory and on that basis routed numbers to the central arithmetic unit CA and orders to the central control CC. Eight bits of an order were allotted to the specification of the operation to be performed and, if a reference to M was required, thirteen bits to an address.

Normally orders were taken from the delay lines in sequence, but one order with address z provided for the central control CC to take its next order from memory position z. This was the unconditional shift of control. The conditional shift of control was based on the central arithmetic unit CA's ability to choose one of two numbers according to the sign of a third number. The first two numbers were the addresses of the orders that were to be executed according to whether the condition on the third number was or was not satisfied.

Numbers were processed in CA serially, the least-significant bits being treated first, and only one operation was performed at a time. When a number was transferred from CA to address w of M, account was taken of the contents of w; if w contained an order (i.e., a word whose first bit was one), then the 13 most significant bits of the result in CA were substituted for the 13 address bits located in w. The addresses of orders could be modified automatically by the machine in this way, leaving the operand part of the instruction untouched.

This last feature of Johnny's order code was crucial, and was invented by him to facilitate programming in the new machines. These new machines would be capable of storing large quantities of data. Von Neumann saw that while the fixed address order codes of the Harvard and Bell machines were adequate for the limited memories of these machines, they would not be efficient for the large memories of the new electronic machines.

Von Neumann's solution to this problem was to invent the modern variable address code. In his EDVAC code variable or virtual addresses are stored in orders. The program is then written so that the machine calculates and substitutes a specific address into an order before each specific execution of that order. This substitution process is controlled by branching when the variable address reaches a preset bound. Thus von Neumann designed his EDVAC code to make possible the recursive loops we are all familiar with. What today we call indexing and relative addressing was accomplished in EDVAC by processing addresses in the central arithmetic unit CA.

It is worth comparing the way EDVAC and ENIAC handled different uses of arithmetic in computing. In ENIAC, the primary arithmetic of solving a problem was done in accumulators, working with the multiplier and the divider square rooter. Function table look-up was accomplished by local arithmetic and switching circuits in the function table units. The master programmer of ENIAC also did arithmetic. It used counters to count the number of times a subroutine was used, and caused a branch when a limit number (preset on switches) was reached. In EDVAC, all these arithemtic functions were centralized in the one central arithmetic unit CA.

In summary, von Neumann was the first to see and exploit the fact that when orders or instructions are stored in a high-speed READ–WRITE electronic memory, they can be manipulated arithmetically and modified by the machine itself. His variable address EDVAC code was the basis of the modern computer software revolution.

I'll make one last point about Johnny's logical design of EDVAC. This concerns the separation of logic from electronics. In ENIAC these were mixed. A gate tube performed the logical operations of "not-and" ("nan"), but it could only drive so much capacitance in the allowed time before an amplifier was needed, and the amplifier was a logical "not." The logical design of ENIAC proceeded *pari passu* with the electronic design. As a consequence, the logical design of ENIAC was not really completed until the circuit design was finished.

In contrast, von Neumann worked out much of the abstract logical design of EDVAC in his draft report. He did this by using idealized switches with delays, derived from the logical neurons of Warren McCulloch and Walter Pitts. This abstraction of logic from engineering enabled him to do the logic of EDVAC without simultaneously doing the engineering, and thereby made it possible for him to essentially complete the design in one draft. This also simplifies the historian's task, for it makes sharper the division between the preliminary design stage (1944–1946) and the final design and construction stage of the stored program computer (1946–1952).

We all knew that von Neumann's logical designs were realizable because he had worked out the building blocks with the group before he wrote the report. I remembered well a discussion of serial adders that took place at one of our meetings of March 1945. Pres and John had designed several serial adders, the simplest of which took ten tubes. Not knowing of these results, von Neumann announced cheerily that he could build an adder with five tubes. We all looked amazed, and Pres said, "No, it takes at least ten tubes." Johnny said, "I'll prove it to you," rushed to the board, and drew his adder.

"No," we said, "your first tube can't drive its load in 1 μsec, so an inverter is needed, then another tube to restore the polarity." And so the argument went. Johnny was finally convinced. But he was not taken aback. "You are right," he said. "It takes ten tubes to add—five tubes for logic, and five tubes for electronics!"

In his First Draft of a Report on the EDVAC von Neumann also proposed the development of a high-speed memory using an electron-beam oscilloscope. He thought such a store would be superior to the delay line store because all the storage cells in a cathode ray tube would be directly accessible.

Late in 1945, von Neumann decided to build a machine at the Institute of Advanced Study based on an electrostatic storage tube to be developed at RCA Laboratories by Jan Rajchman. The rest of the computer was to be designed and built at the Institute. Jan's storage tube was called the "Selectron." In the end the Williams tube electrostatic memory was developed before the Selectron, so the IAS machine used it. One machine of the IAS family, the JOHNNIAC at RAND corporation, used Selectrons. For the story of this and many other topics I have discussed see Herman Goldstine's "The Computer from Pascal to Von Neumann" (1972).

In the spring of 1946, Johnny, Herman, and I worked out the logical design of the Institute for Advanced Study Computer (IAS). Our report, Preliminary Discussion of the Logical Design of an Electronic Computing Instrument, was issued on 28 June 1946.

To take advantage of the gain in memory speed of Selectrons over delay lines, we planned to store the bits of a word in parallel, one bit per Selectron, and process them in parallel. This required more arithmetic equipment than a serial arithmetic unit, but it saved the control equipment needed for timing serial operations. With 40 bit words, two orders could be placed in one word, an important economy. It seemed that in these ways the IAS machine would be an order of magnitude faster than EDVAC and no more complex.

Figure 20 lists the 21 internal orders of the IAS machine. $S(x)$ denotes the word stored or to be stored in Selectron address x. There were to be 4096 words, stored in 40 Selectrons. There was a register associated with this memory, called the "Selectron register." Words were moved from the Selectrons to it, and thence to either the arithmetic unit (for a number) or the control (for a pair of orders). Words were moved from the arithmetic unit to the Selectron register and then into the Selectrons. The arithmetic unit contained a 40-bit accumulator and also a 40-bit register.

The leftmost 12 bits of an order were for an address and the rightmost 8 bits specified an operation. There were two orders in a word, left-hand and right-hand. Correspondingly, address substitutions and shifts of control were of two forms, left-hand and right-hand.

The accumulator could add, subtract, or take the absolute value of $S(x)$. It could be cleared or not before these operations. It could halve or double its contents by appropriate shifts. Multiplication and division involved both the accumulator and the arithmetic register. The contents $S(x)$ could be transferred to the arithmetic register, and the arithmetic register could transfer to the accumulator. The accumulator could transfer to $S(x)$, either totally (for numbers) or partially (for substituting addresses in orders). We

| | Symbolization | | |
	Complete	Abbreviated	Operation
1	$S(x) \to Ac+$	x	Clear accumulator and add number located at position x in the Selectrons into it
2	$S(x) \to Ac-$	$x-$	Clear accumulator and subtract number located at position x in the Selectrons into it
3	$S(x) \to AcM$	xM	Clear accumulator and add absolute value of number located at position x in the Selectrons into it
4	$S(x) \to Ac - M$	$x - M$	Clear accumulator and subtract absolute value of number located at position x in the Selectrons into it
5	$S(x) \to Ah+$	xh	Add number located at position x in the Selectrons into the accumulator
6	$S(x) \to Ah-$	$xh-$	Subtract number located at position x in the Selectrons into the accumulator
7	$S(x) \to AhM$	xhM	Add absolute value of number located at position x in the Selectrons into the accumulator
8	$S(x) \to Ah - M$	$x - hM$	Subtract absolute value of number located at position x in the Selectrons into the accumulator
9	$S(x) \to R$	xR	Clear register and add number located at position x in the Selectrons into it
10	$R \to A$	A	Clear accumulator and shift number held in register into it
11	$S(x) \times R \to A$	xX	Clear accumulator and multiply the number located at position x in the Selectrons by the number in the register, placing the left-hand 39 digits of the answer in the accumulator and the right hand 39 digits of the answer in the register
12	$A \div S(x) \to R$	$x \div$	Clear register and divide the number in the accumulator by the number located in position x of the Selectrons, leaving the remainder in the accumulator and placing the quotient in the register
13	$Cu \to S(x)$	xC	Shift the control to the left-hand order of the order pair located at position x in the Selectrons
14	$Cu' \to S(x)$	xC'	Shift the control to the right-hand order of the order pair located at position x in the Selectrons
15	$Cc \to S(x)$	xCc	If the number in the accumulator is $\geqq 0$, shift the control as in $Cu \to S(x)$
16	$Cc' \to S(x)$	xCc'	If the number in the accumulator is $\geqq 0$, shift the control as in $Cu' \to S(x)$
17	$At \to S(x)$	xS	Transfer the number in the accumulator to position x in the Selectrons
18	$Ap \to S(x)$	xSp	Replace the left-hand 12 digits of the lefthand order located at position x in the Selectrons by the lefthand 12 digits in the accumulator
19	$Ap' \to S(x)$	xSp'	Replace the lefthand 12 digits of the righthand order located at position x in the Selectrons by the lefthand 12 digits in the accumulator
20	L	L	Multiply the number in the accumulator by 2, leaving it there
21	R	R	Divide the number in the accumulator by 2, leaving it there

Fig. 20 Instruction set for the Institute of Advanced Study computer. Register means arithmetic register. [From Burks *et al.* (1946).]

decided not to have orders for square rooting and conversions between binary and decimal, but to program these operations.

This completes my description of the preliminary design of the IAS computer. Its order code and logical design was, I think, superior to that of the machines based on the serial mercury delay line memory.

8. Conclusion

I shall conclude by summarizing briefly the state of the stored-program computer at the end of the preliminary design stage in the summer of 1946. The mercury delay line memory was known to be workable, though not yet designed or built. Von Neumann's logical design of EDVAC was available; the electronic design had yet to be done. The Selectron was being developed. The preliminary logical design of the IAS machine had been done; the electronic design remained.

The final design and construction stage of the development of the stored-program computer was beginning. Several groups were working at this time, and others started later. Much development and construction work remained, mostly electronic, some logical. The history of this stage (1946–1952) would take another long paper.

REFERENCES

Burks, A. W. (1946). Super electronic computing machine, *Electr. Ind.* **5,** 62–67, 96.
Burks, A. W. (1947). Electronic computing circuits of the ENIAC, *Proc. Inst. Radio Eng.* **35,** 756–767.
Burks, A. W., Goldstine, H. H., and von Neumann, J. (1946). "Preliminary Discussion of the Logical Design of an Electronic Computing Instrument." Institute for Advanced Study, Princeton, New Jersey, 28 June.
Eames, C., and Eames, R. (1943). "A Computer Perspective." Harvard Univ. Press, Cambridge, Massachusetts.
Goldstine, H. H. (1972). "The Computer from Pascal to von Neumann." Princeton Univ. Press, Princeton, New Jersey.
Hartree, D. (1947). "Calculating Machines." Cambridge Univ. Press, London and New York.
IBM (1947). IBM electric punched card machines, principles of operation. Electric Multiplier Type 601. IBM Corp., New York.
Mauchly, J. W., Eckert, J. P., and Brainerd, J. G. (1943). "Report on and Electronic Diff.* Analyzer." Moore School of Electrical Engineering, Univ. of Pennsylvania, Philadelphia, 12 April.
von Neumann, J. (1945). "First Draft of a Report on the EDVAC." Moore School of Electrical Engineering, Univ. of Pennsylvania, Philadelphia, 30 June.
von Neumann, J. (1966). "Theory of Self-Reproducing Automata." Univ. of Illinois Press, Urbana.

DEPARTMENT OF COMPUTER AND COMMUNICATION SCIENCES
UNIVERSITY OF MICHIGAN
ANN ARBOR, MICHIGAN

Computer Development at Argonne National Laboratory

J. C. CHU

Richard Hamming in his paper in this volume says: "The history of science is still mainly dates-and-names history and who did it first," and goes on: "We experts in a field usually prefer the classical form of history, while the outsider prefers a cultural history in one form or another." I think he has a good point. Therefore, I shall say a little about the machines, dates, who did it and for what; then a little on human progress and research.

I came to the Los Alamos meeting from the AFIPS Computer Conference in New York, 1976. There, three sessions were devoted to ENIAC—the initiation, the development, and the technology transfer. Sitting there I felt as if I were seeing a movie, "The Birth and Development of Frankenstein." At Los Alamos I felt I was attending the sequel, "The Sons and Daughters of Frankenstein." The daughters, of course, are the software. I shall return to this later in the paper.

In 1949, at Argonne National Laboratory (ANL), Norman Hilbury, Associate Director, Frank Hoyt, Head of Theoretical Physics, and Donald Flanders, Head of Applied Mathematics, decided to have an Institute for Advanced Study (IAS) computer built there to facilitate the computations related to reactor design. Herman Goldstine called me in New York and asked me to go to Argonne to build it. I was delighted to accept.

AVIDAC—Argonne's Version of the Institute's Digital Automatic Computer—was the name dreamed up by Flanders; it was a nearly exact copy of

345

the IAS machine. My job of construction started in early 1950 and was completed in 1951.

In 1950, Alston Householder of Oak Ridge also decided to have a machine for Oak Ridge's own use. Since Argonne already had a computer engineering group, Householder decided to subcontract the work to ANL. We felt that by combining our resources and talents we could perhaps build a computer better and faster. I organized a team to do development work and system design. This team comprised Birge, Kramer, Jacobson, Flanders, Alexander, Merial, and Chu of ANL; Burdette, Klein, Woody, Gerhart, and Householder of ORNL; and Burks of the University of Michigan.

This second computer, the brother of AVIDAC, was named ORACLE — Oak Ridge Automatic Computer and Logical Engine: in those days computers had names instead of numbers. The overall architecture was like the IAS machine, but the engineering design was different. Much faster circuits were used, smaller cathode-ray tubes for memory — which was twice the size of the IAS memory. Magnetic tape 2 in. wide with 42 channels was provided as auxiliary memory. ORACLE was in full operation in the summer of 1953 and was installed in Oak Ridge in October of that year.

In August 1953, Argonne sponsored a symposium on computers; quite a few of the speakers were at the Los Alamos conference also. We talked about transistors and circuits, higher-density tape recording, better and faster internal memories, and of course mathematics and programming. The stage was set for the beginning of an exciting and new industry.

Reminiscing about the past while speculating about the future, a writer of a history of electronic computers could divide his book into five major chapters:

(1) The birth of the monster   1942–1946
(2) The sons and daughters of the monster   1946–1954
(3) The emerging of a new industry   1954–1962
(4) The victors and the vanquished   1962–1974
(5) The world of computers — the New Challenge   1974–1982

Some 25 years ago, many of the people working with computers believed they would fulfill a human need. We believed then that electronic computers are machines that can expand our ideas and transport our minds. Certainly we have proved that it is so during the past 25 years. It is rational for us to believe now that there is no better vehicle than the modern computer to take us to a better civilization if properly used. Scientific progress was made in the laboratories but social progress was made by facing a challenge. Computers provide such a challenge to mankind.

ARGONNE NATIONAL LABORATORY
ARGONNE, ILLINOIS*

* Retired.

The ORDVAC and the ILLIAC

JAMES E. ROBERTSON

1. Introduction

The author will deviate from the usual factual presentation of a technical paper for two reasons. First, he was a graduate student without administrative responsibility during construction of the ORDVAC and the ILLIAC, and hopes to pay proper tribute to the talents of the other members of a team of which he was only one relatively minor member. Second, he wishes to present more than the factual material a dedicated archivist could recover, and will attempt to recall incidents, personalities, attitudes, and some aspects of the technology that differentiate the highly individualistic climate of computer design of those times a quarter of a century ago from the climate of today.

2. Brief History

An agreement was made in January 1949 with the Ballistic Research Laboratories of Aberdeen Proving Grounds, Maryland, to the effect that two computers, the ORDVAC and the ILLIAC, were to be constructed by the University of Illinois, with the two organizations sharing the costs of development. Construction began in April 1949. The ORDVAC was completed in November 1951, was moved to Aberdeen, Maryland, in February 1952, and completed its acceptance tests early in March 1952. The ILLIAC was completed during Labor Day weekend of 1952. The ILLIAC was the sole

347

service computer at the University of Illinois until augmented by an IBM 650 in 1959 and remained in service until 1962.

The logical structure of the ORDVAC and the ILLIAC was patterned after the computer described in the 28 June 1946 report, Preliminary Consideration of the Logical Design of an Electronic Computing Instrument, by Burks *et al.* (1946) of the Institute for Advanced Study. The University of Illinois received helpful information and suggestions from discussions at the Institute for Advanced Study, especially during the early period of construction. Drawings pertaining to the arithmetic unit and memory of the Institute for Advanced Study computer were furnished to the University, and some parts of these drawings, such as the registers, were copied. Many details of the physical layout were also copied.

Although it was first planned to build ILLIAC and ORDVAC from circuit drawings obtained from the Institute for Advanced Study, this intention was later changed, and most of the computers were constructed from circuits designed at the University. The fundamental flip-flop, gating, and cathode follower circuits and the registers, complement gate, and clear drivers were copied from those developed for the Institute for Advanced Study computer.

The six-month period of 1952 between the installation of the ORDVAC at Aberdeen, Maryland, and completion of the ILLIAC in Urbana left the University without computing facilities and led to an early experiment with what would now be called a remote terminal. Programs at Urbana and results at Aberdeen were punched on paper tape and transmitted via the commercial Teletype network for reproduction, again on paper tape, at the other end. Initial difficulties were overcome by sending a University representative to Aberdeen for transportation of tapes between the Teletype machine and the ORDVAC, where these facilities were some distance apart, and for general supervision of tape handling, program checkout, and communication of difficulties. The Teletype machines in use with ORDVAC and ILLIAC were modified so that the pattern of holes punched on the paper tape corresponded to the pattern of ones in the binary code for a hexadecimal representation. As a result, tapes punched for ORDVAC (and later ILLIAC) led to gibberish if printed on a commercial Teletype. This led to little difficulty, except during the Democratic convention in Chicago in 1952. Apparently, in the frequent busy periods, circuits were monitored and transmissions between Urbana and Aberdeen were cut off, due to suspicion of error.

3. Personnel

3.1. Preliminary Remarks

Any discussion of personnel of the design team for ORDVAC and IL-LIAC must begin with a highly personal note by the author. The three faculty members on the design team (Meagher, Nash and Taub) were also members of the committee supervising my Ph.D. thesis which, despite my overwhelming interest in ORDVAC and ILLIAC in 1950–1952, I managed to complete in June 1952. These three have had a significant influence on my personal and professional development, both from the academic point of view and also as supervisors of my design efforts for ORDVAC and IL-LIAC. Each of the three, in his own way, has and deserves my gratitude.

Many of my associates of those days, as fellow graduate students or junior engineers, became and have remained personal friends.

My choice of anecdotes thus depends on recollections dependent on the strength of interactions of personalities of others with mine. There is nothing unbiased about this, and I hope the omissions and misinterpretations will be forgiven by those who may be offended.

3.2. Faculty

Ralph Meagher was chief engineer for the construction of ILLIAC and ORDVAC from the inception of the project. The success of these computers was due to his leadership. His highest standards of professional conduct and meticulous attention to detail led to, for example, the useful life of a decade for ILLIAC, when many computers of contemporary design were failures. My own professional success is, I believe, due to attempts to follow the example he set, but I am sure I have failed more often than not to live up to his high standards.

John P. (Jack) Nash relieved Ralph Meagher of his responsibilities in such areas as personnel management and preparation of technical reports. Jack later became Vice President for Research at Lockheed Aircraft, until his sudden death at Cape Canaveral in 1969 during a visit in connection with an Apollo moon launch. (See Meagher and Nash, 1952.)

A. H. (Abe) Taub is a mathematician whose former associations with the Institute for Advanced Study were invaluable in the early design period of ORDVAC and ILLIAC. When I was developing algorithms for multiplication and division, Abe insisted that I formulate the proposed procedures in mathematical detail. I found the process painful, but, in the end, useful and rewarding. A generation of students in my subsequent courses in arithmetic have benefitted from Abe's advice, but did not appreciate it at the time of their initial exposure. Taub later became head of the Digital Computer Laboratory, following Meagher's decision to become a private consultant, and remained in that position until January 1964.

3.3. Graduate Students, Visitors, and Junior Personnel

Donald B. Gillies was a graduate student whose part in the checkout of the ILLIAC will be described later. He later received his Ph.D. at Princeton, then was engaged in computer design for National Research Development Corporation (NRDC) in England, and returned to Illinois to become a Professor. Don remained a close personal friend until his untimely death of a heart attack in July 1975.

Edwin L. Hughes was concerned with circuit design and testing of circuits and subassemblies. Ed was persuaded to move from Illinois to California in November 1952, by Louis N. Ridenour. Ridenour had been Dean of the Graduate College at the University of Illinois, and had played a decisive part in arranging for the University to acquire computing facilities, including the negotiations with Aberdeen Proving Grounds.

The author was involved with algorithms for arithmetic and with asynchronous control design. He remained at the University of Illinois, where he was responsible for the construction of ILLIAC II from 1957 to 1962 and became a professor in 1959.

David J. Wheeler (1953) was a visitor for the two academic years from 1951 to 1953. As one of the participants in the early development of the EDSAC at the University of Cambridge, he was the only one of us, including the permanent faculty, with any practical experience with stored-program computers. Despite understandable resistance,* his persuasion resulted in advantageous changes in the design of ILLIAC.

Joseph M. Wier was responsible for the ILLIAC memory. He later received his Ph.D. at the University of Illinois and joined Bell Telephone Laboratories, where he has remained since.

Personnel listed in the ORDVAC Manual (see Staff of DCL, 1952) as "associated with the work during the major portion of the total (construction) period are":

K. W. Bartlett	G. W. Michael
E. L. Hughes	J. P. Nash
W. E. Jones	J. E. Robertson
T. E. Kerkering	T. Shapin, Jr.
R. L. Liu	A. H. Taub
H. E. Lopeman	H. M. Walker
R. E. Meagher	J. M. Wier

---

* Resistance to change in the design of a computer in 1951 was a matter of economics rather than human conservatism. The estimated cost of one wired vacuum tube circuit (one 2-input AND or one 2-input OR) for a one-of-a-kind computer was $100. Even for the lowest quality AM radio, the cost was $3 per vacuum tube, and for medium quality mass-produced items the cost was on the order of $10 per vacuum tube. Today, the equivalent of a 4-vacuum tube circuit on one integrated circuit chip can be purchased for 14¢, or less than 4¢ per vacuum-tube equivalent. Large scale integration (LSI) examples for microprocessors, etc., are even more striking. When inflation is taken into account a cost reduction by a factor of several hundred is not unreasonable for the change from vacuum-tube logic to medium scale integration (MSI) integrated circuits.

4. Characteristics of the ILLIAC*

Reference is made to the attached photographs, for which the author is grateful to Professor A. S. Douglas, who took them in 1956. The arithmetic unit consisted of three registers, shown in Fig. 1 and 2, and an adder (not shown). The control was asynchronous, and one design rule was that information should not be stored in transit. For example, a shift required a double rank register with information transferred directly from the permanent rank to the temporary rank during the first step, and returned to the permanent rank with a displacement during the second step. The two upper rows of lights in Fig. 1 indicate the state of the temporary and permanent ranks of the accumulator. The central area, dark in Fig. 1, contains the temporary and permanent ranks of the multiplier-quotient register. The two lowest rows of lights indicate registers to which information is read from memory; the upper complete row is the memory register, which stores an operand for arithmetic; the lower incomplete row holds a pair of single-address instructions. The lower rank of the accumulator was connected directly to the adder on the back side of the computer. The memory register was connected to the adder by way of a conditional complementing circuit. Numbers were fixed-point fractions with the sign bit on the left and 39 nonsign bits to the right of the binary point. Negative numbers were in radix (or twos) complement form.

* See Staff of DCL (1954).

Figure 1   Front view of ILLIAC.

Figure 2   ILLIAC controls and input-output area.

An addition (or subtraction with appropriate complementation) involved the following sequence of events. The first operand was transferred from memory to the accumulator with the clear-add instruction. In detail, the accumulator was cleared to zero, the desired operand was transferred from memory to the memory register, and was then added to zero. The adder sum was then transferred to the upper rank of the accumulator, and finally transferred without displacement to the permanent rank. This process was then repeated for the second operand, except that the accumulator was not initially cleared. A third instruction could then be used, if desired, to transfer the resulting sum directly from the accumulator into the memory location specified.

Execution times of the arithmetic instructions are given in Table I. [See Robertson (1955).] For multiplication, digits of the multiplier were sensed serially. The execution time was dependent on the digit pattern of the multiplier, since a "0" bit required only a shift, and a "1" bit required an addition as well. A conditional correction was required for a negative multiplier. The division method was restoring division.

TABLE I
ARITHMETIC EXECUTION TIMES

Addition–subtraction	72 μsec
Multiplication	642–822 μsec
Division	772 μsec
Shifts (63 digital positions max)	16 μsec per digital position

The bright square to the right of the accumulator in Fig. 1 is the display of one digital position of the memory (the 1024 bits of one cathode-ray tube). The display also appears in the upper left of Fig. 3. Immediately below is the 40 position switch, which permits selection of the digital position desired.

Input and output was by means of five-hole punched paper tape. Information was read into the computer by means of a photoelectric reader (Figure 4) at the rate of 300 characters/sec. Output on punched tape was at the rate of 60 characters/sec. Tape for input was prepared externally on modified teletypewriters (see Fig. 5), which were also used for printing the output. Modification to correct errors was awkward, requiring preparation of a new tape. Tape comparators, as in Fig. 6, were used to ensure that no new errors were introduced in the process.

The primary data transfer mode involved 10 hexadecimal characters on tape for one 40-bit computer word. At Wheeler's insistence, an alphanumeric mode was provided for the ILLIAC. The hexadecimal codes for the equivalents of 10 to 15 were K, S, N, J, F, and L. These were selected to minimize the effort in modifying a Teletype in order that the hexadecimal codes from 0 to 15 should conform to the binary equivalents.

The "console" of the ILLIAC being manipulated by Miss Douglas in Fig. 3 is also visible on the extreme left in Fig. 4. It consists of three telephone switches liberated from World War II surplus, and two push buttons and a neon indicator. The WHITE switch had three positions. The uppermost position caused an instruction to be brought into position for execution; the center position caused the execution to occur. Thus, by manually

Figure 3 Control switches and cathode-ray-tube monitor.

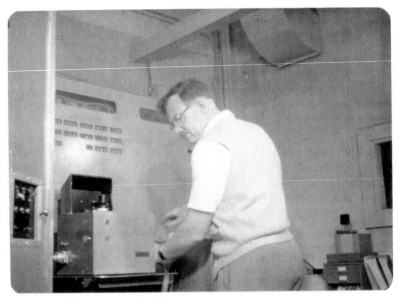

Figure 4 Paper tape reader.

cycling between these two uppermost positions, a program could be executed one instruction at a time. The lower position resulted in a program being run at the computer rate of speed.

The BLACK switch on the console was used in connection with conditional stop instructions. The switch had three positions, with the upper posi-

Figure 5 Teletype unit.

Figure 6   Tape comparator.

tion spring loaded for automatic return to the center position. If a conditional stop instruction were included in a program, the computer would stop on that instruction if the switch were in the center position. Raising and releasing the switch would result in the program continuing to the next stop instruction. The lower position of the switch caused all such instructions to be ignored.

The RED switch provided a rudimentary, but useful, form of diagnostic. One position resulted in normal operation of the computer. The other position resulted in the execution indefinitely of the pair of instructions set into the lowermost register shown in Fig. 1. Addresses of the pair were the same and were obtained from a control counter that counted sequentially through all memory addressed. One commonly used instruction pair provided a quick visual check of the memory. The first instruction complemented the word from memory, the second returned the complement to the original location. With the memory preset to all zeros, the pattern on the monitor switched alternately from all zeros to all ones in all storage locations, in the absence of errors. Errors tended to be preserved and were easily seen as the monitor switch was rapidly rotated through the 40 digital positions.

One of the two push buttons cleared all memory locations to zeros. An instruction consisting of all zeros was a left shift of zero digital positions. Since no action was required by this instruction, nothing was done by the asynchronous control, and the computer came to an unconditional halt. The result was that if a programming error caused a jump into an unused portion of the memory, an unconditional halt occurred immediately. There was no indication of the location of the offending jump instruction, and an early programming diagnostic routine provided for an address search of all locations.

The second push button set the instruction counter and the initial pair of instructions to be obeyed. These brought in a "bootstrap" routine, which, from a few initial words on paper tape, converted the initial instruction pair into a loop capable of reading words from tape into sequential memory locations, and finally brought into memory a rudimentary assembly program. The neon indicator was turned on by an overflow during division, which halted the ILLIAC.

A portion of the control on the back of the computer is shown in Fig. 7.

5.   The ILLIAC Memory

The memory for ILLIAC and ORDVAC was of the electrostatic (Williams-tube) type, with a capacity of 1024 40-bit words with a cycle time of 18 μsec. To describe the fundamental storage process, the "mud-puddle" analogy is useful. Imagine a flat area of thick mud (analogous to the phosphor coating of a cathode-ray tube) and above it, a source of drops of water (analogous to the electron beam). If water is dropped at a particular location a crater is created (analogous to a potential well in the phosphor), and a binary "0" is stored. If the water source is moved slightly (technically known as a

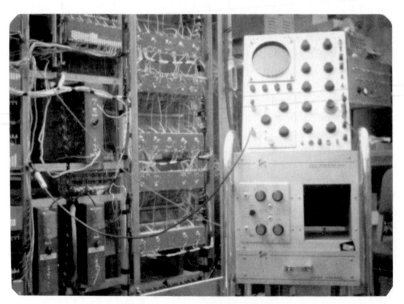

Figure 7   Part of ILLIAC control.

"twitch") and more water dropped, the original crater is partially refilled, and a binary "1" is stored. Sensing of the stored information is achieved by returning the water source to the original location. When water is dropped, more mud will be displaced for the stored "1" following the twitch than for a stored "0" without the twitch. Sensing was destructive, and restoration was necessary. In the electrostatic memory, the slight voltage changes induced by sensing one of the 1024 storage locations were picked up on a metallic screen glued to the outside of the cathode-ray tube. To prevent noise interference from stray electrostatic and electromagnetic fields, each cathode-ray tube was enclosed in a box consisting of alternate layers of copper and mu-metal.

This method of storage has many disadvantages. To use the analogy, the mudholes were gradually refilled either by oozing or by mud splattered from sensing nearby locations. Stored information therefore had to be periodically refreshed, or regenerated. To accomplish this, each "action" cycle, during which information was transferred between memory and arithmetic unit, was followed by at least one regeneration cycle.

One parameter that plagued early ORDVAC and ILLIAC users was called the read-around ratio. This was a measure of the number of times neighboring locations could be sensed before the information at the central location was destroyed. This parameter was originally 10 for ORDVAC and was increased to 30 initially for ILLIAC. In 1953, Taub brought back the word that Ragnar Thorenson at SWAC (National Bureau of Standards Western Automatic Computer, in Los Angeles) was "sensing out in the trash." This meant that the amplified voltage signals from the cathode-ray tubes were not sensed early in the cycle to determine whether a "1" or "0" was stored, at a time when the oscilloscope traces appeared to be clean, but instead later in the cycle when the traces were fuzzy. Joe Wier made the necessary changes, and the read-around ratio increased to 100. This was sufficiently high, so that only a determined (and malicious) programmer could cause an error by this means.

Each cathode-ray tube stored 1024 bits in a 32 by 32 raster, and was associated with one bit of the 40-bit word. Deflection systems of the 40 cathode-ray tubes necessary were paralleled. Alternate rows of the raster were displaced, and rows were spaced to achieve a hexagonal pattern, in order to improve the read-around ratio. Phosphor coatings in the cathode-ray tubes (CRTs) were subject to flaws (analogous, perhaps, to a small rock in the mud puddle), which necessitated careful pretesting and preselection of CRTs. Manufacturers subsequently improved the quality control during formation of the phosphor for CRTs intended for storage. ORDVAC and ILLIAC used 3-in.-diam CRTs, since the ratio of spot size to diameter is smallest for this size. The raster of a particular CRT could be selected for display by means of a 40-position switch, and the intensity of dots in the raster indicated storage locations most active during execution of a program.

An auxiliary magnetic drum memory of 12,800 words was installed several years after the initial completion of ILLIAC.

6. Provisions for Reliability

The concern to achieve reliability affected all phases of design, construction, maintenance, and use of the ILLIAC. Circuit design was worst case; that is, the circuit was designed to function properly for worst-case variations of component values and vacuum-tube emission. Components and vacuum tubes were tested before installation and required to meet more rigid standards than the allowed worst-case variations permitted for design. During turn-on, filaments were warmed up in graduated steps, in order to extend the life of the vacuum tubes, before high voltages were applied.

Permanent malfunctions were usually easy to trace, since the machine was asynchronous. The computer would halt, and a dc voltmeter could be used to pinpoint the faulty component. Intermittent faults, usually due to poor solder joints or internal shorts in vacuum tubes, were more difficult to locate. The tools included a plastic rod and a hammer, which could be used with some delicacy to pinpoint the physical location of the fault.

Careful logs were kept, both for reports of malfunctions by users and for maintenance and repair procedures. Diagnostic tests were scheduled daily, and were also run when the computer was not otherwise in use.

Considerable effort went into the development of diagnostic programs. Read-around tests, which subjected each bit in memory to progressively higher ratios, located and printed the positions with the lowest ratios.

The most elaborate diagnostic for fault detection and isolation was the "leapfrog," written by David Wheeler. [See Robertson and Wheeler (1953).] Individual tests incorporated into the leapfrog are listed in Table II. This program was designed to "leap" through the memory so that every memory location was tested. Elaborate procedures were incorporated to detect and locate memory faults. Five copies of the leapfrog were used, with addresses appropriately modified. Copy 3, called the working copy, conducts the tests in Table II, and also uses copy 2 to manufacture copy 1. As each word of copy 2 is translated to become a word of copy 1, it is also compared with the corresponding word of copy 5, the oldest copy. After manufacture of copy 1 is complete, the program leaps from copy 3 to copy 2, which thereupon becomes working copy 3. If we trace the history of a particular copy at a given position in the memory, we discover it is manufactured (as copy 1), tested for correctness (as copy 2), used (as copy 3), and again tested (as copy 5).* This ensures that the program is always checked before it is used, thus giving the maximum chance that a memory error will be found before it causes the leapfrog to act incorrectly. It also ensures that errors occurring in copies 3, 4, and 5 are also detected.

* Copy 4 is dormant but eventually becomes this copy 5.

TABLE II

INANDIVIDUAL TESTS OF THE LEAPFROG[a]

Name	Effect
Multiplication	A general test of the arithmetic unit, including the use of multiplication instructions.
Division	A general test of the arithmetic unit, including the use of division instructions.
Comparison	Compares copy 2 with copy 5 so that memory errors are detected.
Carry test	Tests the full propagation and collapse of the carry in the adder.
Ones test Zeros test	Tests the functioning of the registers when full of ones or zeros. This essentially tests common driver circuits of the arithmetic unit.
Logical order test	This tests the logical instructions. Every digital position is tested in all conditions.
Shift counter test	This tests every digital position of the shift counter and recognition circuits.
Input–output test	This tests the ability of the input–output unit to read and punch in all digital positions.
Occasional input–output test	This tests the ability of the input unit to ignore certain characters and read correctly a group of characters, and tests the punch while continuously punching.

[a] Note: The first three tests are done 128 times per leap, the next six tests are done once per leap, and the last test once per 128 leaps.

7. Checkout of ORDVAC at Aberdeen Proving Grounds, Maryland (February–March 1952)

The ORDVAC was partially dismantled and shipped from Urbana on 16 February 1952 by commercial truck to Aberdeen, Maryland. Meagher had overcome the objections of the trucking firm, and Tom Kerkering, then a technician, rode in the truck to Aberdeen. Physical installation and wiring required about ten days, and I was summoned to participate in the electronic checkout, and arrived on Thursday, 28 February. Meagher asked me when I had left Urbana, and when I told him, took his pocket slide rule and said, "You averaged 36 miles per hour." (This included the overnight stop.)

My arrival was a day or two premature, so I went to Silver Spring, Maryland, to visit my brother. On 29 February, the night before I was to return, it snowed about six inches, so, early on the morning of Saturday, 1 March, I carefully drove to the nearest service station, had chains put on my car, and drove over back roads to Baltimore. Traffic was snarled on U.S. 40 between

Baltimore and Aberdeen, and I recall sitting in the car, reading the morning paper, for several hours. On arrival at Aberdeen, I found the building locked, and tapped on a window near the ORDVAC installation to be let in. Meagher and Nash had bet that I wouldn't arrive by 3 p.m., and I had just made it by five minutes.

Finding the errors induced by the shipment and reassembly of ORDVAC went smoothly, and on Wednesday, 5 March, the computer passed the original acceptance tests agreed upon the previous fall. I remember overhearing local people saying in amazement, "ORDVAC has passed the acceptance tests"; other computers there had required months. We were not satisifed; the original acceptance tests had been supplanted, in our minds, by the more stringent "leapfrog" written more recently by Wheder. This test indicated errors in the memory, so we spent Thursday locating these, before the formal turnover of ORDVAC to Aberdeen Proving Grounds. During this final testing, several senior officials of the Ballistic Research Laboratory came to inspect their new acquisition and asked for Meagher. Hughes replied "He's the guy over there pushing the broom."

In an off period, Nash and I were looking at one of the Bell Labs Relay computers, when our attention was drawn by the noise of the printing of a teletypewriter. We rushed over and waited expectantly for another printout. This elicited the comment, "You needn't rush, it won't print again until tomorrow."

8. Checkout of ILLIAC (Labor Day Weekend 1952)

In 1952, a digital computer was considered complete when it was first capable of successfully running stored programs. In the case of ORDVAC and ILLIAC, this occurred shortly after wiring connections were made between memory and the arithmetic unit and control. It should be recalled that design changes affecting the operation codes had been made between completion of the ORDVAC and the ILLIAC, and although many programs written in advance for ILLIAC were based on those written for ORDVAC, they had not been debugged. Compatability of programs did not become an issue until later in the decade. Checkout of ILLIAC thus became an alternation between engineering improvements to accept more sophisticated diagnostic programs, which then had to be debugged, and fault indication from the diagnostic programs that isolated malfunctions of the computer. What follows are excerpts from the ILLIAC log book for the period 27 August–2 September 1952, interspersed with my personal commentary.

27 Aug 52 (Wednesday)   "Connections to memory were completed at 3 p.m."

During the 27th and 28th, perhaps a dozen wiring errors, shorts, and faulty tubes were located and repaired or replaced. A simple adder test was run and debugged. A paper-tape reader and punch test was run, and the punch was repaired.

28 Aug 52 (Thursday)   "Started checking read around ratio test 4:20 p.m. Found 2 coding (programming) errors and obtained data 5 p.m. Replaced (cathode-ray) tubes of positions 34 and 37. With 512 word store failures occur at RAR (read around ratio) = 64 (Base 16 ≡ 100 base 10), none at RAR = 32 (≡ 50 base 10). Beginning about 7 p.m., concentrated upon memory."

Between 7 p.m. and 1 a.m., adjustments were made, primarily in the spacing of rows and columns of the raster, twitch direction and duration, and lengths of control pulses, in order to improve the read-around ratio. A test of the read-around ratio at 12:50 a.m. shows three failures in four tests at RAR = 10, and 26 failures in three tests at RAR = 15. These tests were made with a capacity of 1024 words.

28 Aug 52 (Thursday)   "Began checking out leapfrog at 0100. Machine off at 0115."

29 Aug 52 (Friday)   "Division test of leapfrog was recoded from scratch by D. B. Gillies."

Additional adjustments were made to the memory.

30 Aug 52 (Saturday)   "Altered length of twitch in one direction. Seems to markedly improve the readings. No prints at (RAR = 10) and only 1 or 2 at (RAR = 15). 4 or 5 at 20. . . . Life seems sweeter now."

Additional memory repairs and adjustments were then made.

30 Aug 52 (Saturday)   "Ran leapfrog for several (about 6) leaps with intermittent division errors. . . . Traced division errors down to $2^{-37}R_1$."

$2^{-37}R_1$ means digital position 37 of the lower rank of the accumulator.

30 Aug 52 (Saturday)   "Concluded that . . . capacitances from memory and input circuitry were resulting in marginal gating and added 20 (pf) capacitor to grid of TG. Then ran crippled leapfrog from 9:16 to 9:48 p.m. without error."

Two flip-flops in the control, called TC and TG, controlled the basic four-step cycle required for one step of multiplication or division. Addition of the capacitor increased the duration of the gates.

The leapfrog normally jumped from one copy to the next. When arithmetic tests were important, a simple modification resulted in continuous use of a single copy, hence the term "crippled leapfrog."

30 Aug 52 (Saturday)   "Managed to eliminate worst flaws by shifting raster and use of two small magnets in (digital) positions 18 and 39."

Controls were available for shifting the raster simultaneously in all digital positions. To move the raster in a single digital position, independent of the rest, required some ingenuity. We went to a campus drug store and purchased some "tricky dogs." These were plastic replicas of dogs, about half an inch long, mounted on small bar magnets. Magnetization was such that the dogs opposed either a head-to-head or tail-to-tail confrontation. The magnetic field from one of these, when placed near the screen of a cathode-ray tube, was sufficient to move the raster slightly.

30 Aug 52 (Saturday)   "Completed checking out leapfrog except for every eighth sum check which occurs when frog jumps from bottom (largest address) to top (smallest address) of raster. Started leapfrog about 1:10 a.m. Error occurred at 1:12 a.m. Routine continued without error until 2:08 a.m., when division error occurred. Machine off at 2:16 a.m. 31 August, 1952."

From Sunday afternoon 31 August at 3:50 p.m. until early Monday morning, 1 September, the ILLIAC was on for 12.5 hours. During this time, the following three programs were debugged.

1.   Leapfrog debugging was completed. In order to ensure that the paper tape was read correctly, the words from tape were summed as they were read. To avoid bias, the digits of each word were scrambled by shifting. The final word on the tape was a constant whose value was such that the sum of all words was zero. Unfortunately, the final constant, because of the scrambling process, could not be determined from the sum of the other words. Gillies finally found a process that converged; an approximate value gave a sum that led to a better approximation, etc.

2.   The decimal order (instruction) input. This 25-word program was the basic assembly program for the ILLIAC throughout its lifetime. Among other things, it provided for conversion of addresses from decimal to binary and for both fixed and relative addressing.

3.   Calculation of e. The transcendental constant e had previously been calculated to a precision of 2270 decimal digits. The program debugged ultimately led to the calculation of 60,000 digits of e.

All three programs were written by David Wheeler and were debugged by Donald Gillies. The final log entries for the early morning of 1 September (Labor Day) were:

3:07–3:15 a.m.	e	Calculated 2270 digits of e of which 1677 were correct.
3:15–3:47 a.m.	Flaw and read-around tests	Flaws in digital positions #8 and #29.
3:50–4:09 a.m.	e	Calculated 2270 digits of e correctly.
4:12–4:50 a.m.	e	Observed error and quit.

The pattern of alternate engineering tests and program debugging continued during 1 September (Labor Day). Jack Nash turned the ILLIAC on from

9:45 a.m. to 10:55 a.m., during which time he ran the leapfrog for 15 min, ran an eigenvalue code for 15 min, ran a leapfrog again for another 15 min, and debugged the address search routine. Standard procedure for the ILLIAC was to initially clear all words in the memory to zero. An instruction of all zeros was an unconditional halt. Therefore a jump instruction with an incorrect address often led to such a halt. The location of the halt instruction was known; the purpose of the address search routine was to find the faulty jump instruction.

During the afternoon of 1 September, after an hour and ten minutes of engineering tests, there is the following log entry:

4:32–4:40 p.m.   Eigenvector routine with 8 × 8 matrix ran correctly. This routine uses following subroutines: Decimal order input, decimal number input, square root, and single column print.

Difficulties during the afternoon led to changing a cathode-ray tube in the memory at 9 p.m. The final log entries for the day were

9:42–10:45 p.m. e-2 to 4880 places—Checks to 3520 places with ORDVAC calculation.
10:52–11:52 p.m.   Leapfrog with eight special divide test failures.

The ultimate reliability and long life of the ILLIAC, in contrast with many of its contemporaries, was due not only to careful engineering design, but also to the use and follow-up maintenance based on information from the many engineering test programs, which were more stringent than the programs of the users.

A quote from David Wheeler's report #43, The Calculation of 60,000 Digits of e by the ILLIAC, indicates the reliability of the computer two months after its completion.

The calculation was run during the first two weeks of December and should have required thirty-three 55-minute runs. However, two errors on my part in setting various tapes caused us to require an extra 4 full runs. Operators mishandling tapes resulted in about 2 or 3 extra partial runs.

The machine made 4 computation errors resulting in 4 partial runs being invalidated. No errors were made in reading or punching the three quarter of a million characters on punched tape.

Thus the total time required was 40 hours."

REFERENCES

Burks, A. W., Goldstine, H. H., and von Neumann, J. (1946). Preliminary Discussion of the Logical Design of an Electronic Computing Instrument, Institute for Advanced Study, Princeton, New Jersey June.

Meagher, R. E., and Nash, J. P. (1952). The ORDVAC, review of electronic computers, *Joint AIEE-IRE Comput. Conf.* AIEE, February.

Robertson, J. E., and Wheeler, D. J. (1953). Diagnostic programs for the ILLIAC, *Proc. IRE* **41**, No. 10, 1320–1325.

Robertson, J. E. (1955). ILLIAC Design Techniques, Lecture Notes for *Univ. Michigan Summer Conf., June*.

Staff of Digital Computer Laboratory (1952). ORDVAC Manual, Univ. of Illinois, Urbana, Illinois.

Staff of Digital Computer Laboratory (1954). ILLIAC Programming, Univ. of Illinois, Urbana, Illinois.

Wheeler, D. J. (1953). The Calculation of 60,000 Digits of e by the ILLIAC.

DEPARTMENT OF COMPUTER SCIENCE
UNIVERSITY OF ILLINOIS
URBANA, ILLINOIS

WHIRLWIND

ROBERT R. EVERETT

The WHIRLWIND computer was built at the Digital Computer Laboratory at the Massachusetts Institute of Technology between 1945 and 1952. WHIRLWIND was a special machine; the motivation for it was also rather special. It was designed by engineers for engineering purposes and for controlling real-time devices. Real-time control was the motivation behind WHIRLWIND.

WHIRLWIND began as an analog computer. In 1944, a group under Jay W. Forrester at Gordon S. Brown's Servomechanisms Laboratory began work on an airplane stability control analyzer, a device that had been conceived by the Special Devices Center of the Navy, which was run by Luis DeFlorez and had built a number of aircraft trainers. The idea was to build a generalized trainer, which would actually solve the equations of motion and aerodynamics of an aircraft. Putting wind tunnel data into the trainer would cause it to fly like an airplane not yet built. A trainer involved both a cockpit and a very large computer. We set out to build an analog machine and worked at it for some time. The problem lay in achieving the speed of operation, the amount of equipment, and the dynamic range needed to solve this aircraft stability problem. We worked on it very hard and, had we been forced to stick with it, we probably would have built something useful. However, in 1945, Jay Forrester began looking at the new digital computers, talked to a number of people, attended a computer conference and, as I recall it, late that year came back and said, "We are no longer building an analog computer; we are building a digital computer."

365

Things were different in those days. We didn't have a big study group, and when Jay decided to build a digital computer, we all thought that was great. He won the support of MIT and the Special Devices Center, which was also a group of engineers, and we began to build a digital computer in late 1945. At that time the concept of such a machine was already understood. The general ideas and philosophy were available. ENIAC already existed, proving you could make a large electronic machine and make it work. EDVAC ideas were on paper and, perhaps most important but seldom mentioned, radar technology was coming out of World War II activities in tubes and pulse circuits and storage devices that had been developed for moving target indicators. The technological foundation of pulse circuits made possible electronic digital computers. But the task was just barely possible because of limited availability of test equipment and other devices and components. No technical infrastructure existed as we know it today. There were few instruments. We had to go ahead and do almost everything for the first time and when I say *we* I mean not only the Digital Computer Laboratory but everybody in the computer business. Tube life characteristics were unknown. In addition, the MIT group had its own peculiar problem; we were still after an airplane stability control analyzer, a machine that had to work in real time, which required that the machine have enough capacity, speed, and storage space to keep up with real time. You couldn't say, "Well, I didn't quite make it, I'll run a little slower," because there were people in the loop. Furthermore, the downtime had to be kept very low in view of the cost of people and equipment associated with the machine. Failures were very expensive and troublesome. Thus, the double thrust for speed and reliability in a real-time machine constituted the driving force in the WHIRLWIND group.

We began by considering a three-address serial type of machine using what would nowadays be called a read-only memory based on cathode-ray tubes with punched cards in front of them, and a READ–WRITE storage-tube memory. We laid out diagrams for such a machine and did some work on circuits and memory devices. In the summer of 1946, about the time the Moore School at the University of Pennsylvania was running its famous course, we wrote a program demonstrating how we would solve the airplane stability control analyzer job using this serial machine. The program had about 2000 instructions. It was a good thing we never had to check it out, but it showed that the machine was marginal at best. We were also having trouble, particularly with the storage, so we decided to go for a parallel type of machine, which was faster and more flexible, at least for our applications. Further, we decided to build a small machine at first. In the serial machines, one can change the word length to change the machine speed. In a parallel type machine, changing the word length changes the size and therefore the cost. Therefore, we decided to build a small machine, and at a later time, to build a larger machine that would do the larger job.

We selected a word length of 16 bits. That is a nice binary number, but it did not come about arbitrarily. It was determined by asking, "What is the shortest single-address instruction that looks reasonable?" Our analysis of the programs we were interested in showed that 1000 words was tight and 2000 considerably better. That gave us 11 bits and we knew we needed at least 16 instructions; 32 sounded reasonable and that gave us 5 bits more. Therefore, the 16 was not a binary number, it was the sum of two primes. We were well aware that 16 bits was a short word length and that people were worried about roundoff errors. We expected that a great deal of work would be done with double or triple precision, which would slow the machine. We were also concerned about the amount of software overhead that might be needed in multiprecision operations.

As it turned out, the short register was a better choice than we expected. Somebody recently recalled how John von Neumann had made a remark to Julius Stratton of MIT to the effect that WHIRLWIND had such a short word length that John was concerned about its ability to do anything useful. I think John did understand why we did it, but I believe he was more concerned about the word length than we were because he tended to think of different kinds of problems. Jay Stratton understood what we were doing.

By 1947, the logical design of WHIRLWIND had been completed and was issued in a two-volume report. The memory was to consist of specially designed storage tubes, and the machine was to include a test memory of 32 registers of toggle switches, and five registers of flip-flops, which could be inserted anywhere among the toggle switch registers. The organization was relatively straightforward. WHIRLWIND was a stored program machine, but once you get more deeply into it you find that it deviated quite a bit from the standard form. It had a main bus, a repeat-back system for checking transfers, and a very flexible control to permit the addition and modification of instructions.

We were concerned about standardizing pulse shapes, circuits, voltages, connectors, and tubes. We were particularly concerned about vacuum-tube reliability. We expected to use a lot of tubes and expected a lot of trouble with them. Tube failures were generally of three kinds. First was a kind of infant mortality that could be avoided with preburning all tubes. Second were mechanical problems, which could only be circumvented by very careful design and construction. We used special tubes and got a lot of cooperation from the tube companies. We paid $5 or $10 a tube, which was expensive in those days. But we still faced the third problem of gradual decay. As the tubes aged, the cathode emission would go down. Also, some tubes would build up an interface—an insulating layer between the nickel cathode and the emitting oxide—and Jay decided that we should put in a system of marginal checking. All the circuits were designed with safety margins, and, as the tubes aged, these margins would get smaller and smaller. The margins could be measured by changing certain voltages while the machine was run-

Figure 1

ning. Screen voltages were often used to move the operating point within the margin to measure how large the margin was. If the margin became too small, the tube could be replaced instead of waiting for it to go out at some very inconvenient time.

Figure 1 shows the Barta Building at MIT where WHIRLWIND was built. Initially WHIRLWIND occupied about one-third of the top floor. Figure 2 is a picture of the five-digit multiplier we built in 1947 to check out the circuitry and the marginal checking idea. The young man in the saddle shoes is Norman Taylor. The machine multiplied two five-digit binary numbers and checked the result, keeping that up day after day. It underwent marginal checking and preventive maintenance at reasonable intervals starting out every day and subsequently less often. The five-digit multiplier contained about 400 vacuum tubes. It normally ran a few weeks at a time without error and once ran error-free for 45 days. One of the nice things about the computer business in the early days was that it was fairly small. Everybody knew everybody else. Everybody talked to everyone. We all knew what each other was doing. Howard Aiken came to see us one day and we showed him our five-digit multiplier. Jay was very proud of it and told Howard how it had run for 45 days and had done 10 to the 10th multiplications without making a mistake. Howard looked at it and as he was going out the door, he said, "Well, five bits, that's about one digit. Trouble goes as the square of the number of digits, 10 digits, a factor of 100. That's about a half a day; that's not bad," and off he went.

The WHIRLWIND computer was arranged in sections to permit selected voltage excursions in the various sections to help in the check out. One could dial up one of the sections and set test voltage by hand if one wanted to but the excursions could also be set automatically. The checking routine

Figure 2

took about 15 min and was repeated daily. Results of this procedure were very good. We found after we made some changes in the tubes that vacuum tubes were remarkably reliable. Tube failure rates were about 1% per 1000 hours, approximately half of which were located during routine maintenance by marginal checking. Most of the rest consisted of mechanical failures of one sort or another. Gradually deteriorating tubes that were not caught during marginal checking and therefore failed during operation had an effective failure rate of about 0.1% per 1000 hours.

For laboratory use in designing the computer, we decided to develop a set of digital building blocks as test equipment, including clocks, counters, gates, flip-flops, and pulse standardizers, with standardized power supplies —all designed to be plugged together to generate any desired sequence of pulses. We built this digital test equipment in large enough quantities so that someone needing test equipment could have it and go right back to working on the machine, instead of spending time on special test equipment, as had previously been necessary.

The Digital Computer Laboratory also undertook a training program. We had to train everybody for everything including standard soldering. If a person had not been through the soldering course he was not allowed to solder. I never took it, and I assure you, I was never allowed to solder anything either. In addition to the training, there was firm control over all aspects of design and construction. There were good records, and careful drawings, in a word, standards. It was a very carefully engineered and maintained operation; our feeling was that if the whole thing ever got away from us, we'd never catch up with it again.

We decided to build the machine in a two-dimensional array. Figure 3 shows one digit of the accumulator. Everything was spread out two-dimensionally for access to any piece for measurement and repair. All parts were available at all times.

In Figure 4 people are installing equipment in the racks; this shows the scale of the WHIRLWIND computer. Figure 5 shows the arithmetic element. The perforated metal boxes are filament transformers, which were distributed and were adjustable for optimum voltage on everything.

The input routine to start WHIRLWIND was stored in the test storage. There were 32 rows of 16 switches each for the read-only memory. By means of an extra switch for each register the five flip-flop registers could be put in place of any of these 32 switch registers, after which the toggle switches gave the initial conditions for the flip-flops. There were 544 switches in all. One problem was that nobody could set all 544 switches right the first time. The explanation is simple. Looking at the back of the machine, as pictured, you see the highest digit place at the left side, then it moves down to the right. The switches are on the other side so, of course, the sign is on the right, making the whole thing backward. That was just to make it a little harder. We didn't realize the reversal until the first time we set it up; then it was too late to fix.

Figure 6 is a close-up of the operation matrix. Soldering in diodes changed existing instructions or put in new ones. That shadowy figure on the left is Norm Taylor; Gus O'Brien is on the right and the author is in the center.

WHIRLWIND had a peculiarity in its original design. It was desirable to capacitor-couple the gate tubes to the flip-flops. Capacitors don't pass dc, and this was a machine that ran at any speed, including step-by-step. To

Figure 3

Figure 4

Figure 5

Figure 6

keep things working properly the flip-flops had to turn over at fairly frequent intervals, but that did not necessarily occur in normal use. However, the information content of the machine would not be lost if all the flip-flops turned over simultaneously. We solved the problem by using restorer pulses; approximately every 20 μsec the machine would stop whatever it was doing and all the flip-flops would turn over and then all turn back, which would reset all of the capacitors and enable all of the gate tubes to work. Although this worked, it was not one of our better ideas, and before long we went to dc-coupled gates.

There is no specific date on which one can say WHIRLWIND first worked. It started working with test storage in 1949. One row of storage tubes was working with reduced density in 1950, and the entire central machine was working about 1951. A computer, at least in those days, was not something you put together all at once and turned on to find out whether it worked or not. WHIRLWIND evolved gradually over a period of time. Figure 7 shows the control room as of about 1951. Jack Gilmore is on the left, with Joe Thompson, our first computer operator. As you can see, the control room was quite large. It is not the computer. On the left is the marginal checking control, and in front of Jack are indicator lights. To the left of the indicator rack is a synchroscope, which could be connected to probes scattered throughout the computer room for connection to any test point. The control room kept changing; in fact, one could almost make a history of WHIRLWIND with a sequence of pictures showing the control room as it changed over the years.

Figure 7

We used punched paper tape as the primary input for a long time with a Ferranti photoelectric tape reader. Later we added magnetic tape devices.

The five tape transports were built by Raytheon. They were six bits wide. We had the same problems with magnetic tape as everybody else. The tape had blemishes, pieces of dust or other flaws that would push the tape away from the head as it went by and cause a dropout. The principal trouble was from dropouts; we never knew a case of an extra bit appearing. From measurements we found that the dropouts were not very wide, rarely extending beyond two adjacent channels. We ended up ganging the six channels into three groups of two each, spaced half across the tape, one group used for timing and two for data, and under these circumstances the tape units worked very well. As an example of what can be done with very little storage, we wrote a test program to examine the tape dropout problem. This test program ran the tape unit, wrote numbered blocks of 128 lines of all ones, then went back and read the tape block-by-block, and checked it. If all ones appeared, the computer continued. If a zero presented itself, the machine stopped and punched out on paper tape the number of the block and a tape image (which was also six channels wide) of whatever sequences of zeros and ones that block contained. This was all done in 32 16-bit words and shows what can be done if one has very restricted storage.

The tubes used for memory were specially built at the Laboratory. Figure 8 shows a storage tube on the trolley being pumped down. We made them work although I aged a great deal in the process. The storage tubes

Figure 8

were designed for a 32 × 32 array on the face of a mica target. We started
with a 16 × 16 array and gradually built it up over a period of time. Jay Forrester, of course, is on the right; Steve Dodd, chief storage tube engineer, is
in the center; and on the left is Pat Youtz, who was in charge of the tube
shop. There were two of these tubes for each digit, and each tube was put in
a box and trimmed up to have the same characteristics. The tube was replaced by replacing the whole box.

I might mention the contractual and funding matters relevant to all the
Project WHIRLWIND activity. Interest in the aircraft analyzer had dwin-
dled by 1948 and finally disappeared completely. The Special Devices Center had also disappeared, with the WHIRLWIND project being supported by
the Office of Naval Research. The interests of the Digital Computer Laboratory were primarily in control applications, such as fire control, tracking aircraft, antisubmarine warfare, simulation, and air traffic control. A number of
pioneering reports in real-time control areas were written from 1947 on. In
1948, we received support to propose application of digital computers to air
traffic control. However, there was no formal interest by the sponsors in
real-time control; the Office of Naval Research (ONR) was primarily interested in mathematical applications, and was concerned about the amount
of money we spent. We were spending about $1 million/year, which was a
large fraction of ONR's budget, and this created a financial and political
problem. [A book entitled ''The Whirlwind Story'' by Kent Redmond and

Thomas Smith, about to be published by the Digital Press, examines this subject in considerable detail.]

By the beginning of 1950, WHIRLWIND was working, and the Navy decided the time for putting in $1 million a year had passed. Although the Office of Naval Research was willing to continue supporting some computer applications, there was a major contractual crisis. However, as often happens, at this critical juncture an optimum application appeared, one well matched to the concepts that had guided the design of WHIRLWIND. That application was air defense. Aircraft tracking and control needed a computer of the WHIRLWIND capabilities. Air defense had a high priority with money and support. At about that time the USSR had developed atomic weapons and intercontinental aircraft, and considerable attention was being given to air defense. A major threat came from low-flying aircraft. At low altitude, radar range is very short, and information from many radars had to be netted to cover large areas. George Valley at MIT was concerned about radar coverage. He met Jay, and it turned out that what he needed was a digital computer and what we needed was air defense. So Air Force financial support appeared in the nick of time, and we began to devote a large part of our effort to using WHIRLWIND for developing a new approach to air defense. As it happened, a group at the Air Force Cambridge Research Center was working on a means for transmitting radar data over telephone lines. We took their telephone line transmitters and a radar in Lexington, Massachusetts, and hooked them all up to WHIRLWIND, and started tracking aircraft. This development led to a decision in 1951 to develop a computer tracking system for operational use and to form the Lincoln Laboratory to carry out the work. The Digital Computer Laboratory became a division of Lincoln, responsible for the design of the Semiautomatic Ground Environment (SAGE) Air Defense System. (The Digital Computer Laboratory continued to carry out a program of computer applications, using primarily Navy money, and made the machine available to people around MIT for scientific purposes.) From 1951 on, we focused our attention on two areas: (1) adapting WHIRLWIND to real-time-control uses and building facilities for an experimental air defense sector based on WHIRLWIND; and (2) designing the new computer for SAGE.

One of the things that I think we did first was to connect a visual display to a computer. Digital-to-analog converters attached to two of the flip-flop storage registers permitted the machine to select and point the cathode ray tube beam toward any $x-y$ position, after which an intensification pulse would cause a spot to appear on the scope in the place determined by the computer.

Figure 9 shows dots and symbols representing radar data. The T designates the target aircraft, and F the fighter. Below is digital information, which at that time was accomplished by spelling out the characters in dots. We went ahead to build character generators and vector generators for the

Figure 9

air defense operation. Display scopes all worked in parallel. No matter how many displays there were, the same deflection voltages went to all of them, and the computer determined which scopes to intensify to put different pictures on different scopes.

For communication between aircontrol officers and the computer, we developed a light gun as an input device to the computer. Figure 10 shows the light gun in its case. This was one of the early guns. The light gun was a photocell receiver that was triggered by a flash from the cathode-ray display scope. To use it, one put the spout over the place where a displayed spot was expected. When the computer intensified that spot, light was picked up by the phototube and sent back to the computer. Then the computer knew, "Oh, that one," and did what was indicated by the setting of control switches.

Figure 10

The WHIRLWIND computer became the central control for the Cape Cod system (Fig. 11), which was a prototype for the SAGE Air Defense System. To create a first computer-controlled real-time network of radars and interceptor aircraft, we needed drum storage, with two kinds of magnetic drums.

One drum was for auxiliary memory, because the program for the Cape Cod system required 20,000 instructions, and we only had 2000 in the central memory. The other magnetic drum acted as a buffer for radar data and other kinds of information that poured into the system. We didn't have a good interrupt system or the time to handle data on an interrupt basis. So information would be stored on a buffer drum with marker channels, and the computer would read a section of information whenever it had time. We bought those drums from Engineering Research Associates in Minnesota.

There was need in the Cape Cod experimental air defense sector for much terminal equipment, not only from telephone lines but also from many other sources. There were thousands of switches and dozens of phone lines feeding data into WHIRLWIND. In fact, I remember a man from another organization that was working in air defense who visited us one day and was shocked to find that our telephone bill was larger than their total budget.

Figure 12 shows a Cape Cod air controller station in its final version. The large scope is the computer-driven display. The small scope is for digital information. To the left and right are buttons that the operator would push to tell the machine what to do. He is holding a second-generation light gun.

Figure 13 shows the weapons control room as it appeared about 1954. In the foreground is one of the officers. He has two assistants with him and is looking at the aircraft display deciding what to do. To the left of the blackboard in the rear is a small box on a tripod. It contains a photocell over a

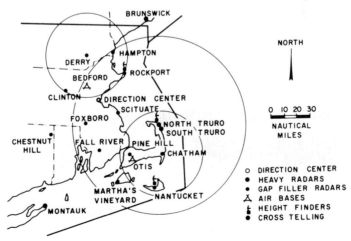

Figure 11 Map of Cape Cod system.

Figure 12

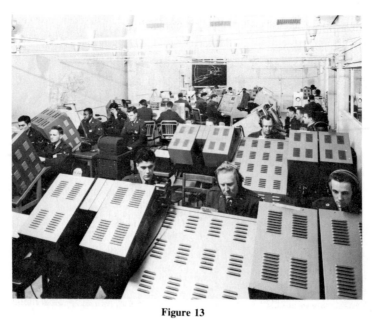

Figure 13

display scope mounted in a horizontal position. This display was used for masking to give the computer special kinds of information. I told Robert Wieser, who built this room, that it looked like a warehouse for old scopes. I don't think he ever forgave me. He maintained the layout was very carefully designed.

There were about 20,000 instructions in the Cape Cod air defense program and we had to do a lot of work on means for writing programs and keeping track of them. There was a lot of pressure on laboratory space. The size of the project operation was going up. At the time WHIRLWIND was built it had a very large staff by the standards of the contemporary computer business. There were some 70 technical staff, 175 persons altogether, and the number began to grow substantially when we started getting into air defense work.

For computer reliability, we had to replace the storage tubes. Because the laboratory had been working for some time on Jay Forrester's random-access magnetic-core memory, which seemed to promise the reliability and speed we needed, we immediately began to develop a full-scale core memory. Figure 14 shows one of the first core planes. It contains ceramic cores in a 16 × 16 array. Cores came from General Ceramics and by the summer of 1952 we had begun to get cores we could actually use.

Figure 15 shows the MEMORY TEST computer built as a test instrument for checking the first core memory. The core memory stack is on the left. The MEMORY TEST computer is famous for two reasons: it is the first

Figure 14

Figure 15

computer to have a core memory, and it is the first computer that Ken Olsen ever built. He is now President of the Digital Equipment Corporation and makes computers by the thousands, but this is his first computer. After it did its work on the core memory, we used it both as a test device to test all of the SAGE peripherals, and as a means for data reduction.

The first full-scale core memory performed so well that we decided to put it into WHIRLWIND, which required building a second memory stack. Core memory had a tremendous effect on WHIRLWIND's efficiency. It approximately doubled the operating speed; it quadrupled the input data rate; and the maintenance time on the storage row fell from 4 hours a day to 2 hours a week. The mean time to failure on the memory rose from 2 hours to 2 weeks, and the entire tube shop was freed to work on the display tubes. We then built a 4000-word memory for the MEMORY TEST computer and subsequently another 4000-word memory for WHIRLWIND. Later we built transistorized memories and, ultimately, a 65,000-word memory, which went on the TX2 computer.

We ran air defense demonstrations about once a week using Strategic Air Command (SAC) aircraft. There was a lot of Air Force support. SAC aircraft acted as targets, and fighter aircraft from Air Defense Command were scrambled against them. General officers came and watched the system work. WHIRLWIND had a character all its own. When there wasn't anything important going on, it could be very temperamental, but if you rushed in and said, "Hey, it's time for the demonstration and General So-and-So is

Central computer	Single-address, parallel, binary computer magnetic core memory = 2048 16-bit words add = 24 μsec, multiply = 40 μsec, control transfer = 16 μsec	35,000 operations/sec
Secondary storage	ERA Magnetic DRUM, 1 × 2048 words, 60 rps	31,000 words/sec
	Raytheon Magnetic TAPE, 4 + 1 units at 125,000 words each	390 words/sec
Input	Ferranti photoelectric 7-hole READER, 2 units	205 characters/sec
	Flexowriter mechanical 7-hole READER	10 characters/sec
Output	Raytheon magnetic TAPE for later printing or punching 2 + 1 units at 53,000 characters each	133 characters/sec
	Flexowriter printer, 1 direct, 2 from tape	8 characters/sec
	Flexowriter punch, 1 direct, 2 from tape	11 characters/sec
	16-in. SCOPE with visible face, and ⎫ graphical points	6200 points/sec
	16-in. SCOPE with computer-controlled ⎬ digits (point-by-point)	200 digits/sec
	Fairchild CAMERA ⎭ digits (special generator)	1200 digits/sec

WORD = 5-bit Operation + 11-bit Address = Sign + 15-bit Fraction

CHARACTER = 6-bit representation of the 50 keys on a Flexowriter,
in arbitrary, Teletype-like code

Figure 16   Terminal equipment characteristics of the MIT WHIRLWIND I computer

here,'' WHIRLWIND would pull itself together and work perfectly, especially if George Valley, whom I mentioned earlier and who was Assistant Director of the Lincoln Laboratory, was around. WHIRLWIND liked George, why I don't know. But when George was around it worked well. So we always tried to get him to come for an important demonstration.

One thing I did in putting together this paper was to resist the temptation to remake any of the illustrations. All are from the old WHIRLWIND records of 20 or 25 years ago. Figure 16 is a chart of WHIRLWIND's speeds and capacities at the time of the Cape Cod demonstrations.

Figure 17 shows the operating reliability, also during the Cape Cod days (about 1953–1954). During that time WHIRLWIND was used for many purposes, both mathematical and experimental, at MIT. It was the machine that Laning and Zierler used for their first algebraic compilers. We also did a lot of work with the machine on air traffic control.

Another of Whirlwind's projects was to compute the tapes for the first digitally controlled milling machine, which was built at MIT and for which Forrester and others hold one of the patents.

Figure 18 shows the WHIRLWIND control room in 1959, just before it was shut down. Under the clock is a hand grenade, attached to a statement

Operating time usable	96.5 %
Average time between failures	10.6 hr
Scheduled maintenance time	1.25 hr/day
Size of system	13,000 tubes

Figure 17   WHIRLWIND system performance.

Figure 18

that the pin would be pulled on 30 June 1959. By that time all the engineers were off the machine, but it was still being operated by technicians. It ran very well but cost about $300,000 a year to keep going. Maintaining the support software was also expensive, so we decided to shut it down.

We expected that that would be the end of WHIRLWIND. But one of the fellows from WHIRLWIND, Bill Wolf, had a software company and decided he wanted the machine. He rented it from the Navy for $1 a year, and actually took it out of the Barta Building and moved it to West Concord, where he set it up again and made it work, much to our surprise. WHIRL-WIND ran for several more years. I think what Wolf wanted was not so much the central machine as all of the terminal equipment that came with it. There had been an agreement between the Navy and the Smithsonian that when the Navy no longer needed the machine, it would be turned over to the Smithsonian. Finally, the Navy got tired of keeping WHIRLWIND on its books and decided to abandon it to Wolf, with the proviso that he deliver the appropriate parts to the Smithsonian. The Smithsonian and Wolf never got together, and eventually — a couple of years ago — Ken Olsen called and told me that Bill Wolf had called him and was scrapping WHIRLWIND, and if Ken wanted any parts to let Bill know. So Ken went over with some of his summer students and trailers and collected all the parts, while I tried to get hold of the Smithsonian. I didn't have much success, but Ken got the machine, kept it in the trailers for a while, and then in a warehouse. Eventually, we took some of it out and made a display, which is now in the Smithsonian.

Figure 19 shows the WHIRLWIND display in the lobby of the MITRE Corporation on the occasion of our farewell-to-WHIRLWIND party, with

Figure 19

many of the WHIRLWIND hands in attendance, a little older than when they worked together in the pioneering days of computers. Jay Forrester is left of center in the second row, with George Valley under the N in WHIRLWIND. We all enjoyed the party so much we had another one in Washington. Figure 20 shows the hello-to-WHIRLWIND at the Smithsonian, with the display as it is there. You can see some of the components. We took one actual digit column out of WHIRLWIND and put a picture behind it to show how the rest looked. The core memory is to the right of the picture. A magnetic drum and other things are also included in the display.

I should like to make a few closing remarks. WHIRLWIND is probably the most documented of the early computers. Not much was published, but for internal reasons, there was a great deal of documentation. For instance, all the staff were required to write biweekly reports; every other Friday near the end of the day each person had to stop what he was doing and prepare a short report on what he had done in the previous two weeks. The reports were all put together and issued as a means of internal communication. There were literally thousands of reports and computation books. All this information has been turned over to the Smithsonian for their archives and is available there. There is also the Redmond–Smith book I mentioned, as well as a complete photographic archive at MITRE. We shall be glad to help anybody who is trying to learn something about WHIRLWIND. In fact, it's rather hard to get WHIRLWIND people to stop talking about it once they start.

Regarding WHIRLWIND's contributions, there were many firsts, stemming, I believe, from our being the first to build a digital computer for real-

Figure 20

time applications. We were the first to face the speed and reliability demands and to solve them. I shall not attempt to name those contributions here, although at the WHIRLWIND display in the Smithsonian you can find a list of WHIRLWIND firsts that has been cleared with others in the field. Two end products resulted from WHIRLWIND. As is well known, it was the predecessor of the SAGE Air Defense System, which in turn is the predecessor of the military C3 systems, the air traffic control system, and other large computer-based systems. Another lesser-known derivative of WHIRLWIND is the minicomputer. Ken Olsen says that WHIRLWIND was the first minicomputer. That sounds strange because it was the largest of the early machines, but in architecture and intent, in order design, in structure, and in use, it is in fact a minicomputer, and the minicomputers today are much more like WHIRLWIND than like other early machines. So if you will be quiet and listen, you will hear a faint rustle, and that is the millions of WHIRLWIND's children coming along in the form of chips to invade our houses and our automobiles and, just like WHIRLWIND, they are going to be smart and reliable and fun to be with.

REFERENCE

Redmond, K., and Smith, T. (1977). Lessons from Project Whirlwind, *IEEE Spectrum*.

MITRE CORPORATION
BEDFORD, MASSACHUSETTS

Reminiscences of Oak Ridge

A. S. HOUSEHOLDER

My own introduction to the high-speed digital computer came shortly after I had arrived in Oak Ridge to join the staff of what was then the Clinton Laboratories. The introduction came in January 1947, at Harvard, on the occasion of the dedication of Aiken's MARK II. This was attended by many of the pioneers, some, like von Neumann, who were already well known and others who would become so. Some were at the Los Alamos meeting.

With the war so recently over, Oak Ridge had not yet adjusted itself to peace, and its mission for the coming era was not yet well defined. Nevertheless, I returned to Oak Ridge fully convinced that an electronic computer would be required. I had only the vaguest notion of for what, and in fact I could hardly imagine that the entire country could use more than half a dozen or so. Still, I began preaching the gospel and was really surprised by the extent to which people showed interest, and the mildness of the opposition. It is true that Alvin Weinberg, who later became Director of what was then called the Oak Ridge National Laboratory, did argue that the use of the computer was becoming a substitute for thinking, and that after enough thought all necessary computing could be done on the back of an envelope. Nevertheless, even he eventually gave his support.

Granted that ORNL should have a computer, the next question was what computer and how to acquire it? From the start the IAS design interested us most. But the idea of building one at Oak Ridge never seemed quite feasible, although I cannot remember exactly why. After all, Argonne hired Chuan Chu to direct the construction of the AVIDAC, and perhaps we could have

385

recruited similar talent. At any rate, I cannot recall that such a proposal was ever seriously considered. Instead, I made numerous trips around the country visiting various establishments, accompanied by one or more of our electronic engineers, looking at what was being done. We were much interested in the RAYDAC, but the asking price of $350,000 seemed totally out of the question. It is interesting to note in retrospect that a RAYDAC* was installed at the naval base at Point Mugu for exactly that price. The UNIVAC seemed more in our price range, $175,000 to begin with, as I recall, but we wanted a strictly scientific computer and the decimal arithmetic and certain other features seemed designed to attract the commercial user so we turned away. We considered briefly the proposed REEVAC,† and the ERA 1101 but discarded both for reasons I no longer remember. And Howard Aiken suggested having GE copy the Harvard MARK IV, and this was considered for a time.

In August of 1949, we hosted the second national meeting of the Association for Computing Machinery (ACM) with a total attendance of about 150, hoping to further our own education. In this we were certainly successful, and thereafter I think that everyone in Oak Ridge agreed that ORNL should have a computer.

Meanwhile, I was becoming increasingly aware of developments at Argonne, largely through my own close associations and friendship with D. A. "Moll" Flanders. I can no longer recall when the proposal was made first, but it was gradually worked out that ORNL would send four of its engineers to Argonne to build a computer under the direction of Chuan Chu. Six months would be spent studying the design of the IAS computer and trying to make improvements, after which construction would actually start. The engineers, some hired for the purpose, were Earl Burdette, Rudolph Klein, Wm. Gerhardt, and Jim Woody. Somewhere along the line the name Oak Ridge Automatic Computer and Logical Engine was decided upon, and I believe it was first suggested by J. W. Givens, who at the time was consultant at ORNL.

During this time F. A. Ficken at the University of Tennessee was consulting at the Gaseous Diffusion Plant at Oak Ridge, and was following developments with some interest, and he suggested one day at lunch that a course on digital computing might be appropriate, so it was arranged that I give such a course in Oak Ridge for University of Tennessee credit. Quite naturally, I was coming to realize that it would be my responsibility to know something about the subject. Hitherto my only contacts with computing had been during the war with naval lead-computing gunsights, a very special-purpose analog computer. So I got busy reading what literature I could find,

---

* Made by Raytheon Corporation.

† By Reeves Instrument Company, but never built.

wrote up my lecture notes carefully, and distributed them widely, soliciting criticisms and suggestions. This led to my book published in 1953.

Meanwhile I had enlisted Wallace Givens as a consultant at ORNL and he became engrossed in the eigenvalue problem for Hermitian matrices. The outcome of this is reasonably well known, but let me digress a bit, and fill in some details that may well have been forgotten.

I should say something about the development of numerical analysis during this period. To begin with numerical analysis *was* INA.* One could hardly exaggerate its impact nor too much deplore its destruction, largely at the hands of a young senator whose political fortune would rise far and then fall abruptly. Among its activities were the organizing of several important symposia during the late 1940s, and that on matrices by Olga Taussky in 1951. At this George Forsythe gave his survey of results to date on the solution of linear systems. The new conjugate gradient method was unveiled. The Jacobi method for finding eigenvalues of symmetric matrices, recently rediscovered and adapted to the large-scale computer by von Neumann and Goldstine, was discussed. And Wallace Givens, in an unscheduled talk, described his method for solving the same problem. This would be among the first computations done on the ORACLE at Argonne in 1953 before it was shipped to Oak Ridge to get under way in the late winter of 1954. The programmer was Virginia Klema (née Carlock). Jim Wilkinson's work in linear algebra, particularly in error analysis, is well known.

I shall not follow the history of the ORACLE except to say that a piece of the arithmetic unit now resides in the Deutsches Museum in Munich, at the request of F. L. Bauer. I do wish to follow briefly two developments, already incipient. First on the Givens method: I believe it was at the ACM meeting at Urbana in 1958 that I first introduced the "Householder matrices" (later so called, but already to be found in Turnbull and Aitken), and suggested that they could be used to reduce computation in the Givens method, and also the unitary triangularization in the course of matrix inversion. Through no fault of my own, my modification has come to be known as "the Householder Method," but, of course, the Householder method is the Householder–Givens, or the Givens–Householder, method. Actually in the original report on his method Givens went far beyond a mere description of the method, and gave a detailed error analysis, in which he developed independently of Wilkinson the technique of backward error analysis.

The other development followed from Olga Taussky's symposium. Givens went from University of Tennessee to Wayne University and hosted in 1957 a second matrix symposium. A number of new names, later prominent, appeared here, but I refrain from naming any. In the summer of 1960, a group gathered in Ann Arbor at one or both of these symposia, and the sug-

* National Bureau of Standards Institute of Numerical Analysis.

gestion arose that it might be about time for another. This was the genesis of the Gatlinburgs, of which there have been seven so far. The first of these was held in 1961. The fourth, in 1969, was the last to be held in Gatlinburg, but the name continues. Gatlinburg V was held in 1972 at Los Alamos, Gatlinburg VI near Munich in 1974, Gatlinburg VII in December 1977, and Gatlinburg VIII is being planned for 1981 in England.

OAK RIDGE NATIONAL LABORATORY
OAK RIDGE, TENNESSEE*

* Retired.

Computer Development at IBM

CUTHBERT C. HURD

When giving this paper at the Los Alamos Conference, Dr. Hurd prefaced his address with the following personal remarks:

> I congratulate the organizers of the International Research Conference on the History of Computing for their foresight, their understanding of the importance of the field, and for their knowledge of the mainstreams of the history of computing, which has allowed them to select the individuals and contributors who are in this room. I am delighted to have been included and feel complimented. A particularly fortuitous outcome of this conference would be a mechanism by which the excellent work of Dr. Henry Tropp could be continued. Under his direction the joint History Project of the American Federation of Information Processing Societies (AFIPS) and the Smithsonian Institution received great impetus and an international flavor. Perhaps AFIPS itself should now come forward with support.
>
> It is particularly appropriate that this conference be held at the Los Alamos Scientific Laboratory not only because of the general scientific contributions of the Laboratory but because of its many contributions to the technology of computing. MANIAC and its successors included ideas of general value, and Dr. Metropolis and his associates were always willing to share those ideas in the scientific community at large. I was among the beneficiaries of those ideas and remember speaking with Dr. Metropolis about them in various places in the world. The development of the Monte Carlo method by Dr. Stanislaw Ulam had great im-

portance in computing and in science. Moreover, the Los Alamos scientists have made direct and early contributions to software, as in SHACO, have used successive generations of computers with skill, have contributed nuclear codes that are generally available such as the Carlson code, and, of course, have contributed to the design of STRETCH.

Next, I want to express my appreciation to Mr. Nathaniel Rochester, a former colleague at IBM and one of IBM's first system engineers. Nat is here today and is assisting me in the presentation of this paper. Also, it is most pleasant to appear on the same platform with Dr. John Curtiss, whose energetic efforts at the National Bureau of Standards beginning in the late 1940s served as an important catalyst to the entire field, and to be again on the same platform with Mr. John Backus. John was one of the early mathematicians in IBM, had an important role with respect to the operation of the SSEC, and is known throughout the world for his pioneering work in compilers, including FORTRAN.

1. Introduction

IBM entered the computer field with the installation of a 701 (Defense Calculator) in the IBM Technical Computing Bureau in New York City in December 1952, and the shipment of the first customer machine to the Los Alamos Scientific Laboratory early in 1953. The 701 was considered an applied science machine because of the participation of that group in IBM in the application planning, programming, sale, and installation of the machines. However, there were immediate commerical data processing applications which offered feasibility proof for later developments.

This paper describes:

(a) some of the characteristics and novel features of the 701 hardware and software, and the technology from which the 701 was developed, including: components such as the Havens dynamic pulse circuit and the eight-tube pluggable unit; subsystems such as the electrostatic memory, the magnetic drum and the magnetic tapes; and the punched card input and output;

(b) the culmination of ideas leading to the 701, including: decades of punched card and relay technology leading to the Selective Sequence Electronic Calculator (SSEC); several hundred Card-Programmed Electronic Calculators (CPC); the beginning of IBM electronics with the 603 and 604; "general-purpose" control panels designed by CPC customers and freely circulated; educational classes conducted at the Watson Laboratory at Columbia University; the increasing participation by universities and government laboratories throughout the world in problem solving with existing equipment and the construction of computers; the Burks, von Neumann, and

Goldstine papers; the association of John von Neumann with IBM; and the explicit decision on the part of IBM in the late 1940s to employ university graduates in mathematics, the physical sciences, and electronics;

(c)   the immediate environment that led to the 701: the clamor of multiple CPC users for a more powerful machine; programming experience and problem solution on the SSEC; test or developmental machines such as the Test Assembly, the Tape Processing Machine, and the Naval Ordnance Research Calculator; the entrance of UNIVAC, ERA, Ferranti, Raytheon, and others with production machines; the reluctance of the sales department and product planning departments in IBM to commit to a large-scale commercial machine; and the need of industry and government as a result of the Korean War;

(d)   relatives and descendants of the 701, including: the first IBM large-scale machine for the so-called commercial market, the 702; the 650, an applied science machine that was quickly adapted to all kinds of applications; the 703; the 704; the 705; and last, STRETCH, which was installed at the Los Alamos Scientific Laboratory as a result of a joint research and development effort initiated in 1956;

(e)   examples of customer requirements that led to punched paper tape, cathode-ray-tube output, the million-bit memory, remote I/O time-sharing; and

(f)   a bibliography as well as copies of some hitherto unpublished papers.

2.   Characteristics and Novel Features of the 701 Hardware and Software

The 701 was formally dedicated at the IBM Technical Computing Bureau, 590 Madison Avenue, New York, New York, on 7 April 1953. Two hundred distinguished scientists, educators, and executives attended the luncheon. Thomas J. Watson, Thomas J. Watson, Jr., Dr. J. Robert Oppenheimer, and I were the speakers. The demonstration problem was of neutron scattering, an unclassified check problem prepared by Bengt Carlson and his associates at Los Alamos Scientific Laboratory. The *IBM Record* [1] of that date gives a list of the guests, details of the remarks, and pictures the principal contributors to the 701 program.

The IBM Type 701 Electronic Date Processing Machine (Fig. 1) consisted of a set of interconnected boxes [2] called the

701 Electronic Analytic Control Unit,
706 Electrostatic Storage Unit,
711 Punched Card Reader,
716 Alphabetical Printer,

Figure 1   701 IBM World Headquarters, 1952.

721 Punched Card Recorder,
726 Magnetic Tape Readers and Recorders,
731 Magnetic Drum Reader and Recorder, and a Power Supply and Distribution Box.

Separate numbers were chosen because there were separate boxes that could, in principle, be ordered separately. Also, it was already intended that there would be a series of improved machines not only in the type 701 central processor itself but in the memory and the peripherals and the numbering system allowed for the naming of such improvements. The name "Electronic Data Processing Machines" was selected after much discussion, and was intended to imply a broader application of the new series than, for example, the name "calculator" as in the Card-Programmed Calculator or than the name "computer," which was then in general use for other large machines. J. W. Birkenstock coined the name and the abbreviation EDPM, which was neither euphemistic nor euphonious. Nevertheless, it was descriptive and we hoped it would counteract the name UNIVAC, which appeared on its way to becoming the "Frigidaire" of the data-processing industry.

The 701 was of the von Neumann type, a binary, 36-bit word machine with parallel arithmetic, three arithmetic registers, and 32 single-address instructions. An unusual feature was the ability to address half-words. Another unusual feature was the use of copy instructions to execute READ and WRITE and therefore allow computing between the reading or writing of the rows of a card for example. Astrahan and Rochester [3] and later Buchholz [4] described this technique with suitable mention of Wilkes. As originally described in February 1951, the machine was to perform about 1000 complete multiplications per second and to contain 2048 words of electrostatic memory. Each of these specifications was improved by delivery time in late 1952 and in the following way. The original multiply time was based on the strict multiply time of 456 μsec plus ten executions at 60 μsec each. An ingenious scheme called the "twelve free games" [5] method of electrostatic memory regeneration in fact allowed the complete multiplication to take place at a rate of about 2000 per second. Moveover, whereas it was originally thought possible to store 512 bits per electrostatic tube, the delivered system in fact stored 1024 bits per tube and thus the later delivered electrostatic storage capacity was 4096 words if two type 706 units were ordered.

A significant innovation of the 701 was the Havens Dynamic Pulse circuit. This device, invented by B. L. Havens of the IBM Watson Scientific Computing Laboratory, eliminated the need for the familiar "flip-flop." It had the property that its output level during each 1-μsec interval was the same as the input level during the previous 1-μsec period; that is, there was a 1-μsec delay through the unit [6]. This circuit was used even more extensively in the Naval Ordnance Research Calculator, for which Havens was the chief engineer. The delay unit was the fundamental component of the eight-tube pluggable unit, which contributed greatly to ease of construction and maintenance and which was shipped to Dahlgren in 1954.

The electrostatic memory used the dot−dash technique of F. C. Williams and was mounted in pluggable storage drawers with two 3-in. IBM 85 cathode-ray-tubes (CRTs) per drawer (Fig. 2). The cycle time was 12 μsec with emphasis on sufficient time for regeneration and reliability. Arthur Samuel joined IBM in 1949 and immediately set to work in Poughkeepsie to design an improved tube. An associate (Mutter [7]) describes the tube.

Each magnetic tape reader and recorder contained two independent magnetic tape units. Each tape unit contained an 8-in. reel of $\frac{1}{2}$-in., oxide-coated, nonmetallic tape. The tapes were 1200 ft long, with seven tracks, recorded at 100 linear bits/in. in a non-return-to-zero type of recording. The tape moved at 75 in./sec controlled by a vacuum tape column.

The magnetic drum reader and recorder contained two physical drums and a total of four logical drums with each of the latter storing 2048 full words. The 13-in. drum rotated at 2929 rpm and was recorded at a linear density of 50 bits/in. Each physical drum was enclosed in an aluminum housing containing 76 removable read−record heads.

The punched card reader read 72 columns or two 36-bit words a row at a

Figure 2   706 electrostatic storage unit.

time, and thus the IBM card held 24 binary full 36-bit words. Cards were read at 150 per minute. Programming was to take care of other than binary representation in the card.

The alphabetical printer printed 120 characters of information at 150 lines/min. Checking was performed by echo pulses.

The card reader punched up to 72 columns at the rate of 100 cards/min with a provision for gang-punching the remaining columns. These latter three devices were all modified from existing punched card equipment. So completely were we enamored of stored programs that the control panel devices on these machines were not used on the 701 but were restored on later 700 series machines (see 705, for example). The availability of the parallel card equipment on the 701 had great significance, of course. It was several times faster than the punched-paper-tape equipment generally available on other large machines. It provided an audit trail at a time when the world was only beginning to use magnetic tape. Last, the card equipment at the front end allowed the conversion of the enormous files of data existing on cards to be converted to tape, and on the back end allowed the detailed printing to which engineering, scientific, and commerical groups were accustomed.

William F. McClelland was assigned by me to manage the mathematics planning and programming for the 701 in Poughkeepsie in January 1951. He had been a mathematician on the SSEC. Working with him and the Rochester Group initially were J. W. Sheldon, Head of the IBM Technical Computing Bureau in New York; W. H. Johnson, Assistant Director of Applied Science; D. W. Pendery, Western Regional Manager of Applied Science; and P. W. Knaplund, E. F. Codd, W. A. Johnson, and J. C. Smith, each of whom was brought in from the Applied Science Field Organization. Other members of Applied Science and Pure Science as well as new recruits were added as the programming and education effort increased.

Notable in my memory is the first 701 assembler by Rochester, the first machine-directed assembler by McClelland, the first "bootstrap" by Codd and Knaplund, SPEEDCODING [8–10] by John Backus and associates, and a then-famous Los Alamos program known as FEJ after its author Floyd E. Johnson.

Apart from the features described above the most important contribution of the 701 was the reliability of operation. It was intended as a production machine by IBM, and it was also intended that the problems to be solved originally on the 701 were problems already being solved on other equipment and schedules were to be met. Thus, there was great talk among the multiple CPC users concerning backup when all of their problems were on one large machine rather than on several smaller machines, and the most persistent question was, "What is the mean free time to error?" Beyond careful initial design, one of the indirect answers to this question consisted of slowing the electrostatic memory down sufficiently to allow adequate regeneration. Next was the use of plastic tape with its easy handling and replacement. Another answer was the employment of the eight-tube pluggable unit (Fig. 3) and the pluggable electrostatic drawer together with the stocking of spares and test equipment immediately at the customer installation and adjacent to the machine room. Moreover, the customer engineers to be assigned to a location participated in the final testing at the factory. Next, the philosophy of construction in separate boxes permitted large amounts of subsystem test in parallel prior to integrated systems test and the replacement of an entire box if necessary. Also contributing to reliability was an arrangement begun in 604 days under which vacuum-tube manufacturers were agreeable to selecting tubes from their product line that met special IBM specifications, with this arrangement later extending to plastic tape produced by Minnesota Mining and Manufacturing Company (3M).

The next major contribution was the schedule and the demonstration that

Figure 3 701 eight-tube pluggable unit.

large and complicated systems of hardware, software, applications programs, customer education, customer engineering education, and installation could be accomplished in a time space of two years. That is, the decision to produce a large machine was made in December 1950. The first
production machine was shipped from the factory in December 1952. Eighteen machines at the rate of one a month followed closely.

Finally, a program prepared for one 701 could be run on another. This
feature was highly useful in checking out programs by customers prior to
their own delivery. That is, IBM offered the machine in New York for program testing but a total of 12 of the 19 machines were delivered west of the
100th meridian. Because of machine interchangeability much of the program
testing was done in the west on a cooperative basis between customers. The
interchangeability was made possible by careful initial design and testing and
by the development of a system of engineering change control and documentation that was quick and efficient. Engineering, Manufacturing, Customer
Engineering, and of course, the customers, cooperated in this program.

3.   The Culmination of Ideas Leading to the 701

In my introduction I stated, "IBM entered in the computer field with the installation of a 701 . . .," but in fact and in some sense IBM entered the computing field in 1914 with the manufacture of a key punch, a gang punch, a vertical sorter, a nonprinting tabulator, and punched cards. A printing tabulator was introduced in 1920, a horizontal sorting machine in 1925, an 80-column card in 1938 along with a subtracting–accounting machine. In 1931, the first of the 600 series of calculators was introduced, the machine that would add, subtract, and multiply. As everyone knows, the first large-scale machine, the Automatic Sequence Control Calculator (MARK I), was built by IBM under Frank Hamilton to Howard Aikens's architecture and presented to Harvard in 1944.

Built somewhat in parallel and with similar technology were the IBM Pluggable Sequence Relay Calculators [11]. Two of these machines were delivered to Aberdeen Proving Grounds in December 1944, and three additional improved machines were built for the Naval Proving Ground at Dahlgren and for the Watson Scientific Computing Laboratory at Columbia University. As of 1947 these machines were faster than the MARK I but smaller in capacity and also had the advantage of relatively high input speed since up to four cards could be read simultaneously at the rate of 100 per minute.

Soon after the completion of the MARK I, work was begun on the Selective Sequence Electronic Calculator (SSEC) (Fig. 4.) under the direction of Frank Hamilton, with co-inventor, R. R. Seeber, who had earlier been on the staff of Howard Aiken of Harvard University. The SSEC was installed in New York in 1947. It completely filled the walls of the first floor and a portion of the basement room which was later to house the 701. It contained 12,500 vacuum tubes, 21,400 electromechanical relays, and was said to multiply 6000 times faster than the MARK I. It was a decimal machine and had the capability of storing and modifying instructions in 8 20-decimal-digit vacuum tube registers or in 150 20-decimal-digit electromechanical storage locations. Expense, of course, was a limitation on the amount of high-speed storage. Moreover, the machine was operated in a duplexed fashion. Because of these limitations, I believe that the machine should be thought of as operating principally from the instructions contained in the continuous cardstock tape. These readers and punches were developed especially for the SSEC, were 66 in number, and to my knowledge were never used again. In addition, there were 36 control panels. The machine helped solve important problems and, of equal importance, attracted a group of young people. The first problem to be solved had been formulated by Dr. W. J. Eckert, IBM Director of Pure Science, and it calculated the lunar coordinates. Another problem that I remember was solved after I had left Oak Ridge to join IBM

Figure 4 IBM selective sequence electronic calculator.

and had been formulated by Dr. Wendall deMarcus. It used the Gauss–Seidel method of performing shielding calculations and was highly successful. The problem I remember most clearly and that had the greatest influence on my later thinking was the Los Alamos hydrodynamic program HIPPO. As I recall, Dr. Robert Richtmyer was in and around New York for many months and worked with the close cooperation of the SSEC staff in order to place HIPPO on the machine. I remember then organizing several meetings to consider how, if at all, modifications of the SSEC could be made to allow the problem preparation to be expedited. The ultimate answer, of course, was a stored program with an adequate amount of high-speed memory.

The next and last forerunner of the 701 was the Card-Programmed Electronic Calculator (CPC) models I and II (Fig. 5). The forerunner of this ma-

Figure 5   IBM card-programmed electronic calculator.

chine had been built for Northrup Aircraft Company in 1948, and I quote from a paper delivered by Toben [12]:

> The solution was important to the guided missile program, and we were able to persuade IBM to convert our IBM Type 405 Alphabetical Accounting Machine into something suitable for the job. They made available an IBM Type 603 Calculating Punch, which was then out of production, and connected it, via cable, to the 405. Forty class selectors and 40 ×-distributors were added to complete the job. The elapsed time from preliminary design to delivery of the machine was only six weeks, and it was so well done that after two years of use we have been able to think of only minor improvements.

Other IBM customers of course heard about the machine at Northrup and asked whether copies might be made available. The result was an announcement in the summer of 1949 with a formal demonstration that I gave in November 1949 [13] in Endicott, New York, at a seminar that was attended, for example, by Richard Clippinger, Donald Flanders, John Curtiss, Richard Hamming, Alston Householder, Frank Hoyt, Herman Kahn, Maria Mayer, Mina Rees, Richard Stark, Abraham Taub, John Tukey, and John von Neumann.

The principal engineers on the CPC were J. Dayger and O. B. Shaeffer, who earlier had built the data acquisition equipment for wind tunnels at the California Institute of Technology, Cornell University, and Chance Vaught. The machine was produced in Endicott, New York. The principal planners were S. W. Dunwell, W. H. Johnson, and D. W. Pendery. The latter wrote the Operators' Manual on a part-time basis while serving as Manager of Applied Science in the west.

The CPC consisted of four individual units interconnected by cables. These units were the 402 Accounting Machine, the 604 Electronic Calculating Unit, the 521 Gang Summary Punch, and the 941 Auxiliary Storage Unit. The latter unit contained 16 ten-digit words of electromechanical storage. At a later time a total of three such storage units could be installed. As William

W. Woodbury, another of the formulators of the program at Northrup, used to say, "The CPC takes 2 numbers, performs an operation, and stores the result." The source or destination of these numbers could be the counters of the 402 assigned in a flexible fashion or could be the number pairs in the 604 using its 37 digits of electronic storage and its 40 program steps and repertoire of program steps, which included add, subtract, multiply, divide, and transfers of various kinds, but also provision for calculation of special functions by iterative procedures by control panel wiring. For example, on the 604 the scheme proposed by von Neumann for producing randon digits could be programmed, namely: Select ten digits from a random number table, square to form twenty digits, save the middle ten, square again, etc. The machine rental was $1500 per month including service for one shift of usage. The additional storage units were rented for $200 per month or at a cost of somewhat more than $1 per month per digit. About 250 of these machines were installed in the 1949–1952 period.

There were several significant results of the CPC program. First, it gave widespread experience in the preparation and solution of problems that frequently required long sequences of operations. These problems were principally in the fields of engineering and science but also began to involve financial calculations and factory production problems. In addition, it was edifying to the IBM sales force to learn that customers would pay a rental of up to $2000 per month for a machine since, for example, the price of the 604 was $600 per month. Of greatest importance, however, in my view, was the beginning of a formal and informal information exchange between CPC customers. This interchange had begun with the computation formus that were inaugurated in 1948 by W. J. Eckert and H. R. J. Grosch and continued throughout 1952 by the Applied Science Department and Department of Education. It was intensified with the design and implementation of the so-called "general-purpose boards." This activity expanded so rapidly that it was decided to publish an Applied Sciences Department series of technical newsletters. Technical Newsletter #1 [14], dated June 1950, contains, for example, a paper entitled A General Purpose 604 Electronic Calculator Control Panel for the Card Programmed Electronic Calculator by B. B. MacMillan and R. H. Stark, Los Alamos Scientific Laboratory. In the same Newsletter are descriptions of three other general-purpose boards, including a paper by B. Oldfield, U.S. Naval Ordnance Test Station: 604 Electronic Calculator Diagrams for the Calculation of sin-x, cos-x, e^x, e^{x2}, Sinh-x, and Cosh-x on the Card Programmed Electronic Calculator. Increasingly these boards were in floating-point and increasingly diagrams of the boards but sometimes copies of the boards themselves were circulated. I should suppose that hundreds and perhaps thousands of persons ultimately became acquainted with problem preparation for the CPC, and major universities also began to use the machine as a research and teaching device. The educational effort by IBM was furthered by Eric Hankam at the IBM Watson Laboratory at Co-

lumbia University, who organized a course of instruction of one month's duration to which persons came from all over the world. The IBM Department
of Education scheduled classes in New York, Endicott, and Poughkeepsie,
and the Applied Science Department organized courses of instruction and
demonstration centers on a countrywide basis.

On a wider scale, the efforts of major universities throughout the world
and government research laboratories were adding impetus to the field.
Much of the early work was done on punched cards [15, 16]. The work of
major universities in Austria, Belgium, Canada, France, Germany, Italy, the
Netherlands, Sweden, Switzerland, the United Kingdom, U.S., and the
USSR all come to mind in one context or another. In addition, in the U.S.
the coordinating and stimulating work at the National Bureau of Standards
and Office of Naval Research merits special commendation. Dr. John Curtiss, Dr. Mannie Piore, and Dr. Mina Rees were not only instrumental in providing governmental support to universities that were engaged in the computing field but also arranged for information exchange among those
universities and between those universities and other government agencies
and industrial organizations and the public at large.

At this point I want to comment on the association of John von Neumann
with IBM. The fundamental papers [17] by some combination of A. W.
Burks, H. H. Goldstine, and John von Neumann of course had a significant
effect on our thinking. Also, I had known John for some time and in 1947 or
1948 had obtained his agreement to become a consultant in Oak Ridge particularly for the purpose of helping with the modeling of the K-25 diffusion
plant. After I joined IBM in early 1949, John and I continued to see each
other and, for example, he gave a dinner address entitled The Future of High
Speed Computing at the IBM Seminar on Scientific Computation in November 1949. Typifying the demands on John's time, a digest of this address
did not reach us in time to be published in the November 1949 Proceedings
but was published in the December 1949 Proceedings instead. At any rate, I
asked whether he could also consult with IBM. He expressed interest but
immediately started to tell me about an idea he had, which he thought might
be patentable. I interrupted, urged him to seek a patent attorney, and stated
that it would not be appropriate for him to consider a consultantship until
that particular question had been resolved. Finally then, an agreement was
reached, dated October 1951, under which Dr. von Neumann was to consult
up to 30 days per year for a modest retainer. He continued this consulting
agreement until he was asked to serve as a Commissioner of the U.S.
Atomic Energy Commission. At that time he expressed concern to me about
the future well-being of the outstanding group of scientists who had been assembled at the Institute for Advanced Study to work on the computer
project. He was uncertain as to the future of the project and asked whether
IBM would wish to interview members of the group. As a result, Dr. Herman Goldstine and Mr. James Pomerine joined IBM. Dr. Goldstine helped

IBM in many ways both in establishing and managing research in Mathematical Sciences and in assisting in the program of cooperation with universities. James Pomerine quickly assumed a position of leadership in the design and construction of HARVEST, a companion to STRETCH. Incidentally, the patent to which I alluded was for a subharmonic oscillator and was the result of harmonic analysis as well as a remark that Harper North had made to John concerning the possibility of building a 1000-megacycle diode. The point of all this is that whereas IBM was the beneficiary of the Burks, von Neumann, and Goldstine publications and was the beneficiary of my informal conversations with John, we did not have the benefit of his direct participation as a consultant on the 701 project. I could, of course, recall many contributions made either informally to me or formally through publications that contributed to the IBM computer program as well as to computer programs throughout the world.

Specifically, the work of the Moore School of Engineering at the University of Pennsylvania and the construction of the ENIAC under Presper Eckert and John Mauchly can never be mentioned too often. I have never known the details of their interaction with IBM, but I did attend with them a luncheon given by T. J. Watson, Jr., on 31 October 1961, for computer pioneers: ''a small group of people inside and outside of IBM who urged upon us the potential of the tape driven large capacity computer for science and industry'' [18]. The IBM Board of Directors was also present at this luncheon.

And last in this section, I shall mention the changing professionalism within IBM in the late 1940s. IBM traditionally had been a manufacturer of electromechanical devices and the founding factory at Endicott, New York, was engaged in the engineering and manufacturing of such devices. The smaller factory and laboratory at Poughkeepsie had been built in the early 1940s in response to a government need and was operated by a 1% profit basis on war materials. Following World War II, R. L. Palmer assembled a small group of electrical engineers and built the 603. He then added to the staff including Nat Rochester, an MIT graduate with experience, for example, in building the memory for WHIRLWIND. Mr. Palmer also engaged individuals with graduate experience including Ph.D.s in the fairly new field of electronics majors in electrical engineering departments. Concurrently, Dr. W. J. Eckert at the Watson Laboratories was attracting a small number of key individuals with experience at the Radiation Laboratory. With the success of the 604, an electronic machine, and the additional startling success of the CPC, Mr. J. J. Kenney set up a separate organization within IBM Customer Engineering to service the electronic equipment and began to employ graduates in engineering from universities first in the U.S. and later throughout the world. At this time also a program of employing individuals with advanced degrees in management was initiated and such individuals were placed both at the factory and in the headquarters. Finally, beginning in March 1949, I was visiting universities for the purpose of engaging mathematicians, physicists, chemists, and engineers for Applied Science. These individuals were to have first and foremost an interest in problem solving and were to serve as a bridge between the customers and the engineering organization. IBM was never parismonious in budgets for this activity, and I shall always remember a telegram which T. V. Learson, then Sales Manager, sent to his Branch Offices saying "Hurd needs fifty men. Help him find them!" By 1950, then, every major operating unit in IBM had employees whose ideas of the potentialities of computing and computers were somewhat advanced.

4. The Immediate Environment That Led to the 701

During the summer and fall of 1950, the tempo of research and development was increasing. Many IBM customers were using the larger computers around the world that were beginning to run. Customers were operating multiple CPC installations and these customers were prepared to make the commitment for a large machine. Competition from other manufacturers was increasing and a number of large-scale and middle-scale computers had been announced and/or delivered. For example, at the First Joint Computer Conference held in Philadelphia in 1951, ten large-scale computers of varying designs and performance were described [19]:

> Specific presentations covered performance of the Census UNIVAC System, the Burroughs Laboratory computer, the IBM Card-Programmed Electronic Calculator, the ORDVAC, the ERA 1101 computer, the Mark III electronic calculator, the Ferranti Mark I/University of Manchester computing machine, the Whirlwind I computer, the EDSAC computer, the National Bureau of Standards Eastern Automatic Computer (SEAC), a review of the Bell Laboratories' digital computer developments, plus a discussion of present and future trends in digital computers by J. W. Forrester.

Additionally, IBM had a desire to assist in the defense effort, and this desire was made explicit by a telegram that Thomas J. Watson had sent to President Harry S. Truman offering the full services of IBM to the government. J. W. Birkenstock had the explicit assignment of determining the manner in which IBM might most fruitfully implement that telegram. For a number of years, Mr. Birkenstock had been serving as an Executive Assistant and was responsible for keeping abreast of developments in what was usually referred to as the electronic area or the magnetic-tape area. Mr. Birkenstock made a round of visits to the Pentagon and became convinced that a "special-purpose" machine might serve the government. On some of these occasions I was present. At the same time, Mr. John McPherson, IBM Vice President and a participator in the activities of the Watson Laboratory and the SSEC, had concluded that a large decimal machine such as NORC would be useful particularly to Naval Ordnance and to the world at large. The IBM Product Planning Department was impressed by the success of the 604, particularly in applications such as utility billing, and desired a machine of modest cost that could outperform the 604. Poughkeepsie engineers were at work testing the Test Assembly and designing the Tape Processing Machine with the hope that it could be produced. During this period of time, I took Mr. Ralph Palmer, IBM Director of Engineering in Poughkeepsie, on a trip for the purpose of allowing him to speak firsthand with some of those who believed in large-scale machines, particularly those that were fast enough for engineering and scientific computations. The whole subject came to a head in the conference room of Mr. Thomas J. Watson, Jr., around Christmastime in 1950. Mr. Rochester had a preliminary design for a machine in his pocket, and I had a list of prospective customers in my pocket. Mr. Birkenstock was convinced by now that a machine like the defense calculator would serve the needs of the defense establishment. Mr. W. W. MacDowell, IBM Director of Engineering, Mr. Ralph Palmer, and Mr. John MacPherson pointed to work already done, which indicated that components already in hand could be assembled to produce a high-speed machine. Every point of view was given a hearing at that meeting. The decision was made to go ahead, and immediately thereafter there was only one point of view with respect to the defense calculator. All departments cooperated completely, as did 400 subcontractors.

The next step was to establish a price. A 604 with 600 vacuum tubes and two boxes was rented profitably at $600 per month. It was known that many of the machines under development elsewhere were expected to contain 1000 vacuum tubes, although it was also known that the UNIVAC with alphabetic representation was considerably larger. An estimate was made of the ratio of the number of tubes expected in the 701 to the number in the 604. An estimate was also made of the relative number of boxes. These ratios were applied to the price of the 604 and the number then doubled to take care of the extra speed of the Defense Calculator and the more limited quantity. This turned out to give a monthly rental of $5500. When I discussed the number with Mr. A. L. Williams, Financial Vice President, he said, "Let's round it off to $8000 per month." This number then was used when Mr. Birkenstock and I separately visited prospective customers with a resulting 30 letters of intent. Upon the completion of the engineering model and fairly detailed cost estimates, it was found the price should have been considerably higher. We finally settled on an average price of about $15,000 per month, and Charles Benton and I started out again to visit the customers with the final result of six firm orders. IBM then took the risk of ordering 18 sets of parts with the expectation that the machine would be successful.

In an earlier section, I alluded to what I consider the heroic schedule from the decision to produce to delivery in less than two years. Here are a few key dates in the program of design and manufacture and installation together with the names of some of the participants:

December 1950	Decision to build a Defense Calculator
January 1951	Pricing
	Applied Science under W. W. McClelland assists Engineering Planning under N. Rochester, Development Engineer. Dr. M. Astrahan and Dr. Werner Buchholz assigned under Mr. Rochester.
February 1951	Initial Specifications
	30 Letters of intent at $8000 per month rental
	J. A. Haddad appointed as Manager of Component Development
	Preliminary design
	Six development groups formed
April 1951	Final specifications
	Preliminary Operators Reference Manual
	Start of software
July 1951	Start of field engineering training
	R. J. Whalen appointed Production Project Manager
October 1951	Completion of preliminary testing of components
January 1952	Release to Production with 4000 sets of drawings
March 1952	Demonstration of Defense Calculator (701) by Rochester and Hurd to IBM Board of Directors
	Machine running except for drum
April 1952	9:30 p.m.–8:30 a.m. availability of machine for testing of programs by Applied Science and Engineering. The largest problem later ran 24 hours/day and was supplied by John Sheldon:
	a differential equation based on work of Thomas–Fermi–Dirac [20]
May 1952	Training for second group of field engineers
	Announcement of $11,900–$17,600 per month
August 1952	First 701 Customer Education, Poughkeepsie, New York. Representatives of 16 customers or prospects. Short shots on machine. Papers by Hurd, Haddad, Ladd, Sheldon, Knaplund, Johnstone, Pendery, Astrahan, Codd, Glaser, McClelland, and Rochester
	Customer discussion of SHARE
December 1952	Shipment of first machine to IBM Technical Computing Bureau, New York City
January 1953	First customer machine to Los Alamos
7 April 1953	Formal dedication
1953–1954	17 machines to: Lockheed Aircraft, National Security Agency, Douglas Aircraft, General Electric, Convair, U.S. Navy—Inyokern, United Aircraft, North American, Rand Corp., Boeing, Los Alamos

#2, Douglas Aircraft #2, Naval Aviation Supply,
University of California at Livermore, General
Motors, Lockheed Aircraft #2, U.S. Weather Bu-
reau

The 701 Technical Computing Bureau helped solve a number of interesting problems and also received many interesting visits. For example, Dr. (now Professor) Thomas Kilburn and Professor F. C. Williams came to call, particularly appropriate in view of their contributions to the 701 and the 704. A portion of the time of the machine and of the staff was reserved for endowed programs of research as proposed by universities. Under this plan a three-layer weather computation was made under the direction of Professor Jule Charney and John von Neumann, then at the Institute for Advanced Study in Princeton. Also, an experimental translation from Russian to English was made in cooperation with Georgetown University under the direction of Professor Dorot. This demonstration was widely publicized and led to a visit by Professor D. Panov of the University of Moscow, who was working on similar ideas. Of great technical interest was a problem proposed by Professor F. J. Murray of Columbia University and a consultant to the Reeves Instrument Company. Reeves manufactured a large analog computer and also operated a service bureau that was used extensively for "real-time" applications. Professor Murray assisted Henry Wolenski and Helmut Sassenfeld of Consolidated Vultee Aircraft Corporation in the simulation of a missile trajectory on the 701. They proved that, within the limits of accuracy required, the 701 could compute as fast as the missile could fly. Such a result, coupled with the later development of software packages which allowed programming in analog language, helped settle the question of the universality of application of the general-purpose computer.

I shall conclude this section with the story of the start of SHARE. Twenty-seven representatives of 15 customers or prospects met for a 701 seminar at Poughkeepsie 25–28 August 1952. The status of the machine was discussed; there were papers on programming systems and utility programs; and each customer was given several short periods at the console of the machine. I well remember the feeling of awe and consternation that each of us had. Here was this big machine that could do so much. It was almost upon us, and we seemed to know so little about how to use it. During one of the evenings a group of the customers met privately and decided that only a co-operative effort of help and information exchange could magnify the individual efforts and lead to success. That informal meeting was formalized a few weeks later in Los Angeles and thus SHARE was born.

SHARE was a model for user groups both with respect to other products in IBM and with respect to many other manufacturers of computers. It has been a teaching device and a reaction device of great help to IBM in its product development.

5.   Relatives and Descendants of the 701

5.1.   *The 650 Magnetic Drum Calculator**

The increasing acceptance of the 701 in late 1952 led inexorably to the need for a medium-size and medium-price computer that, among other things, would succeed the CPC. Mr. Frank Hamilton, builder of the MARK I and the SSEC, had started to experiment with magnetic drums in Endicott immediately upon completion of the SSEC. He had built a number of proto-types and had discussed these with the representatives of Product Planning and the Sales Department. None of them seemed to suit because the em-phasis continued to be on a machine with rental in the neighborhood of $1000 per month that could outperform the Type 604. My interaction with the En-gineering Department in Poughkeepsie had been so fruitful, as had been the interaction of members of Applied Science in general, that I had established what were called Mathematical Planning Groups at the Endicott Laboratory and Poughkeepsie Laboratory. Mr. Elmer Kubie as manager and Mr. George Trimble (formerly of Aberdeen) were the key elements of the Endi-cott group. Dr. George W. Petrie III was the group leader in Poughkeepsie, assisted by Robert Barton, Ted Glaser, and Beryl Smith. A third effort was established at the San Jose Laboratory but not in time to effect the ultimate decision. The three IBM contenders were a revised Hamilton machine under Mr. Ernie Hughes and two machines at Poughkeepsie: the Midget Digit under Messrs. Harper and Furnecke and a second machine called the Wooden Wheel under William Woodbury. The Applied Science Mathemati-cal Planning Group worked with both of these machines. During this time also there were numerous discussions with representatives of Engineering Research Associates (ERA) who, beginning with the ERA 1102, had devel-oped an exceptional drum technology. Dr. Arnold Cohen and Mr. John Combs were among the visitors I remembered from ERA. The discussions concerned whether ERA should build drums for IBM or build a total ma-chine for the middle machine market. Moreover, Mr. John McPherson had visited England and had seen the ACE and was urging a similar design. Also, Consolidated Electrodynamics had built a drum machine that it did not wish to market. Finally, to complicate the whole consideration, it appeared that any use of revolvers or recirculating devices on a drum would cause a patent interference. This question was resolved, however, by the invention of a high-speed drum by Al Brown in Endicott.

The Wooden Wheel deserves special comment because it was an exten-sion and improvement of the CPC with, for example, 1000 words of cathode-ray-tube memory, which was organized and replicated in such a fashion that it had great reliability. We conducted a competition among the machines in which the elapsed time on a certain set of calculations plus the estimated

---

* See Fig. 6.

manufacturing costs formed the figure of merit. On this basis the Wooden Wheel was superior, but to a large extent, I felt, because of the great ingenuity of Messrs. Woodbury and Toben in organizing the control panels that in CPC style constituted the essential internal programming method. Since the machine was to be announced as an Applied Science machine the decision was made in concert with Mr. W. W. McDowell and in the office of T. J. Watson, Jr. The Endicott machine, later known as a 650, was chosen, principally on the basis of its ease of programming and its potentiality for teaching large numbers of persons to program an automatic machine. There then arose the question of price. In this case there was a working engineering model and also considerable cost experience with the 701. The price then depended upon the quantity. Given the competition of the Datatron and a number of other magnetic drum calculators, which were being built principally in the West, we felt that the price should be in the neighborhood of $3500 per month of rental. The Applied Science District Managers from various places in the U.S. each prepared a detailed, by customer name, list of prospects which they considered fairly certain, and this number totaled 200. The Product Planning Department and the Sales Department thought that only an insignificant number could be sold with a rental in the $3000 class. However, the Washington Office of IBM, which had wished for a better solution to the logistics and supply problem, was enthralled by the idea of a modern computer. Mr. MacDonald Smith of the Washington Office pledged to sell and deliver 50 machines. With this forecast, the Type 650 Magnetic Drum Calculator (Fig. 6) was announced on 2 July 1953, jointly by Mr. T. V. Learson and myself. It was a biquinary decimal machine with a price of $3200 per month for 1000 ten-decimal-digit words of storage. It used two address instructions. The multiply time was 9 msec, the divide time 12 msec, and the average storage access was 2.4 msec. Included was a good deal of checking,

Figure 6   IBM 650 magnetic drum calculator.

a "table look-up" operation, and punched-card input at the rate of 200 cards/min and output of 100 cards/min. A control panel was included to assist in reading and punching card columns. The forecast of 250 was indeed met and surpassed in the market described by Applied Science and the Washington Office. Of greater significance, the IBM sales force and IBM customers received the announcement with great enthusiasm. This interest was communicated to Mr. O. M. Scott, the newly appointed Sales Manager. Working with Product Planning and Engineering, he quickly arranged that the 650 could at least read alphabetic information from a card and use that information for later card punching. The orders began to flood. The later attachment of a printer, the RAMAC (disk memory), and magnetic tapes ultimately led to the sale and installation of several thousand machines.

Elmer Kubie and George Trimble wrote the test programs for the 650, the Manual of Operations, and the initial programming aids [21]. These included a description of optimum programming, an interpretive floating-decimal code, floating-decimal subroutines, double-precision arithmetic, complex arithmetic, and a loader. By the fall of 1955, however, customer participation in software development was so great that 14 papers on 650 software were given at a computation seminar in Endicott [22]. The authors of these papers agreed to make available program deck cards, etc., so that other customers could use their results.

Following the announcement of the 650 a discussion occurred whose outcome was, I think, crucial to the future success of IBM. IBM had a policy of instant reward (+ and −). Therefore, because of the successful announcement of the 650, Mr. Watson, Jr., spoke to Mr. Learson and me and proposed that Applied Science become a separate Division. Such a plan would have had the effect, for example, of a separate sales organization, which in some sense would compete with the existing sales organization under Mr. Learson which was already in place around the U.S. and by implication around the world. It also carried the implication of separate planning, engineering, manufacturing, and service, which, of course, had been in effect informally beginning with the Card Programmed Calculator. I accepted the salary increase and the title but not the organizational change. Not because I was wise enough to understand that the changing technology and software could make a general-purpose computer all things to all people, as is now obvious to all. Rather, I selfishly wanted to preserve the direct support and cooperation of the IBM sales force and the IBM customer engineering force. Thus, the Applied Science Division remained as the technical arm of the field organization and ultimately formed the Systems Engineering organization.

5.2. The 702

Concurrent with the program to design, manufacture, and install the 701, the Sales Department, Product Planning, and Engineering Planning continued toward a large-scale machine that was more specifically directed toward accounting and record keeping. A number of joint systems studies were conducted with customers in order to refine the specifications, and the technical developments of the 701 were assessed and reoriented. Charles Hardwick, S. W. Dunwell, Walter Johnson, Werner Buchholz, and C. J. Bashe were the principal participants whose names I remember. In addition there was application information arising from the use of the 701. The installations at Naval Aviation Supply in Philadelphia and at the National Security Agency in Washington clearly had "commercial" overtones, and all 701s were encountering large input and output. The former was in the field of logistics and supply and its most advanced mathematics could have been formulated as a matrix by vector multiplication. The NSA 701 application was completely unknown to us, but a hint was given by the request for the design of a machine that became the 703. Moreover, the Monsanto Chemical Company under the leadership of Mr. Edgar Queenie, Chairman, had a great desire to publish its quarterly results at least as quickly as any other major corporation. The IBM Technical Computing Bureau, under the direction of Dan Mason, undertook to program and check out the work for both the Naval Aviation Supply and Monsanto. The rewards were great in that the programming was accompiished and the lessons were even greater; namely, although possible on a binary fixed word machine, life would be much simpler with an alphabetic, variable field size machine with more flexible and powerful input –output equipment because adequate software had not been developed and was not available then as it is at present. On 25 September 1953, the Type 702 Electronic Data Processing Machine was announced by Mr. T. V. Learson and it was shipped to the customers whose names follow in order of shipment:

1   IBM Poughkeepsie
2   Monsanto Chemical
3   National Security Agency
4   Aviation Supply Office, USN
5   State of California (first shipped to IBM WHQ where it was employed temporarily for customer program testing)
6   General Electric, Hanford
7   Commonwealth Edison
8   Oaklahoma City Air Material Area, USAF
9   Pratt & Whitney
10 Bank of America
11 Chrysler
12 Prudential
13 General Electric, Schenectady
14 Ford Motor

An Applied Science person was assigned to help in each of these installations, as had been the custom with the 701.

5.3. The Type 703

In response to the requests of the National Security Agency, IBM built a machine known as the 703. It was a special-purpose machine that was intended to carry out a high-speed sort based on tape input to about 1000 words of cathode-ray-tube storage. I believe that the algorithm was sort by merge. This machine ran well and was installed, by which time it became apparent that technology then available could produce a machine like the 704 or 705, which was more cost effective even on sorting than the 703.

5.4. The 704 and 705

5.4.1. The 704. Both the 701 and 702 were produced in a limited quantity. Customer acceptance, however, led to the demand for additional machines and Mr. T. V. Learson was given a special task force assignment as Director of Electronic Data Processing Machines for the purpose of defining a follow-on program. My role was that of assisting Mr. Learson through Applied Science in every way possible and also of managing directly the follow-on to the 701.

The main outlines of the 704 program were fairly clear for several reasons. First, there was more experience with the 701. Second, the 701 engineering design team had in its latter stages already begun to think about possible product improvements. For example, John Backus and John Sheldon and many customers were dissatisfied that SPEEDCODING, which was in floating decimal, slowed execution by at least a factor of 10. Dr. Gene Amdahl thereupon developed schemes for including floating-point arithmetic, and at a later time, ideas for including index registers such as had already been described at the University of Manchester. By the time of the Type 701 Computation Seminar to be held in Endicott on 3–6 May 1954, the 704 was almost ready for announcement. In anticipation of that event we had prepared two agendas that differed only in that the so-called type 701A (704) machine whose programming was to be included in one but not the other, these papers to be given by Gene Amdahl and John Backus, respectively. My instructions to my assistant, Dr. G. T. Hunter, were to use the non-701A agenda in the booklets which were to be distributed. I remained in New York to work on pricing and the final announcement. Either by mistake or with a fine prescience the agenda was in fact distributed with the 701A papers included. Almost immediately a telegram was dispatched to Mr. Thomas J. Watson, Jr., signed by all the customers in attendance and probably spearheaded by Dr. H. R. J. Grosch of General Electric Company and Mr. John Lowe of Douglas Aircraft. In essence the telegram said: "Where is Hurd and what is the 701A?" The 704 was announced on 7 May 1954 with the specifications intended for the 701A. The pricing, as I remember it, was based on the forecasting of 50 machines.

The 704 performed a floating-point multiplication in 204 μsec. On non-floating-point operations, it was about twice as fast as the 701. The drum was

12 times as fast in transmission time and the access time was one quarter the 701. There were 73 operations as compared with 32, and of final great importance was the inclusion of index registers. The monthly charge for first shift with service and two electrostatic storage and two magnetic drums was about $30,000 a month. A specific point was made in the announcement that interpretive programs such as the IBM 701 SPEEDCODING systems were no longer needed for floating-point operations, and by this time, I think, John Backus was already at work with help from United Aircraft Corporation and to a lesser extent with other customers on the design of what became FOR-TRAN.

The forecast was greatly exceeded, aided by the early inclusion of magnetic core storage.

The 704 and later the 705 ushered in IBM participation in the world trade market of large machines. Parts for a 704 were shipped to France, and the machine when assembled and tested was installed at the Place Vendome, Paris. As was customary, a portion of the time for this computer was reserved for the use of universities. Professor Maurice Wilkes and Professor A. van Wijngaarden were both kind enough to serve on the advisory committee that selected the problems to be computed. The computing center was operated under the direction of René Rind, one of the first Applied Scientists in IBM in Europe. Somewhat later, a 704 was installed at Adermaston at the United Kingdom Atomic Weapons Research Establishment.

5.4.2. The 705. I am much less clear on the details of the 705 program. I do remember that the formal idea of a kernel was developed by Mr. Irving Liggett, an Applied Science representative who had been assigned to the Planning Group for the 705 and who was later manager of the 705 Test Facility in Chicago. The kernel idea was an extension of the programming that had been done by the engineers and applied scientists in the 701 program to test the effectiveness of various ideas. I also remember that the competition for sales by this time was keen. UNIVAC was having marked success; the BIZMAC was in strong evidence; GE, Bank of America, and Stanford Research Institute were in a cooperative program for the banking industry; Hughes Aircraft and the newly formed Ramo-Woolridge Company were known to be highly competitive in electronics and known to be working on computers. Many magnetic drum calculators were in evidence. Moreover, there was the serious question of improved input and output arising both from 701 users and 702 users.

On 1 October 1954, the IBM Type 705 Electronic Data Machine was announced by O. M. Scott but as a result of the coordinating influence and direction of T. V. Learson. Its main features were magnetic core storage (Fig. 7), increased speed, simultaneous reading and writing of tape, direct memory transfer, a flexible accumulator, a new and flexible card reader, and a record storage unit. The latter, an optional feature, permitted the almost complete overlapping of tape reading, processing, and tape writing. The

Figure 7 Type 705 magnetic core storage.

"new and flexible card reader" used control panels to save main frame memory and processing time. At a rental of about $30,000 per month the forecast was probably for 75 machines. Unfilled orders for the 702 were filled by the 705 and again the forecast was exceeded.

5.5. Magnetic Core Memory

The 704 was announced with electrostatic memory. However, during this general time period there was increasing interaction between IBM and the SAGE program under J. W. Forrester and G. E. Valley of Massachusetts Institute of Technology. In April 1953, the Air Force had authorized the production of SAGE and shortly thereafter IBM was requested to work with the Lincoln Laboratories of MIT on the project. The FSQ-7, which IBM was to build and which was to contain ferrite core memory, was thought not sufficiently far along in production engineering to allow its inclusion in the initial delivery of the 704. These cores, of course, depended upon the fundamental work of J. Forrester and his colleagues. Nevertheless, IBM negotiated a feasibility study with the International Telemetering Group in Los Angeles to understand better the implication of core memory. Also, the 704 was designed in such a fashion that core memory could be field installed at a later time. All 705s were delivered with core memory and as a result of great engineering and manufacturing actively all 704s were delivered with core memory with the resulting increase in reliability.

5.6. STRETCH

The STRETCH program was inaugurated again as the confluence of a number of considerations. First, the engineers under Mr. Palmer and Mr. Haddad wanted to produce a new generation that was as advanced beyond the 704 and 705 as possible. Also, there was the existence of the transistor and its embodiment, for example, in the LARC proposal by UNIVAC at the Radiation Laboratory at Livermore. There was also the TRANSAC by Philco. Prototype transistor computers were in operation at MIT, in the IBM Military Products Division, and in other laboratories throughout the country. Dr. Lloyd Hunter and his associates of the IBM Laboratories in Poughkeepsie had developed a high-performance transistor, a high-performance magnetic core, and in addition, work was in progress on greater speeds of input–output, including a large high-speed disk, and a very large store later known as TRACTOR. A team including Lloyd Hunter, Gene Amdahl, John Backus, Steve Dunwell, Bob Evans, Don Pendery, and me, visited the Lawrence Radiation Laboratory and the Los Alamos Laboratory to discuss these developments and the possibility of a joint effort to develop a new and high-speed machine. Visits were also made to the National Security Administration. These discussions culminated in an agreement in the fall of 1956 under which scientists at Los Alamos were to assist in planning and IBM was to build the fastest machine within its capabilities for a fixed price of $4.3 million. Many organizational ideas including "look-ahead" came from discussions between Amdahl, Backus, Sheldon, and others, including later, Los Alamos scientists. These ideas are described in detail in Dr. Buchholz's book [23] and I shall not repeat them. S. W. Dunwell was named Manager of Project STRETCH and the General Manager also of the later Project HARVEST. Mr. Bengt Carlson was the Director of the Computer Activities at Los Alamos during the design phase, and Dr. Roger B. Lazarus was responsible for the joint design activities. It contained 150,000 transistors and on a sample problem was 75 times faster than the 704.

The machine was delivered to Los Alamos in 1961 and served in a productive fashion until 21 June 1971, when a retirement ceremony was held in Los Alamos. Other machines were shipped to

Bureau of Ships, U.S. Navy
AEC—Livermore
Atomic Weapons Research Establishment, United Kingdom
U.S. Weather Bureau
MITRE Corporation
Naval Proving Ground, Dahlgren, Virginia
IBM
Commisariat à l'Energie Atomique, France

History, or course, repeated. The 701 was delivered before the big research machine NORC. Both the 7090 and the highly successful 1401 were in quantity production before STRETCH and HARVEST were completed. HARVEST was a variant of STRETCH that was built for the National Security Administration.

6. Customer Requirements

As announced and first delivered, the 701 seemed to have somewhat greater input–output capabilities than did other machines because of the parallelism of the punched card. However, it was quickly evident that I/O was inadequate. For example, the aircraft companies, having performed a flutter analysis for a wing loading calculation, required a tremendous amount of printing to describe the results. Similarly, in nuclear calculations the amount of input to describe boundary conditions and the amount of output to describe flux, for example, was large. In retrospect, this was an early indication that "scientific computing" and "commerical computing" were really not dissimilar from the standpoint of input and output requirements. Also, it became evident that there would be chain calculations by the machines and, hence, since machines of other manufacturers used punched paper tape as primary input and output, there was a necessity for a bridge. As one consequence, the 702 that was delivered to the Bank of America had a provision for punched paper tape, which to my knowledge was the first time that any IBM machine ever had such an attachment. An indication of the high input and output requirements for the 701 was a request by North American Aviation to place the 727 tapes that were supplied on the 702 on the 701 to replace the 726 tapes. The reason was that the separate card-to-tape, tape-to-card, and tape-to-printer machines that were supplied with the 702 required a different tape. IBM made the modification to the 701 and supplied such tapes for North American. North American then developed a piece of software that was a sequential monitor for batch operations [24]. This was the first monitorlike piece of software to my knowledge. Another indication of high-volume output requirements was given by the request of the RAND Corp. for a cathode-ray-tube output that was to be attached to the 701. I believe that such a device was first installed on the WHIRLWIND at MIT and that RAND knew about it because of information exchanged in connection with an Air Force contract to train radar operators. I also believe that such a device had been installed on the ORDVAC at the University of Illinois. In any event, Mr. Paul Armer of RAND made the request and later described the machine [25].

This device was later annou nced as the Type 704 Cathode Ray Tube Recorder and made a standard feature of the 704. B. O. Evans of IBM was highly influential in these developments.

Other devices of particular interest are in the communications field. Thus, Dr. H. R. J. Grosch [26] installed card-to-punched-paper-tape devices and later the IBM Transceiver at the Evondale, Ohio, 701 location and in a New York location in order to permit transmission of data. The transceiver was IBM's first communication product and went from punched card to punched card over telephone wires.

At about the same time United Aircraft Corp. was installing a parallel printer, which was located about a mile from the main processor. Next and of great significance was the pioneering work of Professor John J. McCarthy, then at MIT, and his associates at the IBM New England Computer Center at MIT. A "real-time" channel had been developed for Convair Aircraft to be attached to the 701 for missile control. This device was later made available on the 704 for attachment to the Boeing Aircraft wind tunnel. Using the real-time channel Professor McCarthy [27] developed the software that allowed the attachment first of one Flexowriter and later of several to begin his development of the time-sharing concept. I have been told that Professor Strachey in England was working along similar lines and quite independently.

All in all, the period from about 1953 to 1956 or 1957 was characterized by greater emphasis on input–output and included the development of higher-speed printers and higher-speed tapes. The Random Access Memory Automatic Computer (RAMAC) was announced in 1956. A later disk (1301) coupled with the IBM-invented channels on the 709 then led to operating systems and multiprogramming as understood today.

I shall close this section with a description of the efforts leading to the "million-bit memory." The first magnetic core memory supplied with the 704 had a capacity of 4192 36-bit words. Later, a second box of similar capacity was made available. Again, Mr. Paul Armer of RAND telephoned and asked for a price of 33,536 words of such memory. After a modest period of study of the logical implications, power implications, and cost, I telephoned Mr. Armer to say that such a million-bit memory could be installed for $500,-000. I seem to remember that at the time the cost of the first such memory was to be about $1 million but that we would be sharing this cost in a joint research and development mode. Mr. Armer's response was, "We'll take three." Instantly, the informal communication line between customers began to function, and I received other telephone calls. Given this informal but highly effective market study, we decided to rent the memory at $15,000 per month, and this was the start of another successful program.

These few examples illustrate what has been the central fact of the rapid growth of the computer field; namely, devices placed in the hands of users quickly led to new applications, new capacities, new speeds, new peripherals, and new software systems. It would be impossible ever to give too much credit to the users of computers for the ideas that they have contributed.

7. Concluding Remarks

The world of today could profit by a recapture of the spirit of cooperation and the method of cooperation that existed between individuals and between countries in the early days of computing. We were not institutionalized and we were not formalized with organization charts and budgeting and reporting procedures. We were few in number, we knew each other by first name, and a visit or a telephone call from person to person was the fast way to learn. Thus I repeat that I can look around this room and remember what I learned when and where from many of you. The world has another great need—the development of new energy sources, which like the computer field, can grow from almost nothing to 5% of the gross national product in 25 years. Who will be the pioneers?

REFERENCES

1. IBM Record, Vol. 36, No. 2. IBM Corp., New York (April 1953).
2. Principles of Operation, Type 701 and Associated Equipment. IBM Corp., New York, 1953.
3. Astrahan, M. M., and Rochester, N., The logical organization of the new scientific calculator, *Proc. ACM Meeting* p. 79 (2–3 May 1952).
4. Buchholtz, W. The systems design of the IBM Type 701 computer, *Proc. IRE* **41**, No. 10, 1272–1275 (1953).
5. Frizzell, C. E., Engineering description of the IBM Type 701 computer, *Proc. IRE* **41**, No. 10, 1275–1287 (1953).
6. Ross, H. D., The arithmetic element of the IBM Type 701 computer, *Proc. IRE* **41**, No. 10, 1287–1294 (1953).
7. Mutter, W. E., Improved cathode ray tube for application in the Williams memory system, *Elec. Eng.* **71**, 352–356 (1952).
8. McClelland, W. F., Notes on Programming Systems and Techniques for the IBM Type 701 Electronic Data Processing Machines, prepared for the Applied Science Course held during the week beginning 16 March 1953.
9. Hurd, C., IBM SPEEDCODING System. IBM Corp., New York (1953).
10. Rochester, N., Innovations in the Organization of the Defense Calculator. IBM Corp., New York (31 October 1951).
11. Eckert, W. J., *Math Tables Other Aids Comput.* (1948).
12. Toben, G. J., Transition from problem to card program, edited by Applied Science Dept., IBM Corp., *Proc. Comput. Seminar* 128–131 (December 1949).

13. Hurd, C., The IBM card-programmed electronic calculator, *Proc. Seminar Sci. Comput.* pp. 37–41 (November 1949).

14. Applied Science Department, Technical Newsletter #1, IBM Corp., New York (June 1950).

15. Bachne, G. W. (ed.), "Practical Applications of the Punched Card Method in Colleges and Universities." Columbia Univ. Press, New York, 1935.

16. Eckert, W. J., Punched Card Methods in Scientific Computation. Thomas J. Watson Astronomical Computing Bureau, New York (January 1940).

17. von Neumann, J., Collected Works (A. H. Taub, ed.) Vol. 5, pp. 1–235. Pergamon Press, Oxford, 1963.

18. Watson, T. J., Jr., Letter to C. C. Hurd (13 September 1961).

19. Review of electronic digital computers, *Joint AIEE-IRE Comput. Conf.* (February 1952).

20. Sheldon, J. Use of statistical field approximations in molecular physics, *Phys. Rev.* **99,** No. 4, 1291–1301 (1955).

21. Kubie, E. C., and Trimble, G., Technical Newsletter #8, Applied Science Division, IBM Corp., Endicott, New York (September 1954).

22. Technical Newsletter #10, Applied Science Division, IBM Corp., New York (October 1955).

23. Buchholz, W. (ed.), "Planning a Computer System: Project Stretch." McGraw Hill, New York, 1962.

24. Wagner, F., SHARE Meeting for Pioneers, Side I, Tape I, AFIPS–Smithsonian Institution Joint History Project (8 March 1972).

25. Armer, P., Applications of Cathode Ray Tube Readout Device for 701, IBM 701 Computation Seminar, Endicott, New York (May 1954).

26. Grosch, H. R. J., Remote Data Transmission, IBM 701 Computation Seminar, Endicott, New York, (May 1954).

27. McCarthy, H., Memorandum to Professor P. M. Morse A Time Sharing Operator Program for Our Projected IBM 709 (1 January 1959).

IBM
NEW YORK, NEW YORK

The SWAC: The National Bureau of Standards Western Automatic Computer

HARRY D. HUSKEY

1. Background

The SWAC had its beginning at the 19 October 1948 meeting of the Applied Mathematics Executive Council held at the National Bureau of Standards (NBS) in Washington, D.C. This Executive Council served as an advisory body to the National Applied Mathematics Laboratories, which was a division of the NBS.

The Mathematics Laboratories had been established in 1945 through a "suggestion" by the Navy Department to the Director of the Bureau of Standards, Dr. Edward U. Condon. The Navy hoped that the Bureau would establish a centralized national computation facility, equipped with high-speed automatic machinery, to provide computing service to other government agencies and to play an active part in the further development of computing machinery. Dr. Condon complied, setting up the National Applied Mathematics Laboratories, with Dr. John Curtiss as Chief. The Laboratories were to have four main parts: the Computation Laboratory, the Machine Development Laboratory, and the Statistical Engineering Laboratory, all in Washington, D.C., and the Institute for Numerical Analysis (INA), a field station to be located near some university in California.

The success of the ENIAC had excited mathematicians and other scientists to the possibilities now opening before them. No company was yet turn-

419

ing out electronic computers, but several had become interested in trying. University scientists, encouraged by the University of Pennsylvania's success in the field, were also attempting to build computers for their own use. Government agencies, quick to see the potentials of an electronic computer, were eager to acquire one. However, the field was new, there was no background of experience, and no one was absolutely certain what type of computer would best suit his purpose, or even what company was most likely to build a workable computer within a reasonable time. Therefore, government agencies were glad to ask the NBS to assist them in negotiating with computer companies. In early 1948, the Bureau had begun negotiating with the Eckert–Mauchly Computer Corporation and the Raytheon Corporation, and later with Engineering Research Associates.

The computers were slow in being developed. New techniques were being tried and often they did not work as well, or as soon, as had been first thought, or hoped. The personnel of the Applied Mathematics Laboratories became impatient with this slow development, and decided that they could build one faster with the help of the Electronics Laboratory at the Bureau. Also, it had become clear that in order to be able to judge effectively the probability of a new technique working they would need more "hands-on" expertise. Dr. Edward Cannon and the author convinced Dr. Curtiss that this "gamble" was worth trying, and Dr. Mina Rees of the Office of Naval Research backed them up. This was in spite of the advice of a committee, consisting of Dr. George Stibitz, Dr. John von Neumann, and Dr. Howard Aiken, which had been asked by Dr. Curtiss to consider the Bureau's role in the computer field. Their advice had been that the NBS shouldn't really work on computers, but should confine its work to improving components.

In May 1948, the decision was made at the Executive Council to build a machine for the Bureau's own use in Washington. At that meeting it had also been decided that the Bureau should buy three UNIVAC's which were being developed by the Eckert–Mauchly Computer Corporation. One of these was to go to the Census Bureau, one to the Air Materiel Command in Dayton, Ohio, and the third to the INA. Later, due to a security problem that had arisen in the company, it was decided that the military funds could not be used to purchase UNIVACs. This reopened the question of procuring a computer for the Air Materiel Command and for the INA. Thus, at the October 1948 meeting of the Executive Council it was decided that the Bureau should build a second computer at the Institute for Numerical Analysis, which had by now been located in a reconverted temporary building on the campus of the University of California at Los Angeles. This machine was to be built under the direction of the author, who had joined Curtiss's group in January 1948. He had spend the previous year at the National Physical Laboratory in Teddington, England, working under Alan Turing with James Wilkinson and others on the Automatic Computing Engine (ACE) project. He had been offered the job there on the recommendation of Professor Douglas Hartree, whom he had met while working on the ENIAC project.

2.   The Institute for Numerical Analysis

In December 1948, the author transferred to the Institute for Numerical Analysis, and in January 1949, work started on the INA computer. The computer at the NBS in Washington followed the EDVAC (University of Pennsylvania) design using mercury delay lines for memory. The Executive Council, which included representatives of the U.S. Air Force and the Office of Naval Research, felt that the NBS should not build the same type of machine that others were already building, or planning to build. The author had become interested in the possibility of using cathode-ray tubes for storage while in England, where he had seen the work being carried on at Manchester University under Professor F. C. Williams, and the proposal was made that this type of computer be built at INA. As a precaution, the Council wanted it to be designed in such a way that if it didn't work it could be converted to a magnetic drum computer. Of course, we had no doubt that it would work.

Finances were tight. Three hundred thirty thousand dollars had been transferred to the NBS to cover the cost of both the INA computer and the one for the Air Materiel Command (which was to be contracted to the Raytheon Corporation). Dr. Curtiss noted in his 1953 progress report on the Mathematics Laboratories, "The project was handicapped throughout by having much too tight an annual budget"[1].

At INA an empty room was given to the author and he was told to "go ahead." Not only did personnel have to be recruited to assist in designing and constructing the computer, but also machine shop equipment and supplies had to be procured from scratch. Fortunately, the Bureau had just completed a study contract with Eckert–Mauchly so we asked for all the machine tools acquired on that contract to be shipped to Los Angeles. There was also the race against time. After all, part of the justification for the NBS's building its own computers was the slowness of the would-be commerical suppliers in putting workable machines on the market. Consequently, construction of the computer began even while the study of the general machine organization and logical system was still under way. The development of the machine system, circuitry, and building techniques proceeded simultaneously with the actual construction of the machine.

The assembly of the computer was completed by July 1950. It was formally dedicated on 17–19 August. The opening session on the afternoon of the 17th featured speeches by Dr. Condon; Colonel F. S. Seiler, Chief of the Office of Air Research, USAF; Dr. L. N. Ridenour, Dean of the Graduate

School at the University of Illinois; Dr. Curtiss; and the author. The real highlight of the program, of course, was a demonstration of the computer.

The second day consisted of a symposium, opened by Dr. Condon, on the applications of digital computing machinery to scientific problems. Paul Armer, Leland Cunningham, Samuel Herrick, Stanley Frankel, Derrick Lehmer, and Jerzy Neyman were among the speakers. The third day was spent mainly in demonstrations of the SWAC.

3.   Naming the Computer

The name of the computer had undergone several changes during its construction. In a talk that the author gave at the Second Symposium on Large-Scale Digital Calculating Machinery, held at the Computation Laboratory at Harvard University on 13–16 September 1949, the machine was called the ZEPHYR. This name had been chosen to emphasize the modest nature of the effort, "a gentle wind from the west," in contrast to other projects carrying names such as TYPHOON, HURRICANE, WHIRLWIND. Good-natured rivalry with the group at NBS in Washington caused them to suggest SIROCCO (a hot wind from the desert) as a substitute for ZEPHYR.*

In retrospect it was clear that ZEPHYR was not a strategic choice of name. Hence, the very prosaic name, Institute for Numerical Analysis Computer, was used for a time, and appears in an article published in [3]. Early in 1950, someone in the administration at NBS suggested that the names of the computers being built at the Laboratories in Washington and at INA be tied together to the glory of NBS. Hence came the name National Bureau of Standards Western Automatic Computer, which in the style of the times lent itself nicely to being shortened to the name SWAC. Similarly, the NBS computer in Washington was initially called the NBS Interim Computer. Later it became the National Bureau of Standards Eastern Automatic Computer or SEAC. It was constructed under the direction of Dr. Samuel Alexander.

4.   Project Organization and Staff

The project was divided into three major parts: memory, arithmetic, and control. B. Ambrosio, with the help of Harry Larson, was to handle the memory. Bill Gunning visited from Rand Corporation and helped with the memory until he broke a leg skiing. Edward Lacey worked on the arithmetic unit, making use of the type of circuitry developed at MIT on the WHIRL-WIND project. David Rutland worked on the control unit, and we pro-

---

* Independently, H. Zamenek of Vienna, Austria, named the machine built under his direction MAILUEFTERL (gentle wind, also as a joking comparison).

ceeded to put together a computer. R. Thorensen joined the group later and worked on the magnetic drum. Other parts such as power supply and input–output, all being more straightforward (requiring less development), were handled by the group in a less explicit way

By July 1950, the staff consisted of three engineers, three junior engineers, and four technicians, in addition to the author. Everyone knew that what was being done was pioneer work on a new frontier and excitement abounded. A good-natured comradely rivalry developed between the two projects at the Bureau, as well as with similar projects elsewhere. There was a good deal of open exchange of information and techniques, and no one doubted that significant progress was being made on all fronts. The staff worked long and irregular hours uncomplainingly, spurred on by the eager interest of the distinguished internationally known scientists working at the INA. All of them were eagerly looking forward to having such a tool as the SWAC at their disposal.

The computer was to be parallel, using for its memory standard commerically available cathode-ray tubes (in contrast to some projects that were experimenting with specially built tubes). This decision was made both in the interests of time and of money. In fact, components that were mass produced commerically were used wherever possible in the SWAC. The reasoning behind this decision was that they could be easily replaced, were relatively economical, and, in general, could be expected to have more reliability. To further assist in servicing and to decrease the down time for maintenance, it was also decided to have all circuitry on removable plug-in chassis, with spare plug-in units for about 80% of the computer. Thus, in case of the failure of some component the faulty chassis could be removed and replaced by a spare one. This type of construction was especially important in those early days when no one knew just how much reliability one could expect from the components. Laboratory test equipment was constructed so that faulty chassis could be repaired in the laboratory without use of computer time. The majority of the plug-in chassis contained an average of 10 tubes each; however, the magnetic drum circuits, which were built later, were smaller, usually having a single tube per plug in unit.

Besides the 37 cathode-ray tubes used in the memory, the SWAC contained 2600 tubes and 3700 crystal diodes. The average tube life was between 8000 and 10,000 hours. Most tube failures resulted from low emission and intermittent shorts, and not from heater failure.

5. Memory

As noted earlier, the author had visited F. C. Williams and his staff at Manchester University, and observed there the method of storing information in cathode-ray tubes. One of the main appeals of the Williams system was the high speed of computation possible because of random access to memory locations. Numbers could be transferred in parallel instead of by serial pulse trains. However, the machine being designed at Manchester was serial by bit in operation, which meant that information was transferred to or from one tube at a time. In order to take full advantage of the possible speed of the Williams tube storage the SWAC was designed to operate in parallel. That is, information would be transferred in and out of all memory tubes simultaneously. This may have increased the headaches during construction but it did pay off in speed. At the time of its dedication in August 1950, the SWAC was the fastest computer in existence, being able to do 16,000 three-address additions or 2600 such multiplications per second.

The main disadvantage of the cathode-ray type of storage on the SWAC was its relatively small size. The SWAC stored 256 words of 37 binary digits (bits) each. To do this 37 cathode-ray tubes were used, with the various bits of a particular number being stored in corresponding positions of each of the tubes. At first it had been hoped that it would be possible to push the high-speed memory above 256 words (to 512 or even 1024 words). However, memory difficulties prevented this from happening. In this type of memory the individual digits of information were stored as spots of charge that existed over small areas inside the face of the tube. These spots were arranged in a rectangular array on the face of the tube. Two different charge distributions, providing the two states needed to represent a binary digit, could be produced at each spot. These spots had either a dot or a dash appearance, the dot corresponding to a 0 and the dash to a 1. A monitoring tube mounted on the console showed the dot–dash pattern in terms of zeros and ones on any one of the 37 memory tubes depending on an appropriate switch setting.

This type of memory required regeneration. Unless this was done the original charge pattern would tend to disappear over a period of time as the charged spots collected stray electrons. We always knew this would happen, so the memory cycle was made 16 μsec long, with an 8-μsec action cycle followed by an 8-μsec restore cycle. During the action cycle operands were transferred from the memory to the arithmetic unit, results were transferred back to the memory, or the next instruction was transferred to the control unit. In the restore, or regeneration, cycle one of the spots was restored to its initial value. Thus, in 256 restore cycles (about 4 msec) the whole memory would have been regenerated. Under these conditions, information could be stored in the memory indefinitely. A crystal-controlled oscillator regulated both the rate of regeneration of the memory and the synchronization of the control circuitry.

There were two main features of the Williams-tube type of memory that gave us considerable trouble, and prevented us from storing more information on each tube. One of these was the presence of so-called flaws on the inside of the face of the tube, which prevented it from storing information satisfactorily. We found that each particular tube had three or four such spots on it.

These spots turned out to be small carbonized particles of lint. The problem was that we had to build 37 tubes, deflecting all the 256 bits on the faces in unison so that no one of the bits would land on any of these carbonized spots. A storage spot might be alongside one of the flaws, and any slight drift might bring the spot onto it. It was only after it was too late to look for another supplier that we learned that our tubes were being manufactured in a reconverted mattress factory! That no doubt had increased our difficulties substantially; however, all commerically manufactured cathode-ray tubes had some flaws in them. To minimize this difficulty tubes were carefully selected, and the location of the memory array was adjusted so as to avoid bad spots. We also spent a lot of effort producing extremely stable power supplies, so that we could control drift for reasonable periods of time in order to avoid trouble from such spots.

Another major problem with the memory was "spill-over," or redistribution of charge. Each memory access generated a cloud of secondary electrons that "rained down" on the neighboring charged spots. This limited the number of times the neighboring spots could be read before the spot in question had to be regenerated. The term read-around ratio indicated how many times one could look at a given spot before the neighbors were ruined. A program might access spots in a given area of the tube many times before the regeneration occurred. One was between the devil and the deep blue sea—if one adjusted parameters in one direction flaws were less troublesome, but the read-around ratio would collapse. If one tried to improve the read around ratio with sharper focus, then flaws were more of a problem. It was spill-over that kept us from increasing the memory size above 256 words.

Since it was not practical to enlarge the size of the high-speed memory, it became imperative to have auxiliary storage. It was decided to use a magnetic drum for this purpose. At first it was planned to use a magnetic drum built by Professor Paul Morton at the University of California, Berkeley. In those early days drums were made from extruded aluminum tubing. There are stresses in the metal and, as time passes, the material flows. This happened to our drum. Although it was round when delivered to us, it was no longer round by the time we had built circuitry and tried to connect it to the computer. There was much folklore around, such as "haul the tubing around in the trunk of your car for six months so that it would be relaxed." Ultimately we purchased another drum from a commerical supplier and connected it to the computer. The drum used had 4096 words of memory. Average access time per word was about 500 μsec, in contrast to the cathode-ray tube access time of 16 μsec. Transfers to and from the drum were most efficiently handled in blocks of 32 words, which was the number of words on any track on the drum. The transfer would begin with the first number that became available and persisted for precisely one revolution of the drum. The drum rotated at 3600 revolutions per minute, so 32 words were transferred in approximately 17,000 μsec. Since there was no wait time in this mode, the access time per word was about 500 μsec. The drum transfer instruction also allowed for transfers of 8 or 16 words. However, these took the same time as a full 32-word transfer.

6. Arithmetic

The arithmetic unit used three 37-bit registers. A memory buffer register supplied operands from memory. There were 37 binary adders that could add this operand to the contents of the accumulator (the second register). The third register (called R) stored the multiplier and parts of the product during multiplication.

The maximum carry propagation time (through 37 bits) was 6 μsec. Negative numbers were stored in memory as sign and absolute value. Negative operands were complemented in the memory buffer. The timing was synchronous with sufficient time being allowed for maximum carry propagation. This timing very nicely matched the 8-μsec memory access cycle.

At the time of its dedication it was the fastest computer in existence, being able to do a three-adress ($C = A + B$) addition in 64 μsec and a similar multiplication in 384 μsec.

High-current low-impedance circuits were used in the arithmetic unit to give a fast carry so that multiplication would take the minimum time. Multiplication was by repeated addition with shifting occurring on an 8-μsec cycle. The least significant bits were processed first so that carry was at most across 37 bits. The use of high-current circuits caused substantial change in power supply current when operands were all ones versus all zeros. This change was a much as 15 amperes. A neat diagnostic test was discovered after some months of operation. It consisted of multiplying ones by ones for a tenth of a second, then running the diagnostic program the next tenth. Since the power supply filtering was designed only for three phase full wave (equivalent to 360 cycles) rectification, this change in load caused changes in voltage levels of about 20 volts. When the diagnostic routines ran under these conditions, no known failures occurred on general problems.

7. Input and Output

Initial input and output were by typewriter and punched paper tape. The typewriters (Flexowriters) and the tape stations required substantial maintenance and were terribly slow. Therefore, we soon connected an IBM collator (077) and a card punch (513) for input and output. The collator read cards at 240 per minute and the punch punched at 80 cards per minute. Seventy-eight bits (2 words) were read in from each row on the card and 11 rows were used. Substantial computing could be done between rows on the card.

8. Control

The SWAC used eight basic instructions: add; subtract; multiply rounded; product (two-word answers); compare; extract; input; and output. There was a variation of the compare instruction, which compared absolute values.

Two principles were followed in deciding upon this list of basic instructions. The first was that there should be as few instructions as practical in order to simplify the electronic circuitry of the computer, and to permit speedy construction. The second was that the instructions should be sufficiently general to do scientific computation. The SWAC used a four-address instruction. A floating-point interpretive system called SWACPEC was later developed, which made it easier for users to write programs.

9. Other Details

The SWAC was small in size compared to most of the computers of its time. The units were mounted in three connected cabinets, which were made to order by a local manufacturer. The memory and control were on one side and back-to-back with it was the arithmetic unit. The total size of these cabinets was approximately 12 ft wide, 5 ft deep, and 8 ft high. For esthetic reasons the cabinets had glass (shower) doors. The building was made of wood and had fire sprinklers mounted in the ceiling. This led to a good deal of kidding from the INA staff saying that there was something wrong in the relative location of the sprinklers and the shower doors.

The operating console was an ordinary desk with specially built panels mounted on its top surface. The actual operation of the SWAC took place from it. In addition to the memory monitoring tube already mentioned, there were neon lights and another cathode-ray tube that indicated the address in memory involving memory accesses during action cycles. The desk and cabinets were a tan color. The entire computer was located in a room 40 by 30 ft, with power supplies, a motor generator, and an air conditioner located elsewhere.

In the course of operation, certain logical facilities were added to make the operation more efficient. One of the more interesting of these was the addition of a loudspeaker and plug-in arrangement allowing the operator to "listen" to any of the instructions in a problem. For example, an alternate succession of add and subtract instructions produced an 8-kHz note. One of the problems run on the SWAC involved the generation of pseudorandom digits. The corresponding sequence of tones was christened the Random Symphony.

Being afraid of trouble from power line transients caused by other activities on the UCLA campus, from the beginning we expected to use a motor generator on the power line. The Engineering Department offered us a spare alternator. For some reason that we never quite understood (the

Figure 1

alternator was alleged to have the wrong number of poles) the output of the power supplies when using the alternator had more noise then when we connected directly to the power line. Ultimately, we replaced it with a larger regulated system with much more satisfactory results.

We had expected to cool the computer with the Los Angeles air. However, the germanium diodes turned out to be much more temperature sensitive then we had expected, so we added a cooling unit to the air system. By this time the total computer was very well integrated with the building. This only became a problem later when it was decided to move the computer to the UCLA Engineering Building.

10. Applications

By mid-1953, the SWAC was producing useful results 70% of the time that it was turned on, and was doing over 53 hours of useful computing per week. This was before the installation of the magnetic drum.

The SWAC was used in a research computing environment, and therefore the problems run on it tended to be quite large. Solution times as high as 453 hours were reported during its early operation.

Figure 2

The INA was an exciting place as many scientists of international reputation spent a few days, weeks, months, and occasionally a year or more there. It was a crossroads for numerical analysts and early computer scientists. Some of the early problems included the search for Mersenne primes, the Fourier synthesis of x-ray diffraction patterns of crystals, the solution of systems of linear equations, and problems in differential equations. In addition to problems originating from the INA staff, the computer was also used to do problems for other government agencies.

One of the exciting problems in pure mathematics on which the SWAC worked was the study of Mersenne numbers, that is, numbers of the form 2^p-1, where p is a prime. These numbers, when prime, are related to the "perfect numbers" of the Greeks, numbers that are the sum of all their integral divisors excluding themselves. The list of values of p that yielded prime numbers up to that time was $p = 2, 3, 5, 7, 13, 17, 19, 31, 61, 89,$ and 107. Everyone was greatly excited when the SWAC added 521 to the list, and there was a real celebration when 607 was added about an hour later. In all, by June 1953, five values had been added to the list with the use of the SWAC as a result of systematic testing of all primes up to 2297.

Applied problems, such as the study of large-scale circulation patterns in the earth's atmosphere, were also run on the SWAC. In this problem 750,000

Figure 3

pieces of data were processed to yield a similar number of answers. SWAC
spent 325 hours on this problem.

When the NBS ceased to support the INA in 1954, the SWAC was transferred to the University of California at Los Angeles and moved to the Engineering Building. There it continued in useful operation until it was retired in
December 1967, at the age of 17. Parts of the SWAC are on exhibit in the
Museum of Science and Industry in Los Angeles.

ACKNOWLEDGMENT

The author wishes to express his appreciation to Velma R. Huskey for assisting in the preparation of this paper.

REFERENCES

1. J. H. Curtiss, Progress Report on the National Applied Mathematics Laboratories of the
   National Bureau of Standards, p. 73 (April 1, 1953).
2. H. D. Huskey, Semiautomatic instruction on the ZEPHYR, *Proc. Symp. Large-Scale*

Digital Calc. Mach., *2nd*, pp. 83–90, Harvard Univ. Press, Cambridge, Massachusetts, 1951.
3. H. D. Huskey, Characteristics of the Institute for Numerical Analysis computer, *Math. Tables Other Aids Comput.* **4**, No. 30, pp. 103–108 (1950).
4. H. D. Huskey, R. Thorensen, B. F. Ambrosio, and E. G. Yowell, The SWAC-design features and operating experience, *Proc. IRE* **41**, No. 10, pp. 1294–1299 (1953).

DIVISION OF NATURAL SCIENCES
UNIVERSITY OF CALIFORNIA
SANTA CRUZ, CALIFORNIA

Computer Development at Manchester University

S. H. LAVINGTON

1. General Introduction

The design of digital computers at Manchester started in late 1946 with the arrival of F. C. Williams and Tom Kilburn, who were both previously engaged in wartime electronics development at the Telecommunications Research Establishment. The first patent application for Williams-tube electrostatic storage was filed on 11 December 1946. Williams and Kilburn decided to build a small digital computer—the "baby MARK I"—to provide a realistic test for their storage invention. The preliminary design for this machine was contained in a report [1] widely circulated in the U.K. and U.S.A. The baby machine ran a 52-minute program on 21 June 1948, and is believed to be the first stored-program computer to come into operation. From August 1948, this prototype was under intense engineering development and the Manchester MARK I working by April 1949 had an enhanced specification including a larger random-access store, a drum backing store and two B-line (index) registers. A further enhancement concerning programmed input—output transfers was introduced in October 1949. The Manchester project began to attract government interest and the firm of Ferranti Ltd. was given support to build a production version of the university prototype. The Ferranti MARK I, delivered in February 1951, is believed to be the first commercially available stored-program computer.

The early days at Manchester were characterized by a relatively small team of about four people working in an environment where electronic components and other resources were difficult to obtain. Significantly, the prototype MARK I was built in the Electrotechnical Laboratories, where an enthusiasm for hardware innovation tended to outweigh any call for a stable computing service. An idea of the continuous nature of the development may be gained from Table I, which shows the distribution of 57 Manchester computer patents filed during the period 1946–1951. By the end of 1956, the U.K. National Research Development Corporation held 81 computer patents originating from Manchester.

It is very difficult to assess the overall historical impact of the MARK I on computer science development. Certainly, significant Manchester inventions such as address modification would have been developed sooner or later elsewhere if Williams and Kilburn had never existed. Perhaps of clearer significance is the ongoing tradition of large machine design and fruitful cooperation with industry which was established at Manchester by the MARK I project. Over the years this has led to the production of five systems of which the latest—MU5 and its industrial counterpart the ICL 2900 range—was completed in 1975. The fourth Manchester computer was called ATLAS. This grew from Kilburn's MUSE project, started in 1956. The Ferranti ATLAS was developed by a joint University–Ferranti team and at its inauguration in December 1962 was regarded as the most powerful computer in the world. Many ATLAS ideas such as virtual storage and paging have made their impact on present-day computer design.

The following general themes are suggested as a guide to Manchester's overall contribution over the last 30 years:

(1) addressing and store management (index registers, page address registers and virtual storage, common segments, local name-space administration);

(2) fruitful industrial cooperation (the design and production of five large computers and several smaller projects);

(3) compilers and operating systems [the first compilers (1952 and 1954), the compiler compiler, the ATLAS operating system, the MU5 portable operating system];

(4) architecture for high-level languages (MU5).

2. Main Characteristics of the Production MARK I

A comprehensive account of computer development at Manchester from 1946 to 1976 has been given elsewhere [2]. The purpose of this paper is to

TABLE I

	1946	1947	1948	1949	1950	1951
No. of patents filed per year	1	1	7	26	9	13

provide more details of the structure and order code of the MARK I machine. This is described in modern terminology since the original papers and user manuals are written in an obsolete notation, and in any case are often difficult to obtain. Emphasis has been placed on the production version of the MARK I, because it was the definitive expression of ideas contained in the series of University prototypes completed during the period June 1948 to October 1949.

The Ferranti MARK I was a serial, fixed point binary computer with a CPU technology based on EF50 (CV 1091) and EF55 pentodes, and EA50 vacuum tube diodes [3-6]. It had a normal word length of 40 bits treated either as a two's complement number or an unsigned quantity, depending on the instruction. The least significant digit was stored on the *left* ("backward binary").

Two 20-bit instructions were packed to a word, with an instruction format as follows:

Address	B		Function
10	3	1	6

There were eight B-lines (index registers). The main store (random access) consisted of 256×40-bit words arranged as eight 32-word pages on eight Williams tubes. Addressing was to 20-bit boundaries. The main store was backed by 16K (max) of drum storage. The drum, of 30 msec revolution time, was servo synchronized to the main CPU clock, thus allowing extension to multiple drums without special buffering. Phase modulation recording was used. The track address was stored along with each page of information on the drum, and when a page became resident in main store an extra 20-bit line was assigned on each Williams tube to hold the track address of that page. (This was the germ of an idea which later led to page address registers and virtual-to-real address translation of the ATLAS computer.)

Transfers to and from the drum and other peripheral equipment was carried out via 20-bit control words. These had two formats, distinguished by one of the mode bits. For *drum* transfers the format was

Drum Track Address	Mode		Tube
11	4	1	4

Three mode bits then specified reading/writing, read checking/write checking, single-page/double-page transfers. For *input–output* transfers the format was

	Mode	
10	5	5

Four mode bits then specified: output a character; check output buffer; input a character; send a control character (equal to carriage return, line-feed, figure shift, letter shift) to the output device. Input was initially via a 250-characters/sec five-track paper tape reader and output was to a tape punch and printer. Other peripherals were added later.

Central registers in the MARK I were in general implemented via Williams tubes rather than flipflops, thus achieving considerable economy. In order to relate to modern terminology the following notation is used when describing their action:

ACC   the contents of the double-length main accumulator (80 bits)
AM   the most-significant 40 bits of ACC
AL   the least-significant 40 bits of ACC
S   the contents of a store line, equal to the full 40 bits except that B orders used the least significant 20 bits and control transfer orders used the least-significant 10 bits
B   The contents of a B line (index register)
D   the contents of the multiplicand register (40 bits)
H   the digits set up on 20 console handswitches

3. The MARK I Order Code

The order code of the Ferranti production machine had been specified, except for a few minor details, by November 1949 [7]. It is based on the order code for the Manchester University MARK I as it existed in October 1949, since "all the facilities of the University machine shall be reproduced in the Ferranti machine in order that any programmes devised for the existing machine can be transliterated to work with the new machine" [7]. In the following list of instructions the mnemonics are intended to suggest present-day equivalent operation codes, while the teleprinter characters signify the bit patterns actually used by MARK I programmers. The 5-bit teleprinter code, when in letter shift, consisted of the 32 characters

$$/E@A:SI U\tfrac{1}{2}DRJNFCKTZLWHYPQOBG''MXV£$$

and hand coding was carried out in terms of these symbols [8, 9]. Note that since the least-significant digit was held at the left-hand end, the symbols /E@A . . . represented the bit patterns 00000, 10000, 01000, 11000, ...

(a) *Main Arithmetic and Logical Orders*

Mnemonic	Description	Teleprinter code
LDA	load AL (AM cleared)	T/
LDAS	load AL, sign extend into AM	$T\tfrac{1}{2}$
LDN	load AL negatively	TF

STA	store AL	/S
STM	store AM	/E
STMC	store AM and clear AM	/A
SWAP	interchange AM and AL	/I
STAM	store AL, move AM to AL and clear AM	/U
STAC	store AL and clear ACC	TA
CLR	clear ACC	T:
ADD	$ACC := ACC + S$ (signed S)	TC
ADDU	$ACC := ACC + S$ (unsigned S)	TI
SUB	$ACC := S$ (signed S)	TN
ADDM	$AM := AM + S$	/J
LDDU	load D (unsigned multiplicand)	/C
LDDS	load D (signed multiplicand)	/K
MADU	$ACC := ACC + D \times S$ (unsigned S)	/N
MADS	$ACC := ACC + D \times S$ (signed S)	/F
MSBU	$ACC := ACC - D \times S$ (unsigned S)	$/\frac{1}{2}$
MSBS	$ACC := ACC - D \times S$ (signed S)	/D
AND	$ACC := ACC \& S$ (S sign extended)	TR
ORA	$ACC := ACC$ or S (S sign extended)	TD
NEQ	$ACC := ACC \neq S$ (S sign extended)	TJ
SHLS	$ACC := 2 \times S$ (arithmetic shift)	TK
ORS	$S := AL$ or S, $:= AL$	TE
ORSC	$S := AL$ or S, then clear ACC	TS

(b) *B-Line (Index Register) Manipulation*

Mnemonic	Description	Teleprinter code
LDB	load a specified B-line	TT
STB	store a specified B-line	TZ
SUBB	$B := B - S$	TL
LDBX	load a B-line (without modification)	TO
STBX	store a B-line (without modification)	TB
SBBX	$B := B - S$ (without modification)	TG

(c) *Control Transfer Orders*

Mnemonic	Description	Teleprinter code
JMPA	absolute indirect unconditional jump	/P
JMPR	relative indirect unconditional jump	/Q
JGEA	if $ACC \geq 0$, absolute indirect jump	/H
JGER	if $ACC \geq 0$, relative indirect jump	/M

| JGBA | if (last-named B-line ≥ 0, absolute indirect jump | /T |
| JGBR | if (last-named B-line) ≥ 0, relative indirect jump | /O |

(d) *Peripheral and Miscellaneous Orders*

Mnemonic	Description	Teleprinter code
IOTH	I/O transfer using H as a control word	//
IOTS	I/O transfer using S as a control word	/:
NORM	add to AM the position of the most-significant one in S	/@
SADD	add to AM the number of 1s in S— population count	/R
RNDM	load a random number into AL	/W
LDAD	load a page address word into AL	T@
DST1	debugging stop (1)	/L
DST2	debugging stop (2)	/G
TIME	S := clock	/Y
HOOT	pulse the console hooter	/V
STH	S := console handswitches H	/Z
NULL	no operation	T

In the MARK I programming manual [8] the orders were described by means of short equations. For example:

Teleprinter code	Equation	Binary code
T/	$A' = \{S_+\}_0^{79}$	100000
TC	$A' = \{A_\pm + S_\pm\}_0^{79}$	101110
/P	$C' = \{S_+\}_0^{9}$	001101

The hardware designers originally used a simpler notation [3, 4], so that the above three orders would have been expressed as

S, A

A + S', A

S, C

(C was the value of control, i.e., the program counter). Thus, when Tom Kilburn gave a series of four lectures on the University prototype MARK I (8–12 November 1948) the following handout was provided. (Note that this represents the first version of the 20-bit instruction format, which employed five function bits before programmed I/O and drum transfers had been added. This version of the Mark I did useful work on Mersenne primes during the period April–July 1949.)

Code for Charge Storage Computer

Significance as an instruction	Binary code	Code form	Decimal form
s, C	00000	/	0
c + s, C	10000	E	1
s, BO	01000	@	2
s, B1	11000	A	3
s ′, D	00100	:	4
s ′, R	10100	S	5
s, D	01100	I	6
s, R	11100	U	7
s ′, A	00101	H	20
2s ′, A	11101	Q	23
−s ′, A	10101	Y	21
a + s ′, A	00111	M	28
a + s, A	00011	O	24
am + s, Am	01011	G	26
a − s ′, A	10111	X	29
a & s ′, A	11111	£	31
a or s ′, A	00010	½	8
a ≠ s ′, A	01111	V	30
al, S	10010	D	9
am, S	11010	J	11
al,S;(0),AL;Rev. A	10011	B	25
Rev. A	10001	Z	17
Test	01010	R	10
Stop	01110	C	14
am,S;(0), Am	11011	″	27
s ′, A	01101	P	22
al or (al + s), Al	00001	T	16
	01001	L	18
	(00110	N	12
Nothing	(10110	F	13
happens	(11001	W	19
	(11110	K	15

4. Performance

The Ferranti MARK I had a 10-μsec digit period. The basic machine rhythm was designed in terms of 240-μsec "beats," where a beat contained 20 digit periods, together with a 40-μsec "blackout period." Generally speaking, store access (or "scan") beats alternated with ALU (or "action")

Figure 1 The Manchester University MARK I computer as it appeared in June 1949.

beats during execution of an instruction. Control transfer and B-line orders took four beats (i.e., 0.96 msec); accumulator load/store/add logical orders took 1.2 msec and multiplication took 2.16 msec. A contemporary benchmarking exercise rated the MARK I at about the same raw power as the National Physical Laboratories's ACE computer, even though the ACE had a digit period one-tenth as long. The favorable performance of the MARK I was attributed to its random access main memory (ACE had a delay line store) and its relatively fast multiplier.

5. Production Schedule

The first production MARK I was installed in February 1951 and finally dismantled in June 1959. Ferranti delivered nine MARK I or MARK I* machines between 1951 and 1957, to the following organizations:

Customer	Date delivered
Manchester University	1951
Toronto University, Canada	1952
Ministry of Supply	1953
Royal Dutch Shell Laboratories, Amsterdam, Holland	1954

Figure 2 Tom Kilburn (left) and F. C. Williams (right) at the console of the Manchester University MARK I computer.

Figure 3 Some of the Manchester University MARK I design team (left to right): D. B. G. Edwards, F. C. Williams, Tom Kilburn, A. A. Robinson, and G. E. Thomas.

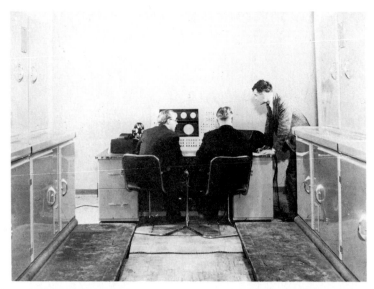

Figure 4 The Ferranti MARK I, installed at Manchester University in 1951. The person to the right is A.M. Turing, who was responsible for early programming development.

National Institute for Application of Mathematics, Rome, Italy	1955
Atomic Weapons Research Establishment, Aldermaston	1954
Ministry of Supply, Fort Halstead	1955
A. V. Roe and Co., Ltd., Manchester	1954
Armstrong Siddeley Motors, Ltd., Coventry	1957

REFERENCES

1. T., Kilburn, A Storage System for Use with Binary Digital Computing Machines. Electrotechnical Lab., Univ. of Manchester (1 December 1947).
2. S. H. Lavington, A History of Manchester Computers. National Computing Centre, Manchester (1975).
3. F. C. Williams, and T. Kilburn, A storage system for use with Binary Digital Computing Machines, *Proc. IEE* **96,** Part 2, No. 30, 183ff (1949).
4. F. C. Williams, T. Kilburn, and G. C. Tootill, Universal high-speed digital computers: A small-scale experimental machine, *Proc. IEE* **98,** Part 2, No. 61, 13–28 (1951).
5. T. Kilburn, G. C. Tootill, D. B. G. Edwards, and B. W. Pollard, Digital computers at Manchester University, *Proc. IEE* **100,** Part 2 487–500 (1953).
6. B. W. Pollard, and K. Lonsdale, The construction and operation of the Manchester University computer, *Proc. IEE* **100,** Part 2, 501–512 (1953).
7. G. C. Tootill, Informal Report on the Design of the Ferranti Mark I Computing Machine, Ferranti Internal Memorandum (November 22, 1949).

8. A. M. Turing, Programmer's Handbook for Manchester Electronic Computer Mark II (1950). (Note: The Ferranti machine was called the Mark II by Turing, to distinguish it from the existing university prototype or Mark I. Turing's nomenclature was later abandoned and the machine became known simply as the 'Ferranti Mark I,' as distinct from the 'University Mark I'.)
9. R. A. Brooker, The programming strategy used with the Manchester University Mark I Computer, *Proc. IEE Suppl. 1–3*, **103**, 151–157 (1956).

DEPARTMENT OF COMPUTER SCIENCE
UNIVERSITY OF MANCHESTER
MANCHESTER, ENGLAND

A History of the Sieve Process

D. H. LEHMER

I spent the two days before the Los Alamos meeting in Moab, Utah, walking around in the red canyons and exploring the paleontology and archeology of the region in order to get in a proper mood to give this particular talk. On the floor of the canyon are little potholes, and if you investigate one of these you will find a whole little world of its own, living, until it dries out of course, in this very restricted environment. That's the nature of the material I am presenting here. It is really arcane, exotic, and also ancient. We are discussing the history of the sieve process. The standard reaction is that every time a person hears the word "sieve" he says, "Oh, primes!" I shall prove that this inference is false. This is a different kind of paper from those about machines. It is the history of a process, not just one machine, and it's based on entirely different principles. There are no sponsoring agencies, for instance, to begin the process; there is no lethal or practical value to the calculations that are contemplated. There are no deadlines to make. There are no reports to write. There is no competition even and there's no teamwork and no distinction, which you usually find in computation environments, between the two sides of the counter that crosses the environment, on one side of which you find the user and on the other side the purveyor of computation. In this case there is no counter.

Let's begin by giving in full generality what we mean by the *sieve process* by means of which we solve *sieve problems*. In a sieve problem you are given two numbers A and B, k integers or *moduli*

$$m_1, m_2, \ldots, m_k,$$

445

k other integers

$$n_1, n_2, \ldots, n_k,$$

and finally a matrix

$$\{a_{ij}\}, \qquad i = 1(1)k, \quad j = 1(1)n_i,$$

and the problem is to find an unknown integer x that satisfies

$$X \equiv a_{i1} \quad \text{or} \quad a_{i2} \quad \text{or} \quad \cdots \quad \text{or} \quad a_{in_i} \pmod{m_i}$$

for $i = 1(1)k$ so that X is congruent to one of these n_i residue classes (mod m_i) specified in rows of our triangular like matrix. The final condition is simply $A < X < B$. The sieve problem is then to find all those integers satisfying the two kinds of conditions, congruential conditions and inequalities. We can also say that the problem is to find the least value of X satisfying these conditions.

There are two extreme cases: One is the case in which $n_i = 1$, which means we have no *or*ing, X being congruent to just one given value with respect to each modulus. This is a very ancient problem, and since we are dealing with history, we should try to recall that historians like to talk about anniversaries that are nice round positive integers less than 2000. The $n_1 = 1$ case goes back to a Chinese gentleman by the name of Sun Tsu. Dickson says first century A.D. so we will set the date at A.D. 76 exactly 19 centuries ago* (I'm sorry about the 19). The fact that Sun Tsu was able to solve this problem wasn't known to Europe until 1856, when someone back in Shanghai discovered a manuscript indicating this, and it now is always known as the Chinese remainder algorithm. Believe it or not, it has 20th century value and a number of engineers have used this particular problem-solving device in design. In fact many design people don't know about Sun Tsu and call it the Czechslovakian system because Professor Svoboda used it in 1955.

The other extreme case occurs when you have not just one of the as in each row, but as many as you possibly can. Of course, you could have $n_i = m_i$, so that every integer between A and B would be a solution. The nontrivial extreme case is the one where $n_i = m_i - 1$. This problem is somewhat more ancient; it goes back to Eratosthenes and we give the date 276 B.C. for that (historians may disagree). Eratosthenes was an Egyptian in the same way that Euler was a Russian and Einstein was an American. He suggested putting in all possible remainders a_{ij} except zero. That gave him the list of primes that everybody seems to remember as the one useful application of the sieve process.

Without presenting more paleographic material let's go back 200 years. We are celebrating the 200th anniversary of the first mechanical realization of the sieve. There are two names here, Hindenberg and Felkel, a German

---

* The talk on which this paper is based was given in 1976. [*Editor's Note*]

and an Austrian. They invented what we now call the stencil method, a stencil being just a piece of stiff cardboard that you lay over a table of cells (you can buy about a quarter of a million cells for 20¢ at the dime store). The stencils had the appropriate holes punched in them and they marked the paper cells underneath through these holes. Next, the stencil was carefully shifted periodically until they exhausted the area of cells that they had in mind. Then another stencil was applied, and so on. Felkel used this method to produce a factor table whose title page mentions the limit 10 million. The table actually runs to 408,000. The Austrian government refused to finance the table beyond that point and finally took all the paper that was needed for the table that had been printed and made cartridges of it for the war against the Turks. That is an example of the frustration that goes with the sieve process.

Actually the stencil method was used many times. Lehmer's* factor table has 48 columns, each row representing numbers larger by 210 than those of the preceding row. My father used the stencil method, all the way back in 1909, to produce the factor table to 10 million.

There is another type of sieve problem called *quadratic* in which n_i is approximately equal to $\frac{1}{2}m_i$. This means that a random X has about a 50% chance of satisfying any one of these congruences and if you have k of these the number X has about 1 chance in 2^k.

This different kind of problem may also be solved by the stencil method. I skip over some comments by Gauss, who showed how this kind of sieve problem arises when you study Diophantine equations.

Going through the turn of the century we finally come to the date 1926. At this time we have the first electromechanical sieve and the device is shown in Fig. 1. This was made in the students' shop in LeConte Hall (University of California, Berkeley), to solve some messy problems that I had been using the stencil method for. The thing we are using here is the other part of Dr. Bigelow's† bicycle. Instead of using the wheels we are using the chain.

It is obvious how that works: The sieve had a relay, some contacts, and circuitry that was very primitive but quite effective. I had a width k of 16 and we were able to eliminate values X at the rate of 60 per second. That doesn't sound very fast today, but remember next time you get some ac hum on your hi-fi set, every one of those little hums is another value of X passed in our search for the first solution X. This sieve has the advantage over the stencil method in that you don't have to plan in advance how far you are going to go and apply carefully one stencil after another. It was a genuine parallel machine.

In order to understand the details a little more thoroughly (I have no

---

* D. N. Lehmer, father of the present author. [*Editor's Note*]
† Refers to a design for magnetic-wire transport: see Bigelow's paper in this volume. [*Editor's Note*]

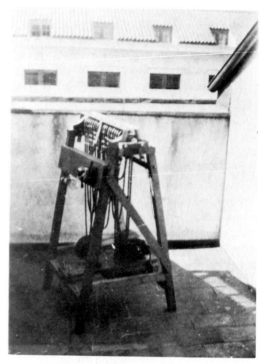

Figure 1

other picture of this early device) let's skip ahead ten years to the next electromechanical sieve (Fig. 2). This is the kind of hardware we used back in 1936. Inside the box (Fig. 3) is 16-mm film and the values of a_{ij} are the little round holes in that leader tape. The motor is missing and some of the tapes have been removed to make it easier to see how it works. There is a 10-sprocketed shaft at the top. We have lowered some of these brushes in order to make a current flow from the brass bar at the top to the shaft. It is being interrupted by these unpunched tapes. A closer look (Fig. 4) shows how easy this sieve was to make: it was made at home on top of a mountain in Pennslyvania. So much for that kind of technology.

We shall have to go back now four years, to 1932, to see the first photoelectric sieve (Fig. 5). That is how it was set up at the Century of Progress Exposition in Chicago. It is made up of gears of different size and so it replaces chains or tapes by wheels. The wheels were perforated at fixed distance from the circumference and bits of toothpicks were inserted in some of the holes to represent the numbers a_{ij}. These are three sets of gears; the set in the middle all have 100 teeth. The various other gears correspond to the 30 moduli m_i. The other interesting feature of this machine is that it was photoelectric and a beam of light entered on one side and tried to run the gauntlet

Figure 2

of the holes to reach a photocell and find the first answer. We had to have an amplifier for this and at the output of the amplifier we had to have a flip-flop. As far as I know this was the first place in which the flip-flop was used in computing. It had just been used in counting cosmic rays and that's where I got the idea. The techniques of those days were quite inferior to what we soon were to have, and we had lots of trouble shielding the amplifier with its

Figure 3

Figure 4

Figure 5

low impedance. Nevertheless, we got a lot of good work out of this sieve back in 1932: Believe it or not, this sieve ran at 5000 counts per second, which makes it the first high-speed computer, I guess. Only comparatively recent computers have been able to execute the same operation at 5000 counts per second.

Our next date is 1946 and this, of course, is the ENIAC. Can we use the high-speed computer to do the sieve process? This was a highly parallel machine, before von Neumann spoiled it. We were able to build a sieve into it. I remember the occasion very clearly. We had a Fourth of July weekend situation when the Lehmer family was allowed to come in and pull everything off the machine and reset the ENIAC for our particular problem. The Lehmer family consisted of myself, my wife, and two teenage kids. We marched in on the Friday about 5 p.m. and started setting it up with an entirely different kind of problem not concerned with interior or exterior ballistics. There was one other person there, a meteorologist named John Mauchly. He was the one who suggested that we ought to use some of the arithmetic units to make a kind of sieve, and I remember that we worked it out in a restaurant just before we went to work.

Thus began a long series of sieve processes in which a high-speed general-purpose computer was used. Many different kinds of results were obtained. The SWAC put out some pretty good sieve programs and I wrote a small paper on the subject. I think the best sieve we ever got was an IBM 7094 sieve by John Brillhart in which 100,000 counts per second was finally achieved. In that case there were chains that were simulated in the memory by pushing bits around. The technique to get the high speed was to combine many moduli into five or six very long chains filling most of the memory.

When I went home from the ENIAC it occurred to me that I ought to build a really high-speed sieve using vacuum tubes, and Paul Morton and I sat down and figured one out. We made one out of counters; we were warned by Eckert that long counters were dangerous and he was certainly right. We built a kind of decoding counter that I haven't seen elsewhere, using a matrix and two short counters feeding into it. The whole thing was a little too short on reliability. We gave up the idea in favor of another kind of a delay line sieve (Fig. 6) where we get the periodicity required for the sieve problem out of a delay line. I was leery enough about delay lines not to use mercury. We found some navy surplus lumped value ones that turned out to be very good. We had 2877 μsec of delay storage in the system. Figure 7 shows the circuit diagram for an imaginary sieve with only four tanks representing four moduli. These tanks feed back and circulate past a coincidence counter. The question of getting the information into the tanks and starting off in parallel has a rather interesting answer. You will see gates along the left side of the diagram. If you set the gate one way the pulse returns to the tank from which it has just left (after reshaping and timing). If you set the gate the other way the output of one tank goes into the next tank below and finally the output of the bottom tank goes up and feeds into the top tank. In

Figure 6

one pulse time we convert all these parallel wheels we have generated into one long wheel. That is the serial *idle mode* and happens every time we get a solution. The sieve stays in this mode until we print the answer X and then the sieve goes back into the original parallel mode. The input data patterns are fed into the sieve in idle mode one pulse at a time monitored by an auxiliary counter that also serves to start the sieve off in parallel at approximate times differing by precisely 2877 μsec.

That's the way the delay line sieve has been operating for ten years now, 24 hours per day. We have no maintenance and since the whole system is just a long piece of wire, nothing ever went wrong to speak of except for occasional counter printer trouble. It was still a very good piece of electronics. The rate for this sieve is one million counts per second.

Figure 8 shows our recent sieve, a shift register sieve that runs at 20 million counts per second. Figure 9 is a close-up of the front panel. We have two counters: one gives the answer X and the other gives the number of times we have had an answer to the problem. There are some problems where the Xs are so frequent that you don't want each one; you just want to know how many they are between limits to get some density ideas. These switches are stop, start, manual, input, and all the other things you would normally put on a very simple electronic device.

Figure 10 shows the big card that holds the hardware program that loads the data, starts it running, prints the answer, and monitors the stack of problems waiting to run.

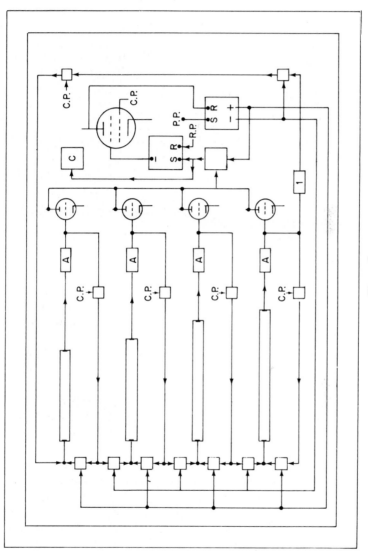

Figure 7

Figure 8

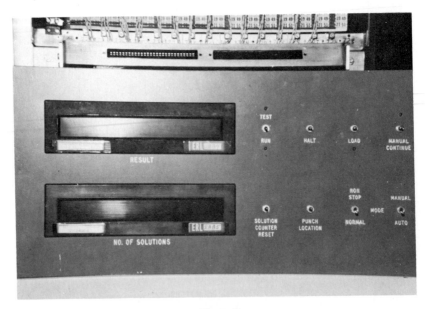

Figure 9

Figure 10

I could have told you about the history of plans that people have made for sieves. For example, Jerry Estrin and his group have some pretty fine plans for making 100,000,000 counts per second possible, but they never did anything about it. I have read in Venkov's book (Venkov, 1970) that they have one of Lehmer's sieves in the Institute for Mathematics in Leningrad. I don't know anything about it. All I can say is that none of my sieves is missing.

[In the discussion on this paper at the Los Alamos conference Professor Lehmer was asked, "What is the interest in this problem—aside from the fact that it is very difficult mathematically?" He replied as follows:]

No, it is not that. It is a powerful tool. The point of the method is this. You are looking for a solution to some problem like $f(x, y) = 0$. That includes a very general class of problems. If you could solve that problem in integers, you would be very famous. If f is a polynomial, with x, y as integer variables, every time x is increased by m, the value of f (not necessarily zero) is unaltered modulo m. It is very quick, as Gauss showed, to go from a problem like $f(x, y) = 0$ to a set of necessary sieve conditions and that's why the sieve method is used so much to solve Diophantine equations in two variables. It is also used in algebraic number theory quite a bit. We have examples of sieve runs that make possible new theorems about the distributions of the values of the class numbers of various algebraic fields. There is a lot to do. A reasonable man, like myself, wouldn't spend 12% of his time, maybe, worrying about building sieves if there wasn't any real use for them.

It's very esoteric, of course, and since I am practically the only man working in this field you can see how widespread the interest in it is.

REFERENCE

Venkov, B. A., (1970). "Elementary Number Theory," p. 25. Wolters—Noordhoff, The Netherlands.

DEPARTMENT OF MATHEMATICS
UNIVERSITY OF CALIFORNIA
BERKELEY, CALIFORNIA

The MANIAC

N. METROPOLIS

1. Introduction

With all the nonlinear partial differential equations pervading this rarefied atmosphere from the very beginning of the Los Alamos project, it was inevitable that the Laboratory would suffer total immersion in computing. I should like to give a brief account of this inexorable fate.

During the war period, accounting machines (IBM) were adapted to highly repetitive but relatively simple calculations. At each stage the latest machines were sought and a gradual expansion continued into the postwar years.

The pressure for ever improved capability has always maintained a high level, so that in the closing year of the war, Los Alamos was seeking computational aid beyond the Laboratory, starting with the ENIAC. Parallel to these two developments, a third emerged in 1948, namely, a program to design, build, maintain, and utilize a computer transcending existing capabilities. This interaction between designer–builders on the one hand and users on the other proved to be a healthy and stimulating one and made for good progress. In due course, the software systems people began to interact with the other two types to the advantage of all. The time period covered here is through the 1950s.

2. The War Years

Initially, theorists did their own computing on desk machines—and at one stage no less a scientist than Feynman was devoting some of his time

457

and not inconsiderable talents to their maintenance, such were the exigencies of wartime. Gradually a group of (mostly) women were ably trained by the remarkable Donald Flanders, affectionately known as Moll. They did the sophisticated computing. It was Dana P. Mitchell who first suggested in early 1944 that accounting machines of that vintage be used at Los Alamos. As a member on leave from the Columbia physics faculty, he was aware of the utilization made by his astronomer colleague Wallace Eckert. In short order an arsenal of IBM's finest was installed under the aegis of Stan Frankel and Eldred Nelson. Not long after, Hans Bethe, head of the Theoretical Division, asked Dick Feynman and me to join that management.

3. Postwar Computation Center

With Alamogordo a part of history a new phase for the computing center began with contributions from Dick Hamming, Preston Hammer, and Dick Stark followed by Bengt Carlson, and Max Goldstein, with Bengt holding the fort for the longest period. Quietly in the background, overseeing that evolution, was Carson Mark, long-time head of the Theoretical Division in the postwar period, whose contributions have been much underestimated.

The sophistication of the computation center was directly related to the progress at IBM and the march of CPCs, 701s, 704s, 709, 7090, 7094 was a continual one, often with several copies. Later, Control Data was to have its day with its 6600s and 7600s.

4. External Resources

The most significant prelude to the MANIAC project was the ENIAC. von Neumann was a consultant at Los Alamos essentially from the beginning; he was also one at the Aberdeen Proving Ground, in particular, at the Ballistics Research Laboratory. In early 1945, he informed Edward Teller, Stan Frankel, and me about the ENIAC, nearing completion at the Moore School of the University of Pennsylvania. He raised the question whether the relatively ambitious computational problems of a thermonuclear nature might be put on that computer. With his great clarity of expression and thoroughness, Johnny described the design and implementation of this fantastic undertaking by the Eckert and Mauchly team. Naturally we were mesmerized by the prospects. A preliminary visit was arranged for Frankel and me, and we were briefed by Herman and Adele Goldstine.

The arrangements made were that we could attempt the first problem on the ENIAC if (i) we prepared the flow diagram, (ii) we programmed it on the computer, (iii) we would then try to debug it, and finally (iv) we would try running it. The reciprocity in the arrangements was that our computations would provide a rather comprehensive test (some 95% of the "control capacity'') on this shakedown cruise. No better opportunity could have been provided a pair of neophytes than this. It was a stimulating way to really learn to thread that electronic labyrinth and, thanks to the malfunctions that were detected, to gain a detailed knowledge of its construction. Anthony Turkevich was to join us in this effort.

In the course of this extended stay at the Moore School, there were many occasions for long conversations with Eckert and Mauchly and some of their staff, especially Arthur Burks, Chuan Chu, and Harry Huskey. The focus was already on the next stage of development, namely, the EDVAC. By the time we left, we had learned much more than we had any reason to suspect. (This exposure to such a marvelous machine coupled in short order to the Alamogordo experience was so singular that it was difficult to attribute any reality to either.)

It is interesting to contemplate how different even global events might have been if some commerical computer company had undertaken the design and construction of an electronic computer in, say, the ENIAC class, that would have been available before World War II. The electronic components used in ENIAC were certainly available.

On one of his many visits to Los Alamos (circa 1947), von Neumann described a suggestion of Richard Clippinger of the Ballistics Research Laboratory that the ENIAC might be converted into a limited stored-program mode of operation instead of its gigantic plugboard mode distributed over the entire machine. The idea was that the so-called "function tables," normally used to store 300 12-decimal digit numbers set by manual switches, could be used to store up to 1800 2-decimal digits that would be interrogated sequentially (including loops), each pair corresponding to an instruction. Thus one could go from one problem to another much more efficiently.

Adele Goldstine at Princeton indeed started to plan the background control to implement this form of control. Halfway through this stage, it was apparent that the control capacity of the ENIAC was insufficient. However, on a visit to the ENIAC in early 1948, in preparation for its use after its move from Philadelphia, I was briefed by Homer Spence, the quiet but effective chief engineer, about some of their plans. He mentioned the construction of a new panel to augment one of the logical operations. It was a one-input–hundred-output matrix. It occurred to me that if this could be used to interpret the instruction pairs in the proposed control mode, then it would release a sufficiently large portion of the available control units to realize the new mode—perhaps. When I mentioned this to von Neumann, he asked whether I would be willing to take over the project, since Adele had lost interest; so with the help of Klari von Neumann, plans were revised and completed and we undertook to implement them on the ENIAC, and in a fortnight this was achieved. Our set of problems—the first Monte Carlos—were run in the new mode. Subsequently, J. Calkin, F. and C. Evans, and J. Suydam were to utilize the ENIAC for an extensive series of problems.

The demand at Los Alamos for larger, faster, and more-sophisticated computers continued unabated. In the postwar years, in addition to the ENIAC, access was gained to the SEAC (NBS) in Washington, the UNIVAC in Philadelphia, and SWAC (NBS) in Los Angeles shortly after they started humming (in the early 1950s). Without exception, the cooperation between the teams sent from Los Alamos and the support staff at the respective sites was exemplary.

5. The MANIAC

We come now to the computer research and utilization program at Los Alamos. In 1946, Stan Frankel and I joined the faculty of the University of Chicago. The plans of President Hutchins to expand the scientific effort were sufficiently ambitious as to considerably delay the construction of several buildings, whose existence was a necessary condition to starting our computer activities. In 1948, Carson Mark, head of the Theoretical Division, proposed that a computer research effort be started at Los Alamos and in-

Figure 1   The arithmetic unit, the high-speed electrostatic memory, and the control unit of the MANIAC. The four central panels constitute the arithmetic unit; the two panels on the outside constitute the controls. Twenty of the forty storage units, operated in parallel, are located above the arithmetic unit, with the remaining twenty in corresponding positions behind them. A monitor unit is included at each end of the memory units.

vited me to have a try. Good computer engineers were rare in those days; they were gradually evolving at about the same rate as cyclotron engineers. It seemed sensible to follow in the footsteps of the project at the Institute for Advanced Study—then in its third year—and accordingly arrangements were made with von Neumann. Since it is always easier to duplicate then to design ab initio, a copy of the arithmetic processor was made in good time. Our engineering staff by then included R. Merwin, H. Parsons, J. Richardson, H. Demuth, W. Orvedahl, and E. Klein.

Development of the cathode-ray (Williams) storage system at Princeton was more time consuming than expected. Owing to the fact that J. Richardson has some preliminary experience with that approach at the University of Toronto, we decided to pursue an independent course for memory, using a 2 in. tube rather than the 5 in. one considered by Princeton. We then went on to plan an independent control system and vocabulary, a quite distinct input–output including photoelectric paper tape reader punch, $\frac{1}{4}$-inch magnetic tape, typewriter, 10,000-word magnetic drum, and a line printer (Analex Model 1). The inclusion of electromechanical devices led to the oracular pronouncement, Whenever electromechanics can be replaced by electronics, do so!

Figure 2   Close-up of the arithmetic unit with Lois Cook (Leurgans), exceptional programmer, coder, operator, and problem analyst.

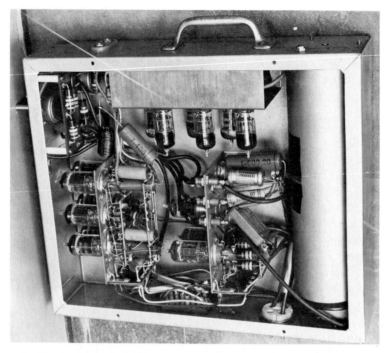

Figure 3 Plug-in memory unit of the MANIAC, a 2-in.-diam oscilloscope tube stored 1024 bits. Forty such units operating in parallel served as the high-speed memory.

Debugging and testing were completed in early March 1952, and the first scientific computations were started. The exhilaration and satisfaction derived from watching the neon lights flickering their way through the calculation more than compensated for the frustrations, delays, and long hours on the way. Published reports of the technical details are available.

The long process of preparing a subroutine library began, including aids such as tracer routines. For this as well as for programming assistance, there were R. Bivins, L. Cook, M. Jones, D. Bradford, E. Alei, and M. Tsingou. Led on by J. Jackson, studies were begun on assembly languages and an assembler was produced; E. Herbst and friends made frequency distributions of vocabulary usage for a comprehensive spectrum of computational problems; M. Wells *et al.* launched the MADCAP studies that led to a high-level language and compiler.

A parenthetical note may be inserted here thay may help reduce further confusion in the literature. MANIAC was the name of the Los Alamos computer and not the name of the Princeton computer. That computer was identified as the Institute for Advanced Study (IAS) computer. MANIAC II is a successor started in 1955 here and MANIAC III was developed at the University of Chicago a few years later.

The problems of the laboratory rapidly took the lion's share of available time. Some of the individuals with "hands-on" the computer included R. Richtmyer, the Rosenbluths, R. Lazarus, L. Nordheim, and E. Teller. In addition, a variety of unclassified problems were run to test the adequacy of the vocabulary as well as for their intrinsic interest.

(a)   First and foremost was Fermi with his pion–proton phase shift analysis [1] along with the nonlinear minimization problem that has led to much research in applied mathematics. Discussions with such a master were perhaps the most satisfying experience of all. H. L. Anderson was to join that effort at a later stage.

(b)   Then S. Ulam and J. Pasta collaborated with Fermi on the problem of nonlinear coupled oscillators with their totally unexpected results, which provoked a global outpouring of just barely countable publications [2].

(c)   Led on by Gamow, we did some of the early numerical experiments on the genetic code [3].

(d)   A. Turkevich and I initiated studies on nuclear cascades to study the interactions of high-energy particles on heavy nuclei, using Monte Carlo techniques [4].

(e)   J. von Neumann instructed us on how to attack two-dimensional flow of two incompressible fluids under gravitational and hydrodynamical forces [5].

(f)   Edward Teller with obvious delight at gaining access to a marvelous toy stimulated us greatly as we tried to learn about equations of state for substances consisting of interacting individual (rigid spheres) molecules using a modified Monte Carlo technique on a plane [6].

(g)   P. Stein investigated a series of problems in the quite different direction of discrete mathematics with emphasis on combinational theory [7].

(h)   The first ideas on significance arithmetic emerged in this period [8].

(i)   M. Wells *et al.* prepared the first program to develop a strategy for "anti-clerical" chess—this was on a 6 × 6 board with the bishops removed. That experience was not only highly amusing but had many implications for subsequent games of strategy.

(j)   Last but not least, S. Ulam and company introduced the notion of "lucky numbers," a generalization of the ordinary prime numbers with many similar properties.

These are, of course, merely samples of the studies identified with the MANIAC. They illustrate the rather wide spectrum of interest; each was to stimulate further intensive studies elsewhere, where the related publications can best be measured in hundredweight. It is perhaps worthwhile mentioning that the problem originators interacted directly with the computer. With the eventual achievement of interactive capabilities and *high-level languages*, there may be a return to what, in retrospect, seem like halcyon days.

REFERENCES

1. E. Fermi, N. Metropolis, and E. Felix Alei, Phase shift analysis of the scattering of negative pions by hydrogen, *Phys. Rev.* **95**, 1581 (1954).
2. E. Fermi, J. Pasta, and S. Ulam. Studies of Nonlinear Problems, Document LA-1940 (May 1955).
3. G. Gamow and N. Metropolis. Numerology of polypeptide chains, *Science* **120**, 779–780 (1954).
4. N. Metropolis and S. Ulam. The Monte Carlo method, *J. Amer. Statist. Assoc.* **44**, 335 (1949); N. Metropolis, R. Bivins, M. Storm, and A. Turkevich, Monte Carlo calculations on intranuclear cascades, *Phys. Rev.* **110**, 185 (1958).
5. A. Blair, N. Metropolis, J. von Neumann, A. H. Taub, and M. Tsingou, A study of a numerical solution to a two-dimensional hydrodynamical problem, *Math. Tables Other Aids Comput.* **XIII**, 67 (1959).
6. N. Metropolis, A. W. Rosenbluth, M. H. Rosenbluth, A. H. Teller, and E. Teller. Equation of state calculations by fast computing machines, *J. Chem. Phys.* **21**, 1087 (1953).
7. R. L. Bivins, N. Metropolis, P. R. Stein, and M. B. Wells. Characters of the symmetric groups of degree 15 and 16, *Math. Tables Other Aids Comput.* **VIII**, 212 (1954).
8. N. Metropolis and R. L. Ashenhurst. Significant digit computer arithmetic, *IRE Trans. Electr. Comput.* **EC-7**, 4 (1958).
9. J. Kister, P. R. Stein, S. Ulam, W. Walden, and M. B. Wells, Experiments in chess, *J. Assoc. Comput. Mach.* **4**(2), 174–177 (1957).
10. V. Gardiner, R. Lazarus, N. Metropolis, and S. Ulam. On certain sequences of integers defined by sieves, *Math. Mag.*, Jan.–Feb. 117–122 (1956).

LOS ALAMOS SCIENTIFIC LABORATORY
LOS ALAMOS, NEW MEXICO

Early Research on Computers at RCA

JAN RAJCHMAN

The way we entered into the computer field at RCA was through the initiative of Col. Simon from the Franklin Arsenal in Philadelphia in 1939. The Germans had a great dominance in the air and the Allies were very poor at antiaircraft fire control. While the guns could shoot the planes, it was very difficult to aim them with the mechanical "directors" of the day, which were much too slow. Col. Simon had the foresight to believe that electronics could provide the required speed. He approached us at RCA to see whether we would be willing to look into the matter.

There appeared immediately two approaches. One, which was what we would call digital, would be based on the then-existing cosmic ray counters, and the other, then called continuous and that we now call analog, would be sort of an imitation of what was done mechanically.

And so we undertook the job. In fact I was the first man to start working on it and I can't remember whether we started before or after the invasion of Poland, but it was just at the very beginning of the war.

My first inclination was to start with the analog approach in imitation of the mechanical directors, but I soon found out that making anything that works with a precision of 1% was practically a miracle, and to do it at any reasonable speed was a double miracle. Since the equations obviously required far more precision than that, I went on the digital approach quite soon. I was soon joined by a few others, including R. L. Snyder, L. E. Flory, and G. A. Morton. Another man by the name of A. W. Vance undertook to

465

follow the analog approach and eventually he developed a machine called the TYPHOON, which did help in some shooting toward the end of the war. But I shall describe the digital approach only because that's the only part that really had an important sequel after the war.

We decided on the binary system right away. We developed arithmetic units based on a shift register accumulator of the type that is still in use today. The only nonlinear device with gain was the vacuum tube, which was very power consuming and expensive. So we tried to minimize the required number of tubes by doing some of the logic through resistive networks. We were, in fact, doing what was later called threshold or majority logic. We made arithmetic units based on such resistive networks, notably a matrix multiplier in which the product was the result of direct matrix switching of the multiplier and multiplicands, without any explicit timing cycles. We thought a lot about the respective merits of synchronous and asynchronous operations, as well as ac or dc coupled circuits.

We also needed a way to generate function tables, as for example for ballistic tables. In modern terminology we needed read-only memories, or "arbitrary function generators" as we called them then. I first tried to use cathode-ray tubes and a mask with curves that were read out by phototubes. I soon was discouraged by the D to A conversion problem and the difficulties to keep all the analog circuitry stable. These difficulties led me to think of the resistive matrix generator described by Burks.*

The resistive matrix is a forgotten device today, but it played a very important role for quite some time. It consists of rows and columns of conductors and coupling resistances between them at selected intersections. When a row is exited, all columns coupled to it will provide a signal and all columns without coupling will have no signal. Hence, the pattern of presence or absence of a resistance can be made to encode the desired function. There are "sneak" couplings between every column and every row since all the resistive couplings are linear. In some sense the resistive matrix is a monster short circuit. In fact, von Neumann remarked on that when he first heard of it and thought it may not work. The trick to avoid the effect of sneak paths is to provide the columns with resistive couplings to ground that are low compared to the coupling resistances. The resistive matrix was used extensively in the ENIAC, for decimal multiplication tables and for many other functions.

We were in the formative years (1942–1943) of digital computers, and we gradually became acquainted with the relatively few who were interested in this field. We had many visitors. Among them was John von Neumann, who came to see us frequently and who became very familiar with our research. We also had frequent visits from Herman Goldstine. We had contacts with the Moore School of Electrical Engineering of the University of Pennsyl-

---

* See paper by Burks in this volume.

vania, essentially our neighbors in Philadelphia (we were in Camden, New Jersey).

It became apparent that digital computers would be much more useful for the war effort for solving urgent computation problems such as calculating ballistic tables than for fire control. The very large number of tubes required made them impractical for field use for which their speed, though high, was still insufficient for real-time computations. On the other hand, their three-order-of-magnitude-greater speed with respect to mechanical computers made them a godsend for lengthy numerical computations.

We thought of the difficulties involved with a computing machine requiring thousands of tubes and the failure rates that it would entail. This led us to invent a single tube capable of performing all the arithmetic. When I explained the principle of the computron, as we called the tube, to Warren Weaver, who was then head of the NDRC, he became fascinated by it and immediately gave us a contract for its development. There were many beams in the tube, each guided by deflecting electrodes and each striking separate targets. The targets of one beam were connected to deflecting electrodes of others. Because of secondary emission, the targets assumed one or another of two stable voltages, without the necessity of any coupling resistances. After the inputs were applied the various intermediary electrodes performing the carry operations trickled successively to their stable potentials and the output appeared in the final electrodes without any explicit timing pulses. We demonstrated the principle with a model having several cells. However, the technoogy was too intricate for a follow-up, as we were attempting in a sense "integration" in the difficult vacuum technology.

During that period the matter as to whether RCA should undertake the building of a complete computing system with many thousands of tubes was considered. Actually, in 1943, the Moore School obtained a contract for starting the building of what became the ENIAC. I recently confirmed that date with Professor Brainerd. We eagerly transmitted all the expertise we had to the Moore School. There were many mutual visits. Also, I remember giving several talks at the Moore School. There was a mood of great patriotism, everything was done for the war effort, and there were no questions asked about authorship or patent rights. A great deal of intangible and undocumented information was transmitted. Two concrete devices from RCA were adopted in ENIAC: the resistive matrix function generator already mentioned and a decimal ring counter that had been designed by Igor Grosdoff.

There was a hiatus in our research, but not in our interests in digital computers, from 1943 until after the war in late 1945. This was the period of EDVAC and an evolution in thinking that gradually resulted in the realization of the great benefits of a truly random access memory. In the fall of 1945, von Neumann suggested that we cooperate in the building of the Institute for Advanced Study computer. The decision was made that we should undertake the random access memory.

Perhaps because of my dislike for analog deflection in a cathode-ray tube (CRT)I conceived a purely digital tube—the Selectron—or the selective electrostatic storage tube. The tube had two orthogonal sets of parallel bars, which controlled an overall bombardment of electrons. By means of these bars, all current could be stopped expect in a given "window." This purely digital addressing mechanism was used to select a location for writing and reading. For storage, electrons were allowed through all windows, bombarded discrete metallic elements, and kept them at one or the other of two stable potentials through a secondary emission mechanism identical to the one used in the computron. We were engaged again in integrated vacumtube techniques. This time we brought research to a successful conclusion, developing not only the tube but the circuits to drive it. I believe this was in late 1949 or early 1950.

The tube Division of RCA at Lancaster produced about 2000 Selectron tubes, the first being available in late 1950 or early 1951. Looking at the project in retrospect, I believe its timetable was remarkably short—only four years from conception to product—particularly when considering that the maximum manpower at the Laboratories was only three persons. Yet considerable technology had to be developed.

Of course, at the time the progress did not seem so fast. It is natural that our friends at the Institute became a bit impatient when we had delaying difficulties, as they were eager to have some definite memory to incorporate in the advancing design of the computer. It turns out that in 1947 or 1948, Professor Williams at Manchester invented a way to use an ordinary unmodified CRT for a random access memory, and Julian Bigelow* decided to use it for the IAS machine. The Selectron was chosen by the group at Rand, who built a so-called copy of the IAS machine—the JOHNNIAC. Bill Gunning and Keith Uncapher at Rand made a superb job of the circuits for the Selectron. In fact, the Selectron memory worked for many years and was still operating well when it was finally replaced by a core memory.

In 1949, I conceived the core memory. It was invented independently by Jay Forrester at MIT. I believe that the story and evolution of the core memory are well known and I shall not dwell on the subject. There was a period in 1949 and 1950 when we were working on the core but still had to devote much time to the Selectron, and our group was still very small. In the 1950s we were engaging in the core memory and other types of magnetic memories. Also, I conceived, with Arthur Lo, the transfluxor, or multiapertured core, which has nondestructive readout and logic switching properties. This development spurred a great deal of research and development in this country and abroad. Eventually the transistor eclipsed most of the uses of tranfluxors. Use of transfluxors abroad continued longer than in the United States because of a much slower development of transistors.

---

* See the paper by Bigelow in this volume.

I shall skip over the great era of the development of commerical computers, in which RCA played an important but alas passing role, and consider for a minute or two today's scene. The hardware has long ceased to be the critical issue in the sense it was in the early days. The spotlight has switched to new disciplines of computer science: languages, software, applications, system of computers, etc. For sure, some of the spotlight is returning to the hardware because of the spectacular success of large-scale integration of circuits made on silicon chips (LSI).

However, I believe that there is one very important hardware problem of long standing that is unsolved: a fast random access mass memory. We depend on mechanical serial access in our mass memories based on magnetic recording. We are forced into tremendously high bit rates because most bits in the series are not the ones we are interested in and because the access channels are so few. There is great complication and expense to match this memory to the semiconductor LSI random access memory, as well as a great deal of necessary ongoing intellectual work to match the two operationally. What is needed is a huge nonmechanical random access memory with a wideband access capability. Electron beam addressed and holographic attempts at mass memory have not yet made the grade. The problem is important, difficult, and very interesting. It is an outstanding challenge to those in the physical sciences and inventive arts.

RCA LABORATORIES
DAVID SARNOFF RESEARCH CENTER
PRINCETON, NEW JERSEY*

* Present address: Consultant, Princeton, N.J. 08540.

Memories of the Bureau of Standards' SEAC

RALPH J. SLUTZ

During the late 1940s, Johnny von Neumann gave several lectures describing the computers that were being developed then. I've always remembered a comparison he gave to make the power of the computers more understandable. He compared 15 minutes of running a particular computer to hiring a group of some 20 people using desk calculators, giving them their instructions, and locking the door on them for about a year—then finding out what went wrong because you had overlooked something in your instructions.

Lest we forget what computation of that sort was like, I shall give a brief excerpt from the memoirs of an early member of the WPA Mathematical Tables Project in New York City. This project was established in 1938 with a very small number of mathematicians and a fairly large number of people from the relief rolls of the Depression. The people who came from the relief rolls were a varied sort, and more than rusty in their arithmetic. Therefore, they were divided into four different groups. One group was to do addition, a second group to do subtraction, a third to do multiplication, and the fourth group to do division and check the results. The people were installed in an abandoned stable in New York City, and the four groups were seated facing the four walls of the room. Each group faced a wall on which there was a large poster giving them their most important instructions, and to keep negative numbers straight each person was given both black and red pencils to work with. The poster giving instructions for the addition group said:

Black plus black makes black.
Red plus red makes red.
Black plus red or red plus black,
   hand the sheets to group 2.

Ten years later, this humble beginning had grown into the National Applied Mathematics Laboratories of the Bureau of Standards under Dr. John Curtiss. Also in the Bureau of Standards was the Electronic Computers Laboratory, under Sam Alexander, which was concerned with the hardware side. At this point I should like particularly to remember Sam Alexander, who was the moving spirit in the Bureau's hardware work on computers, and who should be writing this paper if he were still alive. He always treated me more like a son than an employee, and we had a warm and productive relationship. Sam's group in 1948 had developed several computer components, particularly involving pentode vacuum tubes and pulse transformers. The group had also developed some of the input-output equipment for the Institute for Advanced Study computer. Sam was also acting as technical representative and contracting agent for three to five major computers.

When I joined the group in 1948, computer development everywhere was being ruled by the "von Neumann constant."* Some people have mentioned it as being a part of von Neumann's machine, but as I remember it Johnny developed it as a universal constant—that constant number of months from now until everyone's machine is expected to be completed.

After the ENIAC, many computers had been started, but at that time none had reached the promised land. In fact, the Office of the Air Comptroller of the U.S. Air Force had a major contract for the development of a machine to be used for linear programming analyses of economic problems. This was largely sparked by George Dantzig, who eventually became so impatient with the von Neumann constant that he persuaded the Air Force to contract with the Bureau of Standards to develop a computer with a minimum of complications and quickly, to fill the gap. During the development phase, this was known as the National Bureau of Standards Interim Computer. When it became operational it was renamed the SEAC, for Standards Eastern Automatic Computer, but we who worked on it sometimes prefer the name Interim, because that shaped much of its design. Reliability was of course paramount in the design goals, but simplicity came next in order to reduce the development time. No provision was made for floating-point arithmetic, none for alphabetic input or output, none for magnetic tapes. Instead, the original goal called for input from Teletype paper tape, integer arithmetic throughout, and output to the same Teletype printer that had read the paper tape. At that time one of the most nearly operational memories was the mercury delay line design of the EDVAC project. So with the fine cooperation of the EDVAC people it was possible to purchase from the

* Known in Britain as the Hartree constant [Editor's Note].

EDVAC supplier a cabinet containing the mercury lines and the temperature control system. This of course determined the general shape of the machine. It would be of the general EDVAC structure with delay line memory and synchronous circuitry, but the circuitry in which the Bureau of Standards was experienced was very different from the circuitry being used by the EDVAC group. Thus the circuitry and the detailed logic were worked out entirely independently by the Bureau.

The logic design included integer multiplication, integer division, and logical multiplication. The hardware had two rather unusual features. One of these was that, except for the memory circuits, all of the pulse amplification was performed by a single type of pentode vacuum tube driving step-down pulse transformers. The pentodes gave a well-defined voltage output and relatively low inpedance because of their saturation characteristics. The signal then went to a 5:1 step-down pulse transformer, so the already low output impedance was lowered by an additional factor of 25. Thus the signal lines were of very low impedance and could drive as many as a dozen or more gates as well as long connecting lines without worrying about distributed capacitance.

The other outstanding feature was that all of the logic throughout the machine was done by germanium diodes. This, as I understand it, makes it the first computer to do all of its logic with solid-state devices. It did have vacuum tubes, but they were used solely for amplification while all gating, all clocking, all pulse reshaping were done by germanium diodes.

For short delays, wire-wound delay lines were used, so that a flip-flop was a 1-μsec circulating loop. This made the design and debugging a bit difficult, since there were no static states, but everything was pulsing at a microsecond rate. However, Julian Bigelow at the Institute for Advanced Study project had trained me carefully in the principles of tolerance analysis and its fundamental importance. At the Bureau of Standards we were able to apply these principles so successfully that we achieved a complete separation of electrical and logical design. Alan Leiner, who played the principal part in the final logical design, was able to work with a complete set of building blocks which had well-defined limits. He didn't need to worry at all about the electronics within the building blocks—as long as they were fitted together within timing tolerances and load tolerances, they worked.

This resulted in circuitry which had some 750 vacuum tubes and 10,000 germanium diodes. Of course, this was at a time when there was a tremendous worry about the reliability of vacuum tubes. The program planners had to have frequent reports of the total number of vacuum tubes in the design, but somehow they didn't worry about germanium diodes. It was easier to add 1000 germanium diodes to the design than to add 10 vacuum tubes. Using so many diodes was something of a gamble, for the diodes were a very new device at the time, and we used the old 1N34 whisker diodes. But the gamble paid off. After the machine was debugged, we set up a preventive maintenance schedule that removed every tube and diode from the machine and tested it individually at least once a month. (The diodes were all in plug-in clusters.) With this schedule the failures that were not caught during maintenance time were kept low—each month during computation time we had about one vacuum tube and about two germanium diodes go bad. Thus the balance of reliability was pretty good.

We actually had much more trouble from bad solder joints than we ever had from vacuum tubes, diodes, or delay lines. I can well remember that we established two standard debugging techniques. After about two hours a day of preventive maintenance, we would start a test program running. Then we applied the ''stir with a wooden spoon'' technique, which consisted of taking something like a wooden spoon and going around the computer, tapping everything you could see. If the test program stopped, you had found something. When that test was finally passed, we applied the Bureau of Standards' ''standard jump.'' We were in a building with wooden floors that were not difficult to shake, so the standard jump consisted of jumping up in the air about 15 cm and coming down on the floor as hard as possible. If that test was passed, the machine was ready to tackle a computational program— and even more interesting bugs would show up.

Three particular bugs stand out in my mind. The first was in arithmetic. When the machine was nearly complete and we started running programs we found indeed that $1 + 1 = 2$ and $2 + 2 = 4$, but $4 - 2$ gave different answers depending on what program was used! Some programs gave 2, while other programs gave 3. After considerable sweating we found that $4 - 2 = 3$ whenever the *addresses* of the two numbers differed by 7(modulo 8). Excess carry bits from complementing the negative number were propagating through the three guard bits at the end of the word and carrying into the answer. We changed one wire and so redefined the arithmetic to be more acceptable by human standards.

The first significant problem was done in May 1950, concerning tracing skew rays in optics. This type of computation was used very extensively by the Bureau of Standards for many years. Steady work was also started on linear programming, but it was not many weeks before Nick Metropolis and Bob Richtmyer showed up with a problem from Los Alamos that they wanted to put on the machine. I didn't realize until much later how much of a habit it was for Nick Metropolis to show up with a problem as soon as somebody got a computer running. Anyway, they were perfectly willing to take any time that we would give them, so they got the time from midnight to breakfast. But although the machine was running many problems for the Bureau during the daytime, it just would not run Bob Richtmyer's problem at night. There was trouble after trouble after trouble, and we all took turns being the nighttime debugger. Finally at 4 a.m. one morning I discovered the cause. Since Bob and Nick were real mathematicians, they didn't do things like everyone else and write their code from the bottom of memory up—

they wrote it from the top down, which was possible since SEAC was a four-address machine at that time. This resulted in the instruction word having nearly all ones, instead of the more usual nearly all zeros. And a design error of 0.1 μsec in one of the delay lines of the instruction register caused an occasional bit to be lost when the register was nearly full. So at 4 a.m. I hung on (with loose wires) an additional delay line of 0.1 μsec and it stayed there for about five years until SEAC was moved to another location and so refurbished.

The third flaw was a real hardware flaw. We had a narrow walkway through the middle of the machine and a narrow door for access. In mid-1951 we were having an open house, and my wife came with my children. The machine was open, there were people everywhere, and everything was happening at once, when my wife came hurrying to me in the next room. Our two-year-old son was crawling along the interior walkway toward the power supplies, which were uninsulated since they were inside the cabinet. And my wife couldn't get through the narrow door to rescue him because she was pregnant with our next child.

Well, engineers never seem to be willing to let well enough alone. The original design was four-address, with the fourth address being the location of the next instruction so you could do optimum coding with respect to the timing of the mercury delay lines. However, this meant that the addresses split hexadecimal digits in the input, and so different addresses had different representations. It also meant that there were only four bits to use for instructions, and so there could be no more than 16 instructions. It also meant that the memory would be forever limited to 1024 words, but we engineers had grandiose ideas of putting on a lot more memory—perhaps even as many as 2000 words. So during the design we worked out a scheme of including about seven additional tubes and 10 toggle switches, which could change it to either a four-address or a three-address machine. For some years it would run half of each day in the four-address mode on computational problems, and then the switches were flipped and it ran the other half-day in the three-address mode for testing out additional memories.

With these provisions for future growth, additional instructions were included permitting the use of two instruction counters and permitting the addresses to be relative to either of the instruction counters, thus creating a convenient subroutine jump and return. Other additions were magnetic wire and tape input-output devices. The first was a magnetic wire cartridge that was part of a commercial dictating machine. It took about a second for the wire to come up to speed, so it was only practical for handling "large" records of a hundred or more words at a time, but by leaving gaps of several seconds between such records it was possible to use one cartridge for many records. We then went on to add magnetic tape drives that avoided the problem of servoing the magnetic tape reels by getting rid of the reels. The tape was stored in a kind of two-dimensional wastebasket consisting of a pair of parallel glass plates. The tape was just dumped between the glass plates and it folded loosely any way it wished at the bottom. Three such plates made two wastebaskets for the two ends of the tape, and it worked very nicely for up to about 200 ft of tape, although we did have to use either metallized tape backing or radioactive emitters to discharge the static electricity which built up. The only moving parts were two pinch rollers, one for forward and the other for backward motion.

Another major addition was a set of 45 Williams' tubes for additional and parallel memory of 512 words. Near the end of 1950, a cathode-ray tube (CRT) graphical output was added with a joy stick to simulate aircraft guidance and control. We simulated a radar display by a program in the computer, and used the joy stick to guide a second plane for interception.

During the first year we ran some 50 programs. I have mentioned three: linear programming, optical lenses, and Richtmyer's Los Alamos program. Others of significance that should be mentioned were tables for Loran navigation, optimum statistical sampling plans, wave functions of the helium atom, and design features of a proton synchrotron.

This being a historical volume, I should perhaps say a little something about the historical position of the machine. For myself, I like to think of it as the first machine in this country to break the von Neumann constant. It was demonstrated in April 1950, and was in full mathematical use by May 1950. Thus I suppose you could say it was the first of the von Neumann type, or stored-program type, of computers in this country. But we recognize full well that in England the EDSAC, the Manchester machine, and perhaps the Pilot ACE can lay prior claim on an international basis.

I had thought that SEAC was the first with a remote terminal. In the middle of 1950 we wanted to demonstrate it to the people of the Bureau of Standards, and so put a Teletype a quarter-mile away in a lecture room much larger than the limited space around the computer. A few months later we put a terminal in a Washington hotel several miles away for a general conference. But I have heard that George Stibitz put a remote terminal on the relay computer long before. I do think it was the first to do all of its logic with solid state devices, and perhaps was the first with cathode-ray tube graphical output.

However, much more important than any enumeration of its firsts is the question of whether it fulfilled its design goals, and I think it did. It was designed as the NBS Interim Computer. It grew up to get the less transient name of SEAC, and for a few years it satisfied its design requirement by providing a very significant part of the total United States's computing capacity. In addition to its original design goal, however, we were able to put enough growth potential in it to permit expansion in its instruction set, its memory (to 1500 words), and its input-output devices. With these expansions it went on to be a workhorse computer for the Bureau of Standards for a total of 14 years.

Finally in 1964, 14 years after it came to life, the once shiny new machine could still be polished up to be shiny, could compute far better then when it was new, but was hopelessly outclassed by its successors. But I think the attitude of the many of us who worked on it can well be given by a short poem that Ida Rhodes wrote for *Datamation* magazine at the time that it was retired. She said:

Say it's weary, say it's slow,
Say that luxury ignored it;
Say it's growing old, but know
We all adored it.

ENVIRONMENTAL RESEARCH LABORATORIES
NATIONAL OCEANOGRAPHIC AND ATMOSPHERIC ADMINISTRATION
BOULDER, COLORADO

Early Computers

GEORGE R. STIBITZ

In the late fall of 1937, I was asked, as a "mathematical engineer" at Bell Telephone Laboratories (BTL), to look into the design of the magnetic elements of a relay. Until that time I had had no acquaintance with relays, and I was curious about their properties and capabilities. In particular, the logic functions that the relays embodied were interesting, and it occurred to me that binary arithmetic would be naturally compatible with the binary behavior of relay contacts.

I borrowed a few U-type relays from a junk pile the Bell Labs maintained, finding some with low-resistance windings suitable for operation on a few volts of dry battery. Late in November, I worked out the logic of binary addition of the two one-digit binary numbers, each defined by the state of a manually operated switch. The two-digit output of this adding circuit actuated a pair of flashlight bulbs. With a scrap of board, some snips of metal from a tobacco can, two relays, two flashlight bulbs, and a couple of dry cells, I assembled an adder on the kitchen table at our home.

I took this device to the Labs with me and demonstrated that binary devices like the relays were capable of performing arithmetic operations. Of course, I sketched a schematic for a multidigit binary adder, and pointed out that a relay machine could do anything a desk calculator could do.

The problem of interface between decimal computists and a binary computer next engaged my attention. It seemed impractical to persuade the computists to learn the binary notation, and the alternatives appeared to be those of making the computer convert decimal numbers into binary ones or of making the computer into a decimal device. This last alternative was abandoned at once. However, in its place I proposed a mixed binary–decimal system in which each decimal digit was converted into a binary number. Then all arithmetic operations could be performed by binary adders suitably interconnected.

The circuitry required to carry between binary adders was rather messy, and it occurred to me that if each of the digits were increased by three units before adding, then the sum would be increased by six units, and a sum equal to nine would become a binary fifteen. Any greater sums would be binary numbers of more digits. Thus in the "excess-3" notation, decimal 9 is 111 and decimal 10 is 10000. In this notation, the decimal carry occurs if and only if there is a carry in the excess-3 adder.

An incidental advantage of the excess-3 notation is that the binary complement is the binary form of the decimal complement. A simple reversal of polarity in the relays that represent numbers in excess-3 form produces the decimal complement of the represented number.

The investigations into the excess-3 system and the relays that would embody it took place, as I recall, toward the end of that winter and in the early spring of 1938.

About that time, developments in the theory of filters and transmission lines at the Bell Labs increased greatly the load of computing with complex numbers. There were at least two groups of computists whose work was largely applied to complex arithmetic. For this work, they used standard desk calculators. A complex multiplication—usually carried out to eight or ten decimal places—involved four multiplications and the transcription of two intermediate numbers, besides the two real numbers that constituted the result. A complex division demanded about four times this amount of work.

Several people—notably Mr. Nelson Sowers—suggested that complex arithmetic might be simplified by mechanical coupling of standard calculators. Dr. T. C. Fry, head of the mathematical engineering group, asked me whether the relay computers I had been playing with might be able to handle complex numbers. This event occurred, as well as I can recall, in the early summer of 1938.

For a few weeks, I sketched schematics for a complex-number relay computer. I proposed relay storage of eight-digit numbers in excess-3 notation and switching by way of rotary switches. Output was to be provided by a Teletype printer. The final sketch was assigned to S. B. Williams for evaluation.

Williams decided the circuit was feasible, but suggested the use of the then new crossbar switches instead of individual relays for storage, and relays in place of the rotary switches for transfer of numbers. It was decided to build the computer, with facilities for multiplication and division of complex numbers. Data was introduced directly on binary-contacted keys, in the form of eight-digit real and imaginary numbers and operation (multiply, divide) keys.

Williams designed the equipment for two racks of standard size. Each operation was allowed a "safe" time for relay close or open operations. After debugging, late in 1938 and early 1939, the "complex computer" (now Model 1) was put into service. It was immediately found that the restriction to multiplication and division was unwise, and the circuitry was revised to include addition and subtraction. The ease with which this alteration was made impressed the Bell people, who considered it a proof of the flexibility of the relay machine.

In September 1940, after several months of routine use at the Laboratories, the computer was demonstrated at a meeting of the American Mathematical Society held at Dartmouth College, in Hanover, New Hampshire. Williams designed an interface so that the number signals could be serialized and transmitted over a standard telegraph line. I gave a short paper on the use and design of the computer after which those attending were invited to transmit problems from a Teletype in McNutt Hall to the computer in New York. Answers returned over the same telegraph connection and were printed out on the Teletype.

Among those who attended the lecture and used the computer were John Mauchly and Norbert Wiener.

While the computer was being designed and built, I continued to think of other applications of binary calculation. Because of the simplicity of the basic computing and control elements, I believed that it would be possible to build much more automatic computers. Among those I proposed was one that evaluated polynomials and other rational functions. However, the high cost of the complex computer ($20,000 for design and construction) frightened the Lab administration, and no further computers were built for several years.

Meanwhile the war emphasized the need for large computations, and Dr. Warren Weaver, chairman of the National Defense Research Committee, supported the design and construction of Model 2, a small computer designed to subtabulate data for a D/A "Tape Dynamic Tester" I had designed for testing antiaircraft directors. This tester consisted of a set of several digital servos controlled by data punched on tape, and used to turn either the handwheels or the synchros of antiaircraft directors. The data punched in the tapes consisted of real-time target coordinates (azimuth, altitude, range) and of correct gun orders (azimuth, elevation, fuse).

The tracks used were either synthetic geometric ones or reconstructions of recorded runs. The servos required data samples at 10/sec (later 60/sec) for many minutes of run time. The computer "relay interpolator" read from punched tapes the numerical values precalculated at relatively long intervals (e.g., 1 sec or more) and applied second- or third-order digital filtration to this data. It also punched out on tape the calculated values at the required interval.

This Model 2 was fitted with changeable taped programs that embodied several interpolation or filtering formulas. The arithmetic was linear, and no

multiplier was included, other than what could be obtained by detailed programming of constant multipliers.

It was, however, strictly automatic and could be set to work and left
alone to work as long as it had input data. Much of its work during the years
it was in operation was done at nights and over the weekends, unattended.

The Model 2 computer used a "self-checking" or error-detecting code,
which I had worked out and proposed about 1940. In place of the excess-3
code, I used a biquinary one that gave checking with fewer relays. The computer was not clocked, but advanced after the completion of each step consisting of a transfer of a number. It was possible to interrupt the computer at
any time by inserting a toothpick into any one of the arithmetic relays,
without causing an error. When the obstruction was removed the machine
took up where it had left off and completed the calculation.

In 1940, I circulated a memorandum suggesting the floating decimal or
"scientific notation" as a way of avoiding the need for elaborate investigation of the order of magnitude likely to be met in a long calculation. This
scheme was not introduced into a computer until about 1945, when Model 5
was designed.

Both Models 2 and 3 were detailed and constructed under E. G. Andrews. His group decided to use in Model 3 a true multiplier in which relay
circuits generated the products, digit by digit, of an entire multiplicand for a
given multiplier. Adding circuits added these product terms. Model 3 included multipliers, relay storages, taped programs, taped input data,
punched or typed outputs, and taped data tables (e.g., of ballistic data, trigo-
nometric or other information). Several of the tables contained functions of
two variables. They were read by Teletype readers modified to go either forward or backward.

The function arguments acted as addresses, with subaddresses. A separate control searched forward or backward in the tapes for the required address, read blocks on both sides of it, and calculated the interpolated values
independently of the main computer. Either the main or the memory control
waited for the other when it had completed its task.

I believe that I first worked out and used a coordinate graph for drafting
the computer circuits in the design of Model 2. In this scheme each wire (or
logical variable) was represented by a horizontal or a vertical line, and functions were represented by junctions which were identified by symbols for the
controlling variable (a relay contact, etc.).

Model 3 was delivered to the Antiaircraft Board at Camp Davis, North
Carolina, about 1944, and used for ballistic calculations involved in testing
antiaircraft equipment. It used the biquinary self-checking code, and included an alarm triggered by the checking circuits, which sounded a bell
over Sgt. Stoddard's bed if for any reason the computation was halted.
Again, the computer was designed for full-time unattended operation, although a schedule of preventive maintenance was instituted. It was esti-

mated that Model 3 did work equivalent to about 25 computists with desk calculators.

The next relay computer was Model 5, the product of Williams and Andrews together. I had suggested that several independent elements be combined; we had already used two arithmetic units cooperating in the complex-number machine, and the idea was carried further in Model 5. Several independent "stations" were made, any one of which could work independently on problems of moderate size, while one station could take control of the entire machine if more facilities were required. Program tapes, table tapes, input tapes, and station identification were checked automatically before a station could take control.

On completion of a problem at any station, another station could acquire command. If an error was detected or if commands could not be executed, then control was passed to another problem.

This computer was the first to use the floating-decimal scheme I had suggested some years earlier. It could punch intermediate data to the capacity of a reel of tape, and could read back some of the punched-tape outputs for use later in the problem. It was also provided with a jump instruction, which would transfer control from one tape to another, and back at a later time, if required.

Two copies of this model were built. One was installed at the Aberdeen Proving Ground, and the other at Langley Field of NACA. The Aberdeen unit set a record of 167 hours of up-time in one week. It usually approached this figure; the preventive maintenance was so arranged as to tie up only part of the computer at a time, while the remainder continued to carry the load.

In summary, I should like to point out that the relay computers were first in many ways. I believe (subject to correction by Dr. Zuse) that they were the first working binary-coded computers (1939) and the first to use the excess-3 code (1939). The use of punched-tape interchangeable codes appeared in the Model 2 (1943). An error-detecting code appeared in this same computer. Table-hunting controls and indepedent component computers cooperating on single problems appeared in this computer, as did self-diagnostic signal systems. Floating decimals and a simple jump instruction appeared in Model 5 (1945).

[*Editor's Note:* A complete catalog of Dr. Stibitz's papers, with a biography, is available under the title "An Inventory of the Papers of George Robert Stibitz Concerning the Invention and Development of the Digital Computer." (Dartmouth College, Hanover, New Hampshire, 1973.)]

DEPARTMENT OF PHYSIOLOGY
DARTMOUTH MEDICAL SCHOOL
HANOVER, NEW HAMPSHIRE*

* Formerly of Bell Laboratories, then in New York, New York.

The Start of an ERA: Engineering Research Associates, Inc., 1946–1955

ERWIN TOMASH

It is no secret that cryptography as currently practiced by the major nation-states depends heavily on the extensive use of the electronic computer. A moment's reflection supports the notion that computing and cryptography have a long-standing intimate relationship. But because cryptographic activities have always been shrouded in secrecy, very little information has been released on the extent to which the cryptologic community actually helped to father the electronic computer.

One exception is Brian Randell's paper on COLOSSUS, a special-purpose electronic digital handling device built for cryptographic work by the British in 1943 [1]. Another is Samuel Snyder's report that during World War II similar work was underway in the United States [2]. A section of the U.S. Navy was so engaged and functioned under the official title of Communications Supplementary Activities—Washington. It was commonly referred to as "seesaw" because of its initials. CSAW was headed by Capt. Joseph Wenger, a career Navy officer, and prominent in its hierarchy were reserve officers Howard T. Engstrom and William C. Norris. During the war, CSAW earned a well-deserved reputation for excellence.

1. The Concept

In the summer of 1945, with World War II nearly over, Engstrom and Norris started to think about their return to civilian life. Neither wanted to

485

return to his prewar occupation, and one possibility they considered was to continue to work for CSAW by joining the civil service. Another, suggested by Engstrom almost in jest, was to start a business to build cryptographic analytic equipment. Engstrom and Norris discussed the idea with the other members of the CSAW staff who were facing the same dilemma, and found them receptive. They then broached the subject with Wenger and other senior Navy officers and somewhat to their surprise received a cautiously positive reaction. These officers saw merit in Engstrom's idea because they thought it important to keep the CSAW equipment engineering group intact even if it were outside the government.

Thus, mildly encouraged, Engstrom and Norris set about trying to find finance for their company in the fall of 1945. They were hoping to establish a high-technology company to do government work whose nature could not be divulged to potential investors, and it is not surprising that they found little interest. But they stubbornly continued to try to raise capital. In the winter of 1945, they were joined by another reserve officer, Capt. Ralph I. Meader. Meader was stationed in Dayton, Ohio, where he headed the United States Naval Computing Machine Laboratory (USNCML), a wartime operation, located within the confines of the National Cash Register Company (NCR) [3]. USNCML had produced devices and machines for CSAW and was scheduled to be disbanded. Before agreeing to endorse the Engstrom–Norris project the Navy had asked NCR if they would like to continue working for CSAW. NCR was eager to return to the cash register business and had declined [4].

2. The Know-How

By late 1945, the CSAW group had grown restive and it was clear that unless the new company was formed rapidly its major attraction, the team of skilled, experienced people, would soon be scattered over the United States. The proposed venture was about to founder when John E. Parker was introduced to Engstrom, Norris, and Meader. Parker was an investment banker, an Annapolis graduate, a Washington, D.C., resident, and was known in Navy circles.

During the war, Parker had founded and headed Northwestern Aeronautical Corporation, which manufactured wooden gliders in St. Paul, Minnesota, under contract to the Army Air Corps. In 1945, as the war wound down, businesses everywhere started to convert their plants to peacetime production. Northwestern, which had been established to do war work, faced the more difficult problem of finding a new role for itself. As president, Parker devoted his energies during this period to seeking new directions for his company.

Parker recalls meeting Meader through a mutual friend in Dayton and hearing about the proposed new company from him. He expressed a desire to learn more and subsequently met with Engstrom and Norris, who were able to describe their program only in the most general terms. Late in 1945, a meeting was arranged at the Navy Department at which the senior Navy officials present confirmed their support for the project [5].

Parker agreed to look into the matter and in the days that followed met several times with the founding group. Negotiations went smoothly and it soon became apparent that Parker had found a new direction for Northwestern and that the CSAW group had found a backer. On 8 January 1946, Parker had a new company named Engineering Research Associates, Inc. (ERA) incorporated under Minnesota law. ERA was owned 50% by the founding technical group, headed by Engstrom, Norris, and Meader, and 50% by the founding investor group, headed by Parker. The equity invested was $20,-000. Shares were sold at $0.10 per share, 100,000 shares to each group. In addition Parker and his associates agreed to provide a line of credit of $200,-000. Almost immediately thereafter Engstrom and Norris started to recruit technical staff and arrange for them to move to St. Paul.

A few months later, in June 1946, the Navy Department, without competitive bidding, issued two contracts; one fairly small to ERA and a larger one to Northwestern. ERA had no operating record and under the law was ineligible to receive a major contract award, whereas Northwestern was eligible since it was an established business. Northwestern and ERA had the same management and both were located at the same facility in St. Paul.

The founding of ERA and the receipt of its first contracts involved obvious Navy rule bending. This should not be confused with questions of substance. The Navy was aware of the risks involved and took steps to maintain control and protect the taxpayer. Simultaneously with the contract awards, USNCML was ordered to move from NCR-Dayton to St. Paul, Minnesota, so that when the ex-CSAW group arrived to begin work in the middle of 1946 they found a complete contractor surveillance organization on site.

3. The Start

In 1946, as Northwestern, the infant ERA, and the recently transferred USNCML started to work together, rapid development was taking place in the new field of electronic computers. The importance of these breakthroughs was not lost on the Navy [6]. The question was not what work to give ERA but rather how to contractually define its role. To this question the Navy found a relatively simple answer—task-type contracts. These were annual contracts that called for the contractor to undertake a series of tasks to be defined later. A ceiling expenditure figure for the fiscal year was the major feature of each contract. Northwestern and ERA could, therefore, get started knowing the approximate level of financial support that would be forthcoming.

1946 was also a year of change and movement and new beginnings all across the United States. Engineers and scientists who had worked in war plants or served in the Armed Forces came back to their homes and started looking for work. Minnesotans who looked in the want ads of St. Paul and Minneapolis newspapers had few choices. Only a few ads for engineers and physicists appeared, among them a small one placed by ERA. Eligible applicants were told merely that Engineering Research Associates was a new company doing electronics work. Those who asked for more information were told that ERA was associated with Northwestern and was working on electronic systems for the aviation industry. All readily accepted the story that ERA was also doing what was simply described as "secret government work."

The ads helped recruit a small group of experienced technical people who wanted to return to work in Minnesota, plus a larger group of wartime University of Minnesota graduates. These, added to the nucleus of some 40 seasoned CSAW staff who moved to St. Paul and a few engineers and scientists recruited from other Navy activities, formed the technical staff of ERA [3, p. 130]. As for the organization of the new company, John E. Parker was the President, and Howard T. Engstrom, William C. Norris, and Ralph I. Meader were vice presidents. Technical programs were headed by CSAW veterans, John E. Howard as Director of Development and Charles B. Tompkins as Director of Research.

The ERA organization was straightforward but the organizational setup in St. Paul, with two private sector companies and a Naval station sharing one facility, could hardly have been more chaotic. The task-type contracts served admirably to bring order out of this chaos. The tasks were defined and added one at a time as the situation developed. Serially numbered, starting with Task 1, they varied from training programs (a holding tank of uncleared people), to consulting programs, to building of special purpose electronic data processing devices, to research on data handling and storage techniques. Some represented ongoing programs; others had specific time schedules as short as a few months.

From the start, ERA showed strength in problem solving as contrasted with problem definition. This characteristic arose from the security aspects of the program in which ERA was involved. Cryptologic work has always required that a high degree of compartmentalization be maintained. Because of this, ERA was always assigned specific, concrete projects and each project was told only as much as it needed to know. This policy exacted a price from the customer—primarily in some loss of interplay between equipment user and equipment designer.

ERA also paid a price. From the early days onward, ERA was more specification oriented than user oriented, a characteristic that later hindered its entry into commercial activities and delayed its maturation into a total computer systems supplier. However, the emphasis on hardware and on specific solutions also built strengths. One benefit was the development within ERA of independent project teams capable of handling an entire equipment design from start to finish. Another was that under the ever watchful eye of USNCML, ERA soon developed into a disciplined, efficient supplier of reliable hardware.

At a time when electronic computers were being wired in place by their builders and nursed into operation in the laboratory, ERA machines were being built in modules, tested, dismantled, and moved to remote locations where they were maintained and operated by persons unknown. At a time when electronic computers exhibited mean free time to failure of minutes, ERA was delivering finished equipment with mean free time to failure of hours. ERA may have been hobbled by tight security, but the new company did have the advantage of working with a knowledgeable client who had resources. Under the auspices of the customer, ERA was made privy to much of the computer development work going on around the country and, indeed, the world. ERA designers were able to visit other laboratories and, as security permitted, to welcome visitors to ERA. They modified, adapted, improved, and then made use of whatever was available.

The first ERA tasks involved not only development of special digital machines, but also called for research and development on both data-handling and data-storage techniques. Out of one of these tasks came ERA's maiden paper at a national meeting. At the National Electronics Conference in November 1947, John Coombs described a magnetic storage technique developed for a specialized processor [7]. From another task came important results in addressable, selectively alterable drum storage at what were then high densities and high scanning rates [8]. These techniques paved the way for the drum storage used in ERA's first general-purpose computer. By the end of the first year, the tasks had begun to yield results, and ERA project teams were routinely being assigned development of large-scale calculating devices incorporating hundreds and even thousands of vacuum tubes.

One interesting task directed ERA to conduct an investigation into "the status of development of computing machine components." The finished report provided a useful technical picture of applicable components and techniques, plus a generous quantity of tutorial material by ERA staffers. Dr. Mina Rees, head of the Office of Naval Research Mathematical Sciences Division, suggested that the report be made available in book form. The resulting book* was the most comprehensive reference work of the period.

From a business point of view the two Navy contracts supported the company. Revenues for the fiscal year ending 31 October 1947, the first full year of operations, were $1.5 million, on which a profit of $34,000 was earned. However, with working capital of only $100,000 and a total debt of

---

* *High Speed Computing Devices*. McGraw-Hill, New York, 1950.

$330,000, ERA was seriously undercapitalized for its volume of business. Employment, which had been 145 at the start of the 1947 fiscal year, rose to 420 by the year end.

4. ATLAS

In August 1947, ERA was assigned Task 13. Under this task it was asked to start work on the paper design of a general-purpose computer. Arnold A. Cohen was placed in charge of the logical design. In March 1948, the Navy approved the proposed design, authorized construction of the machine, and assigned it the code name ATLAS after the mental giant in the comic strip Barnaby [2, p. 7]. The ATLAS project called for the development of a 24-bit parallel, magnetic drum store, selective sequence calculator. John L. Hill was appointed to head the engineering aspects of the project.

The assignment of Task 13 to ERA was paralleled by the customer's decision to build a small 6-bit relay model to prove the logic. This model, which used an ERA furnished magnetic drum, was itself useful for a number of years both before and after it surfaced as the unclassified ONR RELAY COMPUTER [9]. The original ATLAS was completed in the fall of 1950. It was moved to Washington in December 1950, installed in eight days, and operated immediately. The machine, which contained 2700 vacuum tubes and 2385 crystal diodes, was operated 24 hours per day with 10% of each day allotted to preventive maintenance. In its first 4500 hours ATLAS had unheard-of performance: unscheduled maintenance amounted to only 4% of the total "heater on" time [10].

With the success of ATLAS, ERA requested permission from the customer to offer the computer for sale. After lengthy consideration the Navy cleared a modified version. Based on a suggestion made by John L. Hill, the machine was named the 1101, which is the binary representation for 13. The 1100 series nomenclature thus started is still in use at UNIVAC today.

The unusual pioneering features of the 1101 are often overlooked. For example, the machine incorporated its own air-conditioning system, had a built-in system of marginal checking, and featured a central maintenance panel. The integral air-conditioning system not only provided the cooling but obviated costly building modifications; the marginal checking capability greatly increased the mean time to failure by isolating incipient faults during preventive maintenance periods; and the central maintenance panel greatly reduced mean time to repair by identifying and locating the area of malfunction.

The corporate characteristics alluded to earlier were also evident. The 1101 was announced in December 1951, without any supporting programs whatsoever and without input–output facilities other than a typewriter, a paper-tape reader, and a paper-tape punch. Indeed, at the time, programming activity did not exist at ERA, although project personnel had done some exploratory work on minimum latency coding [11]. ERA viewed itself as a hardware supplier, and regarded application as being the responsibility of the user.

From a business point of view, ERA's performance after the first year was erratic. The second year, fiscal 1948, had been strong. Revenues had more than doubled and earnings climbed 90%. But, under the frugal defense funding of the Truman administration before the Korean War, revenues and profits declined 20% in the third year. In its fourth fiscal year, just when the company was doing so well technically, revenues declined a further 25% and earnings barely exceeded those of the first year. Employment, which had risen to 652 in 1948, had dropped back to 528 by 1950.

Well before the 1101 announcement, ERA was becoming known in the infant computer industry. In 1949, ERA contracted to do a paper design for IBM on a punch card, magnetic drum computer system intended for business use. ERA's design was to be judged competitively with those of two internal IBM groups. Few, if any, of ERA's technical contributions seem to have found their way into what eventually became the IBM 650. However, two extensive patents came out of the effort, and these were assigned to IBM as sponsor of the project. In addition, a cross-licensing agreement between ERA and IBM gave IBM access to ERA's then-pending patents in magnetic drum storage.

Also in the early 1950s, ERA undertook a wide range of concurrent developments for various customers. These were precursors of today's large-scale data system now implemented in general-purpose computers with hierarchies of storage. One of these systems, sold to the John Plain Company of Chicago, was the first electronic inventory system for a merchandizing application [12]. Another was a system delivered to the Civil Aeronautics Administration in 1953, which accommodated 100 Teletype terminals in an experimental network for storing, searching, and processing aircraft flight plans [13]. A third example was the LOGISTICS COMPUTER delivered to ONR in 1953 [14].

In the same period, ERA built magnetic drum 1102 computers for on-line data reduction and open-loop control of experiments at USAF's huge Arnold Engineering Development Center in Tennessee. Another special order yielded the 1104, a programmable machine with both cathode-ray tube (CRT) and drum storage, delivered to Eglin AFB in 1964 for closedloop control in the BOMARC missile program. Still another development was the arithmetic and control unit for an early track-while-scan air defense system. Other noteworthy early efforts were the Athena ICBM guidance system, an early high-reliability transistorized computer system, and that durable workhorse, the Navy Tactical Data System, which reached new levels of ruggedness in engineering design and construction.

And, more important, early in 1950, several months before ATLAS was even delivered, ERA was authorized to begin work on its successor. This project was Task 29, code-named ATLAS II. Arnold Cohen was again in charge of the logical design and, under his supervision, ATLAS II emerged as a 36-bit machine with a unique two-address logic, electrostatic storage, larger drum memory, facilities for magnetic tape, punch card and paper-tape input–output, and a revised strengthened repertoire of instructions, including the REPEAT command. In sum, a much more powerful machine.

5. The Sale

In 1950, at the start of the Korean War, the first consolidation of the still-tiny computer industry took place. Eckert Mauchly Computer Corp., developers of UNIVAC, had gotten into financial difficulty and were absorbed by Remington Rand Inc. (RemRand). RemRand had already acquired some computer development capability when, in 1949, they successfully recruited a group of senior ERA people to join their Development Laboratories in Norwalk, Connecticut.

ERA's financial problems were by no means as serious as those of Eckert Mauchly, although ERA remained severely undercapitalized. ERA management had three practical alternatives: they could borrow more; sell more stock; or sell out. To someone with Parker's background the answer was evident, and the decision to sell out was only a question of time and price. From 1948 onward, he maintained contact with companies in the industry who might be potential purchasers. IBM, Raytheon, NCR, Honeywell, and Burroughs were among these. In the end, it was none of these contacts that matured. RemRand simply approached Parker through a mutual acquaintance in the investment banking business in the fall of 1951, and serious discussions began immediately. On 6 December 1951, Parker announced to a surprised group of ERA shareholder engineers that he had accepted an offer from RemRand for the purchase of the company. Actual closing of the transaction was delayed until the spring of 1952 by an inquiry by the Department of Justice and the Federal Trade Commission.

Parker recalls that the negotiation with James H. Rand, Jr., head of RemRand, was complicated by the lack of security clearance for any of the RemRand executives. This made it impossible to disclose to them the majority of ERA's computer projects beyond the 1101. The price paid was 73,000 common shares of RemRand worth about $1,700,000 on the New York Stock Exchange. The final valuation of the business was arrived at by multiplying $5000 by the 340 engineers employed; probably the only time since the Civil War that people have been "sold by the head" outside of the professional sports world. A multiple of 85 on their investment was realized by the original ERA investors in a little more than five years.

Late in 1951, IBM announced its Defense Calculator and by 1953 the machine, renamed the IBM 701, was in production. The initial delivery of the 701 took place in April 1953, and six months later, in October 1953, the initial delivery of ATLAS II was made to the government. About a year prior to delivery, in the fall of 1952, with the development of ATLAS II progressing well, ERA requested permission to announce an unclassified version. Approval was forthcoming, and in November 1952, a presentation was made to the top management of RemRand revealing the existence within their company of a machine called the ERA 1103. The astounded executives approved a program to produce two machines and to buy parts for two more. A modest marketing program was also approved.

The 1103 was an immediate success. In a few months the four machines were sold and more were released for production. Eventually, about 20 1103s were built. The success of the 1103 required ERA to face the problems of truly manufacturing a series of machines—something it had not done before. Questions arose regarding machine rental, field service, installation, programming, customer training, and support. In November 1954, in its by now characteristic manner, ERA silently delivered Task 32, a magnetic core memory version of ATLAS II, probably the first delivery of a commercial computer with magnetic core storage [2, p. 8].

6. The Merger

RemRand with its Norwalk, Eckert Mauchly, and ERA operations now had in its employ a significant fraction of the total experienced computer engineering man power in the U.S. But RemRand in 1952 was not a unified company; each of its three electronic units reported to different corporate departments, and no coordinating structure existed between these units.

In St. Paul, sound technological progress continued to be made. For example, transistors were not yet reliable, so in July 1954, ERA commenced work on a machine using only diodes and magnetic core logic. This project was given the code name BOGART after the city editor of the New York *Sun*, John B. Bogart [2, p. 17]. Several of these workhorse ultrareliable nonvacuum tube machines were delivered and they remained in service for years.

In Philadelphia, Eckert Mauchly was continuing its pioneering work on commercial systems. UNIVAC was now a household word, having been used to predict the outcome of the Presidential election of 1952. In the beginning of 1953, John Parker moved to New York to head a newly established Electronic Computer Sales Department. Under his leadership, RemRand placed computers ahead of IBM at such places as General Electric, U.S. Steel, Westinghouse, and Metropolitan Life. But it was a rental and service business; the more Parker succeeded, the more capital RemRand required.

By 1954, despite its head start, RemRand had started to lose ground. IBM announced its 702 and 705 against the UNIVAC I and its 704 against the 1103. RemRand countered belatedly with UNIVAC II and the 1103A. But by

1955, it was clear that RemRand had neither the management nor the fiscal resources to maintain a position of market leadership. James Rand recognized the implications of RemRand's position and, as had John Parker before him, sought a stronger partner. On 30 June 1955, Sperry Gyroscope Co. and Remington Rand Inc., merged to form the Sperry Rand Corporation.

Almost immediately Sperry assigned one of its senior executives to study its newly acquired electronic computer activities. By the fall of 1955, he had recommended that Eckert Mauchly, the Norwalk Laboratories, Engineering Research Associates, the RemRand tabulating machine business, and the Electronic Computer Sales Department be unified into a single electronic-computer division. A few weeks later, on 1 October 1955, William C. Norris, head of ERA in St. Paul, was appointed as the first general manager of a new consolidated UNIVAC Division.

The unification brought together in one business entity the ingredients of engineering, manufacturing, marketing, and finance and started UNIVAC toward its present-day success as a giant business. This success came only after a difficult, sometimes traumatic, period of integration. During the integration period, in a process now recognized as quite normal for dynamic industries, a number of splinter groups left to form their own companies and some of these, in turn, spawned splinter companies. One of UNIVAC's offshoots, Control Data Corporation, is today almost as large as its progenitor.

In retrospect, it is clear that were it not for the stimulus of the Naval cryptographic community, which encouraged two groups of entrepreneurs to form ERA, the nature of that collection of activities we today call the computer industry would be vastly different and almost certainly be less richly varied, diverse, and vigorous.

ACKNOWLEDGMENTS

The author wishes to thank the many ERA pioneers who generously provided the information used in preparing this paper. In particular, the extensive collaboration of Dr. Arnold A. Cohen is most gratefully acknowledged.

REFERENCES

1. B. Randell, COLOSSUS: Godfather of the computer, *New Scientist* (10 February 1977), p. 346.
2. S. S. Snyder, Influence of U.S. Cryptologic Organizations on the Digital Computer Industry, p. 4. National Security Agency (May 1977).
3. K. Draheim, R. P. Howell, and A Shapero, The Development of a Potential Defense R&D Complex (Minneapolis-St. Paul), p. 128. Stanford Research Institute, Palo Alto, California (July 1966).
4. J. Delmont, ERA: Control Data's Forerunner in a Gloomy Glider Factory, *Contact* 3–6 (July 1976).

5. Interview with John E. Parker, Washington, D.C. (26 June 1975).

6. H. D. Huskey, The development of automatic computing, *Proc. U.S.-Japan Comput. Conf., 1st. Tokyo, 1972,* p. 702.

7. J. M. Coombs, Storage of numbers on magnetic tape, *Proc. Nat. Electron. Conf. Chicago, Illinois* **3,** 201–209 (1947).

8. A. A. Cohen and W. R. Keye, Selective alteration of digital data in a magnetic drum computer memory, Abstract of paper presented at IRE National Convention, *Proc. IRE* **36,** 379 (1948).

9. J. J. Wolf, The Office of Naval Research relay computer, *Math. Tables Other Aids Computat., VI* **40** 207–212 (1952).

10. F. C. Mullaney, Design features of the ERA 1101 computer, *Proc. Joint AIEE-IRE Comput. Conf.,* pp. 43–49 (December 10–12, 1951).

11. D. P. Perry, *Math. Tables Other Aids Computat., VI* **39,** 172–182 (1952).

12. W. D. Bell, "A Management Guide to Electronic Computers," pp. 248–258. McGraw-Hill, New York, 1951.

13. A. P. Hendrickson, G. I. Williams, and J. L. Hill, Message storage and processing with a magnetic drum system, *Proc. Eastern Joint Comput. Conf.,* pp. 74–78 (December 1954).

14. R. S. Erickson, The logistics computer, *Proc. IRE* **41,** 1325–1332 (1953).

DATAPRODUCTS CORPORATION
LOS ANGELES, CALIFORNIA

Early Programming Developments in Cambridge

M. V. WILKES

Work started on the EDSAC project in October 1946 shortly after I had returned from attending the latter part of the Summer School held at the Moore School of Electrical Engineering at the University of Pennsylvania. In one of his lectures to that course—delivered in fact before I arrived—Eckert had remarked that the ENIAC was designed in a considerable hurry. The same was true of the EDSAC. No attempt was made to realize the full potential of the technology of the day, particularly in regard to the speed of operation. We did, however, attempt to produce a complete machine, which, while not having any luxuries, would be convenient and easy to use. This, of course, involved gazing into a crystal ball since no one anywhere had, at the time, experience of running programs on a stored-program computer. The building of the hardware was regarded as the first phase of the project; the second was the investigation of programming methods and the solution of practical problems. I have written elsewhere about the period during which the hardware was being put together. In this paper I should like to describe the programming methodology that we developed.

When it first worked on 6 May 1949, the EDSAC was a complete machine with paper tape for input and a teleprinter for output. It had a full repertoire of instructions. We had worked single-mindedly for this day and had made no attempt to give demonstrations with a machine that lacked any of the above features.

At an early stage in the EDSAC project, I gave much thought to the design of the input system and to the way in which the initial loading of a

497

program into an empty machine could be accomplished. I decided to make the basic input operation that of reading a single row of five-hole punched paper tape and placing its binary equivalent directly into the store. A special code in which the digits 0 to 9 were represented on the tape by their binary equivalents was used with a view to simplifying the conversion of numbers from decimal to binary form. In order to avoid the inelegance of having to attach a meaning to a row of blank tape, the most-significant digit was reversed by the input hardware. With an input instruction as simple as that described above, it was necessary that there should be a program in memory before a program tape could be read. A read-only memory, to use a modern term, was therefore provided, and this contained a sequence of *initial orders* that were transferred to the EDSAC memory when the starting button was pressed. The read-only memory consisted of a bank of stepping telephone switches (uniselectors). The initial orders were designed to read a program tape and they therefore defined the form in which orders were punched in exactly the same way as is done by a modern assembly routine. The read-only memory could accommodate about 40 orders so that there was some scope for sophistication in the form that orders were punched, and this was made full use of by David J. Wheeler, who had joined the Laboratory as a graduate student in September 1948 and had made this department of the project his special concern.

The first set of initial orders designed by Wheeler were wired into the read-only memory in the early part of 1949 and were used during the final commissioning of the machine and the early months of its operation [1]. These initial orders required that orders should be punched in the following form. The first character (punched as a letter) constituted the operation code; the next digits represented the address in decimal form. The latter were punched without leading (nonsignificant) zeros and were terminated by S or L according to whether a short or a long word was referred to.

Wheeler perceived that additional facilities were required to enable independently punched sequences of numbers and instructions to be combined together to form a complete program. At first these facilities were provided by a sequence of *coordinating orders* that could be punched at the beginning of a program tape and read in by the initial orders. The reading of the remainder of the tape would then be done under the control of the coordinating orders. This was rather a clumsy arrangement and Wheeler saw that by exercising his not inconsiderable ingenuity he could compress the functions of the initial orders and coordinating orders into a new sequence of initial orders that would just go into the space available in the read-only memory. The new initial orders were wired into the read-only memory in September 1949. They were capable of modifying addresses as punched by adding a base address to them before they were put into the memory. It was then possible to have in a single program a number of sequences of orders or numbers, as the case might be, each numbered from 0 upward, the necessary relocation being performed by the initial orders. For this purpose each address was terminated on the tape by a code letter. Fifteen distinct code letters were available, and each corresponded to a certain location in memory. When the code letter was read the number in this location was added to the address. The locations corresponding to code letters could be loaded during the reading of the tape by making use of *control combinations,* which were groups of characters punched on the tape and which acted in effect as directives to the initial orders. One of the code letters was reserved for relative addressing within a subroutine, and a special control combination punched at the beginning of the subroutine loaded the corresponding location with the address into which the first order of the subroutine was to go. Thus, by an early date, we had in use a system of some sophistication for the reading of orders from the input tape and converting them to binary notation. In Cambridge we did not pass through the stage of punching our orders in octal or hexadecimal form.

Von Neumann, Goldstine, and Burks had addressed themselves to the same set of problems and arrived at equivalent but somewhat different solutions. I did not have the advantage of seeing their report until I visited Princeton during my next visit to the United States, in 1950.

From the very first, I had seen the establishment of a library of subroutines as being of prime importance. Not only would the availability of such a library to draw on save the programmer effort, but library subroutines could, in conjunction with the initial orders, enable the programmer to work at a level above that of a raw binary computer. The importance of a library of tested subroutines took on a new aspect once practical experience had begun to show how difficult it was to write correct programs. Finally, there was the invention by David J. Wheeler of the closed subroutine, which made possible the development of a coherent system of programming based on nested subroutines.

The initial orders were capable of reading subroutines, doing the necessary relocation, and putting them one after another in the memory. This made it possible to store the library subroutines in ready punched form and to copy them mechanically on to the program tape. The initial orders were not, however, capable of inserting the correct addresses into the subroutine calls so as to link the components of the program together. This function was performed by a short library subroutine, written by me, that acted in conjunction with the initial orders and was known as an *assembly subroutine.* Unlike the great majority of subroutines in the EDSAC library it was an open subroutine.

Closed subroutines could have parameters of two kinds, *preset* parameters and *program* parameters. The values of preset parameters were punched on the program tape and incorporated into the subroutine by the initial orders when the subroutine was read. They enabled subroutines to be made more general in purpose and hence reduced the number that needed to be kept in the library, and they also provided a means for passing to a subroutine such information as the position of any auxiliary subroutine that it needed. Program parameters were used for information that might be different on different occasions when the subroutine was called in, and were written immediately after the two orders that constituted the basic subroutine call.

In the summer of 1950, we began to put together a comprehensive report on the programming methods that we had developed. This was in draft by the time I left early in July for my second visit to the United States. The report, in its final form, bore the date September 1950, and it was circulated widely among the small computing community of those days. Through the interest of Professor Z. Kopal, the report in an updated form, but with no major changes, was published in 1951 under the joint authorship of myself, Wheeler, and Gill [2]. This was, I believe, the first book on programming ever to be published. It bore the title, "The Preparation of Programs for an Electronic Digital Computer" and the subtitle "With Special Reference to the EDSAC and the Use of a Library of Subroutines." In addition to a description of the EDSAC from the point of view of the programmer and an account of the programming methods advocated, this book contained the specifications of all the subroutines currently in the EDSAC library (amounting to nearly 90 in all) together with complete coding for half of them.

The book also contained a number of examples of complete programs. Among these was a program for tabulating the integral

$$\text{Ch}(x, \chi) = x \sin \chi \int_0^x \exp(x - x \sin \chi / \sin \lambda) \csc^2 \lambda \, d\lambda.$$

for a series of values of x and χ. This program made use of five closed subroutines from the library, one for integration (using Simpson's rule), one for computing exponentials, one for computing sines, one for printing results in decimal form, and one for dividing, the EDSAC having no hardware divider. In addition, there was a decimal input routine for reading in constants; this was overwritten as soon as it had done its work. Specially written for the problem were a main program or *master routine* and an auxiliary subroutine used by the integration subroutine for computing the integrand. It was remarked that the total number of orders was 300, of which only 98 needed to be specially written. It will be observed that in respect of the use of nested subroutine calls—in this case to a depth of three—the methods then in use clearly foreshadowed one of the modern tenets of structured programming, except that people now usually talk of procedure calls rather than subroutine calls. Of course, everything was done in machine language since high-level languages had not then been thought of. In one further respect, namely, the avoidance of global jumps, the example followed good modern practice. The integrand fell away exponentially and the integration was terminated when the integrand became negligible. This condition was detected in the auxiliary subroutine and the temptation to use a global jump back to the main program was resisted; instead an orderly return was organized via the integration subroutine. At the time I felt somewhat shy about this feature of the program since I felt that I might be accused of undue purism, but now I can look back on it with pride.

The example just described was not made up specially for the purpose. The integral occurs in Chapman's theory of the ionization of a spherical atmosphere by the sun, and I first encountered it in about 1937. I formed a desire then to tabulate it, but with no premonition of the fact that there would be things called electronic computers and that I should be involved with them. A little time after the book was published, I did complete and publish a table [3]. I also published separately an account of the method I used for automatic control of the interval of integration, a feature that I quickly found to be essential [4].

A program structured with the aid of closed subroutine calls is much easier to find one's way about than one in which much use is made of jumps from one block of code to another. A consequence of this is that we found that we did not need to draw elaborate flow diagrams in order to understand and explain our programs. In fact, there is not a single flow diagram to be found in our book. There was a sharp contrast between our practice in this respect and that of other groups who did not base their programming so strongly on the use of closed subroutines.

Editor's Note: The lecture at the Los Alamos conference ended with the showing of a short film featuring the EDSAC that had originally been shown at the first Joint Computer Conference held in Philadelphia in 1951. A brief description of the film and some stills will be found in Wilkes [5]. Information about the EDSAC itself will be found in Wilkes and Renwick [6] and Wilkes [7].

REFERENCES

1. D. J. Wheeler, Programme organisation and initial orders for the EDSAC, *Proc. Roy. Soc. London Ser. A* **202**, 573 (1950).
2. M. V. Wilkes, D. J. Wheeler, and S. Gill, "The Preparation of Programs for an Electronic Digital Computer." Addison-Wesley, Cambridge, Massachusetts, 1951.
3. M. V. Wilkes, A table of Chapman's grazing incidence integral $Ch(x,\chi)$, *Proc. Phys. Soc. B.* **67**, 304 (1954).
4. M. V. Wilkes, A note on the use of automatic adjustment of strip width in quadrature, from report of a Conference on Electronic Digital Computers and Information Processing, Darmstadt, 25–27 October, 1955. *Nachrichtentechnische Faberichte* **4**, 182 (1956).
5. M. V. Wilkes, Early computer developments at Cambridge: The EDSAC, *Radio Electron. Eng.* **45**, 332 (1975).
6. M. V. Wilkes and W. Renwick, The EDSAC (Electronic Delay Storage Automatic Calculator), *Math. Tables Other Aids Comput.* **4**, 61 (1950).
7. M. V. Wilkes, "Automatic Digital Computers." Methuen, London and Wiley, New York, 1956.

COMPUTER LABORATORY
UNIVERSITY OF CAMBRIDGE
CAMBRIDGE, ENGLAND

Part V

The Places

Between Zuse and Rutishauser—The Early Development of Digital Computing in Central Europe

FRIEDRICH L. BAUER

Historical Background

In April 1945, a truck left Göttingen, heading for Bavaria. It carried an instrument that had been built in Berlin during the war for the Aerodynamische Versuchsanstalt (Aerodynamic Research Institution) and had been brought to their Göttingen laboratory a few weeks before. Here it had been put into operation for the first time. But then, the Russian army approached Göttingen. The instrument had the code word V4 (Versuchsmodell 4) and because of the parallel with V1 and V2, the code words for buzz bombs, the man who had built the instrument got permission to bring it "in Sicherheit." The adventurous journey via Hof, München, and Ettal ended at the village of Hinterstein near Hindelang, a small town in the Bavarian Alps, in a province called Allgäu, near the Austrian border. A few days later, North African troops of the French army occupied Hinterstein. They found may things, but not the instrument that was hidden in a cellar. Later, American troops moved in, and two British officers of the Secret Service investigated the instrument with the devilish code name, but found it harmless and drove off, apparently disappointed.

In the winter of 1944–1945, a Swiss soldier was on duty in the Rätikon

505

and Silvretta mountains, at the border to Austria, some 50 miles away from Hinterstein—in fact, Austria has just a width of 50 miles there. Later, he would use the instrument the fugitive from Prussia had built.

This fugitive was Konrad Zuse, born in 1910 in Berlin, raised in Braunsberg, East Prussia. There he had visited the Humanistisches Gymnasium, which was the place where Weierstrass, some decades before, had earned his living. He had studied civil engineering at the Technische Hochschule Berlin–Charlottenburg and had started in 1934 to build a computer that could ease the calculations of statics. V4 was his fourth model; V3, which was destroyed in 1944 in a bomb attack, was the first fully programmable computer when it became operational in 1941. Konrad Zuse is now Doctor Honoris Causa of the Technical University of Berlin and Honorary Professor of the Göttingen University. He was given the 1965 Harry Goode Memorial Award (together with G. R. Stibitz).

The soldier in the Swiss Army was Heinz Rutishauser, born in 1918, who had lost his parents at the age of 16. He had studied mathematics at the ETH (Swiss Federal Polytechnic Institute) and had obtained his doctor's degree. Five years later, Zuse's V4–now called Z4–was working in the Institute for Applied Mathematics of the ETH headed by Professor Stiefel and was programmed by Rutishauser. In 1951, Rutishauser wrote the famous paper "Automatische Rechenplanfertigung," marking the start of compiler construction and of programming languages. Rutishauser in 1958 was one of the founders of ALGOL. Since 1955 he was Professor at the ETH. He died in 1970 of a heart attack.

Zuse and Rutishauser are pivotal points in the early development of computing in Central Europe. The political and economic situation in that region, due to the effects of World War II, was disastrous. Quite naturally, people who wanted to become "in" in computing looked to the United States and/or to England, where immediately after the war great efforts had been started. Rutishauser was sent to Princeton in 1948–1949. So were R. Lüst, A. Schlüter, and E. Trefftz from the Göttingen computer development group. R. Piloty from the Munich group had got experience from MIT; his father, H. Piloty, had visited the U.S. in 1950. A. Walther, from the Darmstadt group, had contact with Aiken.

K. Zuse, however, had been functionally ahead of the Anglo-Saxon achievements until 1944 in a number of aspects—binary coding, floating-point arithmetic, instruction set, input–output conversion. Later, the Princeton design became a landmark. But in 1951 already, Rutishauser took the lead for several years with respect to compilers and algorithmic languages. And in 1945, Zuse designed the Plankalkül. Before discussing this achievement, which I consider to rank with the engineering efforts of Zuse, we have to see how functionalism, formalization, and abstraction has accompanied Zuse's machine design.

Junge Menschen sind zum Glück unbefangen genug, um sich erst einmal mit den verschiedensten Fragen zu beschäftigen and erst dann die ganze Arbeitskraft auf ein bestimmtes Problem zu konzentrieren.

K. Zuse [1]

1. Engineering and Logic

To start with, I should confess that I was always amused by the reason Zuse gives for approaching the computer, after juvenile inventor dreams of city planning, photography, moon rockets (the movie "Frau im Mond" by Fritz Lang appeared in 1929), and calculating vending machines: He was appalled by the mental labor connected with the statics calculations he had to practice.

Starting from existing paper forms, he tried in 1932 to mechanize (verbally) the control flow in a calculation, using a device that could move horizontally and vertically, pick up numbers punched into the form, perform the arithmetical operations, and punch the result. Thus, when he writes [1, p. 38] that his basic idea was to generalize the control in a way that a universal form could be treated, he had a very general idea of a program [German *Rechenplan*] mirroring a formula in a way that shows even the aspects that became interesting only more recently: collateralism of the operands of arithmetic operations and parallel computation. In fact, nothing in Zuse's scheme implies that the work has to be done strictly serially. (It is interesting to note that parallel performance comes up again in 1950 in Angstl's formula-controlled logical computer; see below.) Thus, between 1932 and 1934, Zuse arrived at a point beyond which Babbage had left the scene: the paper form replaced by a (two-dimensional!) array of fields capable of storing numbers —a storage [*Speicherwerk*], a selection mechanism [*Wählwerk*] that connects storage locations with the arithmetic unit [*Rechenwerk*], and a control unit [*Planwerk*], controlled by punch tape, which commands both the selection mechanism (giving addresses) and the arithmetic unit (giving instructions). To increase the storage capacity, several layers of this two-dimensional storage can be used.

We know what came out from this imagination: Work on a mechanical store (Figs. 1–3) was begun in 1936—a patent was filed and granted, DRP No. 907 948, 924 107–when to the dismay of his parents Zuse left his position with Henschel Fluzeugwerke. This mechanical solution was still used in the Z4 and it worked reliably. I saw it working in 1951, at the ETH in Zürich, and, being more electrically minded than mechanically, could not believe it. Compared to a relay solution, there was considerable gain in the volume needed: a store with 1000 cells needed less than a cubic meter. A corresponding relay solution with 40,000 relays would have needed a hall.

Figure 1   The Z1 in Zuse's parents' living room.

Figure 2   Mechanical storage (from Zuse [1]).

Figure 3 Mechanical storage (from Zuse [3]).

Going on, Zuse also developed mechanical logical circuits (Fig. 4) and only later replaced them by relays. This gave him the idea of developing an abstract notation that could be used equally well for mechanical and for relay solutions.

It goes almost without saying that Zuse had used binary representation from the very beginning. The first sketch of 1932 used holes punched in paper, and later pins that could be locked. This binary principle was, because of its reliability, especially important for mechanical solutions. Of course, Zuse had the usual direct binary coding of numbers which Leibniz had used, in mind. He saw, however, the need to express also scale factors, and introduced what he called semilogarithmic form (the scale factor corresponding to the "integer part" of a logarithm), a floating-point representation. Operations with the 7-bit exponent and the 16-bit mantissa were performed separately.

Figure 5 shows a diagram containing the arithmetic unit of Z1 and Z3; the left part deals with the exponent.

The next step of abstraction came when Zuse had to discriminate arithmetic operations. He developed a notation for dealing with propositions. He used

(A, B) for disjunction (logical "or"),
$[A, B]$ for conjunction (logical "and"),

Figure 4 Mechanical construction of the Z1 (from Zuse [3]).

and

$$- A \qquad \text{for negation,}$$

and he wrote

$$[(Lm, Ld), ([Vx, Vy], [-Vx, -Vy]) \Rightarrow Vr$$

to determine the sign of the result ("is positive" being true or false) depending on the signs of the operands (Vx, Vy) and on the choice of multiplication (Lm) and division (Ld). With the help of corresponding circuit elements in relay or in abstract form the circuit is generated from the description. Here are the first roots of manipulating the description in a *Kalkül*, the roots of the *Plankalkül*.

This was in 1937. In his diary, Zuse wrote on 19 June 1937 [1, p. 68] (Fig. 6),

Erkenntnis, daß es Elementaroperationen gibt, in die sich sämtliche Rechen— und Denkoperationen auflösen lassen. . . . Mit dieser Form des Hirns muß es theoretisch möglich sein, sämtliche Denkaufgaben zu lösen, die von Mechanismen erfaßbar sind,* jedoch ohne Rücksicht auf die dazu erforderliche Zeit. . . . Schnellere Erledigung von Vorgängen, z. B. 1. parallele Ausführung von Elementaroperationen, 2.

---

* Note the mentioning of a "thinking machine" defined in a correct way!

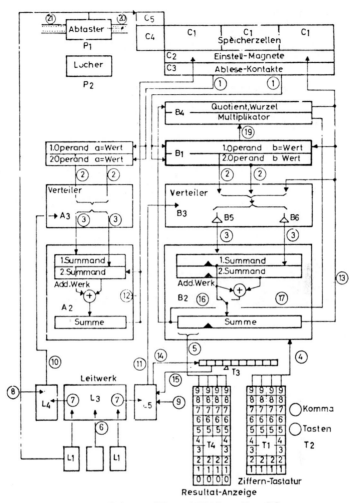

Figure 5 Scheme of Z1 and Z3 (from Zuse [1]).

gleichzeitige Bestimmung langer Bedingungsketten. . . . Die Operationen folgen einem Plan, ähnlich einem Rechenplan . . .

and on 20 June 1937,

Die Elementaroperation heißt: Vergleich zweier Sekundalziffern auf Gleichheit. Resultat ist zweifach variabel, also ebenfalls eine Sekundalziffer.

Zuse produced a short paper on his *Bedingungskombinatorik* (combinatorics of conditions), with the title, hommage à Leibniz, Allgemeine Dyadik. This had the effect that his former mathematics teacher advised him to read first the books of Hilbert and Ackermann, Hilbert and Bernays, Frege, and

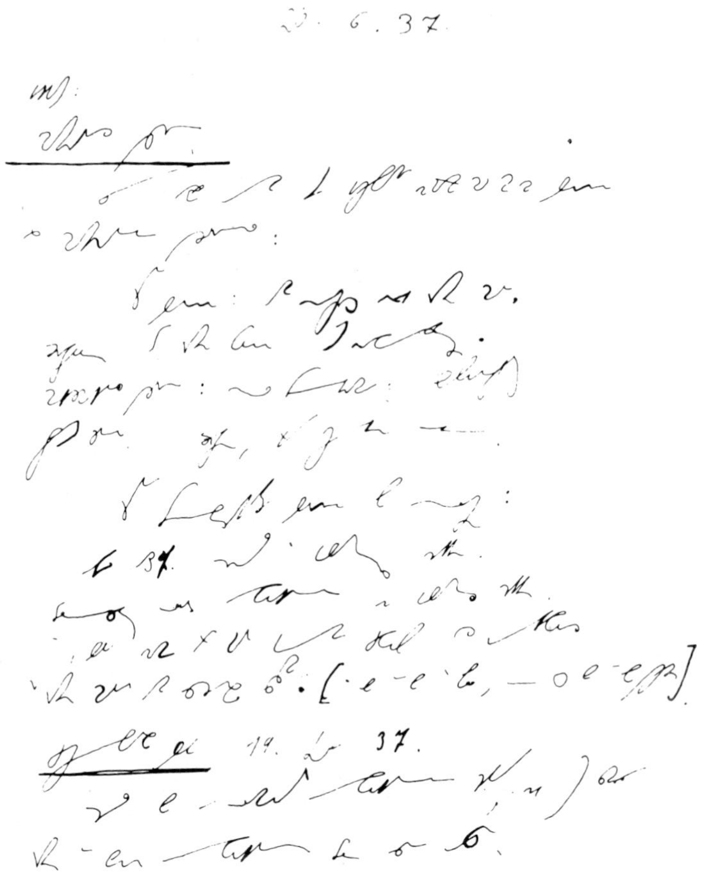

Figure 6 Zuse's diary from June 19, 1937 (from Zuse [1]).

Schröder. Zuse discovered in the propositional calculus, apart from the notation, things he was well familiar with, and others he had not seen before, like de Morgan's law. (He was also not aware of the related work of Piesch [2].) The propositional calculus was, like his own abstract notation, neutral with respect to relay or mechanical realization.

Zuse continued for a while to use mechanical circuits. But levers and bars complicated the constructions.

Oft mußte ich vierzehn Tage lang die Teile auseinandernehmen und wieder zusammensetzen, um nur einen einzigen Fehler zu beseitigen. Dadurch verlor ich viel Zeit [1, p. 70].

2. Wartime Work

Z1, the mechanical construction, approached its final stage in 1938. Work on a relay version Z2 had started in 1937. And, thanks to the abstract description, the same general design could be used for an electronic version. Together with Dr. Schreyer, first studies with electronic circuits, using vacuum tubes and gas diodes, began in 1937; a demonstration model* was shown in 1938 at the Technical University, Berlin, where Schreyer in 1941 got his Ph.D.† The prospect of needing some thousand tubes for a complete computer killed further such attempts in prewar Germany, although Zuse and Schreyer had seen that enormous speed could be obtained. In 1939, the relay version Z2, working with the mechanical store of Z1, was almost finished when Zuse was drafted into the Army. He came back to Henschel Flugzeugwerke in 1940 and could, over the weekends, finish Z2. A demonstration for the Deutsche Versuchsanstalt für Luftfahrt (DVL) was successful, although technical malfunctions of the relays made Z2 unusable for practical purposes. But DVL was interested, and Zuse could continue work on the Z3, which was completed in 1941—the first programmed computer in full operation. It used binary, floating-point numbers, a word length of 22 bits, a storage for 64 numbers, was controlled by eight-channel tape (with 8-bit-instructions), and had input and output conversion to floating-point decimal numbers. It needed 3 sec for a multiplication, division, or taking the square root. It had 2000 relays and a central pulse clock. It was destroyed in 1944 by bombs, together with Z1 and Z2.‡ In 1941, Zuse had submitted the patent application Z391 comprising the full Z3 design. In 1967, the German Federal Patent Court gained ridiculous immortality when finally rejecting the application on grounds of "Lacking height of invention." Work on the Z4 started in 1942, and this computer evaded disaster; it is the one we find later in Zurich. Its storage was again mechanical; its (32-bit) arithmetic and control unit with relays was more sophisticated than the ones of Z3. It still could not alter its program. I shall come back to this question of the "missing wire."

I shall be brief on the engineering side of Zuse's work, but his relay solution for a one-step addition should be mentioned. For the functional aspects we have seen the roots in the "Bedingungskombinatorik." In 1939–1940, during the half-year Zuse was in the Army, he had time for contemplation. Calculation, he found, was not to be done with numbers only; it could be done—see the diary notices from 1937—with logical values, with anything given (*Angaben*, data). Chess, for example—a good example with its net of conditions and cases. Could one day a computer win against a champion? Zuse used the word "Angewandte Logistik" (applied logic) for what was exaggeratingly called "artificial intelligence" later. In 1943, he drafted and built a pilot model of a universal machine based on logical operations§ which was planned to be implemented later electronically; the gain in speed would

---

* Later, a 10-bit parallel adder, using about 100 tubes, was built [1, p. 91; 3, p. 517].
† See also Deutsche Patentanmeldung Sch. 1704. 19 November 1940.
‡ A replica of Z3 has been built for the Deutsches Museum.
§ See Deutsche Patentanmeldung Z 394, 11 October 1944.

compensate for the detail necessary when performing, for example, arithmetic. From a remark made in [4], we can infer that in such a way he hoped to achieve a "Planfertigungsgerät," a compiling device for the Plankalkül. This device should not only produce a program from formula input, but also from problem descriptions like the one of Fig. 7, given in the form of pair lists.

Zuse's partner in the theoretical discussions was Lohmeyer, a student of Heinrich Scholz in Münster. Scholz encouraged Zuse to continue in his efforts. At that time, Zuse worked on a dissertation he wanted to submit at Darmstadt with the help of Alwin Walther; the working title was Ansätze einer Theorie des allgemeinen Rechnens unter besonderer Berücksichtigung des Aussagenkalküls und dessen Anwendung auf Relaisschaltungen [5]. Moreover, first notes were written on which the Plankalkül later was based. Walther, by the way, worked on the coupling and controlling (by tape) of business calculating machines. In the cryptography field, similar attempts were made and special devices, partly analog, partly digital in character, were built. This had no impact on the further development in that geographic area.

The Plankalkül was designed and described while Zuse was, after the war, immobilized in the little village of Hinterstein and later in Hopferau, near the Bavarian Alps. The manuscript, as it was published later [5], was more or less completed in 1946. Zuse, step by step, built up a small company and moved it to Neukirchen, Kreis Hünfeld, in Hessia, near the border of the Soviet occupation zone. The Z4 was renovated, supplemented (among other things, conditional instructions were added), and brought to Zürich. It worked there from 1950 to 1955, and was then moved to the Laboratoire de Recherche, St. Louis, near Basel, a French Aerodynamic Research Institution, where it was in operation until 1960.

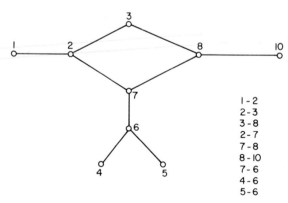

Figure 7   Relational description of a problem in electrical networks, pair list of conducting connection (is 1 connected with 10?).

3. The Plankalkül

It is impossible to give here a comprehensive description of the Plankalkül. Fortunately, an English translation has appeared [4] and can be made available.* There is also a discussion of its features in Bauer and Wössner [6].

In short, the Plankalkül is a highly developed programming language. It allows one to build and describe procedures as well as structured objects. It allows conditional statements and repetitive statements; it has variables and an assignment; it allows one to build compound statements. It allows subscripts. It has parameter mechanisms (input parameter, result parameter) for procedures. It surpasses present-day programming languages by providing operators like the μ operator with the meaning: "The next component . . . for which a certain condition holds," for example,

$$\mu x \ [x \in \underset{0}{V} \ \& \ x = \underset{1}{V}].$$

Among the features most recent programming languages have, only references and pointers are missing; also recursion is lacking.

In order to demonstrate that the Plankalkül was not restricted to numerical processes, Zuse treated two examples at some length that were of "combinatoric nature": checking well-formedness of Boolean expressions and checking chess moves. By and by, Zuse became known among certain circles. In the academic year 1947–1948, Professor Britzelmayr from the University of Munich invited him to speak in his colloquium on formal logic. At this occasion, I heard for the first time about the Plankalkül. I had difficulties in understanding Zuse, and a further complication was caused by the fact that Zuse presented the program for syntax checking of a Boolean expression as a Plankalkül example. The interest of my teacher Britzelmayr was much more centered on this problem than on the Plankalkül as such, and so I was further confused. Moreover, Zuse refused to let any written documents out of his hands. In connection with Britzelmayr, I have to mention another curious event. One of Britzelmayr's students, H. Angstl, devised a mechanical instrument [7] for testing well-formedness of Boolean expressions in parenthesis-free form and even for performing the operations. When Britzelmayr showed me the proposal in the fall of 1950, I saw, with my preference for electrical solutions, that a relay realization would be more appropriate. At the turn of the year 1950–1951, the design was made and later, indeed, a model called STANISLAUS was built with the help of friends[8]. The wiring diagram was set up in such a way that intermediate values were

---

* The Plankalkül. BMFT-GMD 106, 1976 [4]. (Write to: GMD, Abt. Informationswesen, D-5205, St. Augustin 1, Germany.)

pushed down, as we said, into a "cellar." This we will find later in our sequential method for formula translation.

In September 1948, Zuse gave a lecture on the Plankalkül at the Gesellschaft für Angewandte Mathematik (GAMM) meeting in Göttingen; there is an abstract in *Z. Angew. Math. Mech.* [9]. Another short paper was published in *Arch. Math.*, received 6 December 1948 [10]. Zuse says, "die Sache verpuffte jedoch völlig." The Plankalkül was much ahead of its time. But this does not mean that his ideas had no effect. Of course, for the engineer starting in 1949 in Central Europe to build the computer, there had been other problems. But only a few years later, problems of programming were becoming very demanding. In 1952, at several places, including Zurich and Munich, people learned of the Plankalkül. Rutishauser certainly knew about it. He even used the typical Zuse terminology, "Rechenplan" (his paper on "Automatische Rechenplanfertigung"), "Superplan," etc.

4. The "Superplan" for "Formula Translation"

Zuse writes in 1962 [3, p. 520] that he wanted to describe with the help of the Plankalkül devices, which could produce programs (Programmator, [11]). Rutishauser himself has mentioned to me that Zuse had "such dreams," and refers to their possibilities in [12]. Thus, the idea of automatic programming was not invented by Rutishauser. He had, however, the idea that the same computer for which the program is intended could also produce it. He also saw that a little bit had to be done beyond the von Neumann machine in order to simplify this. The ERMETH was designed accordingly. Most important, however, Rutishauser first gave a method for doing it. He presented his ideas at the GAMM meeting in Freiburg, 28–31 March 1951. There is an abstract in *Z. Angew. Math. Mech.* [13]; the paper was published later [12].

Rutishauser could have complained, too, about his efforts being "verpufft." When FORTRAN was started a few years later, people on the other side of the ocean had also not heard of Rutishauser—nor did they know about Böhm, who already in 1952 had presented a sequential method for a restricted class of formulas [14]. Rutishauser gives [12] a description of the principles of the design of the ERMETH.

In Germany, at four places work had started, too, to build electronic computers. These were universities and research institutions. Ahead in time was the Max Planck Institut in Göttingen, directed by Biermann.

There, a magnetic drum store was designed in 1947 by Billing independently of the developments that were carried on at the same time by Booth in England. Billing saw the advantage of combining storage on a drum with serial performance of addition, and built the small serial computer G1 with 470 tubes (finished in 1952) and the larger G2 (finished in 1954). In 1948, Alwin Walther started work, together with Dreyer, on designing a serial computer.

In 1950, N. J. Lehmann at Dresden also started to build a magnetic drum calculator D1 (finished in 1956); and Piloty and Sauer, at Munich, begin with the design of hardware and software of a large parallel computer, the PERM (finished in 1955) (Fig. 8). The PERM had built-in floating-point arithmetic, including a variant for significance arithmetic. Its instructions were composed from up to four (later five) microinstructions. The Swiss ERMETH, started in 1951 under the technical direction of Ambros Speiser, was finished in 1956.

Zuse, who had built first the Z5, a relay computer, started in 1955 with the design of an electronic computer.* It was based on the plans of Th. Fromme's MINIMA. Zuse says that they discussed frequently the question of "the smallest electronic computer" and it was clear that neither a Turing machine nor his "logic machine" would be an economical solution. Fromme had been influenced by van der Poel's ideas [15] (Fig. 9). In the line of the EDSAC philosophy he used an "analytischen Code" (functional bit coding) for the instructions: each bit of the code was directly responsible for a gate opening or closing a connection between parts of the computer. Like the PERM, very flexible programming was possible. The MAILÜFTERL, which Zemanek built in Vienna in 1956–1959, had similar features. The Z22, however, turned out to be a bit larger than minimal; an interesting feature had been added by Güntsch, a "repetitive bit." The ERMETH, by the way, had intriguing features, too: all numbers could be tagged ("Q-Zeichen") and

* In 1955, the ban imposed by the Allies, preventing in Germany among the industrial design of certain electronic devices was lifted. Siemens and Standard Electric started work in 1955, too.

Figure 8 PERM (Munich).

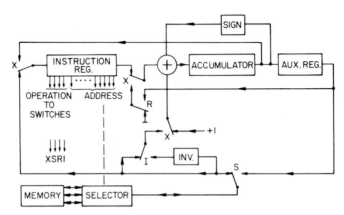

Figure 9   Van der Poel's minimal machine.

there were conditional jumps triggered by the Q. Moreover, there was an extraordinary number ∞ available in floating point computation; this also goes back to Zuse.

It has been stated somewhere that Zuse's machines up to the Z4 (before the supplements for the ETH were made) could not alter their programs and thus he had the first program-controlled modern computer, but not the first stored-program computer.

Zuse has remarked on this [1, p. 99]:

> Since programs are like numbers built from bit sequences, it was obviously to store programs, too. Then one can perform conditional jumps and can calculate addresses. . . . [The] feedback from the result of the calculation to the program flow can be established symbolically by a single wire. I hesitated to do this step.

Zuse saw that this would open Pandora's box. Indeed, the development of programming up to the 1960s made very free use of the possibilities of unrestricted feedback; only later was it observed that this free style of programming was necessarily hazardous and unsafe.

Zuse's approach might have been a shorter way to the modern methodology of programming. The actual development, however, was geared to the stored-program approach, with Rutishauser seeing first that programming programs were possible—an idea coming up independently in the Russian school [16].

5.   Formula Translation and ALGOL

In the early 1950s, the diva computer (French *calculatrice*) was capricious, and everything turned around her. But soon the need for help in programming was felt everywhere. In October 1955, at a conference in Darmstadt, a GAMM Committee for Programming Languages was initiated by Rutishauser [17]. In Munich, special programming techniques with hardware support were developed using "Leitzellen" (memory locations occupied by addresses) and "indirect addressing," invented by Schecher in 1955 [18] and soon copied elsewhere. Special hardware support was also given to facilitate address calculations and automatic subroutine linkage [19]. Under the influence of Rutishauser's "Automatische Planfertigung" and in close contact with him, attempts to create a programming language based on common mathematical ("algebraic") notation and to construct automatic translators were started in 1954 by Samelson and Bauer. Knowing well Angstl's design, Samelson observed in 1955 [20] that in addition to the "Zahlkeller" ["number cellar"—(NC)], where intermediate results were stored in proper order, an "operation cellar"—(OC)—would be in the general case hold operations that had to wait, again in proper order. This means that the restrictions Böhm had accepted were quite unnecessary. We called it the "cellar principle" of sequential formula translation. A patent was filed* describing on several levels machines that would be immediately formula controlled (Fig. 10, from [21]). The machines were to use hardware stacks. They were never built. In fact, the German patent was finally not granted (which brings Samelson and me in pleasant company with Zuse), but the U.S. patent, into which went a full wiring diagram, was issued as No. 3 047 228.

* Deutsche Patentanmeldung 109 4019, 30 March 1957.

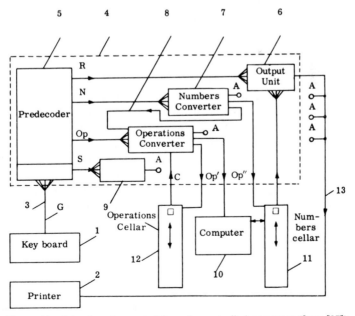

Figure 10 A keyboard operated formula controlled computer (from [27]).

When it became clear at that moment that machines of this sort* were not to be built (they have been built 15 years later as minicomputers), we turned [22, 23] to implementing the cellar principle by a program, a "Superplan" in the terminology of Zuse and Rutishauser. Designing the compiler and designing the language was done in close cooperation with Rutishauser starting in 1956; later Bottenbruch, from Walthers Institute at Darmstadt, joined us. Bottenbruch's speciality was the connection to formal systems of mathematical logic. Our main task in Munich was what today would be called parsing and code generation. Rutishauser was particularly interested in run-time systems. He had worked out a system of procedure linkage and storage allocation that allowed one to bring procedures "through the back door" as parameters into a procedure, it was described in the form of rules to be observed by programmers when writing library programs for the ER-METH [24] and was worked out by Waldburger. The system allowed one to bring into a procedure the same procedure "through the back door"; it had a fully recursive storage allocation. Rutishauser did not publish it, but he was disappointed when Dijkstra, in 1960, published his method which he had found independently. Rutishauser, however, did not know that recursive organization of procedures was already envisaged (in a special case) by van der Poel, who [15, 25] described in 1952 an organization of return instructions that amounts to stacking. On the other hand, he was aware of Schecher's work [19] on automatic subroutine linkage; Schecher in turn did not know of an earlier hardware design by Turing [26].

In the middle of 1957, a detailed description in the form of syntactic charts of the programming language to be used and of the parser and code generator to work on it was ready. Parsing was described by a table of entry symbols against the top symbol in the cellar, giving the transition of the cellar content; in other words, in the form of what Oettinger called later a pushdown automaton. At the first IFIP Congress in Paris in 1959, the method, with the table in the meantime replaced by a function based on precedence, was presented by Samelson to a surprised audience.

During a visit Bottenbruch and I made in the fall of 1957 to the U.S., we found some interest in jointly discussing language efforts further, especially by J. Carr, III, Alan Perlis, and Saul Gorn. In the fall of 1957, the GAMM Committee approved a joint enterprise, and soon the Association for Computing Machinery (ACM) did so, too. The conference, which was then held in Zürich in the first days of May, had Perlis, Backus, Wegstein (who had found techniques for parsing similar to ours), and Katz together with the four mentioned already from the Zürich–Munich–Darmstadt group. In one week, the proposals from the two sides were amalgamated and a report was written [27]. We could agree on everything but the name; Rutishauser dis-

---

* In the summer of 1957, I was consulting at Göttingen while the G3 was being built, and a number cellar went into that design.

liked IAL, International Algebraic Language. The name ALGOL came up at a fall 1958 meeting of the ZMD people at Mainz University, to which place I had moved. Someone said, "Algorithmic language abbreviated gives ALGOL," and the ones among us who had studied astronomy immediately saw the pun. Whether the word really meant "bad luck" for the language was asked frequently later on, in particular when heavy reactions on the side of and conflicts with the leading manufacturer came up [28]. But this was in the 1960s and is outside the time scale of this paper.

By the end of 1958, an ALGOL 58 compiler for the Z22, written by Paul, was working in Mainz, while one for the PERM, written by Seegmüller, was ready in Munich, and one for the ERMETH was finished by Schwarz. Several other computing centers and manufacturers (Regnecentralen Copenhagen, University of Bonn, MAILÜFTERL Vienna, Oak Ridge National Laboratory, Siemens & Halske AG) then joined in and formed the ALCOR group to which the existing general compiler description based on the cellar principle was made available. Thus, the European side went to the ALGOL 60 Conference in Paris, January, 1960, with strong technical experience.

Zuse has repeatedly raised the question of the relation between ALGOL and the Plankalkül. First of all, the Zuse company had had help from the ALGOL people inside and outside the ALCOR group, especially with the compilers for the Z22 and Z23. Certainly, the Plankalkül was not (and may still be not) fully recognized by the computing community. Rutishauser wrote in 1967 that "his notation was quite general but the proposal never attained the consideration it deserved." But this does not mean that Rutishauser neglected the Plankalkül, nor is it true in the case of Samelson and myself. Zuse wrote [1, p. 127]

> Um das Jahr 1955 entstanden die Programmiersprachen FORTRAN und ALGOL. Auch diese waren in erster Linie auf numerische Rechnungen zugeschnitten, entsprechen aber sonst dem Plankalkül. Es lässt sich heute schwer feststellen, wieweit Gedanken des Plankalküls übernommen wurden.

Certainly, FORTRAN was absolutely independent. ALGOL, however, was not (probably therefore it was always better than FORTRAN). The ALGOL procedure concept, the type concept with specifications, the assignment concept was conceptually based on similar ideas in the Plankalkül. Quite frequently, this was done by the European ALGOL members subconsciously.*

On the other hand, Zuse did not see this:

> Ich selbst war um diese Zeit mit dem Aufbau der Firma beschäftigt und konnte nur gelegentlich Gespräche mit den Schöpfern des ALGOL, wie Rutishauser und Bauer, führen. Meist redeten wir aneinander vorbei. Der Grundgedanke des Plankalküls, eine Programmiersprache syste-

---

* In particular, since some of Zuse's sources had been part of the mathematics folklore.

matisch aus ihren Wurzeln aufzubauen, erschien übertrieben oder wurde als Ballast empfunden.

Certainly, for numerical work, and this was mainly the purpose of ALGOL 58, there was neither a need nor an advantage for describing algorithms down to the bit. (The general situation was taken care of in ALGOL 68.) Moreover, the Plankalkül had a horrible notation, absolutely unsuited for the input to a compiler. Zuse admits, "Der Plankalkül hätte noch "compiler-gerecht" zugeschnitten werden müssen" [1, p. 128]. Moreover, Rutishauser had already in 1952 found the convenient notation for a for-clause, which is lacking in the Plankalkül together with many other helpful notational devices. Conceptually the Plankalkül has had its maximal influence on the European ALGOL development; fortunately for ALGOL, it has left no scars on ALGOL notationally (there was other harm done to ALGOL from elsewhere, but this is not our theme).

I hope I have been able to show that the following complaints Zuse made in 1972 [4] are hardly justified:

> The indifference towards the PK [Plankalkül] was somewhat disappointing for me, when the official discussions about ALGOL started in 1955. Some of the participants had sufficient knowledge of the PK to cooperate and in my opinion it would only have been fair if they had openly announced and utilized the ideas anticipated in the PK [4, p. 24].

In any case, Zuse can be assured to the contrary as far as I am concerned.

ALGOL 58, ALGOL 60, and also ALGOL 68, however, were international in development, and did, for example, not reflect (to his dismay) all of Rutishauser's wishes, nor did it list all the sources. It is not even true that ALGOL was a joint European enterprise [1, p. 127]. On the other hand, Zuse's criteria, "to be able to program chess programs, to program artificial intelligence problems, to describe a compiler in its own language" [1, p. 128], are today fulfilled, by ALGOL 68 among others. Thus, Zuse's visionary draft of 1945 has finally left its imprint on programming of today and tomorrow. Maybe, as Zuse said in 1976, "It would have been better *to base hardware and software developments on the philosophy of the Plankalkül.*"

6. Closing Remark

I wanted to show that the early development of computing in Central Europe had two men who were ahead of the general development: Zuse and Rutishauser. Zuse's main impact on the functional side was between 1934 and 1946. Rutishauser's main influence on computing was between 1952 and 1962. Rutishauser was carrying on—sometimes indirectly—ideas Zuse had introduced, and new ones that gave the programming scene decisive impulses. In honoring Zuse as one of the still-living pioneers, we should not forget Rutishauser, who died too early and yet fulfilled his goal.

REFERENCES

1. K. Zuse, "Der Computer, mein Lebenswerk." Verlag Moderne Industrie, Munich, 1970.
2. H. Piesch, Begriff der allgemeinen Schaltungstechnik, *Arch. Elektrotechn.* **33**, No. 10, 672–686 (1939).
3. K. Zuse, Entwicklungslinien einer Rechengeräte-Entwicklung von der Mechanik zur Elektronik, "Digitale Informationswandler" (W. Hoffmann, ed.). Friedr. Vieweg und Sohn, Braunschweig, 1962.
4. K. Zuse, The Plankalkül, BMFT-GMD-106 (1976) (in English).
5. K. Zuse, Der Plankalkül, BMBW-GMD-63 (1972) (in German).
6. F. L. Bauer and H. Wössner, The "Plankalkül" of Konrad Zuse: A forerunner of today's programming languages, *Comm. ACM* [23] **15**, 678–685 (1972).
7. F. L. Bauer, Angstl's mechanism for checking wellformedness of parenthesis-free formulae, *Math. Comput.* **31**, 318–320 (1977).
8. F. L. Bauer, The formula controlled logical computer "STANISLAUS," *Math. Tables Other Aids Comput.* **14**, 64–67 (1960).
9. K. Zuse, Die mathematischen Voraussetzungen für die Entwicklung logisch-kombinativer Rechenmaschinen. *Z. Angew. Math. Mech.* **29**, 36–37 (1969).
10. K. Zuse, Über den Plankalkül als Mittel zur Formulierung schematisch-kombinativer Aufgaben, *Arch Math.* **1**, 441–449 (1948/49).
11. K. Zuse, Der Programmator, *Z. Angew. Math. Mech.* **32**, 246 (1952).
12. H. Rutishauser, Automatische Rechenplanfertigung bei programm-gesteuerten Rechenmaschinen. Mitteilungen aus dem Institut für Angew. Mathematik ETH Zürich, No. 3, Basel (1952). See also *Z. Angew. Math. Mech.* **32**, 312–313 (1952).
13. H. Rutishauser, Über automatische Rechenplanfertigung bei programmgesteuerten Rechenmaschinen, *Z. Angew. Math. Mech.* **31**, 254–255 (1951).
14. C. Böhm, Calculatrices digitales: Du déchiffrage de formules logico-mathématiques par la machine même dans la conception du programme [Digital computers: On the deciphering of logical-mathematical formulae by the machine itself during the conception of the Program], *Ann. Mat. Pura Appl.* **37**(4), 175–217 (1954).
15. W. L. van der Poel, A simple electronic digital computer, *Appl. Sci. Res. Sect. B* **2**, 367–400 (1952).
16. A. P. Ershov, Addendum, *In* "Compiler Construction. An Advanced Course," (F. L. Bauer and J. Eickel, eds.), 2nd ed., pp. 622–626. Springer-Verlag, Berlin and New York, 1976.
17. H. Rutishauser, Discussion remark. *Nachrichtentech. Fachber.* **4**, 143 (1956).
18. H. Schecher, Maßnahmen zur Vereinfachung von Rechenplänen. *Z. Angew. Math. Mech.* **36**, 377–395 (1956).
19. H. Schecher, Programmierung für eine Maschine mit erweitertem Adressenrechenwerk, *In* "Aktuelle Probleme der Rechentechnik" (*Ber. Internat. Math. Kolloq., Dresden, Nov. 22–27, 1955*). pp. 69–81 VEB Deutscher Verlag der Wissenschaften, Berlin, 1957.
20. K. Samelson, Probleme der Programmierungstechnik, *In* "Aktuelle Probleme der Rechentechnik" (*Ber. Internat. Math. Kolloq., Dresden, Nov. 22–27, 1955*), pp. 61–68 VEB Deutscher Verlag der Wissenschaften, Berlin, 1957.
21. K. Samelson and F. L. Bauer, The ALCOR Project, *In* "Symbolic Languages in Data Processing," pp. 207–217. Gordon and Breach, New York, 1962.
22. K. Samelson and F. L. Bauer, Sequentielle Formelübersetzung, *Elektron. Rech.* **1**, 176–182 (1959).

23. K. Samelson and F. L. Bauer, Sequential Formula Translation. *Comm. ACM* **3**, 76–83 (1960) (Translation of [22].)

24. H. Waldburger, Gebrauchsanweisung für die ERMETH. Institut für Angew. Mathematik an der ETH Zürich (1958).

25. W. L. van der Poel, Dead programs for a magnetic drum automatic computer, *Appl. Sci. Res. Sect. B* **3**, 190–198 (1952).

26. A. M. Turing, *Proc. Symp. Large-Scale Digital Calculating Machinery, 2nd* pp. 89–90. Harvard Univ., Cambridge, Massachusetts, 1949.

27. A. J. Perlis and K. Samelson (ed.), Report on the Algorithmic Language ALGOL by the ACM Committee on programming languages and the GAMM Committee on programming, *Numer. Math.* **1**, 41–60 (1959).

28. R. W. Bemer, A politico-social history of ALGOL, "Annual Review of Automatic Programming," Vol. 5, pp. 151–237. Pergamon, Oxford, 1969.

INSTITUT FÜR INFORMATIK
TECHNISCHE UNIVERSITÄT
MUNICH, WEST GERMANY

The ENIAC*

J. PRESPER ECKERT, JR.

1. Some ENIAC Basics

One confusion that has crept into some historical accounts of the ENIAC has been to describe its circuits as being derived from radar technology. As John Mauchly and I have pointed out before, they were in many ways derived from circuits that physicists were using in cosmic-ray and nuclear investigations. The ring counters were the "scaling circuits." Pulse counting and gating were used in many laboratories. Connections with radar came later, particularly with respect to the acoustic delay line storage device proposed for the EDVAC and used in the BINAC and UNIVAC as well as other machines. The attribution of early computer technology to radar is not at all correct.

We thought the most important development problem that we faced in the ENIAC was to provide a control system consistent with and adequate for its intended general-purpose use. And it was about the controls of the computer that von Neumann first asked when he came in September 1944, for his first visit to the ENIAC project. If he had first asked questions like "How fast does it work?" we would have been disappointed. Because he asked about the control logic, there was an immediate rapport.

---

* Dr. Eckert was to have given a paper at the Los Alamos conference but in the end was not able to be present. His script was read by Dr. John Mauchly. The following paper is an edited version of that script, with comments added by Dr. Mauchly.

525

But there is a lot of history to be told about the period before we ever met von Neumann in September 1944. Long before we met von Neumann on the ENIAC project, it was John and I who had to figure out how to arrange for flexible controls that would do all the things that we felt were absolutely necessary for the generality of use that was our goal. We were glad that Leland Cunningham, then working for the Ballistics Research Laboratory (BRL), also had this philosophy and purpose. Unfortunately, it is often said that the ENIAC was built just for preparing firing tables. Cunningham and others at BRL all supported us in making the ENIAC as generally useful as we could contrive to make it within the limited time that conditions of war demanded. Yes, BRL wanted firing tables, but they also wanted to be able to do "interior" ballistics, and all kinds of data reduction, and they went on and on with examples of what they would hope to be able to do with a truly flexible computer. We wince a little when we hear the ENIAC referred to as a special-purpose computer; it was not.

The name "ENIAC," where the "I" stands for "integrator," was devised to help sell the Pentagon that what the BRL was getting would compute firing tables, which were, in 1943, the greatest need of Ordnance. But there was a flexibility of control far beyond the implications of the name.

Now lots of good things in this world have been stopped before they should have been because somebody made bad experiments. If the experiments do not turn out as you hoped, you may easily abandon what you were trying to do. We saw that that might happen to our ENIAC project if we were not very careful. Apparently, MIT and other research centers were ready to advise those who had backed us that vacuum tubes were too risky and that a number of relays operating in parallel, for instance, would be a far better thing to try.

Our main method for guiding a group effort, involving only a dozen engineers, plus technicians and wiremen, was to give everyone a set of rules, a kind of discipline, to work by. By careful analysis of "worst cases," we fortunately did not fall into any deep traps, and our first big project, the ENIAC, did indeed perform as we expected. It was gratifying to see how well it all went together and tested out. The first two "accumulators" that were assembled, once a few wiring bugs were corrected, could and did solve second-order difference equations exactly. This was in the summer of 1944. Then, soon after, Goldstine brought von Neumann in for a demonstration. Also, this successful demonstration of the essential correctness of much of our design took a great load off the shoulders of Dean Pender and J. G. Brainerd. They had been receiving the flak from other institutions, which cast great doubt on whether our electronic methods could succeed.

The original simplified version of the ENIAC would have required about 5000 vacuum tubes—a bit scary for many who had had bad experiences with poorly designed laboratory equipment with only a few hundred tubes. In the end, we wound up with over 18,000 tubes in the ENIAC, almost entirely because of expansion of requirements by BRL. When Cunningham and others at BRL saw what we were planning and how we were going about it, they asked for not one, but three, function tables (read-only switch set memories) for inputting drag functions and other things that might prove handy. And they wanted more accumulators than the 10 we had originally planned for, bringing the total number of accumulators up to 20.

The result of this was to more than triple the amount of hardware to be built, and this of course more than doubled the money needed and the time it took to finish things.

If we had built the ENIAC according to the original proposal, when the contract was first let, it might have taken just about the 5000 that we estimated originally.The cost of $150,000 that we originally estimated became $400,000. All things considered, we had made good estimates, better than some we made in the years to follow.

2. Flexibility, Modularity, and Control

Now we come to the big problem—that of providing flexibility of control. Neither I nor John had any knowledge of Babbage's ideas and had never heard of Lady Lovelace at that time. Neither did we know about whatever Dr. Aiken or IBM was doing at Harvard, nor had we any knowledge of Dr. Zuse. There did not seem much to guide us. I was influenced somewhat by the differential analyzer. We had one at the Moore School, being used by BRL to integrate trajectories. John Mauchly had studied how the extra personnel hired by BRL and working at the Moore School did numerical integrations with desk calculators. John Mauchly was able to provide, in an appendix to the 1943 ENIAC proposal, a diagram suggesting how a set of accumulators might be "hooked up" to achieve the kind of numberical integration cycles needed for a typical trajectory calculation. Both John and I had used desk calculations, John much more than I.

Whatever experience I had gained, and a great deal that John had had before coming to the University, pointed directly to the necessity for "subroutines." Branching and looping were the essence of efficient and compact controls. So the ENIAC had to be equipped to handle a number of subroutines. A large part of the facility for such controls was provided by what we called the "master programmer." It had electronic counters and electronic stepping switches and various ways of controlling "program pulses" so as to produce looping a predetermined number of times, or until a predetermined "condition" was met. Nested subroutines were available through these panels, and interlocking of parallel operations was provided for. Note that the Harvard MARK I as originally built had no facility for proper use of subroutines. There were a few wired-in functions. Later, several paper-tape readers were added to read paper-tape loops, which provided a limited subroutine facility.

I think we are particularly proud of the fact that we did provide this flexibility. Dr. Brainerd obtained the services of mathematicians to study the "roundoff" problem, but nothing that issued from that study affected machine design. The "controls" were our own doing.

The number of quite different problems done on the ENIAC is testimony that it was very far from "special purpose."

We were building a "modular" machine, expandable if one wished, so much of the control had to be decentralized. The level controls of the various panels were stimulated by program pulses that had to get from one part of the machine to another as quickly as the data. We had to be sure that the pulses got from "here to there" in the ENIAC properly timed for their functions. There were terminated shielded lines 80 ft long, and we were quite concerned about transmission problems. The machine actually did work as a machine in which you could carry on *several independent processes simultaneously*. It was a *multiprocessing device as well as a parallel device*. The various programming options available made it a very flexible device, even by modern standards.

The distributed control was dictated by the ease of building and getting it done in good time, since we did not know when we started whether someone would want more of this or more of that. If we had used centralized control, as in our later designs, we would have delayed the design. In some problems we made use of the distributed control system to speed up the operation, and this was intended as a feature of the original design.

There is no point in describing further the many features of the ENIAC controls, since the reports, although not widely published, are quite complete and available for those who wish to learn more. What we are striving for here is to draw attention to the fact that the ENIAC, when viewed 30 years after its completion, had some very modern features—it's just that we did not then use the modern terminology to describe them.

We were also quite aware of the shortcomings of our first attempt. When most of the machine design was already frozen, but much construction and testing lay ahead, we had enough time to ponder these shortcomings. We knew that "setup time" for some problems would be a small part of the time spent on calculations once the set up had been made and verified. That was true for the range tables, for instance. And we had done a few obvious things to allow the overlapping of setup times. The function tables had portable switch panels, on casters, to allow for conveniently changing one function to another in preparation for an upcoming problem, while disconnected from the machine, without interfering with the problem in progress. We conceived of another mode of ENIAC operation, in which the function tables would control "the program." The switch setting then would not represent numerical data for calculating, but arguments fed to the function tables would elicit patterns of program pulses output to prearranged program lines. There were two ways in which this might ease the burden of "patch-cord setups"—(1) if a new program were put on a function table, another program could check or verify the switch settings of the "read-only" portable panel, making it unnecessary to go through the tedious manual checking of the patchcord setups, or (2) a possibly long-term setting of the function table switches might be given a permanent set of arguments corresponding to some permanent set of program functions to be stimulated. Then every time a new set of numbers was read from the card input, a new set of operations would be caused to occur.

The foregoing ideas could be easily implemented on the ENIAC, and we expected that at some time someone would want to do this, so we built the necessary cable to connect "program pulses" into the function tables in place of "digit pulses." Hence there would be no difficulty in doing this when desired. In Aberdeen, Dr. Clippinger later "rediscovered" these uses of the function tables, without knowing that they had already been provided for in the original hardware. A project was set up for operating the ENIAC with a permanent numerical code set. The permanently set up "instructions" were chosen with von Neumann's consultation, and became known as the "von Neumann code for the ENIAC." Although it is sometimes said that von Neumann converted the ENIAC to a "stored-program machine," this is not really correct in view of our provisions for this type of operation. In my view, von Neumann tended to run ahead without proper investigation or careful statements on where ideas he was discussing had originated.

What was done was that a new "function table" was added, instead of using the existing ones, and this made use of new storage devices that could receive code numbers from input cards. I originally suggested this type of storage. The setup time was thus very much decreased, but it greatly reduces the speed of program execution. Additional comments on this mode of operating the ENIAC are to be found in "A Trilogy of Errors in the History of Computing,"* cited in connection with "stored programs."

It should be clear, since we were thinking in terms of controlling programs by feeding coded numbers in from a card reader, that we regarded the instructions to any computer as representable by such codes. It is clear that we already had high-speed storage for certain elements of ENIAC programs already included in the master programmer and various electronic steppers. But at the time that we started building the ENIAC, with the schedule we hoped to meet, we had no time to look for cheaper high-speed storage. Yet, when it was finished, we expected that there would be good reason to build a better computer.

3. Generality

One of the things that has always interested me very much is trying to get as much generality as I can in the things that I do. Therefore, I worry about

* N. Metropolis and J. Worlton, A Trilogy of Errors in the History of Computing, *Proc. 1st U.S.–Japan Conf., Tokyo, 1972*, p. 683.

how the modern microprocessor fits in and still maintains the kind of generality we have had in our designs in the past.

In January 1944, we were very well aware that the ENIAC had some good generality and that it had some poor generality. It took hours to set the original unmodified version but it was better than the Bush Differential Analyzer that usually took days to set up with screwdrivers and lead hammers and so on. MIT was concerned about this, and so built a Bush-type analyzer at MIT, which was interconnected with relays and servos rather than shafts and could be set up rather quickly. It could at that time be set up more quickly than our ENIAC as originally used or our old-style Bush analyzer.

We were also concerned with another thing that we thought was even more basic: that is, we seemed to have too many different kinds of memory in ENIAC. We had fast, expensive memories using flip-flops, we had slower read-only memories that we called "constant transmitters," and we had great big racks of switches called "function tables," which were really more read-only memory but several times slower in action for constants that were not used as frequently. We had a bunch of cables and switches that were set up to route the program pulses in the program sequence where we needed the most speed. When we actually came down to putting programs on paper, we used numbers (or letters) to denote all these things—so all this stuff was described by symbols (or codes).

In late 1943 and early 1944, John Mauchly and I were beginning to have more time to think about "the next machine." And the two problems, "setup time" and "better storage for common purposes," were uppermost in our thoughts. I first thought magnetic disks or drums would answer the storage problem.

Ideas were tossed around, including magnetic core storage, as outlined in the early EDVAC reports. We started to analyze some problems that might be put on an ENIAC, and found that some problems would have been better handled if more money had been spent on "accumulators" and less on "function tables." For other problems, the reverse was true. In building another machine, how would we know what to do? We might know nothing about the type of problems that the user would want to solve now or next year. Problem types might change; new mathematical techniques might also cause changes for the same problem. How could we design a "problem-independent" sort of computer?

It struck me that in the next machine we were not going to know how to do anything right! So, how were we going to get around this dilemma?

4. Storage Problems and Solutions:
   ## BINAC or UNIVAC

In January 1944, I wrote a memo, Disclosure of Magnetic Calculating Machine, which I typed on my home typewriter and then gave to my supervisor for retyping. For some reason it never got typed, but I finally did get my own version back. I had also read a Master's Thesis by Perry Crawford, at MIT, where he had proposed using a disk with some spots magnetized on it for storage of numbers. My memo stated that we could use magnetic disks either erasable or permanently for the storage of information both alterable or unchangeable. The concept of general internal storage started in this memo.

The more I thought about it, the more I realized that a magnetic drum was a mechanical device that would limit our speed, even though the instructions on the drum would reduce the setup time and give us the required flexibility. So, while we would be solving some of our problems, we would not get the really high speeds that we hoped to get by our electronic methods.

Before working on the ENIAC, I had invented a mercury signal delay tank that was an ultrasonic delay line for radar uses. I had also figured out, prior to ENIAC, how to circulate a pulse in a delay line for timing purposes. Without going into further detail now, I then figured out how to recirculate patterns of pulses in a delay line so as to build a memory that had an average "waiting time" of about 1/5000 sec, or 200 μsec, and which could deliver pulses at a rate of several megacycles.

Some may recall that we built a machine called BINAC, with a 4-megacycle pulse rate using delay line storage; this was a kind of early simplified prototype of UNIVAC I. We built many UNIVACs using delay line storage at a pulse rate over two megacycles, before going to core storage in UNIVAC II. Ordnance was asked to fund development of the mercury delay line storage, and we began spending all our spare time planning a machine that would use such storage. But our main obligation was to finish and test the ENIAC, and it took until late in 1945 before that was ready for the big test that Nick Metropolis and Stan Frankel gave it.

My best computer idea, today briefly called "stored program," became to us an "obvious idea," and one that we started to take for granted. It was obvious that computer instructions could be conveyed in a numerical code, and that whatever machines we might build after the ENIAC would want to avoid the setup problems that our hastily built first try ENIAC made evident. It was also obvious that the functions supplied by the Master Programmer in controlling loops and counting iterations, etc., would be achieved very naturally by allowing instructions to be subject to alterations within the calculator. We even thought that Goldstine, who had frequent contact with us, understood all of the uses to which these delay lines could be put. Not so, it seems as it turned out.

Mauchly comments: At the Los Alamos conference I had the chance to check with Harry Huskey, who says he started on the staff of the ENIAC Project about April 1944. I asked him whether, when he first came to the Moore School, he had heard any notions about storing programs in the same storage used for computer data. He said, "Yes. My immediate reaction was,

'Why didn't I think of that?'" But for some reason, Goldstine did not understand this, if I correctly interpret what he says in his volume "The Computer from Pascal to von Neumann."* Goldstine was writing to Gillen to get the new project on mercury acoustic delay lines funded, but at the same time or even later he was writing about schemes to use relays for setting program switches and function tables, all of which could be done from paper tape instead of the way the ENIAC had been set up.

Apparently, while we were racing ahead on plans involving obvious uses of the delay storage device, Goldstine had spent a great deal of time in the hospital with hepatitis, and had failed to get the full impact of the delay storage on control problems. This makes more understandable his apparent belief that von Neumann was the source of ideas that in fact we had generated before Goldstine had met von Neumann at the Aberdeen railroad station. That chance meeting in Aberdeen was the very beginning of von Neumann's high interest in electronic computation. The clearance document for von Neumann's first visit to the Moore School ENIAC project has been found, and his first visit could not have been before 7 September 1944. In my own records, which also became a court document, is confirmation that Eckert and I had a commitment to meet von Neumann about 7 September. I believe that was our first meeting with him.

5. The EDVAC Report of 1945

When we were preparing our progress report on the EDVAC, my January 1944 disclosure was very deliberately included in the Historical Comments of that report. When Metropolis and Worlton wrote "A Trilogy of Errors in the History of Computing" for the first U.S.–Japan Conference in 1972, they cited that report and quoted its description of the magnetic calculator as having the important feature that "the operating instructions and the function tables would be stored in exactly the same sort of memory device as that used for numbers." From that same progress report, Goldstine was able to quote our acknowledgment that von Neumann had helped us in many specific ways. However, he seemed to have missed entirely the import of the "magnetic calculator disclosure" and that its January 1944 date was many months before any of us had met von Neumann (or before von Neumann had obtained security clearance to visit our ENIAC project).

The original was written in January 1944. Apparently it got lost not just once but twice. The first time was while it was waiting to be retyped. But it suffered the fate of many other classified documents in this world—it was put in a filing cabinet, and no one paid any further attention to it. We thought our confidential reports to Ordnance were record enough of what we were

---

* H. H. Goldstine, "The Computer from Pascal to von Neumann." Princeton Univ. Press, Princeton, New Jersey, 1972.

designing. We failed to reckon with the many others who talked about our ideas, never mentioning whose ideas they were, and who, as time passed, more and more came to be regarded as the generators of those ideas.

The typewritten pages were stamped CONFIDENTIAL, but in effect, they were really a well-kept secret until lawyers, going through the files in preparation for a Federal Court trial, unearthed them among the various documents that they thought might be useful as an exhibit.

A retyped copy of the original January 1944 Disclosure is at the end of this paper.

6. Von Neumann at the Moore School

We described our ideas to von Neumann when he came, and you could not have found a more receptive person. He immediately began to concern himself with some of the logical (but not electronic) details of the problem. He was particularly interested in the instruction code for the EDVAC that we at the University of Pennsylvania had proposed. A three-adress instruction code was being discussed; we were going to tell the computer the location of two operands and the location for storing the result. Such an instruction of course included the operation to be performed. Goldstine arranged for as many subsequent visits as von Neumann could make, and from time to time others joined the "discussion group." Dr. Arthur Burks was usually with us. Later, John von Neumann and I struck up a long conversation on whether it was better to have one, two, or three addresses in each instruction and whether it was better to store one or two instructions per location, and things of this type.

I remember going to see the new differential analyzer at MIT. We called it the Caldwell machine. During a meeting, von Neumann and I were sitting in the very last row of an auditorium while talks were being presented. We spent most of the time discussing whether minimum latency coding would be practical for the EDVAC—that is, whether we could arrange the timing of things in such a way as to cut down the waiting time to some needed operand in the proposed mercury tank memory. Von Neumann thought it would be too difficult to be practical. He was not right. Grace Hopper used minimum latency coding and figured out an approximate way of doing this, first with hand charts that she prepared. Later, she used the UNIVAC itself to work out the memory locations.

That was akin to our general philosophy, of course. You should use the computer to do all the tedious dirty work if you possibly can. That was the origin of all the languages, interpreters, and such that have since been developed.

As a matter of fact, we were adversely influenced by von Neumann's opinions in designing the UNIVAC I. It became apparent after we had fixed the design that it would have been better to have put more than 10 words into each mercury tank, made the tanks longer, and used the minimum latency principle. We could have got a much needed larger memory at about the same cost, had we done this, without loss of operating speed.

I also discussed with von Neumann the ideas I had about parallel machines. (At the Institute for Advanced Study in Princeton, von Neumann's workers later built such a parallel machine, which I originally proposed to von Neumann at the University of Pennsylvania.) I was influenced by the Bell Labs Relay machines and my own work on electrostatic storage-tube memory. The problem for us with parallel machines was that we did not at that time know how to build a good parallel storage. We certainly fully understood the concept. I worked on a storage-tube device at the University of Pennsylvania modeled on the ideas of the iconoscope. I showed this work to F. C. Williams, who came over from England when the Moore School Lectures on Computer Design were given in 1946. Williams went back to Manchester and applied for patents on iconoscope ideas, first in England and then in the U.S. I believe IBM took a license under some of those patents.

7. Security Classification and Other Problems

All during the ENIAC and EDVAC project period at the Moore School, the work that John and I were doing was under a security classification of CONFIDENTIAL. We were not allowed to go out and give unapproved talks. It is our opinion that von Neumann adopted many of our ideas and rewrote them with the "neuron notation" of McCullough and Pitts. It has always upset me (and John, too) that von Neumann gave talks on the work we had done on the Moore School ENIAC/EDVAC project, rarely if ever giving any credit to the University or to the people who had actually produced the ideas. (He has been quoted as saying that when ideas are discussed within a group, no one can assign authorship—really!)

As to the classification problem, he may have supposed that by translating from electronic circuit terms into neural notation, government security was no longer a concern. From our standpoint, the classification operated to let others discuss and disperse our ideas while Mauchly and I could not do the same.

Von Neumann refused to correct the misunderstandings that he gave to others, even after the group at the University of Pennsylvania (including Dean Pender, John Mauchly, and myself) repeatedly registered our request that he do so.

We were going to have a joint project involving the University of Pennsylvania, which would work on input–output circuits, and the Institute for Advanced Study at Princeton, which would work on the central computer, and Princeton University, which would work on software. Unfortunately, this arrangement could not be carried through because von Neumann's way of taking credit for the work of others caused a disagreement between Dr.

Harold Pender, Dean of the Moore School of Electrical Engineering at Pennsylvania, and Dr. John von Neumann, of the Institute.

At this time, von Neumann created other problems by bringing the RCA Laboratories at Princeton into an otherwise academic group for collaboration. He wanted to consult with commercial companies such as RCA and IBM. (He later did consult with IBM.) It is our understanding that he collected considerable consulting fees, and we can only believe that the ideas that he discussed as a consultant included our ideas.

All of these things seemed unfair to John Mauchly, Dr. Pender, and myself. (Dr. Zworykin asked John Mauchly to join with the RCA Laboratory, but this would have required John to sign the standard RCA patent agreements. Von Neumann said that there would be no patent agreements at the Institute.)

I did recruit a number of people to work for von Neumann at Princeton. I was trying to carry out a part of the agreement that we had tried to make, but I never joined in with his group as originally planned, because of the problems everyone (except Goldstine and Burks) had with von Neumann.

8.   My Last Contact with von Neumann

My last contact with von Neumann occurred in 1955, just before we finished the design of the UNIVAC LARC. Actually, we fell into the middle of a disagreement between Edward Teller and von Neumann on a particular point. Teller took the position that he wanted to get all the memory in the LARC (Livermore Automatic Research Computer) that their budget would allow. This turned out to be 20,000 rather large words (we later built a LARC with 30,000 words for the Bureau of Ships.) Von Neumann contended that putting anything more than 10,000 words in a computer would *always* be a waste of money, and he felt Teller should not waste the government's money by contracting for a LARC with more than 10,000 words. Teller prevailed, which was not surprising since he was more directly interested in the project than von Neumann. This was a second item, along with minimum latency coding, on which von Neumann's practical advice was poor and probably led to a number of incorrect computer design ideas that many proceeded to follow.

Today we have machines with high-speed, fast-access storage of over a million words. I can remember reading an article by Richard Bellman many years ago in which he was stressing the need for much larger fast storage of this size or larger.

Mauchly comments: A final remark: Both Eckert and I have tried to fill in some items of history that are unfortunately missing or not likely to be found in the literature. I think the moral of all this is to alert the historians and others that you have got to be careful about the attributions, and the interpretations of words which change with time. Some of the computer ideas were so obvious—for instance, that of putting timing tracks on a drum or disk. We thought that was very obvious. Note that it is included in the January 1944 Disclosure. It seems possible that it has something to do with the patent claim on which Technitrol may have collected some money at a later time.

Addendum

Editors' Note: In view of some of the statements in the paper relating to priorities of invention it seems desirable to reproduce the relevant parts of the discussion which followed Dr. Mauchly's reading of the paper at the Los Alamos Conference.

Dr. Hurd: Von Neumann became an IBM consultant for 30 days a year, and I always spent that 30 days each year with him, so we talked about many things. I never heard him make the claim that he invented stored programming. I heard him describe many times meetings with a group of other people which included John [Mauchly] and Presper [Eckert] in which he made statements like, "I went to the board and wrote down maybe summaries of these conversations or ideas," but I never really heard him make the claim. I think it is perfectly consistent with some of the things you have said.

On the second point [storage], during those days of consulting there was a question about the amount of high-speed memory versus the amount of low-speed memory. He was always pushing us towards small amounts of core memory and large amounts of magnetic drum memory to back it up, which, when you are able to program in your head about a hundred instructions as he could, maybe is the way to do it. But that it was not the way to do it for the market was then apparent.

Dr. Mauchly (in reply to a question about "the iconoscope and the connection with F. C. Williams"): Eckert and I and Kite Sharples and Brad Sheppard and others were asked to arrange a series of lectures on automatic computer design (in the summer of 1946). The lectures were funded by the government, and government workers were eligible to come to them. Also, others like Maurice Wilkes and F. C. Williams came from England. We tried to make the lectures cover many aspects of computer desires. We had Aiken as one of the speakers. We could not get von Neumann. On iconoscopes for storage, Eckert had many ideas, and talked to the attendees about such possibilities. F. C. Williams arrived after the series had begun, but he and Eckert had private conversations on how CRTs might be used.

It may be of interest to mention that Eckert delayed the choice of fast storage for our UNIVAC I until the last possible moment. He and Hermann Lukoff and others at Eckert Mauchly had developed a very reliable CRT store at the same time that Brad Sheppard and others had developed the mercury delay line into a reliable device. It was a very close race. The staff under John Curtiss at the Bureau of Standards was aware of these CRT tests and developments.

A complete logical diagram of a character at a time (bytes) computer was developed to be used with the CRT storage if it had worked well enough. All the memory tubes were steered to a memory location in parallel for read-out or -in, on a character or byte at a time basis to reduce the number of amplifiers and computer gate circuits required. Such a machine, had we built it, would have been several times faster than UNIVAC I and could have been built in the same time frame.

Disclosure of Magnetic Calculating Machine

A simplified method of constructing a numerical calculating machine is proposed in which some of the mechanical features of an ordinary mechanical calculating machine are retained and combined with certain electronic and magnetic devices to produce a speedier, simpler machine as well as providing additional features of utility, ruggedness and ease of repair.

A continuously rotating shaft called the time shaft, driven by an electric motor, has at least some of each of the following discs or drums mounted on it:

a) Discs or drums which have at least their outer edge made of magnetic alloy capable of being magnetized and demagnetized repeatedly and at high speed. Suitable coils and other apparatus are provided to convert electrical pulses or other wave shapes into spatially distributed magnetized sectors on the periphery of these discs, the position and/or phase of these magnetized sectors providing a method of storing, in some usable code, those characters or digits which must be used later or indicated. It should be noted that the direction of magnetization of the sectors is unimportant and may be in any direction relative to the motion or a combination of directions, this being a well known technique. This is analogous to the use of a magnetic tape to record sound except that here linearity is of little importance.

b) Discs or drums having edges or surfaces engraved in such a way as to cause voltage to be induced in a coil arranged near the disc. In any case either the disc or pole piece of the coil should be a magnet. This disc would generate such pulses or other electric signals as were required to time, control and initiate the operations required in the calculations. This is similar to the tone generating mechanism used in some electric organs and offers a more permanent way of storing the basic signals required than would be afforded by the alloy discs referred to above.

c) Discs or drums carrying characters, usually the digits 0 to 9, which can be illuminated by a light modulating device, say a neon gas discharge lamp, and so arranged that at any desired phase of the rotating shaft, corresponding to the positions of the characters, they can be flashed thus making one of the characters on the disc visible. This stroboscope principle is to be used as the high speed indication device in this calculator.

Addition, subtraction, multiplication and division would be carried out by processes of successive addition, such as is well known in mechanical calculation machines. The alloy discs or an auxillary alloy tape could be used to store function data such as a sine table. A multiplication table might be included in this manner to appreciably speed up the process of multiplication by the method of accumulation of partial products used in mechanical calculators.

The original data or numbers might be put into the machine by means of the usual keyboards, tapes or cards. These same types of tapes or cards could be used to record the calculated results.

In the above operations some means must be provided to switch the various signals from one circuit to another. This can be done rapidly by using electronic tubes as switches. A great economy in the numbers of these switching tubes can be effected by putting all the digits of a particular number on the same disc and taking them off serially through the same switching tube. This is to be contrasted to taking the n digits of a number off through n pick-up coils and through n switching tubes.

It has the advantage of reducing the number of tubes required but slows down the operation and may require the mechanical shaft system to be extended so that the alloy discs rotate slower and in synchronism with the indicator discs to allow any of the numbers on the discs to be indicated concurrently or serially. In addition to the above switching operations electronic tubes will be used to count and/or discriminate the pulses used in the system to allow composition of pulse groups from two or more sources and their deposition into other channels. Clearly the power circuits for such a system may be electronic tubes, selenium oxide rectifiers or similar devices.

The use of the binary number system is favored by such an apparatus since the switching circuits are no more complicated and the required pulse groups for representing the number are simpler. The counter circuit is also simpler and more reliable. Either discs of the etched or alloy type may be used to remember combinations required in the conversion from the decimal to the binary system and the reverse if such a system is used.

If multiple shaft systems are used a great increase in the available facilities for allowing automatic programming of the facilities and processes involved may be made, since longer time scales are provided. This greatly extends the usefulness and attractiveness of such a machine. This programing may be of the temporary type set up on alloy discs or of the permanent type on etched discs.

The principal virtues of such a machine are largely due to the alloy discs which allow numbers to be stored indefinitely and to be put on and taken off by a conveniently controlled electric circuit, and that none of the mechanical parts have to accelerate or decelerate during the operation of the machine. The advantages of the electric control are not only that it allows rapid operation but that the design is simplified and capable of more readily being extended and interconnected to other apparatus.

Several economies of operation result. It should be cheaper to build, because the precision of the electric parts is much smaller than the equivalent mechanical parts. Maintenance should be reduced because of the reliability and long life of the electric parts, the residual mechanical parts having only very simple bearing surfaces capable of giving long life. The coil structure used to magnetize the alloy discs may be separate from those used to reproduce and demagnetize them, although in the interest of simplicity it should be possible to produce all these operations with the same coil assembly. An economy over card and tape machines may be effected since no materials are normally used up in the operation of the machine, only electric power is consumed.

[Copied on 1 February 1945 from three typewritten sheets dated 29 January 1944.]

UNIVAC DIVISION
SPERRY RAND CORPORATION
BLUE BELL, PENNSYLVANIA

The ENIAC

JOHN W. MAUCHLY

1. Introduction

In starting to write this contribution to the history of ENIAC, many things come to my mind that seem to be missing from the various accounts of this history that I have seen. I can't cover them all but I shall try to cover those that I feel are the most important.

First, I want to note a large deficiency in the transmission of information, whether on technical details of operation or on history. We were very well aware, from the start of the ENIAC project at the Moore School in 1943, that problems of reliability were extremely important, so we went all out to conquer them if we could. Eckert was a superb engineer on this score—in all his work and in the direction of others, reliability was his first consideration. As far as Eckert knew, and as far as the rest of us on the ENIAC Project knew, we had succeeded quite well. Before the ENIAC had completed its tests in Philadelphia and was moved to Aberdeen it would often work for hours or days at a time without error. Dr. Goldstine and others have quoted runs three days long without error. Considering the speed advantage that ENIAC enjoyed in comparison with any prior computing methods or devices (100 to 1000 times faster), these periods of a day or so would accomplish computations that would otherwise have required a year or more.

For more than a year, ENIAC was in fact the *only* working computer having such capability and speed, which was the major consideration for keeping it working in Philadelphia for a year before having it moved to Aber-

541

deen. Some of the problems done on it would not have been attempted by any prior method. One such problem was the one that Nick Metropolis and Stan Frankel brought from Los Alamos to Philadelphia. It was to be used as the shakedown test for the ENIAC. This real "humdinger" was highly classified at the time. The test was run over a period of months, and there was no doubt—the ENIAC had been thoroughly tested, and passed to everyone's satisfaction.

2. Rules That Should Not Be

One terrible example of the deficiency relates to the ENIAC at Aberdeen. Recently, at a computer meeting in New York City, Dick Clippinger told some of us that the ENIAC performed very poorly at Aberdeen when he was there. For some months the uptime was under 50%. This was shocking. In Philadelphia, we learned to expect fairly high uptime, usually over 90%. Dick Merwin and H. J. Gray, the Moore School engineers who went to Aberdeen to reassemble the ENIAC when it was moved, tested it thoroughly, and never reported any situation comparable to that which Dick was now, after almost three decades, reporting. Naturally, I had to know more about his experience. "It was very bad," said Dick. "We were lucky to get anything useful done at the end of the day, after spending most of our time troubleshooting. When we turned the machine on in the morning, all sorts of things seemed to go wrong." That last statement astounded me. "Why did you turn it off?" I asked. Dick answered, "Those were the rules."

Why? One explanation was that the rule was to save electricity. Another was that any unattended hot electrical device required a guard for fire precautions, and this expense was not authorized. Whatever the reason for the rule, it was applied to the ENIAC, as a matter of routine it would seem. Whoever made such a rule probably made it for some good reason, but without knowing a thing about the ENIAC and its value as a scientific tool, nor the cost of the time taken by the Clippinger group to restore operation each morning.

We had learned early in the game that vacuum tubes with heaters inside cathode sleeves were likely to suffer from thermal expansion and contraction when the heaters are turned off and on. Consequently, we had the heaters on a separate circuit, and they were normally on at all times, regardless of the other power needed by the ENIAC. Thus we came to expect over 90% uptime in Philadelphia with ENIAC, and the Moore School engineers who later reassembled and tested it at Aberdeen never reported that they had any difficulty getting similar performance.

Here seems a clear case not only of stupid rules stupidly applied, but failure somewhere to transmit information vital to the proper operation of a calculating instrument that was, in its time, unique in the whole world. I later found out that Merwin and Gray, while getting the ENIAC back into operation at Aberdeen, did *not* abide by the "turn-off rule" but kept power on 24 hours a day. They obtained over 90% uptime in their tests.

3. Our Classified Work

Eckert and I were working on classified projects at the Moore School, and this was a new kind of world brought about by the need for military security in technical work. I had grown up in a community of scientists and was used to open discussion and publication. Now everything had changed. And we weren't sure we knew all the rules, nor what penalties might be visited on us for violating rules.

One could not discuss one's own work with others, whether friends or staff, at the University unless they too were "cleared" for the same project. They were probably cleared for something, but if for a different project, that was not enough. We had a designated secure area in which our work was to be done, and other projects had similar areas, separate from ours. We did not discuss our project work outside the project area, unless sure we were not being overheard. At a restaurant, lunch or dinner conversation was circumscribed. Posters advised that "the enemy may be listening." Many others will have experienced what I have just described.

In Dr. Brainerd's office there was a rubber stamp that said CONFIDENTIAL, and there were rules as to how to keep documents which were so classified. In general, the various engineers just tried to handle their work and the papers they created in accordance with the "rules," and kept all technical talk within the project staff.

My reason for dwelling on the problem of military security as we experienced it is that it had a rather profound effect on how the ideas that we were generating were disseminated. Normal avenues of publication seemed closed to us for an indefinite time. Although the ENIAC was publicly announced in February 1946, and visitors were given a rather elementary demonstration of its speed, we understood that the "circuits" remained classified. We were glad that Professor Hartree was invited to visit the project in 1946 and that an excellent description of many of the ENIAC unclassified features (gleaned from a user's point of view) were written up by him [1]. But that did not lessen our apprehension regarding what we might say, since the circuits were, we were told, still classified. Later, a partial declassification was said to have taken place but even then I was told that the Signal Corps still desired that some of the circuits remain classified. The safest thing seemed to be not to publish. The patent applications that we expected to file could not be jeopardized if nothing were published, and this was a further incentive to refrain from publishing.

4. Work at Ursinus

My ideas about the feasibility of electronic calculation date back to the days in which I was teaching college physics at Ursinus, and reading the journals such as the *Review of Scientific Instruments,* in which circuits were published for "binary scalers." I also took my serious students, such as John deWire (now in nuclear work at Cornell), on trips, for instance to the Bartol Research Foundation, where such circuits were used for cosmic-ray measurements. Also, we went to Washington and visited my friends Larry Hafstad and Merle Tuve, who had a working high-voltage laboratory for nuclear experimentation. (That is where the Meitner atomic fission experiments were first verified in the United States.)

At Ursinus College, some of the students remember my building small models of experimental digital circuits using some gas tubes as well as vacuum tubes. Some of these still exist and work. All of this predates a visit I made to Ames, Iowa, where I found it impossible to persuade Dr. Atanasoff that his projected machine did not realize the potential speeds of electronic calculation that I had in mind. He said he had not succeeded in making flipflops reliable.

5. At the Moore School in 1941

Having taken a defense training course in electronics at the Moore School in the summer of 1941, and having joined the teaching staff that fall, I had hoped to find a sympathetic atmosphere for the development of fast electronic computers in the engineering environment. Almost immediately, I was swept, along with others at the time, into project work for the military, to be carried on side by side with teaching undergraduates. But since the Moore School had a differential analyzer that was then taken over by the Ballistics Research Laboratory (BRL), it became a focal point for various projects to aid the BRL in computational tasks which became ever more urgent.

Eckert's very first contribution to the projects on which we later collaborated occurred during that summer of 1941. He was a laboratory instructor for the defense course, and, day after day, I took the opportunity to talk to him about my ideas on electronic computing. He was not only sympathetic—he was very encouraging. Then, and later, it was the knowledge that Eckert saw no technical obstacles to the realization of fast electronic computing that sustained my own confidence that it could be done.

6. The ENIAC Contract

Not everyone at the University was as encouraging as Pres Eckert. The best advice I received during the first year or so as I was trying to gain converts was that of Dr. Carl Chambers—"Write it down!" What I wrote is now reprinted in Brian Randell's "Origins of Digital Computers" [2] and so is available to any who may wish to read such things. Once Dr. Goldstine had seen my "memo" he asked for a proposal. Eckert and I stayed up the night before 9 April 1943 (and then missed breakfast) preparing a proposal for Goldstine and Brainerd to take to Col. Simon and others at a meeting in Aberdeen. Dr. Oswald Veblen was present, I am told, and helped crystalize putting the project on a contract basis between Ordnance and the University of Pennsylvania.

We got an early start in that we immediately began looking for engineers to man the ENIAC project, even before the official date, 1 June 1943, on the contract. In another sense it was a late start—in 1942 I had been told that there was no use starting the computer I had proposed, because the war would be over within a year!

The first contract was for just six months, to get us started. In a way, this limited the risk for everyone. To me, the planning that we accomplished in the first six months was incredible—but that's what we had to do to meet our schedule. The planning was done hand-in-hand with education. Our engineering staff was constantly meeting to go over what we were expecting to do and how we should go about doing it. First we had to get a reliable design for a decade ring counter. But at the same time, all of the staff were given Eckert's rules for ensuring reliability. We were training all of the engineering staff in a philosophy of design that could not be found in any book or learned in any college course.

One simple but fundamental example from those early days can be cited —a pulse, no matter for what use, had the same physical definition in almost all situations throughout the ENIAC machine. Some pulses were used to control operations and others to signify data, but all were to conform to standards that specified the amplitude and width variations that were to be allowable. Thus a pulse representing an algebraic sign for some data, or one representing a digit value, could be fed into a control circuit and be expected to function just as any control pulse might function.

When the first six months rolled by, our progress was evident to those who wanted the contract extended, and I can recall no question as to the series of extensions. But we did have to write progress reports and they constitute quite a history of the design work that had to be done for the project to be successful. We described the tests that had been made on various counter circuits, and on many other things, and the reasons various decisions had been made as we went along. Historians may some day find the information in those reports and discover that some of the speculations that others have indulged in through the years have been in error.

The reports that we wrote were classified for reasons of national security. The number of copies produced was not very large. So, even after various declassification steps were finally processed after the war years, there were no widely available copies of those reports. Some of them may have been obtainable in microfilm eventually, but the cost of such copies was not the only unfavorable element—one would also need a microfilm reader to find out what we had written. Many of us working on the ENIAC project eventually found ourselves unable to locate our own personal copies. Grist Brainerd told me his copy had long ago disappeared. So these reports are not easy to refer to, but I believe they are not "extinct."

7. Reasons for a Decimal ENIAC

It has been said more than once that we were "wasteful" in using a decimal rather than a binary system in the ENIAC. We carefully considered whether we would gain by using binary throughout, and carefully estimated how many tubes we might use one way or the other. We found that we might use fewer tubes with the decimal system, given the other features that were planned. Remember that this was to transmit the numerical data "in parallel," so parallel gating was part of the plan. For binary there would be over three times as many gates and power transmitting tubes in each accumulator as for decimal. Our estimates showed that we might use even more tubes for a wholly binary system. But that was not our primary reason for choosing the decimal system: it was very much a secondary reason. The primary reason was that we thought the users would be better off not having the additional complication of radix conversion every time they wanted to check whether the calculation was going right. We knew that fundamentally the whole machine was binary in all its details, and so it was really a matter of how and where the conversion took place. The numbers in any accumulator could be read out in decimal directly whenever the operator chose to stop the machine.

8. The ENIAC Stores

I have read many an account of the way in which "instructions" for a problem were given to the ENIAC, and quite a few make our method sound rather primitive. Well, it was, if you think that we should have stored all elements of the necessary instructions in the way that we now are used to. But at the time, with fast storage requiring a number of tubes per digit, and considering the pressure to produce the fastest calculator as quickly as we could, we had to do the best with whatever seemed the most available methods.

Taking a superficial view, ENIAC may have seemed like no more than a giant plugboard. Cables ran from place to place over the entire 80 ft of panels that housed various arithmetic and functional devices with local controls. These had to be shielded cables and rigid "trays" with many shielded conductors, some with "data pulses" and others with "program pulses." These pulses were rather sharp, often at 100,000 pulses/sec rates. For any new problem almost all of these cabled connections had to be changed, because they determined the sequence of operations performed and selected the data on which those operations were performed. This provided a program sequence that was as rapid as the arithmetic and functional units required. But it allowed no flexibility whatsoever.

A device that we called the master programmer provided program storage that could be altered by the program itself at electronic speeds. This supplied our electronic arithmetic units with controls fast enough to take full advantage of the arithmetic speeds. In modern terms, the branching and looping capabilities provided in the ENIAC required that we have electronic stepping switches and electronic counters that contained program information which was altered by the program itself. Thus, in the places that were crucial to the ENIAC's flexibility and speed, parts of its program were stored in fast devices which were altering the program sequences as required. Clearly, we were already providing "stored program" in the most important phases of control.

Eckert's paper in this volume says more about the origin of the "stored-program concept." Here let me just say that the fast memory was not cheap and the cheap memory was not fast. I have often been asked, "How big was the ENIAC storage?" The answer is, Infinite. The punched-card output was not fast, but it was as big as you wished. Every card punched out could be read into the input again, and indeed that is how Metropolis and Frankel managed to handle cycle after cycle of the big problem from Los Alamos.

So, punched cards were cheap, but the rate of punching or reading was 100 cards/min, and the cards had to be put in and taken out by people.

On the fast end of the scale, a flip-flop could respond in approximately a microsecond, but cost several tubes, including pulse formers and gates. It may be interesting to compare how much fast storage we devoted to data and how much to program. There were 20 accumulators, each storing a 10-digit decimal number and its sign. Regardless of how many tubes may have been used, let us simply state that there were less than 700 bits of high-speed data storage in the ENIAC. On the other hand, there were 20 decades of iteration counters and 10 "ring-of-six" program stepper switches in the master programmer, and each accumulator had one decade for a program counter in its distributed control. Roughly, then, we could estimate that about 150 bits of fast electronic storage were available for "program control"—that is, for storage of those parts of the program that had to be altered quickly.

I think that is an interesting way of looking at the very first large electronic computer ever to be built—more than 20% of its high-speed storage was for storing program information. Eckert's paper tells how we fretted over the question as to what percentage would be appropriate in subsequent machines.

9. Other Shortcuts

Our way of handling the "control" or program storage is just one example of the various "shortcuts" we took in order to get from nothing to a working ENIAC in $2\frac{1}{2}$ years. One of the more reasonable shortcuts was to leave the input and output of the whole business in the hands of IBM. That took a large load off of us and was entirely reasonable from the standpoint of BRL in Aberdeen. Hollerith methods were already part of the everyday scene for them. For instance, the results from range computations on the differential analyzer at the Moore School were immediately punched into 80-column cards and tested for errors by differencing on an accounting tabulator. Hence the IBM card input and output for the ENIAC was for the BRL a very compatible arrangement.

For buffer storage between the accumulators and the card equipment we chose some very reliable relays to which we were introduced by the Bell Laboratories. Needless to say, both the IBM and the Bell Lab personnel were very curious about what was going on at the Moore School, for all they could get from us at the time were very carefully framed specifications as to what they should supply.

When we received the IBM units, Harry Huskey and I started to check them out to see whether they met the specifications. One did, and the other didn't. For a while, we couldn't figure how this had happened, but in the end the explanation was that the modifications that the drawings specified had been made on an IBM punch of a different type than that called for. Once we understood what had happened, the punch was adapted properly, and there was no further problem in the input or output.

10. Legal Decisions Are Not Scholarly Judgments

The ENIAC patent application was involved in various interferences. Also, it was delayed in part because there were some questions as to whether "public use" was a bar to issuing the patent.

In a New York federal court the judge decided the patent should be issued, and it was issued in 1964. A federal court in another district came to a different conclusion in 1974, and the patent was declared invalid. I can't go into all the complications of the trial, but it was a kind of omnibus affair in which the ENIAC patent was only a small part. Nevertheless, it became a permanent casualty to a legal decision.

Although there were 30,000 documents brought to that trial, much of what they contained was unlikely to have been considered, and some documents were certainly ignored because they were not relevant in the eyes of the adversaries. However, they might be very relevant to the history we are interested in. One example of that is given in Eckert's paper: A long-lost Moore School disclosure was found showing that Eckert and I were planning on stored programs long before von Neumann had heard of the EDVAC project.

Another example of a legal judgment is the ABC machine, the Atanasoff-Berry computer, the design of which was never completed, but for which there exists a proposal which Brian Randell has included in his "Origins of Digital Computers." Because I visited J. V. Atanasoff for just two or three days in 1941, the 1974 decision of Judge Larsen was that I had derived all my notions about building electronic computers from Atanasoff. Yet the same judge, one page later in his decision, said that Eckert and I were the true inventors of the ENIAC.

Anyone who is interested in learning what I learned during my Iowa visit can read Atanasoff's proposal which Brian Randell reprinted in his book. The time I spent in trying to persuade Atanasoff to use flip-flop and scaling circuits instead of his mechanical commutation was to no avail. As I mentioned earlier, he rejected this approach because he had never got a flip-flop to work reliably.

It is unfortunate that the ABC machine was not completed, and that Atanasoff never gave to the patent attorneys the information that they requested so that a patent application could be filed. When I joined the Moore School in 1941, I wrote to him suggesting that he might join us and possibly have a better chance of developing his ideas, but he chose not to do this. He did no further work in computer development that I know of, although at the Naval Ordnance Laboratory a large budget was put under his direction for this purpose at the end of the war.

11. Conclusion

We should all be grateful to Randell for providing the reference material that, in many cases, had never been published. I hope that from a reading of the papers presented at the Los Alamos conference we shall all gain an improved understanding of the way in which our various contributions have intertwined and interacted to evolve the vastly improved calculating instruments needed to aid in man's many ways of probing the universe.

REFERENCES

1. Hartree, D. R., The ENIAC, an electronic computing machine, *Nature* (London) **158,** No. 4015 (1946).
2. B. Randell (ed.), "The Origins of Digital Computers; Selected Papers," Springer-Verlag, Berlin and New York, 1973.

UNIVAC DIVISION
SPERRY RAND CORPORATION
BLUE BELL, PENNSYLVANIA*

* Retired.

Computers in the University of London, 1945–1962

ANDREW D. BOOTH

During the early 1940s I was concerned with the determination of crystal structure using x-ray diffraction data [1]. The production of electron density maps for structure analysis involves very heavy calculations on large quantities of numerical data, and the state of the art in the early 1940s was such that the limits of human ability in this area were reached at structures containing not more than about 10 crystallographically distinct atoms. The determination of a 10-atom-type structure involved, in the early 1940s, about six weeks of experimental work followed by anything up to three years of hand computation for a group of human "slaves" and, even during wartime, I was trying to design equipment to mechanize parts of the crystallographic process. The results of one of these attempts [2] is shown in Fig. 1, which represents a small digital machine for the evaluation of structure factors. At the conclusion of hostilities, I moved for a short time to the British Rubber Producers' Research Association at Welwyn Garden City, which was under the inspired directorship of the late John Wilson, M.C., C.B.E. John Wilson was a lifelong friend and was enthusiastic for my project to build automatic machinery for mechanizing the whole process of x-ray structure determination. He provided funds for a succession of projects, the first of which was for a completely automatic but mechanical method [1, pp. 76–80] for calculating the structure factors just mentioned. The complex equipment was built, and an example of one unit is shown in Fig. 2.

By 1945, I had become interested in the possibilities of digital computation, and again received the support of John Wilson, even though I had by

551

Figure 1 Digital machine for the evaluation of structure factors.

this time transferred my allegiance to Birkbeck College in the Physics Department under the late Desmond Bernal. With the help and encouragement of these farsighted scientists, I started on the construction of a relay calculator for the automatic computation of all of the elements required in x-ray crystal structue analysis. This work was accomplished during the period of 1945 to early 1946. Our work on the relay structure factor calculator was

Figure 2 An example of the equipment for x-ray structure determination.

nearly complete at the end of 1945. Its circuits included what would now be called a many–one and a one–many function table for decoding and executing instructions. I invented this particular device without any knowledge of work that was going on elsewhere, but before its final completion the publicity that the machine attracted led the late D. R. Hartree to visit my laboratory, and it was from him that I learned of the exciting developments which were going on in the field of electronic computation in the U.S.

Desmond Bernal was also intrigued by this work and, as a result of his efforts, he secured funds for me to visit the U.S under the auspices of the Rockefeller Foundation. During this visit, I looked at the work of a number of groups, including that of von Neumann and Goldstine at Princeton, J. W. Forrester at MIT, Howard Aiken at Harvard, Eckert and Mauchly in Philadelphia, and Morris Rubinoff at the Moore School. At the conclusion of the visit, the Rockefeller Foundation offered me a fellowship to work at an institution of my choice in the U.S. My choice fell immediately on the von Neumann group at the Institute for Advanced Study at Princeton, not because I had seen anything of the hardware of their project, which I had not, but because the rigorous logic and precise thought of von Neumann attracted me: it had none of the airy imprecision of some of the other workers.

On my return to the United Kingdom, work on the x-ray calculator was suspended, and my research assistant, Miss Kathleen Britten (now Professor Kathleen Booth) and I devoted ourselves to exploring the joys of logical design on the von Neumann principle. This design was directed entirely toward serial operation and was really an exercise in mathematical enjoyment rather than anything of a practical nature. It was, however, at this same period (late 1946) that I became seriously interested in the problems of large-scale storage and conducted an analysis of the physical phenomena that might be used for storing information. The results of my analysis, later confirmed and refined during my stay at Princeton, led to a rejection of the mercury delay line, which was then well known, and practically all of the transient phenomena such as secondary emission storage and charge storage on discrete capacitors. I identified magnetic processes as the only ones that, in my opinion, had any potential for large-scale long-term storage. I also sketched out various embodiments of the magnetic principle, ranging from disks to drums, but took no steps to construct any of them.

During my stay at Princeton (March–September 1947), I developed an even greater appreciation of the virtues of von Neumann and of his mode of thought. I concluded that the electronic technology at Princeton was so far ahead of that available to me at that time, and that the equipment involved was so costly, that there was no hope of my producing a fully electronic machine in a short time; neither for that matter was there any hope of acquiring the Selectron tube that was to be the storage organ of the original Princeton machine. Miss Britten and I divided our efforts. I designed a 21-bit parallel binary arithmetic and control unit using Siemens high-speed relays while at the same time she developed programs for this device [4], one of which is shown in Fig. 3. Having designed the relay machine, Kathleen Britten tested some of the circuits for me, and I went on to investigate the ways in which I could build a magnetic storage organ and completed both the electronic and the mechanical design for such a system by May or June of 1947 [3].

On our return to the United Kingdom, and using the facilities of the Brit-

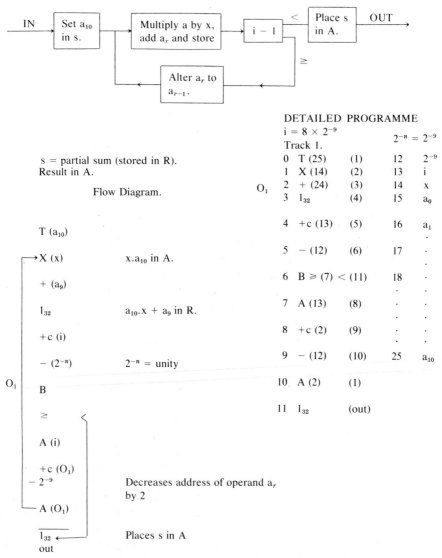

Figure 3 The first program for ARC written by K. Britten

ish Rubber Producers' Research Association since no laboratories were available at Birkbeck College, we started on the construction of our machine. My first experiments on magnetics involved the use of a thin oxide-coated paper disk extracted from a Mail-a-Voice recording machine. The notion was that, under centrifugal force, the disk would remain approximately flat and that the Bernoulli-effect forces would keep it in proximity to a reading and recording head. However, experiments revealed gross instabilities, and having neither time nor resources to work upon the elimination of these, I turned to a second alternative, which was the magnetic drum. A simple drum was constructed and nickel plated. An important feature of the system was that we used a prerecorded clock track and a counter and coincidence sensing system to identify position on the drum. We also used a gap between the finish and the start of the continuous 256 clock pulse set to reset the clock counter to zero when the drum was started up. This was only one of a number of reset methods which we used subsequently.

I worked on this system and completed an input–output device for use with the drum. This system was attached to the relay arithmetic unit which, by this time, was operational and so the ARC was born. Some extracts from my 1947–1948 diaries are shown in Table I and I draw attention to two which are of significance. The first is for Wednesday, 18 February 1948, when Mr. D. M. O'Donnel Livsey, a patent agent, was consulted with reference to the ARC machine. The information supplied to him included a description of the magnetic disk store and the drum equivalent thereof. The ARC machine was operational by 12 May and was demonstrated to Sir William Palmer, then the Chairman of the Board of the British Rubber Producers' Research Association. Just a few days later, we also gave a demon-

TABLE I

Extracts from 1947–1948 Diaries

1947	
Tuesday, 18 March	Considering possibility of new memory organ
Wednesday, 19 March	Wire and paper memory
Thursday, 23 October	Shifting register working
Wednesday, 12 November	Coincidence circuit complete and working
Saturday, 22 November	Worked on pole piece design
Tuesday, 16 December	Full accumulator working
1948	
Thursday, 1 January	Got memory working
Monday, 5 January	Saw F. C. Williams [at Manchester]
Wednesday, 18 February	O'Donnel Livsey . . . re patents in A.R.C.
Thursday, 19 February	256 pulses on! [i.e., 256 words of drum storage (2-in.-diam nickel plated drum)]
Wednesday, 12 May	Work on m/c-debugged completely. Sir William Palmer, Mr. Dickie [& others] came to see m/c-impressed
Sunday, 23 May	Met Weaver and Pomerat. To W.G.C. showed m/c

stration to Warren Weaver and Gerard Pomerat of the Rockefeller Foundation, who were visiting the United Kingdom at that time. The ARC system and the store are illustrated in Figs. 4 and 5.

Our staff at that time consisted of two people—myself, working on the electronic side of the machine, and Miss Britten, working on programming and generally maintaining the relay circuits.

With ARC completed, I turned my attention to the development of a fully electronic version of the machine, SEC, and for reasons of simplicity adopted the serial mode using shift register techniques [5]. This was something that no other project, as far as I know, had attempted. The Wilkes machine, and its prototype EDVAC, used mercury delay lines as shift registers. My charge-storage-type shift register proved to be the prototype of most of the shift registers developed and used in the future, and the basic design is still in general use.

The ARC machine worked in the one address mode, but we soon realized when we came to construct SEC that the magnetic drum, with its mean random access time of 0.01 sec could be much speeded up operationally by the adoption of a two-address code and in fact, as shown in our book [6], the design of a two-address machine using shift register techniques is actually simpler than that of a single-address machine using a control counter. The SEC was completed with the assistance of a research student, Mr. N. Kitz.

Figure 4 The ARC system.

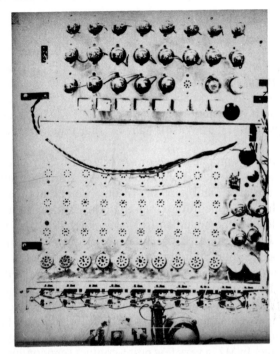

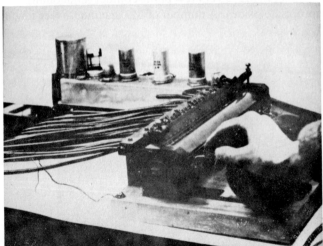

Figure 5   The ARC store.

The electronic hardships that we suffered were considerable. The only tube that was available to us was the VR102, a revolting version of the 6SN7 double triode in which one of the grids was brought out to a top cap with consequent clumsiness of the associated wiring. With the assistance of the Rockefeller Foundation, however, I was able to acquire a large stock of 6J6 tubes and, with these, we constructed the first of the APEXC series of machines (Fig. 6). The research student involved in this project was Dr. B. Zacharov, who has since had a distinguished career both in computing and in instrument design and is now (1978) Director of the University of London Computer Centre (ULCC). A number of APEXC machines were built, among them one for Birkbeck College, one for the British Rubber Producers' Research Association, and one for the British Rayon Research Association to which Mr. J. Wilson had, by that time, moved as Director of Research.

The late John Womersley, one of the original ACE pioneers, had moved from the National Physical Laboratory to the British Tabulating Machine Company by this time, and knowing of our project, approached me with a proposition that we join forces and that the British Tabulating Machine Company undertake the manufacture of our machines. This they did, the resulting series being named HEC (Hollerith Electronic Computer.)

The Birkbeck group continued in existence until 1962, when I left the country. We produced a large number of machines. From APEXC we developed the machine called MAC, shown in Fig. 7, and later a more sophisticated and stylish version which was called M2. These were all tube machines and employed semiconductors only in the function table, for which we used selenium diodes, costing only a fraction of a penny—all we could afford at the time. In M2, a very few point-contact semiconductor diodes were used in appropriate places. A number of M2 machines were made, and I used

Figure 6 The first of the APEXC series.

Figure 7 The MAC machine.

this machine as a means of supporting my research students and laboratory during the latter part of my sojourn at Birkbeck College. A number of my students worked on these projects, and their names deserve a place in the history of computers: John Cleave, now at the University of Bristol, who did pioneer work in the field of machine translation; Michael Levison, who worked on machine linguistics and is now at Queen's University, Kingston, Ontario, Canada; Martin Prutton, who has left the computer field, but is an authority on semiconductors; and Andrew Colin, who became, in due course, director of one of the British University Computing Laboratories.

My history is now more or less complete, and I will only remark that, on coming to Canada with its North American expertise, we rapidly constructed a totally semiconductor version of the M2. This was called M3 and

Figure 8 The M3 machine.

shown in Fig. 8. The architect of victory for this machine was Mr. Ken Cameron, who built the machine and debugged it in a period of 10 months for his master's degree [7]. M3 is still working in Saskatchewan, as is one of the M2 series donated to the Moose Jaw Technical Institute. The M3 has been extended in a number of directions and has worked for well over 10 years without serious malfunction or any real servicing. I believe that this is probably the only machine directly descended from the original that is still operational, and I believe it significant that my original design has proved capable of receiving, without adaptation, multiple inputs, analog–digital converters, and even a core store.

REFERENCES

1. A. D. Booth, "Fourier Technique in X-Ray Organic Structure Analysis." Cambridge Univ. Press, London and New York, 1948.
2. A. D. Booth, Two calculating machines for x-ray crystal structure analysis, *J. Appl. Phys.* **18,** 664–666 (1947).
3. A. D. Booth and K. H. V. Britten, "General Considerations in the Design of an All-Purpose Electronic Digital Computer," 1st and 2nd ed. Institute for Advanced Study, Princeton, New Jersey, 1947.

4. A. D. Booth and K. H. V. Britten, "Coding for ARC." Institute for Advanced Study, Princeton, New Jersey, 1947.
5. A. D. Booth, A magnetic digital storage system, *Electron. Eng.* **21**, 234–238 (1949).
6. A. D. Booth and K. H. V. Booth, "Automatic Digital Calculators," 1st ed., pp. 32, 104. Butterworths, London, 1953.
7. K. E. Cameron, The Design of the M3 Computer. M. Sc. Thesis, Univ. of Saskatchewan (1964).

LAKEHEAD UNIVERSITY
ONTARIO, CANADA*

---

* Retired.

A Programmer's Early Memories

EDSGER W. DIJKSTRA

Not being a trained historian, I assume myself unable to conduct an objective historical study. Therefore I shall not even pretend objectivity in any sense: I intend to record from my personal memory what somehow seems relevant or typical to me, leaving it to the professional historian to sort this out, and to select and to ignore in accordance with *his* professional standards.

In September 1951, I attended as a private person in Cambridge, England, the Summer School on Programme Design for Automatic Digital Computers, the same Summer School that, one year earlier, had been attended by A. van Wijngaarden, then the Head of the Computation Department of the Mathematical Center in Amsterdam. In connection with a letter of recommendation that I needed for a government grant of f200 (then $50) in support of that trip, I met van Wijngaarden during the summer of 1951. Being asked what I had done, I showed him two recent discoveries, one being a nomographic technique for finding the one real root of a special class of nth degree equations that I had encountered, the other being a technique for converting from decimal to octal with a mechanical desk calculator. On the strength of that he offered me a job as a programmer before I had left him; as a consequence of other commitments I had to wait until the end of March 1952 before I could accept his offer.

When I started to work at the Mathematical Center I found there B. J. Loopstra and C. S. Scholten, continually rebuilding a relay machine, called the ARRA. During most of 1947, van Wijngaarden had been abroad, study-

563

ing in the U.S. and the United Kingdom; during a short stay in Amsterdam, however, he had attracted Loopstra and Scholten, who joined the Mathematical Center on 1 August 1947.

None of us was formally trained as a mathematician. Van Wijngaarden was officially a graduate in mechanical engineering, but in the meantime one with extensive experience in numerical work; Loopstra and Scholten were supposed to study experimental physics at the University of Amsterdam and I still studied theoretical physics in Leiden. Our common background was that we came from two of the then most famous secondary schools of the country, van Wijngaarden and I from the Gymnasium Erasmianum, and Loopstra and Scholten from the Vossius Gymnasium. I mention this because I firmly believe that that background, which included a solid training in five foreign languages, has had a great influence on the way in which we worked. Such a binding element was very welcome, for in other cultural aspects we diverged widely: measured by my mildly conservative standards, the other three were at that time radicals on the verge of anarchy, and Scholten, a capable pianist, could even stand the music of certain modern composers!

Concurrently with the early developments at the Mathematical Center in Amsterdam, in the Hague, and later in Delft, W. L. van der Poel developed first the PTERA and then the ZEBRA, but although the distance between Amsterdam and the Hague is negligible, there was surprisingly little contact between those two groups, all the more surprising because in those postwar years of extreme poverty and general shortage of everything, one could raise the question whether for such a small country two mutually independent efforts at computer development was not a little bit too much. The lack of contact can partly be explained by a difference in background: van der Poel came from a different type of secondary school, he spoke and wrote a different kind of Dutch, and communications was, indeed, difficult.

When I joined the Mathematical Center in March 1952, the ARRA was believed to be approaching completion. It was a binary relay computer with a word length of 30 bits. The fixed-point arithmetic unit that contained the usual two 30-bit registers had been completed first; with a small relay memory it had been driven for some time via uniselectors from a plugboard. In 1951, the uniselectors and the relay memory had been replaced by a 1024-word drum. It had an instruction code of 16 instructions, among which were two for multiplication and two for division, i.e., both with and without rounding. The conversion from binary to decimal representation was built in; the single type instruction that caused a number to be typed was further controlled by a 30-bit code word that specified the layout. Programs were stored with one instruction per word, viz, in the least significant half. The most significant halves of the first 64 words that contained the standard input program were used in such a way as to present the code words for all possible number formats.

The machine, however, was so unreliable as to be practically useless. It was officially put into operation with all the pomp and circumstance that was deemed necessary; for the demonstration program that it had to execute at that exciting moment, for safety's sake the printing of a table of random numbers had been chosen, and as far as I can remember that has been the most ambitious program that, in spite of valiant efforts, it has ever executed successfully.

In late 1952, what was euphemistically called "a major revision" was decided. As a matter of fact, a totally new, this time largely electronic, machine was built, that had only the word length and the name ARRA in common with the previous effort. For the purpose of this discussion I shall refer to it as ARRA II. On 1 November 1952, Loopstra and Scholten were joined by G. A. Blaauw, who came from Howard H. Aiken's laboratory in Harvard. Whereas the old relay machine had worked with "operation complete" signals, Blaauw introduced the clocked machine; besides that he introduced selenium diodes, proper documentation techniques, and plug connections so that faulty units could be replaced. Blaauw's competence, his technical input, and his devotion to the job at hand were highly appreciated. It was not surprising, however, that a few years later he would leave us again: in the irreverent, godless society we formed, the devoutly Christian Blaauw did not fit too naturally.

Design, development, and construction of ARRA II took 13 months; in December 1953, it performed its first programs and for the next $2\frac{1}{2}$ years, until mid-1956, it was in continuous use. It, too, had the familiar two-register, fixed-point serial arithmetic unit, a store of 1024 words, eventually divided over 32 tracks of 32 words each, with two instructions stored in each word. Simple additions were performed in (slightly over) one drum revolution of 20 msec, multiplications and divisions took (slightly over) five drum revolutions. It had a nice symmetric instruction code of 25 instructions, with six instructions involving the A-register only:

$$(A) := (A) + (n) \qquad (A) := (A) - (n)$$
$$(A) := (n) \qquad\qquad (A) := -(n)$$
$$(n) := (A) \qquad\qquad (n) := -(A)$$

and a similar set for the S-register. Only in multiplication, division, and double-register shifts were these two registers treated on a different footing: conditional jumps were conditional on the sign of the last number written into store; conversion was no longer a special instruction—two fast multiplications by 10 were provided instead.

Its functional description (Report MR12, 1953) was the first report I produced as employee of the Mathematical Center. The first sentence states that the ARRA II is an automatic digital computer. The second sentence is worth quoting. Its English translation is:

In the sequel this machine will be described as far as is relevant for the person that *uses* the machine: we shall describe *what* the machine does, and not *how* the machine works. (Italics as in the original Dutch text.)

The sequel indeed defines the net effect of each instruction without any reference to the internal mechanisms accomplishing it. In retrospect I think it highly significant and telling that I then felt called upon to introduce my text in that fashion, italics included. It is surprisingly modern when we compare it with the following quotation—alternatively we may conclude that progress is, indeed, very slow!—from Wirth (1976):

> Hence, we conclude that the first criterion that any future programming language must satisfy, and that prospective customers must ask for, is *a complete definition without reference to compiler or computer*. (Italics as in the original.)

Wirth stresses the profound difference between a language (definition) and its implementation, and urges programmers to distinguish clearly between the two—in exactly the same way as the functional description of the ARRA II sharply distinguished between the instruction code and its "implementation," i.e., the machine that could obey it.

For me, that second sentence has a deep psychological significance: the nonoperational definitions of the semantics of each single instruction provided the impenetrable interface that I needed between me as an emerging programmer on the one hand, and the machine builders Loopstra, Scholten, and Blaauw on the other. And that sentence's inclusion at that crucial place in the report strongly suggests that in that environment at that moment, such explicit separation between abstract specification and physical realization was a novel idea, something that is not surprising when we see that 23 years later Wirth has still to argue the very same point on the next level of language. Another indication of some novelty is that, nearly before the stencil ink was dry, this report was nicknamed The Appalling Prose. It was written with the thoroughness of a legal document, and my hardware friends teased me with it, also because I needed a lot of teasing in those days. (But it only needed revision when they changed the machine!)

The machine had a double selection, one for instructions and one for numbers. The motivation for that was twofold. First, by disconnecting the number selection from the first two tracks, the standard input program could be protected from inadvertent overwriting. Second, track selection was the only place in which relays had not been thrown out, and as a result, a track change in one of the selections caused an additional delay of one or two revolutions; by doubling the selection the number of track changes was reduced. This reduction was not as effective as hoped: note that the machine had no B-register* and it had, therefore, to change its instructions in store.

---

* The original Manchester name, now index-register [*Editor's Note*].

The replacement by a more reliable and faster electronic track selection was the first major improvement of the machine. A further improvement of its reliability was obtained by replacing the selenium components by germanium diodes.

After about half a year of use the original standard input program contained in two protected tracks was replaced in 1954 by a standard input–output program occupying five tracks. The change is significant. Clearly, reliability problems had plagued us. The original input program would assemble words from paper tape and store them on consecutive locations, the address of the first location to be filled being given by a leading control combination on the tape. In the second version this control combination had to be punched twice and the input program checked in addition, each time a word had been stored, that the address of the store instruction had been correctly increased by one. Besides that, such a piece of paper tape could be read in two modes, either storing or comparing for checking purposes.

The output took place via an electric typewriter of which 16 keys could be operated by means of magnets. The decoding tree selecting the proper magnet was built with relays that retained their position until the next type instruction was given, and in between, a special "echo instruction" could read back into the machine the number of the last selected magnet. Short of actually reading the typed page, this was the most complete check on the output operation that could be envisaged. I designed a very ingenious process—of which I was therefore very proud—in which the conversions from binary to decimal and the conversion back from the decimal echos to the original binary were merged to the extent that they shared the same multiplication by 10. This rigorous total check on both the conversion and the actual magnet selection became standard practice on ARRA II and its next three successors and was abandoned only when the lineprinter hardware did not provide anymore for the echo reading. In case of a discrepancy, the machine would type the number again in the same position of the next line.

Today such precautions may seem exaggerated. But in the preface of a 200-page table of interpolation coefficients, van Wijngaarden and I proudly stated [van Wijngaarden and Dijkstra (1955)]:

> The whole table has been produced by the electronic computer ARRA. The program included complete mathematical checks including the signals sent out to the typewriter. The sheets are reproduced by photo-offset.

I think that our pride was justified—the only error ever found was in the hand-typed preface! This was indeed an achievement with a machine whose major shortcoming was that its not-too-reliable drum memory was not protected by a parity check. It is, by the way, a sobering thought that practically no computer today could produce those master sheets with the same trustworthiness and printing quality. So much for progress. . . .

The machine was in continuous use; during the night, often unattended for long periods, it worked on a very time-consuming project of integrating wave equations for research in theoretical chemistry. In order to increase the probability of useful work in spite of an unreliable memory, I rewrote with Scholten that program entirely. The operation x := x + 1 was originally coded—in modern notation—as

```
A := x;    A := A + 1;    x := A ;
```

we replaced it by:

```
repeat A := x; A := A + 1; y := A ;
       A := -x; A := A + y; A := A - 1 until A = 0 ;
repeat A := y; x := A; A := -y;
       A := A + x until A = 0 .
```

I remember that night mainly because, as the hours went by, much to Scholten's amusement, I got more and more cross with that program's original author, hurt as I was by all its clumsiness. Scholten and Loopstra, who also acted as maintenance engineers for the machine, were grateful: the transormation was highly effective and from then onward they hardly received any more calls for service at night.

In the first half year of ARRA II's operations its builders were still busy improving it. Then, in May 1954, a contract with Fokker, our national aircraft industry, was signed to deliver to Fokker the FERTA, an improved version of ARRA II. Apart from more elaborate shift instructions, it was basically the same machine. Seven months later, in December 1954, the FERTA performed its first test computations; it was delivered on 1 April of the next year, less than a year after the contract had been signed.

The Fokker plant, where the FERTA was installed, was not too easily reached. Blaauw and I did the debugging of the hardware during the winter of 1954–1955. Blaauw, who had been in the U.S., was rich enough to have a car, at least some sort of car: in an nth-hand Standard Vanguard he would drive from the Hague, where he lived at the time, to Fokker near Schiphol. I lived as a student in Leiden, and would leave my room at seven o'clock in the morning and cycle towards the highway, where I would hide my bicycle and climb up to the road where Blaauw would pick me up. It was a grim winter, but the combination of an old Canadian army coat and the fact that Blaauw was a punctual man made this possible. One night, at about half past ten, when we wished to return, the old Vanguard, the last car on Fokker's otherwise deserted parking lot, refused to start. I do remember that it had started snowing; I don't remember how we came home: presumably Blaauw himself fixed another bug that day.

It is sometimes hard to remember how poor we were in those days. When I entered the service of the Mathematical Center at the age of 21 with the best possible credentials, my salary was f11 (about $3) per day. Three years later, when the FERTA was transferred to Fokker, the successful transaction was concluded by a dinner with the directors of Fokker's Aircraft Industry. I shall never forget the main course: chicken boned by the waiter at our table. And I still remember the regret with which I saw so much perfect chicken meat being returned to the kitchen: in those days I was not only poor, I was hungry. But, somehow, we did not seem to mind: we worked like mad; we were never in doubt about the immediate usefulness of our work; we lived in a state of continuous excitement and had a tremendous amount of fun.

In retrospect the ARRA II with which I worked for nearly $2\frac{1}{2}$ years was an ideal machine for getting introduced to the subject. We wrote all the usual things like floating point and multilength routines, routines for elementary functions, and what not. Its decent order code and its slow but fairly homogeneous store were an incentive to do a nice job. Its limited size and speed saved us from overambitious projects and its unreliability was a sobering reminder.

I must mention a demonstration program I wrote for it at the occasion of the International Mathematical Congress that was held in Amsterdam in 1954. It faked the ability "to learn to type a digit": after each digit was typed the environment had to signal whether the machine had typed "the desired digit" or not. If, for instance, a "3" had been chosen as desired digit, it would eventually type almost always a 3. It was then possible to withhold the "appreciation": gradually the 3s would be replaced by other digits. It was a simple one-page program concocted within an hour; it generated pseudorandom numbers and had a few thresholds determining the speeds of "learning" and "forgetting" and the frequency of "errors." During its exhibition I got alarmed by the enthusiasm it evoked among the impressed visitors who were misled into believing that we were seriously simulating learning processes. Eventually I tried to explain that we were only faking, but I was not very successful, because their enthusiasm had carried our visitors too far away: it was a frightening experience.

By the end of June 1956, fifteen months after the delivery of the FERTA, Loopstra and Scholten had completed their next machine, the ARMAC, a new machine for which I had again written the functional description, designed the program notation, and written the basic communication programs. For the third time the entire road from conception to a fully documented and working machine had been covered in less than $1\frac{1}{2}$ years. Clearly we were getting experienced!

In view of our previous equipment the ARMAC was an exciting *monstrum*. It was exciting because on certain computations it could be 50 times as fast as the ARRA II, which was instantaneously dismantled when the ARMAC was put into operation. Personally I remember the awe with which we looked at it when it performed its first production program, a computation of transverse movements of railway carriages. Another reason for remembering that occasion was that the program had been written by M. C.

Debets, bound to become Mrs. Dijkstra a year later. The word length of the ARMAC was 34 bits, two instructions per word and an instruction code of 30 instructions. Its main store consisted of a drum of 112 tracks of 32 words. The first 512 words of store were intended to be realized by ferrite cores; eventually this was only done for the first 32, the so-called "fast page." Besides the fast page the machine was equipped with a 32-word ferrite-core buffer: as soon as control switched to a new drum track, the computation came to a grinding halt for the duration of a revolution of the drum (which rotated at a speed of 75 revolutions/sec), during which the new track was copied into the high-speed buffer, and from then onward instruction fetch was again instantaneous. The device, a one-page virtual memory *avant la lettre,* was extremely effective. It was also very tricky: the machine had still no B-register and, therefore, had to modify only the copy in the buffer. Needless to say, a full description of that wonderful feature, complete with warnings for all the pitfalls, occupied several pages in the manual. It was a time when all standard routines were elaborately polished until they fitted exactly on a single 32-word page.

The ARMAC had a parity check on the memory and, as far as speed and reliability were concerned, it was a great improvement over its predecessor. The fact that its programmer had to be highly conscious of the existence of the individual tracks was a step backward; the high penalty of buffer refilling furthermore made many more advanced programming techniques, although logically possible, too unattractive in terms of efficiency to be considered seriously. Autocoders and compilers were plainly out of question. In retrospect this has been a blessing: it has forced us to skip the stage of infancy of what was then called "automatic programming," and when we got our next machine, the EL-X1, we could approach the problem of compiling ALGOL 60 without the burden of misleading experiences.

As far as programming was concerned, the ARMAC period was one of consolidation of our practice of running the Computation Department. The manual, for instance, states as one of the strict rules of the house that each program should be "restartable," i.e., without the need for reading it in another time: no more saving of a few instructions by means of initializing some locations during program input.

I recall from that time one failure on my side that is indicative of the progress of the art of programming that would materialize during the next decades. Let in N successive storage locations be given a permutation of the numbers from 1 through N, which is *not* the alphabetically last one: write a program that will transform that permutation into its immediate alphabetical successor. I remember that I tried to solve this problem for more than two hours and then gave up. In the early 1970s, when I needed a simple example for an introductory programming course, I suddenly remembered that problem and solved it without pencil and paper in 20 minutes, and what is more I also did not need more than 20 minutes to explain my solution next morning to my novice audience. I myself was very impressed by this palpable proof of progress and tried to drive home that message by faithfully reporting my failure of some 16 years earlier. They were not impressed: they concluded that if I had not been able to solve that problem, I could not have been a very bright student. But I remember my failure so well that I still know how I failed. I was still thinking in terms of individual instructions, some of them being jumps: I programmed without sequencing discipline and had not the syntactical grasp provided by the repetition clause. I did not even know what a loop was, I only knew that as a result of jumping around, instructions could be executed many times. To add to the confusion I was mentally coding for a machine that, for lack of a B-register, had to modify its own instructions in store, thereby blurring the difference between the constant program and the variables. In view of our primitive way of thinking about the programming task, it is in a sense a marvel that in spite of it we still designed so many nontrivial programs.

Three months after the completion of the ARMAC, in September 1956, the specifications for a next machine, the EL-X1, were drafted. Its detailed design was ready by the end of the year, and another year later, at the end of 1957, the prototype X1 performed its first computations. Again, it was done in less than 18 months. The EL-X1 was really exciting. It was a fully transistorized machine that would have ferrite cores as its main memory, and it was ten times as fast as the ARMAC.

This time the design and production of the standard input–output program was a totally new challenge, and it was so for two reasons. The one reason was that the hardware required the standard input–output program to be wired in. I designed the program as carefully as I could, paid equal care to the ARMAC program that was used to derive from my hand-punched version the punched-paper tapes that were going to control the semiautomatic wiring machine. It was the first time in my life that a considerable investment was made in the hard wiring of a 25,000-bit program that I had been unable to test. I am grateful for the experience, as it taught me that the flawless production of such a program is not a superhuman task. The other reason was that, following a suggestion from A. W. Dek, the X1 was equipped with a real-time interrupt which signalled the completion of I/O commands. When this was first suggested it frightened the wits out of me as soon as I realized that it would make the machine a nondeterministic one without reproducible behavior, and I managed to delay by my fear the final decision to incorporate the interrupt for a few months. Eventually I was flattered out of my resistance, and this double inability to test my program before it went into "production" gave a new flavor to the task.

I remember my first contribution: when trying to design the status-saving and status-restoring protocol in such a way that I could prove its correctness, I discovered that with the proposed means for enabling and disabling the interrupt it was impossible to do so. After Loopstra and Scholten had checked my argument, that part of the instruction code was changed in accordance with my recommendations.

After that programming task had been completed in early 1958, I did not program for a while. I was absorbed by writing my thesis on that last effort, translating my thesis from Dutch into English and, besides that, the running of the Computation Department took more of my time, due to temporary absence of its Director, who had had a serious road accident. Preliminary discussions, based on ALGOL 58 and eventually leading to ALGOL 60, were started. Besides that, it would last until March 1960, until the Mathematical Center would get its copy of the EL-X1, the first copies being granted to more impatient customers.

On the 28 October 1959, I defended my thesis, with A. van Wijngaarden acting as my Promoter. Four days later, on 1 November, we started the discussion on how to implement ALGOL 60, of which the final definition reached us in January 1960. Harry D. Huskey had just spent a few sabbatical months at the Mathematical Center, working on an algebraic compiler, but his style of work differed so radically from mine that, personally, I could not even use his work as a source of inspiration; the somewhat painful discussion with my boss, when I had to transmit to him that disappointing message, is remembered as one of the rare occasions at which I banged with my fist on the table. During my 1959 summer holiday in Paterswolde I had given my first thoughts to the question how to implement recursion; in the early months of 1960 we discovered how, in combination with that, to do justice to the scope rules of ALGOL 60. After the interface with the run-time system had been decided, J. A. Zonneveld and I wrote the compiler while Marlene Römgens and Fiek Christen wrote under my supervision the routines of the run-time system. In March the machine arrived and in August our implementation was operational. Our first test case had been something like begin real a; a := 7 end; our fourth test case had been a recursive summation procedure, via the call-by-name mechanism and Jensen's device called to perform a double summation. The combination of no prior experience in compiler writing and a new machine without established ways of use greatly assisted us in approaching the problem of implementing ALGOL 60 with a fresh mind.

Our implementation of ALGOL 60 marks the end of the period of growth that I intended to cover; it also marked the beginning of a new one. Finally I was beginning to consider myself as a professional programmer, and, thanks to the beard I grew during the ALGOL 60 project, I was even beginning to look like one. It marked the beginning of the period during which the programming activity would begin to evolve from a craft to a scientific discipline. In December 1960, I bought my first car, a Volkswagen I could barely afford. I had a wife, one and a half children, a telephone, a piano, and a car: the son, whose wanderings had sometimes worried his parents, showed at last the symptoms of a respectable citizen.

REFERENCES

van Wijngaarden, A., and Dijkstra, E. W. (1955). Report R294. Computation Department, Mathematical Centre, Amsterdam.

Wirth, N. (1976). Programming languages: What to demand and how to assess them, ETH Report (March).

BURROUGHS
NUENEN, THE NETHERLANDS

Early History of Computing in Japan

RYOTA SUEKANE

I shall start this paper with a short note on the history of punch-card machines in Japan and then go on to relay computers and to electronic computers.

Knowledge of Hollerith punched-card machines reached Japan as early as 1892 with the publication in Japan of the *Statistical Bulletin,* which reported on the American census of 1890. This is mentioned to illustrate the quickness with which information about science and technology was being disseminated in Japan. For economic reasons, the taking of a census in Japan was postponed until 1920, although the census law was passed in 1905. In the interim period, the Japanese government was preparing for the taking of a census.

The first Japanese punched-card machine was designed and constructed by Mr. Kawaguchi in 1905. This machine was an elementary manual one with a low level of performance. A follow-up to this machine was stopped when the census was delayed. The second machine was designed by Mr. Takahashi of the Electrotechnical Laboratory (ETL Technical Report No. 146, 1922) in 1920. Ten units of this machine were produced for use in the first census of Japan. But all of these machines were destroyed by the famous earthquake of 1921 in Kanto. At the same time, the first Hollerith punched-card machine and verifier were imported by the Census Bureau. Before 1941, about 1000 punched-card machines were imported.

There was no other Japanese effort to develop punched-card machines because the production of the machines and cards was not successful. In

575

1954, however, they were produced by IBM Japan. The early Japanese effort was made because Hollerith machines were available only on a rental basis, not for purchase, and were difficult to import.

As it became clear that the production of punched-card machines, as well as the cards, was difficult, the idea of using relays as components for calculation and control emerged, instead of the electromechanical punched-card machine.

This is one stream. In 1938, Mr. Shiokawa of Fuji Electric invented a relay binary circuit and Dr. Ono, professor of mathematics at Tokyo University, conceived the idea of using a binary system in his statistical computer in 1939. This statistical relay computer was actually completed in 1951 with the cooperation of Dr. Yamashita, professor of electrical engineering at Tokyo University. This delay was due to the intervening war effort, which not only stopped research but also created a shortage of materials. Two sets of the statistical relay computer were produced by Nippon Electrical Company and Fujitsu Company, and were installed at the Census Bureau and the Municipal Office of the City of Tokyo. Dr. E. Deming showed great interest in this machine. Its input was from a manual keyboard, and the output was to an electromechanical counter that was photographed by a camera.

In 1951, there was an International Computing Center conference arranged by UNESCO, in Paris, attended by Dr. Yamashita. At that time it was believed that only about 10 computer centers would be sufficient for the entire world. After this conference, he went to the U.S. and learned from Dr. Aiken that relay computers were more reliable than vacuum-tube computers. In spite of this knowledge, he involved himself in the vacuum-tube computer project, TAC (Tokyo Automatic Computer), which was started in 1952, influenced by the UNESCO conference. That computer was completed in 1959.

Information about ENIAC reached the Japanese by a story in *Newsweek*.* In 1948, news of IBM's SSEC was reported in the *Scientific Asahi* by Mr. Ando, who was manager of IBM Japan. These two reports were to encourage tremendously Japanese computer pioneers. Another important source of information was a library established by the U.S. in Tokyo, the Civil Information and Education Library of General Headquarters. There we found the *Proceedings of the IRE* and the *Proceedings of the IEE*, the *Annals of the Harvard Computation Laboratory* (MARK I, MARK II), *High Speed Computing Devices*, and *Programming of EDSAC*. We went there with hungry stomachs to satisfy our mental hunger. The famous report of von Neumann, Goldstine, and Burks was not there. It came to Japan in the form of microfilm at the request of Dr. Jo of Osaka University to Illinois University in 1952 and was circulated in Tokyo and Osaka.

Dr. Hamada, head of the Research Laboratory of Toshiba Company, was

* *Newsweek* (December 18, 1946).

also a promoter of the TAC project. He was a friend of IBM's T. J. Watson and was influenced deeply by him. Mr. Watson showed Dr. Hamada Pascal's computer. This visit was made before World War II.

Professor Wilkes's book* had a great influence on the designers of early Japanese computers, such as TAC, the computer at Osaka University, and the ETL MARK III and MARK IV. Due to a misprint in the book, it took us a week to learn that the op code LF should have been LD. The design of ENIAC did not influence us much because it was a decimal, special-purpose machine.

TAC was an ambitious machine, using a cathode-ray tube (CRT) as its memory element. It took seven years to complete. This experience, however, was the origin of the invention of the parametron, which was made of ferrite cores. The Japanese designed a number of parametron computers, but the quick progress of transistors made them obsolete.

Japan at this time was experiencing a shortage of dollars, which made the import of goods very difficult. For the early computer builders, this meant that they had a difficult time getting germanium diodes and such measuring devices as the synchroscope, which were not being produced in Japan.

Let us turn now to another stream in the development of relay computers in Japan. Dr. Nakajima of Nippon Electric Company published his theory of contact circuits in 1936. According to his memorial article, he was helped by a paper by Dr. G. Birkhoff on lattice theory in the *Annals of Mathematics* in 1935. He found that his theory, which was based on the concept of impedance 0 (zero) and infinity, was Boolean algebra itself. From the time of Nakajima's paper, there was a group of mathematically minded electrical engineers in Japan with a strong interest in contact circuit theory and mathematical logic. Dr. Nakajima's theory treated combinatorial circuits. This was extended to sequential circuits by Dr. Ohashi of ETL in 1941. In 1949, Dr. M. Goto made his theory to solve logical equations. In 1951, Dr. Y. Komamiya of ETL applied Dr. Goto's theory of logical equations in the design of binary computing circuits, such as the full adder, carry generator, and the conversion circuits between the decimal and binary systems. (See ETL Technical Report No. 526, 1951.)

In contrast to Tokyo University's electronic computer based on the EDSAC and using a CRT memory, we (Dr. M. Goto, Dr. Komiyama, and R. Suekane) started a relay computer project because of our tradition of contact circuit theory, its reliability, and ease of design. We completed the ETL MARK I in 1952 as a pilot model of a bigger machine and completed the ETL MARK II in 1955. These machines were binary internally and were equipped with decimal-to-binary and binary-to-decimal conversion circuits. The MARK II used about 20,000 relays of a special design. It had floating-point

* M. V. Wilkes *et al.*, "The Preparation of . . . Digital Computer." Addison-Wesley, Cambridge, Massachusetts, 1951.

arithmetic and fixed-point arithmetic. Memory capacity was 256 words, but three paper-tape reader punches were also used as memory. It had special registers that could perform bitwise Boolean operations or change the form of number representations. The construction of MARK II was done by Fujitsu Company. This company also produced a commerical relay computer, the FACOM 128B, which used a biquinary system and a crossbar memory of 500 words. The MARK II and the FACOM 128B were in operation for more than ten years.

There is much more to be said about the early history of computing in Japan, just because the facts are not known to the world. But at this point we shall make some short comments on electronic computers.

Before 1960, the Japanese effort was concentrated on producing electronic computers of her own design. While they continued to do so, Japanese firms also began making technical agreements about 1960 with American companies, stemming both from the difficulty with software and the problems of producing peripheral equipment.

Throughout all of this, one must understand the influence on the Japanese of the ubiquitous abacus (soroban), which is deeply rooted in education and in business. Last year more than five million abaci were sold; their use is taught in elementary and middle schools by private teachers. And it is used for both business accounting and scientific calculations. This fact, combined with the inability of the Japanese to produce punched-card machines, may explain why business automation was delayed in Japan. With the spread of electronic calculators, however, this situation is changing.

In 1970, the Information Processing Society of Japan formed a committee to study the history of computing in Japan. Several interviews were conducted to get a taped record of conversations with eminent members of the computing community. This committee was disbanded in 1973 because the association lacked the space to store these tapes and associated documents.

Another effort related to the history of computers was made by the National Museum of Science and Technology, by Mr. Ishibashi. Part of the MARK II computer developed by the Electrotechnical Laboratory and other early computers are on exhibit there. But it has no long-term project on the history of computing. There is, however, a continuing effort by a journal called *Computopia* to interview a wide circle of people in the Japanese computing community. This is being conducted by Mr. Kenji Usui.

FACULTY OF ENGINEERING
YAMANASHI UNIVERSITY
KOFU, JAPAN

From Mechanical Linkages to Electronic Computers: Recollections from Czechoslovakia

ANTONIN SVOBODA

My belief, as everyone must have one, is that one has to learn from somebody and then add maybe some hard work and some talent of one's own, so that perhaps one day one will learn something by oneself. I should like to acknowledge especially the people from whom I learned to be a computer scientist. My motivation was sometimes envy, sometimes love, always curiosity.

As a young man I believed that I would become a theoretical physicist; until 1936 I was completely unaware of any computer. In 1937, I had to start to do something for the war effort. I met Dr. Vand. He was my first teacher in a certain way. He rediscovered the principle of a mechanical differential analyzer, and he added one parameter to the system. When you move the axis by a certain distance from the center of the spinning disk you can get the variable, its first derivative and its second derivative. Within the Czechoslovakian Ministry of National Defense, Vand and I designed an antiaircraft gun control system.

Hitler crossed the border of Czechoslovakia on 15 March 1939, and the Ministry sent us abroad, anywhere, to work this system against Hitler. Now, next thanks to SAGEM,* which is a very big concern in France, and thanks to M. Pasquet, who I hope is still living, we got a position with the Ministry of War. The Ministry wanted to build that antiaircraft system based on the differential analyzer in the improved version by Dr. Vand. But we needed some additional tricks and this is where my first linkage computer was designed. Even here I don't know whether I had not an impulse from Dr. Vand. Now, naturally I had to escape from France because Hitler closed in. By a twist of fate, instead of landing in England, where I was going, I entered the U.S. in 1941 and later I became a staff member of the Radiation Labora-

---

* SAGEM: Societée d'Application Générale d'Electricité et Mécanique, Paris.

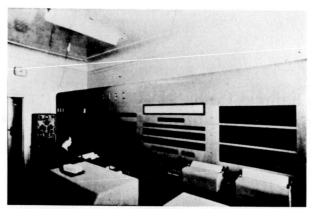

Figure 1 View of SAPO.

tory. I expected that they would need me to apply the advanced "Svoboda" approach to shooting but it was far from the truth. They had something much better. I joined the group of the analog computers connected with MARK 56 antiaircraft control. The analog computer had two sections. The linear part, which was called OMAR, was done by linear potentiometers of high precision, so that the precision was better than one-thousandth. But then, because the linear assumptions were not correct the linear theory had to be corrected by nonlinear corrections. This concept of division into a linear and a nonlinear part was created by the members of the group: Dr. Hurewicz (de-

Figure 2 Detail of SAPO.

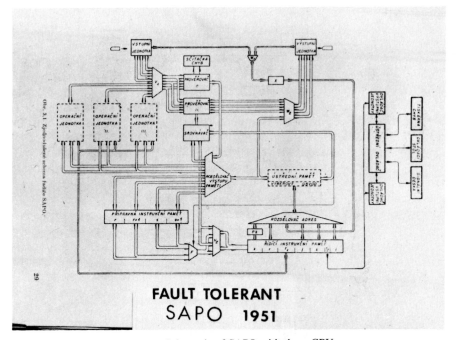

Figure 3 Schematic of SAPO with three CPUs.

ceased); Dr. Phillips, professor of mathematics at Stanford University; and Dr. Dowker. The Radiation Laboratory didn't ask me to design the theory of that device, but they asked to produce a mechanical solution for the nonlinear part of the system. Computing linkages generating functions of one or two variables were supposed to be used. A well-behaved function is given with just two independent variables: Produce a mechanism with nonlinear scales for those variables that produces this function as an angular motion (nonlinear scale) with high accuracy. For instance, the ballistic function is such a function. And, it is a surprise that you can do it with the precision better than one per mil, which, I should say, fills the practical purpose here.

Now, I had first meetings with my computer teachers: Professor Howard Aiken, Professor V. Bush, and Professor Caldwell were working rather close to me. At that time I was meeting them, discussing problems with them and, naturally, learning. This is the point that I want to stress, that we all, I am happy to say, have to learn from somebody. And, the explosion that we are today witnessing in the field of science is just due to the fact that this learning is being done. We have quite a bit of material for us that is growing fast, and we learn from more and more persons and this is why we achieve more and more.

The Radiation Laboratory series was published at the end of the war and

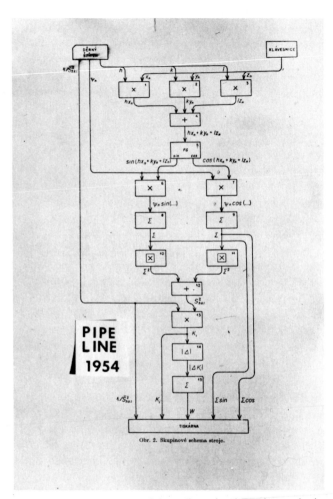

Figure 4 Pipeline processor of three-dimensional Fourier synthesizer.

it still is a learning medium in many ways. When we send probes to Mars we still have something to do with radar, with servomechanisms; while the hardware is a little bit changed today, it is certain that the problems of wave forms are still with us. At the end, I should like to say the epitaph of my analog career was the number 27 of the Radiation Laboratory series, "Computer Mechanisms and Linkages," where tricky, mathematical methods of linkage computer design are described. I am happy to say that it has been reprinted in paperback.

When the war was over, I was feeling very conceited because I had been sent by the Ministry of War in Prague to fight Hitler. During that time I had published more than one hundred patents for the war effort during a short period of time. I was going to Czechoslovakia, a free country, for a short visit. I wanted to show my son to my parents in Prague. In 1946 and 1947

Czechoslovakia was relatively free and I asked for a grant to go West to learn digital techniques much better than I knew then. I wanted to visit all the eminent leaders in the field of computers in the world. The learning again started with a visit to the Eckert facility using IBM punch cards at Columbia University. I saw scientific computing being done by punch cards. I saw the first relay multiplier and I believe Dr. Stibitz's work is somehow behind it. I was certainly learning a great deal.

When I visited the Institute for Advanced Study, I had a most rewarding experience. I met many people who are my friends today. Maybe I should say better that I am their friend. Dr. von Neumann, Adele Goldstine and Dr. Goldstine, and Dr. Bigelow all gave me a lot of material in the form of reports and suddenly I understood even why von Neumann was striving in a certain direction. Don't forget, the central processing unit (CPU) at that time was quite expensive and what was happening was to find out how to use the most expensive part of the system to the best advantage. Then in England, I visited Cambridge University; I didn't visit it only once, so I can't be certain exactly when this trip was made. There Professor Wilkes taught me his methods of microroutines and his control of large computers. Then I visited Dr. Turing, who that day in particular was not very well. He wanted me to come in the afternoon and I should have loved to. We had had a very nice sitting in the morning, but, I noticed he was really quite ill, so I told him I had some business to attend in the afternoon. I did not go back that afternoon to see him and to this day I am still sorry. Now, I shall go back to my

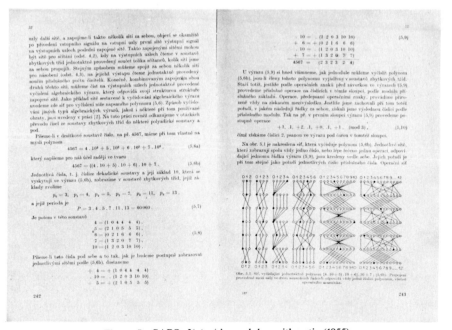

Figure 5 SAPO: Valach's modular arithmetic (1955).

first teacher, Dr. Vand. I met him again in 1947 when visiting England. The twist of fate which brought me to the U.S. brought him to England (1940). But, he left his credentials with me and when asked by authorities about his name and biography, he said he was an expert of the Ministry of War in Paris. He was sent to prison immediately. One day he had a brainstorm and asked for some paper, pencil, and a slide rule and designed the schematic of our antiaircraft gun control system. Then suddenly, he was persona grata and he ended up as chief of research of the Unilever at Liverpool, and when I met him in 1947 he had just prepared his wedding. I was asked to be his best man and that is how I know how a wedding is done in England.

After this was all over I realized that I now had enough information to design my own computer and the sketching of the machine SAPO began to emerge in my mind as I was traveling back from England to Prague. I should have liked to return to the U.S. but there was a takeover by the Communists in 1948 and this made a return impossible at the time. However, in Prague I was promoted to a position in the Department of Mathematical Machines in the Academy of Sciences. This later, in 1951, became the Research Institute for Mathematical Machines, from which there came many machine designs. Early on, soon after my return to Prague, I designed a calculating punch that used an algorithmic trick to make division go fast. SAPO was a fault-tolerant computer and was followed by EPOS, which also was fault tolerant and was

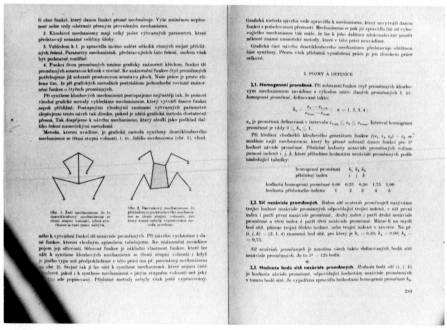

Figure 6 SAPO: Valach's linkage function generator with three independent variables (1954).

Figure 7 *Mathematicke Stroje* **1–13** (*Mathematical Machines*. Publishing House of the Academy of Sciences, Prague, Czechoslovakia). Translation of some Czech papers at the Library of Congress, Washington, D.C.

multiprogramming and time sharing. It had two CPUs and scratchpad and data-masking. One kind of work we did with SAPO was tracing of skew rays for photographic lenses. There was a pipeline processor for three-dimensional Fourier synthesis used for crystal structures with up to 40 atoms in the molecule. And Valach extended my work on linkages to three independent variables. All this, and more, is in a series of 12 volumes, "Information Processing Machines," from the Publishing House of the Prague Academy of Sciences (see Figs. 1–7).

And last—life with computers, by computers, and for computers goes on at UCLA, where I am working on fault detection and fault tolerance for arithmetic and computers.

COMPUTER SCIENCE DEPARTMENT
UNIVERSITY OF CALIFORNIA
LOS ANGELES, CALIFORNIA

Central European Prehistory of Computing

H. ZEMANEK

Bella gerant alii,
tu, felix Austria, nube!

[Let others make war,
you, lucky Austria, marry!]

The quoted principle [1] was overoptimistic in its time: Austria was involved in wars. And it does not seem probable that it would work today (although young people have a similar, but oversimplified slogan these days); at least, it was not heard that the present (Austrian) Secretary General of the U.N. had tried to resolve a United Nations problem by means of wedding.

But the quoted principle did work in its time: the aggregation, for instance, of Hungary, Bohemia, and Austria was managed by a double wedding in Vienna in 1515. And if one thinks this principle over, then it seems to indicate a different and (maybe) more lucky philosophy of activity and success in Central Europe. Indeed most of the stories in this paper are not really stories of success, of economic success. But one should be careful with judgments.

Describing the life of John von Neumann, Herman Goldstine writes [2, p. 168]:

Out of the repression and intellectual sterility that were the hallmarks of Habsburg rule, there grew up suddenly most remarkable groups of scientists of whom von Neumann and Eugene Wigner were examples in Hungary, Banach in Poland, and Feller in Yugoslavia. Prior to this

587

period there had, of course, been other great scientists in the Austro–Hungarian countries such as Sigmund Freud, Georg von Hevesy and Theodore von Karman, but in general Central Europe was not an ideal climate under the Habsburgs.

Certainly, rapid development and expansion at that time was as difficult as it has become in America. To develop a scientific or technical idea into a commercial success that would give full credit to the inventor was achieved by only few people. But neither was there a sudden genesis of remarkable scientists nor was there intellectual sterility. On the contrary: A careful investigation and evaluation would prove a constant growth of many schools of important scientists and engineers, and it would show an intellectual intensity and productivity which compares very well with any of the top intellectual centers in Western Europe or America.

The Habsburgs ruled a metanational, multilingual compound of countries, a forerunner of a United Europe, in which very small minorities that disappeared in the succeeding national states might have survived. The cross-fertilization of all those bigger and smaller groups was one of the reasons for the mental power and intellectual fertility of Central Europe under the Habsburgs.

Of course, it cannot be the intention of this paper to give a general review or description of the climate in which scientists like Boltzmann and Mach, engineers like Ghega* and Negrelli† set milestones for developments there and abroad, and out of which developed scientists like Ludwig Wittgenstein, Richard von Mises, Abraham Wald, Kurt Goedel, Karl Popper, Oskar Morgenstern, Karl Menger, Hans Feigel, Franz Alt, Erwin Reifler, Ernest Weber, and Heinz von Foerster—to name but a few Austrians close to our profession. It rather is limited to short versions of eight selected stories supporting the above statement about the Central European climate and contributions, whose intention will be to complement other papers in this volume and—this broadens the scope of the subject considerably—to stress the programming aspect of information processing.

My problem is one of selection. There is a great deal of material I could give, but for reasonable brevity I will confine myself to eight topics, presented in the form of eight short stories.

---

* Karl von Ghega (born 1802 in Venice, died 1860 in Vienna): He was a road engineer and he built the first railway over the Alps (1842–1854), connecting Vienna and Trieste.

† Alois Negrelli von Moldelbe (born 1799 in Trentino, died 1858 in Vienna): He was also a road engineer, working for instance in Tirol and in Lombardy. His plan for the Suez Canal was accepted in 1856, and he directed the work until his death. At the opening 1869, Lesseps took all the credit and did not even mention Negrelli. So Negrelli's daughter went to the court in Paris, had Poincaré as her lawyer, and succeeded in winning recognition that the canal was Negrelli's intellectual property.

Story 1. Broesel (fl. 1680–1690?):
Programmed Weaving

The punched card comes from the Jacquard weaving loom. I believe that information processing still has some things to learn from weaving that we have neglected because mathematics and logic delivered to us such powerful tools. But weaving, in contrast to mathematics and logic, which are sequential by nature, is a highly parallel process, and the study of weaving tricks and problems might yield new ideas for us.

We know that Jacquard had his card-programmed loom ready for industrial production around 1807, and we know that he had predecessors, particularly Vaucanson, who constructed a tape-controlled loom in 1745. There were earlier pioneers, for example, Falcon and Bouchon around 1728 in France and Cartwright around 1787 in England.

Now my colleague Professor Adolf Adam [3] has discovered in a weaving museum in Upper Austria near the three-country corner of Germany, Bohemia, and Austria a weaver's programming device built in 1740, but in all probability invented between 1680 and 1690, perhaps by a man of whom we know only the name: Broesel, which means little Ambrose.

The device is a closed loop of a linen strip (Fig. 1). The program consists of little wooden bars that control the loom. Whether a closer investigation can produce more facts and details on its method, application, and history remains to be seen. I should like to try.

Figure 1 Programming unit of the Broesel machine.

Story 2.   Maelzel (1772–1838):
Programmed Music

Music is a programmed structure, and musical notation is a programming language. On a second level, there is the so-called program music, the composition that executes a program, a story, an event, or a period of time. A battle is an event that requires a special program from the appearance of the armies on the battlefield to the victory, and battle music has been very popular, and very spectacular, for centuries. Another feature that music has in common with the computer is the need for a central clock—the conductor in the case of music; but how does he get the correct speed? Are the speed indications like largo or presto precise enough? The classic composers felt very unhappy about wrong performance speeds. My next story is about a man who designed a program for a battle symphony for Beethoven and who introduced the speed regulator for music, the metronome.

Johann Nepomuk Maelzel [4] was born on 5 August 1772, in Regensburg (Bavaria) and came to Vienna in 1792 as a piano teacher and organ mechanician. He invented the big music machine based on the organ, the panharmonium (Fig. 2), and he became the showmaster of the Vienna Congress 1814–1815. He traveled around Europe in the following years with music machines and Kempelen's famous chess playing Turk [5] built by Wolfgang von Kempelen. In 1828, Maelzel crossed the Atlantic and traveled with his show through the U.S.; he died while en route home by ship from Havana on 21 July 1838.

In order to get a publicity hit for his panharmonium, Maelzel convinced Beethoven to accept his program for a stereophonic battle symphony for two automata celebrating Wellington's victory over the French army near Vitoria in Spain on 21 June 1813 [6].

Maelzel collected army songs and trumpet signals, listed the restrictions on his music machines, and made a sketch of the architecture of the symphony. Beethoven finally agreed and delivered the score, his opus 91, within an astonishingly short time, so that Maelzel could program the drums of his machines. But time passed fast in Napoleon's era; Maelzel soon realized that putting the pins on the drums would take too much time. He went back to Beethoven and convinced him to transcribe the composition for two orchestras and he volunteered to organize an "all-star festival" (as we would say today). He got everybody who had a name and a rank in the musical life of Vienna to accept a role in a performance for the benefit of the victims of the battle of Hanau. For this purpose, he was able to get the main hall of the Vienna University (today Old University, Academy of Sciences). Salieri conducted, for instance, the artillery. (Beethoven, already having difficulties with hearing, conducted the whole enterprise.)

The first performance on 8 December 1813 became a tremendous success, in fact, the biggest triumph of Beethoven during his life; the battle symphony had to be repeated on 12 December and six times in 1814.

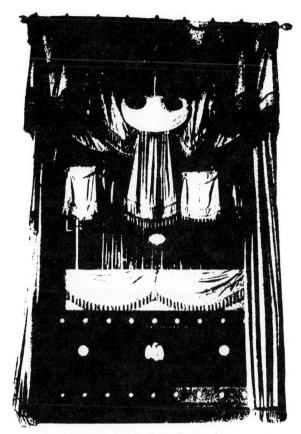

Figure 2 Maelzel's panharmonium.

But since the symphony had been transformed into a normal composition, there was, in Beethoven's mind, no more place for a mechanician. He paid back to Maelzel the 50 guilders he had invested in the enterprise and considered him out of the game. Maelzel was very upset, because he had hoped to earn enough money for a trip with his machines to Amsterdam and London. So he stole the orchestra score and had the work performed twice at Munich on 16 and 17 March 1814. Beethoven, who soon heard about that, was furious. He feared that Maelzel might ruin his chances in London—he saw good prospects for this composition in England and he had dedicated it to the Prince of Wales (who never responded to Beethoven's letters). So Beethoven filed a suit against Maelzel (which was terrible in its wording— Maelzel certainly had questionable features in his character, but he never could have been as bad as Beethoven described him).

Maelzel was, however, already in Amsterdam, and there he was faced with a shocking discovery: a Dutch mechanician had found the solution for the chronometer [7]—the metronome with a sliding weight at the top of the

pendulum. The inventor, a German-born man by the name of Diederich Niko-
laus Winkel (1777–1826), asked him to support the invention. Maelzel generously agreed. But what he did was to get a patent in London and Paris and
to start mass production of metronomes without even mentioning the name
of Winkel. So this poor man was very angry, and he wrote articles for the
professional musical journals describing the truth about the invention. Maelzel continued to produce metronomes.

In 1817, he came back to Munich and Vienna: in Munich, Maelzel convinced Beauharnais to lend him the Kempelen chess player. In Vienna,
Maelzel made peace with Beethoven; each paid half of the lawyer's costs
and Beethoven published the Maelzel metronome measures (MM) for all
movements of all his symphonies. They had a gay evening in the Black
Camel in Old Vienna and they sang a canon on Maelzel, the melody for
which is the second movement of the Eighth Symphony. The Black Camel,
by the way, is connected to the camelia: because its name comes from the
first owner Kamel—and a member of this family was a friend of Linné, who
named the flower after this friend.

In 1819, Winkel went to the Academy of Sciences of Amsterdam to complain again about Maelzel, who was not ashamed to come to Amsterdam,
and to work there his machinery and to request settlement of Winkel's
claims. An academy committee investigated the history of the invention;
they found that Maelzel had contributed only the scale; everything else
clearly was the invention of Winkel. Maelzel was requested to sign a declaration that he would, immediately, mention Winkel and pay royalties. Maelzel signed, but never acted. So until today, the metronome is Maelzel's metronome.

Winkel decided to beat him in his main field, the orchestrion business; in
1821 Winkel invented an orchestrion, which was able to compose by means
of a stochastic element (a wheel which stops after rotation at 0 or 1, deciding
whether the next two bars will be taken from the variation played now or
from the next one on the drum). This orchestrion is called componium [8]. It
was displayed in Amsterdam (1822), Paris (1824 and 1829), and London
(1830), where, however, due to the death of King George IV, nobody wanted
to hear the machine. It was a total fiasco, and in addition, Winkel found out
that his customs documents were not in order. He tried to smuggle the machine (6 ft high and 4 ft wide) through customs, who—of course—caught
him. The machine remained for a year in a wet customs warehouse and was
badly damaged. Winkel died, poor and discouraged. Between 1840 and 1850,
the componium was repaired by the famous magician Robert Houdin. Later,
it came to Belgium—where it still is, in the Museum of Musical Instruments
of the Conservatoire Royal de Musique, and where I managed the third repair by Mr. Krcal from the Vienna Museum of Technology.

Maelzel traveled through Europe with his machines and with the chess
player [5] to which he added, by the way, a device pronouncing "chess"

built with the technology of Kempelen's Speaking Machine [9, 10]. In 1825, he crossed the Atlantic and showed the machinery in the U.S. In Richmond, Edgar Allan Poe saw it several times and wrote his famous essay, Maelzel's Chess Player.

After the death of Maelzel a few chess players in Philadelphia bought the machine in 1840, repaired it, and displayed it to their friends and the public. They published a description and put the machine into the Chinese Pavilion in Philadelphia. When this building burned down on 5 July 1854, the chess player was destroyed after a life of 85 years.

Story 3. Petzval (1807–1891):
Programmed Calculation

Josef Petzval [11] was born on 6 January 1807 in a town in the Tatra mountains, Szepes-Bela in Hungarian and Spisska-Bela in Slovak. Petzval became a university professor in Budapest in 1835 and in Vienna in 1837, where he remained active for 40 years. He died on 17 September 1891. As a typical Austrian he can be said to have been Slovak, Hungarian, and Austrian, which may be confusing, but it is correct and in order (for an Austrian). Petzval was an applied mathematician, but also a physicist and engineer. He lectured on many subjects, for instance, on analytical mechanics, celestial mechanics, ballistics, differential equations, tone systems, and the theory of striking swords.

This is the story of his contribution to optics, namely, the calculation and production of the first precise photographic lens—one for portraits in 1840 and one for landscapes in 1856. The problem included complicated numerical calculations and, naturally, there was no computer.

So Petzval had to find another device, but obviously before this he had to design an algorithm and to resolve the programming problems. The calculation of lenses was and is called dioptrics, and in his time it used power series. Petzval had to establish a set of linear equations, the number of which depends on the intended approximation; so the fifth-order approximation required 8 equations, the seventh-order 27 equations [12]. In addition, with increasing order of approximation, the number of calculated decimals also had to be increased. Petzval, as an applied mathematician, did not want only to get the result of the approximation, but also a measure for the deviation from the ideal.

The input of the calculations depended on certain constructional decisions and on the properties of the glass used, so that a lot of experiments and measurements had to be made in order to get the input.

The device that Petzval had to use was of course the programmed calculation of human beings, a technology that seems to exist at least since the end of the 18th century and which, I think, might deserve some research work, if one is interested in the history of programming.

In the last century, however, human calculators already represented quite a financial problem, certainly one beyond the means of a university professor. The help came from the army. The story is that Petzval used to complain that he knew how to calculate a precise lens but could not afford to carry out the necessary calculations. He did so during a dinner where a member of the Habsburg family was present, Archduke Ludwig, the Director of the Austrian Artillery. In his bombardier corps, Ludwig had experienced specialists for the programmed calculation of shooting tables. Very probably, Ludwig recognized the military importance of precise photographic lenses and so he lent Professor Petzval ten calculating bombardiers, and Petzval mentions two of them by name, Oberfeuerwerker Löschner and Oberfeuerwerker Hain. The crew seems to have worked for several years.

I have tried to get protocols of those calculations, but without success. The heritage of Petzval, including his books and notes, was moved to Budapest before World War I and during the wild period at the end of World War II they disappeared. They must still exist, because several of the books appeared on secondhand book markets, but the appeals of the Hungarian authorities to render the whole material available were for obvious reasons unsuccessful.

Petzval not only established the theory and the calculations, he got the lens made. In May 1840, he gave the tables and many drawings to the Viennese optician Voigtlaender. Voigtlaender produced the first camera with the Petzval lens before the end of that year. This camera is now in the Vienna Museum of Technology. The lens was exactly as the calculation had predicted, and it reduced taking a photograph from many minutes to a few seconds. Petzval had revolutionized photography. But there was no contract with Voigtlaender, who did not pay any royalties to Petzval and who gave him almost no credit for the invention. A long struggle developed. When in 1856 Petzval demonstrated a landscape lens in Vienna and had it produced by another Viennese optician, Voigtlaender, who had meanwhile moved to Germany, manufactured that second lens immediately too, based on the equations and tables that Petzval, not realizing the economic importance, had handed over to him. The name of Voigtlaender is internationally known; the Austrian inventor is practically unknown.

Petzval, by the way, in his report on the dioptric theory, uses the term "thinking machine" [12], as far as I know for the first time, and moreover in a correct sense:

> Analytical optics is not a science, in contrast to pure mathematics, which aims at the perfection of a big and powerful thinking machine, without any consideration of the processed material—while analytical optics discusses the properties of certain artefacts. So pure mathematics has its value in itself while analytical optics gets its value only in view of the useful purpose of its artefacts. [*Author's Note:* This is not a fully literary translation of the quotation.]

Story 4. Schaeffler (1838–1928):
Plug-in Programming

Otto Schaeffler was not born an Austrian. Like many other famous Viennese—Beethoven, Brahms, Maelzel—he came from abroad [13]. He was born on 15 October 1838, in Unterheimbach, east of Heilbronn, Germany. His parents sent him to the seminary of Blaubeuren near Ulm, but the boy wanted to become a mechanic. So he left the seminary at the age of 15 and entered a mechanic's shop in Stuttgart. His ability for this profession was confirmed immediately: he received an award of second class in the first year and an award of first class in the second year, the latter for designing an electromotor. In 1855, he traveled to Vienna and continued to learn there in mechanics shops for four years; then he went to London for another four years. In 1863, he settled in Vienna for life.

He knew when to take a chance: when the Austrian Post Administration in 1867 bought for 40,000 Austrian guilders the patent rights for the Hughes printing telegraph, which was internationally accepted at the Second International Post Congress in Vienna in the following year, Schaeffler cooperated with the American inventor so successfully that he was able to start a local production of Hughes telegraphs. Soon he was exporting them to Serbia and Roumania, to Italy and Switzerland, and even to Japan. Schaeffler established his own factory, and an advertisement in 1871 offered all kinds of telegraph equipment, railway signaling systems, and physical measurement apparatus. The main customer was the Post Administration, which in 1871 closed its own Central Telegraph Workshop (founded by the German inventor and telegraph officer Steinheil in 1850) and turned to private suppliers. Schaeffler succeeded in getting the main contract, installed a contract workshop in the Post Administration building, and ran the business of Post Telegraph and Telephone supply and maintenance until 1896, his successors until 1913. He supported the projects of the Post engineers, and he let them publish and earn all the glamour while he produced and sold. So there is little trace of his work in the technical literature; I had never heard his name during my studies and I had a lot of work collecting the facts about him. The result is fascinating.

At the Vienna World Exhibition of 1873 and at the Paris World Exhibition of 1878, Schaeffler showed, apart from his Morse and Hughes telegraph equipment and his railway signaling systems, a stock exchange printer of his own invention. His stand was one of the best at both events; he received Gold Medals and France made him "Chevalier de la legion d'Honneur" and "Officier de l'Academie."

In 1880, Schaeffler married a Viennese, and, in 1883, he became an Austrian citizen. Between 1874 and 1895 he filed 18 patents; in 1885, he fought the Bell patent with partial success. In 1884, he moved into a new factory where he employed 80 workers (plus six in the contract workshop at the Post

Administration). He was known in Vienna as a progressive entrepreneur: no children's work, no Sunday work—not normal in those days. He financed health and help insurance for his employees and cared that they got medals for being 25 years in their profession (from the "Gewerbeverein" of Lower Austria).

In 1896, Schaeffler came home with a big surprise for his wife: he had sold his factory to Czeija & Nissl, who from then on carried the name United Telegraph and Telephone Factories Czeija, Nissl & Co (now merged into ITT Austria).

Schaeffler died in 1928, at the age of 90, unknown, no longer as rich as at the end of the previous century, but after a life full of success and satisfaction.

What are Schaeffler's achievements? I shall select the two most important for us—a binary code and a programming patent.

In 1874, he invented a printing telegraph, a quadruple system like the Baudot, but mechanically more sophisticated. The Hughes telegraph had two synchronously rotating fingers, one in the sender and one in the receiver. By a pianolike keyboard the operator selects a letter and thereby offers a contact to the rotating finger in the corresponding direction. Since the receiving finger is in the same direction at this moment, the receiver can print the correct letter. The Baudot and the Schaeffler printing telegraphs use a five-bit binary code. But while the Baudot operator must learn the code and apply it to a five-key board, Schaeffler has a Hughes-like piano keyboard for 26 letters (or signs and numerics) plus letter blank and sign blank; below the keyboard there are gliding bars like in a teletypewriter of our days which produce the code. Schaeffler's code is a reflected binary code [14]! What F. Gray patented in 1953 for pulse code modulation (PCM), Schaeffler had applied in his telegraph in 1874, and for a similar reason: reliability. He had contact fingers sensing on five cams consecutively all combinations; the right one triggered printing. The code is described in a letter by the Austrian Post employee J. N. Teufelhart, inserted there as a footnote and telling that Schaeffler found the code by combining wooden bars like dominos with the different combinations until he had the best solution. The Baudot apparatus was successful, the Schaeffler apparatus was not; the Post Administrations were not interested in too much proliferation of telegraph systems. And Schaeffler soon turned to the next subject, where he saw and got his next big chance: the telephone.

Graham Bell and Elisha Gray had shown their inventions in 1876 at the Philadelphia World Exhibition. The first American telephone network was opened in Detroit two years later. Vienna followed in 1881: a private company got the license for a telephone network within a 10-mile circle around St. Stephen's Cathedral and they started in December, the same year, with 154 subscribers. Schaeffler constructed and built telephone stations, but first he supplied the exchanges: for 500 subscribers in 1882, for 2400 in 1884, to which he added a second of the same capacity in 1890, and a third for 3000 in 1892. In a report by J. Hopkinson, a member of the Royal Society of London, dated 1893 [15], the Vienna network is classified as faster, better and less expensive than the networks of London, Paris, and Berlin (except for some noise in the lines). In 1895, the Post Administration bought the Vienna network (which now had 18,500 subscribers) for 1,300,000 Austrian guilders, so that the Austrian telephone was completely nationalized.

In 1889, Hermann Hollerith got his patent for the punched-card system. The Director of the Austrian Census Office, Professor Inama Sternegg, an important statistical and economic scientist of his time, wanted to apply the Hollerith system to the Austrian census of 1890. How he came to this idea and how he found Schaeffler we do not know. But I found out that Hollerith was in Vienna during his honeymoon trip and the time fits well enough to assume that he met one or both of them and explained the technology of his invention and its merits.

Schaeffler agreed to import and to service the Hollerith machines, to care for the power supply, to organize trial runs, and to try them on smaller tasks like cattle censuses and hospital statistics. In the spring of 1891, Emperor Franz Joseph I visited the Hollerith operation [16] (Fig. 3), which processed 28 million punched cards by 12 machines through 667 days, carrying out al-

Figure 3   Austrian census.

most 100 million counting steps. The Emperor was very satisfied with his visit, and after completion of the work, Schaeffler received a very high distinction (Ritterkreuz des Franz-Josephsordens).

Programming of punched-card operations was extremely clumsy on Hollerith's early machines. An electrician had to wire the interconnections between sensors, counters, relays, and their contacts. Schaeffler, the experienced telephone exchange specialist, saw the way for the remedy: apply the exchange technology, plugs and plug-in cables. On 20 May 1895, he got the Austrian patent [17] for this idea. He wired from the different elements around a bar (so that the programming board could be bent out and the electrician given access in case of trouble) to contact plates of metal: 77 counters, 100 relays, 240 punched-card hole sensors, and 5 batteries are accessible and can be programmed—neighboring elements by plug-in cables (claim 7) and groups of sensors by metal sheet forms (claim 9). This patent clearly was the beginning of technical programming carried out by the census employees—no electrician required [18].

In the 30-year period prior to 1908, only five national censuses had been carried out on Hollerith machines, the American of 1890 and 1900, the Austrian of 1890 and 1900, and the Russian of 1895. But in spite of such a modest list the idea of punched-card census elaboration received much attention and the reports on the Austrian census before the Congress of the International Statistical Institute [18] had probably more impact on government statisticians in Europe than the American operation.

Story 5.   Torres y Quevedo (1852–1936): A Specification Language

The subject of my fifth story is a specification language and I mention the first true chess player. The biography is of Leonardo Torres y Quevedo, who was born in the Province of Santander in Spain and who lived and died in Madrid; but his idea of a specification language was turned down in Vienna.

Torres y Quevedo was born on 28 December 1852, in Santa Cruz de Inguna, Province of Santander [19]. Like Konrad Zuse, Torres studied building technology but never practiced his profession, because he got so interested in calculators and automata. Torres built a cable car over the Niagara river on the Canadian side, which is still in operation, but who among our Canadian colleagues knows that this tourist attraction was built by a computer inventor? Torres worked on wireless telecontrol for balloons and ships and invented many analog calculators as well as a very interesting digital calculator operated by a typewriter. In 1912, Torres built the first real chess player, with a king and a rook against the king of the human opponent. The second model of 1920 was less general but had a very nice appearance; Norbert Wiener played against it at the Paris Conference of 1951 [20], and I had the pleasure to play against it at the World Fair of Brussels in 1958. The automaton then was displayed by his son Gonzales; Leonardo Torres had died on 18 December 1936.

My story concerns a formal language for the definition of mechanical drawings and, therefore, of mechanical constructions. Indeed, it looks very much like a programming language for the numerical control of machine tools. Torres submitted his paper to a meeting of the International Association of Academies of Sciences that took place in Vienna in 1907. Copies of the paper were sent out from Vienna to 20 academies [21].

The language describes a device piece by piece, giving position, form, and measures, for instance, for sphere, cylinder, excentric disk, or cogged wheel. It indicates the orientation of the piece, refers to its fitting, defines transmissions, and marks symmetries rather than denoting the same information two or more times (Fig. 4).

The language uses mainly letters, numerics, and punctuation, but also analog symbols (e.g., most simple drawings), which could be, however, produced by a typewriter, say by a special ball of the IBM 71 typewriter.

As an example, Torres shows a device for the multiplication of two complex numbers, which he had published in 1906 [21]. He gives on the left the drawing and on the right the 31 equations that define the drawing and include as well the box of the device. Torres did not want to replace the drawing but to complement it by the equation for precision and as a reading aid.

He did expect objections against his language; very probably he was not too astonished to be turned down by the academies. His arguments in defense of the abstract definition are very modern and could be used for any specification language for programming systems.

Story 6.   Tauschek (1899–1945):
Bookkeeping System

After World War I, little was left of the punched-card activities in Austria. The now-small country had to fight hard for its survival, and recession hit the newly developing economy. But the scientific and engineering substance was there. In spite of the missing economic background, new developments began, also in punched-card technology.

Gustav Tauschek was born on 29 April 1899 in Vienna [21]. Immediately after high school he was called to the army, and he never could afford to study systematically at the University of Technology as he wished so much. He became a messenger at the Austrian National Bank, and in this job he could see how inefficiently administration and bookkeeping were working. He started to dream of automatic bookkeeping. His first invention, however, was a machine for engraving the loop patterns of money bills. He got a patent and—for the first time in his life—so much money that he could afford to work out his ideas, to turn his dreams of automatic bookkeeping in working devices. He soon found that there was no hope of getting his machines

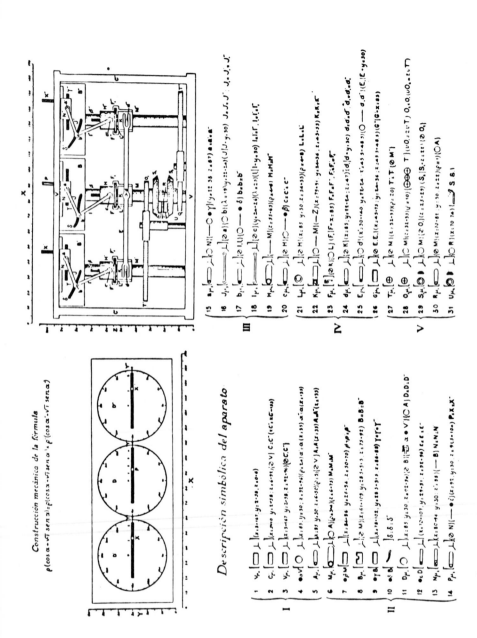

Figure 4 Torres equations.

produced in Austria; he went to Germany in 1928. But there after a short, hopeful period, the reaction was the same. After spending several hundred thousand Reichsmark for Tauschek's development, the Rheinische Metall- und Maschinenfabrik in Soemmerdo decided not to go into production of the Tauschek system. So he returned to Vienna in 1930 and continued to make new inventions. As soon as IBM became interested in his work, things improved; Tauschek got a working contract with IBM that ran from December 1930 to December 1935. He could from now on live for his inventions. Altogether, he sold 169 of his patents to IBM. Tauschek died on 14 February 1945 in Zurich.

Tauschek had educated himself, so he was little biased by what already existed: He found his own ways. He did not improve existing punched-card machines; he started from a systems point of view. He aimed at having one manually performed entry act, while all subsequent processes should run automatically except for those human interferences that cannot be avoided or are on a higher level.

Tauschek defined "automatic accounting" as "distribution and recording of the single entry on different accounts, where the entry is on a punched card, while the account is on a section of a large paper tape, with the address marked by punched holes." His card had 75 positions, in the upper part only —the lower part of the card could be used as input or output document. The code was n holes for digit n, i.e., 6 holes for the digit 6. This code is used for step-counting procedures. The throughput of his automatic bookkeeping system was 4000 cards/hour (Fig. 5).

He also invented the system elements, for instance, a reading machine in which the incoming digit or letter is compared to an optically stored form, and the form is recognized where no light passes. Other elements were a special card sorter and a special card mixer. Here the speed was up to 20,000 cards/hour. Finally, Tauschek also invented a magnetic store on steel plates based on Poulsen's invention of the telegraphon.*

Tauschek invented also many other things, for instance, a motor-driven sledge, and he worked also on cryptographic problems (coding pictures) and on secret observation by means of tubes (a forerunner of fiber transmission); those ideas were prepared for patenting, but not actually filed.

Story 7. The MAILUEFTERL

Of course, I want to say a few words about the contributions made in Vienna under my direction. I might come back here to the Austrian principle

---

* The telegraphon (télégraphone) is an invention of Waldemar Poulsen, a Dane, shown at the Paris World's Fair of 1900 (U.S. patent No. 661 619); it was the first magnetic recording device. It used a steel wire around a cylinder. This was the origin of the tape recorder; high frequency for recording and deleting was invented in Germany by Braunmühl and Weber in the 1940s.

Figure 5   Tauschek's accounting machine.

of marriage, because the computer we built at the University of Technology between 1956 and 1958 [23] was not only one of the earliest European fully transistorized computers—it was a real marriage between ideas and structures originating all over Central Europe (Fig. 6). It is most remarkable in at least one respect: it was built almost without funds and more or less against the will of the university. We did get some money as Fig. 6 shows, most of it late; but practically all hardware was a gift from industry, particularly from Philips, who gave us 3000 transistors, 3000 cores, and 5000 diodes (Fig. 7).

Its hardware had a number of innovations that were patented, but I want to speak mainly about its architecture and about our programming efforts. I want to make one comment, however. For our core store, we got, free of charge, ferrite cores—selected ferrite cores, but the selection was such that

ZUSE FROMME HERSFELD	SIEMENS (MUNICH)	ITT (STUTTGART)	PHILIPS
			3000 TRANSISTORS
	EQUIPMENT		3000 CORES
			5000 DIODES
PERM BAUR (MUNICH)	1954 – 1961 MAY 56 – MAY 56 MAILUEFTERL		VAN DER POEL VAN WIJNGAARDEN (HOLLAND)
ETH (ZURICH)	FRIENDLY VIENNESE MAY BREEZE NO WHIRLWIND OR HURRICANE		KOERNER PRIZE $ 1 K
UNIVERSITY OF TECHNOLOGY ROOM ETC. NO BOSS	AUSTRIAN INDUSTRY MATERIAL	E.R.O. U.S. ARMY $ 16 K	AUSTRIAN BANKERS $ 20 K

Figure 6 Austrian marriage: the network of MAILÜFTERL sources and resources.

somebody else got the center of the distribution, while what we got free of charge were the tails of the distribution. So we had to find a principle by which to bring cores with rather unequal parameters to safe operation. We found it and we got a patent for it: rather than throwing the cores back from 1 to 0, we threw the rest of the cores to 1, and this idea under our given circumstances compensated for the differences between the cores. The reliability of the matrix was as high as if we had had the first selection [24].

Figure 7 The computer MAILÜFTERL.

The name of MAILUEFTERL is derived from a joke I made when I first announced our project at the historic conference in Darmstadt in 1955 [25]. "We are not going to have a WHIRLWIND, TAIPHOON, or HURRI-CANE," I said, "But we shall have a nice Viennese spring time breeze (MAILUEFTERL)," because the transistors we got free of charge were intended for hearing aids and so had a very low cutoff frequency. But my people developed circuits that finally allowed a clock frequency of 133 kHz, and that was not so low for the time.

The instruction code of the MAILUEFTERL had very great flexibility (Fig. 8).

A machine word had 48 bits and each 4-bit group could also express a decimal numeric in Stibitz code. The first group in each word was a flag group in which the first bit distinguished alphanumeric or instruction words, the second bit distinguished numeric or alphabetic words, the third bit was the proper flag bit, and the fourth bit was a check bit used only for storage from write to read.

The instruction word again was organized in independent sections. The first group expressed 15 different conditions, so that any instruction could be made dependent on the fulfillment of a condition. The next group allowed a selection between 16 main operations like decimal or binary addition, logical connections, and transport instructions. The next three bits allowed the choice between eight auxiliary operations like negation of one input—which yielded of course subtraction—decimal and binary left and right shift, clear accumulator, and set and remove flag bit. The following nine bits were func-

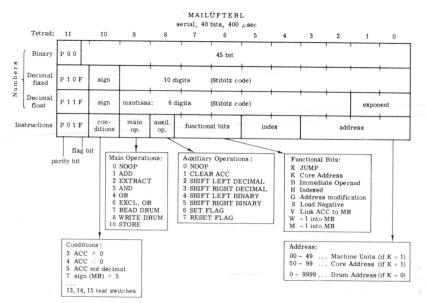

Figure 8 The MAILÜFTERL code.

tional bits, each of which triggered some kind of action in addition to the previous part of the instruction, for instance, negation of one input of the accumulator (which yielded of course subtraction), address not on the drum but elsewhere, Schein address, index operation, or add or subtract 1 in the multiplicator register (very useful for multiplication and division, which were programmed operations but with very few instructions).

The first real calculation was a problem of musical theory, more exactly a problem of 12-tone music: how many all-tone series exist? After a computation time of 60 hours the computer had printed 1928 such series, which is half of the total (the other half is symmetric to the first).

The computer was subsequently equipped with an ALGOL compiler and with a compiler for a logical language designed in parallel to ALGOL and supplementing it, namely LOGALGOL [26]. This language handled chains of bits and was used, for instance, for a program to minimize Boolean expressions. We also programmed on the computer what we had built as hardware devices: the three basic cybernetic models—the artificial tortoise after W. Grey Walter, the homeostat after W. R. Ashby, and the mouse in the maze after C. E. Shannon.

The computer MAILUEFTERL was moved four times: in 1961, from the university to the IBM Laboratory, a spectacular trip of a computer through Vienna; then from the second to the fifth floor in the same building; then into a warehouse; and finally last year from there into the Vienna Museum of Technology, where it now belongs to the Computer Department. There we have, by the way, installed a European version (with Austrian accents) of the history wall as shown for several years in the Manhattan IBM headquarters. We followed the Eames & Eames structure as documented in "Computer Perspective" [27], but the majority of the items are different and many are European or local.

Story 8.   Vienna Definition Language

Let me conclude with a paragraph on a programming subject which might appear to be too recent even for computer history. But as far as Vienna is concerned, the Vienna Definition Language is a closed chapter. It belongs to this paper insofar as it extends history of programming to definition languages and abstract machines.

The gap between natural and formal languages appeared to me first in my cybernetic period. Within the science of the behavior of animals, Pavlov's experiments with the conditioned reflex of dogs are a famous highlight. They resulted in a simple and clear model of a type of behavior, so simple and clear that Grey Walter could implement this model with practically no alternations in electronic circuits. The result was the famous artificial tortoise [28]. Between 1958 and 1960, we had in Vienna a Hungarian behaviorist and neurologist, Dr. A. Angyan, who knew both the Eastern and Western schools of conditioned-reflex behavior, and we decided to develop an advanced model including as much knowledge as possible, but restricted to one pair of conditioned reflexes. This artificial tortoise was produced in Vienna in five different variations, one of them for a New York hospital and research institute [29].

The development was a fight against the imprecision of natural language. The two schools of conditioned reflexes used, of course, natural language for their papers. But a model with 6 state variables and, consequently, 64 possible states, in each of which the reaction to a stimulus could be different, is a very complicated logical system. Only a lengthy trial-and-error process brought us from the natural language description of the many details of reactions to a structure described by switching algebra matching optimally the facts found by the two schools.

The problem of defining a programming language is even worse. Natural language is not an adequate means to handle it, and still one had to use it for defining formal languages in mathematics and for programming before better tools were invented.

For the definition of the syntax, John Backus had conceived a set of precise production rules that could produce all well formed expressions and programs of ALGOL; this was given in a paper for the International Conference on Information Processing, 1959, in Paris [30].

The definition of the semantics of a programming language can be a standard compiler, but only as long as only one type of computer is under consideration or decisive. As soon as there is a family of computers, like the IBM System/360, one needs an abstract definition of semantics. The IBM Laboratory in Vienna undertook the formal definition of PL/I which had to cover all members of the 360 family. But no method was known in 1964 and nobody had yet tried to define formally the semantics of a programming language of the size of PL/I.

As a preparation for the task, we organized the IFIP Working Conference on Formal Language Definition Languages in September 1964 [31], in Baden, near Vienna, thus creating a model for IFIP Working Conferences that has been followed since then by more than 15 IFIP Working Conferences.

The Baden conference gave to the members of the Vienna Laboratory not only a clear picture of the state of the art, but also personal contact with the most important scientists working in the field.

During the succeeding five years, the Vienna Laboratory produced a complete formal definition of PL/I in three versions, each one an improvement and an extension of the previous one. The idea was to build an abstract machine with well-defined states and transition functions on which the elaboration of a program with specific data becomes a clear process independent of the compiler. The sequence of states through which the abstract machine runs is the precise definition of the semantics of the language. The specification language of this abstract machine made use of the notion of abstract objects so that only the necessary was expressed and anything not necessary (like the specific arrangement of the symbols of the programming language) could be avoided [32]. The method has become known as Vienna Definition Language (VDL) [33]. Several efforts were made to improve method and language, but since 1975 no more work has been done in Vienna on this problem. In this sense, VDL has become history.

Conclusion

In conclusion, I hope to have shown that small as Austria may be today and as little the economic importance Central Europe may have and have had, there has been a steady flow of contributions to automata, computers, and programming, which has had its important share in the international promotion of our field. Professor Antonin Svoboda is a landmark for the Prague line and John von Neumann for the Budapest line.

Furthermore I hope that I have been able to give a few facts that were interesting and new, and that I have been able to give an impression—although only by highlights and short stories rather than systematically and thoroughly—of the steady stream of innovation that came from this part of the world. It deserves attention by the historians of computing, even if the economic use was made elsewhere and if the inventors remained unknown or left Central Europe. Austria, we used to say, has an excellent climate for Nobel Prize winners (of which Austria has quite a number), because one hardly hears that anyone has died there. That could also be said about information processing pioneers. But that would be, of course, a great exaggeration.

REFERENCES

1. Attributed to King Matthias Corvinus (1443–1490), *In* W. Stirling, "Klosterleben Kaiser Karls," Vol. V. Leipzig, 1852.
2. H. H. Goldstine, "The Computer from Pascal to von Neumann." Princeton Univ. Press, Princeton, New Jersey, 1972.
3. A. Adam, "Von himmlischen Uhrwerk zur statistischen Fabrik" p. 139. H. O. Munk, Vienna, 1973.
4. H. Zemanek, A life story of J. N. Maelzel (to be written).
5. C. M. Carroll, "The Great Chess Automation." Dover, New York, 1975.
6. E. Forbes, "Thayer's Life of Beethoven," Chap. 26. Princeton Univ. Press, Princeton, New Jersey, 1949 and 1970.
7. A. Chapuis, "Histoire de la boite à musique et de la musique mécanique," Chaps. IX and X. Editions du Journal Suisse d'Horlogerie et de Bijouterie, Scriptar SA, Lausanne 1955.
8. H. Zemanek, Das Componium von Winkel, *Elektron. Rech.* (*Munich*) **8**, No. 2, 61–62 (1966).
9. H. Zemanek, Wolfgang von Kempelen, *Elektron. Rech.* (*Munich*) **8**, No. 1, 5–6 (1966).

10. W. von Kempelen, "Mechanismus der Menschlichen Sprache" J. V. Degen, Vienna, 1791. Reprint, Grammatica Universalis 4, Frommann Verlag, Stuttgart, 1970.

11. L. Erményi, "Dr. Josef Petzval's Leben und Wissenschaftliche Verdienste" W. Knapp, Halle a.d. Saale, 1902.

12. J. Petzval, "Bericht über die Ergebnisse einiger dioptrischer Untersuchungen." C. A. Hartleben, Budapest, 1843.

13. H. Zemanek, Otto Schäffler-Wiener Pionier der Lochkartentechnik, *Elektron. Rech.* (*Munich*) **12**, No. 3, 133–134 (1970); Datenverabeitung vor 100 Jahren-Otto Schäffler, *Elektrotech. Masch.* (*Vienna*) **90**, No. 11, 543–550 (1973); Nachrichtentechnik und Datenverarbeitung zur Makartzeit, *Jahrb. Österreich. Gewerbevereins, Vienna* 71–92 (1974).

14. M. Rothen, La télégraphie et quelques autres applications, *J. Télégr.* (*Bern*) **4**, 247–254 (1878).

15. J. Hopkinson, Befund über das Wiener Telephonsystem. Verlag der Wiener Privat-Telegraphen-Gesellschaft, Vienna, 1893.

16. Visit of Emperor Franz Joseph I to the Census Office Punched Card Operation, *Wiener Z.* No. 106, 4 (May 10, 1891).

17. O. Schäffler, Neuerungen an statistischen Zählmaschinen, Austrian Patent 463 182 (20 September 1895, priority of 30 May 1895).

18. H. Rauchberg, Die elektrische Zählmaschine und ihre Anwendung insbesondere bei der österreichischen Volkszählung, "Allgemeines Statistisches Archiv," pp. 78–126, 131–163 Laupp'schen Buchhandlung, Tübingen, 1892; Description de la machine électrique servant au dépouillement du recensement autrichien de 1890, *Bull. Inst. Internat. Statist.* **6**, 19 (1892).

19. H. Zemanek, Leonardo Torres y Quevedo, *Elektron. Rech.* (*Munich*) **8**, No. 6, 217–218 (1966); L. Rodriguez Alcalde, Torres y Quevedo y la cibernética. Los Sabios del Mundo, Entero no. 21. Ediciones Cid, Madrid, 1966.

20. Les Machines á calculer et la pensée humaine, *Colloq. Internat. CNRS 37th, Paris,* January 1951. C.N.R.S., Paris 1953. In this volume: G. Torres y Quevedo, Les travaux de l'école espagnole sur l'automatisme, pp. 361–381; Présentation des appareils de Leonardo Torres y Quevedo, pp. 383–406.

21. L. Torres, Sobra un sistema de notaciones y símbolos destinados a facilitar la descripción de las máquinas, "Revista Ingeniería." J. Palacios, Madrid, 1907; H. Zemanek, Eine formale Sprache aus dem Jahre 1907 von L. Torres y Quevedo, *Elektron. Rech.* (*Munich*) **10**, No. 1, 5–6 (1968).

22. J. Nagler, In memoriam Gustav Tauschek, *Blätter Techn.* (*Vienna*) **28**, 1–10 (1966).

23. H. Zemanek, Mailüfterl, ein dezimaler Volltransistor-Rechenautomat, *Elektrotech. Masch.* (*Vienna*) **75**, No. 15/16, 453–463 (1958); H. Zemanek, *et al.*, Mailüfterl, *Digital Comput. Newsletter* **10**, No. 1, pp. 14–15 (1958); N. S. Blachman, Central European computers, *Comm. ACM* **2**, No. 9, 14–18 (1959); I. L. Auerbach, European electronic data processing, *Proc. IRE* **49**, No. 1, 330–348 (1961); H. Zemanek *et al.*, Mailüfterl, *Digital Comput. Newsletter* **13**, No. 3, 24 (1961).

24. K. Bandat, Zur Störreduktion in Ferritkern-Matrizenspeichern, *Elektron. Rech.* (*Munich*) **2**, No. 4, 177–182 (1960).

25. H. Zemanek, Die Arbeiten an elektronischen Rechenmaschinen und Informationsbearbeitungsmaschinen am Institut für Niederfrequenztechnik der Technischen Hochschule Wien, *Nachrichtentech. Fortsch.* (*Vienna*) **4**, pp. 56–59 (1956).

26. P. Lucas, Requirements on a language for logical data processing. Information processing, 1962, *Proc. IFIP Congr. 62nd, Munich August 27, to September 1, 1962* pp. 556–560. North-Holland Publ., Amsterdam, 1963.

27. C. Eames and R. Eames, "A Computer Perspective." Harvard Univ. Press, Cambridge, Massachusetts, 1973.

28. W. G. Walter, "The Living Brain." Duckworth, London, 1953.

29. H. Zemanek, H. Kretz, and A. J. Angyan, A model for neurological functions, *Symp.*

Informat. Theory, 4th, London, 1960 (C. Cherry, ed.), pp. 270–284. Butterworths, London, 1961.

30. J. W. Backus, The syntax and semantics of the proposed international algebraic language, *Proc. Internat. Conf. Informat. Proc., UNESCO, Paris, June 15–20, 1959*, pp. 125–132. Oldenbourg, Munich, and Butterworths, London 1960.

31. T. B. Steel, Jr. (ed.), Formal language description languages for computer programming, *Proc. IFIP Working Conf., Baden/Vienna, 1964*. North-Holland Publ., Amsterdam, 1966.

32. P. Lucas and K. Walk, On the formal description of PL/I. "Annual Review in Automatic Programming," Vol. 6, part 3, pp. 105–182. Pergamon, Oxford, 1969.

33. P. Wegner, The Vienna definition language, *ACM Comput. Surv.* **4,** No. 1, 5–63 (1972); A. Ollengren, "Definition of Programming Languages by Interpreting Automata," Academic Press, London, 1974.

IBM AUSTRIA
VIENNA, AUSTRIA

Some Remarks on the History
of Computing in Germany

KONRAD ZUSE

Studying the history of computing, we realize that there is a history of the philosophy of this history, too. From my own subjective point of view I can say that today I watch the computer development in another way than 10 or 20 years ago. While writing this paper I finally realized that there are different philosophies behind the different developments, especially in comparison with my own. But I shall concentrate mainly on the developments in Germany connected with my own work.

First, I should like to mention that in Germany the development of calculating machines began in 1623. Contrary to the general opinion that Pascal and Leibniz were the first in this field, recent historical research has shown that the German Schickard was their forerunner by some 30 years. We have to thank Professor von Freytag-Löringhoff, who revealed the nearly forgotten work of Schickard in Tübingen and who reconstructed the machine.

Today we know that the program-controlled computer began during the last century with Babbage. But he was so far ahead of his time that his machine was nearly completely forgotten. So in Germany when I started in 1934 nearly nobody knew him or his work. I was a student in civil engineering in Berlin. Berlin is a nice town and there were many opportunities for a student to spend his time in an agreeable manner, for instance with the nice girls. But instead of that we had to perform big and awful calculations. Also later as an engineer in the aircraft industry I became aware of the tremendous number of monotonous calculations necessary for the design of static and aerodynamic structures. Therefore I decided to design and construct calculating machines suited to solving these problems automatically. The work proceeded almost parallel to, but quite independently of, the developments in the United States by Stibitz, Aiken, Eckert, Mauchly, and others. It is interesting that during the pioneer days the computer development was represented by engineers and scientists who were not specialists in the field of calculating machines. At that time nobody knew the difference between hardware and software. We concentrated ourselves on purely technological matters as well as on logic design and programming. So I was unprejudiced and free to try new concepts.

In order to illustrate the opinion of the manufacturers of calculating machines at that time, I should like to mention a telephone conversation that I had in 1937 with one of them. He told me that it was, indeed, wonderful that I as a young man had dedicated some time and effort to the development of new ideas, and that he wished me all the best for possible other inventions, but stated that in the techniques of calculating machines all feasible solutions were already exhausted. Therefore, it would be absolutely hopeless to come up with any new ideas. In addition, he asked me whether my machine was based on the "sequential addition principle" or on the "one times one table." To this I replied that for my machine this was of no importance whatsoever. Here you should know that at that time the specialists of calculating machines were divided into two schools of thought, each applying either principle. According to the opinion prevailing at that time, only a lunatic could make a statement that this difference was irrelevant for his design. Nevertheless, this manufacturer came to my workshop and I was finally able to convince him that in a machine operating on the binary principle, this was indeed irrelevant.

The development of my interest and activities is shown diagramatically in Fig. 1. In 1934, as a student, I started to form my first ideas and designs on paper. In 1936, I began with the hardware and constructed the models Z1, Z2, and Z3. The first two were only test models; they had all the features of the later computer but did not work satisfactorily. The Z3 was completed in 1941 and was the first fully operating model.

In 1939, due to the perfectly private state of my workshop and due to the lack of official sponsorship, I became a soldier at the beginning of the war. The manufacturer, who assisted me, wrote a letter to my major requesting leave for me to complete my work on an important invention. He wrote that I was working on a machine useful for the calculations and designs in the aircraft industry. My major looked at this letter and said "I don't understand that. The German aircraft is the best in the world. I don't see what to calculate further on." Half a year later, I was freed from military service, not for work on computers but as an engineer in the aircraft industry.

The year 1945, with the end of the war, cut off hardware development in

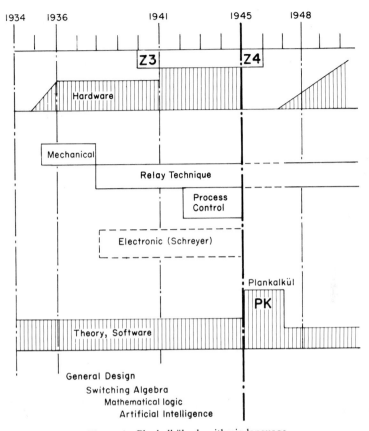

Figure 1   Plankalkül, algorithmic language.

Germany. We were able to save only the model Z4, which we transported from Berlin in an adventurous odyssey to Bavaria, where it was hidden in a small village in the Alps.* And because of the unfavorable postwar conditions nothing could be continued before 1948.

In the course of this work several technologies were tested and used. At that time calculating machines normally were small units to be put on a desk. So I was psychologically prejudiced and started with mechanical constructions. But I made a step from the traditional decimal calculating machines to real binary switching elements. This was, I think, the only attempt to make a mechanical machine based on a two-positional principle. But this technology did not work well with the exception of the storage unit, and I decided to change to the electromechanical technology with its well-proven relays.

Two additional lines of hardware development may be mentioned, a

---

* See the paper by Bauer in this volume.

model for process control and the electronic calculating devices of Schreyer. I shall discuss both later on.

The lower part of Fig. 1 shows the parallel development of theory and software. Right from the beginning I tried to base the whole development on a new and solid theoretical foundation. At first, the analogies between switching circuits and the calculus of propositions were discovered and a switching algebra was set up. General considerations concerning the relations between calculating and thinking followed. I realized that there is no border line between these two aspects and by 1938 it was already perfectly clear to me that the development would progress in the direction of the artificial brain. At that time I knew scarcely anything about the working method of the human brain. Even today we do not know exactly how it works. But I did not see the problem from the technological point of view, but more by analyzing the information process connected with "thinking." I took these ideas very seriously and this may have influenced my whole philosophy of the further development. At that time there was practically nobody to discuss with me the consequences of the possible innovations following this line. Even ten years later, when after the war I became acquainted with the pioneer work on the other side of the Atlantic, I sometimes had the impression that they were playing with computers as children play with matches without overlooking the whole scope of the new field. But these ideas were elaborated on paper only.

The interruption of hardware development in 1945 allowed me to concentrate all my attention on theoretical considerations, and to develop a universal algorithmic language, which I called "Plankalkül." The background and the situation of that time were the reason for the special philosophy behind it. Later on, this led to some differences and perhaps to some misunderstandings with my colleagues, for instance, Bauer and Rutishauser. But I am very pleased to see in the paper of Bauer in this volume that they studied seriously the Plankalkül.

Table I shows the models built in Germany from 1935 to 1945. There is the mainline, beginning with the models Z1 to Z4. These were universal computers for numerical calculations. They all operated in the binary system and, with the exception of Z2, with floating-point arithmetic. The program was read from punched tape. I used an eight-channel input code and one-address instruction code. S1 and S2 were special models for process control.

Schreyer built some test models in electronic technology.

The logical computer L1 was a test model in relay technology for programs with bits as operands.

I used an abstract representation for switching diagrams, which could be transferred into an arbitrary hardware. We applied it to mechanical elements with metal sheets and slots, connected by pins, to electromechanical relays and to electronic circuits. The idea of using pneumatic and hydraulic switching elements was only pursued on paper.

TABLE I
MODELS CONSTRUCTED BY ZUSE UNTIL 1945

| Model | Year | Technology[a] | | Binary system | Point Fixed Floating | Program |
		Arithmetic unit	Storage			
Z1	1938	M	M	+	Floating	Punched tape
Z2	1939	R	M	+	Fixed	Punched tape
Z3	1941	R	R	+	Floating	Punched tape
Z4	1945	R	M	+	Floating	Punched tape
S1	1942	R	R	+	Fixed	Rotary switches
S2[b]	1944	R	R	+	Fixed	Rotary switches
Schreyer	1938	E				
Schreyer	1944	E		+	Fixed	
Log. 1	1944	R	R	Logical Computer		Punched tape

[a] Legend: M, mechanical technology; R, electromechanical relay technology; E, electronic technology.
[b] Process control.

Unfortunately, I never published my ideas concerning this matter. Later on I learned that there were some papers, two in German by Piesch and Eder, and one in English by Shannon. But I missed there the consequent confrontation with the calculus of propositions. For us the terms "and," "or," and "not" belonged to our daily language. We really worked with them and made the step to apply the mathematical logic to the computer design. I translated the logical rules systematically into switching algebra. For instance, the principal of duality gave new insights into the working of switching diagrams.

For propositional formulas it means: change all "and" into "or" and invert and negate every elementary proposition to get the negated proposition. The analogous rule for contact circuits reads: change all serial connections into parallel and invert and change all "on" contacts into "off" contacts and invert to get the switching diagram representing the inverse of the given circuit. As a result of this practice the logic represented by the hardware was very sophisticated, using contrived microprogramming depending on complicated conditions, conditional branching, and so on.

So, switching algebra was consequently applied in all the computers we constructed. When Schreyer changed to the electronic technology, he first had only to design the switching elements corresponding to the three propositional operations: conjunction, disjunction, and negation. After that he was able to translate one-to-one the already proven diagrams for the electromechanical machines. The machines Z1 to Z4 correspond to this concept but, contrary to Babbage, they used coded addresses and a selecting unit. Both the computer of Babbage and my machines had no conditional orders or feedback in the program unit.

The first computers in Germany were exclusively designed for numerical calculations, and the limited financial basis and short time available for the construction did not allow any special features. Besides that, the users of the computer did not see the necessity for a more sophisticated logical design in those days. But on paper there was no limit on further ideas, even during the war.

The idea of general calculating or information processing, as we say today, induced me to consider that the program, too, is information and can be processed by itself or by another program. This general concept was elaborated in all consequences in the Plankalkül. In hardware it means that we not only have a controlling line going from left to right, but also from right to left. I had the feeling that this line could influence the whole computer development in a very efficient but also very dangerous way. Setting up this connection could mean making a contract with the devil. Therefore, I hesitated to do so, being unable to overlook all the consequences, the good as well as the bad.

So I first concentrated on theory. This led to the Plankalkül. It is interesting to follow the further development. My colleagues on the other side had no scruples about the problem I just mentioned. John von Neumann and others constructed a machine with a storage for all kinds of information including the program. This idea may have been trivial, as soon as the programs were binary coded and there existed storage for any binary coded information. This requirement was already fulfilled by the machines Z1 to Z4 and others (See Fig. 2). Besides this, the idea of storing the program was already mentioned, for instance, in one of my patent applications in 1936. Other pioneers may have had the same idea rather early. I think it was the special organization of the machine of John von Neumann that opened the door for universal calculating. He gave the signal "all clear" for the scientists but for the devil, too. This concept was adapted to the situation around 1945 and was very efficient, especially for numerical calculations.

My own designs for future machines on paper were more structured, with instructions stored independently and special units for the handling of addresses and subroutines nested in several levels. I believed that other pioneers, too, have been in a similar situation. Most of the theoretical work on paper, published or not, goes far beyond the machines really constructed.

Now let's return to the situation in Germany during the war. In our situation the only realistic way to process a program by itself was to build a separate computer for this purpose. Thus, the construction of the computers for numerical calculations could be continued without drastic modifications. We called this type of machine "Planfertigungsgerät," that means, a special computer to make the program for a numerical sequence controlled com-

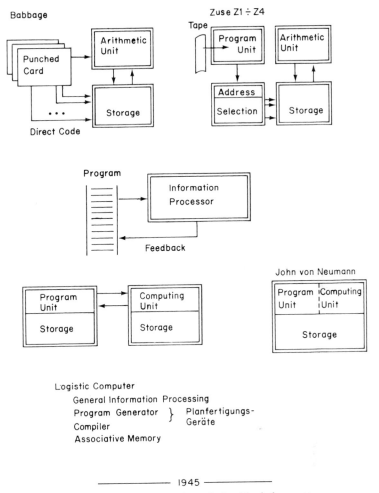

Figure 2   Plankalkül, universal algorithmic language.

puter. This device was intended to do about the same as sophisticated compilers do today. But in 1945 we had to stop this interesting development.

I intended to proceed in the following steps:

(1)   Converting algebraic formulas written in traditional form into a sequence of orders for the computer.

(2)   Inserting subroutines in a main program in several levels including the changing of corresponding addresses.

(3)   Developing programs for determinants, matrices, etc., of different order and arrangement of non zero elements. This means mainly the processing of addresses.

(4)   Analyzing whole technical systems like frameworks for constructional engineering and others and setting up the program for the numerical calculations for such a system with varying parameters like measures and forces.

This led to rather complicated and sophisticated evaluations, using the calculus of relations, predicates, etc.

After this general review I want to discuss some details.

Figure 3 shows the block diagram of the models Z1 to Z4. We have a punch, operated by hand to make the program tape. The program unit is tape controlled and gives orders to the computing unit and the addresses for the selecting unit of the storage. Input and output units were directly connected to the arithmetic unit. Input of both numbers and operations was from a keyboard, and for output numbers were displayed on banks of lights. Inside the machine numbers were represented by sign, digit, exponent, and mantissa. The work done with this machine during 1941–1943 included solution of linear equations up to third order, solution of quadratic equations, and evaluation of determinants with complex elements for aircraft flutter calculations.

I mentioned earlier the special-purpose computers S1 and S2. In an aircraft factory, guided missiles were being manufactured on an assembly line.

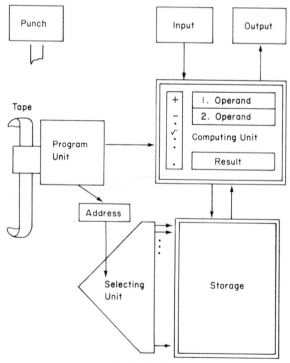

Figure 3   Model Z1 ÷ Z4.

These missiles had to fly very precisely in order to be remotely controllable. Therefore, every missile had to pass a special measuring station, where the deviations from the aerodynamic symmetry were measured at about 100 points with measuring clocks. These data were the input for a computer, programmed by rotary switches, which calculated the necessary corrections of the positions of the wings. A sequence of some hundred additions, multiplications, etc., was executed automatically. This computer was in operation around the clock for two years during the war. In a second version the measuring devices were read automatically via rotary switches, which transferred their positions into the computer. Today we speak of analog to digital conversion and process control.

Now let's take a look at the work of Schreyer. I already mentioned that the switching algebra allowed us to design a computer in abstract diagrams, which could be transferred into a special hardware technology, for instance electromechanical relay circuits. Following this idea, Schreyer first designed and constructed the circuits corresponding to the operations of the propositional calculus. Today it is commonplace to speak of NOR and AND circuits, etc. But please remember that the first electronic calcualtor, the ENIAC, built some years later, worked by simulating decimal gears. Schreyer could not use the semi conductor technology at that time (1937), as we do today. He used a special type of tube with two parallel grids with the same characteristic. See Fig. 4.

It was interesting for me to learn from the paper of Randell* that in the COLOSSUS similar ideas were applied. This used circuits corresponding to the propositional operations, too.

During the war Schreyer built a ten-digit parallel binary calculator (Fig 5) specialized on transferring a three-digit decimal number into a ten-digit binary number. The model was ready for tests in 1944. We submitted the concept of an electronic computer with 2000 tubes to the German Government Research Authorities, but their reaction was negative. We would never have attempted to construct a computer with 18,000 tubes, and I admire the heroism shown by Eckert and Mauchly.

Most of the machines we constructed in Germany until 1945 were destroyed by air raids. Only the model Z4 could be saved. In 1950, after some improvements, it was leased to the Eidgenossische Technische Hochschule in Zurich, Switzerland. It was so reliable that it was customary to let it work through the night unattended. I remember the good cooperation with Stiefel, Speiser, and Rutishauser.

Not until 1950 could we continue the development of computers after an interruption of some years. Together with two friends I started the ZUSE KG near Bad Hersfeld, Hessen. At first, the optical industries were our customers, then the Authorities for Land Surveying and the Universities. Be-

* Paper included in this volume.

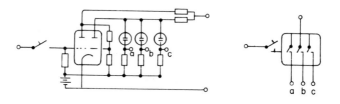

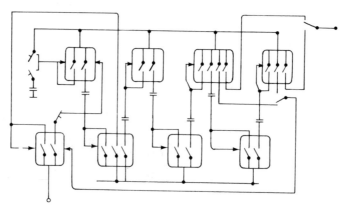

Figure 4   Schreyer electronic relay circuits.

sides the last there was no sponsoring or assistance by the government. A series of new models followed, but this is less interesting for the purpose of this paper. Perhaps I may mention the development of an automatic plotter with high accuracy about 1958. Today the name of ZUSE KG is cancelled and my former factory is owned by Siemens AG.

Independent of this development and without any knowledge of each other, Dr. Dirks during World War II constructed a computing device for commerical purposes using a rotating magnetic storage. This was a forerunner of the later-developed magnetic drum and disks. It would be interesting to study the priorities in the field of rotating magnetic storage devices, especially in comparison with parallel constructions in other places. About 1947 another German pioneer, Dr. Billing, constructed a magnetic drum for use in a computer.

I shall now give some details of the algorithmic language Plankalkül. I have said already that with the end of the war we had to stop our hardware work, so I concentrated on theoretical investigations. I can give only a general survey here: anyone who would like to know more may study the new edition recently published in English by the German Ministry for Technology (BMFT), under the title "The Plankalkül" (BMFT–GMD 106, 1976).

	Step			
Schreyer ✗ 769	1	①	7	LLL
Electronic	2	④ ⑥	x 10	LLLo / LLLooo
Computer	3	⑤ ②	70 + 6	LoooLLo / LLo
Decimal to			76	LooLLoo
Binary conversion	4	④ ⑥	x 10	LooLLooo / LooLLooooo
	5	⑤ ③	760 + 9	LoLLLLLooo / LooL
	6	⑦	769	LLooooooooL

Input
① ② ③

④ x 2^1

⑤ x 2^0

⑥ x 2^3

Adder

Output

⑦ ⊗ ⊗ ⊗ ⊗ ⊗ ⊗ ⊗ ⊗ ⊗ ⊗

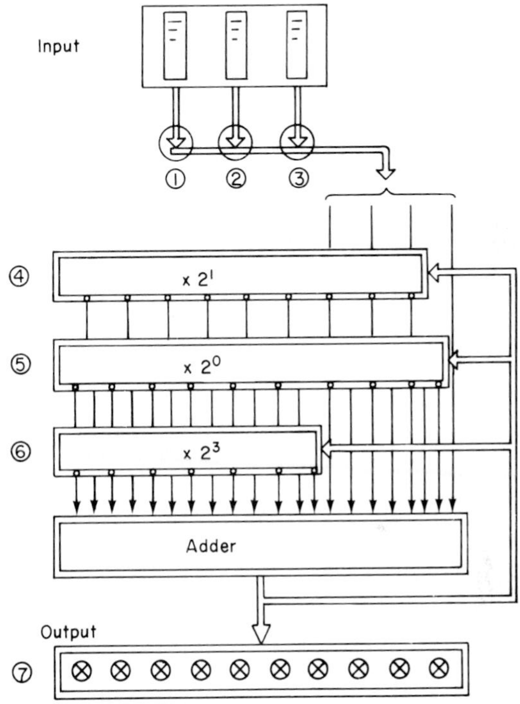

Figure 5 Schreyer ten-digit parallel binary calculator.

The first principle of the Plankalkül is: data processing begins with the bit. Even today I have difficulties with some of my colleagues in justifying this assertion. During the past 20 to 30 years the priority of numerical calculation has only slowly been overcome; and in this time, in conventional computers the bit has been tolerated only as a Boolean object for controlling conditional branching and so on. In contrast, the Plankalkül is fundamentally based on the bit. To express logical relations I used the notation and results of the propositional and the predicate calculus. Any arbitrary structure may be described in terms of bit strings; and by introducing the idea of levels we can have a systematic code for any structure, however complicated, and can

	R(V	, V	) $\Rightarrow$ (R		, R	, R)
V	0	1	0		1	2
S	$m\times\sigma$	$n\times\sigma$	$(m+n)\times\sigma$	1.n	0	
	Input:	V	list with m elements		V	list with n elements
		0			1	
	Output:	R	list with $m+n$ elements		R	binary number	R	predicate
		0			1		2	

If the program P3.7 has this input–output specification, then

	R3.7(Z	, Z	) $\Rightarrow$ Z	
V	9	11	12	
S	1.n	$m\times\sigma$	$n\times\sigma$	1.n

means: the result R of the program P3.7 applied to the objects Z and Z is assigned to Z . (Z ,
                                                                                                                    1   9   11   12   9
Z , and Z are local objects.)
11   12

Objects of a program

V   Input values
Z   Local values (Zwischenwerte)
R   Results
C   Constants (reference level 0)
i, j Local values for the variation of indices and so on
x, y Bound variable used in the predicate calculus:

	$\Rightarrow$ corresponds to	:=	
	$Z + 1 \Rightarrow Z$		
	$\rightharpoondown$ corresponds to	IF . . . THEN . . .	
	for instance		
	$V > V \rightharpoondown V \Rightarrow R$		
	0 1 0 0		
FIN	end symbol		
Z $\rightharpoondown$ FIN	conditional end symbol		
0			
W( )	iterative program section		

Fig. 6   Input–output specification (Randauszug).

identify any of its components. Figure 6 shows the main syntactic features of Plankalkül, where So refers to the bit level. Every program is a module in itself. There is a "Randauszug," or "input–output specification," which gives the relations of the program module to the environment.*

Subroutines are defined in the following way: every result of an arbitrary program can be used as a function of some variables. So this language gives

* The paper by Knuth and Trabb Pardo in this volume contains a section on Plankalkül, which describes the language in more detail and will be found helpful if read in connection with the present paper. [*Editor's Note*]

the exact logical content of the program but not additional information concerning the details of the implementation such as

"Call by value,"

and

"Call by reference."

The objects of a program may be input values (variables), local values, results, constants, and auxiliary values for controlling interative processes or bound variables for the operators of the predicate calculus.

We also have some special symbols for statements, conditional orders, and iterative cycles. There is also an end-symbol, FIN, which corresponds in a limited sense to the GO TO of other languages. But according to the modular organization of the Plankalkül there is no danger of applying it in a confusing manner.

It was interesting for me to test the efficiency and the general scope of the Plankalkül by applying it to chess problems. I learned to play chess especially for this purpose.

This field seemed to me suited for the formulation of rather sophisticated data structures, nested conditions, and general calculations. Figure 7 shows some special types of data structures defined for this purpose.

Let us take a look, for instance, at the "field occupation." For the description we need a list of 64 specifications of the type of occupation of any point and so on.

$A\Delta 1 = S1.3$	Coordinate
$A\Delta 2 = 2 \times S1.3$	Point
$A\Delta 3 = S1.4$	Specification of occupation
$A\Delta 4 = (A\Delta 2, A\Delta 3)$	Occupation of a special point
$A\Delta 5 = 64 \times A\Delta 3$	Field occupation
$C\Delta 5$	Field occupation at the start
$A\Delta 6 = 64 \times A\Delta 4$	Field occupation as $A\Delta 5$, but supplemented by the point coordinates
$A\Delta 9 = (A\Delta 5, So, S1.4, A\Delta 2)$	Actual situation of the game
K0 $\underline{A\Delta 5}$	Field occupation
K1 $\underline{S0}$	"White has the move"
K2 $\underline{S1.4}$	Conditions for castling
K3 $A\Delta 2$	Aiming point of the last move
$C\Delta 9$	Situation at the start
$A\Delta 11 = (A\Delta 2, A\Delta 2, S0)$	Specification of a move

Fig. 7 Data types (Datenarten) for chess programs (extract).

I will give only a general impression of what programs written in this language look like. The program is called PΔ160 and evaluates whether the white king is in checkmate or stalemate. The input is a "field occupation" and the output are two bits, one for each of the wanted predicates. Then follows a kind of comment, which is not a part of the proper program.

Figure 8 gives some preliminary comments on the meaning of the objects used.

Figure 9 shows the actual program. You see there some operators of the predicate calculus like "this one," or "those which," and some conditional orders.

The arrangement of the formulas gives the impression of a two-dimensional language, but this is not really so. This form facilitates the reading of

		Input–Output		
		R(V) $\Rightarrow$ R , R)		
	V	0	0	1
	A	Δ5	0	0

V	V	Field occupation
A	Δ6	

V	R	"The white king is checkmate"
S	0	
	0	

V	R	"The white king is stalemate"
S	1	
	0	

V	Z	Point occupation
A	0	
	Δ4	

V	Z	List of the pieces attacking the white king
A	1	
	□×Δ4	

V	Z	Number of the pieces attacking the white king
A	2	(A9 = natural number)
	9	

V	Z	"The white king is checkmate or stalemate"
S	3	
	0	

V	Z	"No white piece, except the king, is able to move"
S	4	
	0	

Fig. 8   PΔ160: conditions for checkmate or stalemate.

PΔ160

(1) Evaluation of the point, occupied by the white king (Z).

0

(2) Formation of the list of the pieces attacking the white king (RΔ129, Z).

1

(3) The number of the attacking pieces influences the further evaluations.

(4) If the king is not attacked (Z = 0) or the king is able to make an evading move (RΔ148),

2

then the program is finished (FIN).

(5) If the king is attacked by more than one piece (Z > 1), then we have checkmate or stale-

2

mate (Z). [The case of an evading move is already taken into account by (4).]

3

(6) If the white king is attacked by one piece (Z = 1), then we have checkmate or stale-

2

mate if

(7) the attacking piece cannot be captured by white without discovering check (RΔ142)

(8) and in the case of free points between the attacking piece and the king (RΔ19)

(9) there is no white piece being able to move to one of these points (RΔ152).

(10) Investigation, if there are white pieces, except the king, being able to move (RΔ150). If this is not the case, then Z is positive.

4

(11) Condition for checkmate (R).

0

(12) Condition for stalemate (R).

1

Fig. 8 *Continued.*

the program for the user. For implementation it can be stretched into a linear representation without changing the structure of the program.

Behind the Plankalkül there is a special philosophy based on my early conviction, that there is a steady way from simple numerical calculation to high-level thinking processes. In order to test the universality of this language I applied it for several unusual fields. Thus, for instance, I made some steps in the direction of symbolic calculations, general programs for relations, or graphs, as we call it today, chess playing, and so on. Here you will miss the normal numerical calculations like linear equations. Some general considerations showed me that these are rather trivial in comparison to the other fields selected by me for further investigation. This later on led to some misunderstandings, when 10 years later just these numerical calculations became popular. The Plankalkül was critized as a special logical language going too far ahead of the problems then to be solved.

So my concept may have been too advanced at that time. But looking at the present situation I come to the conclusion that it would have been better to base the hardware and software development of the computer on the philosophy of the Plankalkül from the beginning. Surely, we can be proud of the achievements of our pioneer activity; nevertheless, data processing is not

(1)

$$x' \begin{bmatrix} x \in V \;\land x\; = --+- \end{bmatrix} \Rightarrow Z$$

V		0			0
K			1		
A	Δ4	Δ6	Δ3		Δ4

(2)

$$\hat{x} \begin{bmatrix} R\Delta129(V\;,x\;,Z\;)\land x \end{bmatrix} \Rightarrow Z$$

V		0	0			1
K			0	0	1.3	
A	Δ4	Δ6	Δ2	Δ2	0	□×Δ4

(3)

$$N(Z\;)\Rightarrow Z$$

V	1	2
K		
A	□×Δ4	9

(4)

$$Z = 0 \lor R\Delta148(V\;) \to \begin{bmatrix} (-,-) \Rightarrow (R\,,\,R) \end{bmatrix} \quad FI\overline{N}$$

V	2	0		0	1	
K						
A	9	0	Δ6	0	0	

(5)

$$Z > 1 \to \begin{bmatrix} + \Rightarrow \overline{Z} \end{bmatrix}$$

V	2	3
K		
A	9	0

(6)   (7)

$$Z = 1 \to \begin{bmatrix} \neg R\Delta142(V\;,Z\;) \end{bmatrix}$$

V	2		0	1
K			6	0.0
A	9		Δ6	Δ2

(8)   (9)

$$\land \neg R\Delta19(Z\;,Z\;)\Rightarrow R\Delta152(V\;,Z\;,Z\;) \Rightarrow Z$$

V		0	1	0	0	1	3
K			0.0		0	0.0	0
A		Δ2	Δ2	Δ6	Δ2	Δ2	

(10)   (11)   (12)

$$R\Delta150(V\;)\Rightarrow Z \quad\mid\quad Z \land \neg Z \Rightarrow R \quad\mid\quad Z \land Z \Rightarrow R$$

V	0	4	3	4	0	3	4	1
K								
A	Δ6	0	0	0	0	0	0	0

Fig. 9   PΔ160.

yet fully emancipated. There is some confusion and trouble in the field. I think some problems cannot yet be solved satisfactorily. On one side there are sometimes too many mathematicians influencing computer science in a worldly innocent manner. On the other side, relatively primitive methods and programming languages are still applied in practice.

To conclude, I shall say something about my more recent ideas. In the years from about 1948 to 1964 I was occupied with organizing the development of the ZUSE KG. Unfortunately, as a manager I had hardly the time for profound theoretical considerations. But in the last 10 years I have been able to continue my life as a scientist again. The main objectives are new investigations on the Plankalkül in comparison with other algorithmic languages. According to my subjective opinion the Plankalkül is not only interesting from a historical point of view but is also of great significance for solving present-day problems. The situation in the field of algorithmic languages is rather confusing. Structured programming is only a partial solution. Some features of the Plankalkül may help to solve the problems.

Another field of my research is "self-reproducing systems." But I see the problem not from the mathematical point of view, as, for instance, von Neumann did, but as an engineer. It may be better that there is almost no support for such ideas. Perhaps the devil is behind it, too. But speaking about this would go far beyond the scope of this paper.

Almost from the beginning of my work in the field of computing I had the idea of parallel information processing, for instance, with cellular automata. This induced me to apply this idea to theoretical physics. I developed some ideas concerning the "Rechnender Raum," meaning something like "calculating cosmos." This general idea is of increasing interest in other places, too, for instance, in the U.S. I am convinced that such investigations will gain broader attention in the future also from physicists. But most of these ideas are as crazy today as the idea of the computer was 30 to 40 years ago. Therefore, it is my fate to perform these investigations on a very limited scale. Nevertheless, I feel happy to be a pioneer until the end of my days.

HÜNFELD, WEST GERMANY

The Origins of Digital Computers: Supplementary Bibliography

B. RANDELL

Introduction

This bibliography is intended as a supplement to that appearing in "The Origins of Digital Computers: Selected Papers" (B. Randell, ed.). Springer-Verlag, Berlin and New York 1973. It therefore concentrates on the period from Babbage to the invention of the stored-program electronic digital computer in the mid-1940s, but also contains items relating to earlier work on mechanical calculation and on devices incorporating sequence control mechanisms. The bibliography covers events up to about 1949, when the earliest stored-program computers became operational, but no attempt has been made to cover the explosive growth in the literature on electronic computers that occurred after 1946, when a large number of computer projects were started in the U.S. and elsewhere based directly on the plans for the EDVAC or IAS computers. All the items listed have been inspected, sometimes somewhat cursorily, by the author.

In what follows we attempt a brief survey of some of the more interesting groups of items in this bibliography, giving special attention to those that add significantly to the information given in the set of chapter introductions in "The Origins of Digital Computers." We also give brief comments on some of the larger bodies of historical material that particularly merit study by historians of science. One such body of material, that arising from the so-called ENIAC patent suit, is described at some length in a separate Appendix. In

629

general, however, the patent literature is not covered in this bibliography. It is to be hoped that before long someone with the necessary skills and experience will undertake the task of surveying this literature for material relating to the origins of digital computers.

General Works

In the last two or three years there have appeared a number of very useful books on the history of calculators and computing. The best known, at least in the English-speaking world, is one from the office of Charles and Ray Eames, edited by G. Fleck, entitled "A Computer Perspective." Quoting from the review by D. E. Knuth in *Historia Mathematica:*

> The style of presentation is aimed at a popular audience and it is a fascinating way to present history; it depicts the spirit of the times, giving isolated details rather than stating a large number of organized facts. But it is also useful as a guide for scholarly research, since the picture credits and index at the rear of the book are quite complete.

The other books are as yet not available in English. This is particularly to be regretted in the case of that by Apokin and Maistrov, which incorporates a wealth of material on East European calculator and computer developments. In contrast, Adam's book includes interesting material on early work in Austria and Germany, namely, that by Schäffler on punched-card machinery, and the little known pre-Jacquard automatic draw loom known as a "Broselmaschine." The one other book is in fact the proceedings of a conference to mark the 350th anniversary of Schickard's calculating machine. Relevant papers from this book are listed separately in the bibliography under the names of the authors—Howlett, Reinecke, von Freytag Löringhoff, von Mackensen, and Zuse.

Charles Babbage

The supplementary bibliography contains a fairly large number of additional items relating to Charles Babbage, including contemporary commentary on his machines and further biographical material. One of the most interesting items is the book by Losano, which incorporates material from yet another cache of Babbage papers, namely, those that we now find were left behind in Italy after his visit there in 1840. Even more surprising are the extracts from secret police files containing reports by the agents who shadowed Babbage and his traveling companion, although these give little information of importance.

The amount of extant Babbage material is indeed considerable. The British Library has a large number of volumes of his correspondence, the Science Museum Library his drawings and most of his notebooks (others being at the Scientific Periodicals Library in Cambridge), the Museum of the History of Science at Oxford the important set of papers that he bequeathed to H. W. Buxton, and the Royal Observatory Library at Edinburgh his library. At least one other collection of Babbage letters, etc., is known to be in the hands of a private collector, Mr. A. W. Van Sinderen. All of this material merits much more study than it has had so far—indeed it seems incredible that no scholarly biography of Babbage has yet appeared.

Another item relating to Babbage is the paper by Metropolis and Worlton, entitled "A trilogy on errors in the history of computing." This provides much more evidence to contradict the view that Babbage's work was almost forgotten after his death and rediscovered only after the electronic computer had been invented. It shows that a considerable number of descriptions of his work appeared over the years, although some authors evidently had a much clearer appreciation of the difference engine than of the analytical engine. As many of these further descriptions as could be obtained are included in the supplementary bibliography.

Vannevar Bush

The original bibliography contained only a few items relating to Vannevar Bush. Of these, the most important was his 1936 survey paper "Instrumental analysis," the first half of which covered mechanical and electromechanical digital calculators. This included the proposal that a set of standard punched-card devices be connected together and provided with a control device, so producing "a close approximation to Babbage's large conception." There was nothing else in the bibliography to indicate that Bush had carried this idea any further, but it was noted that Norbert Wiener's book on cybernetics, published in 1948, contained the claim that he had submitted a report to Bush in 1940 recommending the development of a program-controlled electronic binary computing machine. It will be seen that this long-lost report has now been found and is listed in the present supplementary bibliography as Wiener (1940). However, it turns out that this report contains little of substance with respect to a program-controlled computer.

Much more important is the evidence now found that after preparing his "Instrumental analysis" paper, Bush went on to do some preliminary design work himself on a program-controlled electronic digital computer and that this work led to a research program at MIT, the Rapid Arithmetical Machine Project, sponsored by NCR. Bush apparently documented his ideas in a set of memoranda written during 1937 and 1938, which would constitute the earliest known proposal for a program-controlled electronic computer. Unfortunately, these memoranda cannot be found and their contents are known only from references such as those made by Radford (1939) and Crawford

(1939). Bush himself in his later years either had forgotten, or consciously played down, the significance of his prewar work on digital electronics (see Bush, 1970). Perhaps this was because the work was abandoned in about 1942 and, as far as is known, did not have any influence on the ENIAC project, which started shortly afterwards. However, Professor Wildes's study of the Electrical Engineering Department at MIT makes it clear that immediately after the war, people there made a deliberate and successful effort to resume the work on digital electronics, an effort that led to the development of the WHIRLWIND computer. It is believed that much material on this work has been collected by the Smithsonian Computer History Project—one awaits the analysis of this material with interest.

Cryptanalytic Machines

In the past few years, after many years of almost complete silence, a number of books and papers have been published about the work on cryptanalysis carried out in Poland, France, and Britain before and during World War II and on its impact on the course of the war. Several of these works that contain mention or description of computers, or computerlike devices, used for cryptanalytic purposes, particularly those developed at Bletchley Park, are included in the bibliography—see Brown (1975), Calvocoressi (1974), Kahn (1974), Kozaczuk (1975), Whiting (1975), and Winterbotham (1974). Of these, the book by Brown is of particular interest because of the claims it makes about Alan Turing's work on the design of cryptanalytic machines. Much more detail about wartime work with which Turing was associated is contained in a lengthy paper by the present author on the COLOSSUS, a paper made possible by the partial declassification in 1975 of this special-purpose electronic computer, which was put into operation in 1943. This paper gives details of the careers of the people involved, of how the basic concept of COLOSSUS was arrived at, and how the first machine was designed and built, and then a MARK II version designed and manufactured. One other paper that is listed is that by Jensen, which describes a number of largely electromechanical devices developed in Germany during World War II for cryptographic purposes.

Other Items

Two other books of great interest to the author are the biography of the Spanish pioneer Torres y Quevedo, by Rodriguez Alcalde, and the compilation of material on the difference engines of George and Edvard Scheutz (Losano, 1974). It will be seen from the index that a number of other items relating to difference engines and early calculating machines are also included. Two important items concerning early sequence control mechanisms are those by Vaucanson and the annotated translation of a 13th-century Arabic work that contains detailed descriptions of an amazing collection of mechanical automata. There is also a small set of papers describing a curious 19th-century machine for composing random Latin hexameters!

At the other extreme of the time period covered by this bibliography there are, for example, papers on BINAC, a group of papers on the first postwar computer developments in Britain that were published in the *Radio and Electronic Engineer* (by Booth, Clarke, Wilkes, Wilkinson, and Williams), and an excellent analysis by Carpenter and Doran of von Neumann's and Turing's 1945 reports.

Finally, mention should be made of the paper by Klir concerning the work by Bernard Weiner in the 1920s on an electric calculator, which mentions that Weiner went on to work on the design of a fully automatic computer; attempts to find out more about this prewar work have so far met with no success.

BIBLIOGRAPHY

A. Adam, "Von Himmlischen Uhrwerk zur Statistischen Fabrik." O. Munk, Vienna, 1973.
  A wide-ranging survey, starting with early astronomical instruments, ending with the use in Austria of early Hollerith equipment. Contains extensive discussions of Schickard's calculating machine, automated drawlooms, including the little-known "Broselmaschine" (1680–1690), and of Schäffler's developments of Hollerith's machines.

R. R. Adler, Mr. Babbage's calculating engine, *Machine Design* **30**(3), 125–129 (1958).
  Brief but well-illustrated account of the difference engine and analytical engine.

I. A. Apokin and L. E. Maistrov, "Rasvitie Vyichislitelynih Mashin." Nauka, Moscow, 1974.
  An account of the history of digital computing from the earliest aids to calculation to the modern computer. Chapter 1 includes discussion of the abacus in China, Europe, and Russia. Chapter 2, on mechanical calculators, discusses the work of Jakobson, Tchebichef, and Odhner, as well as Schickard, Pascal, and Leibniz. Chapter 3 covers tabulating machines and electromechanical desk calculators. The next chapter, "The birth of electronic computing," which names M. A. Bonch-Bruevitch as having invented an electronic trigger circuit in 1918, one year before the independent work of Eccles and Jordan, describes such projects as the Harvard MARK I, the Atanasoff–Berry computer, ENIAC, and EDVAC. Chapter 5 describes early stored program computers, and states that the first Russian computers were the MESM (Lebedev and Rameen, 1948) and BESM (Lebedev, 1952). The final four chapters discuss transistorized and integrated-circuit computers, computer applications, and the future of computer technology. A large number of references are listed, to both Russian and English language sources.

R. C. Archibald, Bibliographia de Mathematicis X: Charles Babbage (1792–1871), *Scripta Math.* **3**, 266–267 (1935).
  A brief bibliography.

A. A. Auerbach, J. P. Eckert, Jr., R. F. Shaw, J. F. Weiner, and L. D. Wilson, The BINAC, *Proc. Inst. Radio Eng.* **40**, 12–29 (1952).

A detailed description, with many circuit diagrams, of the BINAC, which is described as "the first computer of its type to be completed successfully in the United States." It is stated that the BINAC was built to solve an (unidentified) specific problem, for which a small amount of input/output was required relative to the amount of computation, but that it contained all the necessary elements for solving a great variety of problems. A sample program is given, but no mention is made of the status of the system, or when it became operational.

C. Babbage, Observations on the application of machinery to the computation of mathematical tables, *Mem. Astron. Soc.* **1** (2), 311–314 (1825).

A paper, which was read on 13 December 1822, speculating on the value of removing the restrictions of the difference engine to functions with some order of difference being constant.

H. P. Babbage, "Memoirs and Correspondence of Major-General H. P. Babbage." Privately printed, London, 1910b.

In the section dealing with his childhood, H. P. Babbage describes visits to his father's workshop, where he learned to handle tools and draw machinery, and got to know the workmen there including Jarvis, the draftsman responsible for the drawings of the analytical engine. Most of the book is devoted to his military career in India. It states that during a visit to Britain in 1854–1855 he studied mathematics, met Scheutz and his son, documented their difference engine using the mechanical notation, and worked with his father on cryptanalysis and on assembling a small model of the difference engine. He was back in London in 1871 when his father died, and retired to England permanently in 1874. A brief summary is given in the book of his work on the analytical engine after his father's death.

J. Bernstein, "The Analytical Engine." Random House, New York, 1963.

A popular introduction to computers, and discussion of the work of Babbage, Aiken, Stibitz, Eckert, Mauchly, von Neumann, and others.

A. D. Booth, Two calculating machines for x-ray crystal structure analysis, *J. Appl. Phys.* **18**, 664–666 (1947).

The first of these wartime machines appears to be based on a planimeter mechanism, and is entirely analog in operation. The second machine, the "cosine adding machine," incorporates a digital counter.

A. D. Booth, Computers in the University of London, 1945–1962. *Radio Electron. Eng.* **45** (7), 341–345 (1975).

A well-illustrated description of the sequence of calculating devices and computers developed by the author, starting in the early 1940s, originally for the analysis of x-ray diffraction data. One wartime device involved a mechanical counter, the others being analog devices. After the war he started to build a relay calculator. "Our work on the relay structure factor calculator was nearly complete at the end of 1945. Its circuit included what would now be called a many–one and a one–many function table for decoding and executing instructions." The author states that before the calculator was completed he learnt via Hartree of work elsewhere, particularly in the U.S., on electronic computers. He spent some months with von Neumann's group in 1947, and on return to Birkbeck College worked on the logical design of IAS-type computers, and developed various magnetic storage devices. He states that his first computer, the ARC, which was built from relays and incorporated a magnetic drum store, was completed in May 1948. Subsequently an electronic version, the SEC, was built and then the whole APEXC series of computers. A commercial version of this series, the HEC series, was manufactured by the British Tabulating Machine Company.

B. V. Bowden, Charles Babbage, father of the mechanical brain, *Sci. Digest* **49**, 82–88 (1961). Condensation of Bowden (1960).

D. Brewster, History of mechanical inventions and processes in the useful arts, *Edinburgh J. Sci.* **1** (1), 141–151 (1824).

P. Drath, The relationship between Science and Technology: University Research and the Computer Industry 1945–1962. Ph.D. Thesis, Victoria University of Manchester, 1973.

The thesis concentrates on the cooperative development of a series of computers by Ferranti and the Electrical Engineering Department at Manchester University, Starting in 1949, but contains one chapter of the origins of the digital computer, and the backgrounds of the first postwar British computer projects.

E. Droz, From jointed doll to talking robot, *New Scientist* **14**, 37–40 (1962).

A well-illustrated and careful account of the development of mechanical automata, concentrating on the work of Vaucanson, von Knaus, and the Jacquet–Droz family.

J. M. Dubbey, Charles Babbage and his computers, *Bull. Inst. Math. Appl.* **9**(3), 662–669. (1973).

A very interesting essay on the mathematical thinking that lay behind much of Babbage's work. Contains separate sections on notation, the calculus of functions, the difference engine, he analytical engine, and algebra. It states that his ideas on algebra "were decisively influenced but characteristically he has received no credit for them at all."

C. ..ns, Pioneers of Computing: An Oral History of Computing, Compiled by Dr. Christopher Ev. with the Support of the Science Museum and the National Physical Laboratory (in pro).

.. a growing series of tape cassettes, each providing a one-hour recorded interview with a .r pioneer. The interviews are very well done, and the quality of the recording and ..ed .xcellent. Some 20 or so interviews have been taped to date, and a number of edited .. .repared, those of D. W. Davies, T. Kilburn, J. Pinkerton, F. C. Williams, and K. .. pioneers who have been interviewed to date for this series include A. W. M. .. Eckert, J. W. Forrester, I. J. Good, G. M. Hopper, J. W. Mauchly, D. Michie, .. .n. Copies of the cassettes are to be available from the Science Museum.

.. "Über die Entwicklung und das Wesen des Maschinenrechnens." Zella-Mehlis,

.. .et of 14 pamphlets, totalling 60 pages, each giving a well-illustrated account of .. history of manual or machine calculation. Includes coverage of the work of .. .hott, Leibniz, Perrault, Poleni, and Leupold.

.. .mputer Perspective." (By the Office of Charles and Ray Eames). Harvard .. .e, Massachusetts, 1973.

.. .ed book based on an IBM-sponsored exhibition. Although aimed at a .. .ains a vast amount of information, relating directly or indirectly to the .. is not readily available elsewhere. Hundreds of rare photographs and .. An excellent book, which does a very fine job of attempting to por-.. .ual background against which the modern computer evolved.

.. .hine arithmétique, *Les Études Classiques*, Namur **20**, 181–191

.. .ivities and attitudes in inventing, defending, and trying to perfect .. .hine.

.. .ical Construction of the Machine for Composing Hexameter

.. .ning of the machine, and of the repairs required to make it .. .ied out.) The report reveals that the machine incorporated .. f wires projecting radially from it. Each wire represented .. .t each drum had a fixed set of words encoded on it. These .. .nts and then used to control the display of a set of six .. an acceptable hexameter Latin verse. Each drum was

Contains a two-page account of Babbage's difference engine, based on an account by Baily. It starts, "The extraordinary machinery invented by Mr. Babbage, and now constructing under the patronage of Government, has excited so much interest in every part of Europe, that we have been anxious to gratify the curiosity of our readers by any details respecting the nature and progress of the machine."

A. C. Brown, "Bodyguard of Lies." Harper, New York, 1975.

A massive account of the "cover and deception" operations used by the Allies in World War II, which contains an account of Turing's wartime work on the design of a cryptanalytic machine used for breaking the ENIGMA cipher. It is implied that this machine was in some way related to Turing's prewar concept of a universal machine, but other statements seem to contradict this implication.

D. J. Bryden, George Brown, author of the Rotula, *Ann. Sci.* **28**, 1–29 (1972).

Scholarly account of the life of George Brown, and of his Rotula, which was a simple aid to addition, involving a single carry wheel.

V. Bush, "Pieces of the Action." Morrow, New York, 1970.

A series of somewhat autobiographical essays in which Bush states that he had little to do with the invention of the digital computer, and does not mention his prewar work in digital electronic calculating devices, though a description is given of the Rapid Selector project.

M. Butler, A historical background, *Nucl. News* 26–30 (April 1968).

A popular account of the development of digital computing and computers, containing a useful list of references and summaries of the logical design of ENIAC and the IAS computer.

P. S. C., Mr. Babbage and his rivals. *Mech. Mag.* **23**(614), 119 (1835).
See S. Y. (1835).

P. Calvocoressi, The ultra secrets of station X. *Sunday Times* pp. 33–34 (24 November 1974).

A detailed personal account of wartime work at Bletchley Park on the analysis of information obtained by decoding German radio messages, which considerably supplements the information given by Winterbotham (1974). It states that the cryptographers "were incidentally helped by machines called bombes which were prototype computers."

B. E. Carpenter and R. W. Doran, The Other Turing Machine, Rep. 23. Massey Univ. Computer Unit, Palmerston North, New Zealand (August 1975).

Provides an excellent analysis in modern terms of the original design for ACE given by Turing in his 1945 report, and a comparison of this report with the slightly earlier EDVAC report by von Neumann. It points out that, in contrast to the von Neumann report, which is incomplete, with neither the I/O mechanisms nor the details of the central control being spelled out, "Turing's paper, on the other hand, is a complete description of a computer, right down to logical circuit diagrams, with an exhaustive thirteen-page analysis of the physical properties of the memory, and a cost estimate of £11,200." Among the topics listed as discussed in Turing's report, but not found in that by von Neumann, are address mapping, instruction address register and instruction register, microcode, hierarchical architecture, floating point arithmetic, hardware bootstrap loader, subroutine stack, modular programming, subroutine library, link editor, symbolic addresses, and the ability to treat programs as data.

A. Chapuis and E. Droz, "Automata. A Historical and Technological Study." V. T. Batsford, London, 1958.

Translation of Chapuis and Droz (1949).

G. Chroust. "Bibliography for the History Wall Data Processing." IBM Laboratory, Vienna, 1974.

Bibliography listing the artefacts, photographs, books, and articles displayed in the exhibition "The History of Data Processing" at the Museum of Industry and Technology, Vienna.

R. Church, Review of Sadovskii, I. E. Topics from the history of the development of mechanical mathematics in Russia. *Math. Rev.* 12(2), 69 (1951).

According to this review Sadovskii's paper deals mainly with the work of Tchebichef on a machine with automatic multiplication and division (1881) and with Odhner's machine (1878), as well as various analog devices.

R. Clark, Barbara Froena Domi Promittunt Foedera Mala. "Somerset Anthology" (P. Lovell, ed.), pp. 96–102. Sessions, York, 1975.

An article written in 1951 about a machine for composing Latin hexameter verses and its inventor John Clark (1785–1852). The title of the article is one of the verses produced by the machine, which had recently been restored. It describes how the machine was exhibited in London in 1845 as "The Eureka" and quotes a letter from a visitor to the exhibition as stating, "Clarke is a strange simple looking old man; Babbage said the other day that he was as great a curiosity as his Machine!" A photograph of the machine, showing one of its pegged cylinders, accompanies the article.

S. L. H. Clarke, The Elliott 400 series and before, *Radio Electron. Eng.* 45(8), 415–421 (1975).

"At the end of the war Elliotts [were] developing an electronic digital computer intended to be the centre of the most sophisticated fire-control system of its day." This was the 152, which had a fixed program store, and 100-μsec multiplier. The paper goes on to describe the later Elliott machines, including the 152, Nicholas, 401, 402, 403, and 405.

H. T. Colebrook, Address of Henry Thomas Colebrook, President of the Astronomical Society of London. . . . On presenting the honorary gold medal to Charles Babbage, Esq. F.R.S., *Mem. Astron. Soc.* 1(2), 509–512 (1825).

"The invention is as novel, as the ingenuity manifested by it is extraordinary. . . . . It substitutes mechanical performance for an intellectual process: and that performance is effected with clarity and exactness unattainable in ordinary methods, even by incessant practice and undiverted attention."

L. J. Comrie, Untitled article, *The Observatory* 51, 105–108 (1928b).

Record of presentation by Comrie of a paper "The application of the Brunsviga–Dupla calculating machine to double summutation with finite differences," and the ensuing discussion, which includes the comment, "I should like to congratulate Comrie not only this considerable advance towards the practical solution of the Babbage problem, but also on the vigilance which enabled him to discover in the Dupla a latent and unsuspected capability."

L. J. Comrie, Modern Babbage machines. Bulletin, Office Machinery Users Assoc. Ltd., London (1932b).

A 29-page article on difference engines and techniques. The first part of the article discusses the history of purpose-built difference engines (Babbage, Scheutz, Wiberg, Grant, and Hamann), including that built by A. J. Thompson, using four Triumphator calculating machines. The major part of the article discusses the use of various standard calculating machines as difference engines, including the Brunsviga–Dupla, the Nova–Brunsviga IVA, various Burroughs bookkeeping machines, and the National Cash Register (Ellis) accounting machine.

L. J. Comrie, Inverse interpolation and scientific applications of the national accounting machine. *J. Roy. Statist. Soc. Suppl.* 3(2), 87–114 (1936).

Comrie's introduction to the section dealing with the use of the National Accounting Machine surveys the history of special-purpose difference engines, and indicates his preference for using standard commercially available equipment.

L. J. Comrie, G. B. Hay, and H. G. Hudson, The application of Hollerith equipment to an agricultural investigation, *J. Roy. Statist. Soc. Suppl.* 4(2), 210–224 (1937).

Detailed description of an application using the various items of Hollerith equipment, including a multiplying punch, tabulator, and sorter.

J. Connolly, History of Computing in Europe. IBM World Trade Corp. (1967).

A 117-page account, containing a mass of information about the growth of the punched-card industry, and of the emergence of a computer industry in Europe. Nearly half of the report consists of a detailed chronology, covering the years 1880–1967, which concentrates on the activities of Hollerith, the British Tabulating Machine Co., Deutsche Hollerith Maschinen GmbH (Dehomag), Powers–Samas, Cie des Machines Bull, and (especially) IBM. The report, although written in a rather casual style, is obviously based on detailed data from the companies concerned, although no references are given. Among the scientists and engineers whose work is described are Herman Hollerith, Charles Babbage, James L. Powers, Otto Schäffler, Gusta Tauschek, Frederick Bull, Ralph Lorant, James Bryce, and Konrad Zuse.

P. O. Crawford, Jr. Instrumental Analysis in Matrix Algebra, Part V, pp. 60–65. B.Sc. T MIT, Cambridge, Massachusetts (1939).

Sketches the design of "an automatically controlled calculating machine" capabl forming a variety of matrix calculations, and incorporating means for scanning digita resented on punched tape, for adding, subtracting, multiplying, and dividing two n for storing and printing or punching the data. A punched tape was to be used for s trol, which would specify the selection of the numbers to be operated on, the c performed, and the disposal of the result. It is stated that "many of the detail system similar to that suggested by the above have been considered by Bus memoranda, and that the problem to be considered] was that of developing tem and a control system." Later on it states, "electronic calculating cir posed by Bush would be desirable, although the electrical operation of would be suitable for preliminary work."

P. O. Crawford, Jr. "Automatic Control by Arithmetical Operations, bridge, Massachusetts (1942).

"It is the purpose of this thesis to decide the elements and ope for performing one of the operations in the control of anti-aircr prediction of the future position of the target. . . . In this intro ing the operations occurring in automatic calculating is describ tronic switching elements, devices for multiplying two numb recording numbers, translating mechanical displacements ing numerical data into mechanical displacements." The proposals for an arithmetical predictor, which, in additi primitive form of magnetic disk store.

L. B. C. Cunningham and W. R. B. Hynd. Random *Roy. Statist. Soc. Suppl.* 8(2), 62–85 (1946).

Contains a description and photographs of a designed by Shire and Runcorn.

C. R. Curtis, "Mechanised Accountancy. B Bookkeeping, Together with a Survey of t

Contains illustrations and detailed dis accounting machines (Burroughs, Nati Samas and Hollerith punched-card sys machine, or "ten thousand register Powers–Samas. "The Campos mac than any other known device, and error."

S. E. De Morgan. "Memoir o mans, Green, London, 1882.

Contains a few brief mentions Lady Lovelace "to see Mr. Babbage

Contains a two-page account of Babbage's difference engine, based on an account by Baily. It starts, "The extraordinary machinery invented by Mr. Babbage, and now constructing under the patronage of Government, has excited so much interest in every part of Europe, that we have been anxious to gratify the curiosity of our readers by any details respecting the nature and progress of the machine."

A. C. Brown, "Bodyguard of Lies." Harper, New York, 1975.
    A massive account of the "cover and deception" operations used by the Allies in World War II, which contains an account of Turing's wartime work on the design of a cryptanalytic machine used for breaking the ENIGMA cipher. It is implied that this machine was in some way related to Turing's prewar concept of a universal machine, but other statements seem to contradict this implication.

D. J. Bryden, George Brown, author of the Rotula, *Ann. Sci.* **28**, 1–29 (1972).
    Scholarly account of the life of George Brown, and of his Rotula, which was a simple aid to addition, involving a single carry wheel.

V. Bush, "Pieces of the Action." Morrow, New York, 1970.
    A series of somewhat autobiographical essays in which Bush states that he had little to do with the invention of the digital computer, and does not mention his prewar work in digital electronic calculating devices, though a description is given of the Rapid Selector project.

M. Butler, A historical background, *Nucl. News* 26–30 (April 1968).
    A popular account of the development of digital computing and computers, containing a useful list of references and summaries of the logical design of ENIAC and the IAS computer.

P. S. C., Mr. Babbage and his rivals. *Mech. Mag.* **23**(614), 119 (1835).
    See S. Y. (1835).

P. Calvocoressi, The ultra secrets of station X. *Sunday Times* pp. 33–34 (24 November 1974).
    A detailed personal account of wartime work at Bletchley Park on the analysis of information obtained by decoding German radio messages, which considerably supplements the information given by Winterbotham (1974). It states that the cryptographers "were incidentally helped by machines called bombes which were prototype computers."

B. E. Carpenter and R. W. Doran, The Other Turing Machine, Rep. 23. Massey Univ. Computer Unit, Palmerston North, New Zealand (August 1975).
    Provides an excellent analysis in modern terms of the original design for ACE given by Turing in his 1945 report, and a comparison of this report with the slightly earlier EDVAC report by von Neumann. It points out that, in contrast to the von Neumann report, which is incomplete, with neither the I/O mechanisms nor the details of the central control being spelled out, "Turing's paper, on the other hand, is a complete description of a computer, right down to logical circuit diagrams, with an exhaustive thirteen-page analysis of the physical properties of the memory, and a cost estimate of £11,200." Among the topics listed as discussed in Turing's report, but not found in that by von Neumann, are address mapping, instruction address register and instruction register, microcode, hierarchical architecture, floating point arithmetic, hardware bootstrap loader, subroutine stack, modular programming, subroutine library, link editor, symbolic addresses, and the ability to treat programs as data.

A. Chapuis and E. Droz, "Automata. A Historical and Technological Study." V. T. Batsford, London, 1958.
    Translation of Chapuis and Droz (1949).

G. Chroust. "Bibliography for the History Wall Data Processing." IBM Laboratory, Vienna, 1974.
    Bibliography listing the artefacts, photographs, books, and articles displayed in the exhibition "The History of Data Processing" at the Museum of Industry and Technology, Vienna.

R. Church, Review of Sadovskii, I. E. Topics from the history of the development of mechanical mathematics in Russia. *Math. Rev.* 12(2), 69 (1951).

According to this review Sadovskii's paper deals mainly with the work of Tchebichef on a machine with automatic multiplication and division (1881) and with Odhner's machine (1878), as well as various analog devices.

R. Clark, Barbara Froena Domi Promittunt Foedera Mala. "Somerset Anthology" (P. Lovell, ed.), pp. 96–102. Sessions, York, 1975.

An article written in 1951 about a machine for composing Latin hexameter verses and its inventor John Clark (1785–1852). The title of the article is one of the verses produced by the machine, which had recently been restored. It describes how the machine was exhibited in London in 1845 as "The Eureka" and quotes a letter from a visitor to the exhibition as stating, "Clarke is a strange simple looking old man; Babbage said the other day that he was as great a curiosity as his Machine!" A photograph of the machine, showing one of its pegged cylinders, accompanies the article.

S. L. H. Clarke, The Elliott 400 series and before, *Radio Electron. Eng.* 45(8), 415–421 (1975).

"At the end of the war Elliotts [were] developing an electronic digital computer intended to be the centre of the most sophisticated fire-control system of its day." This was the 152, which had a fixed program store, and 100-μsec multiplier. The paper goes on to describe the later Elliott machines, including the 152, Nicholas, 401, 402, 403, and 405.

H. T. Colebrook, Address of Henry Thomas Colebrook, President of the Astronomical Society of London. . . . On presenting the honorary gold medal to Charles Babbage, Esq. F.R.S., *Mem. Astron. Soc.* 1(2), 509–512 (1825).

"The invention is as novel, as the ingenuity manifested by it is extraordinary. . . . . It substitutes mechanical performance for an intellectual process: and that performance is effected with clarity and exactness unattainable in ordinary methods, even by incessant practice and undiverted attention."

L. J. Comrie, Untitled article, *The Observatory* 51, 105–108 (1928b).

Record of presentation by Comrie of a paper "The application of the Brunsviga–Dupla calculating machine to double summutation with finite differences," and the ensuing discussion, which includes the comment, "I should like to congratulate Comrie not only this considerable advance towards the practical solution of the Babbage problem, but also on the vigilance which enabled him to discover in the Dupla a latent and unsuspected capability."

L. J. Comrie, Modern Babbage machines. Bulletin, Office Machinery Users Assoc. Ltd., London (1932b).

A 29-page article on difference engines and techniques. The first part of the article discusses the history of purpose-built difference engines (Babbage, Scheutz, Wiberg, Grant, and Hamann), including that built by A. J. Thompson, using four Triumphator calculating machines. The major part of the article discusses the use of various standard calculating machines as difference engines, including the Brunsviga–Dupla, the Nova–Brunsviga IVA, various Burroughs bookkeeping machines, and the National Cash Register (Ellis) accounting machine.

L. J. Comrie, Inverse interpolation and scientific applications of the national accounting machine. *J. Roy. Statist. Soc. Suppl.* 3(2), 87–114 (1936).

Comrie's introduction to the section dealing with the use of the National Accounting Machine surveys the history of special-purpose difference engines, and indicates his preference for using standard commercially available equipment.

L. J. Comrie, G. B. Hay, and H. G. Hudson, The application of Hollerith equipment to an agricultural investigation, *J. Roy. Statist. Soc. Suppl.* 4(2), 210–224 (1937).

Detailed description of an application using the various items of Hollerith equipment, including a multiplying punch, tabulator, and sorter.

J. Connolly, History of Computing in Europe. IBM World Trade Corp. (1967).

A 117-page account, containing a mass of information about the growth of the punched-card industry, and of the emergence of a computer industry in Europe. Nearly half of the report consists of a detailed chronology, covering the years 1880–1967, which concentrates on the activities of Hollerith, the British Tabulating Machine Co., Deutsche Hollerith Maschinen GmbH (Dehomag), Powers–Samas, Cie des Machines Bull, and (especially) IBM. The report, although written in a rather casual style, is obviously based on detailed data from the companies concerned, although no references are given. Among the scientists and engineers whose work is described are Herman Hollerith, Charles Babbage, James L. Powers, Otto Schäffler, Gustav Tauschek, Frederick Bull, Ralph Lorant, James Bryce, and Konrad Zuse.

P. O. Crawford, Jr. Instrumental Analysis in Matrix Algebra, Part V, pp. 60–65. B.Sc. Thesis, MIT, Cambridge, Massachusetts (1939).

Sketches the design of "an automatically controlled calculating machine" capable of performing a variety of matrix calculations, and incorporating means for scanning digital data represented on punched tape, for adding, subtracting, multiplying, and dividing two numbers, and for storing and printing or punching the data. A punched tape was to be used for sequence control, which would specify the selection of the numbers to be operated on, the operation to be performed, and the disposal of the result. It is stated that "many of the details of a calculating system similar to that suggested by the above have been considered by Bush [in unpublished memoranda, and that the problem to be considered] was that of developing a data scanning system and a control system." Later on it states, "electronic calculating circuits of the type proposed by Bush would be desirable, although the electrical operation of a mechanical machine would be suitable for preliminary work."

P. O. Crawford, Jr. "Automatic Control by Arithmetical Operations. M.Sc. Thesis, MIT, Cambridge, Massachusetts (1942).

"It is the purpose of this thesis to decide the elements and operation of a calculating system for performing one of the operations in the control of anti-aircraft gunfire, that is namely, the prediction of the future position of the target. . . . In this introduction, equipment for performing the operations occurring in automatic calculating is described. This equipment includes electronic switching elements, devices for multiplying two numbers, finding a function of a variable, recording numbers, translating mechanical displacements into numerical data, and for translating numerical data into mechanical displacements." The thesis goes on to give detailed design proposals for an arithmetical predictor, which, in addition to the units mentioned above, used a primitive form of magnetic disk store.

L. B. C. Cunningham and W. R. B. Hynd. Random processes in the problems of air warfare, *J. Roy. Statist. Soc. Suppl.* **8**(2), 62–85 (1946).

Contains a description and photographs of a special purpose relay computer based on that designed by Shire and Runcorn.

C. R. Curtis, "Mechanised Accountancy. Being a Review of the Latest Methods of Mechanical Bookkeeping, Together with a Survey of the Machines Used." Griffin, London, 1932.

Contains illustrations and detailed discussions of the use of a wide variety of then-current accounting machines (Burroughs, National, Underwood, Remington, etc.), of the Power–Samas and Hollerith punched-card systems, and the Campos machine. Apparently the Campos machine, or "ten thousand register machine," had recently been placed on the market by Powers–Samas. "The Campos machine eliminates the human element to a greater known extent than any other known device, and therefore, reduces to an absolute minimum the possibility of error."

S. E. De Morgan. "Memoir of Augustus De Morgan, with Selections from his Letters." Longmans, Green, London, 1882.

Contains a few brief mentions of Babbage, and an account of a visit paid in the company of Lady Lovelace "to see Mr. Babbage's wonderful analytical engine."

P. Drath, The relationship between Science and Technology: University Research and the Computer Industry 1945–1962. Ph.D. Thesis, Victoria University of Manchester, 1973.

The thesis concentrates on the cooperative development of a series of computers by Ferranti and the Electrical Engineering Department at Manchester University, Starting in 1949, but contains one chapter of the origins of the digital computer, and the backgrounds of the first postwar British computer projects.

E. Droz, From jointed doll to talking robot, *New Scientist* **14**, 37–40 (1962).

A well-illustrated and careful account of the development of mechanical automata, concentrating on the work of Vaucanson, von Knaus, and the Jacquet–Droz family.

J. M. Dubbey, Charles Babbage and his computers, *Bull. Inst. Math. Appl.* **9**(3), 662–669. (1973).

A very interesting essay on the mathematical thinking that lay behind much of Babbage's work. Contains separate sections on notation, the calculus of functions, the difference engine, the analytical engine, and algebra. It states that his ideas on algebra "were decisively influential, but characteristically he has received no credit for them at all."

C. Evans, Pioneers of Computing: An Oral History of Computing, Compiled by Dr. Christopher Evans with the Support of the Science Museum and the National Physical Laboratory (in progress).

This is a growing series of tape cassettes, each providing a one-hour recorded interview with a computer pioneer. The interviews are very well done, and the quality of the recording and editing is excellent. Some 20 or so interviews have been taped to date, and a number of edited recordings prepared, those of D. W. Davies, T. Kilburn, J. Pinkerton, F. C. Williams, and K. Zuse. Other pioneers who have been interviewed to date for this series include A. W. M. Coombs, J. P. Eckert, J. W. Forrester, I. J. Good, G. M. Hopper, J. W. Mauchly, D. Michie, and J. Wilkinson. Copies of the cassettes are to be available from the Science Museum.

F. M. Feldhaus. "Über die Entwicklung und das Wesen des Maschinenrechens." Zella-Mehlis, Thun, 1928–1930.

A very useful set of 14 pamphlets, totalling 60 pages, each giving a well-illustrated account of some aspect of the history of manual or machine calculation. Includes coverage of the work of Pascal, Morland, Schott, Leibniz, Perrault, Poleni, and Leupold.

G. Fleck (ed.), "A Computer Perspective." (By the Office of Charles and Ray Eames). Harvard Univ. Press, Cambridge, Massachusetts, 1973.

A profusely illustrated book based on an IBM-sponsored exhibition. Although aimed at a popular audience, it contains a vast amount of information, relating directly or indirectly to the origins of computers, that is not readily available elsewhere. Hundreds of rare photographs and documents are reproduced. An excellent book, which does a very fine job of attempting to portray the social and intellectual background against which the modern computer evolved.

J. Fonsny, Pascal et la machine arithmétique, *Les Études Classiques, Namur* **20**, 181–191 (1952).

A discussion of Pascal's activities and attitudes in inventing, defending, and trying to perfect his design for a calculating machine.

C. Foster, Notes on the Mechanical Construction of the Machine for Composing Hexameter Latin Verses. (8 March 1951).

A detailed report on the functioning of the machine, and of the repairs required to make it operational. (These were in fact carried out.) The report reveals that the machine incorporated six wooden drums, each with rows of wires projecting radially from it. Each wire represented (by means of its length) a letter, so that each drum had a fixed set of words encoded on it. These drums would be turned random amounts and then used to control the display of a set of six words, with the hope that it would form an acceptable hexameter Latin verse. Each drum was therefore a rather sophisticated form of pegged cylinder, used to represent data as much as sequencing information.

N. Foy, "The I.B.M. World." Methuen, London, 1974.
Chapter 2 contains some information, not readily available elsewhere, on the activities of IBM in Europe before and during World War II.

R. A. Frazer, On the Present Need for Automatic Calculation in Practical Mathematics. Memo 3005.0.75, Oscillation Sub-Committee, Aeronautical Research Committee, N.P.L., Teddington, Middlesex (13, May 1937).
Proposes a design for an electromechanical calculating machine, intended for matrix calculations. It was to incorporate a number of interlinked desk calculators, and a specially designed means for representing matrices, in which each digit of each element was to be represented by the lateral position of a sliding rod.

C. Freeman, C. J. E. Harlow, J. K. Fuller, and R. C. Curnow, Research and development in electronic capital goods, *Nat. Inst. Econ. Rev.* **34**, 40–91 (1965).
Contains a good summary of the origins of computers and of the growth of the computer industry.

J. Fyvie, The calculating philosopher, "Some Literary Eccentrics," pp. 179–209. Constable, London, 1906.
A popular account of Babbage's life, based on his autobiography, which shows very little sympathy for his work on calculating machines.

W. D. Gardner, Will the inventor of the first digital computer please stand up? *Datamation* **20**(2), 84, 88–90 (1974).
An article prompted by Judge Larson's ruling in the ENIAC suit that includes an account of an interview of Atanasoff.

F. J. Gruenberger, A short history of digital computing in Southern California, *Comput. News* 145.23–145.31 (1958).
Informal account of digital computing activity in the Los Angeles area from 1942 to 1957. Describes the growth of the use of punched-card calculators and early digital computers, but gives little technical detail. Valuable for the many dates and names of the people involved.

J. E. Hofmann, "Leibniz in Paris 1672–1676." Cambridge Univ. Press, London and New York, 1974.
A scholarly account of the period when Leibniz "conceived his decisive ideas in mathematics," when his "philosophy, founded on mathematics and the natural sciences, was formed," when "his most significant and fundamental insights in psychology dawned" and when he completed his revolutionary calculating machine. Valuable for its discussion of Leibniz's life and mathematical research, even though few technical details are given of his work on the calculating machine.

B. D. Holbrook, Bell Laboratories and the Computer from the Late 30's to the Middle 60's, Computing Science Technical Rep. No. 36. Bell Laboratories, Murray Hill, New Jersey (1975).
A very useful account covering both analog and digital computers, and hardware and software developments. Of particular interest is the discussion of the relationship of the work on early relay-based digital computers to the digital techniques used in prewar telephone switching —it is stated that facilities for storing and sequencing semipermanent subroutines in the Bell Labs Model V computer were based on the facilities provided for telephone number translation in the No. 5 crossbar dial system.

S. H. Hollingdale, Charles Babbage and Lady Lovelace—two 19th century mathematicians, *Bull. Inst. of Math. Appl.* **2**(1), 2–15 (1966).

An excellent account of Babbage and Lady Lovelace. Especially valuable for its discussion of the stages by which Babbage arrived at the idea of general programmed sequence control, and for its careful analysis of Lady Lovelace's program for calculating Bernoulli numbers.

J. Howlett, Charles Babbage and his computer. "350 Jahre Rechenmaschinen" (M. Graef, Ed.) pp. 34–42. Carl Hanser, Munich, 1973.
A useful summary and analysis of Babbage's work, based on the standard sources.

C. L. Hull, An automatic correlation calculating machine, *J. Amer. Statis. Assoc.* **20**(15), 522 –531 (1925).
Description of an electrically powered special-purpose mechanical calculator which would compute the sum of a set of products of numbers read from two perforated tapes. The machine could operate unattended, and when it stopped the result would be read from a dial. Little detail is given of the multiplier, but it is implied that the multiplication is performed by repeated addition, and that operands can have three decimal digits.

W. S. Hunt, Research Notes on Charles Babbage: Birth, Death, Residences, Family, Education, Achievements and Descendants (unpublished).
A collection of manuscript notes documenting extensive searches for primary historical evidence on Babbage, which has been deposited at the Marylebone Public Library. The collection includes extracts for correspondence (held at the Public Record Office—Ref. CREST/174 pp. 310–319) relating to Babbage's attempts to build a workshop in Dorset Street in 1842.

A. Hyman, Letter to the editor, *Computer Weekly* p. 8 (11 December 1975).
Letter giving, apparently for the first time, complete details of the place and date of Charles Babbage's birth—the author states that the information was obtained while preparing an as yet unpublished monograph for the Science Museum.

Ibn al-Razzaz al-Jazzari. "The Book of Knowledge of Ingenious Mechanical Devices" (D. R. Hill, ed. and translator). Reidel, Dordrecht, 1974.
A well-annotated and illustrated translation of a 13th-century Arabic text, which describes a number of surprisingly complex mechanical automata, some of which incorporated pegged cylinder sequencing mechanisms. These mechanisms are in general driven by waterwheels, and themselves control the movements of model figures.

W. Jensen, Hilfsgeräte der Kryptographie (Unpublished—submitted to the Technischen Hochschule, München as a Ph.D. Dissertation, but later withdrawn) (1952).
A detailed description of the various special-purpose devices, using photoelectrical tape readers, and electromagnetic relays, used for cryptographic purposes in Germany during World War II.

D. Kahn, The ultra secret, *The New York Times Book Review* p. 5 (29 December 1974).
Review of Wintherbotham (1974), which criticizes his account of the breaking of ENIGMA, and summarizes the contribution of the Polish cryptanalysts. Kahn states that the COLOSSUS was designed to solve machine ciphers used by various branches of the German armed forces.

D. W. Kean, The computer and the countess. *Datamation* **19**(5), 60–63 (1973).
A popular, but nevertheless detailed, account of the life of Lady Lovelace, and of her inter-actions with Charles Babbage concerning the analytical engine and a gambling scheme.

J. Klir, An invention that might have accelerated the development of mathematical machines, *Tech. Dig.* **5**(5), 39–41 (1963).
A brief article on the patent that Bernard Weiner obtained in 1923 for an "electric computer and typewriter," built from relays. It is stated that the machine had fixed built-in "programs" for the basic arithmetic operations, $\sin x$, a, etc., which are described in the patent. A final paragraph gives a brief biography of Weiner, and states that a special department was set up at the Vitkovice Iron Works "where Weiner worked in developing his idea and designing a fully auto-

matic computer. This work was stopped for good by the German occupation. Weiner . . . perished in 1942.''

H. E. Kneiss, First Electronics Research Lab. rediscovered, *NCR Dayton* **6**(3), 1–3 (11 April 1973).
Brief illustrated account of the Electronics Research Laboratory where Desch and Mumma led the work on the NCR Electronic Calculator Project.

S. G. Koon, Hollerith tabulating machinery in the business office, *Machinery* **20**, 25–26 (1913).
A brief survey of commercial applications of the Hollerith system, including photographs of installations at the Southern Pacific R. R. Co., the Carnegie Steel Co., and the Cleveland Electric Illuminating Co.

W. Kozaczuk, The war of wits, *Poland* **6**, 10–11, 34–35 (1975); **7**, 32–34 (1975).
A detailed account of the work of Polish cryptanalysts on the ENIGMA cipher, claiming that in 1937 they had ''cryptographic bombes,'' which were ''complex electronic units with tens of thousands of subassemblies and details (and) a special system of electrically connected revolving drums.''

F. Kreindl, Jacquards Prinzip bereits 200 Jahre alt? *Sonderdruck Melliand Textilber. Heidelberg* **2**, 1–2 (1935).
A description with photographs of a drawloom incorporating a wooden sequence control mechanism involving small wooden pegs fixed to a piece of canvas, thus being somewhat akin to a pegged cylinder mechanism. The author suggests that this ''Broselmaschine'' was invented by a member of the Ortner family, of Muhlviertel in Upper Austria, in or before 1740, and that the invention was made independently of Bouchon and Falcon, Jacquard's precursors. It is stated that the machine is exhibited at the Heimatsmuseum in Haslach, Upper Austria.

E. R. Larson, Findings of Fact, Conclusions of Law and Order for Judgement. File No 4-67 Civ. 138, Honeywell Inc. vs. Sperry Rand Corporation and Illinois Scientific Developments, Inc. U.S. District Court, District of Minnesota, Fourth Division (19 October 1973).
A fascinating 319-page document, giving Judge Larson's findings concerning the validity of the ENIAC patent, and of possible infringements of this patent. Three separate chapters detail the findings concerning the earliest public use made of ENIAC, the attempts to commercialize the machine, and the influence of Atanasoff on Mauchly, all causing various aspects of the ENIAC patent to be invalidated. In particular Judge Larson states that ''Eckert and Mauchly did not themselves first invent the automatic electronic digital computer, but instead derived that subject matter from one Dr. John Vincent Atanasoff.'' Other chapters cover such topics as the relationship of various ENIAC patent claims to work on electronics at RCA, IBM, and elsewhere, and the preparation and distribution of von Neumann's 1945 report on EDVAC.

J. Last, Digital calculating machines. *Chartered Mech. Eng.* **9**(11), 572–579 (1962).
An important paper, containing descriptions of many mechanical details of most of the major early calculating machines (Pascal, Morland, Stanhope, Thomas, Bollée, Steiger), accounting machines (Burroughs, Felt, etc.), and early punched card machines (Hollerith and Powers), and brief details of the work of Babbage and Scheutz.

S. Lavington, ''A History of Manchester Computers.'' N.C.C. Publ., Manchester, 1975.
This very useful booklet summarizes the history of five successive computer projects at Manchester University, during the period 1946–1975. The early pages give information, from primary sources, on the development of the first computer at Manchester, and on the roles of F. C. Williams, T. Kilburn, M. H. A. Newman, A. Turing, and others. Profusely illustrated.

T. C. Lewis, ''Heroes of Science: Mechanicians.'' Society for Promoting Christian Knowledge, London, 1884.
Pages 302–340 constitute a popular account of Babbage's life and work, based in large part

on his "Passages from the Life of a Philosopher." It provides an adequate account of the principles of the difference engine, but no details at all of the analytical engine.

W. B. Lewis, "Electrical Counting: With Special Reference to Alpha and Beta Particles." Cambridge Univ. Press, London and New York, 1942.

Contains detailed discussions of various trigger circuits, and binary and decimal counters,
using gas-filled or hard vacuum valves. "The technique of electrical counting has grown as an
essential aid in research in nuclear physics, and this book owes much to those who have pursued this science at the Cavendish Laboratory. The central chapters of this book . . . will I
hope be of interest to many who have occasion to use valve circuits, but who may not be concerned with nuclear physics."

M. G. Losano, Charles Babbage e la programmazione delle machine da calcolo, *Atti Accad.
delle Sci. Torino* **106**, 25–37 (1971/72).

Discusses Babbage's ideas on what would now be called program control. Derived mainly
from "Passages from the Life of a Philosopher."

M. G. Losano, "Babbage: La Macchina Analitica, Un Secolo di Calcolo Automatico." Etas
Kompass Libri, Milan, 1973.

Contains hitherto unpublished papers and letters by Babbage whose originals are preserved
in the library of the Academy of Sciences of Turin. The most interesting document is a French
translation of a letter written to Plana, presumably in 1834 or 1835. It discusses the current state
of the design of what became the analytical engine, although at this stage it was more akin to a
digital differential analyzer and the idea of program control by Jacquard cards had not yet
arisen. The book also includes extracts from the Turin police files concerning the surveillance of
Babbage and his traveling companion/guide Fortunato Prandi, a suspected revolutionary.

M. G. Losano, "Scheutz: La Macchina alle Differenze." Etas Libri, Milan, 1974.

Contains articles on the life of George Scheutz by Losano, and on his difference engine by
Merzbach, together with Italian translations of a number of original documents and papers, including several by Babbage and his son. An extensive bibliography by C. F. Bergstedt is also
included.

M. G. Losano, Le radici Europee dell'elaboratore elettronico, *Le Scienze* **89**, 57–72 (1976).

An illustrated account of four European contributions to the computer, namely those of
Leibniz and Pascal, of Charles Babbage, of Scheutz, and of Zuse. The section on Scheutz is
particularly detailed.

R. Malik, In the beginning—Early days with ACE, *Data Syst.* 56–59, 82 (1969).

A very useful discussion of the situation in Britain immediately after the war, when work
was starting at NPL, Manchester, and Cambridge. It concentrates on personalities and attitudes,
but includes a number of quotations from Turing's 1945 report proposing ACE. Turing's wartime work is hinted at, in a paragraph which mentions that the work was closely analogous to
that "carried out by Bell Labs on the 10 L predictor." The final sections of the paper describe
the various efforts at NPL at building an electronic computer, culminating in the completion of
Pilot ACE in late 1950.

R. Malik, Only begetters of the computer, *New Scientist* **47**(710), 138–139 (1970).
Brief interviews with J. P. Eckert, Grace M. Hopper, and K. Zuse.

R. Malik, "And Tomorrow the World: Inside I.B.M." Millington, London, 1975.

Chapter 1 contains a highly idiosyncratic and somewhat intemperate account of the origins
of computers, which nevertheless contains some interesting items and comments about Turing,
Zuse, von Neumann, and others.

C. Manby, "Scheutz' Difference Engine and Babbage's Mechanical Notation." William
Clowes, London, 1856.

Excerpt minutes of proceedings of the Institution of Civil Engineers, Vol. XV, Session 1855 –1856, at which H. P. Babbage presented his description of the Swedish machine. Charles Babbage is quoted as saying, "The principle of calculation by differences is common to Mr. Scheutz's engine and to my own; and is so obviously the only principle at once extensive in its grasp and simple in its mechanical application, that I have little doubt it will be found to have been suggested by more than one antecedent writer."

E. C. Mayne, "The Life and Letters of Anne Isabella, Lady Noel Byron." Scribner's Sons, New York, 1929.
The epilogue, by Mary, Countess of Lovelace, contains a brief biographical sketch of her husband's mother, Ada Augusta, Countess of Lovelace.

N. Metropolis and J. Worlton, A trilogy on errors in the history of computing, *Proc. USA-Japan Comput. Conf., 1st, Tokyo, October 3–5, 1972* pp. 683–691. AFIPS Montvale, New Jersey, 1972.
An important paper containing careful analyses of the extent to which the developers of the early computers and relay calculators were aware of Babbage's work, and accounts of the development of the stored program concept, and the early history of the MANIAC. Evidence is presented that "awareness of Babbage's work has suffered no long gaps . . . what is surprising, then, is not that some people were *aware* of Babbage's work, but that others were *unaware* of his work." The discussion of the development of the stored program concept claims that Clippinger, rather than von Neumann, was the originator of the idea of controlling ENIAC by a sequential program stored in function tables.

R. Millington. What did you do in the war Daddy? *Computing* **10** (3 June 1976).
A popular but nevertheless useful article giving brief details and anecdotes about a number of little-known digital and analog calculators built in Britain during World War II. The digital devices mentioned include ones developed at TRE for cryptanalytic purposes, and relay calculators designed by Shire and Runcorn, and by Barnes (also at TRE) and Petherick at RAE (Farnborough).

G. G. Mollenhoff, John V. Atanasoff, DP Pioneer, *Comput. World* **8,** 1, 13 (13 March 1974); 15–16 (20 March 1974) 9–10 (27 March 1974).
A fairly extensive account of the life and work of Atanasoff, based on personal interviews with him.

B. Morgan, Total to Date: The Evolution of the Adding Machine; They Story of Burroughs. Burroughs Machines, London (1953).
A well-illustrated popular account of the origins and growth of the Burroughs Corporation, and its British offshoot.

Sir Samuel Morland, "The Description and Use of Two Arithmetick Instruments." London, 1673.
Although full details are given of the use of the machines, no details are given of their mechanisms.

G. W. Patterson, The first electric computer, a magnetological analysis. *J. Franklin Inst.* **270,** 130–137 (1960).
Discussion and analysis of Marquand's electrical binary logic machine.

H. Pengelly (ed.), "A Memoir of William Pengelly of Torquay, F.R.S., Geologist." Murray, London, 1897.
Pengelly was a friend and admirer of Babbage. A number of the extracts from Pengelly's correspondence reprinted in this memoir mention meetings and correspondence with Babbage.

(Porter?). A Treatise on the Origin, Progressive Improvement and Present State of the Silk Manufacture, Lardner's Cabinet Cyclopaedia, Vol. 48. Longman, Green, London, 1831.

A book referred to by Lady Lovelace. Part 3, Chapter 4 (pp. 232–261) on figure weaving contains a detailed description of the operation and use of the Jacquard loom, and of various improvements made to it by British inventors. "In the course of the very few years which have elapsed since its first introduction into this country, the Jacquard Loom has entirely taken the place of every other method of figured silk weaving. . . ."

Publicola (pseud.). Mr. Babbage's calculating machine. *Mech. Mag.* **17**(466), 256 (1832).

A letter to the editor prompted by a review of Babbage's book "On the Economy of Machinery and Manufactures," which had appeared earlier (No. 464, 30 June 1832, pp. 213–220). Cynically asks why, despite the understanding the book shows of the planning and execution of complex engineering works, Babbage has still not completed his great calculating machine.

J. Pugh, "Calculating Machines and Instruments." Science Museum, London, 1975.

Revised and updated version of Baxandall (1926). Since 1926 the Science Museum's collection has more than doubled in size. However, in this revised catalog only minor changes have been made to the very useful descriptions written by Baxandall, and the items added to the collection listed in an appendix.

A. Quetelet, Notice sur Charles Babbage, Associé de l'Académie, *Annu. Acad. Roya. Sci. Lett. Beaux-Arts De Belgique* 149–165 (1872).

Detailed reminiscences of meetings and correspondence with Charles Babbage by one of his friends of long standing. M. Quetelet mentions meeting Lady Lovelace in 1851, and their unachieved plan to collaborate on the writing of an introduction to probability theory.

W. H. Radford, "Report on an Investigation of the Practicability of Developing a Rapid Computing Machine." MIT, Cambridge, Massachusetts, 1939.

Describes one year's work on a project funded by NCR to assess a machine proposed by Dr. V. Bush. "The rapid arithmetical machine is to be an extremely flexible device for automatically and quickly performing extended and complicated computations involving all combinations of the four fundamental arithmetical operators." The machine was to have "a master control unit" that would receive its operating directions by some such means as punched tapes or magnetic coding on steel strips, although "in the case of a machine designed to handle restricted types of problems, the control unit might advantageously be arranged in the form of a key or plug board." It would appear that the Bush memoranda discuss such aspects of the proposed machine—Radford's report is largely concerned with a detailed account, including circuit diagrams, photographs, and experimental data, of the various electronic components that had been developed, such as triggers, counters, and registers.

B. Randell, The COLOSSUS, this volume.

"The partial relaxation of the official secrecy surrounding COLOSSUS has made it possible to obtain interviews with a number of people involved in the project. The present paper is in the main based on these interviews, but supplemented by material already in the public domain. It attempts to document as fully as is presently permissible the story of the development of COLOSSUS. Particular attention is paid to interactions between the COLOSSUS project and other work carried out elsewhere on digital techniques and computers, and to the role that those involved with COLOSSUS played in post-war computer developments in Britain."

H. Reinecke, Neuere entwicklungen mechanischen rechenmaschinen, "350 Jahre Rechenmaschinen" (M. Graef, Ed.), pp. 43–50. Carl Hanser, Munich, 1973.

A survey of the development of mechanical calculating machines in the 19th and 20th centuries.

C. J. Richardson, "A Popular Treatise on the Warming and Ventilation of Buildings," 3rd ed. John Neale, London, 1856.

Pages 90–102 describe the self-regulating central heating system installed at Charles Babbage's house in Dorset Square in 1837. Plate 16 shows the layout of the house and Plate 17 an "ingeniously-contrived" mechanism for controlling water flow in four circulation loops, apparently invented by Babbage himself.

D. Riches, An Analysis of Ludgate's Machine Leading to a Design of a Digital Logarithmic Multiplier. Dept. of Electrical and Electronic Engineering, University College, Swansea (June 1973).

An interesting analysis of Ludgate's design, and a comparison of it with modern counterparts. Speculative drawings of the mechanism of Ludgate's machine are provided, and detailed designs are given for multipliers similar to that described by Ludgate, but using logarithms to base eight and base four, rather than base ten.

R. D. Richtmyer, The post-war computer development, *Amer. Math. Monthly* **72**(2), 8–14 (1965).

Discusses how the modern stored-program computer evolved following the development of ENIAC. A brief account is given of the ENIAC converter code, which allowed manually set function tables to be used to represent programs, and an accumulator to be used as an instruction counter. The idea of the converter code is attributed to von Neumann.

L. Rodriguez Alcalde, "Torres Quevedo y la Cibernetica," Los Sabios del Mundo Entero No 21. Ediciones Cid, Madrid, 1966.

A 209-page biography, which, although intended for a general readership, contains much information not available elsewhere. A number of photographs of Torres and his family, and of various of his machines, are included.

J. L. Rogers, The Sumador Chino. Comm. ACM **3**(11), 621–622 (1960).

Illustrated description of a strange instrumental aid to addition reminiscent of Napier's rods, found by the author in Mexico.

C. J. Scriba, Review of "Maistrov, I. E. and Cenakal: V. L.: A very old calculating machine," *Math. Rev.* **40**(3), 456–457 (1970).

Provides a fairly detailed précis of an account of a calculating machine "built by an otherwise unknown Hebrew clockmaker and mechanic Jewna Jacobson at Neiswiez, province of Minsk, Lithuania, probably not later than 1770." The machine could perform addition, subtraction, multiplication (by repeated addition), and division (by repeated subtraction) on numbers of up to nine digits. "It is obvious however from signs of usage, that the machine was mostly— and for a long time—employed for the computation of numbers with no more than five digits."

E. S. Shire and S. K. Runcorn, "An Apparatus for the Computation of Serial Correlations and its Use in Frequency Analysis," Rep. No. 7, Selected Government Research Rep., Vol. 5: Servomechanisms, pp. 98–121. HM Stationery Office, London, 1951.

Based on a RRDE Research Report, January 1945. Describes an apparatus involving two paper-tape readers, and a multiplier built from relays and uniselectors.

D. E. Smith, Among my autographs, *Amer. Math. Monthly* **29**, 114–115 (1922).

A brief article based on a letter written by Babbage following a visit he paid to the widow of Laplace in 1840.

M. G. Stevenson, Bell Labs: A pioneer in computing technology. Part 1: Early Bell Labs computers. *Bell Labs Record* **51**, 344–351 (1973).

In addition to a summary of the development of the Bell Labs Series of relay computers, describes a tape-driven relay-based automatic message accounting system, first installed in 1948, and a variety of analog computers and calculating devices.

R. T. "Mathematical and Scientific Library of the Late Charles Babbage of No. 1, Dorset Street, Manchester Square." Hodgson and Son, London, 1872.

A 191-page sale catalog, including sections on pure mathematics, astronomy, mechanics, optics, electricity, pneumatics, and mathematical tables. Over 2000 items are listed, some consisting of whole sets of books or papers. A few items relate to Babbage's work on calculating machines, including a book about Sir Samuel Morland.

J. Timbs, "Stories of Inventors and Discoverers," 2nd ed. Lockwood, London, 1863.
Includes an account of Babbage's machines (pp. x, 134–145) and also brief sections on automatic and speaking machines, the automaton chess-player, Sir Samuel Morland and his inventions, and Jacquard and his loom.

J. Todd, John von Neumann and the National Accounting Machine, *SIAM Rev.* **16**(4), 526–530 (1974).

L. Torres y Quevedo, Ensayos sobre Automatica—Su definicion. Extension teorica de sus aplicaciones, *Real Acad. Ciencias Exactas Fiscias Naturales, Revista* **12**, 391–418 (1913).
Original version of Torres y Quevedo (1914).

F. G. Tricomi, Un Precursore delle Moderne Macchine Calcolatrici: Charles Babbage (1792–1871), *Atti Accad. Sci. Torino* **106**, 17–24 (1971/72).
A summary of Babbage's life and his work on calculating machines, and in particular his visit to Turin in 1840, mentioning that letters and papers relating to this visit were still retained at the Academy of Sciences in Turin.

H. Tropp, The effervescent years: A retrospective, *IEEE Spectrum* **11**(2), 70–79 (1974).
An account of American computer developments based on interviews with the pioneers. It covers the work of Stibitz, Aiken, Atanasoff, Eckert and Mauchly, and von Neumann, and discusses the role of U.S. companies such as IBM and NCR.

R. C. Tumbleson, Calculating machines, *Elec. Eng.* **67**(10), 6–12 (1948).
"Essentially full text of paper which appeared in Federal Science Progress (Washington, D.C.) June 1947, pages 2–7." A popular account of Babbage's analytical engine, which surveys American electromechanical and electronic computer developments. Provides an unusually clear summary of the method by which ENIAC was programmed.

H. D. Turner, Charles Babbage F.R.S. (1792–1871), *Res. Appl. Ind.* **14**(9), 342–352 (1961).
A brief illustrated account of Babbage's work on the difference and analytical engines. It quotes a letter written by Babbage to Arago in December 1939 explaining his use of the Jacquard-card technique.

J. Vaucanson, "Le Mécanisme du Fluteur Automate." Guerin, Paris, 1738.
A fascinating 15-page account of the mechanisms used in the automaton flute player. The descriptions of the means of blowing and fingering the flute, and of the pegged cylinder used for controlling the sequence of actions, are very detailed but somewhat difficult to follow, since no diagrams are included.

B. von Freytag Löringhoff, Wilhelm Schickard und seine Rechenmaschine von 1623, "350 Jahre Rechenmaschinen" (M. Graef, Ed.), pp. 11–20. Carl Hanser, Munich, 1973.
An account of Schickard's life and work.

L. von Mackensen, Zur Vorgeschichte und Entstehung der ersten digitalen 4-spezies-Rechenmaschine von Gottfried Wilhelm Leibniz, *Akten des Internat. Leibniz-Kongr., Hannover, 1966* ii, pp. 34–68. Franz Steiner, Weisbaden 1969.
After a lengthy introduction discussing early aids to enumeration and calculation, including the work of Schickard and Pascal, this gives an extremely detailed account of Leibniz's work on calculating machines.

L. von Mackensen, Von Pascal zu Hahn: Die Entwicklung von Rechenmaschinen im 17 und 18

Jahrshundert, "350 Jahre Rechenmaschinen" (M. Graef, ed.), pp. 21–33. Carl Hanser, Munich, 1973.
    Among the inventors discussed are Pascal, Schickard, Leibniz, Leupold, Braun, and Hahn.

C. R. Weld, "The Eleventh Chapter of the History of the Royal Society." Richard Clay, London, 1849.
    In addition to the reprint of the chapter from Weld's book, this booklet, which appears to have been edited by Charles Babbage, contains reprints of two articles by De Morgan. The whole relates to Babbage's disputes with the government over the difference engine. De Morgan's verdict is that the government was to blame for the eventual abandonment of the difference engine.

W. C. White, Evolution of electronics, *Electronics* **25**(9), 98–99 (1952).
    "History of electronics industry is charted as a family tree in which roots represent basic research and branches represent resulting types of commercial tubes."

C. Whiting, "The Battle for Twelveland." Corgi, London, 1975.
    A popular account of Anglo–American intelligence operations within Germany during World War II with one brief chapter on the ENIGMA cipher. It claims that a "new Post Office computer," which was used to strip a numerical additive from the enciphered code, was operational at Bletchley Park by February 1940.

N. Wiener, Memorandum on the Scope etc., of a Suggested Computing Machine. Unpublished memorandum, now in the Institute Archives, M.I.T. Libraries (1940).
    A proposal, sent to Vannevar Bush, apparently on 23 September 1940. The 12-page memorandum is mostly about finite difference techniques for the solution of boundary value problems in partial differential equations. It suggests the construction of a special purpose electronic calculator which would mechanize a four-point relaxation procedure, using a binary adder and a tape scanning mechanism involving four reading heads and one writing head. Various possible technologies are mentioned, but magnetic recording is preferred. A final brief and vague paragraph suggests the possibility of "electronic machines capable of performing rapid sequences of operations such as addition and multiplication on the data read off, before printing the result on the binary scale."

K. L. Wildes, The Digital Computer—Whirlwind (unpublished).
    This is part of a draft of a study of the MIT Department of Electrical Engineering and Computer Science. Based on original documents, it provides considerable details of the early work on digital electronics at MIT started by Bush, and then continued by Radford and Overbeck under the sponsorship of NCR. Crawford's associated work on electronic digital fire control devices is also covered, as is the postwar work on the (soon abandoned) Rockefeller Electronic Computer Project and the WHIRLWIND Project.

M. V. Wilkes, Early computer development at Cambridge: The EDSAC, *Radio Elec. Eng.* **45**(7), 332–335 (1975).
    Describes the origins of the Mathematical Laboratory at Cambridge, the author's attendance at the 1946 Moore School Lectures, the development of EDSAC, and the early programming techniques used. Numerous illustrations, many taken from a 1951 film demonstrating how EDSAC was used.

J. H. Wilkinson, The pilot ACE at the National Physical Laboratory. *Radio Elec. Eng.* **45**(7), 336–340 (1975).
    Provides a detailed account of the trials and tribulations involved in developing the Pilot ACE Computer, whose first successful public demonstration was in December 1950. It describes how the design was based on that of the "test assembly," a prototype design by a team led by Harry Huskey, which was in turn based on what Turing described as version V of his

original 1945 proposal for an automatic computing engine. It states that the term "engine" was chosen "in recognition of the pioneering work of Babbage on his Analytical Engine," and that Turing was already at work on version V in May 1946, when the author joined NPL.

F. C. Williams, Early computers at Manchester University, *Radio Elec. Eng.* **45**(7), 327–331 (1975).

An article, which is both informative and entertaining, about the original 1948 prototype computer built to demonstrate the CRT storage system, the larger 1949 computer (which incorporated index registers and a drum store), and Ferranti MARK I.

M. R. Williams, The difference engines, *Comput. J.* **19**(1), 82–89 (1976).

An excellent account, starting with Müller's 1786 proposal, and ending with an account of the use made by Comrie and others of commercially available desk calculators and accounting machines as difference engines. Brief accounts are given of proposed or completed difference engines by Deacon, Grant, Ludgate, Bollée, Hamann, and Thompson. Much more complete accounts are given of the work of Babbage and of George and Edvard Scheutz, based on a great variety of early documentary sources. Brief explanations of the workings of their difference engines are included.

F. W. Winterbotham, "The Ultra Secret." Weidenfeld and Nicolson, London, 1974.

The first book to be published about the information that was obtained during World War II by "breaking" German messages in such ciphers as ENIGMA, which by implication claims that there was an electronic computer at Bletchley Park in 1940.

J. R. Womersley, 'ACE' Machine Project. Memorandum to NPL Executive Committee, NPL, Teddington, Middlesex (19 March 1946b).

A brief overview of, and expression of strong support for, Turing's plans for the ACE. It states that Turing's plans are based on those for the EDVAC. "Some of the basic ideas are given in Professor J. von Neumann's 'Report on the EDVAC,' a secret report of the Applied Mathematics Panel of the NDRC, but it contains a number of ideas that are Dr. Turing's own and are to be found in a paper published by him in the *Proc. Lond. Math. Soc.* 1937."

M. Woodger, J. R. Parks, and D. Lewin, The foundations of computer engineering, *Radio Elec. Eng.* **45**(10), 598–602 (1975).

Transcript of a discussion concerning, inter alia, the origins of the stored program concept.

C. E. Wynn-Williams, Electrical methods of counting, *Rep. Progr. Phys.* **3**, 239–261 (1937).

Surveys current work on the design of electronic counting circuits. The final section discusses relay-based auxiliary apparatus for controlling an electronic counter, for decimal-to-binary conversion, and for printing.

C. E. Wynn-Williams, The scale of two counter, *Year Book Phys. Soc.* pp. 56–60 (1957).

A marvelously evocative account of Wynn-Williams's work at the Cavendish Laboratory, and later at Imperial College, on thyraton-based counters. He explains how an electronic ring counter was first built in 1930, and in the next year, a binary counter capable of recording events occurring at 1/1250-sec intervals. By 1935 basic electronic counters had been provided with ancillary equipment, using relays and uniselectors, for binary–decimal conversion, timing of runs, and automatic printout. A second version of this apparatus at Imperial College was provided with the means by which it could be operated remotely, by telephone. "Finally, just before war broke out, a programme device was added, which could control experimental conditions and carry out cycles of pre-arranged runs by remote control of the equipment." All of this work was carried out with the minimum of funds and facilities—the resolution time counter was measured using "a glorious system of rubber bands, workshop nails, the inevitable Cavendish string, resistance wire, wooden laths and a long piece of strong catapult elastic" and the typewriter was a homemade affair using "a sixpenny toy printing set."

S. Y. Calculating Machinery, *Mech. Mag.* **23**(624), 317–318 (25 July 1835).
   This letter, and that of P.S.C. (1835) were written in support of Babbage and his plans for a machine capable of calculating and printing mathematical tables automatically. They were written in response to brief and unsubstantiated claims, noted in earlier issues of the magazine, of other people to have invented automatic calculating machines, claims which by implication were pouring ridicule on Babbage's efforts.

H. Zemanek, Spanische automaten: Leonardo Torres y Quevedo (1852–1936), *Elektron. Rech.* **8**(6), 217–218 (1966).
   A brief illustrated article about Torres y Quevedo and his various electromechanical devices, including the arithmometer, and both chess players.

H. Zemanek, Datenveranbeitung von 100 Jahren: Otto Schäffler (1838–1928) ein zu Unrecht vergessener österreichischer Pionier der Nachrichten- und Lochkartentechrick, *Elektrotech. Maschinenbau* **90**(11), 543–550 (1973).
   A well-illustrated account of Schäffler and his work.

H. Zemanek, Otto Schäffler (1838–1928)—Ein vergessener Österreicher, *Jahrb. Österreich. Gewerbevereins* 71–92 (1974a).
   A valuable account of the life and work of Otto Schäffler. Contains an extensive bibliography, and numerous illustrations, including several relating to his improved method of "programming" a tabulating machine by incorporating a telephonelike switchboard.

H. Zemanek, John Vincent Atanasoff: Ein Amerikanischer Computer-Pionier Bulgarischer Abstammung. *Elektron. Rech.* **16**(3), 91–92 (1947b).
   A brief account of Atanasoff and his work on a special-purpose electronic computer.

K. Zuse, The working program-controlled computer of 1941, *Honeywell Comput. J.* **6**(2), 49–58 (1972).
   A partial reprint, and translation of, Zuse (1962).

K. Zuse, Die ersten programmgesteuerten Relais-Rechenmaschinen, "350 Jahre Rechenmaschinen" (M. Graef, ed.), pp. 51–57. Carl Hanser, Munich, 1973.
   A brief summary of the author's work, concentrating on the Z3, Z4, and special-purpose machines.

K. Zuse, The Plankalkul, Report 106. Gesellschaft für Mathematik und Datenverarbeitung, Bonn (1976).
   An English translation of the 200-page document written by Zuse in 1945 on his concept of an algorithmic language. It is accompanied by translations of a 1944 paper by Zuse entitled "Statements of a theory of general calculation" and a commentary written by Zuse in 1972 which summarizes his prewar and wartime work, and serves as an introduction to the main document on the Plankalkül. In this commentary Zuse states that during World War II he designed "several theoretical models which utilized logical instructions, program selection, address computation, and the facilities of my Conditional Calculus. I already realized then that computers must also be able to store programs as well as data. But to me this capability seemed to be such a self-evident requirement then, that I omitted to apply for a patent for its realization."

Anonymous, Mr. Babbage's calculating machine, *Mech. Magazine* **10**(263), 64 (23 August 1828).
   "Mr. J. F. W. Herschell, who has been entrusted by Mr. B. to superintend the progress of this great undertaking during a tour which he is now undertaking on the continent, informs us that though the work continues in active and steady progress . . . a very long time must elapse, and a very heavy further expense be incurred, before it can be completed. We are glad, however, to learn that no suspicion of failure has yet arisen."

Anonymous, Mr. Babbage's calculating machinery, *Mech. Magazine* **18**(488), 173–175 (1832).
    Reprint of an article in Partington's "British Encyclopaedia," which surveys calculating machines developed prior to Babbage's difference engine, explains the operation of the engine, and describes a successful demonstration of the small prototype difference engine.

Anonymous, Mr. Babbage and his calculating engines, *Mech. Magazine* **21**(578), 391–392 (6 September 1834).
    Apparently based on an article in the *Edinburgh Review* **120**. Summarizes present problems over the difference engine, and calls for the Government to "appoint proper persons to inquire into and report on the proper state of the machinery; to ascertain the causes of its suspension; and to recommend such measures as may appear to be most effectual to ensure its speedy completion."

Anonymous, The Eureka, *Illustrated London News* (19 July 1845).
    A brief account of the machine for composing hexameter Latin verses. It states that the machine produces about one line of verse a minute—"during the composition of each line, a cylinder in the interior of the machine performs the National Anthem."

Anonymous, Disputes in the Royal and Royal Astronomical Society, *Mech. Magazine* **62**(1649), pp. 242–246, 267–271 (1855).
    Commentary with extensive quotations on a number of pamphlets concerning Babbage, most notably "Address of the Right Honourable the Earl of Rosse, etc. . . . Royal Society, Thursday Nov. 30, 1854 (printed by Taylor & Francis, London)."

Anonymous, The calculating machine of M. Scheutz. *Mech. Magazine* **64**(1705), 343–346 (1856).
    Incorporates a reprint of the paper by Charles Babbage addressed to the Royal Society, describing the origins and development of the Scheutz difference engine, and recommending that it be awarded one of the Society's gold medals.

Anonymous, "Specimens of Tables Calculated, Stereomoulded and Printed by Machinery." Longman, Green, London, 1857.
    The 11-page preface provides a detailed account of the history of the development of the Scheutz difference engine, its public exhibition in England and France, and its sale to the Dudley Observatory. This is followed by an account prepared by Mr. Gravatt of the method of using the machine.

Anonymous, The late Mr. Babbage, *The Times* (23 and 30 October 1871b).
    An obituary, with a follow-up article giving further details on Babbage's parentage and early youth.

Anonymous, The late Mr. Babbage, *Illustrated London News* p. 423 (4 November 1871c).
    A factual obituary and engraved portrait. "The death of Mr. Charles Babbage the eminent mathematician and inventor of 'the calculating machine,' was announced last week. . . ."

Anonymous, Mr. Charles Babbage, *The Illustrated Times*, p. 267 (28 October 1871d).
    An obituary notice, which describes in some detail Babbage's efforts at constructing a difference engine.

Anonymous, Our obituary record, *The Graphic* p. 495 (18 November 1871e).
    A very favorable obituary notice for Charles Babbage.

Anonymous, Mechanical tabulation, *Engineering* **74**, 165 (1902).
    Brief article describing method of operation of the Hollerith tabulating system, and its use for the 1900 U.S. census.

Anonymous, "60 Jahre Brunsviga." Brunsviga-Maschinenwerke Grimme, Natalis and Co., Braunschweig, 1931.

A 98-page illustrated booklet, containing brief sections on the history of desk calculating machines, current models of the Brunsviga, and on the Trinks–Brunsviga Museum, as well as much material on the manufacture and worldwide sales of Brunsviga.

Anonymous, Tercentenary of Wilhelm Schickard (1592–1635), *Nature* (*London*) **136**, 636 (1935).
Brief biographical note, concentrating on his work on astronomy.

Anonymous, BINAC demonstrated, new electronic brain, *J. Franklin Inst.* **248**(4), 360–361 (1949b).
Account of a demonstration of BINAC at the Eckert–Mauchly Computer Corporation in Philadelphia, at which solutions to Poisson's equation and square and cube roots of numbers typed in by the audience were calculated. Only brief details are given of BINAC, which is stated to be a twin computer system, with each computer incorporating 700 vacuum tubes, in which numbers and instructions are held in mercury delay lines.

Anonymous, Three N.C.R. pioneers cited by Smithsonian for electronics work, *NCR Dayton* **6**(3), 1, 3 (1973).
Brief illustrated accounts of the careers of Joseph Desch and Robert Mumma, who worked from 1938 to 1942 on the NCR electronic calculator, and Don E. Eckdahl, leader of the MADDIDA (magnetic drum differential analyzer) project, which was completed in 1949.

Appendix

The litigation between Honeywell, Inc., as Plaintiff and Sperry Rand Corporation and Illinois Scientific Developments, Inc., as Defendants, in which the validity of the ENIAC patents was challenged, resulted in the accumulation of huge amounts of material of great historical value. The statistics of the case are staggering. The litigation commenced in May 1967, and it was not until October 1973 that Judge E. R. Larson issued his verdict. In the interval there was a total of 135 days of court hearings, involving testimony or sworn depositions from over 150 witnesses. The transcripts of the hearings total approximately 20,000 pages. However, even this is only the tip of the iceberg, since the Plaintiff submitted over 25,000 pieces of evidence and the Defendants over 6000, ranging in size from a single letter to a whole filing cabinet full of documents.

The case is summarized in a 420-page document by Judge E. R. Larson entitled "Findings of Fact, Conclusions of Law and Order for Judgment" (Larson, 1973). One finding that has attracted a lot of attention is the one stating that "Eckert and Mauchly did not themselves first invent the automatic electronic digital computer, but instead derived that subject matter from one Dr. John Vincent Atanasoff." It is my understanding that here the term "automatic electronic digital computer" has the original definition given in the ENIAC patent, which was not challenged by the Plaintiff— there is no implication that the term necessarily matches the modern conception of a stored-program electronic digital computer.

Atanasoff's prior work is just one of the reasons given for invalidating the ENIAC patents; other arguments, for example, are based on the finding that the patent applications were delayed too long after the ENIAC was made available for public use. The "Findings of Fact . . . ." therefore cover matters concerned with the completion and use of ENIAC as well as its origins and relevant prior art. With regard to prior art, the main work investigated in addition to that of Atanasoff is that by Dickinson, Phelps, and others at IBM, by Desch and Mumma at NCR, by Bush, Radford, and Overbeck at MIT, and by Zworykin and Rajchman at RCA. In addition to that on ENIAC, considerable material relating to EDVAC, BINAC, and UNIVAC was amassed.

I initially gained the impression that, of all the documents in the case, only the "Findings of Fact, . . ." were available to the public. However, Judge Larson has indicated that the complete files are available in Minneapolis for purposes of historical research. Moreover, at his instigation, Mr. H. Halladay, of Dorsey, Windhorst, Hannaford, Whitney, and Halladay, the leading attorney for the Plaintiff, very kindly lent me his personal microfiche copy of the entire transcript and the Plaintiff's computerized lists. A brief description of this material follows.

The most readily usable aspect of the transcript is that each witness gives an account of his or her own career. In the case of the principal witnesses the amount of biographical material, together with technical details of scientific and engineering achievements, is considerable. Mauchly's testimony, for example, covers over 700 pages of the transcript. Other pioneers who gave extensive testimony include J. V. Atanasoff, A. A. Auerbach, R. Clippinger, J. R. Desch, A. H. Dickinson, J. P. Eckert, S. P. Frankel, H. P. Goldstine, J. C. Mark, N. C. Metropolis, C. N. Mooers, F. E. Mumma, B. E. Phelps, J. Rajchman, E. Teller, and S. Ulam.

However, it is the various computerized lists that provide the major means of access to the contents of not only the transcript but also of all the trial exhibits. One such list is the Plaintiff's "computerized brief," which is itself over 4500 pages long. It consists of a large number of "event statements," each typically consisting of a single sentence. In general, each such statement is accompanied by:

(1) the Defendants' reply, which often denies the validity and/or relevance of the Plaintiff's statement;
(2) comments by the Plaintiff on this reply;
(3) the Defendants' post-trial argument, usually rather more detailed;
(4) the Plaintiff's response to the defendants' argument;
(5) the Defendants' final argument. This, and the preceding argument, are in many cases quite lengthy, with extensive quotations from testimony and exhibits;
(6) Plaintiff's list of exhibits related to the particular event statement with (usually) brief indication of contents of each exhibit, together with extensive cross referencing to relevant pages of the transcript whenever the exhibit was offered in evidence, objected to, discussed, etc.;
(7) Plaintiff's summary of supporting testimony, crossreferenced, to-

gether with any other relevant testimony, to appropriate transcript page numbers.

This formidable, highly structured, but readable document naturally concentrates on the various points at issue in the trial, and so does not attempt to summarize or analyze all of the information contained in the testimony or exhibits. Other simple forms of index go some way to performing this function. These include a 7500-page master KWIC index to Plaintiff's summaries of source documents, together with much smaller subsidiary KWIC indexes to summaries of testimony and to the subject matter description of each trial exhibit. There are also other indexes consisting of straightforward alphabetized listings of exhibits, organized in various ways.

It is in all an impressive demonstration of the power of computer techniques to facilitate use of what would otherwise be an absolutely overwhelming mass of information. The computerized lists enable one to obtain a good idea of the contents of the trial exhibits. Thus these lists, and the trial transcript, which together occupy almost 200 microfiche cards, are an extremely valuable source of historical information. I understand that the exhibits themselves are in the main still in custody in Minneapolis, where they can be inspected, but that some have been returned to their owners. Enquiries concerning this material should be addressed to Mr. Halladay.

INDEX

Babbage: analytical engine
Adler, 1958; Babbage (H.P.) 1910; Losano, 1971, 1973; Timbs, 1863; Tumbleson, 1948; Turner, 1963; Wilkinson, 1975
Babbage: difference engine
Adler, 1958; Babbage, C., 1822; Brewster, 1824; Lewis, 1884; Losano, 1974; Publicola, 1832; Timbs, 1863; Turner, 1961; Weld, 1849; Williams (M. R.), 1976; S. Y., 1835; Anon, 1828, 1832, 1834, 1871d
Babbage: influence of
Dubbey, 1973; Metropolis and Worlton, 1972
Babbage: mechanical notation
Babbage (H. P.), 1910b; Manby, 1856
Babbage, H. P.
Babbage (H. P.), 1910b; Manby, 1856
Barnes, R. C. M.
Millington (n.d.)
Bell Laboratories Computers
Holbrook, 1975; Malik, 1969; Stevenson, 1973
Bell Laboratories Computers: Model V
Holbrook, 1975
B.E.S.M.
Apokin and Maistrov, 1974
Bibliographies
Chroust, 1974; Losano, 1974
BINAC
Auerbach *et al.*, 1952; Larson, 1973; Anon, 1949b
Bletchley Park
Brown, 1975; Calvocoressi, 1974; Kahn, 1974; Randell, 1976; Whiting, 1975; Winterbotham, 1974
Bonch-Bruevitch, M. A.
Apokin and Maistrov, 1974
Braun: calculating machine
Von Mackensen, 1969
Broselmaschine
Adam, 1973; Kreindl, 1935
Brown, G.
Bryden, 1972
Brunsviga–Dupla calculating machine
Comrie, 1928b, 1932b; Anon, 1931
Bryce, J.
Connolly, 1967
Bull, F.
Connolly, 1967
Burroughs: calculators
Morgan, 1953
Bush, V.
Bush, 1970; Crawford, 1939; Radford, 1939; Wildes (n.d.)
Calculating machines
Apokin and Maistrov, 1974; Feldhaus, 1928–30; Last, 1962; Morland, 1673; Rogers, 1960; Scriba, 1970
Calculating machines: descriptive catalogues
Pugh, 1975
Calculating machines: design
Last, 1962

Ten thousand register machine
    Curtis, 1932
Thompson, A. J.
    Comrie, 1932b; Williams (M. R.), 1976
Torres y Quevedo, L.
    Rodriguez Alcalde, 1966; Zemanek, 1966
Torres y Quevedo: arithmometer
    Torres y Quevedo, 1913; Zemanek, 1966
Turing, A. M.
    Brown, 1975; Carpenter and Doran, 1975; Lavington, 1975; Malik, 1969, 1970, 1975; Randell, 1976; Wilkinson, 1975; Womersley, 1946b
Vaucanson, J.
    Droz, 1962
von Neumann, J.
    Bernstein, 1963; Carpenter and Doran, 1975; Larson, 1973; Malik, 1975; Metropolis and Worlton, 1972; Richtmyer, 1965; Todd, 1974; Tropp, 1974; Womersley, 1946b
Weiner, B.
    Klir, 1963
WHIRLWIND
    Wildes (n.d.)
Wilkinson, J.
    Evans (n.d.)
Williams, F. C.
    Evans (n.d.); Lavington, 1975
Zuse, K.
    Connolly, 1967; Evans (n.d.); Malik, 1970, 1975
Zuse: computers
    Losano, 1976; Zuse, 1972, 1973, 1976

COMPUTING LABORATORY
UNIVERSITY OF NEWCASTLE UPON TYNE
NEWCASTLE UPON TYNE, ENGLAND